American Health Crisis

The publisher and the University of California Press Foundation gratefully acknowledge the generous support of the Barbara S. Isgur Endowment Fund in Public Affairs.

American Health Crisis

One Hundred Years of Panic, Planning, and Politics

Martin Halliwell

UNIVERSITY OF CALIFORNIA PRESS

University of California Press
Oakland, California

© 2021 by Martin Halliwell

Library of Congress Cataloging-in-Publication Data

Names: Halliwell, Martin, author.
Title: American health crisis : one hundred years of
panic, planning, and politics / Martin Halliwell.
Description: Oakland, California : University of Cal-
ifornia Press, [2021] | Includes bibliographical references
and index. | Summary: "Despite enormous advances in
medical science and public health education over the last
century, access to health care remains a dominant issue
in American life. U.S. health care is often hailed as the
best in the world, yet the public health emergencies of
today very often echo the public health emergencies of
yesterday: the Great Influenza Pandemic of 1918–19 and
COVID-19; the displacement of the Dust Bowl and the
havoc of Hurricane Maria; the Reagan administration's
antipathy toward the AIDS epidemic and the lack of
accountability during the water crisis in Flint, Michigan"
—Provided by publisher.
Identifiers: LCCN 2020037071 (print) | LCCN
2020037072 (ebook) | ISBN 9780520379404 (cloth) |
ISBN 9780520976719 (ebook)
Subjects: LCSH: Public health—Political aspects—
United States. | Emergency management—United States. |
Medical policy—United States.
Classification: LCC RA395.A3 H3437 2021 (print) |
LCC RA395.A3 (ebook) | DDC 362.10973–dc23
LC record available at https://lccn.loc.
gov/2020037071
LC ebook record available at https://lccn.loc.
gov/2020037072

Manufactured in the United States of America

30 29 28 27 26 25 24 23 22 21
10 9 8 7 6 5 4 3 2 1

I know we can be better than we are....We can also be infinitely worse, but I know that the world we live in now is not necessarily the best world we can make.

—James Baldwin, 1984

Contents

Preface

This book explores a deeply contested arena of politics and culture in its assessment of US federal responses to critical health episodes over the course of a turbulent century. In these pages, I interleave three arguments that together offer a layered and expansive approach to modern and contemporary health crises. The first argument is that we need to combine thematic and historical perspectives to understand the nature, scale, and consequences of health crises. To this end, I plot the book around six crisis concepts—Disaster, Poverty, Pollution, Virus, Care, and Drugs—that might easily be newspaper headlines and continue to test the resilience of health services and diverse communities across the United States, from New Hampshire to Utah and from Alaska to Florida. These six chapters are bookended by two years, 1918 and 2018, that are especially instructive for assessing the health needs of the nation, revealing how seemingly distinct crises are often just the most visible phases of a longer arc.

Public health responses in the early twenty-first century are much more sophisticated than they were in the closing months of World War I when the Woodrow Wilson administration was looking to expand the remit of the US Public Health Service. But I do not seek to revive the "grand march of science" model that *Life* magazine celebrated in January 1950 during the so-called golden age of medicine, and I do not want to emulate John Burnham's long historical account, *Health Care in America*, of 2015 that shows how the health care infrastructure has become ever more intricate across a sequence of eras.[1] Instead, my six chapters trace patterns of repetition and inertia in health care provision as well as chart periods of progressive reform in which legislators, advocates, and medical leaders have tackled thorny issues of access, inclusion, and parity that continue disproportionately to affect the nation's most vulnerable communities. This underpins the emphasis of the book's two halves on different kinds of vulnerabilities, and it informs my second argument: that we need a more historically informed understanding of the environmental and infrastructural pressures that make some communities and individuals especially vulnerable to health crises.

In the following chapters, I hope to show how a study of modern and contemporary health crises prompts some far-reaching questions. Such a study raises organizational questions about how robust and flexible health care systems are and biopolitical questions about what role governments and local authorities should play in safeguarding and enhancing the well-being of families and communities. I also read health crises as episodes of differing scales that pose economic questions about budgetary priorities and effective service delivery; ontological and sociological questions about identity, belonging, and rights; ethical and pragmatic questions about the willingness or ability of authorities, groups, and individuals to act responsibly in pressure situations; and questions about language and representation, such as how health crises are structured rhetorically, how they are documented historically, and how they are remembered culturally. This nexus of questions shapes my third argument. In order to better prepare to face future health crises in which environmental and epidemiological issues relating to vulnerable communities and fragile habitats are likely only to intensify, we need to develop more situated concepts of public health and health citizenship as key facets of what University of California sociologist Robert Bellah calls a moral ecology.

In addressing these questions, the book brings into dialogue political, historical, medical, scientific, and cultural sources through eighteen case studies in which different health narratives converge, some of them macronarratives at the federal level, some micronarratives emerging out of local stories. This is with the twin aims of assessing the shifting scales of crisis across space and time and of foregrounding the human dimension of health crises that can easily disappear in a blizzard of high-level statistics. My case studies reveal geography to be a major factor in how crises are experienced and managed, while their historical range enables me to discuss eighteen US presidencies, from Woodrow Wilson to Donald Trump, that span the Great Influenza pandemic of 1918–19 and a dramatic rise in opioid-related deaths in the late 2010s, during a particularly polarizing phase in the national health care conversation.

There is a debate to be had about how much the US president influences health policy: sometimes legislation is pushed through at the president's behest within a program of change; at other times it emerges from congressional business at arm's length from the executive branch, often after lobbying by special interest groups or critical coverage in the media. With this in mind, the chapters give more space to the eight Democratic US presidencies falling between 1916 and 2020, during which the moral commitment to improve national health has often surfaced, in contrast to the Republican predilection for small government. However, I do not ignore Republican-led health policies or the efforts of Republican administrations to deal with health emergencies, neither do I think Democratic administrations have always been better at ameliorating crises or ensuring their health policies are sustainable in the long term.

The Lyndon Johnson administration is pivotal to understanding the arc of public health policy across these hundred years, partly because it represents the book's midpoint and partly because the period 1964 to 1966 is often upheld as the zenith of the federal government's moral responsibility to the nation's health via programs designed to be responsive to underserved communities and intended to embody participatory democracy. This is most explicitly evident in the middle case studies in chapters 2 and 5 on Great Society reforms, but the legacy of the mid-1960s also informs my discussions of the Vet Center community health model toward the end of the fifth chapter and the Affordable Care Act in the conclusion. I do not wish uncritically to portray the mid-1960s as a utopian phase or the "apex of modern American liberalism" though. This is a myth historian Julian Zelizer rebuts in his 2015 book *The Fierce Urgency of Now* by arguing that "this period of liberalism was much more fragile, contested, and transitory" than is often remembered.[2] On this view, Richard Nixon's contention at the close of the 1960s that Johnson's reforms came at too great a national cost is reflected by less partisan commentators, such as the pediatrician Julius Richmond (later surgeon general and assistant health secretary in the Jimmy Carter administration) who saw great value in the Johnson administration's Community Action Program but also believed that coordination of health care at federal, state, and local levels lacked cohesion.[3]

The federal level is my primary horizon, set against a recognition that health crises are planetary and affect some countries more often and more intensely than others, even as interconnectedness in the early twenty-first century means that disease outbreaks often cross borders rapidly. US federal responses are, at times, shaped by global health conditions, the health security systems of other countries, and the governing role of the World Health Organization (since its inception in 1948), but my intention here is to balance domestic health policies and localized experiences that in certain phases weave in these transnational threads. The conclusion gathers up these threads via a model of health citizenship that stems from my reading of Robert Bellah's two collaborative books, *Habits of the Heart* (1985) and *The Good Society* (1991).[4] This is with the aim of developing a community-facing model of public health that might strengthen resilience in the face of future crises and can assist governments and communities to move beyond the "panic and planning" cycles that my case studies reveal.

The book emphasizes the importance of health citizenship as a key facet of a broader moral ecology that requires political leaders to be responsive to public health priorities. Yet this is no easy task. In the final months of writing this book, the COVID-19 pandemic had spread across all fifty US states and nearly two hundred countries, after first emerging in central China in December 2019. It is too early to fix a historical perspective on what is widely seen as the worst public health crisis in a century. However, as I discuss at the end of chapter 4 and in the coda, the Trump administration's initially slow and then erratic response to the pandemic, together with the president's hope in late February 2020 that a "miracle" might eradicate the virus two weeks before he announced a national emergency, are clear signs that these panic and planning cycles not only illustrate the American past but also the likely American future.[5]

For many of the book's primary sources I discuss domestic policy documents held at the thirteen National Archives and Records Administration presidential libraries, from Herbert Hoover to George W. Bush, plus the independent Woodrow Wilson and Calvin Coolidge libraries in Staunton, Virginia, and Northampton, Massachusetts. I have also consulted holdings in the History of Medicine division of the National Library of Medicine in Bethesda, Maryland; the Records of the Public Health Service, 1912–68 (Record Group 90) at the National Archives, College Park, Maryland; and the papers of the Committee on Drug

Addiction and Narcotics at the National Academy of Sciences archives in Washington, DC.

To complement these federal-level sources I draw on regional archives, national and local newspaper reporting, and firsthand and documentary accounts that, when read together, are a reminder that the national story cannot ignore those whom health crises affect the most. I flank these historical sources, on the one side, by statistical reports and longitudinal surveys that offer a detached scientific perspective and, on the other, by creative and imaginative written and visual texts that give legibility and visibility to crises by offering personal and shared stories, sometimes during a state of emergency and sometimes in the rearview mirror and with historical parallels in mind. This range of texts allows me to balance the empirical and experiential aspects of health and illness and to consider the diverse medical, political, and cultural sources that contour their public understanding. It also enables me to examine health crises from the outside in and from the inside out, so as to address what the editors of the 2012 *Precarious Prescriptions* volume call "the pursuit of health as [it is] experienced and fought out within multiple arenas of everyday life."[6]

Introduction

1918

Woodrow Wilson, Crisis,
and the Arc of Public Health

On July 1, 1918, during a summer that saw the United States Armed Services sending more troops to strengthen the western front in Europe, President Woodrow Wilson released a short but consequential executive order concerning the US Public Health Service. While most eyes were focusing on the war effort, Wilson was looking to streamline and professionalize the nation's domestic affairs. On the recommendation of his surgeon general of public health, Dr. Rupert Blue, Wilson ordered that "all sanitary or public health activities carried on by an executive bureau, agency, or office, especially created for or concerned in the prosecution of the existing war, shall be exercised under the supervision and control of the Secretary of the Treasury."[1] The development of a public health service began 120 years earlier when President John Adams established a Marine Hospital Service to raise funds to care for sick seamen and to build hospitals in river and port cities by taxing sailors' wages 20 cents per month. The role of the service within the Treasury Department broadened in 1870 in an effort to improve sanitation and curb infectious disease by means of quarantine and disinfection. It was retitled the Public Health and Marine Hospital Service in 1902, and its name was shortened to the Public Health Service ten years later. Wilson's executive order of July 1918 went further than ever before to ensure the service had a central role in the life of the nation and would work collaboratively with state and local health departments, as Congress had approved it should in 1902 when it also passed the Biologics Control Act to regulate vaccines and antitoxins.[2]

However, all was not well in summer 1918, even though US and French troops were counterattacking the Germans in the European war zone. At home, members of the American Public Health Association (now approaching its fiftieth year) viewed the improvement of public health in idealistic terms, not just for "the strenuous times" of war "in which we are now living" but also for building "robust citizens of tomorrow."[3] Secretary of the Treasury William Gibbs McAdoo (Wilson's son-in-law) was not so idealistic. McAdoo wrote to President Wilson a few weeks before the article appeared in the *American Journal of Public Health* to warn him that "the situation regarding public health work in this country is serious and is steadily becoming worse...due to an acute shortage of sanitary and medical personnel and an impending disintegration of the Federal, State and local health organizations."[4] High on the list of problems was poor inner-city sanitation, a critical issue that led Theodore Roosevelt to sign the Pure Food and Drug Act and the Federal Meat Inspection Act in 1906, the same year that Upton Sinclair (an advocate of "new hygiene") graphically portrayed the unsanitary conditions and poor health of Chicago meatpackers in his muckraking novel *The Jungle.*[5] Opinions were divided on who was accountable for public health: Wilson believed that local authorities should take primary responsibility for sanitation and hospital conditions, whereas some medical leaders thought this was the moment to launch a national health department.[6]

Wilson's first year in the White House appeared to be quiet on the medical front, yet a number of health-related issues were escalating behind the scenes. For example, in December 1914 Congress passed the Harrison Narcotics Tax Act to prevent the distribution of opium and curb cocaine addiction by limiting the opium content of domestic products. The Harrison Act was not what the American Medical Association (AMA) had hoped for in its mission to eradicate quackery and improve health care and medical education, including AMA's endorsement of the landmark Flexner Report, *Medical Education in the United States and Canada*, which pressed for a modernization of facilities.[7] Rupert Blue and AMA leaders worried there was a degree of "uncertainty and indefiniteness as to just what the [Harrison] law really means and how its provisions will be applied," especially as the law enforcement and public health aspects of the legislation seemed to be in tension with each other.[8] This period of uncertainty with respect to the new law lingered for four years, until a 1919 amendment prevented physicians from prescribing narcotics to addicts, followed by the Anti-Heroin Act five years later that outlawed the chemical synthesis of narcotics.

Perhaps the most urgent of the health challenges was the spread of venereal disease in the armed forces. The response to this challenge was the Chamberlain-Kahn Act of July 1918, the formation of a new Division of Venereal Diseases in the Public Health Service to oversee extra-cantonment zones for the treatment of venereal disease, and federal grants for the forty-eight states, including a fifth of $4 million of new appropriations directed toward improving sex education.[9] The health education campaign included a 1918 War Department film *Fit to Fight* (which blended "clear statement, impressive emotional appeal, inspiration, action, moral incentive, and...genuine entertainment"), "Keeping Fit" exhibits targeted at teenage boys (these 1919–22 Public Health Service and the American Social Hygiene Association exhibits were seen by over two million Americans), a surgeon general's warning of December 1918 that the "scourge" was likely to spread if demobilized soldiers did not show restraint ("the time from now on is the most critical of all"), and interventionist measures aimed at women who could be examined involuntarily if suspected of carrying a sexually transmitted disease.[10] These campaigns were fueled by fear and anxiety, leading Montana lawmakers to respond to the Chamberlain-Kahn Act by stating that "syphilis, gonorrhoea and chancroid" are "contagious, infectious, communicable and dangerous to the public health" and by making it "unlawful for anyone infected with these diseases...to expose another person to infection."[11]

Such responses suggested that crisis, or at least the fear of crisis, was the key stimulus for the Wilson administration to invest in health programs. In this respect, Wilson's July 1, 1918, executive order reprised President Grover Cleveland's annual message of 1894 delivered in response to a series of hookworm crises in the South. In this speech, Cleveland proclaimed that "the inauguration of a national board of health," in collaboration with local health boards, was a necessity as a "precaution against contagious disease and in the interest of the safety and health of our people" and a source of "constant and authentic information concerning the health of foreign countries and all parts of our own country."[12] In 1879, Rutherford Hayes introduced a temporary National Board of Health to help track disease following a yellow fever outbreak in Mississippi, but this experiment lasted for only four years due to disagreements about whether the governance of health should sit at the federal or state level.[13]

Cleveland's picture of a disjointed system was at odds with the growing optimism that modern medicine could eradicate disease. Coordinated planning was necessary, such as the Treasury Department's effort to give manufacturers involved in the war effort free smallpox and typhoid fever vaccinations for their workers.[14] However, each time a reform group argued for a federal public health department (such as a 1912 campaign by the Committee of One Hundred on National Health), their proposals failed to gain traction in Congress, even though President William Taft had championed a Bureau of Health in 1910 for "the preservation of public health."[15] In fact, despite periodic calls by the White House and reform groups for an "omnibus health agency" that could work in tandem with the Public Health Service, it was not until 1953 that the Department of Health, Education, and Welfare was formed in an effort to "give the human problems of our people the highest priority."[16] This cabinet-level initiative followed earlier attempts at government reform: during the Hoover administration to more tightly coordinate federal public health activities; in the mid-1930s to interlink health and welfare in the hope that this would lead to what President Franklin Roosevelt called "complete coordination of the Government's activities in the health field"; and a proposal in the aftermath World War II to form a department of health, education, and security.[17]

It is difficult to argue that Franklin Roosevelt's vision of "complete coordination" has ever been realized, despite the aims of the organizers of a July 1938 National Health Conference to put momentum behind Roosevelt's goal of a "national program of action" and to enhance health promotional campaigns, such as the National Negro Health Week that had been an annual event since April 1915.[18] A year after the conference, Bertram M. Bernheim, a professor of surgery at Johns Hopkins University, claimed that despite advances in laboratory science "modern medicine has outgrown the structure erected to house it." To fix this, Bernheim argued that "a national public health policy" was required that could be "directed toward all groups of the population" by means of a "functional consolidation of all federal health and medical activities, preferably under a separate department."[19]

The lack of long-term federal strategy that Bernheim bemoaned is a major reason why health reform has tended to be piecemeal in the century since 1918. The Chamberlain-Kahn Act, for example, laid the groundwork for research into venereal disease at the Hygienic Laboratory in Washington, DC, a precursor to the more expansive National Institutes of Health that was formed in 1930. Yet health was not the primary focus of the legislation. Instead, it sought to police prostitution in an effort to ensure that contagion did not spread through the US Army, reinforcing President Wilson's proclamation that soldiers should be "good men" who are "fit and straight in everything and pure and clean through and through."[20] And, at a time when the American Association for Labor Legislation was pitching for a better insurance deal for sick workers, Wilson simply instructed Rupert Blue to inspect sanitary conditions to gauge how the nation was "safeguarding the health of workers" compared to Europe.[21]

Unsurprisingly, the Wilson administration had its eye on social hygiene in light of antispitting laws in the 1890s to prevent the spread of tuberculosis, on quarantine practices on the Texas-Mexico border to contain smallpox, and on better public education to ensure that citizens were responsible in their health habits.[22] In 1909, the Army Medical Department claimed sanitation to be "a new science" that would vanquish germs if practiced rigorously. This germ theory circulated widely until advocates of "new public health" such as Canadian bacteriologist Hibbert Winslow Hill started to argue in the early 1910s that medical science should pay as much attention to healthy carriers as it did to germs and dirt.[23] However, not all health issues were out in the open, so much so that in 1918 the editor of the *Municipal Journal* pressed Surgeon General Blue to communicate more effectively to the American people the aims of the Public Health Service.[24] It was odd, for example, that there was no national reporting of influenza in spring 1918, following detection of the virus in rural Kansas. A local doctor notified the Public Health Service of the February outbreak, but not until the virus had spread to thirty cities in late spring did it arouse attention—and then not seriously until a second wave in August and September hit the Northeast, carried by soldiers returning to Boston after serving in Europe.[25] Chapter 4 focuses on the influenza pandemic of 1918–19, but the crucial point is that the juxtaposition of careful planning based on principles of hygiene, medical scientists eager to speak to the public, and a seeming federal disregard toward early cases of influenza, is emblematic of what this book calls "panic and planning" health cycles.

As an uncontrollable fear leading to a kneejerk reaction, panic is not the legitimate province of responsible governance. This is especially the case in the twentieth century when "so much government infrastructure and information stand between populations and unfettered panic," as a 2013 *New York Times* opinion piece, "A Brief History of Panic," describes it, by looking back to panic reactions to waves of yellow fever in the late nineteenth century. Thus, a dual focus on panic and planning can help us to evaluate the effectiveness of health policies as well as to understand better the evolving relationship between federal politics, medicine, and the media over the hundred years of this study.[26] This triangular relationship is often fraught though, given that acute emotional responses are as often fueled by the misplaced words of public figures or incendiary news headlines as they are by legitimate safety warnings or carefully researched health journalism.

Crises can lead to swift action by shortcutting bureaucratic inertia and providing an opportunity to think how to improve coordinated responses in the future. Yet they can also reveal base fears about loss, invasion or disgust that can erupt in different kinds of panic response: a heightened level of general anxiety, a loss of control due to an acute stress reaction, or the kind of panic buying and hoarding that epidemic outbreaks can often trigger.[27] Rather than leading to rational yet responsive measures, crises can provoke what Stanley Cohen has called a "much deeper and more prevalent condition" that stems from fantasies and fears or what "A Brief History of Panic" describes as a "a swirl of confusion and frustration."[28] To untangle these discourses, and set against New York governor Andrew Cuomo's view that "the fear, the panic" is often a "bigger problem" than the actual emergency, it is crucial to interlink historical, psychological, sociological, and cultural aspects of health crises to see how public fears have reemerged—as this book shows—often in repeat mode.[29]

1918 AND NEW PUBLIC HEALTH

With the war raging in Europe, 1918 was an important year for American health for two further reasons. The first was the modernization of the hospital system. The director of the American College of Surgeons between 1913 and 1924, John G. Bowman, was keen to ensure hospitals would never be breeding grounds for cross infections, but in 1919 Bowman also made a grand moral statement about patients receiving honest care as a right rather than as a privilege.[30] This view aligns with the federal government's move to recruit additional doctors and nurses to the armed forces, to make preventive medicine more effective, and to ensure that hospital ships were better equipped so that the "wounded or sick, the officer, bluejacket or marine will be tenderly and efficiently looked after," as the president's physician, Cary T. Grayson, described in a 1916 speech on advances in the US Navy's Medical Corps.[31] John

Burnham argues in his 2015 study *Health Care in America* that this drive to modernization was both technological and organizational, leading to more systematic medical records, new research and treatment facilities, and better training opportunities.[32] Though this did not prevent variability of conditions and standards among hospitals, 1918 saw the opening of the Johns Hopkins School of Hygiene and Public Health in Baltimore, which developed immunology and virology programs and provided research training for physicians and administrators.[33]

The second progressive move was to offer better care and health education for children as part of a "Modern Health Crusade" that the National Tuberculosis Association helped kick-start in the first decade of the century.[34] Its volunteers worked alongside women's reformist groups (such as the National Congress of Mothers and the General Federation of Women's Clubs) and the American Red Cross (of which Wilson was the first honorary president from 1913) at a time when the nation was looking to conserve its natural resources, which included infants and children.[35] A landmark 1909 White House Conference on the Care of Dependent Children set the groundwork for the formation of the US Children's Bureau in 1912, a federal agency focused on improving infant mortality rates, teaching "hygiene in elementary schools," ensuring parents took "community responsibility" seriously, and enforcing the child labor regulations that Wilson signed into law in 1916.[36] Children's health was so important that the Children's Bureau designated 1918 Children's Year to raise awareness of high infant mortality, to increase birth registration, and to expand state medical services.[37] Herbert Hoover, Wilson's director of the US Food Administration, championed children's health in war-torn European countries via his new role as head of the American Relief Administration. But Hoover was not a fan of the Children's Bureau, nor the direct use of federal funds for aid, as mandated by the Promotion of the Welfare and Hygiene of Maternity and Infancy Act of 1921 (this scheme lapsed in 1929 after sustained criticism on behalf of the AMA).[38]

It is clear that in 1918 health politics often had a moral cast. For example, when Woodrow Wilson addressed the AMA in June 1912, the year of his first presidential campaign, he pictured physicians as the "guardians of communities not only with regard to those general sanitary problems which are summed up under the head of sanitation and general hygiene...but of a great many moral problems also."[39] This view of physicians as guardians contrasts with the moralistic emphasis of social hygienists on cleaning up vice and with laboratory medical science that typically requires more resources and patience than can be afforded in the face of crises. Wilson recognized these deep tensions at the close of his speech: "the whole problem of modern society is infinitely complicated, just because it is variously specialized, and it should be our object to avoid the separation of interests...so that heat, hostility, and friction may be taken out and all the sweet and wholesome processes of life may be restored."[40] This description might seem fanciful at a time when an arms race was mounting in Europe and with discourses of eugenics and population control circulating at home.[41] Wilson's emphasis on public health and his belief that it is "our duty to see that endeavor is not swallowed up by the government" echoed the optimism in medical advances and techniques of containment practiced under previous administrations (such as the control of yellow fever when it reemerged in Louisiana in 1897 and 1905), now bolstered by the AMA's advocacy work, the annual publication of vital statistics, the development of local health units, routine school inspections, and the work of public health nurses who were thought to carry "the lamp of knowledge into the front line trenches."[42] Some health officials were concerned that inevitably "public health would become enmeshed in politics," but most thought that efficiency and scientific reason would triumph over narrow interests.[43] Such optimism took its impetus from Progressive-era speeches such as one given in 1906 by New York health commissioner Eugene H. Porter, in which he convinced a meeting of insurers that "we are living in the midst of a great remaking of medical history" that would see a new dawn for the nation.[44]

President Wilson did not move as quickly as the AMA and others would have liked. Following a meeting in Atlanta in November 1916, the president of the Southern Medical Association, Robert Wilson Jr., wrote to the US president to say that "a department of public health with a cabinet head is one of the most pressing needs" confronting him in his second term. He also recommended the development of a "preparedness policy" to address the fact that 600,000 Americans were dying annually from "unnecessary diseases" (malaria, polio, tuberculosis, typhoid fever) and five million a year were sick. Robert Wilson's letter credited the federal government for passing "constructive legislation," but Wilson also tacitly criticized the administration for its lack of a coordinated health policy when it came to "sanitary preparedness."[45] There was no evidence that the Southern Medical Association received a reply from the US president to its conference invitation, let alone its recommendations, which is surprising given that New York City had faced another outbreak of polio just a few months earlier. In fact, it was not for two more years that high-level coordination began to emerge, following the July 1918 executive order when William McAdoo beseeched Woodrow Wilson to increase spending and to better integrate national health services in his claim that "adequate protection of the health of the civil population is essential to winning the war."[46]

Arguably, this two-year period—between 1916 and 1918—is emblematic of other episodes in the twentieth and early twenty-first century when chances were squandered to better prepare the nation for potential health crises. There is always the benefit of hindsight in stating what could have been done better, but in 1918—and in other cases discussed in these pages—signs of a health crisis loomed on the horizon even as Wilson was preparing a blueprint for world peace. Crises can escalate suddenly and can throw into sharp relief inadequacies in leadership and support systems, but there are usually warning signs about the interplay of human and environmental factors that make some communities more vulnerable than others. On the surface, 1918 was a triumphant year. Internationally, the United States emerged from World War I more favorably than European countries: loss of life among US troops was 116,000 (53,000 in combat, 63,000 to disease) compared with 750,000 soldiers and 600,000 civilians in Britain. This was, in part, because the US Army Medical Department had prepared itself for the conditions of war, including extra personnel, a Medical Reserve Corps, and with assistance from the American Red Cross. Yet the fledgling health care infrastructure was under strain on the domestic front. A series of seasonal polio crises in major cities and the influenza pandemic of 1918–19 were major shocks to a federal government that firmly believed modern medicine and purposeful politics would only strengthen Progressive-era optimism.

Instead, I would argue that this 1918 moment is illustrative of a series of subsequent health crises in which panic, planning, and politics intertwine. While my focus is on the rhythm and recurrence of panic and planning cycles, the political sphere is an important third vortex. When it operates effectively, political leadership can mediate between a rationalistic and efficient administrative view of planning (which can often neglect the humanity of the citizens it serves) and emotionally charged rhetoric that can win over hearts and minds (but in some circumstances can scramble senses). This is not to say that such mediation is easy or that a public health approach and the economics of governance align easily. In 1918, for example, the Wilson administration and

Congress, which were focusing their energies on winning the war effort, only acted when confronted by a crisis that could no longer be ignored.

It is pure speculation to ask how many lives might have been saved had the influenza pandemic been curbed in late summer 1918 or had an effective vaccine for polio emerged in the 1920s, but when the president and first lady visited US soldiers at the American Hospital of Paris just before Christmas 1918, Wilson's response and the news coverage masked these health crises, as well as medical personnel shortages back at home.[47] Wilson was concerned about the wounds of the 1,180 hospitalized US soldiers in France, but he found this group to be "without exception in excellent spirits," noting that "only a few of them looked really ill." He pressed on the soldiers how grateful the nation was for their service.[48] There was an element of festive stagecraft in the president's visit, and reports of the exchanges made no mention of shell shock or of the emotional toll of warfare, just physical wounds to the legs and lower body.[49] Nevertheless, Wilson's "very human" response (according to the *New York Herald*) suggested that he cared genuinely about health issues. However, it is also fair to say that prior to the war his political and legislative priorities impeded the development of a health system that could better prepare the nation for domestic and international crises.

This inaugural moment of 1918 set the terms for the sequence of health crises over the next hundred years, a moment that Cary Grayson foreshadowed when he spoke to the Southern Medical Association in late 1916: "We question ourselves on the measure of our preparedness. Some believe we are ready, but there are others who realize that there is much to be done."[50] It is unclear from President Wilson's papers whether he became more attentive to the influenza pandemic after his own bout of debilitating flu in spring 1919, but it is likely that memories of his visit to the American Hospital of Paris prompted him to ask Congress in December 1920 to approve "a more complete programme" of veterans' health care.[51] The establishment of the League of Nations Health Organization in Paris in 1919 (a precursor to the World Health Organization) was an indirect legacy of Wilson's foreign policy, but his second term was sparse when it came to domestic health topics. For example, he made only passing mention in March 1921 of the role of the Public Health Service in quarantining and "disinfecting" European immigrants to reduce the risk of disease spreading, a heated topic with rising numbers of new immigrants arriving from Eastern Europe.[52] The lack of policy detail was in part because Wilson's health was failing in

1920 and in part because he maintained the ideal of immigrants loyally embracing American values rather than recognizing diverse groups with differing belief systems. Given that he had started to prioritize domestic social programs, if Wilson had stayed stronger and his decision-making more assured, he might have developed a coordinated federal health program, though he remained wary of radicalism and did little to change segregation practices or to address injustices African Americans faced.[53]

HORIZONS OF HEALTH GOVERNANCE

In its fitful response to pressing national health issues, the Woodrow Wilson administration set the horizon for uneven federal health policies over the ensuing century. This erratic focus on coordinated governance is often triggered by a natural disaster or epidemic threat, but sometimes it is spurred by a special cause such as Herbert Hoover's interest in children's health (shaped by his orphan childhood in Iowa) or Franklin Roosevelt's sponsorship of the "March of Dimes" polio campaign (linked to his own adult poliomyelitis). Special interests also span John F. Kennedy on mental retardation (stimulated by the developmental and medical challenges his sister Rosemary experienced) and First Lady Rosalynn Carter on mental health gained through her volunteer work at Georgia Regional Hospital and the treatment Jimmy Carter's cousin received at Milledgeville State Hospital.[54]

In fact, personal stories weave through the national history of public health. Sometimes these experiences lead directly to change, such as Betty Ford's candor in 1974 about her mastectomy, which prompted many women to seek early breast screenings. These motives do not always help the national agenda though, while other stories are hidden away when arguably the public should know. We could look to the mysterious death of the "calm man" Warren Harding in August 1923 (probably from a heart attack or due to food poisoning after he had received treatment for neurasthenia in his mid-thirties) or the efforts of Roosevelt's surgeon to keep his deteriorating physical health away from newspapers as he sought a fourth term in 1944.[55] Or we could look to medical racial injustices such as the Tuskegee Syphilis Study conducted by the Public Health Service in Alabama from 1932, in which African American patients were denied penicillin in the name of medical observation, or to the case of Henrietta Lacks, a Virginian unsuccessfully treated for cervical cancer at Johns Hopkins Hospital in 1951, whose cancer cells were cultured to create the immortalized cell line HeLa without the patient's informed consent.[56] These stories pivot on state secrecy, medical protocol, public disclosure, and the privacy of one's own health. They also point to a deep tension between what Daniel Sledge calls *public health*, in which the federal government takes "an overt and central position" (though not always a consistently funded one), and the *health of individuals*, which flourishes or withers (often depending on socioeconomic status, regional location, and educational opportunity) under the "auspices of a complex and disjointed system."[57] Yet there is confusion between the remit of institutions of public health and the health of individuals, leading Nancy Tomes to argue that citizens are often hazy in understanding the *public* dimension of public health, while those working in this arena often feel "misunderstood and unappreciated."[58]

Leaving aside the social and political dilemmas of the early twentieth century for a moment, there have been numerous attempts to develop a comprehensive health security system following the Social Security Act of 1935. But these plans prove difficult to pass through Congress due to partisan wrangling about how expansive or minimal the subgovernmental structure of health care provision should be, and because for some citizens nationalized health care looks like socialized medicine through the back door.[59] The ideological freight of publicly funded health systems in Europe and Canada is a major reason why the US government has worked only sporadically on health care reform, but this is not the only story. Developing Woodrow Wilson's view that medical practitioners are also "guardians of communities," the ideal of American health care carries a deep moral valence. As political economist Uwe Reinhardt observes, health economics and legislative procedures often mask or distort the social and moral aspects of health care, relating to what Reinhardt calls "distributive ethics."[60] Yet these aspects have nonetheless surfaced (albeit in imperfect form) in the landmark health reforms of the Social Security Amendments of 1965, the Americans with Disabilities Act of 1990, and the Patient Protection and Affordable Care Act of 2010.

Fifty years after Wilson's struggle to foresee the benefits of a coordinated health system, Lyndon Johnson embodied this moral task in his vision of a Great Society that had health and education (as well as civil rights and consumer rights) at its core. These twin pillars were, for just over a quarter century, from spring 1953 until late 1979, brought together in the Department of Health, Education, and Welfare.[61] In addition to taking responsibility for the administration of the US Public Health Service, the health department expanded in size and scope in the mid-1960s. Its officials were tasked with improving health education, initiating urban health programs, and implementing interventions to eradicate smallpox, measles, and rubella via the National Communicable Disease Center, a branch of the Public Health Service, formed in 1946 in Atlanta with the aim of tackling malaria and other communicable diseases (in 1970 it was renamed the US Center for Disease Control).[62] As I signaled in the preface, President Johnson played a central role in the campaign to make the system more responsive. This included the passing of the Comprehensive Health Planning and Public Health Services Amendments of November 1966 in an effort to move federal health services away from a "piecemeal" approach and "broaden the base" of state and local health programs to tackle rural and urban poverty and to improve access for all races and in all regions (the subject of chapter 2).[63] Speaking to Congress, Johnson cast disease as "the cruellest enemy of individual promise" and stated that "medical progress" makes it "less and less tolerable that illness still should blight so many lives." Johnson shared with his health secretary, John W. Gardner, a belief that the solution would be to combine better medical care, more effective administrative procedures, and what the president called "a spirit of creative change," which in unison would safeguard not just "better-than-average health" but the "best of health."[64]

However, because federal health care costs rose sharply in the mid-1960s, in part because of the introduction of Medicare and Medicaid to support the elderly and poor, these reforms strained against economic realities. Elected as Johnson's successor in November 1968, Richard Nixon expressed anger about what he believed was the federal government meddling in state governance and the freedoms of citizens. Following his comment in July that Johnson's reforms had done "grave and permanent damage to the economy," Nixon displayed his belligerent side in January 1971 when he called the welfare system a "monstrous consuming outrage" as he looked to disinvest in Johnson's community health program.[65] Backlash politics are not unique to Nixon, of course. They have had a long lifespan when it comes to health care, such as in 2017 when the spiraling costs of insurance premiums in some states left the Affordable Care Act open to attack by Republicans who favored a marketized model to replace a hybrid public-private system that included federal subsidies and an individual insurance mandate. That congressional Republicans attempted unsuccessfully in 2017 to push through Congress a series of repeal and replace bills under the header of "budget reconciliation" (rather than developing a bipartisan health reform bill) raised the hackles of Democrats who saw it as a cynical move that sought to replace a rights-based framework with a market calculus.

To address these acute issues, in its focus on the federal response to health crises as they have arisen in the century since 1918, this book presents a set of eighteen case studies that span the geography of the United States.[66] Sometimes the terms *crisis* and *emergency* converge in public life. We could look to the global spread of the Zika virus in 2015–16 or the dangers posed by recent hurricanes that have heightened the threat to habitat and health in the South and Southeast since Hurricane Katrina hit the Gulf Coast in 2005. Globally, *crisis* and *emergency* often align, such as the World Health Organization's authority to declare a "public health emergency of international concern," as was the case for Ebola in 2014, Zika in 2016, and the coronavirus COVID-19 in early 2020 (a topic with which I close the book).[67] However, I maintain a distinction between the two terms. Domestically, only the President of the United States or the US Secretary of Health and Human Services can declare a national health emergency, though governors can call state emergencies and mayors can call municipal emergencies in accordance with their own health codes.[68] The calling of an emergency at the federal level is in line with the principles of the Disaster Relief Act of 1974, the National Emergencies Act of 1976 (which led in 1979 to the formation of FEMA, the Federal Emergency Management Agency), and the Stafford Disaster Relief and Emergency Assistance Act of 1988.[69] Calling a national *public health emergency* pushes the departments of Health and Human Services, Homeland Security, Defense, and Veterans' Affairs to coordinate activities and redirect existing resources under the auspices of a National Disaster Medical System. In contrast, the phrase *national health crisis* is a less categorical term with a wider bandwidth that spans environmental disasters, organizational predicaments, institutional failure, and the spread of infectious disease. It is with this broad range of crisis concepts in mind that the book divides into two: the first three chapters evaluate health crises that emerge primarily from environmental pressures of floods, poverty, and pollution, whereas chapters 4 to 6 turn to systemic crises of organization and treatment, focusing on epidemics, health care, and drugs.

The six chapters adopt both thematic and historical approaches to health crises to emphasize resonances between types of crisis experiences and the longer, sometimes occluded, narratives that do not fit into neat period categories. Health crises often reveal far more about social institutions, belief systems, and cultural patterns than it seems at first glance, but it is important to stress that these crises are not singular in kind and do not have a typical duration. In fact, there is often a mismatch between the recognition of crisis at the national level and the experience of that crisis among regional and local communities. This is obvious if we take a few brief examples. As chapter 1 explores, the Great Mississippi Flood of 1927 caused crises in different regions of the Midwest and South over a number of months, yet its repercussions linger to this day as rising water levels and hurricanes pose a perennial threat to southern communities. The influenza pandemic of 1918–19, the subject of chapter 4, lasted a few months or nearly two years, depending on how we document it, but the virus had different contact points and consequences as it spread, as did a series of polio epidemics that hit cities unpredictably over the course of forty summers. And, as I discuss in chapter 5, the prognosis of war trauma is difficult to determine, but its symptoms often linger throughout a veteran's life and require integrated modes of therapy and support. This is the reason why my eighteen case studies have differing temporalities: some focus on the moment a crisis comes to national attention; others follow a longer arc that charts its emergence and afterlife.

The idea of crisis itself is not a universal, even though the World Health Organization defines different grades of crisis with respect to how destabilizing they are and their level of emergency threat.[70] My case studies show that there is always something revelatory about a crisis, even if the moment of clarity is quickly lost, but they also raise questions about who has the authority to label a crisis—and to what end. Activists might evoke a crisis to make visible hidden health problems or to demand that authorities invest more health dollars; government officials may call for a state of emergency to bypass regular constitutional procedures or in an effort to assume greater powers; and health organizations may reach for the term when resources are tight or when they detect a looming epidemic. Yet, moments of evasion or silence when authorities do not speak out are often as politicized as the decision to call out a crisis. This is especially the case because the rhetoric of crisis is often in tension with its revelatory potential, as is evident in Donald Trump's obfuscating habit of using the word *disaster* in an idiomatic sense regardless of the magnitude of the matter.[71] We might take this as an instance of what leftist critic Naomi Klein calls a "shock doctrine" in which apocalyptic language becomes a smoke screen for "pro-corporate policies" that intensify vulnerabilities by widening rather than narrowing economic divides. Adopting such a perspective might also lead us to agree with Klein that we are now in a state of perpetual crisis: "ours is an age when it has become impossible to pry one crisis apart from all the others. They have all merged, reinforcing and deepening each other, like one shambling, multi-headed beast."[72]

Serious studies need to resist mistaking hyperbole for reality of course, because this mistake can easily lead to what Timothy Clark terms the "derangements of scale" in that it skews one's ability to calibrate concepts accurately.[73] The danger of casting health threats in apocalyptic language is that these terms tend to exaggerate or enflame a critical situation that demands speedy yet deliberative action, using data to model the scale and likely trajectory of the crisis in order to devise a proportionate response. Such an impulse to label just about everything a *disaster* no matter its scale is a version of what sociologist Stanley Cohen calls a "panic discourse," or what psychologist Albert Ellis describes as an urge to "awfulize" (in which irrational emotions mask or distort purposeful plans) and "catastrophize" (where a fantasy of impending doom plays out as negative wish fulfilment).[74]

The fact that this discursive level carries so much psychological freight is one reason why the chapters move intertextually between different types of source material with the aim of better calibrating the rhetoric and reality of crises. To this end, I draw on government documents and newspaper accounts as crucial historical sources for my case studies. In addition, I span a range of cultural texts in which writers, filmmakers, artists, and musicians have explored the experiential language of crisis to reveal how the broad sphere of public health should be as much about thoughtful reflection as about intervention.

CRISIS CYCLES AND COMMUNICATION CHANNELS

The six chapters of the book address each of the decades in this hundred years of public health, but the crisis cycles have arguably moved faster since the 1970s at a time when economic conditions were giving rise to what German economist Wolfgang Streeck calls a "conflict of distribution."[75] Debates about equal distribution of resources go back to the early days of the Republic, but they have become more strained in recent decades, due in part to an erosion of confidence in national leadership and increasing polarization in Congress. These crisis cycles also link to the shift in the 1970s to a more disorganized and fragmented phase of capitalism, at a time when major news outlets were extending their coverage by hiring journalists to probe complex social, political, and cultural factors beyond mere reporting.[76]

Public figures on the right assert that state deregulation and market choice are the answers to better health care. Yet the crisis of late capitalism plays a major role in the most recent of my case studies, linked to environmental crises in the first half of the book and sustained challenges to health provision, coordination, and delivery in the second half.[77] Connecting these case studies are two major trajectories. The first three chapters are viewed through the lens of "geographies of vulnerability" in which the locality shapes the trajectory and contours of the health crisis. In chapters 4 to 6 I switch the focus slightly to "states of vulnerability" in order to examine the structures of and access to a health care system that rarely seems robust enough to serve the needs of such a vast and diverse nation. To explore the politics of these intersecting trajectories, I draw on the concept of vulnerability from the environmental humanities as a psychosociological predisposition toward stress and debility that often accompany health crises, in contrast to "fragility," which is a term frequently used to describe economically unstable or conflict-affected countries.

Johnson's health care reforms mark the midpoint in this hundred-year study, but the subsequent period, between 1968 and 1975, is equally consequential. From the final year of the Johnson presidency to the aftermath of Nixon's resignation in the wake of the Watergate scandal, the economic system underwent a critical phase of development—what Wolfgang Streeck describes as "inflation, state debt, market debt, structural unemployment, falling growth, rising inequality."[78] The sustained economic boom of the late 1990s when President Clinton balanced the national budget heralded a return to the optimism of the mid-1960s, but this upbeat mood was short-lived and masked creeping health and economic inequalities that have become more visible in recent years.[79] Most conservatives and many liberals accept that market forces are now "the chief mechanism for the distribution of life chances."[80] However, demands for a fully publicly financed system, such as calls for "Medicare for All" by progressive Democrats and Independents, pose testing questions for capitalist health care as well as revealing how a vertical approach to public health deployed by governments in times of crisis is in tension with a horizontal approach that could strengthen health systems more holistically.[81]

Another aim of the book is to examine the role of national and regional media in communicating and shaping health crises. This focus is partly because the media acts as a filter between public health awareness, medical reports, and federal legislation, but also because the media helps to label a crisis, although often at a point when only rearguard action is possible. Scholars at the Disaster Research Center have argued that "media accounts reporting instances of panic flight reactions at disaster sites are common," but they also note that such stories are "sometimes *acted upon*, not only by individuals but also by officials responsible for community disaster planning and response."[82] An obvious case is when in 1998 an unfounded theory spread that the MMR (measles, mumps, and rubella) vaccine given to infants can increase the risk of childhood autism, following the publication of a controversial article in the *Lancet*. Although in 2010 the *Lancet* fully retracted the article, the rumor was hard to check once it had entered the public realm, leading Donald Trump to perpetuate it in conspiratorial tones during the presidential primary race of 2015–16.[83] However, rather than adhering to the view that the media uncritically promulgates panic myths in search of headlines, my book follows Jon Lee's *An Epidemic of Rumors*, his account of the SARS epidemic of 2002–3, by looking at how a health crisis escalates at the discursive level and the routes by which it spreads.[84] Spanning a hundred years allows me to reflect on how changing media technologies—from print to radio to television to social media—have transformed public health education at accelerating speeds and on expanded platforms. An independent press via print, broadcast, and digital media can help to make a crisis visible, sometimes helpfully through objective reporting, agenda setting, and in amplifying hidden voices, sometimes critically in exposing cover-ups and challenging vested interests, and sometimes unhelpfully in terms of scaremongering, misjudging scale, or turning a complex health issue into an easily digestible story.[85]

With so much emphasis on the visual spectacle of crises, an attendant danger is to ignore or underreport less visible health issues such as the "stealth epidemic" of diabetes and obesity rates that rose 63 percent among teenagers and 54 percent among children between 2000 and 2010.[86] The media is sometimes quiet on emerging health issues—in the early months of the 1918 influenza pandemic or in response to initial cases of HIV/AIDS in San Francisco and New York City—and at other times information with little substance is recycled. On this count, Alison Bashford argues how "the touch of words" is "required for panic to become a phenomenon beyond the individual and beyond the local"—what Jackie Orr in *The Panic Diaries* (2006) calls the "contagions of suggestion" in contrast to "reasonable truths."[87]

Certainly, in the first two decades of this century the public has access to more health information and greater "touch" via television, the internet, and social media, together with advances in telehealth and wearables. In recent years, mobile health (mHealth) services offer portable platforms for promoting health literacy and healthy lifestyles and for enhancing communication between patients and health care providers. However, health information at the broader digital level is often unfiltered, or its messages move so quickly that it is sometimes tricky to distinguish professional advice from folklore and rumor, such as with the practice of masking, which—as the book's cover image depicts—was as resonant during the influenza pandemic of 1918–19 as it is during the current COVID-19 pandemic. This can result in an echo chamber effect in which misinformation is repeated until it becomes dogma, pushing the World Health Organization to tackle "infodemics" that often accompany disease outbreaks.[88] Whereas social media as a bottom-up platform can help tackle misinformation, raise awareness of crisis support, and promote sexual health, it does not necessarily lead to better self-care or bind together a community. In fact, it can lead to social fragmentation or feelings of isolation, especially among teenagers and young adults for whom social media use is the highest.[89]

On this basis, *American Health Crisis* considers two modes of public health information. One is a formal channel that has its source in the federal government through the Public Health Service and the Centers for Disease Control and Prevention as units of the US Department of Health and Human Services. The other is a range of health messages from nongovernmental associations, agencies, practitioners, public figures, advocacy groups, patient and ex-patient groups, cultural practitioners, research institutes, university programs, and news channels. These narrow and broad platforms have their own, sometimes conflicting, health agendas. However, where liberals and progressives are in broad agreement—and the reason why this broader bandwidth is crucially important—is that the federal government does not necessarily act in the public's best interest when it comes to health care.[90] Polarizing politics in Congress and on network news channels in the early twenty-first century appear to support Theda Skocpol's idea of a "boomerang effect" in which one administration strives to undo the achievements of the previous one. This leads to what Jonathan Engel calls a series of "small, incremental measures" followed by "substantial steps back" in which health programs are terminated "in a flurry of tax-cutting devolution and states' rights rhetoric."[91]

I do not want to over rely on Skocpol's idea of the boomerang effect because it ignores the longer arc of public health, both nationally and internationally, conceals lines of continuity between administrations, and tends to impose a macrolevel framework that can blur regionally resonant issues. National governments are compelled to act when crises are widespread or destabilizing enough that they cannot ignore them. Yet this national scale should not ignore localized health episodes that reveal hazardous geographies and vulnerable communities, including the Buffalo Creek Flood that devastated a group of West Virginia mining communities in 1972 (chapter 1), lead-contaminated water that debilitated residents of Flint, Michigan, in 2014–16 (chapter 3), and opioid use in Ohio and New Hampshire (chapter 6), which were the second and third worst affected states in the country for opioid-related deaths in 2016–17. These chapter 3 and chapter 6 episodes made the national news because they provoked divergent ideological reactions from Republicans and Democrats in the presidential election year of 2016, serving to overlay acute local needs with grand political gestures.

This book does not seek to identify an ideologically neutral space for public health, but instead it steers between two divergent progovernment and antigovernment concepts. On the progovernment side, it is possible to view public health initiatives as an aspect of what the Stanford legal sociologist Michele Landis Dauber calls "the sympathetic state" in her study of the FDR administration in its New Deal commitment to reforming welfare. On the antigovernment side, Harvard anthropologist Paul Farmer (based on development work he conducted in Haiti and Rwanda) argues that the state often enacts "structural violence" on vulnerable communities via systems of governmentality and surveillance.[92] My six chapters make use of these concepts of sympathetic state and structural violence while recognizing that the semiotics of "sympathy" and "violence" are as mutable as they are polarizing.

Importantly, I map a space between these two concepts by developing what sociologist Robert Bellah calls "the middle range between the local and the global level" in which public health advocacy, education, and intervention arguably can best operate at the interface of social institutions and civic participation, with a commitment to open debate and tolerance for disagreement.[93] In their 1991 book *The Good Society*, Bellah and his collaborators at the University of California argue that this middle range—"the bonds of human institutions and culture"—is often "a void in awareness, a gap in our thinking at the crucial point."[94] With the recognition that public health often provokes "uncomfortable conversations" (to cite the subtitle of Michael Stein's and Sandro Galea's 2020 volume *Pained*), an understanding of these voids and gaps points us to how a fuller conceptualization of health citizenship can keep "public discourse alive in America."[95] By responding to Bellah's search for this middle range as an aspect of the common good, my chapters examine the rhetoric and language of health crises as well as how citizens and communities interact with health care institutions. I then turn in the conclusion to Bellah's notion of "moral balancing" as a lodestone within an ecology of public health that might offer long-term resilience in the face of future crises, before closing the book with some thoughts on the early months of the COVID-19 pandemic that provide a chastening corrective to overoptimistic public health models.

As we look back over the century since Woodrow Wilson started to piece together a federal plan, it is difficult to find more than a few consecutive years when American health and the US health care system seemed not to be in a critical state. There were crisis moments even during the so-called golden age of medicine following World War II. For example, Jonas Salk's polio vaccine is a supreme symbol of the modern nation's conquest over disease, but the vaccine was a long time in coming and controversy beset its trial and mass rollout, as chapter 4 discusses.[96] In recent years, the US Public Health Service Commissioned Corps has adopted an expansive role in response to disaster situations, such as the 9/11 attacks and Hurricane Katrina, and in contributing to preventive measures against international health threats, such as the spread of the Ebola virus from West Africa in 2014. Yet it is also possible to argue that the Public Health Service tends to work in vertical or response mode and does not always deliver the health education messages or receive the level of federal funding that might safeguard and improve national health long-term.[97] These cultural dimensions of public health deepen what I present here as a historical and political study of the American health crisis as it has evolved over the last hundred years.

PART ONE

Geographies of Vulnerability

Environmental Health Crises

CHAPTER I

Disaster

Mississippi Flood, Buffalo Creek, Hurricane Katrina

It is nothing new to say that flooding is a global phenomenon, and one steeped in crisis. The unpredictability of floods is a major reason why health and habitat are regularly in peril around the globe: from storm surges in Haiti caused by Hurricane Matthew in 2016 to the tsunamis that battered Sri Lanka and Indonesia in 2004 and 2018; from the flash flooding in Venezuela in 1999 that led to 30,000 deaths to a trio of tropical cyclones that hit the Bangladeshi coast out of the Bay of Bengal in 1970, 1991, and 2007. Disaster planning can reduce the chance of repeat occurrences for coastal communities and those living on floodplains, but fragile infrastructures in these areas invariably affect the poor most acutely. It is not always the case that floods hit vulnerable communities, but those already underserved by medical facilities and support services most often feel the health consequences of flooding. This is certainly the case for this chapter's focus on the Southern Flood, which I view through the lens of what the German sociologist Hans-Georg Bohle has called "geographies of vulnerability."[1] Bohle's phrase raises a set of questions relating to health, habitat, and "the interplay of geospatial, social, cultural, and economic" factors that shape what the Centers for Disease Control and Prevention (CDC) classify as "natural disasters," though, as my three case studies demonstrate, the natural and social aspects of disasters are nearly always entangled.[2]

Dramatic examples of flooding run through American history. These include the Californian storms of 1861–62 that saw central and southern regions under water for nearly six months; the Great Galveston Hurricane of 1900 that killed more than six thousand Texans in a single day (as novelist Erik Larson recreated in his novel *Isaac's Storm*, seen through the eyes of the meteorologist Isaac Cline); and high winds and flash floods caused by a cluster of tornadoes that hit Tupelo, Mississippi, and Gainesville, Georgia, in April 1936 that killed more than 450.[3] Predictions about the growing prevalence of weather disasters in the twenty-first century are ominous, but floods have long held a unique place in the environmental history of the South and in its popular culture. The many songs that speak to the dangers of water—from "Wasn't That a Mighty Storm" of 1900 to "Rising High Water Blues" (1927) and "High Water Everywhere" (1929) to "Terrible Flood Blues" and "Southern Flood Blues" of 1937—show how pervasive flooding is in southern life. This pattern stretches back to the eighteenth century when South Carolina was vulnerable to storm surges from the Atlantic Ocean, and as it was again in September 2018 when the slow-moving Hurricane Florence hit the Carolinas.[4]

It is in the twentieth and early twenty-first centuries that the Southern Flood has resonated most forcibly and with increasing rapidity, as signaled by declarations of public health emergencies by the Department of Health and Human Services in the face of hurricanes Katrina (2005), Sandy (2012), Harvey and Irma (2017), Florence and Michael (2018), Dorian (2019), and Laura (2020). A wave of publications on risk reduction and emergency management has not lessened the dangers of "natural disasters," but because floods are always rich in dramatic symbolism and complex meanings they cannot simply be couched in terms of preventive plans and recovery procedures.[5] In this respect, while floods literally cover the land they also paradoxically reveal more than they hide. Mississippi novelist William Faulkner recognized this in his 1939 tale "Old Man." Early in the story, Faulkner's narrator describes the flooded Mississippi River in dualistic terms: it has a "flat and motionless steel-colored sheet" surface caused by heavy sedimentation, "from beneath which came a deep faint subaquean rumble which... sounded like a subway train passing far beneath the street and which inferred a terrific and secret speed."[6] Faulkner's description of a hidden reality that has a "secret speed" is useful for thinking through the public health consequences of flooding. These effects offer what environmental historian Ari Kelman calls "a chance to measure humanity, to catalog its strengths, and, as importantly, to witness its limitations."[7] Whatever their scale, floods cover the land in "spatially complex" ways, to use geographer Mark Monmonier's term, but they have a habit of testing systems of social justice, the adequacy of health services, and the effectiveness of authorities in providing culturally responsive aid.[8]

There is a debate to be had about the relationship between flooding and southern exceptionalism that, as Martyn Bone notes, feeds into "narratives of decline and endurance, invasion and resistance that have shaped southern identity for decades."[9] Topography is crucial for understanding the health consequences of floods, posing questions about local hazards and the ability of emergency responders to work effectively in pressure situations and in spaces that are often difficult to access. Disaster mythology can obscure the actual lived experience of a crisis and its aftermath, but, conversely, we cannot understand the sequence of events simply in terms of evacuation plans or damage costs.[10] Floods have an intense materiality that can not only destroy property but also can create a deep emotional and ontological charge in their threat to family, home, and identity. This is a prime reason why it is important to consider the interplay of historical and imaginative accounts. It is equally as important to recognize that disaster stories are bound by certain generic conventions in which the actual experience of floods is often either overplayed or underplayed for dramatic effect, creating what Kate Parker Horigan calls a deep tension between "exceptionality and familiarity."[11]

In order to map the intersections between lived experience, disaster health services, and government responsibility, this chapter analyses the health consequences of three southern floods viewed through the filter of the historical record, journalistic and autobiographical accounts, imaginative reflection, and memories of events that linger long beyond the rising waters. My first case study is the Great Mississippi Flood of spring 1927 that covered 25,000 square miles across seven states in the South and Midwest, led to between 250 and 500 deaths, and established the politics of flood relief for the rest of the century. The second example, the Buffalo Creek Flood, is less prominent in national memory, partly because of its location in a white working-class region, but it nonetheless devastated a group of mining communities in Logan County, West Virginia, in February 1972. The Buffalo Creek tragedy has been called the "ground zero" of disasters that posed questions about the culpability of a local mining company and public authorities as well as the need for health and welfare services to recognize a range of debilitating psychological symptoms, collectively dubbed Buffalo Creek syndrome.[12] The massive flooding in Louisiana and Mississippi caused by Hurricane Katrina in August 2005 has been widely documented, but it remains instructive for my third case study in assessing its health effects along the Gulf Coast, as well as what Michelle Obama calls the "wrenching exposure of our country's structural divides."[13] Winds and floods caused close to 1,600 recorded fatalities in Louisiana, yet residents of New Orleans, many of them African American, experienced complex physical and mental health symptoms relating to infection, trauma, and displacement that raised the stakes of the earlier floods with respect to social disruption and psychological distress. These three southern floods not only illustrate the "panic and planning" cycles outlined in the introduction, they also take us into the heart of the "geographies of vulnerability" theme of the book's first half because issues of fragility and disposability weave through the regional and historical specificities of the case studies.

The level of vulnerability of a population made homeless, forced to evacuate, or experiencing injury, disease, and death as consequences of flooding can be measured by what the authors of the 1994 book *At Risk* call the "access model" with respect to the tangible resources available to an affected community. Just as importantly, the *At Risk* authors note that vulnerability is a double-facing concept. It can reveal a group's exposure to harm but also a "people's capacities to resist, avoid [or] adapt" both during and after the experience of disaster.[14] In response, this chapter not only interlinks a variety of source texts, some of them empirical and others imaginative renderings and recreations, but it also addresses race as a pivotal concept in the history of southern floods. This topic has led literary critic Patricia Yaeger to argue that the "throwaway bodies that mire the earth" in the wake of floods and hurricanes are also "disposable bodies denied by white culture" and prompts Karin deGravelles to identify "third-worlding" perceptions of politicians and journalists when it comes to seemingly remote hurricane-hit communities.[15] However, it is important not to just see the humanitarian consequences of flooding in terms of vulnerable victims awaiting aid, for agency can emerge from tragic episodes as an index of a community's own health resources.

CHANGING WINDS:
THE GREAT MISSISSIPPI FLOOD, 1927

The month after Richard Nixon resigned his office of US president in August 1974, following his efforts to dismantle the health care and welfare reforms of the mid-1960s, satirical singer-songwriter Randy Newman released *Good Old Boys*, a concept album that explores the myths of the Deep South. Newman's West Coast satire is both cruel and kind to the region. The album shuttles between local and national perspectives, filtered through the viewpoint of southerners who are sometimes at a loss for words to articulate the meaning of their place and time. Although on first listen it appears to perpetuate stereotypes of a backward and divided South, the opening track of the album's second side, "Louisiana, 1927," scales back Newman's satirical edge.

Perhaps softened by the fact that he spent his childhood in New Orleans, the song returns almost half a century to the Great Mississippi Flood that more than any other natural or social phenomenon since the Civil War redefined the region. The result of heavy and persistent rain from August 1926 through April 1927, the flood saw 640,000 people over 16.5 million acres along the Ohio and Mississippi Rivers homeless and displaced as it stretched nearly 600 miles from Cairo, Illinois, in the heart of the upper Midwest beyond New Orleans and into the Gulf of Mexico. Newman conveys this loss in the face of an unprecedented environmental crisis that saw double an average year's rainfall in a five-month period, causing the levees (that were more a patchwork of dams than an integrated water-control system) to strain and break against the rising waters. Moreover, Newman also captures the hidden health implications of what Herbert Hoover, President Coolidge's secretary of commerce and the leader of the relief effort, called the "greatest peace time calamity."[16]

Following an elegiac string prologue that evokes the music of the Old South, Newman's vocal enters to piano accompaniment and a spare bass that capture the bewilderment of a poor resident of Evangeline Parish, Louisiana, who in a cracked voice describes the disappearance of his home, now submerged under six feet of water. Given that Newman could have picked or invented another place in the Delta, it is significant that it is not somewhere geographically closer to the Mississippi River (the main town in the parish, Ville Platte, is 50 miles from the river's western bank). Instead, he chooses a parish that shares its name with Henry Wadsworth Longfellow's 1847 popular narrative poem "Evangeline," which relates the expulsion in the previous century of French descendants, the Acadians, from Nova Scotia. Whereas Longfellow's poem has an epic questing theme—the heroine spends her life searching for her fiancé Gabriel after being exiled from Acadia by British troops—Newman's song is marked by regional loss and disorientation. They are both tragic stories. After traveling to the Deep South, Longfellow's Evangeline eventually finds Gabriel, now an old man close to death, in an alms house in Philadelphia. In Newman's song, Evangeline, despite being a recently founded parish, is sharing in the collective regional trauma of a natural disaster with a nonnatural twist. A spare song of fewer than two hundred words, "Louisiana, 1927," via its stark date and the immensity of the flood, carries similar historical and mythical freight to Longfellow's "Evangeline."

The song is both historical and ahistorical. Rather than reinforcing the precise context of the title, it begins colloquially—"What has happened down here is the winds have changed"—as the unnamed inhabitant of Evangeline documents the rain and river water that submerge the parish streets. His cadence is marked by repetition—"rained real hard and rained for a real long time"; "the river rose all day, the river rose all night"—that inflects what seems to be the inevitability of a flood that uprooted communities miles from the Mississippi River. Striking a pragmatic tone, he comments that while "some people got lost in the flood" others "got away alright," although where and in what shape we do not know. The second verse pictures the flood as an invasive force breaking through "clear down to Plaquemines," a parish 150 miles southeast of Evangeline that was devastated when engineers blasted the Caernarvon levee on April 29, 1927, in an effort to save New Orleans from severe flooding. Hidden in these colloquial words is a complex historical and geographical story that profoundly affected the livelihood of many river communities such that the relief effort and the legislative action that led to the passing of the Flood Control Act of 1928 proved insufficient, or at least belated.

This geographical reference marks a subtle shift as it quietly evokes civil rights violations in Plaquemines during the middle years of the century that resulted in the disenfranchisement of African American voters in the parish until 1967.[17] The second verse also makes us rethink the song's opening lines, which introduce us to President Coolidge and a "little fat man with a notepad in his hand," a figure that could either be an unnamed federal bureaucrat or Hoover himself who as chair of a special presidential committee led the American Red Cross relief effort in late April 1927, and for nearly four months traveled in a Pullman railcar through the South. Whatever the identity of these two figures, political intrusion from the north preoccupies the speaker, tinged by a sense of bewilderment that nothing was happening nationally until a fierce storm over the Easter period forced Coolidge to act.[18]

That is not to say that Hoover's efforts were unappreciated, especially in comparison to Coolidge, who did not visit any southern towns himself despite being the honorary president of the American Red Cross and calling the mission "one of the finest chapters in American history."[19] The president was keen not to establish a precedent of leading the disaster-relief effort or to acknowledge that the flood control plan that stemmed from the Mississippi River Commission (est. 1879) might have been refined years earlier. In this vein, the *Times-Picayune* reported that Coolidge "believed the attention of the country would be centered more forcibly on the disaster" if he visited the region.[20] In contrast to Coolidge's reluctance to release funds despite a significant federal surplus, Hoover's role as a figurehead for the relief effort enhanced his reputation. This included high praise from the state of Mississippi for his role in

> heartening the people, directing the work of rescue, organizing, planning to alleviate the immediate sufferings if the sick, the hungry, the homeless, restoring hope in the future by establishing credit, turning his genius for economics and humanitarianism to the problems of restoring a desolate people and country to prosperity and productiveness, working day and night, unceasingly with devotion, patience, insight, sympathy and wisdom.[21]

This praise chimed with newspaper reports of the previous spring in which Hoover's organizing skills were bolstered by a "nationwide confidence in his ability and capacity."[22]

Despite his focus on commerce, Hoover's work in directing the relief effort in Belgium during the war honed the pragmatic approach he adopted as the director of Woodrow Wilson's Food Administration, while his childhood as an orphan in Iowa and Oregon helped shape his commitment to children's and public health. These elements are evident in his March 1929 inaugural speech in which Hoover proclaimed that a "public health service should be as fully organized and as universally incorporated into our governmental system as is public education. The returns are a thousandfold in economic benefits, and infinitely more in reduction of suffering and promotion of human happiness."[23] Hoover focused primarily on the economic costs of the flood—an estimated $400 million—but he realized that health was an integral part of the story set against a battle against environmental hardship.[24] It featured in the second stage of what he described as a four-part flood narrative of rescue, care, reconstruction, and future prevention, but it is also a running theme through these four stages. Such a view may seem to be a manifestation of Hoover's "humane efficiency" and may make us think twice about his reputation as a champion of small government.[25] That did not mean he thought the federal government should simply offer relief whatever the crisis. So, when drought hit the South in 1930–31, Hoover and congressional Republicans argued that state, local, and private funding (rather than federal appropriations) were the only legitimate channels for aid.[26]

Not everyone saw the relief effort in heroic terms. Sally Bell, a New Orleans resident who would have remembered the 1915 hurricane that killed 275, wrote to Hoover three days before he visited the city. She spoke highly of him but also challenged him to live out the promise of President Theodore Roosevelt by building appropriate outlets and spillways, given that the water had been rising for thirty years. Her suspicion that a lobby group of levee board engineers was blocking these plans tempered her view that Hoover could bring a "real sense of relief" to the area. Overall, Sally Bell's letter was ambivalent about whether Hoover could actually help reengineer the levee system, given that calls for congressional help in managing the Mississippi River went back to the 1830s and 1840s.[27] Nearly a century and many flood years later, businesses in New Orleans were fearful that a quick patching-up of the levees would not reduce the ongoing risks. The president of the Louisiana Manufacturers Association, George Long, for example, wrote to his two senators on April 26, copied to Hoover. In the first letter, Long issued an appeal: "We in New Orleans to-day, do not know whether we are going to be ruined or not. We are preparing for and anticipating the catastrophe, as we have never done before." In the second, he expressed gratitude to Hoover, but also stated plainly that:

> it is my regret particularly that President Coolidge himself cannot be here and see, as well as feel, the strain the city is under and the despair of those people in such sections near which it is suggested the levee might be cut in order to save the city of New Orleans.[28]

Some papers outside the region, like the *Seattle Post-Intelligencer*, went further by accusing Hoover of exploiting the Delta folk and preying on disaster "like a foul buzzard," primarily, it claimed, to advance the interests of "Wall Street bandits."[29] Though some locals claimed the Red Cross "did a grand job of supplying the disaster needs," the lyrics of the popular blues song "Red Cross Blues" (1933) criticized the racial politics of the relief effort. Coded criticism can also be discerned in the taut plainspoken idiom of "Louisiana, 1927." Lacking a panoramic perspective, Randy Newman's character trails off after two verses and a chorus as if he cannot evaluate the flood, nor why it had caused so much damage and division.[30]

The flood had already covered three million acres of arable land by the time a coordinated relief effort began in the Delta after April 22.[31] The bewilderment Newman's character experiences might emanate, then, from the sense that the government should have acted quicker given that 50,000 acres of land were flooded in southern Illinois on April 15 and levees had broken in Missouri and Arkansas by April 17. Either that or disbelief that the *Times-Picayune* was reporting on May 9 that displaced residents of Plaquemines were in high spirits and glad "that New Orleans is safe" despite their homes being underwater.[32] This reading of the song is more plausible than the view that it is a direct criticism of the flood relief effort for which the American Red Cross raised over $17 million in donations, a fund-raising drive that did the service much good in the process—as well as aiding Hoover's 1928 presidential run. In fact, during their eighty-day relief effort, the Red Cross had multiple goals: to provide food and clothes for displaced residents in 154 relief camps (or "tent cities"), seed and feed for livestock, functional farming equipment, basic furniture, and to make repairs to buildings "to the point of sanitary shelter."[33] However, Newman's satire might derive from the fact that the Red Cross field headquarters did not move from Memphis to New Orleans until May 25 (where it remained until July 9) or from criticisms that relief was too basic.[34] A retired lieutenant wrote along these lines in mid-May to complain that the emergency supply of white bread was insufficiently nutritious to help the disaster victims in the long term. "Why insult a body already injured, mentally and physically, with food which will not sustain human life," he asked, "for if there is ever a time these people need normal health, it is *now*."[35]

Hoover noted with pride that locals were returning to their homes after the floods had abated "in a better physical condition" than they had been in when they arrived at the aid camps. He seemed to be unaware of the spread of venereal disease within the tent cities that led the Red Cross to call in the American Social Hygiene Association to lecture refugees on sexual hygiene.[36] Hoover's confidence in the power of engineering, efficiency, and self-help was undiminished, but Newman's satire pivots on human neglect, especially because on April 29 Hoover agreed to dynamite the Caernarvon levee at Poydras in St. Bernard Parish to protect New Orleans from massive flooding. This plan to create a breach would have been sound had not the imminent danger from flooding already passed, though it seems that Hoover was unaware of this.[37] So, hints of paranoia in Newman's song might link to a disregard for underserved communities of St. Bernard and Plaquemines who had recently suffered from a hurricane (in 1915) and now witnessed water pouring through their streets and arable lands.

This series of events, though more explicable in hindsight, did not go unrecognized at the time, given that some were calling the flood a "man-made disaster" rather than an unavoidable natural occurrence. For example, a July 1927 article in *Survey Graphic* claimed that planners and developers had disturbed the river's equilibrium: "we have done practically everything we could to force the Mississippi to make us trouble, and nothing effective to prevent floods."[38] The massive relief effort masked over the fact that these devastating events might recur unless stakeholders started to treat the river as an integrated system rather than chopped up into local interests. Hoover's prime focus was on business, reconstruction, and transportation (he persuaded rail authorities to offer free rides during the worst months and cheap fares for goods), yet he also endorsed the health work of the Red Cross and its drive to raise funds to ensure that displaced families received food rations, blankets, and vaccinations.

National newspapers that spring ran headlines like "Hoover: First Aid to the Distressed" as the Red Cross extended its reach by venturing into communities once the flood waters had started to ebb, where they treated typhoid, smallpox, diphtheria, and pellagra, a disease that had been spreading across the South since 1906 and now seemed to be moving quicker due to diarrhea and vitamin deficiency.[39] Over 115,000 residents received inoculations for typhoid and over 22,000 for smallpox, while the Red Cross distributed brewer's yeast, condensed milk, and tinned tomatoes and beans as antipellagra food across eight Mississippi counties.[40] It is surprising that health issues were rarely headline news in regional newspapers given the disruptions to public water supplies and sewerage systems. There were some exceptions. Greenville's *Daily Democrat-Times* followed the advice of the state board of health in urging residents to "boil all water 20 minutes." The *Clarksdale Register* declared "Health Conditions at Burk Basin Are Regarded Serious" on its April 20 front page due to the unsanitary conditions in refugee camps that heightened the risk of malaria and typhoid, and Jackson's *Clarion-Ledger* ran the headline "Urgent Call for Typhoid Serum" on April 24. A *Chicago Defender* reporter based in Vicksburg described tent cities as "Jim Crow camps," despite the relative safety of the lower Mississippi port town that Charlie Patton described as "a higher mound" in the 1929 blues song "High Water Everywhere." The *Chicago Defender*, the nation's leading African American newspaper, was keen to expose systemic racism, but regional reporting typically focused on the success of the Red Cross in pulling 70,000 displaced people "out of the mud" rather than the unequal treatment of black Mississippians in relief camps.[41]

When Hoover reflected on the Great Mississippi Flood in his memoirs of the early 1950s, he barely mentioned race and labor as crucial elements of the flood narrative, especially in places like the cotton port town of Greenville, Mississippi, 150 miles south of Memphis. In his 1997 book *Rising Time*, John Barry documents a dramatic episode of early morning April 21 when the levee at Stops Landing broke eight miles to the north of Greenville due to a breach 4 miles upriver that formed a channel half a mile wide into which the river poured.[42] Greenville's African American residents supplied the backbreaking work as they tried to repair the levee. Their white supervisors behaved like slave-owning plantation masters despite oversight by William Percy, head of the flood relief committee and chair of the county Red Cross, whose decision to evacuate black sharecroppers to Vicksburg 70 miles downriver was met with resistance by white landowners. Many workers were simply washed away when the Stops Landing levee broke, thousands were stranded, and when the Red Cross set up a facility on the levee it was more a detention facility to retain black labor than an aid camp.

Efforts to bring sufficient aid to the town were fraught with conditions worsening due to inadequate sanitation, diminishing food sources, and water moccasin snakes in the flooded streets. This caused what Percy called "panicky people" to pour both out of and into Greenville, the former predominately white ("frantic mothers with their children") and the latter black: he wrote that for "thirty-six hours the Delta was in turmoil, in movement, in terror."[43] This view was confirmed by regional reporting such as a front page column on April 22 in the *Times-Picayune* that Clarendon, Arkansas, normally 50 miles from the river's west bank, was now seeing refugees, "many of them only partly clad," running toward high ground "screaming and weeping" some "for joy, others from hysteria" as the rising water submerged houses.[44] That same April 22 issue noted that "wild rumors" and "unfounded reports" were flying around the Delta; it was sometimes hard to distinguish factual reporting from hearsay as newspapers tried to keep up with events as the flooding moved downstream.[45]

When Hoover visited Greenville by train a few days later it seemed to be largely a publicity stunt. After working in both the Harding and Coolidge administrations as commerce secretary, Hoover understood the power of the word, whether it was in the press or using the new technology of radio to the federal government's ends in kick-starting the Red Cross appeal. In Hoover's determination to put a positive spin on the relief effort—with statements such as "the Red Cross has spread out such a net of protection over the flooded area that today there is practically no hunger and no lack of shelter"—he actively suppressed stories of abuse on the levee and within aid camps, based on the promise that he would help African Americans in the region if he was elected president.[46] Sensing both civil unrest and concerns about the levee breaking again, the mayor of Greenville and the local senator repeated their demand for free labor from African American residents. This second attempt to raise the levee in early June was successful, yet racial tensions in Greenville were hard to heal; historians see this as one reason why so many African Americans from that part of the Delta migrated northward. Race does not feature explicitly in Newman's "Louisiana, 1927," but the refrain "they're tryin' to wash us away" speaks to the loss of home that resonated in places like Greenville—a town that has preserved these stories by housing its 1927 Flood Museum in a surviving preflood brick building that was originally a blacksmith's workshop dating back to the 1840s.

Hoover emerged triumphant from the episode, whereas Coolidge's belated attempt in October 1927 to offer a national flood control plan did him political damage in the face of so much chaos in the Delta. In contrast to William Faulkner's dualistic view of the river in his 1939 tale "Old Man," Richard Wright's 1938 novella Down by the Riverside captures this sense of regional gloom and despondency by showing that the dangers of the flood are on its surface rather than in its depths. Wright was living in Memphis by 1927, but he would have been aware of both regional and national coverage of the flood given he was born near Natchez and went to school in Jackson. For example, the Natchez Democrat depicted black Mississippians "pouring" into the town's Red Cross camp and refugees in Greenville "clinging to house tops and trees or seeking a haven on Indian mounds"; Time magazine simply declared "Catastrophe: Deluge."[47] Wright had moved to Chicago by the time Down by the Riverside was published in 1935, a year that the Mississippi River again flooded, causing 2,500 families to leave their homes and requiring the Red Cross to once more mobilize in Memphis.[48] This near repeat led President Roosevelt to establish a Mississippi Valley Committee under the Public Works Administration in 1934, to sign a new Flood Control Act in June 1936, and to call for an engineering conference to focus on effective control of headwaters.[49]

Down by the Riverside is a story of what Chicago sociologist Robert Park called the "marginal man," the difference being that Park was writing about migrants, whereas Wright's character, Brother Mann, is marginalized and psychologically tormented in his own environment as he wonders, "what could be on the ground, what landmarks the water hid."[50] Mann makes the decision to remain in his flooded cotton town with his sick pregnant wife instead of evacuating when the boats come: "He had figured that the water would soon go down. He had thought if he stayed he would be the first to get back to the fields and start plowing. But now even the mule was gone."[51] This decision, though understandable, proves fatal. Mann, who himself is suffering from a bout of flu when the story begins, attempts to row his wife to the hospital in a stolen boat on a river that is barely recognizable to him with its swells and submerged debris.[52] Despite his efforts, by the time Mann reaches the hospital, his wife has died. There, he finds himself caught between the white racist owner of the boat (who he kills in self-defense on his river journey) and a callous army (Mann is shot near the river's edge after the army forces him to rescue the boat owner's family in the flood relief effort).

Wright's story is especially bleak as Mann, his wife, and unborn baby all die. It suggests that Mann's initial hesitation to leave precipitates a flood of encounters and actions over which he has little or no control. It is notable that the final image is of his hand "sprawled limply outward and upward. Trailing in the brown current."[53] As a fable, *Down by the Riverside* depicts a racially and economically divided community—the exact opposite of the heroic effort that Hoover and the American Red Cross projected through 1927–28, but that the often militant *Chicago Defender* criticized for its racial politics.[54] Wright's tale identifies the mythic weight of the flood in the spiritual allusions of its title, though the flooded river proves far from redemptive for the beleaguered protagonist, and the narrative pictures the Red Cross as out of reach despite their volunteers "vaxinatin everybody, black n white" and conflict seeming to lurk around every corner.[55] Mann's invisible heroism and inability to see clearly are in stark contrast to the gleaming silver cup Hoover received from "the colored people of Arkansas," now displayed in his presidential library in West Branch, Iowa, next to a diorama of the flood relief. In a reading of *Down by the Riverside*, in tandem with another flood short story by Wright, "Silt" from 1937, William Howard claims the reader is pushed to see that racism "is as powerful and unpredictable—and as much to be feared—as the violence of nature itself."[56]

Of course, Wright was reflecting back on the flood when the country was deep in economic depression and its agrarian communities were facing a new set of economic and health crises (as chapter 2 discusses). Lines like "fear flowed under everything" speak both to the flood crisis and the fault lines of race and class that had been downplayed in the national press during the 1920s and could only be seen in snatches in reports of the flood relief.[57] Such convergence was especially true in the arena of health, a subject that operates at both physical and psychological levels in *Down by the Riverside*: the death of Mann's wife and child exacerbates his feelings of displacement and disconnection for a town he chooses not to leave. This leads William Howard to muse that Wright's "removal of the sentimental pillow leaves the reader with only the nightmare, deprived of the comforts of consolation of hope, and as unsheltered from the harsh realities of Southern life" as his character Mann.[58] In portraying the tribulations of the flood, Wright echoed Will Percy's visceral description of the river's trail of "slime and desolation."[59] However, it is only amid other moments of economic crisis and health inequality—the mid-1930s in *Down by the Riverside* and the mid-1970s in "Louisiana, 1927"—that it is possible to fully recognize the social and racial injustices that the flood laid bare. It is with this broader perspective in mind that I now turn to two later moments in the history of the Southern Flood, the first of them two years before Newman's satirical elegy.

LOSS OF COMMUNALITY: THE BUFFALO CREEK DISASTER, 1972

The flood that captured the interest of reporters, sociologists, health officials, and psychiatrists in 1972 differed markedly from the Mississippi River Flood of forty-five years earlier. It was, for a start, an inland flash flood away from any major watercourse. The Buffalo Creek Flood not only decimated sixteen working villages in Logan County, West Virginia, but it also proved instructive for assessing the effects of environmental disasters on the physical and mental health of a poor rural community situated over 60 miles south of the state capital, Charleston.

The incident occurred in the early morning of February 26, 1972, when a makeshift system of three dams constructed by a local coal-mining firm disintegrated and gave rise to a contaminated deluge of coal, slag, and dirty water that poured through Buffalo Creek Hollow.

Whereas the Mississippi Flood was uncontrolled and had a cascading effect on the waterways down the Delta, the Buffalo Creek disaster was, as Yale sociologist Kai Erikson says, small scale enough to be an illustrative case "of the contours and dimensions of other catastrophes that take place on a scale so wide that they are hard to get the measure of."[60] Erikson's assessment was shaped by the time he spent in the local community in the aftermath of the flood as a consultant for a major law firm that was representing the community in their fight for compensation. Offering a different perspective from the emphasis of researchers working at Ohio State University's Disaster Research Center on sociological variants of disaster in rural and urban communities, Erikson claims that human reactions to occurrences of similar magnitude are not so different whether the crisis is "a toxic spill, an oil spill, an earthquake, [or] a cloud of radioactive fallout." This generalization pushes Erikson toward considering the mythic qualities of the flood that he describes in predatory terms: the water seemed to pursue local inhabitants like a "living creature" hunting down many of their sixty-year-old frame cabin houses—language that heightens the psychological register that William Faulkner and Richard Wright use to explore the drama of the Mississippi River Flood.[61] Reflecting on the Logan County flood a year later, two scholars of the Disaster Research Center drew on Erikson's account, but they resisted his emotive language because it played into a "panic myth" that conflicted with the fact that most Buffalo Creek residents stayed put rather than fleeing.[62]

The breach in the creek was the result of fifteen years of slag deposits in Middle Fork Hollow that had formed a substantial barrier (forty-five feet high and six hundred feet wide) upstream from Saunders, the nearest of the Buffalo Creek villages, northeast of the Kentucky border. Behind the pile of slag had grown a fourteen-acre settling pond containing 132 million gallons of contaminated water hemmed in by three dams. The Buffalo Mining Company was prohibited from dumping this black sludge in nearby rivers, and the theory of a settling pond was that the sediment would sink to the bottom so that the cleaner water could be filtered off. If the waters of the Mississippi River in 1927 seemed to be black (as Wright depicts in *Down by the Riverside*), then this water was pitch black: residents described it as "a black ocean," and a journalist pictured the refuse dam and reservoir as a "pool of gravy in a mound of mashed potato."[63]

The nation's fourth largest coal producing company, Pittston, acquired the Buffalo Mining Company in 1970 in spite of its checkered safety history. Inspections in the early weeks of 1972 led to no concrete action until daybreak February 26, when the Logan sheriff's office issued warnings about rising water. This came too late. By 8 a.m., two of the three dams collapsed from the softened slag heap due to a combination of rain and snow causing a tidal wave that poured into the narrow creek, accompanied by smoke and explosions as it completely obliterated the village of Saunders. In three hours, the flood killed 125 people, injuring a thousand more and making four thousand homeless, covering the valley in coal debris and sludge.[64]

The temptation is to focus exclusively on the dramatic flooding of February 26, 1972, but Erikson also analyzed its aftermath in both psychological and sociological terms. The total and partial submergence of the sixteen villages along the creek provoked feelings of bewilderment, destitution, and apathy as well as for some residents a desire to start over—what Erikson calls "old mountain strengths" in his 1976 book *Everything in Its Path*. The "unbroken line of settlement" of the villages formed, in Erikson's mind, a linear community that was united in a common way of life, but this belied the fact that the population had dropped significantly from out-migration due to limited opportunities beyond coal mining.[65] This economically fragile existence led Erikson to muse in a later edition of *Everything in Its Path* that such disasters "probe" the landscape, rooting out the most vulnerable populations, not because of an angry God but due to the fact that "the most disadvantaged...are most likely to be located in harm's way."[66] This expression of a geography of vulnerability not only links the Buffalo Creek disaster to the displaced communities of the Mississippi Delta in 1927 but also to the aftermath of Hurricane Katrina in 2005, as the third case study reveals.

Just as vulnerable working communities suffer the most material loss relative to their income in the face of such disasters, so they are arguably more susceptible to emotional harm whether it is in the form of anxiety, depression, or psychological complications linked to physical ailments and material loss. However, the "loss of communality" and a dismantling of the "furniture of self" propels Erikson's study.[67] This is not to privilege one survivor's story over others but to give voice to a region that is largely invisible in the national news cycle. Published

four years after the flooding, *Everything in Its Path* attempts to recon-
nect with those who left the region out of necessity or out of personal
choice when a substantial court settlement was eventually agreed two
years later. It was less a natural disaster that, however bewildering, can
be put in its place, and more that human failure had left this working
community living in "a peripheral region" distrustful that anyone was
looking out for them, particularly as mining companies had been exploiting their workers in West Virginia and Kentucky for decades.[68] On
this count, the Buffalo Creek Flood is a more obvious illustration than
the Mississippi River Flood of disaster as plunder based on greed and
a lack of care.

Perhaps inspired by his father Erik Erikson's efforts to identify psychological polarities that can explain life stages, Kai Erikson starts
from generalities—a people "wounded in spirit" and a community that
"seems muted and dulled"—before introducing specific stories.[69] Erikson himself conducted the oral interviews that feature in *Everything in
Its Path*, but he was aware of his outsider status as a Yale sociologist
and son of the famous child psychologist. He was wary about translat-
ing the idiom and idiosyncratic phrasing of the testimonies of the Appalachians, yet he also felt strong empathy for the Appalachians as an
underserved community and a "resource colony" of timber and coal,
to use a more recent phrase to evoke the subjugation of poor working
communities.[70] Erikson realized that he could not fully understand the
events from a detached and singular perspective. It was not that he lost
his objectivity, but just as the psychologist Robert Coles recognized in
his "Children of Crisis" developmental field studies of the 1970s, so Erikson realized the mountain culture of the West Appalachians was facing the historical threat of economic erosion even before the flood hit.
This makes *Everything in Its Path* both a moving account and a serious
inquiry that balances historical, sociological, and psychological views
in an effort to assess the strength of feeling of the residents but without
Erikson himself (figuratively) getting washed away in the flood.

Everything in Its Path also captures the relief effort that followed the
events of the morning of February 26 provided by eight hundred National Guardsmen, mobile medical units, Civil Defense helicopters (to
provide evacuation relief), the Red Cross (care shelters), the Salvation
Army (free meals), other mining communities (water supplies, rescue,
and cleanup), and public health nurses who administered precautionary
typhoid vaccinations. Some injured and sick residents received treatment at the eighty-two-bed Man Community Hospital, but it was the

Man elementary school, acting as a temporary morgue, where displaced villagers gathered looking for lost relatives.[71] An engineering-led effort to remove the debris followed, plus the release of $20 million of federal funds from the Office of Emergency Preparedness, signed off by President Nixon who was on a diplomatic trip to Shanghai at the time.[72]

A range of health problems emerged that spring in an Appalachian community whose workers were prone to heart disease, cancer, hypertension, and diabetes. It was not easy to keep in good health with pneumoconiosis (or black lung) a common complaint, though local medical societies did not recognize black lung until it had reached an advanced stage, even after the introduction of a federal Black Lung Program in 1970 and the Black Lung Benefits Act of 1973 that focused on disability benefits for miners.[73] The passing of the federal Coal Mine Health and Safety Act and the formation of the Occupational Safety and Health Administration in 1969–70 were efforts to exert pressure on mining companies to be more responsible, though the trigger for this legislation was seventy-eight deaths from an underground explosion at the Farmington mine in northern West Virginia in November 1968.[74] The newly formed Mining Enforcement and Safety Administration assumed oversight of equipment safety and working conditions in the mid-1970s, yet progressive massive fibrosis remained—and still remains—a looming threat for miners, despite the introduction of more effective health checks and X-ray procedures.

In fact, members of the local Black Lung Association were especially concerned that the federal legislation denied rather than provided health benefits for miners suffering from breathlessness and constant coughing, given that health insurance claims submitted by miners were routinely problematic. This led fifty Logan County miners to march in protest to the local Social Security Administration office in January 1971 to highlight the mismanagement of social security medical tests.[75] This example of health citizenship and the patchy public health education in Logan County are factors sidelined by Erikson in his at times impressionistic account of Appalachian communities and the trauma of the flood. So too does it ignore the lack of a timely and meaningful response from the White House. It is significant that Nixon in a July 1972 address focused on the "massive destruction" of Hurricane Agnes that hit the Atlantic coastline the previous month, but he did not mention the Buffalo Creek Disaster at all.[76] Nixon proposed additional disaster relief measures in the wake of Agnes, the costliest storm in US history at the time, with five states declared disaster areas. Yet Congress did not entirely ignore the flooding of Buffalo Creek: the episode informed two pieces of legislation, the Flood Disaster Protection Act of 1973 and the Disaster Relief Act of 1974, which sought to improve aftercare and counseling services for survivors.[77]

There was another side to the events that centered on citizens' efforts to hold the Pittston Company accountable for what they were claiming was an "act of God," but which a 1975 documentary film argued strongly was an "act of man."[78] An investigation by the local governor began in early March 1972 to determine causes and were followed by a congressional hearing in May that sought to ascertain to what extent it was a natural or a "man-made" disaster, given that the three-dam system had been constructed expediently.[79] The hearing included an engineering survey, short interviews with residents, and testimonies from Pittston officials, plus one survivor, Denny Gibson, a Pittston miner and resident of Saunders before the village was submerged. The interviews included statements such as "it is virtually impossible to describe what one sees in something like this" and that the victims "were black from sludge and covered in oil," but most were actually little more than brief third-person summaries, and the congressional record fails to convey individual voices.[80] The hearing concluded that the third dam (constructed to protect the first two) "should never have been built in the first place," and it stressed the need to safeguard "the health and safety of all our citizens" through a "vigorous law-enforcement program." Yet despite this strong rhetoric, the officials at the hearing ultimately did not know if the blame should be at federal, state, or company level.[81]

Because the hearing did not include any "survivors, environmentalists, coal miners, [or] public interest advocates," the local community formed its own Citizens' Commission to investigate the causes of the disaster more fully and to ascertain how to protect mining communities in the future.[82] This commission conducted a series of public hearings and interviewed as many local survivors and mine workers as possible. It gathered enough evidence "to charge the company and certain government agencies with outright negligence" and expose what they concluded was a display of "indifference, callousness and insensitivity to human life."[83] Their report presented damning evidence of neglect on behalf of Pittston and local authorities, but it also had a strong activist dimension in encouraging citizens to protect basic rights and to "transform King Coal, the tyrant, into Citizen Coal, the servant for all."[84]

Gerald M. Stern led the lawsuit for the Washington, DC, firm Arnold & Porter against Pittston on behalf of the commission and won a $13.5

million settlement in June 1974 for the 625 survivors, the compensation ranging from $117,000 to $6,650 per person. Stern captures the
landmark case in his 1976 book *The Buffalo Creek Disaster*. It begins
with reflections on his post-law-school work on voter discrimination
cases in the Deep South in the early 1960s and as a "survivors' lawyer," both with respect to the Buffalo Creek survivors and his work
four years later when he represented the "Scotia widows" following
an underground mine explosion in eastern Kentucky that killed fifteen
miners.[85] The 2008 reissue of *The Buffalo Creek Disaster* opens with a
foreword from former lawyer and US president Bill Clinton, who com-
mends Stern for conveying the "severe mental anguish, as well as physical harm and financial loss" of the survivors that seemed not so distinct
from other forms of posttraumatic stress disorder. Developing one of
Erikson's key themes—the combination of individual trauma (a "state
of shock") and collective trauma (a "loss of communality")—Clinton
compares this experience to that of soldiers returning from active service in Iraq and Afghanistan.[86] Though Clinton's reference to contemporary warfare is a rhetorical flourish, it justifies the $6 million in psy-
chological damages that Stern won on behalf of 150 Logan County
families, bolstered by the psychiatric reports on the disaster that underpinned the case. Echoing the theme of vulnerability in *Everything in Its
Path*, these accounts—published in the *American Journal of Psychiatry*
and informed by Robert Jay Lifton's trauma work with Vietnam-era
veterans—explore the "unresolved grief, survivor shame, and feelings
of impotent rage and hopelessness" that marked what was by then being called "Buffalo Creek syndrome."[87]

The psychiatric studies were based on initial interviews with fifty survivors conducted in June 1973. The studies led to the assessment that 80
percent of survivors were experiencing "traumatic neurotic syndrome"
and in many cases ego damage and "personality reorganization."[88] Erikson describes this in health-oriented terms as "ugly scars, not only
on the landscape, but on the minds of everyone who experienced it."[89]
Common symptoms included volatility, sleep disturbances, hallucinations, grief, despair, psychic numbing (an aspect of Lifton's study of
Vietnam-era veterans), apathy, and obsessions about the weather linked
to a sense of pending disaster especially on rainy nights. On this point,
one survivor described his family as "a family of fear. Fear of rain,
storms, winds, or hail."[90] Apocalyptic thinking and catastrophizing
were common motifs in the interviews, accompanied by a sense of inadequacy and isolation, plus feelings of wariness and vigilance among

families who scattered in the flood. The symptomology of repetition was a common refrain; it was clearly difficult for survivors to move on, especially for those living in trailer camps surrounded by their damaged habitat, and feelings of rage punctuated gloomy and introspective moods. Until after the court settlement there were few emotional outlets for the survivors, especially when federal plans to build a modern highway through the valley (itself a controversial proposal for some residents) and new water and sewage systems took far longer than was originally estimated.[91]

The danger of this kind of psychiatric assessment and Erikson's *Everything in Its Path* is that they were both in the service of the legal case. At a distance from these accounts, an independent psychological investigation, published as *Prolonged Psychosocial Effects of Disaster*, conducted follow-up interviews in 1976 after the case had concluded. This 1981 study did not detect the intense symptomatology of earlier interviews, suggesting that reparation and reconstruction of the valley helped ease the Logan residents' pain, along with faith-based and friendship groups that had a more tangible effect than formal therapy.[92] More scathing, though, were three critiques that claimed that ulterior, albeit benevolent, motives skewed these outsider accounts. Two of these critiques were in the form of reviews published in 1978 in the sociological journal *Social Forces*. The third was an impassioned 1999 essay in the *Appalachian Journal* that argued Erikson's study was flawed on three counts: it lacked regionally sensitive longitudinal data; it peddled romantic stereotypes (Erikson depicts rural residents "tuned to the rhythms of nature"); and it portrayed the community's residents as victims rather than identifying pockets of resourcefulness and activism such as the Citizens' Commission.[93] What Erikson called "loss of communality" was mirrored in the language of "psychic impairment" that characterized the survivor interviews conducted by Robert Jay Lifton and a team at the nearby University of Cincinnati.[94] However tricky it is to dismiss Erikson's sensitivity to the victims or to devalue the validity of the psychiatric interviews, these insider critiques reveal the difficulty of producing neutral accounts of disasters, when neither pure objectivity nor close empathy offer an easy methodological path forward.[95]

If Randy Newman's "Louisiana, 1927" is a barbed elegy to the victims of the Great Mississippi Flood written from a historical distance, then a near equivalent is the West Virginian rock band American Minor's song "Buffalo Creek," which lends musical form to what Erin Eldridge calls the political and economic factors behind "coal violence."[96] The electrifying title track of American Minor's 2004 EP captures the shock of the flood through its powerful blues vocals and the screaming lead guitar, which channels the violence done to the Buffalo Creek communities thirty-three years earlier. In doing so, it self-consciously references both Southern Rock and the blues as well as the lyrics of Sin-Killer Griffin's 1934 song "Wasn't That a Mighty Storm" about the deadly Galveston floods of 1900. Unlike Doug and Ruth Yarrow's 1970s labor folksong "The Buffalo Creek Flood," American Minor do not dwell on the culpability of the mining company nor the reparation claims in court, focusing instead on the loss of the family of an unnamed Logan County resident and on shifting between viewpoints in an effort to capture this communal tragedy. Opening in biblical mode, the lyrics capture the inversion of nature and the health consequences of the slurry deluge: "The sky was as black as the water / And you could choke on the breeze."[97] We see coal miners' daughters clinging to trees and urging the homeless singer to escape as his mother vanishes in the flood. "Staring like a dead man," he sees villagers disappear "one by one," before the band members join in for the chorus to breathe life into the victims' anguished yell "we ain't got no place to go." This phrase recalls the panic in the initial hours of the disaster and, thirty years later, seems to have a secondary therapeutic function in commemorating a shared history of strife and survival.

In its expression of dispossession and anger, American Minor's song shows how the events of 1972 continue to strike a painful chord in the region, given that in October 2000 a massive slurry spill in nearby Martin County, Kentucky, posed a major environmental health hazard and once again raised questions of company liability.[98] The band members themselves joined the out-migration of thousands of West Virginians by relocating to Illinois in 2002, but "Buffalo Creek" is also a song about not giving up in spite of the state's ongoing economic hardships. Many West Virginians lacked sustainable health care insurance, and they faced the nation's highest rate of opioid addiction in the 2010s.[99] Contemporary health challenges are intense in Logan County, as indexed by the loss of a dedicated hospital. The Man Appalachian Regional Hospital (formerly the Man Community Hospital) closed permanently in 2001 and was demolished in 2012, following a fire that made the abandoned building a health hazard.

American Minor's "Buffalo Creek" serves to memorialize the defining incident for Logan County, just as West Virginian author Denise Giardina does in her 1992 historical novel *The Unquiet Earth* and Canadian artist Kevin Ledo does in his powerful 2014 mural of the flood.[100] Ledo painted *Buffalo Creek Memorial* on the street-facing brick wall of a preflood building in the town of Man, 15 miles down the valley from the now extinct Saunders, depicting a young woman holding her child against the backdrop of the black creek and collapsing houses. Based on the story of the nine-month-old Kerry Albright, who survived the flood when his mother threw him to higher ground before herself drowning, the mural is a counterpart to American Minor's song in its juxtaposition of grief and hope, as a dove hovers above the ruins shrouded by a blood red sun. The street-art style of Ledo's mural is a folk counterpart to the somber slate memorial a mile and a half away in the town of Kistler, which records the 125 lives that were lost in the flood, including three unidentified infants, two boys and one girl, whose bodies were not claimed.[101] The public health challenges in the West Virginia–Kentucky border region remain daunting, especially the pollution caused by mountaintop removal practices and recent mining disasters such as that at Montcoal mine in 2010, which led to twenty-nine deaths. Nonetheless, the hope embodied in Ledo's mural echoes the final display board of the coal-mining exhibition in Logan County's Museum in the Park, emblazoned with the header "Disaster Sparks Change."[102]

"SHE LEFT US TO SALVAGE": KATRINA, RACE, AND DISPLACEMENT, 2005

In its many renditions, "Louisiana, 1927" captures not only the Great Mississippi Flood but also the second national trauma of the early twenty-first century. This event fell less than four years after the tragedy of September 11, 2001, and, according to philosopher Lisa Eckenwiler, it heightened the nation's "sense of vulnerability to catastrophic events."[103] Perhaps the most powerful of these musical renditions was by New Orleans soul singer Aaron Neville; he covered Randy Newman's song in 1991 with gospel styling and then reprised it in a duet with India Arie on September 2, 2005, for the NBC benefit show *A Concert for Hurricane Relief*, four days after Hurricane Katrina had devastated his city. Neville's recorded version mutes Newman's satire and restores the dignity of the southern worker, signaled by the substitution of "farmer" for "cracker" in the line "isn't it a shame what the river has done to this poor cracker's land." Neville's and Arie's sorrowful televised performance conveyed the mass property damage of Katrina, their vocal cadence capturing the rise and fall of the waters that had irreparably harmed the city, prompting Neville to move to Nashville until 2008.

Aaron Neville was far from the only translator of "Louisiana, 1927" following Katrina. Performers adjusted and varied the song's idiom and lyrics, including an extended version by local jazz vocalist John Boutté, who shifts subtly between the floods of 1927 and 2005. Boutté's lyrics update Plaquemines to "Lower Nine," referencing the major flood damage experienced by the Lower Ninth Ward, a poor east New Orleans community bounded by the Mississippi River to the south and the Industrial Canal to the north. He also changes "cracker" to "creole" to strengthen the song's racial commentary and politically improvises by updating the line about Coolidge to "President Bush flew over in an airplane / With about 12 fat men with double martinis in their hands."[104] Such versions of the song offer lines of cultural continuity across eighty years and suggest that the region is far from being "postsouthern" in that Katrina uncovered "systemic racism" that had in reality never gone away.[105] These new versions sharpen the view that Gulf Coast communities are more vulnerable when human health is subordinate to the economic imperatives of tourism and oil, or when the poor management of the wetlands and coastal resources compromises environmental health.[106]

These various inflections of "Louisiana, 1927" exemplify the situatedness of many accounts of Hurricane Katrina when compared to the outsider reports of the Buffalo Creek Disaster. That Katrina was an insider's disaster was due to two factors. First, because of the unique geography of the city: what the *Times-Picayune* editor Jed Horne calls "a saucerlike landscape, much of it below sea level" that severely limited access to the disaster zone from the outside.[107] Second, because power outages meant national television coverage of the unfolding drama was initially patchy, and the media faced reporting restrictions when the body search began. However, when the well-meaning New Orleans mayor Ray Nagin started to make ill-informed statements about the number of drowned residents and the accessibility of shelters, it was clear that the insider experience could also be misleading.[108]

Katrina was one of three hurricanes to hit the Gulf Coast in 2005, but it was by far the most consequential of the trio. The statistics are stark. Over 1,800 lives were lost and 1.5 million made homeless (compared to 640,000 in the Great Mississippi Flood); 170,000 homes were destroyed; 90,000 square miles were badly affected; the damage was estimated at over $80 billion; and it put 80 percent of New Orleans under water. The magnitude of this damage could not have been predicted, even though the National Hurricane Center had been tracking the storm's intensity for days, and it had already hit land on August 25 in southern Florida. The flood protection system of New Orleans experienced major malfunctions (the levees reconstructed after the 1927 Mississippi Flood failed in over fifty places), and the fact that the relief effort was neither immediate nor carefully coordinated compounded the distress of locals.

Katrina was a major disaster whatever perspective one adopts, and only local volunteers emerged with credit. Just as the failure of authorities to act responsively exacerbated the symbolic force of the two earlier floods discussed in this chapter, so in 2005 the government at all levels faced criticism for failing to provide adequate preventive measures for a creaking levee system and for not attending immediately to the relief effort. Marking a decade after Katrina hit New Orleans on August 29, 2005, the *New York Times* noted that the city had "become a global symbol of American dysfunction and government negligence."[109]

That New Orleans has long experienced high levels of poverty, particularly among African American residents, and a reputation for poor health are clear reasons why resilience in the face of the hurricane and floods should not have been taken for granted.[110] With over three-quarters of the city experiencing storm damage, zones of safety were few. Evacuation was only relatively easy for residents with their own cars who left early enough, and refuge sites at the Superdome and the Convention Center were soon overcrowded, with the Superdome housing more than 24,000 residents in stifling heat before the evacuation process started on September 1. The health care infrastructure faced massive strain when half of the city's hospitals became inoperable—seniors found themselves trapped in flooded nursing homes, and many medical records were washed away.[111] An estimated 40 percent of the deaths in the city were due to drowning, but physical illnesses from dehydration, food poisoning, and diarrhea were also widespread. Vaccination supplies against typhoid quickly became urgent, and reports of looting and violence heightened the vulnerability of sheltering women and children—though these reports were often racialized when it came to the motives of residents searching for supplies.[112] Volunteers were resourceful in turning public and private buildings into makeshift shelters, but it took two days for most emergency supplies to arrive, and the relief effort relied on a mixture of local health workers, the Public Health Service, the National Guard, the Red Cross, Salvation Army, and individual volunteers.[113] Despite the recent implementation of a National Response Plan, the Federal Emergency Management Agency (FEMA) did not send workers in significant numbers until after the worst of the storm surges had hit, even though the Louisiana governor had declared a state of emergency on August 26, three days earlier.

The blame did not lie (or just lie) with FEMA, because its leaders were awaiting instructions, even though some Republicans were quick to blame the agency as they saw it as an arm of big government. FEMA's response to tackling storm damage on the Gulf Coast was arguably creditable, yet its leadership was questionable, pushing FEMA director Michael Brown to resign a fortnight later.[114] The Republican administration and the Department of Homeland Security (DHS) also faced blame for not taking the National Response Plan seriously enough so soon after 9/11. Nonetheless, only a month before, DHS released an "Individuals with Disabilities in Emergency Preparedness" report that began by recognizing that the country was now "much more conscious" of its vulnerability to natural disasters and acts of terrorism; the report went on to establish principles relating to communication, transportation, health, public-private coordination, and technical assistance.[115] In fact, this report expressed an acute awareness of the needs of those with disabilities when confronted with fire or flood, the dangers of "disorientation, post-traumatic stress disorder and depression" among families made homeless by recent hurricanes, and the importance of reestablishing independent living with adequate health care access.[116] The media did not spare Democrats either. CNN's Anderson Cooper questioned why Louisiana senator Mary Landrieu was praising politicians when dead bodies were floating in the streets of the Mississippi Gulf Coast town of Waveland and as first responders were struggling to be effective in the submerged streets of New Orleans.[117]

President Bush was directly in the firing line, despite his proclamation of May 15 that emphasized the "importance of planning ahead and securing our homes and property in advance of storms."[118] Bush's reaction to the immensity of Katrina, as parodied in John Boutté's version of "Louisiana, 1927," was at best sluggish (to begin with the president thought that local and state efforts would be sufficient) and at worst irresponsible (he did not cancel or rearrange visits to Texas, Arizona, and California during the worst days of the storm surges).[119] It was not until August 31, back at the White House, that Bush spoke about the damage. Claiming that he had asked his pilot to fly Air Force One high "over the gulf coast region so I could see firsthand the scope and magnitude of the devastation," he proclaimed it "one of the worst natural disasters in our Nation's history."[120] Bush outlined the FEMA recovery efforts and stressed three priorities: to save lives, to sustain lives, and to rebuild infrastructure. There is nothing in the speech that one would not expect, including an expression of thanks for the Red Cross and Salvation Army, two organizations that Bush would later call "armies of compassion."[121] But it was his conviction, as he elaborated on September 1, that the "storm is a temporary disruption that is being addressed by the Government and by the private sector," which made it seem like business as usual, with an emphasis on capability rather than a focus on lives.[122] The fact that this speech reduced an unprecedented disaster to what the *New York Times* called a "long laundry list" meant that not only was the speech one of Bush's worst as president, but it also showed that his moral compass was well off.[123] This was compounded by an insensitive comment by his mother, former first lady Barbara Bush, five days later that poor evacuees who made it to Houston were better off than they were before.[124]

The president's tone changed when he visited Mississippi and Louisiana on September 2 and 5, yet the refrain "we're going to clean all this mess up" made it sound like a mopping up procedure rather than a life-or-death mission, and his claim that a resourceful nation would help build an even "greater city" of New Orleans seemed like a cliché.[125] He received a great deal of criticism from the Congressional Black Caucus and the NAACP, and the fact that Bush hid behind the four-year anniversary of 9/11 a week later spoke to the mood of a president who struggled to find the most appropriate words. It was not just the 9/11 memorial service that Bush hoped would remind the nation about the need to come together in the face of national loss. Journalist Paul Martin Lester argues that both Hoover and Bush staged public relations opportunities with children to mask over the enormity of the disasters. Lester takes two photographs—one of Hoover accompanied by children at a relief camp in Natchez, Mississippi, in April 1927, the other of Bush in a classroom of elementary-age kids in DeLisle, Mississippi, in October 2005, two months after Katrina hit the Gulfport area—and argues that their visual effects work in reverse, with Bush's approval rating plummeting to 38 percent just as it had risen in the wake of his immediate response to 9/11.[126] In an anniversary speech, Bush acknowledged that coordination could have been improved, and, reflecting back from a five-year vantage point, he realized that the political capital he gained from 9/11 had vanished by fall 2005; the legacy of Katrina "lingered for the rest of [his] time in office."[127] The Bush administration and Congress never fully addressed accountability, particularly when the court threw out a case against the US Army Corps Engineers in 2008 because there was not enough evidence to convict despite the barrier failures. Nonetheless, given the chaos at governmental and operational levels, the Katrina episode fueled what Henry Giroux critically calls the "biopolitics of disposability" with respect to the lower Delta region.[128]

The political disaster was not as profound as the consequences for residents of New Orleans and others on the Gulf Coast who experienced what Raymond Scurfield calls "post-Katrina storm disorder." This hit hardest the poor, those lacking health insurance, and minority groups.[129] A few thousand people decided to stay in New Orleans, and many returned a month later. However, some evacuees remained in Baton Rouge, Houston, and Dallas, while university authorities permitted students to transfer their college credits from Tulane and Loyola universities to accommodating institutions in Texas and Georgia.[130] Hospitality did not take the edge off the experience of homelessness and trauma though. These feelings were at least as intense as the 1927 and 1972 floods, especially for residents of the Lower Ninth Ward who lived close to the river and at a lower level than much of the city. The fact that the flooding affected poor African Americans disproportionately to the demographic was a form of double trauma in which social vulnerability and race-based injustice exacerbated the plight of those who evacuated as well as those who chose to remain.[131]

FEMA established a Crisis Counseling Program for a two-month period after the storms, and the agency collaborated with mental health advocacy groups to identify state support facilities.[132] But evacuation studies have proposed that FEMA and local authorities could have been more attuned to "culturally sensitive logistic planning" and to the distress of displacement, which was particularly tough on mothers and their children who found it difficult to focus on their studies in the classroom and maintain grades.[133] Many evacuated children in overcrowded Houston classrooms displayed symptoms of heightened anxiety when Hurricane Rita approached the Gulf Coast only three weeks after Katrina. Rita caused significant property damage, leading to 120 deaths and three million evacuees from southwestern Louisiana and southeastern Texas. This repeat threat so soon after Katrina felt very real for evacuated families, and it hastened the regional work of the Head Start program, which focused on displaced children, supported by $15 million in emergency funding that was released in September.[134]

The realities of displacement give some indication of why the health consequences of Katrina were so dire. If the disaster had three acts—"a hasty evacuation, a shocking return to the ruined city, and an arduous path toward the restoration of former lives"—then the cumulative collateral damage for those trying to return to their homes ran deep.[135] *Times-Picayune* reporter Chris Rose's powerful account *1 Dead in Attic* documents what he witnessed in the second week of September when he returned to a surreal, ruined, and virtually empty city.[136] Based on columns written in the immediate aftermath of Katrina through the following winter, Rose captures the bewildering range of emotions that disaster victims often experience, even as he tries to retain his journalistic objectivity. One poignant column from December 6 is simply titled "Despair." It tells the story of a New Orleans woman and her Atlanta boyfriend who returned to the city with hope, only to find their relationship under strain when confronted with "no house, no car, no job, no prospects."[137] They decide one night to commit suicide together. He follows through on the pact, but she does not and ends up in the hospital "in another part of the state...learning how to deal." Rose hears from her friends that she "still has hope," a conviction that may or may not be enough to ensure her survival.[138] This story resonates with Rose's own: he writes fourteen months later how he was losing weight, had cut himself off from his family, and had reluctantly accepted a prescription for antidepressants.[139]

"Despair" is just a snapshot of the escalating suicide rates in the city. A local newspaper estimated that within ten months suicides had tripled; other reports suggest that the trauma on individual and collective levels was close to being an epidemic.[140] The adverse health effects on low-income families were profound, with an estimated 50 percent of residents requiring mental health support two months after the flood. And the impact of the damage did not recede quickly. Within five months, symptoms of posttraumatic stress disorder (PTSD) were detected in 30 percent of residents in the New Orleans metropolitan area and 12 percent in the remainder of the disaster zone.[141] After three years PTSD levels had not significantly decreased, and after five years suicide rates in New Orleans were double what might have been expected.[142] The work of Harvard sociologist and health care policy specialist Ronald C. Kessler, who had led the National Comorbidity Survey in the early 1990s and was now working on behalf of the Hurricane Katrina Community Advisory Group, was especially important for providing health data that aligned with traumatic symptomatology, as outlined in the fourth edition of the *Diagnostic and Statistical Manual of Mental Disorders* (*DSM-IV*). Although statistics from these health surveys revealed dire states of health among residents, Kessler's research indicated that suicidal ideations and impulses were significantly lower in "the post-Katrina sample who were able to develop a belief in their ability to rebuild their life and a perception of inner strength." This assessment suggests that hope, a belief system, and the comforts of home were all important factors in sustaining "positive cognitions."[143]

Ronald Kessler's work informed a federal hearing of 2007 that addressed the lack of mental health care in southern Louisiana and Mississippi, despite telehealth support from the Red Cross and the FEMA-funded Mississippi Project Recovery. Led by a DHS Subcommittee on Disaster Recovery, this was the sixth in a series of hearings that had considered the post-Katrina recovery process, housing policies, FEMA's public assistance program, roads, and coastal erosion.[144] There were elements within what the subcommittee chair Mary Landrieu described as a compelling story that "this country needs to hear and absorb," namely, that "our country's disaster response mechanism lacks the muscle and the flexibility necessary to prevent and ward off disasters as well as to facilitate the long-term recovery of impacted communities."[145] Landrieu believed that the "severe emotional and mental impacts" were the lasting legacy of the flood that lingered long beyond the restoration projects.

Based on Kessler's work and surveys of first responders, local police officers, and children affected by the floods, the findings heard that not only were instances of PTSD and depression higher than expected but also inpatient facilities were in short supply due to the extreme flooding of University Hospital and Charity Hospital. These two hospitals had very different fates. The University Medical Center replaced the damaged University Hospital ten years later using FEMA funds. In contrast, Charity Hospital, whose patients included a high proportion of African American and indigent residents, was permanently closed due to flood damage, though the fenced-off shell of Charity currently casts a shadowy reminder of its historic importance over the city's medical district (it originally opened as a public facility for the poor in 1736).[146] Along with 11,000 medical staff, an estimated 2,500 patients were trapped inside local hospitals during and after the storm, of which 147 died. A startling statistic was that only 22 of 196 psychiatrists were still practicing in the city after Katrina, by which time waiting lists to see a mental health professional extended up to three months, a shortage that was exacerbated by the closure of Charity's psychiatric facilities.[147] Spanning testimonies by health workers, the hearing learned about the urgency of long-term investment in mental health support, training for counselors and volunteers, screenings for teachers and children, and services in family-friendly settings such as in schools and preschools.[148]

A wave of literature on disaster response in the years following Katrina often cites a lack of preparedness and delayed response as cautionary lessons, though this does nothing to lessen the disaster.[149] Around 55 percent of evacuees returned to the city by 2008, but better prospects in Houston and Memphis mean that the loss of community is still felt strongly in parts of New Orleans away from the tourist areas of the French Quarter and Warehouse District. And even within these areas it is hard to divorce the logic of tourism from urban politics, given that contractors sought cheap labor from Mexican migrants during the rebuilding period and also that insufficient affordable housing remains an endemic problem in New Orleans.[150]

Some flood narratives are optimistic despite the wreckage, such as the eyewitness footage of rap artist Kimberly Rivers Roberts in the 2008 documentary *Trouble the Water* (combining video footage of the storm and mainstream media reports), who found that evacuation from the Ninth Ward had a positive effect on her life even though she and her husband lost their house.[151] Cultural accounts of Katrina that are marked by loss—a loss of community or a loss of selfhood—are often fused with a survivalist spirt, even if this is only provisional. One example is the end of Jesmyn Ward's 2011 Katrina novel *Salvage the Bones* (from which this section title is drawn), in which a black working-class Mississippi family await, either in hope or in vain, the return of their dog China who has been washed away in the floods. Though Ward's town of Bois Sauvage is fictional, the Delta location links to her own flood experiences growing up in DeLisle, Mississippi, the town President Bush visited for a photo op at the elementary school two months after Katrina. In Ward's powerful literary account, rather than succumb to "the mother that swept into the Gulf and slaughtered," her already strained Mississippi family strive to find new meaning out of loss.[152]

Two of the most incisive visual accounts that probe Katrina's causes and consequences are New York filmmaker Spike Lee's HBO documentary *When the Levee Broke: A Requiem in Four Acts* (aired on the first anniversary of Hurricane Katrina) and four years later *If God Is Willing and da Creek Don't Rise*, which explores the city's fate, the exploitation of the region (including the Deepwater Horizon BP oil spill in the gulf), and the dismissed case against the Army Corps of Engineers.[153] Lee's documentaries are visual memorials and critical interventions that seek to incorporate multiple viewpoints across an extended timeline. In this effort to capture a variety of experiences while striving for a collective voice, Christopher Lloyd reads *When the Levee Broke* as a negotiation between a survivalist spirit and a long southern history of racial violence, especially in its montage of dead bodies floating in the water.[154] Lee resists premature reconciliation though, even as he tackles a loss of social hope in the city and the economic and racial problems that Katrina brought to the surface.[155] On this level, the film echoes the rhythm of survival and mourning in Aaron Neville's rendition of "Louisiana, 1927." Yet it also encapsulates Anissa Wardi's opinion that these floods link "environmental degradation, toxic geographies, racism and classism" as well as what Jacob Remes calls "disaster citizenship," a version of community solidarity that can emerge out of tragedy.[156]

In the years following the hurricane, New Orleans received significant reconstruction funds, including $71 billion from the federal government, $14.5 billion of which helped repair the levee system. However, what Katrina revealed was that little had been learned from previous flood crises about the need to improve emergency services and long-term planning in order to provide adequate care for evacuees and the homeless.[157] This is the reason why the United Nations has, since the mid-2000s, called on countries to significantly reduce disaster mortality by 2030 and observe the goals of the biennial Global Platform for Disaster Risk Reduction, which began in 2005 as a forum for sustainability strategies.[158] The World Health Organization realizes that disaster health plans cannot be a one-size-fits-all approach because recovery procedures need to be attuned to the locality on both cultural and environmental levels.

These three case studies show that crisis intervention also needs to be phased. At the community level, there is increasing awareness that public health workers should adopt a "multisectoral approach" to deal with the health impacts of disasters and to reduce future risks, including an assessment of the vulnerability and resilience of populations.[159] Practical steps to help evacuate a disaster zone require coordinated action, but so too does follow-up and creative outreach within communities, rather than waiting for disaster victims to seek help themselves.[160] This is in addition to a commitment to remember that victims of such disasters are victims because they are blameless not because they are helpless. In fact, as Hans-Georg Bohle argues, people living in vulnerable geographical areas by necessity develop a sense of agency as they "seek to cope with the shocks and stress that threaten their livelihoods."[161]

If the Hurricane Katrina memorials of New Orleans—the more famous one on Canal Street designed in the shape of the hurricane that contains eighty-six unclaimed bodies (as a "healing space for reflection") and the other on the city side of the Lower Ninth Ward, comprising a section of a home painted red and a series of blue poles to mark the rising floods—offer two healing spaces, then these three defining Southern Floods, taken together, should offer another lesson for change.[162] It is clear that the floods that pushed rivers in Louisiana to record levels in August 2016 will not be the last—what Jesmyn Ward describes in mythical terms as the "next mother with large, merciless hands, committed to blood."[163] Climate change champions like former US vice president Al Gore have argued that steadily rising ocean temperatures will inevitably increase the frequency and the force of hurricanes in the coming years, as Katrina showed in shifting from Category 1 to Category 5 as it moved across the Gulf of Mexico.[164]

In fact, it took just one year after these record flood levels in Louisiana before the Category 4 Hurricane Harvey battered the Texas Gulf Coast in late August and early September 2017, producing twenty-seven trillion gallons of rain in a two-week period. Harvey especially affected Harris County, Texas (the home of Houston and where 16 percent of Texans live) and its surrounding counties where flood insurance covered only 17 percent of damaged households. An estimated 27 percent of houses in Harris County were thought to have experienced flood damage, with suburbs like Meyerland to the southwest, Memorial to the west, and North Cypress to the northwest suffering major property damage from watercourses that rose to dramatic levels as rescue teams struggled to find access.[165] Even though Houston is 50 miles from the Gulf of Mexico and a wealthier city than New Orleans with a much better transport infrastructure, it is open to debate whether the lessons of Katrina had been learned, given that Harvey created an "unprecedented and catastrophic event" and caused $200 billion worth of damages (nearly double that of Katrina).[166] The local volunteer effort received praise for its heroism, supported by the Red Cross, Salvation Army, and the Star of Hope homeless service, 25,000 officers of the National and State Guard, and hundreds of federal medical staff stationed in Dallas and Austin, at a time when Houston city and Harris County hospitals were evacuating patients due to the flooding. Yet on organizational and infrastructural levels, critical questions could again be asked, especially because Houston mayor Sylvester Turner's decision not to order an evacuation of the city to provide flood sufferers with "a degree of normalcy" was at odds with the earlier evacuation instructions of the Texas governor Greg Abbott.[167]

That aside, the oil city of Houston had for years arguably put business interests ahead of developing better flood defenses. One could look to the fact the Army Corp of Engineers' North Atlantic Coast Comprehensive Study Report, designed to enable coastal communities to understand flood risks, did not stimulate financial aid to the gulf states to build better hurricane barriers. Through the first half of 2017, FEMA faced significant understaffing, budgetary cuts, and lacked a director. And the tone of the US president was again questionable as Donald Trump seemed eager to exploit the crisis for political gain, using an emergency situation to cloak a controversial pardon of the recently convicted Arizona sheriff Joseph Arpaio.

The Southeast Texas Regional Advisory Council had established a Catastrophic Medical Operations Center in Houston for such regional disasters, but it was clear that hospitals could not cope with the rising waters, while sixteen hospitals in affected areas were forced to close.[168] The public health story was secondary to the spectacle of flash floods, as pictured in a series of front-page headlines in the local *Houston Chronicle* that stretched to nearly four weeks from August 25 ("Harvey's a Menace") through September 18 ("Harvey Transforms Park's Landscape"), with dramatic scenes of the flooding dominating the newspaper's visuals. Yet the cleanup operation was as troubling as the storm itself. Toxic waters were a major health risk as a breeding ground for mosquitos and fire ants, while the "mental strain of displacement" faced by Houstonians was little different from the trials of victims of earlier floods.[169]

For Louise Walker, who had recently moved from New Orleans to Houston, finding herself trapped inside a flooded apartment felt like Katrina all over again as Harvey gave rise to isolation and fragmentation and the disruption of health services.[170] There were some welcome medical innovations though, such as a mobile health app emocha, which enabled out-of-reach health workers to remotely watch tuberculosis patients take their medication.[171] The racial politics of the Houston flooding in 2017 were a little closer to neutral than New Orleans in 2005. Around 43 percent of property damage in Harris County was to Hispanic households, 25 percent to white, 23 percent to African American, and 6 percent to Asian households—statistics that are roughly in line with the city's demographics. That is not to say the suffering and loss was either class or race neutral though, especially as the cost of repair to homes hit minority families harder, some of whom could not afford adequate insurance cover.

A closer comparison to Katrina, with respect to the vulnerability and disposability, is Hurricane Maria, which battered the Dominican Republic, Puerto Rico, and the Virgin Islands in mid-September 2017, three weeks after Harvey. The federal response to the devastation that Maria caused to Puerto Rico was virtually zero until the media goaded President Trump into traveling to the island (he only visited San Juan, the most affluent area of Puerto Rico). This was a week after networks described the Category 5 storm damage as an apocalyptic disaster to a US territory suffering from the failure of its fragile infrastructure already under strain from high levels of unemployment and health problems, including rates of HIV/AIDS four times that of the mainland. The extent of the public health disaster was unclear for many months. There was a chasm between the official death toll of sixty-four and a survey conducted by Harvard University that estimated a 62 percent increase in mortality rates over three months following landfall on September 20. A four-hundred-page economic and disaster recovery plan submitted to Congress in July 2018 (endorsed by the Puerto Rico governor Ricardo Rosselló) put the death toll at close to 1,500, before the official death toll of 2,975 was announced in late August, based on independent research, making it a deadlier disaster than Katrina.[172]

The mainstream media moved on swiftly at the close of the hurricane season, despite fundraising efforts such as the "Deep from the Heart: The One America Appeal" concert, held at Texas A&M University on October 21 sponsored by the five former living US presidents (it raised $31 million for disaster relief in the face of Harvey, Irma, and Maria).[173] Nevertheless, the forgotten victims of Hurricane Maria haunted the new-year 2018 issue of *New York* magazine, its cover depicting two rigid and disembodied feet on a hospital bed, foreshadowing the many hundreds of empty shoes that residents placed in front of the San Juan capitol building that summer as a memorial to the thousands of lost lives.[174] When Mayor Carmen Yulín Cruz spoke on the one-year anniversary of Maria she rejected the view of the Trump administration that the recovery effort was "a good news story" based on initial reports of a low death count, stating that this was instead a "people died story" and blaming federal neglect that was "silently approved" by Puerto Rican officials. Governor Rosselló took this opportunity to admit the recovery effort was not swift or coordinated enough, but the White House did not apologize. In fact, President Trump continued to dispute the scale of the loss of life in the aftermath of Maria, compounding his comment on his visit to San Juan when he underplayed the impact on the island in contrast to a "real catastrophe like Katrina."[175] Trump's response to Puerto Rico is a prime example of what Karin deGravelles calls "third-worlding," and it is also why a group of University of Puerto Rico activist professors frame the disaster in colonialist terms in their foreword to Naomi Klein's 2018 book *The Battle for Paradise*.[176]

Echoing Mississippi novelist Walker Percy's theory of hurricanes as a clearing away of malaise, Al Gore noted a decade before Harvey and Maria that there is "a quality of vividness and a clarity of focus" that arrives with a once-in-a-lifetime disaster like Katrina. Such visibility is central to a fuller understanding of the public health implications of these three disasters. This moment can fade quickly though, "like a passing summer storm," before the instigation of intelligent, responsive, and sustainable plans and a full assessment of the health rights of vulnerable communities.[177] Even though flooding now seems to be what the *New York Times* calls "the new normal," the three floods of this chapter offer vivid lessons about rights, resilience, and preparedness, providing resources to authorities interested in lessening the risk of global vulnerability within a "flooded future."[178] Yet there is also the danger of historical forgetting that means it is likely that panic will strike again when the next disaster hits.

CHAPTER 2

Poverty

Dust Bowl, Urban Ghetto,
Indian Reservation

Hurricane Katrina was both a devastating assault on Gulf Coast communities and an episode in a long American narrative that links extreme weather, fragile habitats, racial politics, and what President George W. Bush called "deep-seated poverty."[1] In the weeks and months following Katrina's landfall, the Department of Homeland Security's disaster recovery team estimated that "a quarter million houses in New Orleans and surrounding parishes [were] no longer fit to live in."[2] The poorest residents, many of them African American, faced a stark choice: abandon their city for a new life in a neighboring state or return to risk homelessness and destitution. Among reports that addressed the neglect of poor Louisianans and Mississippians, the U.S. *News and World Report* drew parallels between Katrina and the victims of the Dust Bowl in the 1930s, many of whom left their battered homes to migrate westward. The liberal news outlet the *Huffington Post* made a similar comparison when Hurricane Sandy hit New Jersey's seaboard in late October 2012 (after it had wreaked damage on six Caribbean islands), just a fortnight before PBS premiered filmmaker Ken Burns's two-part documentary *The Dust Bowl*.[3] The claim in 2012 was that just as overfarming had damaged the agrarian ecosystem of the Great Plains in the years prior to the droughts of the 1930s, so overdevelopment along the low-lying wetlands and sandbars of the Atlantic Coast made the local habitat more vulnerable to the intense winds of Hurricane Sandy.[4]

Floods and droughts are persistent threats to poor Americans, but so too are endemic health conditions exacerbated by crowded urban environments and in rural regions that have limited medical services. Those below the poverty line are not the only ones to face chronic health conditions, but those on meager wages too, at the edge of that line. In his 2004 book *The Working Poor*, David Shipler claims that economic status is the primary factor in determining health.[5] At the time of the 2011 edition of *The Working Poor*, the poverty line was $10,890 for individuals and $22,350 for a family of four based on Census Bureau statistics (in 2018 this had risen slightly to $12,060 and $24,600 respectively). This threshold is set at three times the cost of a minimum diet and fixes eligibility for the National School Lunch Program and the Food Stamp Program, two federal subsidy programs that in 2012 had thirty-one and forty-six million claimants respectively. (In 2018, these statistics were thirty million and forty million, though this drop is due more to shifting eligibility criteria than a decline in true poverty levels.)[6]

Despite moves to improve nutritional access (such as the efforts of former South Side Chicago resident and first lady Michelle Obama to ensure that school meals are nutritious via the Let's Move! campaign), Shipler argues that many poor families in the South and Midwest, where life expectancy is below the national average, remain "food insecure." The Social Science Research Council calculated this concept of "food insecurity" at 14.5 percent nationally in 2012, leading Shipler to muse that "being poor in a rich country may be more difficult to endure than being poor in a poor country, for the skills of surviving through poverty have largely been lost in America."[7]

In 1997, the year that Shipler conducted many of his interviews that underpin the first edition of *The Working Poor*, President Clinton was calling for "One America in the 21st Century." This manifesto pledge built on Clinton's commitment to environmental justice, to raise the profile of economically disadvantaged minority groups, and to close regional disparities in health care access by 2010.[8] The mid-1990s witnessed the passing of progressive health legislation, including workers' portable health insurance and the Children's Health Insurance Program (CHIP), intended to protect children of families earning just enough to disqualify them for Medicaid. Yet inequality arguably worsened in the 1990s. Based on what Timothy Noah calls the "great divergence," the relative income of the top 1 percent compared to other workers has doubled in the thirty-five years since Michael Harrington gave voice to the invisible poor in *The Other America*, his acclaimed study of the social causes of poverty.[9]

Published in 1962, Harrington's *The Other America* offered a damning portrait of the socioeconomic conditions that pushed fifty million Americans under the poverty line. A long *New Yorker* review of *The Other America* by Dwight Macdonald brought the attention of the Kennedy administration to Harrington's argument that these conditions had improved little since the Great Depression and that, trapped by stigmatizing language and a lack of economic opportunity, "the American poor are pessimistic and defeated, and they are victimized by mental suffering."[10] The publication of *The Other America* appeared soon after CBS journalist Edward R. Murrow's television documentary *Harvest of Shame* exposed the plight of migrant workers—what Murrow called a "*Grapes of Wrath* for 1960" in which John Steinbeck's protagonist Tom Joad was a symbol of all migrant workers.[11] Murrow and Harrington asserted that the hostile economic forces that led two million residents of the Great Plains to migrate west in the 1930s had not abated thirty years later despite New Deal reforms, even if the extreme weather and harsh agricultural conditions of the Dust Bowl were no longer headline news. In fact, social theorist Irving Howe's preface to the 1993 reprint of *The Other America* lamented the fact that average wages had dropped even further in the 1980s. The trigger for Howe's comments was the Reagan administration's reduction in entitlements that eroded the measures that Lyndon Johnson sought in the War on Poverty of the mid-1960s, measures that in part responded to the stark conditions outlined in Harrington's landmark book.[12]

Harrington did not focus explicitly on the correlation between ill health and poverty. However, the connection between the two had been recorded twenty-five years earlier in a National Health Survey conducted during fall and winter of 1935–36 and overseen by the Public Health Service and the newly formed National Institutes of Health. Comprising five months of interviews with 2.5 million people living in eighty-three cities across nineteen states, this was "the most comprehensive study of its kind in American history" at a cost of $4 million funded by the Work Projects Administration. The data was less comprehensive on rural health, comprising 14,000 interviews across twenty-three counties; nevertheless, it became an important source for assessing the adequacy of health services over the following two decades. The survey noted that for families on or just above the relief line, "it is apparent that inadequate diet, poor housing, the hazards of occupation and the instability of the labor market definitely create immediate health problems," and it concluded that illness rates increase as income decreases.[13]

My three case studies return to the National Health Survey in their focus on periods when the relationship between poverty and health was high on the national agenda: the Dust Bowl of the mid-1930s, the inner-city ghetto of the mid-1960s, and the Native American reservation during the late 1990s. In doing so, I deepen the focus on the social determinants of health from the first chapter, revealing how sympathetic federal policies only partly mitigate—and do nothing to excuse—the structural violence enacted on the communities that inhabit these spaces.

To show how this dynamic plays out historically, the first case study turns to the health implications of Roosevelt's New Deal policies that opposed the deregulation of farming and heavy industry that occurred during the Coolidge and Hoover administrations. My second example reveals how "the ghetto" was a common stigmatizing label after World War II—as a noun to describe a segregated built environment and as an adjective to signify the psychology of poor urban minorities, most often African Americans. And the third case study explores how the Indian reservation in the late century became a prime symbol of social deprivation and disease in spite of—or because of—federal legislation over land rights, housing, and health care.[14] Just as the first chapter traced how racial politics are deeply rooted in the history of the Southern Flood, so these three case studies show how economic deprivation not only intersects with racial categories but also how it shapes regionally specific notions of ill health.

Tensions between local health needs, the responsiveness of regional health services, and federal provision reveal that health is nearly always politicized when it comes to the nation's poor. That is not to say in the wake of Harrington's critique that the health of the poor was off the agenda in the mid-1960s. Far from it. Following attempts by Roosevelt and Truman to shift the moral compass on social welfare, in July 1965 Johnson signed into law Medicaid as a secondary plank of the Social Security Act Amendments. These amendments updated the New Deal welfare and health care commitments as examples of what Richard Couto calls a "heroic bureaucracy" that was geared toward addressing social inequality.[15] On this score, Medicaid offered open-ended medical assistance for the very poor and disabled via a mix of federal and state funds. In December 1967, the president stated Medicaid "deserves special notice and gives me special pride," and in late December 1968 a series of public hearings were held in major cities to assess the regional effectiveness of Medicaid with the hope that the hearings would provide "the additional thrust" toward the realization of medical protection for poor families.[16] That these hearings occurred so late in the Johnson administration (after Richard Nixon had won the 1968 election) was an end-stage intervention based on fears that Nixon would diminish entitlements given that he had publicly criticized Johnson for overspending on welfare. Congressional investment in Medicaid has had a checkered history ever since, pivoting on questions about its long-term financial sustainability, but through a series of adjustments it has become an irreducible aspect of federal health care commitment, even though more than twenty states resisted Medicaid expansion in the 2010s.[17]

Here I develop from the first chapter my focus on the intersection of federal health policy and the regional experience of health crises, especially for communities experiencing income inequality, viewed through the lens of historical sources, sociological studies, firsthand accounts, and imaginative reflections. A number of these sources are written by "insiders" rooted in the culture of the region, though often with a critical distance from it, such as the Oklahoma folk singer Woody Guthrie, the New York City–based psychologist Kenneth B. Clark, and the Spokane–Coeur d'Alene Indian writer Sherman Alexie. Location and lived experience are of equal importance here. For example, whereas Harrington frames *The Other America* in national terms, the focus is localized in *Dark Ghetto: Dilemmas of Social Power*, Kenneth Clark's 1965 field study of postwar Harlem life, and *A Raisin in the Sun*, Lorraine Hansberry's sociological play of 1959 set in South Side Chicago. These studies diagnose national and local crises, but the danger is that in amplifying social and psychological conditions the texts at times tilt over into polemic or even stigmatize poor communities as desperate and in need of a helping hand. The countervailing danger, however, is that without such interventions authorities can shrug their shoulders in the belief that equitable local health provision is neither a priority nor their primary responsibility, only taking note belatedly when the kinds of disasters discussed in chapter 1 happen.

Even with dramatic headlines like "Black America's Exploding Health Crisis" and "Indian Health Care: A National Tragedy," the discourse of health crises at the intersection of race and poverty is not always self-evident, although the health crises examined here did prompt purposeful responses from the Roosevelt, Johnson, and Clinton administrations—the first two, at least, with lasting consequences.[18] My three case studies link the physical and psychological health of underserved communities to how alienated labor and economic violence are often refracted through the figure of the ghost, a spectral trope that aligns with the geographies of vulnerability of the book's first half. The figure of the ghost is never neutral, especially with respect to its racial inflections (as the second and third cases outline), but it is instructive in configuring the troubling topic of health and poverty as well as linking the historical and cultural sources that shape this chapter. The geographies here are diverse—the Texas and Oklahoma panhandles and southwestern Kansas in the 1930s; the ghettos of Chicago and New York City in the 1960s; Indian reservations in South Dakota and the Pacific Northwest in the 1990s—but each case study reveals how the economic base is a primary determinant of what early century journalist Hollis Godfrey called the "culture-medium of disease."[19]

DROUGHT AND DESPAIR IN THE DUST BOWL, 1935–1937

Health was a major reason why eastern settlers migrated to the Great Plains, a region that stretches without obvious borders from the Dakotas in the north down to No Man's Land in western Oklahoma and the semiarid expanse of the Texas Panhandle. The winds that blew with devastating force through drought-damaged farms in the 1930s were at the turn of the century thought to offer a healthier climate for urbanites suffering from neurasthenia and asthma, bringing fresh air down from the Saskatchewan prairies. Theodore Roosevelt set the example of moving westward to improve his health when he bought a ranch in Dakota Territory in 1883. Clean air in a "high, dry atmosphere" was also the motivation for Dr. George Waller Dawson when in 1907 he journeyed the thousand miles from Owensboro, Kentucky, to Dalhart, Texas, to improve his respiratory health and the lingering effects of childhood polio.[20] Dawson initially tried his hand at ranch farming but, on running into financial problems, he returned to his earlier career by opening a medical facility in Dalhart. He called this the Trans-Canadian Sanitarium, the only such facility within a ninety-mile radius until 1927.

The town of Dalhart grew rapidly in the early twentieth century on the junction between two major railroads that brought a constant supply of patients to Dawson's sanitarium. The sanitarium offered steam heating, X-rays, "and other Modern appliances," as it boasted in newspaper advertisements across northern Texas and the neighboring states.[21] In his evocative book *The Worst Hard Time* (2006), Timothy Egan intersperses Dawson's story with those of other residents of the Texas and Oklahoma panhandles, noting the high volume of minor surgeries that Dawson undertook at the sanitarium, an estimated two thousand operations between 1912 and 1929. However, only six years later, after Dawson had again tried to make his livelihood as a farmer, he lost virtually all his assets in the face of drought, dust storms, and the insolvency of a local bank.[22] With his health once again precarious, Dawson wrote to his son in May 1938, in the aftermath of a particularly fierce dust storm, to say "we are all so discouraged and ready to go."[23]

Dawson is just one example of the three million residents of the Great Plains whose livelihoods were ruined by a painful combination of drought and capitalism: what one commentator in 1934 called a mixture of the absence of rain, wind erosion, and a "grab-and-kill land policy" only a "little above the level of economic idiocy."[24] One of the most haunting visualizations of the impact of these deleterious natural and human factors on agrarian life is Pare Lorentz's 1936 environmental documentary *The Plow That Broke the Plains*. This Farm Security Administration-sponsored documentary focuses on "the great plow-up" that saw the Great Plains overfarmed for more than two decades—a trend that arguably began as far back as the first Homestead Act of 1862, which required a portion of all homesteads be plowed regularly. Lorentz's film takes a more contemporary view. He pictures the mechanized plow as a military tank, pillaging the land and destroying its resilience, such that when the first of four droughts came to the region in 1930–31 the topsoil just turned to dust.

In order to help working families on the plains in April 1935, the Department of Agriculture launched the Soil Conservation Service to promote responsible farming practices, and in early 1936 the Federal Emergency Relief Administration (FERA) offered subsidies to Dust Bowl farmers in order to lower production and prevent further soil erosion.[25] FERA meant that for the first time federal aid for health care outstripped state and voluntary funding, though both this and the Department of Agriculture's publications on responsible farming are examples of rearguard federal action.[26] That is not to ignore the tangible benefits offered in 1934–35 by the Drought Relief Service in purchasing starving cattle from otherwise often fiercely self-reliant plains farmers, but this intervention did not reduce the environmental threat after years of overgrazing.[27] George Dawson's son recalls he was "greatly disturbed" on returning to Dalhart from Houston in the mid-1930s "to see what the drouth and wind had done to that once beautiful land...[it] had become virtually a black, hideous desert.... The people seemed benumbed by their misfortune and to be simply holding on with dwindling hope."[28]

Abandoned ghost towns were a lasting legacy of drought and dust, with 30 percent of the population in the Oklahoma and Texas panhandles migrating west or dying.

There was a lingering sense that plains folk were not only experiencing hard times but also an erasure of life at the profoundest level. The haunting photographs of the Great Plains by Dorothea Lange, Margaret Bourke-White, and Arthur Rothstein, many of them sponsored by the Farm Security Administration (FSA), evoke the psychological toll of seeing homes and livestock buried under dust. There was no diagnostic psychiatric category at the time to explain this experience. While the physical effects of the drought are clear in photographs such as one Rothstein took in Mississippi County, Arkansas, in 1935 of a malnourished child with bowed legs due to rickets, soil erosion and the erosion of selfhood were often entwined, as Lange and Paul Taylor evoked in their 1939 photo-essay book *An American Exodus: A Record of Human Erosion*.[29] New Deal politics are inseparable from photographs such as Rothstein's *A Young Boy in a Dust Storm* and Lange's *Migrant Mother* in helping to make the case for federal aid in the face of what Taylor called the "human debris" of enforced migration.[30] These naturalistic photographs also sought to "destroy" what Bourke-White called "the aura of sentimentality that still befogs issues in the South," to make the "faces" of the region "come alive."[31] There is much to discuss about the role of FSA-sponsored photography in probing, or even staging, the impact of adverse economic and environmental conditions on the health of panhandlers. For example, Lange called her photographic subject a "hungry and desperate mother...with her children huddled around her." But my focus here is the intersection of poverty and poor health, specifically dust pneumonia and despair, a condition that the *New York Times* described in 1937 as one that "numbs and paralyzes and obliterates."[32]

The survivalist mentality of Great Plains' communities might have not been required to such an extent. Governor Roosevelt of New York had spoken in October 1932 about safeguarding social justice during his campaign as the Democratic presidential candidate. He argued that the "jungle law of the survival of the so-called fittest" has no place in a modern nation that should work toward the "protection of humanity and the fitting of as many human beings as possible into the scheme of surviving."[33] The health of the nation is only implicit in this speech, but Roosevelt's expression of moral responsibility toward "as many human beings as possible" shaped his belief that the federal government was more than an administration—it had an ethical commitment to the

American people, including aid for the needy and equitable health care. In his "Forgotten Man" radio address six months earlier Roosevelt described "a real economic cure" in dramatic medical terms, as one that could kill "the bacteria in the system" rather than just treating "external symptoms."[34] And in this October speech he went on to argue that industrial overproduction and deregulated credit (favored by Coolidge and Hoover) needed constraining by means of a pact between the government and the people.

In this speech, delivered to his "old friends of Detroit and of Michigan" on an early October Sunday, Roosevelt addressed health directly, arguing that his political philosophy was aligned to the opinion of the Public Health Service that six million schoolchildren did not have enough to eat "and were prey to disease."[35] His emphasis was on ill-health prevention and the causes of poverty, a condition that the 1935–36 National Health Survey revealed had a strong correlation with poor health, following a 1932 report of the Committee on the Costs of Medical Care that studied the sickness rates of 15,000 families across ten cities.[36] Roosevelt outlined a detailed national plan, including compensation for workplace accidents, home care for seniors, and special education for young people with developmental disabilities. Only an active commitment to public health and a recalibration of economic policy could, he thought, improve a patchy medical infrastructure that disenfranchised those living in rural areas.

One of the most persuasive aspects of this speech is that Roosevelt pictured working-class Americans as the deserving poor. Michele Landis Dauber points out a moral distinction between "deserving" and "underserving" in Roosevelt's vision of a "sympathetic state," but there was an important political dimension too, because he was looking for electoral votes in his campaign to challenge Hoover's policy of deregulation that led to the overharvesting of the Great Plains.[37] Roosevelt held the moral edge over Hoover's business ethos, despite Hoover's long-standing commitment to improving children's health, and he followed through on the promise during his residency in the White House, though not speedily enough to beat the drought and dust. From 1933 onward, FERA offered a safety net for those suffering job losses, and the Social Security Act was the first federal legislation to offer insurance for the jobless and elderly. This 1935 act led the president of the American Public Health Association, E. L. Bishop, to claim that the country was at "the crossroads of opportunity" if it could only grasp "the spirit of highest idealism."[38]

Yet there were few measures taken during the first two years of the Roosevelt administration to safeguard the welfare of farming folk. This is surprising given the first major drought hit the Great Plains at the beginning of the decade, nearly three years before Roosevelt took office, and diseases like pellagra, malaria, and rickets were common in southern regions. Although the 1930–31 drought prompted a debate in Congress about what form disaster relief should take, it led to a state of emergency in Arkansas and Kentucky and to the Red Cross pledging $5 million in aid. This move was not without controversy. The Red Cross director refused to receive and distribute federal funds because the organization was not a public agency, even though the US president had been the de facto American Red Cross president since the days of Woodrow Wilson.[39] That is just one reason why Tony Badger argues the Depression exposed "the inadequacy of the nation's system of health care," especially for the rural poor, many of whom had no electricity or access to the new technology of radio.[40]

The major ecological disaster of the 1930s, which the *New York Times* called a "conspiracy of earth and wind," often overshadows the human story of countless families.[41] The medical journalist Irving Cutter, writing for the *Chicago Daily Tribune*, pointed to the specific conditions faced by residents of Colorado, Kansas, Oklahoma, and Texas, states in which dust-related health complications were distinct from city dirt and rural health issues in the East.[42] More than fifty dust storms hit the region in 1932–33, but the worst of the storms arrived in spring 1935 over a six-week period. The most devastating was "Black Sunday," April 14. Cutter described "clouds of soil laden air from the west—often several miles skyward—containing considerable silica." A Kansas woman saw "swirling whirlwinds of soil," dust particles seeping through house walls, and herself being covered in dirt. An Oklahoma farmer's wife spoke of dust filling "our eyes and noses and throats" and of her husband's "bronchial trouble" aggravated by the constant dust.[43] The flat semiarid landscape and high winds of the Great Plains meant it was not easy to prevent inhalation of airborne topsoil night and day, not just within working hours. Inhaling dense concentrations of silica caused "gritty irritation of mucous surfaces" and led to the "rapid growth of bacteria" in the nose and throat.

Folk singer Woody Guthrie, a native of Oklahoma who moved to Pampa in the Texas Panhandle in 1929 before migrating to California in 1937, captured this mood on his 1940 album *Dust Bowl Ballads* when he wrote fatalistically about strong winds and friable earth.

On the album's opening track, Guthrie described the events of Black Sunday as "the worst of dust storms that ever fills the sky," leaving a "dreadful tack" in its wake, not just in the region but "through our mighty nation."[44] He was responding, in part, to the largely futile efforts of farmers to prevent dust from invading houses and killing their animals. On the relief front, the Red Cross staffed six emergency facilities across three states, and in Kansas workers made dust masks from cheesecloth to distribute to neighboring areas. Yet the wet cheesecloth may have exacerbated the symptoms the Red Cross team tried to treat, including "coughing jags and body aches," fever, nausea, and "chest pains and shortness of breath" that often led to death.[45]

Guthrie's *Dust Bowl Ballads* is instructive because it reveals more than one regional narrative. The black blizzards of dust seemed unavoidable, and health support was patchy, particularly as many rural health units faced funding cuts and thirty-five county health departments closed in 1932 in drought-stricken areas.[46] However, as Guthrie sang on "Dust Pneumonia Blues," it was possible for some to outrun the dust by joining the two million plains folk who chose to move west. His duo of songs "Dusty Old Dust" and "Dead from the Dust" (the first made it onto *Dust Bowl Ballads*, the second did not) document the deleterious social conditions that the dust and wind intensified, but also the medical and ecological emergencies it caused. On "Dead from the Dust" Guthrie warns that "my people cut down by the dust from the mines" have been undermined by the greed of the "fact'ry boss" who seemed willfully ignorant of the pollution that fouls up "our skies."[47] These links between labor and health are explicit in Guthrie's notes to "Silicosis Is Killin' Me" that muse on air pollution and the "deadly poison" faced by many miners lacking in masks and adequate safety precautions.[48] Cultural historian Will Kaufman argues how Guthrie frequently used his guitar as a machine against corruption, inequality, and self-interest. Yet at other times, such as his 1939 (unreleased) song "Poor, Hard-Working Man Blues," he highlighted the threat that machines posed to laborers: "a combine machine come out then / And done the work of a hundred men. / One man run the combine, Ninety-nine went a-begging." Just as this kind of industrial practice endangered the well-being of workers, so greedy bankers and the state's seeming disregard for rural communities undergird Guthrie's music of the 1930s and prewar 1940s.

Dust was only half of the equation though. The other half hinged on anxiety and despair. Dorothea Lange captured this mood in her 1936 photograph *Migrant Mother*, in which the mother's anxious gaze is framed by the heads of two children turned in toward her. This intimate portrait mixes a familial scene with an epic quality that embodies Lange's idea that powerful photography can push the viewer to find "the simple to be complicated, the miniature to be enormous, the insignificant decisive."[49] Given the lack of comprehensive medical data of the time, it is hard to assess how widespread such anxiety and despair was, or to what extent anxiety and despair was pathological, though in the case of *Migrant Mother* it was staged in order to raise the visibility of enforced migrancy. Nonetheless, the historian Gerald Johnson argues that the sustained assault on work and habitat brought to the surface deep and often despairing feelings, as evidenced in imaginative and documentary sources from the mid- to late 1930s.[50] We could look to the desperate figure of Tom Joad's neighbor Muley Graves in Steinbeck's *The Grapes of Wrath* (1939), who refuses to leave his patch of land even after his house is bulldozed and his family has departed. Muley's initial anger ("I was gonna go in an' kill a whole flock of people") gives way to dazed aimlessness ("An' I got wanderin' aroun'. Jus' walkin' aroun'. Never went far. Slep' where I was") and a loss of selfhood in which he sees himself as an "ol' graveyard ghos'" (a phrase he repeats three times), living in the shadows of abandoned buildings, a disenfranchised squatter on his former land.[51]

Even though we might interpret Steinbeck's depiction of Muley Graves and the Joad family as a tool for raising public sympathy toward federal relief, these feelings of despair carry through to the depoliticized Depression-era text *An Empire of Dust* (1940), which offers an "intimate study" of the "everlasting dust menace."[52] Written in the first person by Lawrence Svobida, a young Nebraskan who moved to southwest Kansas in 1929 with the dream of becoming a successful wheat farmer, its early sections are full of resolve. Svobida strives to fulfill his dream for nearly a decade in spite of a throat infection, drought, flood, hail, and blight, even as his moods swing between determination and despair. Perhaps because a large number of residents remained in Meade County (the county had better medical facilities than many rural areas), Svobida pictures those who leave their homesteads as "no Argonauts setting forth in a spirit of high adventure to pioneer new frontiers, but hordes in despair, haunted by famine and disease" that leave behind "ghost towns."[53] This view does not make his life any easier. Only one of his seasonal crops (in 1931) proves successful, and after weathering seven barren years he succumbs to "dust sickness," which undermines his "robust constitution."[54] In 1939, he finally accepts it is a "losing battle," by which point he depicts himself as a desperate, almost abject, creature like Muley Graves: "with youth and ambition ground into the dust, I can only drift with the tide," one of the dispossessed "horde" he had earlier dismissed.[55]

These expressions of deep-rooted despair are in contrast to the resilience upon which Roosevelt focused after returning from an eleven-day drought inspection trip to the Dakotas, Nebraska, and Iowa in late August and early September 1936 as he geared up for his reelection campaign. The president claimed that he would "never forget the fields of wheat so blasted by heat," but in his Labor Day Fireside Chat radio broadcast of September 6, he emphasized the "self-reliance," "tenacity," and "courage" of the farmers of the Great Plains over and above a congressional commitment to issue federal loans for those worst hit.[56] On his tour, Roosevelt spoke with farmers, attended a Drought Conference in Des Moines, Iowa, and witnessed "drought devastation in nine states."[57] Roosevelt was passionate about farming and spent his vacations in rural Georgia, but the president did not set foot in the heart of the Dust Bowl, except very briefly in 1938, much to the chagrin of many southerners.

The despair that Svobida expressed in *Empire of Dust* was not exclusive to men living in the Dust Bowl. A southwestern Kansas farm woman, Martha Schmidt Friesen, kept a diary through the second half of the 1930s, the entries from 1936 to 1937 focusing on the encroachment of dust storms on the farmhouse. Most of her matter-of-fact diary entries are about her farm life in Kendall (near the Colorado border), particularly as she refers to herself in the third person as "she" or "Mo." When she expresses emotions they come with a force, such as an entry from March 1937: "first thing after breakfast she cleans dust then she gets bluer and bluer cries & cries & cries some more."[58] In another entry, she refers to herself as a "shadow," suffers from dental pain, and feels intense loneliness when her grown-up daughters migrate to Oregon. Similarly, in her Dust Bowl letters of 1935, Caroline Henderson wrote of the "physical torture, confusion of mind, [and] gradual wearing down of courage" she saw around her and her husband's Oklahoma Panhandle farm.[59] And despair, both domestic and migratory, is one of the subjects of Sanora Babb's *Whose Names Are Unknown*, a Dust Bowl novel that reflects the emotional power, geographical span, and naturalistic style of *The Grapes of Wrath*. Although Babb had broad experience of Great Plains life—she was raised in eastern Colorado, educated in Kansas, and worked in California tent camps for the Farm Security Administration—*Whose Names Are Unknown* remained unpublished until 2004, sixty-five years after Babb (an Oklahoman, unlike Steinbeck) submitted her manuscript to Random House.[60]

Set in Cimarron County, Oklahoma, in the mid-1930s, the focus of *Whose Names Are Unknown* is the domestic tribulations of a farming couple, Julia and Milt Dunne. The narrative reveals how the pattern of survival and periodic despair inflects their working-class lives, but also a lack of access to basic health facilities, reflecting the fact that the New Deal reforms were slow to come to Oklahoma.[61] For example, when Julia Dunne gives birth prematurely to a stillborn boy, her screams of "terrifying finality" contrast to Milt's belief that had they lived in town "we could have had him put in one of those incubators. He didn't last long because we didn't know what to do."[62] Milt's stoicism gives way to desperation when he goes outside to bury the "unborn and helpless" baby; he feels "a hard loneliness and despair breaking up in him, crashing against the walls of his being. It was the boy and everything unnoticed and unknown to him." He manages to compose himself after the makeshift burial ceremony, but this phrase, "everything unnoticed and unknown," is testament to the determining factors—linking environment to economics to health—that Milt can barely articulate.

The lack of medical support for these figures is unsurprising given their rural locations, but Babb's character, Julia Dunne, muses on "the strange phenomenon of dust" in her diary entries, noting that hospitals were refusing "to operate on anyone unless it's life or death."[63] This psychological dimension tallies with the 1935–36 National Health Survey that revealed chronic sickness was 87 percent higher among relief families and was not just of a physical nature.[64] The survey lacked detail about demographics and mental health and could do no more than gesture toward this conclusion. Nevertheless, one senses from the 1937 *New York Times* feature, "When Biting Dust Sweeps Across the Land," that the image of a dust-clad house says as much about the missing people as the structure itself: "most of the farmhouses seem abandoned, stark and gaunt, with dust banked higher than their window sills.... There is a dead plum thicket buried so that only its topmost twigs rise above the dust. The only living things are the Russian thistles."[65] Additionally, *New York Times* writer Harland Miller thought that the "brief agony of the traveler" driving through the dust clouds is nothing compared to the agony faced by "an inhabitant of this scorched, stripped, inundated circle of land." It is easy to overplay the psychological toll or cast those badly affected as passive victims rather than hardworking laborers and farmers getting by in the worst of circumstances. Nevertheless, the harsh environmental conditions of the Dust Bowl brought to the surface what James T. Patterson calls "old poverty" and exposed how meager were regional health facilities. Access to basic services was substantially worse on the Great Plains than the national estimation that a private nurse visited only 1 percent of relief families, rising to 12 percent for families with a yearly income over $3,000 ($1,348 was the average national income in 1935).[66]

As the country started to recover slowly from economic depression in the second half of the decade, Roosevelt tried to tackle poverty in far-reaching ways. The passing of the July 1935 National Labor Relations Act promised better protection for workers' health; the Social Security Act signed five weeks later stressed the need to expand medical research, to help states develop appropriate health services, and to provide welfare "for aged persons, blind persons, dependent and crippled children" via a Social Security Board.[67] However, the Social Security Act did not provide an adequate system of health insurance, and the availability of loans to pay for medical care remained uneven through to 1938 when the idea of a national health program started to take shape, albeit cautiously. That year a minimum wage was legislated for the first time, and the Farm Security Administration sought to improve rural health care services, based on evidence that failing farms gave rise to often-undetected ill-health issues.[68] Areas hardest hit by the droughts took much longer to recover than others, as reflected by the "disquieting picture" of the region in a 1936 federal report *The Great Plains of the Future*, even as the report clung to the belief that the renewal of human and natural resources was still possible for the region.[69] Regardless of Roosevelt's own ambivalent position on national health insurance, his administration's New Deal reforms sought to safeguard the poorest from deprivation, and the FSA made a concerted effort to support migrant workers' health after 1936. Yet bronchial complications, lower rates of fertility, and the lingering depression of plains folk who lived through the droughts of the 1930s was a lasting legacy of the Dust Bowl.

THE POSTWAR GHETTO AND URBAN HEALTH, 1959–1965

In her 1959 critique of economic and racial entrapment, Chicago playwright Lorraine Hansberry's play *A Raisin in the Sun* depicts the multiple health challenges faced by an African American family living in the "Black Belt" of South Side Chicago. After World War II, sociologists began to assess the demographics and housing conditions of urban ghettos like the South Side (the name for this thirty-block area proved to be so stigmatizing that residents made efforts in the 1930s to change it to Bronzeville). This research followed pioneering studies early in the century such as Jacob Riis's *The Battle with the Slum* (1902) and Hollis Godfrey's *The Health of the City* (1910), two important texts that charted "the close connection between the slum and disease" such as tuberculosis, "whose spread is greatly assisted by overcrowding and bad air."[70] Godfrey's theory that the slum or ghetto was a "culture-medium of disease" in which a "lack of space, air and light" exacerbated poor health, is exemplified in Hansberry's theatrical portrayal of the Younger family's South Side apartment in *A Raisin in the Sun*, with its one outside window next to which a wilting plant struggles for life.[71] A Commission on Race and Housing of 1955–58, put together by an independent citizens' group across twelve cities, revealed how inflated rental policies were a common trap for minority families like the Youngers and that the "spreading blight" of slums meant it was difficult for many to escape.[72]

A Raisin in the Sun is a sociological play that dramatizes the intersection of race and class within an ecological view of the city, though we see only a restricted view of Chicago through the eyes of a struggling black family. Its focus also reflects an impassioned speech at the 1938 National Health Conference by Florence Greenberg, a Chicagoan from a steel-working family, who invited the delegates to see "a sick Chicago, a Chicago of dirt and filth and tenements."[73] Hansberry gained this sociological interest in part from her political activist father and via a series of probing texts, including the 1939 epidemiological report *Mental Disorders in Urban Areas*; St. Clair Drake and Horace Cayton Jr.'s *Black Metropolis* (1945) on the intersection of race, class, and economics in the development of Chicago's South Side; and E. Franklin Frazier's *Black Bourgeoisie* (1957), which explores how psychological responses (self-hatred, guilt, delusions) stem from economic roots. Hansberry's middle-class upbringing in Chicago did not correlate with the dark cramped apartment of *A Raisin in the Sun*, but she was acutely aware that poor sanitation and high-density residences damage health. One example of this involves Bonnie Bullough, a public health nurse working on the South Side in the 1950s, who made house calls to places where rats killed children and in one case "chewed the hand of a small black newborn infant in a dug-out basement under a dilapidated row house."[74] With emergency care an hour away by bus, officials told Bullough that nothing could be done about the rats, leading her to conclude that "poverty, discrimination, and an inadequate health care delivery system [are] an impossible combination."[75]

A Raisin in the Sun does not directly represent slum deprivation, even though it portrays the Youngers' apartment as a "rat trap" and implies that the daughter Beneatha's plan to become a doctor is partly driven by her desire to make broken bodies whole.[76] Instead, the play subtly links class, space, and health. Lena and her husband migrated to Chicago from the South seeking new opportunities, but the realities of urban living hollow out Lena's now deceased husband, and her son Walter Lee talks about the empty future in terms of existential dread "hanging over there at the edge of my days. Just waiting for me—a big, looming blank space—full of *nothing*. Just waiting for me."[77] Instead of leaving feelings of sickness behind them, racial zoning and a lack of decent jobs means it sticks to the male Youngers. Lena's husband used to slump on the couch and stare vacantly at the rug, unable to focus on her or devise a sustainable plan, whereas Walter sees himself as a "giant" in a world of ants and a "volcano" ready to explode, although it is likely this explosion will lead not to positive change but a shriveling up of his being.[78] The play does not confirm that Walter is suffering from poor mental health, but his lack of self-respect, habitual drinking, and unfeasible aspirations make this an underlying theme. A Raisin in the Sun also taps into the discourse of pathology that was often linked to the health of postwar African American men, a discourse that led Stokely Carmichael and Charles V. Hamilton to picture ghetto life in the mid-1960s as racial dynamite: a "vicious circle created by the lack of decent housing, decent jobs, and adequate education."[79] Reflecting on her South Side childhood in the late 1960s and early 1970s, Michelle Obama echoed this sentiment, saying that she often heard the word "ghetto" dropped "like a lit match."[80]

The discourse of pathology at the axis of health and poverty is at the heart of this second case study, the timeline of which runs from the first performances of A Raisin in the Sun in 1959 through to 1965, a year that President Johnson's under secretary for health, Wilbur J. Cohen (later HEW secretary), estimated dwarfed any other year in terms of health legislation.[81] The challenges of ghetto living had been tackled before the war in the didactic 1938 Living Newspaper play One Third of a Nation, a title taken from Roosevelt's second inaugural address.

The play and the 1939 Paramount film adaptation championed the little man who continued to struggle in the face of failed promises of the 1937 Housing Act to improve urban living conditions in inner-city tenements. Despite new housing opportunities for middle-class Americans in the boom years of the 1950s, Lyndon Johnson was facing much the same urban crisis a quarter of a century later. After raising the aid budget for the poor from $1 billion in 1963 to $4.2 billion in 1964, Johnson addressed Congress in March 1965.[82] In this important speech on the nation's cities, he called for action at the "highest level of government" to tackle physical and social urban decay that "casts a pall of ugliness and despair on the spirits of the people."[83] Johnson did not frame the "urban snake pit" in racial terms; in fact, he did not address race at all in this speech, instead focusing on the rehabilitation of slums, some of which were receiving aid from the Ford Foundation's Gray Areas Program.[84] It was clear that more coordination and funding was required for community services, as well as better data and documentation about life in deprived urban areas.[85] To see how these challenges played out for poor urban African Americans I turn to Kenneth Clark's *Dark Ghetto*, published two months after Johnson's speech to Congress and serialized in the *New York Post* in August 1965.

Dark Ghetto was born out of Clark's work from 1962 to 1964 as chair of the activist group Harlem Youth Opportunities Unlimited, commonly known as HARYOU. His 1965 book relates directly to HARYOU's two-year sociological study *Youth in the Ghetto: A Study of the Consequences of Powerlessness and a Blueprint for Change* (1964), but Clark inverted HARYOU's theme of powerlessness in his subtitle to *Dark Ghetto: Dilemmas of Social Power*.[86] There are lines of continuity between what *Youth in the Ghetto* describes as "a picture of despair, hopelessness, and futility" and Clark's critique of "the pathologies of American ghettos." But his stance as an "involved observer" in the "laboratory" of Harlem enabled him to blend his training in psychology at Howard University with his childhood experiences "within the walls" of Harlem—his family moved multiple times in the 1920s "in a desperate attempt to escape its creeping blight."[87] Clark tries to balance two imperatives in *Dark Ghetto*: first, a "disciplined preoccupation" based on interviews and structured observations and, second, active participation in "the lives of the people."[88] Only by adopting a dual perspective on Harlem life did he believe it was possible to detect how "the normal channels of economic mobility and opportunity" in other neighborhoods are typically "blocked" by a lack of opportunity. HARYOU workers shared Clark's belief that this was ingrained for many midcentury urban African Americans who felt economically trapped, lacked adequate health and welfare structures, and could see no obvious way out of the ghetto.[89]

In order to address the developmental challenges of young African Americans, Kenneth and Mamie Clark cofounded the Northside Center for Child Development in 1946, located at 150th Street in upper Harlem. Clark's work at the Northside Center influenced the development of *Dark Ghetto*, as did the personal observations on ghetto life of the New Yorker James Baldwin, whose 1948 essay "The Harlem Ghetto" captures "the sense of congestion" that he felt growing up in New York City during the 1930s.[90] Published when Baldwin was only twenty-four (the year he left for Paris), "The Harlem Ghetto" pictures the congestion in imprisoning terms: "rather like the insistent, maddening, claustrophobic pounding in the skull that comes from trying to breathe in a very small room with all the windows shut."[91] Baldwin, who Clark affirmed as a close friend in the early 1960s, not only explored the concept of pathology but also observed that hatred (including self-hatred) often stems from "desperately constricted" outlets. Baldwin returned to this theme in a 1960 *Esquire* essay, "Fifth Avenue, Uptown," by starkly juxtaposing two visions of Fifth Avenue: the "renowned and elegant" avenue of the Upper East Side and the "filthy, hostile" avenue that marked the mid-rise housing project and "stunted city trees" of Riverton.[92] This anthropomorphic gaze lends expression to what Baldwin calls "stunted maturity," a point echoed seventeen years later in Clark's description of "emotional illness."[93] Based on these accounts, an inferiority complex deleteriously affects personality development that can often stem from a lack of opportunity and support. This recognition led Ralph Ellison, another literary explorer of ghetto life, to call postwar Harlem a ruin: "its crimes, its casual violence, its crumbling buildings with littered areaways, ill-smelling halls and vermin-invaded rooms...are indistinguishable from the distorted images that appear in dreams."[94] There was nothing to suggest greater access to medical facilities would itself resolve squalor or anxieties, yet it seemed to do so, given that Clark estimated Harlem children needed psychiatric and counseling services at twelve times the national average.[95]

The complementary dualism that Clark outlines in his introduction to *Dark Ghetto* is also a deep tension. His sociological eye strains against his emotional connectedness as he mounts a case for increased federal funding to support community health and well-being. *Dark*

Ghetto evokes the "devouring qualities" of damage and instability that Clark believed stemmed from the experience of unemployment and inadequately embedded services.[96] He amplifies his analysis by his fondness for emotive journalese, exemplified by his claim that these critical conditions are a "decay at the heart of American cities." In fact, he argues the ghetto is "all-encompassing" and little different from the "total institutions" of the asylum and prison that Erving Goffman aligned three years earlier for their surveillance practices.[97]

If these bleak comparisons could not entirely be justified given that Harlem and Bronzeville were both experiencing a renaissance in black artistic creativity, it shows that Clark's view of the ghetto was not as panoramic as it might have been despite the development of new facilities.[98] For example, the Lafargue Mental Hygiene Clinic on West 134th Street was from 1946 to 1958 a "unique prism" for addressing the "psychic costs of antiblack oppression," while the Southside Community Committee in Chicago tried to energize citizenship activities, tackle juvenile delinquency, and channel the energies of South Side arts and writing groups.[99] There were no quick solutions to what Ralph Ellison called the condition of invisibility, even when "psychiatry came to Harlem" (to evoke the title of a 1946 essay by Richard Wright) within the walls of the Lafargue Clinic, which was cofounded by Wright.[100] Clark went further in his belief that deprivation infiltrates the consciousness of residents, while the stark juxtaposition of wealthy and poor communities reinforced for many poor urbanites that they were living in what cultural geographer Kevin Robins (echoing Ellison's description) has called "abandoned zones of the city."[101] Clark and others raised the problem of the lack of access to health services for African Americans with Robert F. Wagner Jr., the New York mayor. Wagner eventually responded sympathetically or, at least, politically given his need for the local black vote: in 1962 Wagner helped finance race-neutral psychiatric facilities at the Harlem Hospital and in 1964 an aftercare facility, the Harlem Rehabilitation Center.[102]

These health care initiatives went some way to breaking the perception of total neglect, but they did not shift the dial far for those who wished to relocate. Lorraine Hansberry dramatizes this dilemma of relocation in *A Raisin in the Sun* when an insurance windfall kindles the social aspirations of the Younger family. On receiving the money, they feel torn between moving to the all-white suburb of Clybourne Park or living without light and hope in their "rat trap" of an apartment—even before Walter's wife declares she is pregnant with a second child and

Walter squanders his share of the inheritance on an ill-considered business deal.[103]

There is an undercurrent to Clark's and Baldwin's accounts that couches the ghetto experience in masculinist terms. This experience pivots on "disorganization," a concept that was often framed in psychosociological language. For example, E. Franklin Frazier wrote in the 1940s that the major social problem facing black families was disorganization that made "life among a large proportion of the urban Negro population…casual, precarious, and fragmentary. It lacks continuity and its roots do not go deeper than the contingencies of daily living."[104] And it resonated with postwar discourses of crime and delinquency and the psychiatric categories Abram Kardiner and Lionel Ovesey used in their 1951 book *The Mark of Oppression*, in which personality damage is a pervasive trait, particularly among the male subjects of the book's twenty-five case studies. But the masculinist strain is also there in the disorganized language and erratic actions of Walter in *A Raisin in the Son*, in the exclusively male pronouns used by Clark and Baldwin, and in the implication that frustration and anger delimit the outlook of disenfranchised midcentury black men. The discourse of disorganization is also deleterious and antitherapeutic. Kardiner and Ovesey recognized this when they noted in the 1962 republication of *The Mark of Oppression* that the links they had drawn between race, poverty, and stigma were "too painful to accept" by some readers.[105] The authors did not abandon the discourse of urban pathology, but they realized that in the eleven years between the book's two editions the civil rights movement had showed that it was possible to shift ingrained inferiority complexes through social transformation. This new tone resonated with the obvious love of community that Clark displays in *Dark Ghetto*, a dimension often overlooked when simply taking a diagnostic view of the ghetto as an urban crisis.

The polemic of *Dark Ghetto* is an intrinsic aspect, even though Clark did not generate a crisis in order to gain the attention of political leaders. Like Edgar May's *The Wasted Americans*, also published in 1964, *Dark Ghetto* makes a case for investment in poor urban communities at a time when the federal focus was on alleviating rural poverty, as set out by President Johnson in his two-day tour of Appalachia in April 1964 and his January 1966 message to Congress. It was clear that poverty was not just an economic category, especially as the National Advisory Commission on Rural Poverty report *The People Left Behind* estimated that rural poverty affected fourteen million Americans in which region, race, education, and housing are significant factors.[106] The Medical Committee for Human Rights recognized the intricate link between health access and poverty when it sent a team of health workers in summer 1964 to rural parts of the Deep South to help expand medical capacity.[107] This initiative supplemented the efforts of southern activists like Fannie Lou Hamer, who used her own experience of medical injustice in Mississippi (including an enforced hysterectomy in her hometown of Indianola) to fight for civil rights both in her region and across the nation. Writing of the 1964 Summer Project, which helped to galvanize political awareness in the South, Hamer compared the "race problem" of Mississippi with urban slums in the North, claiming "the sickness in Mississippi is not a Mississippi sickness. This is America's sickness."[108]

Even though *The People Left Behind* report covers migration between rural and urban areas, arguably the War on Poverty solved neither the pressing issue of urban deprivation nor the long-term health consequences of malnutrition, nor the triggers for race riots despite the focus of the Kerner Report on this third topic.[109] Released by the National Advisory Commission on Civil Disorders in February 1968, the Kerner Report amplified some of the themes of *The Negro Family: The Case for National Action*, the title of the Moynihan Report of three years earlier that took a sociological perspective on African American family life and employment prospects. Prior to the Kerner Report, media outlets seemed reluctant to probe the relationship between race and urban conditions in favor of incendiary events: for example, a July 1967 *Life* cover features an aerial photograph of a twelve-year-old black boy lying prone in the street after being shot during the Newark riots of summer 1967.[110] The Kerner Report arguably had a long-term transformative effect on newspaper coverage of African American social and welfare issues. But the report's criticism of federal programs and the media for failing urban minorities "played into right-wing claims that liberal policies [had] created disarray in the cities," regardless of the efforts of the Office for Economic Opportunity (OEO) to "help cool" civil disturbances.[111]

Despite these federal initiatives and the aim of *Dark Ghetto* to raise consciousness about the inner-city experiences, Clark became increasingly frustrated with the white liberal establishment. Arguably, the Johnson administration's War on Poverty and the Community Action Program made little lasting impact on the socioeconomic conditions of areas labeled ghettos, though the plan for community action was to ensure maximum feasible participation of low-income residents and to give them a voice in planning. However, it would be wrong simply to criticize what the administration called the broad-ranging effort to mobilize "considerable talent and energy...to affect change in the lives of those we serve."[112] The president claimed that 1966 would be "the year of rebirth for American cities" following the Housing and Urban Development Act of August 1965.[113] The newly formed Department of Housing and Urban Development (HUD) sought to improve the "crisis in the cities"—"the general welfare of people living in urban slums and blighted areas," recreational and transportation facilities, and ill health—by expanding housing and job opportunities via its new Model Cities Program.[114] The Department of Health, Education, and Welfare also focused on urban renewal by establishing neighborhood service centers to meet the needs of low-income areas, an Inner City Training Program that gave "policy officials exposure to urban problems from the point of view of the recipient, and the worker at the street level," and a Juvenile Delinquency Program for "more effective communication with ghetto youth."[115]

Despite this multifaceted approach and interagency cooperation, there were frustrations and failures. For example, following acts to improve air and water quality in 1963 and 1965, Johnson sought to pass legislation to tackle inadequate sanitation and threats to children's health through the Rat Extermination and Control Bill of July 1967, a bill that the House turned down despite persistent concerns about rats and pestilence that went back to the Woodrow Wilson era. Although some of this frustration was due to high numbers of Republicans in Congress voting against progressive reform bills (87 percent of Republicans voted against the Rat Extermination Bill), this was far from the only issue. Some Great Society initiatives lacked coordination and realism; the Model Cities Program was unfulfilled; the goals of OEO were never fully clear; and many programs remained underfunded, especially when Congress became resistant to overspending due to escalation in Vietnam.[116] Catching this new congressional mood, in summer 1968, Richard Nixon castigated Johnson for his "guns and butter philosophy," which he believed was leading to "serious economic disorder."[117]

For these reasons, the mid-1960s is not simply a high-water mark for American health, or, if it is, then this horizon was only to be glimpsed. Whether these urban programs succeeded in embedding responsive structures and facilities in local urban communities is open to debate. In March 1967, President Johnson was calling urban and rural poverty "unfinished business" even as he clung to the ideal of a "total strategy against poverty" that must "break through on many fronts."[118] Similarly, the US surgeon general's report of that year praised some public health initiatives, but it bemoaned "the failure of health programs to make the total impact needed to meet present and foreseeable crises in our urban communities."[119] And at the regional level, at a public Medicaid hearing in December 1968, Evelyn Zisserson of the Committee on Urban Opportunity, argued that despite the successes of the Chicago Head Start Program in funding blood, sight, and hearing tests and dental care for children, community health programs in poor neighborhoods were not implementing measures to ensure that young patients did not feel rushed, confused, or frightened when they visited a clinic.[120]

The fact that the "cruel and present reality" of poverty persisted through the decade despite the introduction of these programs validates Kenneth Clark's sense of frustration with the failed promises of the Johnson administration and aligns with the administration's own view that the staffing and coordination of these programs was sometimes lacking.[121] Participatory democracy remained an ideal for Johnson, but federal programs struggled to get close enough to the communities. This is in sharp contrast to Clark's urban fieldwork as well as racially inflected studies such as Gerald Suttles's *The Social Order of the Slum* (1968), based on a detailed study of West Side Chicago. Given this contrast and the fact that the cultural and political legacy of *Dark Ghetto* is as important as the text itself, this case study concludes with three examples that extend Clark's analysis of the relationship between urban deprivation and ill health.[122]

Simply increasing the number of doctors and hospitals was to sociologist William Julius Wilson insufficient for improving the quality of ghetto life. In his 1987 book *The Truly Disadvantaged*, written while he was working at the University of Chicago, Wilson argues that access to public medical programs such as Medicaid remained a crucial factor, and that a "progressive reform coalition" was the only political option to guarantee mobility for the urban poor.[123] Wilson's view echoed the shift late in Martin Luther King Jr.'s life from race relations to economics, leading King to work with the Poor People's Campaign in an endeavor to confront the roots of inequality.[124] King moved to Chicago's West Side in January 1966 to refocus the work of the Southern Christian Leadership Conference on northern cities. Two months later, on March 25, he commented at a contentious Medical Committee for Human Rights convention that "injustice in health care is the most shocking and inhuman" of all types of inequality, and he went on to assert, "it is more degrading than slums, because slums are a psychological death while inequality in health means a physical death."[125]

In these actions and statements, King yoked together national and local agendas. He spoke about a lack of congressional funding that could underpin the Great Society programs; he sought to influence the 1966 municipal election in the hope that this would improve the deal for Chicago's poor; and he tackled racial discrimination in employment practices and among the city's bank lenders. When King visited the all-white neighborhood of Marquette Park on August 5, 1966, to protest housing discrimination (six days after a fractious civil rights demonstration there), he faced verbal abuse and a volley of bricks, a reaction that confirmed his view that race relations in the urban North were as fragile and fraught as the semirural South.[126] King's philosophical view was that only a "radical redistribution of economic power" could alleviate "slum shock" (what he called the experience of "denial, discrimination, and dismay") and fix inequality at the root, at a time when the poverty rates of black Chicagoans had risen by 6 percent since 1960, from 33 to 39 percent.[127]

King's view on poverty and health was shared (if not his integrationist philosophy) by Black Panther Huey P. Newton. Four years after King's assassination, Newton was arguing that grassroots programs such as community health clinics and alcohol support facilities might "satisfy the deep needs" of urban minority groups, "but they are not solutions to our problems. That is why we call them survival programs, meaning survival pending revolution."[128] Survival is a basic part of this equation, but so also is a respect for health as a basic right. At a time when poverty among African Americans was nearly 25 percent higher than among whites, this was not the political equivalent of providing the withered plant in Lena Younger's kitchen enough light to metabolize.[129] Instead, this was "survival pending a revolution," as the Panthers showed in 1972 when they amended their founding document of 1966 to include "free health care for all black and oppressed people... to guarantee our basic survival." Rapidly assembled free health clinics staffed by volunteer workers underpinned the Panthers' rights-based philosophy and also echoed the values of the Medical Committee for Human Rights, rather than standing at a radical distance from it.[130] Even if the revolution never happened, or not in the way either King or Newton envisaged, their examples showed how community organization could be a partial antidote to living a ghostly existence within the "invisible wall" of the ghetto in that it could help prevent its inhabitants being "trodden and crushed by the iron feet of poverty."[131]

A second study that was influential in shaping the role of the community in tackling the causes and consequences of poverty in deprived rural areas appeared as *Race and Authority in Urban Politics* in 1973, based on field studies in Chicago, New York City, Detroit, Los Angeles, and Philadelphia. The book does not explicitly address questions of health, but it responds to critiques of Johnson's War on Poverty by arguing that many of these criticisms ignore or underestimate the role of Community Action.[132] This is an example of a study that allows for the possibility that responsive and accessible facilities can help alleviate slum shock, even though a 1973 report based on the Chicago Regional Hospital Survey of the mid-1960s gave a very bleak assessment of the city's health facilities and criticized the AMA for being "a bloodsucking leech coiled around a lancet."[133] The main difference between *Race and Authority in Urban Politics* and *Dark Ghetto* was that Clark thought federal aid was helpful if not always necessary for improving the infrastructure of community health. In contrast, *Race and Authority in Urban Politics* captured the radical mood of the early 1970s in proposing that grassroots community action has the power to make a difference on its own terms. An example of this is Free Breakfast for School Children, an initiative that began in Oakland, California, in January 1969, as one of the Black Panthers' survival programs. By 1970, these health programs had spread to a number of cities, including Chicago, alongside free clinics and racially sensitive health information distributed in a weekly newspaper, at a time when Nixon was looking to scale back federal-sponsored community health initiatives.[134] This example shows how it was possible to combat what Alondra Nelson calls "medical discrimination" by devising community answers to what seem like intractable urban problems.[135]

The third example is the work of the French-born American-based sociologist Loïc Wacquant. Studying under Pierre Bourdieu, Wacquant also took his lead from William Julius Wilson while doing comparative fieldwork in Chicago's South Side in the 1980s, extending a tradition of Chicago sociology that goes back to Robert Park's study of urban behavior in the 1910s.[136] Wacquant found inspiration in the work of the Chicago School of Urban Sociology, together with Erving Goffman's critique of incarceration and Bourdieu's idea of a reflexive sociological method that Wacquant deployed to examine the intersections between race, economics, and habitat. In his 2008 book *Urban Outcasts* and related essays, he reflects on his efforts to inhabit a space in which he could appraise the ghetto from the inside out to mitigate his outsider's perspective. This stance is based on his decision to live "at the edge of the poor black neighbourhood of Woodlawn" near the shore of Lake Michigan. He describes this area as a "quasi-urban lunar landscape, with its unbelievable decay, misery, and violence, backed by a totally hermetic separation between the white, prosperous and privileged world of the university and the abandoned African-American neighbourhoods all around it."[137]

This stark juxtaposition, as captured in his 2009 essay "The Body, the Ghetto, and the Penal State," reveals lines of continuity with Clark's *Dark Ghetto*, a text that Wacquant uses to assess the ghetto as "a mechanism of ethnoracial domination and economic oppression."[138] There are also resonances with the Great Society antipoverty programs such as OEO's 1966–67 pilot project in Chicago's South Side designed to "motivate, train, and place in jobs hard-core, male Woodlawn school dropouts." Offering a middle way between a top-down federal approach and bottom-up grassroots initiatives, the Woodlawn Organization ultimately failed to reach its goal of maximum feasible participation, though it did help reduce crime rates. Jill Quadagno describes this process as a "ghettoization of urban politics," which, despite the grand federal aims of the War on Poverty, was both badly coordinated at the local level and actually served to reduce "political support for funds to cities" by limiting what might have been accomplished with a less racially inflected policy.[139] Such polarization reflected the congressional hearings of late 1968 when Arkansas senator John McClellan launched an attack on OEO programs for misusing public funds and, in the case of Woodlawn, for providing an opportunity for street gang fraud by the local Blackstone Rangers.[140]

In the face of such roadblocks to change one could argue that in the early twenty-first century a ghetto mentality has reentrenched due to the widening economic gulf between rich and poor and by subtle mechanisms of social exclusion, a structural inequality that Black Lives Matters activists have highlighted in the late 2010s. Wacquant uses the terms "hyperghetto" and "ethnoracial prison" to describe such intense urban marginalization.[141] With increasing numbers of African Americans going to prison (a 2009 report estimated that 30 percent of African American men who did not finish high school were in jail by their mid-thirties), Wacquant argues that federal policies, at least since the Nixon years, have led to "the *hyper*incarceration of (sub)proletarian

African American men from the imploding ghetto."[142] Cuts to health services and entitlement programs, rising urban crime rates, and localized police brutality mean the health infrastructure remains insecure and inadequate for many poor urban neighborhoods at the turn of the 2020s, despite the efforts of the Clinton and Obama administrations to emulate Johnson's aspiration to close the health gap for those near and below the poverty line.[143]

RESERVATION HEALTH BLUES, 1997–1999

Sherman Alexie emerged in the 1990s as a distinctive voice among contemporary North American writers, receiving acclaim for his literary explorations of the economic, social, cultural, and medical forces that impinge on the well-being of indigenous groups. Avoiding the language of victimization and marginalization except to critique it, Alexie often draws on tragicomedy to probe alcoholism, depression, and mood disorders, all health conditions that were shaped by his experience of growing up on the Spokane Indian Reservation in eastern Washington in the late 1960s and 1970s. This focus can be traced to two surgical procedures he underwent as an infant to correct congenital hydrocephalus and a phenobarbital prescription he was given as a child to treat a series of epileptic seizures. He later suffered insomnia and mood swings before receiving a diagnosis for bipolar disorder in 2010, a condition he believes he inherited from his mother. This biographical aspect works alongside Alexie's evocation of traditional Indian rituals such as the vision quest and the Ghost Dance, which feature in this third case study and its focus on the late 1990s when the sustained health crisis faced by poor Native Americans surfaced on national and regional levels, particularly in South Dakota.[144]

Alexie's focus on "the rez" as a place of deprivation and imagination in equal measure does not make the Pacific Northwest a unique region. The *Washington Post* ran a piece in December 1997, for example, on the Oglala Lakota Sioux living on the Pine Ridge Reservation, in South Dakota, nearly a thousand miles southeast of the Spokane reservation, proclaiming that there are "a thousand ways to die young here."[145] The historical memory of the clash between the Oglala Sioux and a US Calvary Regiment on December 29, 1890, shaped this view, in which 150 Lakota died at Wounded Knee while defending their indigenous rights. A sparsely populated and predominantly rural state with nine Indian reservations, much of South Dakota encompasses what the British photographer Kalpesh Lathigra calls the "vast endless landscape" of the northern Great Plains.[146] Focusing on contemporary social pressures, this 1997 *Washington Post* article documents high infant mortality, the risk of freezing during bitter Dakota winters, and high suicide rates among what it calls the "heavy hearted and the hopeless." Statistics from the Harvard T. H. Chan School of Public Health underpin the article by comparing the Lakota Sioux with the national population mean and others living in vulnerable habitats. This argument proposes the "deep isolation" of Pine Ridge is not categorically different from the slums of Washington, DC, or Baltimore, but with a more fragile infrastructure—a point that echoes Fannie Lou Hamer's argument in the mid-1960s that Mississippi was a national index rather than an isolated case of regional deprivation.

It is not just deprivation on reservations that concerns the *Washington Post* staff writer Jon Jeter but high levels of homelessness, unemployment, and unwanted pregnancies (he does not mention a series of enforced hysterectomies reported by Lakota women while receiving prenatal and neonatal treatment at Bureau of Indian Affairs medical facilities). Taken together, these factors can lead to a ghostly existence beset with both physical and mental health challenges, an ontological state that echoes Sherman Alexie's experiences as a child growing up in a single-parent family during the 1970s in a small and unfinished federal-aid house on the Spokane reservation.[147] Located in one of the most economically challenged counties, the Pine Ridge reservation's poverty level is significantly higher than the national average for Native Americans. Health and housing statistics for the Oglala Sioux are more typical but equally stark: the 1995 Census Bureau estimated only 20 percent of houses on reservations had proper water pipes and refrigerators, and many lacked telephones.[148] With patchy medical facilities, health education on South Dakota reservations was sparse in the 1990s despite high alcohol intake, high-fat diets, widespread smoking, and a lack of driving safety.

The Pine Ridge Indian Hospital was the main institutional resource for the sick and ailing. Located in the southern part of the reservation, this two-story structure was the largest Indian medical facility in the northern plains, eighty miles from any other hospital in southwestern South Dakota and northern Nebraska. Although the hospital was welcomed when it opened its doors in 1892, from its earliest days it encountered environmental, infrastructural, and cross-cultural problems, and the fact that it has only forty-five beds and sixteen physicians for a local Indian population of 46,000 (based on 2011 statistics) offers a sense of scale.[149] Yet the *Washington Post* article did not echo Alexie's bleak portrait of a 1960s Indian Health Service hospital, which opens his second novel, *Indian Killer*: "The sheets are dirty.... Anonymous cries up and down the hallways.... Walls painted white a decade earlier, now yellow and peeling."[150] Instead, Jeter saw reason for optimism with the opening in the mid-1990s of ancillary and mobile health facilities as part of the Pine Ridge Service Unit.

These progressive measures were aided by the health advocacy work of the Native American Community Board (founded in South Dakota in 1985 to raise the profile of women's health) and the Food Distribution Program on Indian Reservations (a branch of the federal Food and Nutrition Service), which introduced fresh vegetables and other healthier options for those under the poverty line in the mid-1990s, replacing low-nutrient canned and processed foods that tended to increase eating disorders.[151] However, this did little to offset the prevalence of alcoholism on the reservation, despite moves in the early 1970s to develop an Indian Alcoholism Program by the American Indian Commission on Alcohol and Drug Abuse.

This trend was in large part due to alcohol sales just two miles away from the Pine Ridge Reservation in the northern Nebraskan town of Whiteclay on former Sioux territory. Liquor and beer were in plentiful supply in Whiteclay for those living on the dry reservation. Assistant secretary for Indian affairs Kevin Gover (a member of the Shawnee nation) acknowledged that Whiteclay was a problem in 1999, but his response was that the residents of Pine Ridge should be responsible and "need to choose not to drink" rather than implement regulatory measures.[152] For decades, what a local author calls the "armpit of Nebraska" exacerbated physical and mental health problems faced by the Oglala Sioux—young and old, male and female—so much so that in summer 2006 local organizers set up a roadblock in Whiteclay to prevent alcohol coming onto the reservation. And, after much debate, in late 2017, the Nebraska Supreme Court banned the sale of alcohol in Whiteclay.[153] Rather than ending with a focus on alcoholism though, Jeter concludes the *Washington Post* article on the topic of suicide as illustrated by the story of a sixteen-year-old Sioux boy who impulsively shot himself in the head while playing in a reservation house with younger children. This incident is shocking in itself, but so too is the lack of counseling for the children who witnessed the suicide at close range.

By the late 1990s, only modest progressive change had occurred in

Indian health care since September 1976 when President Ford signed the Indian Health Care Improvement Act, which guaranteed Medicaid and Medicare provision for Native Americans around or under the poverty line. Yet this federal reform masked over what a 1973 fieldwork film called a regional health crisis due to the scarcity of doctors and inadequate medical facilities for the scattered Sioux communities, even though the Rosebud Sioux Reservation had benefited from a federal grant in the mid-1960s to facilitate Head Start, sanitation aid, and adult education programs.[154] The twenty-minute film *Health Care Crisis at Rosebud*, made at the University of South Dakota, called for more funding and increased trust between white doctors and Indian patients, and a year later a mental health report concluded that many local tribes "desperately need assistance in adapting to their unavoidable inclusion in Caucasian American society."[155] What the film does not adequately capture are high rates of cancer and birth defects among the South Dakotan Sioux due to the contamination of water supplies from mining and radioactive waste.

It is easy to see parallels between ill health and poverty conditions on the Great Plains at the height of the Great Depression and those of tribal communities in the 1990s. There are marked differences though—culturally divergent health practices, alcohol dependency, and diabetes-related illnesses on reservations—but the mood of despair unites "When Biting Dust Sweeps across the Land" and "Reservation's Despair Takes Greatest Toll," despite the two articles appearing sixty years apart. The 1997 *Washington Post* piece contains snatches of optimism about more responsive Indian Health Service facilities. Poverty on the Pine Ridge Reservation remained a particular concern though, so much so that President Clinton chose to visit in July 1999, a month after the publication of the first-ever surgeon general's report on mental health and the first White House conference on the subject, organized by Tipper Gore.[156] The briefing notes for this June 7th White House Conference on Mental Health reveal that Clinton was meant to mention a dedicated initiative for young Native Americans to combat rising suicide rates, but the final cut of the speech only referenced suicide in general terms.[157]

The presidential visit to Pine Ridge may have been prompted by the fact that it was just over a hundred years since the Wounded Knee Massacre, a blatant infringement of indigenous rights. The Native American Graves Protection and Repatriation Act that President George H. W. Bush signed into law in November 1990 acknowledged this implicitly in demanding that objects removed unlawfully be returned to lineal tribal descendants. During his three-hour visit to the Pine Ridge Reservation, Clinton did not address reparation or the federal government's stealing of the Black Hills from the Sioux nation, even though the Bureau of Indian Affairs (BIA) suggested it was a timely moment to do so.

Clinton's visit was nonetheless well received. The local *Rapid City Journal* acknowledged its historic importance, noting that the president would find both an "area of extreme poverty" and one rich in culture and custom.[158] In his ten-minute address to the tribal president Harold Salway and a large gathering in front of Pine Ridge School, the US president affirmed that "we are all related" in Lakota, *Mitákuye Oyás'iŋ*, and promised tax incentives and easier access to mortgages for the Lakota people in an effort to improve their housing environment. Clinton revived President Johnson's idea of economic opportunity as an engine for improving health, yet this was arguably a missed opportunity to show the federal government cared about the conditions faced by Native Americans at a moment when Bill and Hillary Clinton were prioritizing the health of children, mothers, and workers. In fact, President Clinton did not mention health at all in a speech about housing projects, sustainable energy, communication technologies, and local tourism. The *Indian Country Today* report of Clinton's visit conveys some skeptical local voices, but the president's vision of a federally funded economic Empowerment Zone as part of his New Markets strategy targeting poor regions of the country promised infrastructural hope over the next decade.[159]

The most progressive aspect of Clinton's speech was his acknowledgment that Native American rights had been ignored historically. He recalled his White House invitation to tribal leaders five years earlier, the first time a US president had extended an invitation since 1822, eight years prior to the highly controversial Indian Removal Act. It was not until August 1927, a week after he broke the ground on the Mount Rushmore presidential memorial, that Calvin Coolidge became the first US president to make a formal visit to an Indian reservation. Significantly, Coolidge chose to visit Pine Ridge during his Summer White House residency in the Black Hills. A local South Dakota journal believed that this was the president's effort to study "our ways and our industries, imbibing our spirit, and learning to estimate our place among the people making up our great nation," but Coolidge was intent on affirming citizenship and promoting to the eight thousand Sioux living on the reservation the value of work and education.[160] Speaking of the diversity of Indian life, its many languages, tribal laws, and changing attitudes, Coolidge noted that "the Indian problem," as he called it, is a "many-sided question, complicated by puzzling complexities." He ignored past atrocities and controversial politics, steering a course between a white-friendly version of native life and a recognition that "the Indian problem" was the shared responsibility of federal and tribal governments. Health was only a minor theme of this speech, relating to the need to increase the number of hospitals, physicians, and nurses as well as more federal funds that could help the Sioux "to live in better homes and observe the regulations that are necessary in the home to prevent disease."[161]

There was little recognition in Coolidge's paternalistic speech of the strong correlation between poverty and illness. Nonetheless, the occasion happened soon after the Indian Citizenship Act of 1924. It also formed a prelude to *The Problem of Indian Administration*, a 1928 federal report that begins with the lines "an overwhelming majority of the Indians are poor, even extremely poor" and that "maladjustment and poverty" are the vicious circle in which many tribal communities find themselves.[162] Health is a primary category in the Meriam Report as it was named, after Lewis Meriam, the director of the Institute for Government Research. Following a 1912 Public Health Service report that surveyed an estimated one-eighth of Indians, the Meriam Report (partly funded by the Rockefeller Foundation) demonstrated that governments and physicians were now taking seriously the correlation between poverty and ill health, especially high infant mortality rates and the spread of tuberculosis and trachoma on reservations.[163] Recognizing the need for a better system for tracking births and deaths, the report recommended the immediate improvement of diets, healthier conditions in schools, more medical personnel, and the building of public health clinics.[164] The authors strove to avoid a moralistic tone, yet the report stated boldly, "the health work of the Indian Service falls markedly below the standards maintained by the Public Health Service," and it called on the US government to inject $5 million to compensate for a lack of appropriations.[165]

The 1928 Meriam Report was more consequential in terms of educational needs and land allocation than in expanding facilities to deal with chronic and persistent health conditions, despite President Hoover pledging $3 million in 1930 in part to build more hospitals on tribal lands.[166] The report laid out the health pressures that have haunted Native American groups both before and since. It also sat on the cusp of the assimilationist and self-determinist philosophies that Coolidge and Hoover each tried to balance, before the Indian Reorganization Act of 1934 propelled the "Indian New Deal" toward a philosophy of tribal self-governance, following major crop and livestock losses during the early years of the Great Depression.[167] Epidemiological and anthropological studies of the mid- to late 1940s began to shape a deeper understanding of the social and health challenges tribal groups faced. These included an American Medical Association field project focusing on infectious diseases among Navajo and Hopi tribes in the Southwest and the introduction of "radio medical traffic" by which physicians used short-wave radio to communicate with residents of small isolated Alaska Native villages (in 1948 the US Congress appropriated an Alaska Health Grant to coordinate between the Public Health Service and the Alaska Department of Health).

In truth, though, it was a mixed postwar health legacy. The Office of Indian Affairs (that in 1947 became the Bureau of Indian Affairs and in 1955 the Division of Indian Health within the Public Health Service) began to take nutrition and health education more seriously after the war, but the low-grade nutritional value of these relief supplies meant that type 2 diabetes rates rose on reservations to twice the national mean by the 1990s. Other warning signs were high incidents of rape, which affected one in three native women, and fetal alcohol syndrome, which (since the 1970s) is thought to lead to early-onset cognitive and developmental disabilities, as explored by California writer Tommy Orange in his acclaimed 2018 novel *There There*.[168]

That is not to say there were no progressive gains, just that the politics of integration versus self-determination were delicately poised. The 1960s and 1970s can be seen as a series of missed opportunities despite John F. Kennedy affirming the nation's "moral obligation to our first Americans" in his presidential campaign of 1960, a pledge that led to more doctors (an estimated 30 percent rise nationally) and to better equipped hospitals.[169] This impulse was visible in Senator Robert Kennedy's mission to deepen the Johnson administration's War on Poverty (despite disagreements between Johnson and the younger Kennedy) by tackling rural unemployment, which at the time was around 50 percent at Pine Ridge compared to a national unemployment figure of 3.5 percent.[170] Robert Kennedy affirmed his brother's social covenant in a 1963 address to the National Congress of American Indians in Bismarck, North Dakota, a speech in which he emphasized the toxic mix of "poverty, under-education and disease." And in May 1968 during the Democratic primaries, Kennedy visited the Red Cloud Indian

School just outside the town of Pine Ridge—the same day a front-page column in the local *Rapid City Journal* focused on protestors from southern states making their voices heard in Washington, DC, as part of the Poor People's Campaign.[171] His visits to the Dakotas in 1963 and 1968 were attempts to redress what Johnson in a March 1968 speech to Congress stereotypically (but meaningfully) called "the forgotten Americans," even if these visits were inadequate recognition of largely invisible health issues.[172] Illness and disability among the Oglala Sioux were twice as common as for white Dakotans, even though a 1969 tribal study indicated that Public Health Service clinics and the Pine Ridge Hospital were well used and complemented traditional forms of healing.[173] Johnson stated that "partnership—not paternalism" was the way forward. However, whether Kennedy would have positively influenced the economic and health fortunes of the Sioux is a matter of speculation; his commitment to Native American causes was cut short less than three weeks after visiting Pine Ridge when he was assassinated in Los Angeles before being named the likely Democratic presidential candidate.[174]

Another missed federal opportunity occurred a decade later. A report on mental health conditions among American Indian and Alaska Native groups, compiled in early 1978 by one of the task panels of President Carter's Commission on Mental Health, was sensitive to poverty conditions and fragmented health services, and it recognized that a diagnosis of mental illness needed to navigate between tribal beliefs and medicalized biology.[175] However, when Carter lost the 1980 presidential race to Ronald Reagan, this report—and the commission as a whole—led nowhere consequential in policy terms. Early in the Reagan presidency, Congress replaced the Mental Health Systems Act of October 1980 with the Omnibus Budget Reconciliation Act that apportioned reduced budgets to individual states that would then decide how best to spend their shrinking health dollars. Therefore, when Clinton addressed the gathering at Pine Ridge in July 1999, there was much ground to be regained in health care provision, and it was disappointing that he did not acknowledge this in his speech.

Developing a theme of the 1978 task force report, the risk of viewing the intersection of poverty and ill health among Native Americans only in terms of federal health policy is to ignore the often-uneasy relationship between modern medicine and tribal healing. This is a major feature of Nancy Lande's 2005 book *Words, Wounds, Chasms*, a study based on fieldwork on Montana reservations far to the west of

Pine Ridge that reflects more generally on Indian Health Service units staffed very often by white physicians supported by Native American nurses and ancillary workers. Lande argues that biomedical models are inherently ethnocentric and rarely recognize radically different systems of language, culture, and belief.[176] In contrast to a biomedical model, she promotes an interconnected sociolinguistic approach that attends to differences in the language and kinship ties of tribal groups as well as what a 1991 book on tribal mental health calls a need for "cultural congruence."[177]

These cultural markers of health also apply to the Oglala Lakota (or Shannon) County where two outpatient Indian Health Service clinics in the small towns of Kyle and Wanblee support health on the reservation, together with small part-time units like the Porcupine Clinic, halfway between these two outpatient clinics. Despite a lack of funding and very basic facilities, the Porcupine Clinic is committed to community health and employs bilingual staff to increase access to those tribal elders who speak very limited English. Health information about diabetes, smoking, and mental health is now readily available at these clinics as well as advice on nutrition and the rights of patients. This can be traced back to the work of the Oglala Lakota journalist Tim Giago, who raised consciousness of reservation health issues when he moved in 1992 from editing the weekly reservation publication the *Lakota Times* (founded in 1981 as an independent news outlet) to launch *Indian Country Today*. In a series of articles in these two papers, Giago made clear that better communication networks are as important as facilities for the improvement of health services, and he points to the community role played by radio stations, such as Pine Ridge's KILI, which broadcasts from Porcupine.[178] Culturally attuned initiatives like the Red Road approach to alcohol treatment, introduced in 1999 by Gene Thin Elk, a Rosebud Sioux of the University of South Dakota, is an example of an emphasis on "wellbriety" and the vitality of traditional medicine. It replaces the twelve-step Alcoholics Anonymous journey with the figure of the circle (drawn from iconography of the Medicine Wheel) and uses sweat lodges rather than interventionist drug programs or medication-assisted treatment.[179] The aim of the Red Road is to teach the right path and empower the Lakota in the face of addiction and feelings of powerlessness that, in part at least, have economic roots.

The fact that both Barack Obama and Hillary Clinton campaigned at Pine Ridge (one of the few blue counties in South Dakota) during the Democratic primaries of early summer 2008 indicates that health and poverty remained key issues a decade after President Clinton's expression of a "shared vision." Hillary Clinton failed to win the majority of South Dakotan votes on June 3 (though Bill Clinton had returned to Pine Ridge a fortnight earlier), but this is not to suggest that all the hopes of summer 1999 failed to materialize. The introduction in 1999 of the REACH U.S. Program (short for Racial and Ethnic Approaches to Community Health across the United States) implemented better measures for assessing health risks and more responsive funding for research into diabetes, HIV/AIDS, cancer, and cardiovascular disease, though a decade into the program the REACH U.S. directors acknowledged that "large-scale community based surveys and surveillance systems deigned to monitor the health status of minority populations are limited."[180] Even Obama's commitment to raise funds for the Indian Health Service in excess of inflation (13 percent in 2010, 9 percent in 2011, 14 percent in 2012) had only limited impact on improving the level of provision of the Indian Health Service that catered for around 30 percent of American Indians and Alaskan Natives.[181]

Nonetheless, Obama's pledge in 2010 to address "gaping health care disparities" to modernize the Indian health care system and to reduce the number of uninsured American Indians, as enshrined in his renewal of the 1976 Indian Health Care Improvement Act (this time with no expiry date), feels like a utopian moment in the rearview mirror. The prospect of significant cuts to Medicaid after 2020 proposed by the Trump administration and congressional Republicans could adversely affect tribal communities for decades. Sherman Alexie spoke out angrily against Trump's budgetary postures of 2017 and disregard from those entitled to Medicaid, calling it "total exploitation, with everything up for grabs. Health care, gone. Destroy the environment in search of more profit. State-sponsored violence. Targeted incarceration.... The whole country is becoming a reservation."[182] By this Alexie means that the social disadvantages Native Americans have faced for years were now more prominent across the nation due to an intensified disenfranchisement of the poor, a point that the Nlaka'pamux First Nations writer Terese Mailhot echoes, though she rejects being seen as a "hopeless illustration" and rebukes Alexie's sexual exploitation of native women.[183]

Returning to Bill Clinton's visit to Pine Ridge in July 1999, we again see the clashes between tangible and intangible factors that echo the health and existential issues of the previous two case studies. In his run for a second term in 1996, Clinton focused equally on improving housing and protecting sacred sites as a means to "preserve Indian religious practices," suggesting he understood that well-being was both material and spiritual.[184] He prioritized technological solutions in his July 1999 speech but understood the erosion of well-being can turn healthy individuals into living ghosts, to recall one of Alexie's themes and the arcs of two books by younger indigenous writers: Elissa Washuta's *My Body Is a Book of Rules* (2014) and Terese Mailhot's *Heart Berries* (2018), in which the authors grapple with their own bipolar disorder, anorexia, and PTSD.[185] Had Clinton acknowledged the health challenges and high suicide rates among young Native Americans—and that many Lakota only seek hospital treatment as a last resort—erosion might have been a more prominent theme of his address. Clinton gestured toward this point five years earlier, in April 1994, when he invited two hundred tribal leaders to the White House. This 1994 speech focused equally on heritage, family, community, religious freedom, and economic empowerment. However, at its center is the ghostly image of the American Indian child with "poor health and inadequate education," a disempowered image that nevertheless spoke to the lack of opportunity on many reservations, which returns me to the start of this case study.[186]

Alexie's hauntings, as captured in his 2017 memoir *You Don't Have to Say You Love Me*, are a mix of personal and inherited fears. These include his heavy-drinking and (possibly) bipolar mother Lillian who contracted Parkinson's disease and cancer late in life; the alcohol-related death of his "bottle-blind" father; his grandfather who died in combat in Okinawa, Japan, when his father was only six; the violence on the Spokane Indian Reservation that he saw as a child; and the historical violence against Native Americans that he images as "an Indian baby, shredded by a Gatling gun, lying dead and bloody in the snow."[187]

This theme of violence and unspoken trauma is captured in the often lighthearted rites-of-passage film *Smoke Signals* (1997), based on early 1990s stories by Alexie, but it is better represented in the 2002 Pine Ridge movie *Skins* (both films are directed by the Cheyenne-Arapaho filmmaker Chris Eyre). Rather than presenting *Skins* as a coming-of-age story of Rudy Yellow Shirt, the themes of inebriety, violence, illness, and poverty draw from the Oglala Lakota College educator Adrian Louis's 1995 novel of the same name that deploys a similar tragicomic mode to Alexie's fiction. The Pine Ridge Hospital takes on the proportions of a character in *Skins* and contrasts unfavorably with the VA hospital in Hot Springs and the better-equipped Indian hospital in Rapid City (both predominantly white towns). The reservation hospital fades in and out of focus as Rudy teeters on the brink of ill health and, at times, psychosis, as a Vietnam veteran in his early forties and a reservation policeman still trying to grow up. For much of the story Rudy lives a ghostly, alienated existence that he believes is cursed after encountering a black widow spider as a child.[188] Yet Rudy eventually finds direction in an act of protest at the site of the Mount Rushmore presidential monument, which he considers "nothing more than graffiti on a large scale" that scars stolen Sioux land. However, his attempt at activism is tempered by a recognition that deliberately dropping a five-gallon can of red paint down the granite face of George Washington would do little to "focus worldwide or even statewide attention upon the dismal state of American Indians."[189]

Alexie engages with the idea of protest even as he is aware of its cultural and political complications. The correlation between the Alexie family's poor health and ghosts of Alexie's tribal past contrast to his interest in the Ghost Dance popularized on the plains in the 1880s. He often uses the Ghost Dance as a metaphor of collective resistance and a channel for ancestral spirits, although he recognizes its sacred significance needs to be set beside the persistence of poverty, ill health, eroded rights, and state violence. The Ghost Dance is not just a historic ritual. Not only is it a form of health citizenship, but also in February 1973 the American Indian Movement (AIM) reprised the massacre at Wounded Knee when a standoff between its occupying members and federal agents returned violence to Pine Ridge.[190] Led by the Rosebud Sioux medicine man Leonard Crow Dog, AIM revived the Ghost Dance in an effort to conjure ancestral ghosts as a ritual of remembrance and an act of self-determination.[191]

In all three of this chapter's case studies, the figure of the ghost appears as a manifestation of deep economic disparities. It emerges especially in regional writing where health services are scarce or inadequately responsive, but it also highlights misconceptions about race and region that have proven difficult to shake despite major civil rights reforms. When the "urban outcasts" that Loïc Wacquant identifies appear in the media or in public reports they are frequently reduced to bare statistics or associated with crime and disorder, while in remote communities they are often disregarded as a "low-use segment of the population" (a phrase discussed in the next chapter).[192] These ghosts often connect survivors to the victims of ill health, as we see in Lorraine Hansberry's A Raisin in the Sun when Walter Lee half intuits that he and his dead father are in danger of becoming spectral by succumbing to a pathological condition they can barely detect, let alone articulate.

Becoming citizen-activists in the codelivery of community health is one way of banishing a ghostly existence and in challenging the deficit model of identity that is often implicit in the language of deprivation. But this form of citizenship might simply mask over structural violence and failures of the state to provide adequate health services. It is important to remember that ghosts do not always evoke diminishment as emblematized by the late nineteenth-century Ghost Dance before the state violence at Wounded Knee pushed the tribal ritual underground. Ghosts can arouse fear and can easily take offense when neglected, but ghosts can also convey messages from the past and offer vital resources for the present and "strategies for survival" in the future, to evoke the subtitle of Danielle Raudenbush's 2020 book on urban poverty.[193]

As a coda to this chapter, I want to turn to the figure of the ghost at the crossroads of health and poverty, as conjured in October 2009 during a nine-minute performance of Bruce Springsteen's song "The Ghost of Tom Joad." Joining Springsteen on stage at Madison Square Garden was Tom Morello, lead guitarist of Rage against the Machine, a group that has pushed a revolutionary agenda against the neoliberal stranglehold over individual and collective freedoms, symbolized by the scrawled red lettering on Morello's guitar that read "Arm the Homeless." Springsteen introduced the song as an homage to the "fathers of folk music" in its references to unemployment, loss of home, and "the bloodfight over decent health care." The song first featured as a pared-down acoustic track on the 1995 *The Ghost of Tom Joad* album, which Springsteen released a few months before he criticized the Clinton administration for failing working families by overfocusing on the middle class, and its lyrics offer a spectral link between Steinbeck's Depression-era character and the late century experience of poverty.[194] Just as Springsteen reanimates Woody Guthrie's 1940 Steinbeck-inspired ballad "Tom Joad" and Michael Harrington's 1962 critique *The Other America*, so we can listen to "The Ghost of Tom Joad" as a counter-memory that gives shape to invisible lives. In the final two minutes of the Madison Square Garden performance, this is sonically animated when the four synchronized guitars and Springsteen's impassioned vocal give way to Tom Morello's trance-like guitar solo. Mixing distortion and melody, Morello's guitar brings viscerally to life the anguish and survivalist spirit of all the other nameless Joads.

CHAPTER 3

Pollution

Nuclear Fallout, Water Contamination,
Climate Change

April 22, 1971. On the first anniversary of Earth Day, the nonprofit group Keep America Beautiful launched a television advertisement that became famous for its central character, the Crying Indian. In the opening scene, we see a Cherokee paddling a canoe down a sun-dappled river, but his tranquility is soon disturbed as the camera cuts to scraps of newspaper and debris floating by the boat before pulling back to reveal the canoe dwarfed by an industrial wasteland. When we next see the Cherokee, he is in silhouette, partially blocking the sun that filled the opening scene with brightness and color. He moors the boat on a refuse-strewn shoreline and walks to a busy freeway where a bag of trash thrown by a child from a speeding car greets him. This clash of cultures prompts a somber narrator to speak for the first time: "Some people have a deep abiding respect for the natural beauty that was once this country. And some people don't." We see the Cherokee's reaction in profile. He looks down at the litter, then we see him in full-face as he turns to the camera with a tear running from his right eye—an image environmental historian Finis Dunaway calls perhaps "the most famous tear in American history."[1] As the music reaches a crescendo, the voice returns, "People start pollution. People can stop it," before the ad closes on a plain black leaflet with a white title, "71 things you can do to stop pollution," and a New York address to which viewers are invited to write for a free leaflet.

In twenty-seven words and at just over a minute in length, the 1971

Crying Indian ad campaign captured a moment in which industrialists and environmentalists were locked in a battle to determine the fate of Nature in the late twentieth century. Launched in 1953, the nonprofit organization Keep America Beautiful began working closely with the Advertising Council in 1960, including a 1967 anti-litter ad featuring every American child's favorite dog Lassie. Keep America Beautiful promotes itself in the final frame of the Crying Indian ad as working toward "the public good." This sentiment echoes Lady Bird Johnson's belief that the beautification of the natural environment can therapeutically "create harmony" and "lessen tensions" in society, at a time when the Lyndon Johnson administration was ramping up its environmental health protection programs, based on the president's view that pollution is "one of the most pervasive problems of our society."[2] Surprisingly, the Keep America Beautiful group was made up of not of card-carrying environmentalists but of large manufacturers, including the Coca-Cola Foundation, McDonald's, Nestlé, and PepsiCo—not companies one might associate with ethical waste management.[3] Perhaps this is the reason that the ad centers on an everyday instance of litter throwing rather than tackling factory emissions or corporate greed, with the implication that influencing consumer behavior would help fix the problem rather than passing environmentally friendly legislation that would regulate corporate responsibility. This is not to ignore the dystopian imagery of its scene of industrial effluence, but the ad does not really address the environmental or health consequences of pollution.

The Crying Indian is clearly distressed at the loss of his home, but the ad underexplores his travails at a time when the 1970 film *Little Big Man* was challenging Eurocentric versions of American history by highlighting the sustained historical injustices faced by the Cherokees. Instead, it depicts the figure as a nineteenth-century "noble savage" whose natural habitat suddenly vanishes, leaving him stranded on the edge of a busy twentieth-century highway. The Cherokee's tear is a symbol of authenticity, but a complex interplay of economic and environmental factors shapes his sorrow: it is a sign of psychological distress, an emulation of the wounded planet, and a rending of nature and society that the French philosopher Bruno Latour associates with the rift that divides modernity from premodern notions of interconnectedness.[4] Despite echoing the themes of the first two chapters regarding the social determinants of ill health, Finis Dunaway argues the sincerity of the ad is wholly manufactured, partly because the Cherokee is played not by an actor with Native American blood but rather by the popular Western film actor Iron Eyes Cody, born of an Italian American family.[5]

Although the Keep American Beautiful group lost the support of environmental activists in the mid-1970s over the introduction of disposable drink containers, the emotional impact of the ad persisted. It resonated closely with the rhetoric of Richard Nixon's January 1970 State of the Union Address, especially when the president asked if "the great question of the seventies is, shall we surrender to our surroundings, or shall we make peace with nature and begin to make reparations for the damage we have done to our air, to our land, and to our water?"[6] Nixon dodged the question of who was to blame. Instead, he stressed the need for "better management" of nature and "a new quality of life" that could balance personal opportunity and what he called a "new federalism."[7] This view led to the extension of the 1963 Clean Air Act and the launch of the Community Health and Environmental Surveillance System, with the aim of assessing the relationship between pollution and ill health, the burdens of "exposed communities," and the benefits of pollution control.[8] It is unlikely the ad influenced the Clean Water Act Amendments of 1972 or the Safe Drinking Water Act of 1974. Yet it appeared frequently on television networks at a time when the quality of the air and contaminants in drinking water were cause for concern, and a dramatic fire on the Cuyahoga River near Cleveland, Ohio, was fresh in the memories of midwesterners. In contrast to the clear flowing river at the start of the ad, *Time* magazine described the polluted Cuyahoga River as "chocolate brown, oily, bubbling with subsurface gases, it oozes rather than flows."[9]

The powerful imagery of the Crying Indian resonated with others who were striving for environmental justice. These included the antinuclear group Friends of the Earth (formed in New York in summer 1969) and Lenore Marshall, the poet and cofounder of the National Committee for a Sane Nuclear Policy (SANE), who in a spring 1971 Wilderness Society article warned of "the nuclear Sword of Damocles" that meant "nothing, no matter how remote, is immune."[10] The messaging of the ad was reprised in the mid-1970s and again in the late 1990s in another Keep America Beautiful commercial that depicts the face of the Cherokee pasted on a billboard poster by the side of a litter-strewn bus shelter. This April 1998 ad appeared at a moment when debates about climate change were polarizing congressional leaders, nine months before the death of the ninety-four-year-old Iron Eyes Cody at an age considerably in advance of most Native American men.[11] Notably, the 1998 ad has no voiceover, just a closing caption in lower case on a black screen: "back by popular neglect." In its design, it mixes what Jennifer Thomson calls the two elisions of health and environment—"human health as a marker of structural environmental oppression and the assertion that the planet has a fever"—as well as developing the geographies of vulnerability trajectory of the first half of this book.[12]

With this juxtaposition in mind, this chapter spans the 1930s and 2010s, focusing on instances when the relationship between pollution and health was prominent in the national conversation. It is tempting to document the long fight to preserve planetary health and the rise of the environmental movement that coincided with the first Keep America Beautiful ad. However, in its longer arc, as Miriam Kaprow argues, the environmental justice movement is "an impermanent coalition that gathers people into temporary interaction" around a particular cause rather than in terms of sustained action.[13] For this reason, my case studies focus on three paired moments when environmental crises prompted searching public health questions: airborne radioactive fallout in 1953 and 1979, water pollution and lead poisoning in 1935 and 2016, and the intersection of ecological and human vulnerabilities that was particularly apparent in 2006 and 2017.

The three cases develop the environmental and economic pressures of the first two chapters via a range of diverse yet specific locations in Utah, Pennsylvania, Washington, DC, Michigan, Alaska, and Florida. My first two studies focus on basic elements of life and vectors of disease—air and water—that in their "clean" form are never free, as Nixon reminded Congress in 1970. The third case study pivots on two influential films fronted by the former vice president, Al Gore, *An Inconvenient Truth* (2006) and *An Inconvenient Sequel: Truth to Power* (2017), which as a pair make visible the ecological threat of climate change during the George W. Bush and Donald Trump administrations. It is hard to identify many values that Nixon and Gore share in common, yet they both argue, in Nixon's words, that "through our years of past carelessness we incurred a debt to nature, and that debt is now being called."[14] This is a rare example of resonance across party lines. More often than not, a pro-business Republican view embodies skepticism toward the theory that human activity is the prime cause of climate change, whereas Democrats often (yet not always) put faith in evidence-based science that posits human pollution as the major cause of global warming.

There are strong lines of continuity here from the first two chapters with respect to public health challenges at the fulcrum of environmental and economic pressures, but the socioecological focus also demands a shift in causality. Whereas flood damage and malnutrition are visible in the harm they cause, even if they hide deeper economic and racial realities, the relationship between environmental risk and those individuals or communities most vulnerable to ill health is often invisible. The head of the US Environmental Protection Agency during the Carter administration, Douglas M. Costle, developed this theme of invisibility by proposing "most health-related regulation in the environmental field must be written with even less direct evidence of the linkage between environmental contaminants and their victims."[15] In this April 1980 speech, Costle valorized the importance of scientific knowledge, but he was also concerned about invisible health damage caused by pollutants where there might only be circumstantial evidence. Writing thirty years later, Rob Nixon has argued that what he calls "slow violence" to citizens often happens "out of sight," but this is often "incremental and accretive." It has a multiplying effect over time "where the conditions for sustaining life become increasingly but gradually degraded," especially for typically poor communities that live near hazardous waste or within environments with suspect water and air quality.[16] Set against these largely invisible health threats, this chapter links debates about the Anthropocene (a geological term first used in 2000 by the Dutch atmospheric chemist Paul Crutzen) to the argument that during the Cold War it became apparent that "humans will almost certainly be the architects of our own destruction."[17] This, as the first case study shows, links nuclear tests in Nevada in the early 1950s to the moment of Costle's speech in the wake of a nuclear reactor failure at Three Mile Island, Pennsylvania, at a time when environmental protests were increasingly visible. In tracing environmental health concerns across an eighty-year period, the chapter aims to assess whether the Anthropocene is a relevant climate-sensitive concept for our epoch about survival in a world of toxic waste, unstable territories, and rising oceans.

As the first two chapters show, determining the causal relationship between a harmful environment and ill health is tricky, especially if one is looking to identify ultimate responsibility or seeking reparation for the victims of structural violence. This has prompted conservative critics such as the epidemiologist Elizabeth Whelan in her 1985 book *Toxic Terror* to underplay looming environmental calamities in her claim that scientific critiques overlook the fact that at the national level the United States is getting healthier.[18] The fact that Whelan provides hardly any evidence to underpin this claim is an example of science being at the service of, or even reduced to, ideology. Even in cases when there is substantial evidence of harm or permanent damage to personal health, it is tempting to telescope out into conspiracy theories about the dangers of the industrial-military complex, as President Eisenhower called it in his Farewell Speech of 1961, and what a decade later Barbara and John Ehrenreich called the "medical-industrial complex."[19] The 2004 volume *Landscapes of Exposure* notes that, even in balanced accounts, it is hard to avoid some degree of speculation, because uncertainty is inherent in the "formation of many environmental health problems, starting with the time lag between exposure and possible health effect."[20] Uncertainty, of course, does not help when it comes to policies and planning. The blurred line between probability and possibility raises questions about cause and effect and the veracity of truth claims about the state of the environment that have become increasingly polarized in recent years. The Trump administration stands out in ignoring the warnings of climate change experts, notably a United Nations–endorsed intergovernmental report compiled by scientists from forty countries, including the United States. At existing carbon emission levels, this October 2018 report strongly predicted rising sea levels and climate risks to "health, livelihoods, food security, water supply, human security, and economic growth," with predictions tracked through to 2040.[21]

In recognizing these scientific, medical, financial, and political entanglements—what Lady Bird Johnson called "a tangled skein of wool" in which "everything leads to something else"—this chapter focuses on cases that highlight the relationship between declining health and environmental pressures within what Steve Lerner describes as "contaminated communities."[22] The twin aim is to highlight the vulnerabilities faced by these geographically dispersed communities and to test the notion that public health operates at its most effective in what Robert Bellah terms "the middle range between the local and the global level" by creating collaborative spaces in which health citizenship can flourish.[23] On this model, a more responsive public health culture should involve institutional reform, democratic participation, and a commitment to speak out when partisan beliefs and business interests are prioritized over long-term community health needs. In pursuing these entanglements, I examine the physical and psychological health effects of pollution in historical and near-contemporary cases, set against pervasive fears about air pollution, water purity, and global warming.

A STRANGE BREEZE: NUCLEAR FALLOUT AND CANCER SCARES, 1953, 1979

On December 8, 1953, toward the end of Dwight Eisenhower's first year in the White House, the president addressed the United Nations General Assembly at its headquarters in New York City. Dubbed his Atoms for Peace speech, Eisenhower pledged the nation would "help solve the fearful atomic dilemma" and "devote its entire heart and mind to finding the way by which the miraculous inventiveness of man shall not be dedicated to his death, but consecrated to his life."[24] It had been eight years since President Truman ordered the US Armed Forces to drop atomic bombs over Hiroshima and Nagasaki, killing around 80,000 instantly in Hiroshima, and another 60,000 from related health complications within the year.[25] When Truman authorized the development of a hydrogen bomb in 1949 despite reservations of his foreign-policy advisors George Kennan and Dean Acheson, the mounting arms race between the United States and the Soviet Union led many to believe that a new and even more deadly war was approaching.[26]

Domestic Cold War fears eased a little in the mid-1950s buoyed by a healthy postwar economy, public faith in the experienced leadership of Eisenhower, and optimism in medical advances such as the rollout of Jonas Salk's polio vaccine. While many adults would have remembered the devastating mental and physical health effects of the bombs dropped over Japan, described by journalist John Hersey in his August 1946 *New Yorker* piece "Hiroshima," it was a leap to imagine that such a large-scale story of annihilation could play out on home soil. However, as Joseph Masco argues, the bomb "inverted the definitions of health and security, remaking them from positive values into an incremental calculus of death."[27] Consequently, domestic health fears escalated rather than diminished beneath the surface of a once-again prosperous nation; even "the privileged ones," as Robert Coles called upper-middle-class and wealthy children, displayed anxieties and deep-set fears during the 1950s.[28]

The expansion of print and broadcast media brought public health deeper into the home, especially via middle-class magazines like *Ladies' Home Journal*, *McCall's*, and *Redbook*. Health advice columns offered remedies but they could also stir domestic anxieties, while other health issues remained shrouded in secrecy, especially those relating to reproductive health, mental illness, and cancer treatment. While public health was an important fact of civil defense preparedness and air pollution was being taken seriously in Washington, DC, by 1955 (the Air Pollution Control Act was signed in July), pockets of concern about fallout from aboveground atomic testing in the Southwest were muted.[29] Eisenhower was keen to advance his UN proposal for easing global tensions and to explore peaceful uses of atomic energy, but the president did little to address domestic health threats of the nuclear tests despite the warning of Lewis Strauss, special assistant to the president on atomic energy.[30]

In this first of three case studies on the relationship between environmental strain and ill health, I focus on two years of the long Cold War. The initial year is 1953 when reports surfaced about deaths among livestock in Utah, Nevada, and Arizona, the tristate region within 250 miles of the Nevada Test Site. The second is 1979 when President Carter established an interagency task force to provide a fuller picture of the health implications of nuclear fallout, given that sketchy public knowledge in the 1950s meant that this health crisis was not widely known at the time. By 1979, there was better recognition of the deleterious effects of air pollution, regulatory scrutiny of nuclear power and radioactive waste, and a realization that the postwar socioeconomic boom had led to "a great acceleration" in the fragility of the natural environment.[31] More than just a "long-delayed postscript" to the early Cold War, the late 1970s was consequential for another reason: the partial meltdown of the nuclear reactor in March 1979 on Three Mile Island, twelve miles from Pennsylvania's state capital Harrisburg, caused a wave of media and public reaction that reinforced the environmentalist cause.[32]

The two years, 1953 and 1979, are helpful for determining the long-term health effects of fallout, but this case study is one of cover-ups and delayed disclosures that reveal fissures within Cold War public health and an ambivalent attitude to specialists. Most prominently, theoretical physicist Robert Oppenheimer publicly voiced his Cold War concerns in a January 1955 *See It Now* interview with journalist Edward R. Murrow. Based on his work as the first director of the Los Alamos Laboratory, New Mexico, from 1943 to 1945 and as the director of Princeton's Institute for Advanced Studies since 1947, Oppenheimer acknowledged that "geneticists don't know enough" to be sure about the long-term health effects of radiation. Oppenheimer recognized that the Atomic Energy Act of 1946 had tried to articulate a middle ground between national security secrets and the free interchange of scientific information, but he called for the sharing of scientific evidence when it is known and a degree of honesty when it is not. Nearly ten years before the *See It Now* interview, on October 25, 1945, only a week after resigning his position at Los Alamos, Oppenheimer warned the recently elected President Truman about nuclear risks, and the following May he wrote to the president to express his concerns about the effectiveness of testing. By that time, the FBI had begun surveillance of Oppenheimer on the suspicion that he was a communist spy, but also arguably because he was an outspoken public figure—views that hardened in the 1950s and led to the revocation of his Atomic Energy Commission (AEC) security clearance in May 1954.[33] Given this turn of events, Oppenheimer had concerns about granting Murrow an interview. He nevertheless expressed his reservations about the nuclear program and the dangers that hydrogen bomb development posed. He admitted that he was "not unworried" about the aboveground tests in Nevada, and he voiced concern about secrecy and a lack of honesty, given that the AEC was claiming that radioactivity from fallout was negligible and no cause for alarm.[34]

Oppenheimer's initial feelings of awe on witnessing the first detonation of a nuclear bomb at the Trinity Test Site in New Mexico in July 1945 swiftly gave way to profound reservations about its lethal and potentially uncontrollable power.[35] What is surprising is less that Oppenheimer was outspoken about nuclear dangers and more that his views largely went unheeded during the Truman presidency. The mood changed to an extent in 1952–53 with the release of a report from a panel chaired by Oppenheimer that stressed that nuclear disaster was an imminent danger and that vigilance was necessary to avoid catastrophe.[36] In recommending a course between government complacency and public hysteria, the Oppenheimer Panel report informed Eisenhower's Atoms for Peace speech and the administration's proposal for a 1953 public-relations campaign, Operation Candor.[37] Although never officially launched, Operation Candor emphasized nuclear preparedness and national safety via radio and television commercials as a means to control public emotion and to prevent panic setting in.[38] Few officials seemed perturbed by reports of burns to cattle and sheep in the vicinity, for example, and there was little recognition of the health risks of overground nuclear tests. The AEC did note in a July 1953 report that "fall-out levels were somewhat higher than those recorded in past operations," but also that the levels were not "high enough to create a human health hazard," even though it admitted livestock died coincidentally with the tests.[39]

The test sites were located in relatively remote arid locations in New Mexico and Nevada, yet there was no clear sense of the circumference of the contamination zone or long-term effects on air and water quality. It is unclear whether further disclosure would have heightened or quelled public fears; however, it is clear that the health risks of those living in the region would have been better appreciated had independent examinations of animals been conducted in the vicinity. A lack of robust precautionary measures and independent testing led environmentalist Philip Fradkin to view the whole episode as an AEC cover-up in that it willfully ignored the sustained exposure faced by local communities. Looking from a fifty-year perspective, the Utah poet Corrinne Clegg Hales extends this revisionist view in "Exposure," fourteen poems published in her 2002 collection *Separate Escapes*. The scathing middle poem of this section, "Covenant: Atomic Energy Commission, 1950s," depicts a vigilant yet fearful Cold War nation looking toward Russia for "unambiguous tragedy," only to miss "the atom bomb sneaking in through the side door, blowing / Like a tumble weed across the desert...breathing / Its isotope-ridden breath into air ducts of hospitals, / Schools, high-rises."[40] This ghostly imagery is a legacy of the Cold War and, more broadly, of the Anthropocene.[41]

Invisible fallout affected local farmers especially. They suffered major financial challenges due to a significant loss of livestock, particularly in Iron County in southwestern Utah, downwind from the Nevada Test Site. Nuclear explosions began at the Nevada site in January 1951, and officials were quick to reassure residents that there was "no danger from or as a result of AEC test activities."[42] Prevailing winds meant that communities in Utah to the east had greater reason to be concerned about fallout than did Las Vegas residents living one hundred miles to the southeast. However, there was little meaningful coverage in the *Deseret News* and the *Salt Lake Times*, two widely read newspapers of Salt Lake City, 250 miles north of the communities downwind from the test site.[43] The local *Iron County Record* did include a few cautionary accounts. One of these was by University of Utah student Ralph J. Hafen (a resident of St. George, Utah, near the Utah-Arizona border), who felt "morally obligated to warn people of the irreparable damage that may have occurred or may in the future occur" after witnessing a test blast on March 24, 1953, eight weeks before the dirtiest explosion, Shot Harry.[44] Hafen was worried about the unknown dangers of plutonium on lungs, eyes, and reproductive systems, but even when Geiger counters were registering fallout in Cedar City and St. George days after Shot Harry, an *Iron County Record* editorial concluded its report by repeating AEC reassurances.[45]

That year witnessed further inspections of farm animals as local veterinarians reported to the Public Health Service (PHS) damage to livestock. This PHS report concluded that the deaths of 4,500 sheep and births of stunted lambs was either the result of fallout or malnutrition, given that the area was experiencing an intense drought in spring 1953 at the time of the livestock inspections. It appears that AEC leaders pushed the malnutrition theory, despite studies of tissue samples within controlled conditions conducted by the Utah biologist Paul B. Pearson (who was working for the AEC) suggesting otherwise.[46] When local farmers filed legal suits in 1955–56 following another round of explosions at the Nevada Test Site in spring 1955, the AEC withheld some of the available data from the court to protect liability.[47] The Public Health Service was not as convinced of the malnutrition theory as the AEC, because PHS radiologists had detected suspicious levels of thyroid radioactivity in the region, although it was difficult to reach consensus as to whether nuclear fallout was the primary cause.

Prominent scientists like Hermann Muller and Linus Pauling were arguing in the mid-1950s that no level of radiation was safe for human health, but President Eisenhower maintained in 1959 that "to my knowledge, there has been no suppression of information on fallout" despite the fact that stories in *The Reporter* and the *Saturday Evening Post* in 1957 suggested otherwise.[48] The administration gave airborne toxins more scrutiny from 1954 via the Air Pollution Engineering Branch, a second Air Pollution Control Act in 1955, and from 1961 through a new Division of Air Pollution. Questions of environmental health were even more pressing in the early 1960s when reports were filed that contested the AEC's position on nuclear drift, such as a four-year study of leukemia levels in southern Utah conducted by the PHS radiologist Edward S. Weiss. This study focused on the dental and thyroid health of two thousand schoolchildren born in 1953 in an effort to document mortality rates from cancer in Iron County and Washington County over a fourteen-year period.[49] There was some evidence of a rise in instances of leukemia in these two counties during 1959–60, and yet the AEC judged the report inconclusive. Weiss published a portion of his research in the *American Journal of Public Health* in 1967, but his PHS report remained an internal document until a five-month congressional hearing in 1979 (led by the Utah senator Orrin Hatch) revealed that the AEC had both withheld and skewed evidence.[50] In the middle of this hearing, President Carter decided to set up an inter-agency task force to "study the compensation of persons who may have developed radiation-related illnesses as a result of exposure to nuclear weapons tests."[51] Completed in February 1980, the report of the task force coincided with a new wave of court cases that tended to favor the plaintiffs, including a successful lawsuit filed in 1982 by over one thousand Utah farmers who collectively claimed government negligence.[52] In assessing this sequence of events in the mid-1980s, historian Howard Ball identified a double nuclear problem: fallout affecting farmers, livestock, and crops was compounded by "the government's coercion of local agriculture agents and pathologists," revealing "the dark side of nuclear technology" that was deeply damaging both to regional health and to public trust.[53]

New York photojournalist Carole Gallagher pushed Ball's inquiry further by arguing that one reason that so little was done in and after 1953 was that the AEC viewed scattered communities of Nevada and Utah as part of a "low-use segment of the population," picking up on the myth that the area was an empty space.[54] She adopted the phrase "low-use segment" from a recently declassified AEC memo she discovered in 1979, and it became a keynote for her 1993 book *America Ground Zero*. Gallagher's is a study of the long-term health of working-class residents affected in both fathomable and unfathomable ways, published the year that negotiations began on a comprehensive nuclear test and when declassified information came to public attention about human radiation experiments using plutonium injections.[55] She was self-consciously an outsider in these small western communities, but she tried to listen carefully to the "long silenced" voices, choosing to include stories from "as many different life situations and points of view as possible."[56] Gallagher was not working in a vacuum in trying to make the invisible visible though. One insider who unmasked an AEC cover-up was mathematician Harold Knapp, who conducted studies in 1962–66 (on behalf of the AEC) in an effort to assess the level of radioactivity making its way into the human body via milk from cattle. Knapp's tests revealed the AEC underestimated the amount of radiation downwind from the site and did not heed scientific warnings that mutations from radioactivity were "cumulative and permanent."[57] Knapp's findings were revealing, yet the AEC curbed his attempts to speak out on the premise they would be "potentially detrimental" to the testing program.[58]

Testing was consigned to underground sites when, in August 1963, President Kennedy signed the Partial Test Ban Treaty, but the damage was already done 2,500 miles to the southwest. This was despite Governor Nelson Rockefeller's New York Task Force on Protection from Radioactive Fallout recommending in the late 1950s that the federal government more effectively communicate the dangers of windborne fallout, and that states should work on survival tool kits.[59] So, when Gallagher started her decade-long project in the early 1980s to reveal the hidden stories of the Nevada Test Site downwinders, she sought to capture in word and image connections between working folk, their habitat, and the health risks faced by future generations.[60] These long-term risks did not only center on Nevada and Utah; the fallout drifted as far as Idaho, Montana, and South Dakota according to a 1997 National Cancer Institute report that documented regional instances of thyroid cancer.[61]

Set against this new domestic cancer threat, through the 1950s the National Cancer Institute worked with the American Cancer Society and the American Association for Cancer Research to determine more precisely the chemical causes and effects of cancer. Yet there were different views on effective treatment—for example, when it came to stomach ulcers—and medical treatments using radiation left practitioners open to charges of negligence for failing to offer a full briefing to patients about risks.[62] This was a different yet related ethical issue from nuclear-testing safety and radiation protection, especially as there was limited understanding in the 1950s of the side effects of cobalt radiation treatment, even though there was a long history of treating cancer by combining radiation treatment and aggressive surgery. Cancer awareness groups argued that radical mastectomies to treat breast cancer did unwarranted violence to many female patients, but not until the 1960s and 1970s were aggressive cancer treatments better regulated, underpinned by fuller biomedical data.

The subject of cancer often triggered fearful responses that left many citizens placing a high degree of trust in medical authorities at a time when the National Institutes of Health and the University of Chicago were conducting radiotherapy research, but cancer also raised questions about the robustness of occupational health and growing environmental concerns.[63] The topic of leukemia went public the year that Susan Sontag published an account of her own cancer in *Illness as Metaphor* (1978), coinciding with scientific accounts of the therapeutic possibilities of bone marrow transplants. In February 1978, the *Boston Globe* released a report on the ill-health effects of working conditions on nuclear carriers in the Portsmouth Naval Shipyard in Maine, which the Boston physician Thomas Najarian corroborated when he published two scientific pieces that November.[64] This evidence deepened the following year with the publication of research conducted by the Communicable Disease Center on four thousand nuclear site military workers following the Smoky nuclear test of August 31, 1957, which revealed a spike in instances of leukemia and respiratory cancer.

Polarizing views of the nuclear benefits and dangers emerged in the 1960s but came into full force in the mid-1970s when activist voices grew in volubility. One of these was African American poet Audre Lorde, who, less than two months after being diagnosed with breast cancer, expressed the need to combat silence and censure, "even at the risk" of the message being "bruised and misunderstood."[65] The "harsh and certain" diagnosis of breast cancer left Lorde aware that speaking out loudly was the only alternative to "sitting in the corner mute as bottles" while "our children are distorted and destroyed, while our earth is poisoned."[66] For Lorde, this involved the channeling of anger and a reevaluation of the natural world through the act of imaginative writing, to give a "name to the nameless so it can be thought."[67] She wrote in the mid-1980s about the "nuclear madness" that was "devastating" islands in the South Pacific, and the detrimental health effects of atomic fallout on newborn babies of Micronesia, and in a 1990 speech, she linked nuclear proliferation directly to "ecological disaster," two years before her own death from liver cancer.[68]

Lorde's 1980 *The Cancer Journals* was groundbreaking, especially in the courage she displays in discussing her mastectomy. Yet the environmental sources of cancer remained fear provoking to many, even though by the late 1970s treatments had to be "palatable to the patient" rather than just effective.[69] Despite these "better-tolerated therapies," it was easier to blame cancer on lifestyle choices such as smoking (as did the 1964 Surgeon General's Report *Smoking and Tobacco Use*) than on pollution or fallout. In 1980, Richard Peto called for dispassionate responses to environmental triggers for cancer, arguing that often the epidemiology of cancer was distorted, with industrialists downplaying and environmentalists overplaying its risks.[70] But the threat of invisible toxins did not make for scientific calm or ideologically free public health information at a time when Carter's health secretary Joseph Califano was declaring smoking to be "public health enemy number one."[71]

One of the most significant moments in the hardening of environmental activists toward the hazards of nuclear energy was the Three Mile Island incident of March 1979 in Middletown, Pennsylvania, near the state capital of Harrisburg, when 90 percent of a nuclear reactor core malfunctioned. The incident followed a 1974 report on the Shippingport Atomic Power Station in the western part of the state (the plant opened in 1958), which revealed "levels of radioactivity in the environment in excess of normal 'background' levels" over a fifteen-year period.[72] The plant owner, the AEC, and the EPA all rebutted the potential ill-health effects of the Shippingport emissions. But the two incidents not only worried Pennsylvanians, they also burst the bubble of some who thought nuclear power was the solution to the energy crisis, especially as Three Mile Island coincided with a congressional hearing into the health dangers of fallout from the open-air testing of twenty years earlier.[73]

The emergency phase of the possible radiation leak at Three Mile Island Nuclear Generating Station lasted from March 28 to April 9, 1979, and provoked a strong reaction from the public and journalists. This included a warning in the *New Yorker* that revived existential fears of the Cold War in its claim that nuclear power "is alien and dangerous to earthly life, and can, through damage to life's genetic foundation, break the very frame on which the generations of mankind are molded."[74] Radiological studies of xenon and iodine emissions later confirmed the official view, but they also provoked significant distress for residents, potentially heightening the risk of leukemia and in utero complications. On April 1, in a show of support, President Carter and First Lady Rosalynn Carter visited the control room of the nuclear station and held a press conference in Middletown, eight days before Pennsylvania governor Richard Thornburgh called an official end to the crisis.[75] Yet the response by protestors was stark. Police arrested eleven at a Philadelphia antinuclear rally on March 30; Carter's dinner in Milwaukee the night before his Pennsylvania trip was disturbed by activists; and protestors confronted the president with "Stop the Merchant of Atomic Death" banners outside his Washington, DC, church on the morning of the visit to Middletown.[76] Such was the intensity of the public reaction, fueled by reports that radioactive iodine had contaminated local milk supplies, the Three Mile Island news story ran for a year, even though the President's Commission on the Accident at Three Mile Island (the Kemeny Report), published on October 30, 1979, placed the blame on human error rather than technological malfunction.[77]

The coincidental release of the high-profile Columbia movie *The*

China Syndrome on March 16, 1979, only twelve days before the Three Mile Island meltdown, exacerbated nuclear fears and mistrust of authorities. Starring Jane Fonda and Michael Douglas (who also produced) as a frustrated newsreader and a suspicious cameraman, the film focuses on the clash between broadcast media and a cover-up on behalf of white-collar workers and executive managers over an unstable California reactor. Despite the locations being 2,600 miles apart, and one a quasi-fiction and the other a worrying reality, officials in each case insisted there was no public danger.[78] In the case of Three Mile Island, Governor Thornburgh at least tried to steer a course between preventing a panic scenario and acting responsibly in the face of potential health dangers, advising families living within a ten-mile radius of the reactor to stay indoors and instructing pregnant women and preschool children living within five miles to evacuate. In contrast, the lack of a responsible authority figure in *The China Syndrome* and the absence of a robust emergency procedure at the plant meant that the moral high ground of the narrative is claimed by a reporter and cameraman (played by Fonda and Douglas) who defy orders to gain the attention of their broadcaster and viewers. Given that the movie only accidentally coincided with the Three Mile Island malfunction, Michael Douglas said he was "very wary of capitalizing in any sense on a tragedy"; he even canceled an appearance on Johnny Carson's *Tonight Show* to avoid speaking about the parallels. The more outspoken Jane Fonda was less willing to hold back though, and with local antinuclear groups increasing in number—including protests at Diablo Canyon Power Plant, which inspired *The China Syndrome*—the nation started listening attentively to the nuclear threat in the spring of 1979.[79]

The Kemeny Commission report concluded in the fall that radiation from the plant had "a negligible effect on the physical health" of workers and locals and psychological stress was "short-lived." However, a telephone survey conducted by the Pennsylvania Department of Health three months after the initial Three Mile Island crisis, together with a trio of follow-up surveys conducted in 1980, revealed a strong correlation between self-reported psychological distress and those living within fifteen miles of the plant—a radius that included nearby Middletown and the state capital Harrisburg. Symptoms were particularly evident in mothers of preschool children and pregnant women.[80] The nature of the surveys meant it was tricky to dig deeply into contributory factors, but there appeared to be a strong incidence of distress among the plant workers, their families, and those with chronic health conditions who felt more vulnerable after the incident. Other studies, including an investigation by the Pennsylvania Department of Health, suggested stress remained a background health issue for between 10 to 20 percent of residents more than nine months later. This included an increase in the use of alcohol, sleeping pills, and tranquilizers, although it was unclear to what extent this was a direct consequence of the incident.[81] Further follow-up studies, including a 1990 National Cancer Institute study, agreed that radioactive risks were low, but also revealed that some residents remained anxious for years after. This anxiety reemerged especially when the plant reopened in 1985, partly because by the mid-1980s the safety of other reactors was being questioned and partly because poor families who could not afford to move could do little to eliminate the threat.[82]

The media played a significant role in conveying the danger of the initial incident at a time when details of the AEC cover-ups were surfacing, but also transformed the inhabitants living within range of Middletown into "biological citizens," to evoke the subtitle of a study of the Chernobyl nuclear disaster that occurred seven years later.[83] No deaths followed the Three Mile Island incident, and there were no signs that emissions had harmed residents or had drifted downwind to Philadelphia. Nonetheless, responses from activists (who held demonstrations in front of the State Capitol in Harrisburg) and high-profile figures like Jane Fonda (who called for national protests) marked a strong contrast between this postscript moment of 1979 and the largely silent fallout of 1953. On September 24, 1979, a month before the release of the Kemeny Commission report, Fonda amplified the nuclear threat in front of the Three Mile Island reactors alongside Tom Hayden, her activist husband and former SDS (Students for a Democratic Society) leader.[84] This followed the couple's participation at a No Nukes rally outside the US Capitol on May 6 that took its intellectual impulse from *No Nukes: Everyone's Guide to Nuclear Power*, Anna Gyorgy's consciousness-raising book that shaped the philosophy of the antinuclear group the Clamshell Alliance by emphasizing that the "health dangers of nuclear power are inseparable from environmental dangers."[85]

Speaking in the US Senate on October 9, 1979, Massachusetts senator Ted Kennedy made a comparison between the Three Mile Island incident and the Nevada nuclear tests of the early 1950s in his effort to pass a Radiation Exposure Compensation Act. However, a group of musicians that formed that summer had a greater impact on public opinion.[86] Calling themselves Musicians United for Safe Energy

(MUSE) and led by Californian Jackson Browne, the group organized a series of No Nukes benefit concerts at Madison Square Garden in September 1979 to heighten awareness of the nuclear threat, to raise funds to help local antinuclear groups, and to draw attention to the human cost of radiation. The sentiments of the No Nukes organizers were broad and simple: Browne stated that nuclear energy has "been sold like a drug. Like a mirror that will lie to you," and Graham Nash of supergroup Crosby, Stills & Nash said that nuclear power companies are "threatening my life personally." The concert centered on a group rendition of John Hall's folksong "Power," which contrasts "atomic poison" with "the warm power of the sun" and the "restless power of the wind."

Another strident antinuclear song of that year, Bruce Springsteen's "Roulette," was not performed at No Nukes even though Springsteen was one of its most charismatic acts, perhaps because its fast-tempo punk construction strained against the peace and love vibe of the concert. Springsteen's song pictures a family living in the shadow of Three Mile Island in a state of fear in a "house full of things I can't touch," not knowing whom to trust as they try to escape pending disaster. This sentiment tallies with sociologist Kai Erikson's reading of the Three Mile Island incident, in which he describes the environment as "alive with dangers, a terrain in which fresh air and sunshine and all the other benevolences of creation are to be feared as sources of toxic infection."[87] In Springsteen's song, the "restless power of the wind" of the antinuclear anthem "Power" transforms into a "strange breeze" that carries ghostly threats as local residents play roulette with their health. Its angry tone chimed with what a *Philadelphia Inquirer* report called an "undefinable fear" in the weeks following the incident, prompting residents to stock up on guns and food supplies in an effort to turn an intangible fear into "things they can comprehend."[88] In this respect, the MUSE concerts were a forum to make the intangible visible and audible. Via topical songs such as Hall's reggaefied "Plutonium Is Forever," renditions of Bob Dylan's early songs, and a revival of the countercultural spirit of the 1969 Woodstock Festival, the MUSE concerts intensified public pressure against the construction of new nuclear plants and stimulated a more active form of citizenship.

The focus of the No Nukes songs was not health per se, yet the MUSE movement was as interested as Audre Lorde in collective transformation, turning the power of fear into life-giving energy. It would be too easy to propose a causal link between the antinuclear cultural expressions of 1978–79 and a rising interest in public health; despite the protests of the Clamshell Alliance and No Nukes, antinuclear activism in the 1980s left a mixed legacy. It is also difficult to measure the effect of the Kemeny Commission recommendation that news reporters should strive to "place complex information in a context that is understandable to the public," and that local media should act responsibly "to clear up rumor and explain the conditions" of nuclear plants in an effort to ensure the public have a balanced view of nuclear power.[89] President Carter tried to bridge the polarizing views of the No Nukes movement and America's Electric Energy Companies (with the tagline "Nuclear Power. Because America Needs Energy") in a December 7, 1979, speech that echoed his 1976 campaign pledge that nuclear power was a "last resort" but also that "we cannot shut the door" on it.[90] Yet fears about krypton gas being vented into the Philadelphia air during the clean-up operation at Three Mile Island ran in the media the following spring, at a time when Carter was establishing a radioactive waste management program "to protect the health and safety of all Americans" and a Nuclear Oversight Committee to tighten up regulation and governance.[91]

The production of nuclear electricity accelerated through the 1980s, but so too did the momentum behind the nuclear freeze movement with strong backing from labor unions, religious groups, and organizations such as the American Nurses Association and the American Public Health Association. President Reagan was initially hostile to antinuclear protests. These included a large Central Park peace rally in June 1982 and doomsday theater posters displayed in multiple cities during Ground Zero week of mid-April 1982 that read "if this were Ground Zero a one-megaton nuclear explosion would instantly destroy virtually everything within two miles of this spot" (a thousand times the radiation level of Three Mile Island, as the *Pittsburgh Post-Gazette* reminded its readers).[92] Despite the reluctance of the executive branch to engage, the movement did have an impact on foreign policy when early in Reagan's second term he pushed for nuclear disarmament in his negotiations with the Soviet Union.[93] This White House pivot coincided with a new wave of nonviolent activism at the Nevada Test Site that helped to refocus public attention on the nuclear moment forty years earlier, filling the southwestern landscape with a different kind of power based on "peacemaking, politics, and prayer."[94] And when Three Mile Island eventually closed in September 2019, forty years after the reactor failure, it was for purely economic rather than environmental reasons.[95]

HEAVY WATER: URBAN CONTAMINATION SCARES, 1935, 2016

As an essential resource and a precious commodity, water often provokes strong feelings. It is especially resonant in the early twenty-first century when the sustainability of fresh water has become a major concern for residents in the arid Southwest, for environmental activists, and for eco-sensitive writers like Paolo Bacigalupi, whose futuristic novel *The Water Knife* (2015) explores the health consequences of corporate corruption when the Colorado River dries up.[96] The first chapter showed how the material and symbolic qualities of water blend in the face of disaster, sometimes awakening survivalist instincts to protect property and family and at other times prompting acts of selflessness toward the most vulnerable. The topic of public water is particularly panic provoking when linked to scarcity, additives, and contaminants. It is starkly illustrated by the 2014–16 water crisis in Flint, Michigan, but it was recognized a half century earlier when a 1961 surgeon general's report called "water the no. 1 natural resource problem."[97] This issue was reprised in 2019 by the California senator Kamala Harris when she called future water shortages an "existential threat" for "communities of color," foreshadowing the theme of structural racism that featured in Harris's August 2020 nomination speech for vice president.[98]

The geographer Tom Perreault proposes that the arena of hydrosocial relations poses profound questions in three areas: *environmental* questions about sanitation and safety, *labor-based* questions about farming and fishing, and *social* questions related to equity and rights— three sets of questions that transform geographies of vulnerability into hydrosocial territories, defined in terms of water control and access.[99] A 2016 special issue of *Water International* on hydrosocial territories demarcated a middle space for water control between the poles of providers and consumers, showing how communities provide a structural fulcrum "for economic redistribution, cultural recognition, political legitimacy, and democracy." This communal pivot point aligns with Robert Bellah's idea of a conceptual and ideological "middle range" and offers a more nuanced perspective on hydrosocial relations than do Cold War–style conspiracy theories and panic narratives about water being a vector of mass duping.[100]

However, it is important not to ignore conspiracy theories about water control that arguably emanate from an early Cold War episode in the wake of the Public Health Service decision to add fluoride to water supplies in 1950 in an effort to improve the nation's dental health. Early experiments with water fluoridation in Grand Rapids, Michigan, and Newburgh, New York, in the mid-1940s showed that fluoridation reduced "the amount of cavities children get in their baby teeth by as much as 60% and lowered tooth decay in permanent adult teeth nearly 35%."[101] These early trials led to a wave of other authorities adding fluoride to water supplies over a three-year period, prompting Eisenhower's health secretary Oveta Culp Hobby to state in 1955 that "the adjustment of the fluoride content of public water supplies is a safe, effective, and economical procedure for the partial prevention of tooth decay."[102] Yet, fluoridation led to both critique and panic. Conservative lobbyists argued that fluoridation was an example of the "government-imposed administration" of mass medication that infringed on "the public trust," civil liberties, and the individual's right to choose.[103] Homeopathic and natural health groups went further in arguing that it was a covert case of socialized medicine. In addition, the newly formed anticommunist group the John Birch Society even suggested that fluoride had the capacity to brainwash Americans as part of an invisible anticommunist plot—a view that Stanley Kubrick satirized in his 1964 film *Dr. Strangelove* by suggesting that fluoride was insidiously corroding national resolve.

These conspiracy theories grossly exaggerated the potential threat. Tests in Grand Rapids and Newburgh revealed no evidence that low levels of fluoride were dangerous, especially at the ratio of one part fluoride to a million parts water (1 ppm). A group of national bodies supported fluoridation of domestic water supplies at this safe level as a means to prevent tooth decay, spanning the Public Health Service, the American Public Health Association, the American Medical Association, the American Dental Association, and the National Research Council. There was no robust body of research at the time to disprove those who worried that fluoride-rich water might have long-term negative physical and physiological effects that countered its medicinal benefits of strengthening tooth enamel. In high doses, fluoride led to mottling of the teeth, as noted in the mid-1910s and as verified by experiments on rats in 1931, while an *American Journal of Public Health* article of 1935 suggested that even relatively low concentrations of 0.8 to 0.9 ppm could lead to mottling.[104]

Given the public health aspect of these debates, those who argued about fluoride in the early Cold War years oscillated between advocates who highlighted its health benefits (such as the profluoride Committee to Protect Our Children's Teeth 1957 publication *Our Children's Teeth*) and oppositional voices that argued fluoride toxicosis leads to gastric, intestinal, and cognitive complications, and even cancer (such as in the antifluoride book *The American Fluoridation Experiment* by Frederick Exner and George Waldbott, the former who claimed that fluoridation was "totalitarian medicine" at a congressional hearing in 1952).[105] PHS sanitary engineers and nutritionists such as Frederick J. Stare thought that opposition arguments were "grossly misleading," but there were nonetheless disagreements about whether fluoride was itself dangerous or because it reacted corrosively with lead pipes and pipe solder.[106] By 1956, ten states were not endorsing fluoridation, and medical societies in a further eleven (in the West and South) were not reporting on endorsement of fluoridation.[107]

Cold War fluoride debates brought to the surface extreme views, but a long-held concern was that the underground system through which domestic water supplies flowed was a cause of ill health, a pressing issue that the Eisenhower administration recognized in its stream pollution abatement projects. As early as 1902, a primer on *Hygiene and Public Health* moved from declaring water "a prime necessity of life" to detailing the concerns that lead pipes might react with soft water (lead was used more often than iron due to its ductility).[108] Its authors claimed the dangers were minimal because the resultant lead oxide "rapidly dissolves again," but nevertheless recommended that tin pipes are used when lead poisoning is suspected even though the joints of tin pipes are more problematic than lead.[109] Noting a greater danger from sewers and contaminants than from lead piping, the book switches to the topic of water purification to reduce impurities like silica, which has a corrosive reaction with lead.[110]

Hygiene and Public Health does not comment on emerging evidence that lead pipes could be a major public health risk, potentially leading to stillbirths and an increase in infant mortality via in utero exposure. More recently, Werner Troesken argues that understanding the health risks of lead proved to be no simple matter in the early century due to "an array of environmental variables, including atmospheric pollution, a water supply's chemical and organic content, water treatment techniques, water temperature, and the broader geophysical context."[111] In his book *The Great Lead Water Pipe Disaster* (2006), Troesken shows

United States concurred, putting "research, finances, education, and administration" over explicit environmental issues.[121]

Some officials went further by pointing out that stream pollution was the problem rather than the piping system itself. One of these was the Cincinnati-based PHS sanitary engineer H. R. Crohurst, who argued in 1935 for the benefits of a "full-scale demonstration unit" on the Potomac River in the nation's capital to demonstrate effective governance and to stimulate "public demand for the adequate control of stream pollution."[122] The fact that it would cost $15 million was challenging at the height of the Depression, but faced with rising local cases of dysentery Crohurst shifted the focus to root causes rather than reactive plans. The Crohurst case suggests that the federal government was unmoved by the professional view on waste management of a public health engineer, and yet a broader focus on environmental issues might have distracted from what two chemists in 1936 were calling the "epidemic" of lead poisoning.[123] The Lead Industries Association argued for the versatility and safety of lead pipes even though the epidemic was due primarily to standing water in lead pipes in which the ppm was regularly higher than the PHS safety limit. The recommendation that these levels could be dramatically reduced by periodic flushing, and that the water would then be ready for drinking or cooking, seemed either optimistic or myopic in the light of a 1936 report that lead content in New York City pipes was forty times higher than this safe limit.[124]

Fast forward fifty years to 1986 when newly constructed American houses were being fitted with polyvinyl chloride (PVC) and cross-linked polyethylene (PEX) rather than lead pipes. This move followed the Safe Drinking Water Act of 1974 that sought to establish minimum standards for drinking water purity at the state level, and an amended act of 1986 that mandated lead-free pipes in new housing construction and warning labels on lead solder. However, low levels of lead (8 percent or below) continued to be used as a material in new pipes until 2011. This EPA regulation did not protect residents of older houses from having lead pipes, with unsafe levels of lead detected in a number of eastern states in the early 2000s, including toxic levels in more than half of Washington, DC, homes fitted with lead pipe systems.[125] From the 1960s onward, lead poisoning was designated a particular hazard for children, heightening concerns that contamination of domestic water supplies could lead to cognitive impairments.[126] Thus, questions about toxins and sanitation dovetailed with parental concerns about child safety and some of the "most elemental principles" of public health, such as efforts in the mid-1970s to eradicate all radioactive elements from drinking water.[127] These core principles have led the sociologist Phil Brown to argue that environmental health is the collective responsibility of a range of services and sectors rather than just one, bolstered by community research and citizen science alliances based on principles of democratic participation.[128]

This is why a contaminated water supply was central to the social justice agenda of legal clerk Erin Brockovich and her Californian law firm in the early 1990s when she found evidence of a Californian water supply contaminated with a carcinogen. The case against the Pacific Gas and Electric Company's covert use of the cooling agent chromium 6 made the 2000 film *Erin Brockovich* starring Julia Roberts a powerful dramatization of citizen science in action.[129] The domestic water contaminant in this case was hexavalent chromium, though one could argue that as a Kansan working for a Los Angeles law firm Brockovich was an outsider in the central Californian town of Hinkley rather than a facilitator of community research. Perhaps a better example of lay observation and citizen science is Sandra Steingraber's *Living Downstream* (1997), which interleaves sensitive reflections on her own diagnosis of bladder cancer in the late 1960s with her professional biological concerns about invisible and carcinogenic waterborne pollutants that often threaten health in complex combinations rather in unidirectional cause-and-effect sequences.[130]

The clearest example of the invisible threat to public supplies was the water crisis in Flint, Michigan, an episode that intensified concerns in the city over waste and water that Andrew Highsmith traces back to the mid-twentieth century and that Anna Clark traces forward to the "urban tragedy" of the 2014–16 water crisis.[131] The episode began on April 25, 2014, when Flint switched its water supply from the Detroit River to the Flint River to enable Genesee County to build a new sixty-three-mile pipeline from Lake Huron that would bypass Detroit to the north. The irony of this crisis was that the new pipeline was at the heart of the plans of county and city authorities to launch a "blue economy" to attract businesses that required water. Flint's water system suffered from deep infrastructural problems though, with around 40 percent of water from Detroit leaking out of its "old, crumbling" pipes. When the suppliers switched over in April, what flowed under the streets of Flint was contaminated river water with high acidic levels from untreated industrial waste that reacted with the city's lead water pipes, exposing an already at-risk population to greater health risks.[132] Authorities largely ignored early complaints from residents that their drinking water was dirty and that it emitted a bad smell, even though efforts had been made to depollute the Flint River in 2012 to increase its flow. When an outbreak of Legionnaires' disease over a period of seventeen months (leading to ninety-one cases and at least twelve deaths) prompted city officials to revert to the Detroit system in October 2015, the 30,000 corroding lead supply pipes were already contaminated, and the water was deemed unsafe to drink without a contamination filter system.[133] By February 2016 the lead content in some homes was seven times higher than the EPA safe limit, and seven months later the environmental engineer Marc Edwards (via the Virginia Tech Flint Water Study) calculated that it was actually far higher than this in five thousand Flint homes.[134]

It took sixteen months between evidence that *E. coli* bacteria was present in the water supply to the point when President Obama, speaking in Detroit on January 20, 2016, declared the public health crisis in neighboring Flint a state of national emergency, following Mayor Karen Weaver's emergency declaration the previous month.[135] The president authorized FEMA to spend $5 million to improve conditions for Flint residents over a three-month period, although these federal funds might have been larger had the situation been officially labeled a disaster rather than an emergency. Perhaps inevitably, the relief operation was deeply politicized at the start of a national election year. Presidential candidate Bernie Sanders blamed Michigan's Republican governor Rick Snyder for not acting sooner or more decisively (despite Snyder pledging $234 million in state aid). Sanders took a characteristically high moral tone, but he felt vindicated when Snyder's officials were charged with involuntary manslaughter, given that *Legionella* was detected in the water system a year before the supply was switched back to the Detroit source. This exposed more than ten thousand Flint children to toxins even after bottled drinking water was distributed. These ill-health effects on Flint's vulnerable children intensified local and national attention, though it took a few years before a full assessment of the long-term neurotoxic effects of lead exposure on Flint's children.[136]

The politicization of the episode rolled out on the national stage when Hillary Clinton, Sanders's rival in the Democratic primaries, highlighted the crisis as part of the prioritization of health causes in her campaign. Clinton called on the American people to be "outraged" by the episode. She used emotive rhetoric in her primary debate with Sanders: "We've had a city in the United States of America where the population which is poor in many ways, and majority African American, has been drinking and bathing in lead contaminated water and the governor of that state acted as though he didn't really care."[137] She noted the fact that she had worked on reducing lead contamination during her term as New York senator in the 2000s, but the *Washington Post* thought she was using the crisis as a cynical publicity stunt.[138] Sanders and Clinton were both impassioned when they met for a primary debate in Flint in early March. Sanders spoke of being "flattened" by the local stories of residents and that it was primarily an economic issue, while Clinton focused on mothers and children as well as a lack of trust in local government.[139] A few weeks later Clinton was making grand promises to eliminate the national lead threat within five years; recalling her husband's executive order of February 1994 that focused on environmental justice for poor and minority communities, Clinton envisaged a public-private Flint WaterWorks program.[140] It is easy to be cynical about these campaign pledges, but they align with Clinton's commitment to children's health following her work in the late 1990s on the President's Task Force on Environmental Health Risks and Safety Risks in Children. She promised to launch a commission on childhood lead exposure in her 2016 campaign, though she might have emphasized racial politics more, given that research revealed that 60 percent of young children with elevated lead levels were African American.[141]

Whereas Clinton remained vocal about the need to address the local crisis in Flint and the national regulation of domestic lead and the need for a replacement program, her political adversary Donald Trump was slow to address the subject. On January 19, he admitted the situation was a "shame," but repeated "I shouldn't be commenting on Flint," perhaps to protect Governor Snyder, who he claimed had a "very difficult time going." Trump's primary rival, the Texas senator Ted Cruz, was more vociferous, calling it a tragedy and a failure of government on every level, but there was much less proactivity among Republicans, as witnessed in the more tepid responses during Republican primary debates in Houston in late February and Detroit in early March. When Trump finally visited the Flint Water Treatment Plant, eight months after the Clinton-Sanders debate in the city, media outlets saw it as a cynical public-relations stunt to woo African American voters.[142] This time Trump called the Flint crisis a "horror show" and bragged that it would have never happened under his presidency. While visiting the Bethel United Methodist Church in Flint, Trump made a crude joke about the city losing its car manufacturing and clean water supply to Mexico, leading his host, an African American pastor, to remind him that a church was the improper venue for a political speech in which he wandered off subject to attack Hillary Clinton. In all this political wrangling it was easy to forget the material quality of water, and it took one of Trump's most notorious supporters, the outspoken right-wing radio host Alex Jones, to evoke historical water fears. In his fact-light and frequently incendiary (and now widely banned) internet show InfoWars, Jones revived the Cold War water conspiracy theory, claiming the "anti-government" anger that working-class Americans were channeling could not be stemmed regardless of the "amount of fluoride in the water" or "brainwashing of the children in public schools."[143]

Cultural responses to the Flint crisis on the other side of the political aisle from Alex Jones included the anti-Trump diatribe of polemical Flint resident Michael Moore in his stand-up show *The Terms of My Surrender*. Rather than probing the postindustrial infrastructural challenges of *Flint*, or tackling inequities in the health care system as he had in his documentaries *Roger and Me* (1989) and *Sicko* (2007), the closing segment of Moore's twelve-week Broadway show of summer and fall 2016 used the water crisis to rail against local and state authorities for their disregard for the residents of Flint. In his show, he casts Governor Snyder as a "murderer," whose home he hoses down with Flint water in his politically motivated documentary *Fahrenheit 11/9*, released ahead of the 2018 midterms. Moore sees the Flint episode as a "prologue to Trump's America" in its duping of the working class, based on Trump's blithe promises about job creation and expedient love for the region. Moore wrote in early 2016 that the contamination of Flint was a "racial crime" given its African American demographic, and in his stand-up routine he framed this in economic terms, arguing that a local crisis has become a national one: "Now we all live in Flint, or some version of Flint."[144]

The water crisis was also the subject of the 2017 Sony Pictures made-for-television film *Flint*, which links local activism in the city to national politics, including in its trailer a May 4, 2016, speech in Flint when President Obama described the crisis as "a tragedy that should have never happened in America."[145] The film's targets are Governor Snyder (represented in the film by the emergency manager Jerry Ambrose and the state's Department of Environmental Quality, which lacked adequate data to assess the crisis) and Karen Weaver's predecessor as mayor, Dayne Walling, who is portrayed as duplicitous and irresponsible. However, *Flint* also focuses on the positives of community action and citizen science for tackling often-invisible hydrosocial relations and for raising consciousness about the realities of this urban crisis.

Airing on *Lifetime* on October 28, 2017, the film was based on a January 2016 *Time* cover, "The Poisoning of an American City," accompanied by a heart-tugging image of an African American boy with scaly rashes. *Flint* focuses on the health story of the city's residents, especially Melissa Mays, LeeAnne Walters, and Nayyirah Shariff, a trio of Flint women who raised public awareness of the crisis in the winter of 2015–16 when the water supply in Walters's home reached the frightening level of 100 ppb.[146] In its link to the *Time* story, *Flint* shares an intent with civilian-activist films like *Erin Brockovich*, the 1982 antinuclear movie *Silkwood*, and the 2020 anticorporation film *Dark Waters*, while its emphasis on race, gender, and economics contributed to the conversation that led Flint City Council in June 2020 to declare racism itself to be a public health crisis.[147]

Flint has a conventional narrative arc, yet it is a reminder of the power of community and the potency of imagery to capture the scale of the crisis at both macro- and microlevels. Its opening sequence includes shots of the polluted river, and for its publicity image it depicts a bottle of dirty brown water, with a yellow sticky label bearing the name "FLINT" and the slogan "WATER IS LIFE." More poignantly, the closing credits include a shot of a Black Lives Matter march to remind us that racial justice is particularly at risk in what environmental sociologist Dorceta Taylor calls "toxic communities."[148]

This imagery resonates with the 1971 Crying Indian advertisement with which the chapter began, but it has a much more purposeful activist thrust by linking health risks to what Black Lives Matter activists called the "state violence in the form of contaminated water" that is routinely inflicted on predominantly black communities.[149] The question of racial justice links to a broader recognition that access to clean water is a basic human right and also that it was difficult for residents to rebuild trust in authorities once the immediate hazards had ebbed, especially when lead levels in Michigan's water system remained variable through 2018 alongside other cities like Newark, New Jersey. It also links the prolonged yet indecisive White House debate about corroding water pipes in the mid-1930s to concerns seventy years later when lead levels in Washington, DC, soared again, leading a congressional report to call out a new "public health tragedy."[150]

CLIMATE CHANGE POLITICS AND ENVIRONMENTAL
FRAGILITY, 2006, 2017

What Tom Perreault calls the "question of scale" shapes this third case study on the impact of climate change on human and planetary health during a "crisis of global disturbance," as the biologist Brock Dolman labeled it in the 2007 ecodocumentary *The 11th Hour*.[151] Climate change is an emotionally charged topic, especially when short-term national priorities ignore profound environmental questions, with believers in the deleterious effects of global warming such as former vice president Al Gore pitted against deniers like Republican Oklahoma senator James Inhofe.[152] I have thus far focused on the health of working communities in the Southwest, East, and Midwest, but this section explores two extreme topographies, Florida and Alaska, which are particularly susceptible to environmental stress, to illustrate how climate change debates play out both regionally and nationally.

This chapter has shown how environmental stresses often give rise to pressing public health challenges, especially when linked to air and water, but I am cognizant of Jennifer Thomson's view that "toxic assaults" on the planet should not simply be translated into humanistic terms, even if they expose economic, racial, and human rights injustices.[153] In navigating this line between planetary and human health, I discuss here two high-profile documentaries fronted by Al Gore that have raised public awareness of global warming: the 2006 film *An Inconvenient Truth* and the 2017 *An Inconvenient Sequel: Truth to Power*. The gap between these two years is narrower than the preceding pairs discussed above to highlight the increasing acceleration of environmental threats. However, I also recognize the danger of privileging the visibility that public figures bring that sets these examples apart from the citizen science alliances discussed above. For example, *The 11th Hour* would not have generated an audience without Leonardo DiCaprio as the film's narrator, linking to the aim of DiCaprio's foundation (established in 1998) to protect "earth's inhabitants." Similarly, Al Gore's role as presenter and promoter helped *An Inconvenient Truth* to gross $50 million, a global box-office profit that part-funded his Climate Reality Leaders Project with its focus on environmental education and community organization. Despite his privileged position—and his generalized focus on middle-class rather than working-class Americans—it is important to note that Gore has conducted advocacy as a private citizen rather than as a senator or vice president, and his cause is informed by grassroots groups and ethically oriented companies that realize the need for planetary care does not stop at national borders.

Gore's environmental awareness stemmed from his life as a Tennessee teenager when his mother read to him Rachel Carson's newly published *Silent Spring*. The book had a transformative effect on him, especially Carson's account on how flies in the Tennessee Valley quickly developed a resistance to dichlorodiphenyltrichloroethane (DDT), a synthetic insecticide manufactured in northern Alabama after the war and sprayed on agricultural crops until 1972, when DDT's environmental and human health risks triggered a ban by the newly formed Environmental Protection Agency.[154] Studying at Harvard in the late 1960s, Gore found inspiration in the carbon dioxide research of the environmental scientist Roger Revelle, whose warming-planet theories were in tension with other Cold War figures who were worried more about a nuclear winter.[155] Gore's intellectual interests developed in the wake of a 1979 National Academy of Sciences report (which linked rising levels of carbon dioxide to climate change) and shaped his legislative work as a Tennessee senator in the 1980s, sparking him to organize the first congressional hearing on climate change in the "greenhouse summer" of 1988. That same year the United Nations formed an Intergovernmental Panel on Climate Change, and the media started to pay attention following a widespread drought, fires in Yellowstone National Park, and heat-related deaths, leading *Forbes* magazine to announce a "Global Warming Panic."[156] Gore ramped up his environmentalism as vice president: he chaired the Earth Summit of 1992, pushed for a global treaty to reduce CO_2 emissions (the Kyoto Protocol of 1997), and launched the GLOBE program (Global Learning and Observations to Benefit the Environment) on Earth Day 1995 to raise green awareness among children.[157]

Whereas Second Lady Tipper Gore became a prominent mental health advocate in the 1990s, Al Gore's environmental causes took a broader perspective on planetary health in line with his view that the late century rise in cases of mental illness are linked to "spiritual loss" and a rise of rampant materialism.[158] He outlined this spiritual view in his 1992 book *Earth in the Balance*, in which he mixes pagan Gaia principles with the beliefs he acquired at a young age at his family's Baptist church. Gore frequently goes beyond denominational beliefs though, describing his "smorgasbord of religious experiences" and a "spiritual imagination" that enables him to behold "the myriad slight strands from earth's web of life."[159] He also plays on the meaning of balance as something precarious yet achievable by yoking ideas to action and by not letting belief blindside scientific evidence.[160] The metaphor of balance is matched by the idea of renewal (what he calls "a new common purpose") at a time when the Gores were recovering from a near fatal road accident of their young son Albert.[161] This tragic experience redoubled Gore's commitment to environmental causes and intensified his regard for human health at individual and systemic levels. This commitment is exemplified by his support for a Patient's Bill of Rights to increase medical access and protection for patients and in his promise to increase federal spending on Medicare and Medicaid during his failed presidential run of 2000.

Gore has consistently kept nature front and center. In some instances, such as in the Clinton-Gore 1992 manifesto *Putting People First*, nature is humanized in an effort to "leave our children a better nation," but at other times nature is a "central organizing principle" in its own right, with an ecology and health of its own.[162] Rather than echoing the apocalyptic imagery of activist Bill McKibben's *The End of Nature* (1989), in 2002 Al and Tipper Gore maintained the hope that a mix of federal investment, public advocacy, and scientific research can offer meaningful direction for the new century, symbolized by their idealistic vision of education as a linking of hands and hearts to create "vibrant connections."[163] That hope is also there in the closing chapter of *An Inconvenient Truth*, titled "Crisis = Opportunity," in which Al Gore includes the Chinese characters 危机 above the word "Crisis," following the example of John F. Kennedy's use of the double-jointed term.[164] All of Gore's spiritual expressions link closely to science, and the solutions he proposes to prevent the leap "from denial to despair" are technological: solar panels, geothermal power stations, energy-efficient light bulbs, green roofs, hybrid cars, hydrogen fuel-cell buses, and wind power. Clinton and Gore were often criticized by the likes of Green Party candidate Ralph Nader for being RepDem hybrids and market-bound technocrats, yet Gore emphasizes smart energy solutions that do not erode an already fragile planet.[165] Seeing health as intrinsic to an ecosystem that demands respect and care at this critical phase of the Anthropocene, the closing words of *An Inconvenient Truth* (before his call to action) are humanistic—"It is our only home. And we must take care of it"—set against imagery that reminds us that the earth is just a "pale blue dot" within a huge cosmos.[166]

The film of *An Inconvenient Truth* pivots on an extended lecture by Gore that mixes hard scientific data, satellite photography, a

Simpsons-like cartoon sequence, and audience-friendly visual technology to highlight its twin messages of the perils of global warming and the need to change habits. Gore is careful not to play party politics (the film was released in a year when some speculated he would make another presidential run), though he does attack a reckless pro-Republican business culture. His primary focus is on preserving planetary health in the face of a projected sharp rise of CO_2 from fossil fuels and glaciation recession in the world's colder regions. Thus, in line with his philosophy of balance, he does not retreat into nostalgia but instead seeks smart solutions as lasting resources for the future.

Despite his faith in science and belief in technological solutions that might halt or even reverse global warming if all nations act ethically and with vigilance, it is hard to say that Gore steers away from disaster politics. Take the photographs and video footage of melting glaciers in *An Inconvenient Truth* for example. Here, Gore shows images of disintegration in the arctic north and a cartoon polar bear who cannot find an ice float thick or stable enough for safe haven (*Time* magazine depicted a polar bear on a small raft of ice on its cover image of April 3, 2006, with the headline "Be worried. Be very worried"). Such illustrations can be read as alarmist, but his reasoned delivery and personal yet rational tone tempers his ecological warnings within a rhetorical strategy that he (and director Davis Guggenheim) use to combat what Gore in 2007 described as "the prominence and intensity of constant fear" and "persistent confusion about the sources of that fear."[167] His aim is to stimulate activism rather than provoke panic, driven by the fact that the per capita release of gases from fossil fuels is substantially higher in the United States than any other nation. Gore is also keen to include global examples to challenge a nationalist mindset; he does not ignore fragile American geographies but frames the national challenge in moral terms within a planetary ecosystem that requires co-responsibility.

The topographies of Alaska and Florida feature in the two *Inconvenient Truth* films as spaces in their own right that are vulnerable to warming permafrost and rising seas, but they are also metonyms of an endangered planet viewed through the filter of arctic ecologies and the delicate ecosystem of the Everglades. Alaskan environmentalist Nancy Lord notes these cold and hot places are markers of home: "the Kansas farmer and the Florida vacationer don't need to care about desperately swimming polar bears or Inupiaq hunters falling through the ice to be concerned about what's happening at the top of the world."[168] However, rather than seeing planetary threats in anthropocentric terms, the film focuses on vulnerable habitats in their own right and extinction threats to the polar bear and the Florida panther.[169]

Gore has been outspoken about the threats to Alaska since the 1980s. In March 1989, Senator Gore decried the crude oil spillage when the *Exxon Valdez* tanker ran aground in Prince William Sound on Alaska's southern coast, arguably because the tanker's captain was drunk at the wheel. At 10.8 million gallons, this was the second worst oil spill in US history, affecting more than one thousand miles of coastline over the course of the following year.[170] Dubbed "North America's worst environmental catastrophe," Gore joined the demand that the Exxon Corporation intensify its cleanup efforts, especially when its president, Lawrence Rawl, was slow to respond publicly and Exxon appeared to lack a crisis management strategy.[171] The spill not only endangered fish, coastal birds, and marine animals, but the resulting pollution also led to a number of human health concerns. These included rashes from oil exposure, accidental ingestion of oil, mental health problems, and a rise in drug and alcohol use among inhabitants of small isolated villages, including the indigenous communities of Tatitlek and Chenega Bay, whose basic subsistence was in jeopardy during and long after the cleanup.[172] In addition to opposing offshore drilling, in August 2000 Vice President Gore expressed concern that the Arctic National Wildlife Refuge in northeastern Alaska (est. 1960) was under threat from inland oil and gas developments with the laying of the Trans-Alaska Pipeline system in the 1970s.[173] To illustrate his worries Gore gives examples of arctic, polar, and subarctic regions under threat. Two of these are a time-lapse photograph of the retreating snow line of Columbia Glacier in Prince William Sound undergoing glacial recession and a double-page photograph in the accompanying book of sunlit "drunken" spruce trees, taken north of Fairbanks, with branches pointing awkwardly from weakened roots caused by the melting permafrost. He argues global warming is bad for business too, as the number of days the Alaskan ice is firm enough for trucks to drive on had declined from over two hundred days in 1970 to under a hundred in 2000.[174]

Democratic Alaskans largely respect Gore's views but, as a state that often votes Republican in local and national elections, there were a number of dissenting voices. These voices included 2008 vice presidential nominee and former Alaska governor Sarah Palin, who claimed that Gore was unnecessarily alarmist or was exaggerating facts for his own ends, such as the theory that the fast movement and recession of the Columbia Glacier is the result of natural not human forces. In fact, local conservative climate skeptics in Fairbanks built two ice sculptures of Gore's face in 2009–10, the second of which blew truck exhaust through the mouth of "Frozen Gore" to symbolize him speaking hot air.[175] Gore and Palin had a barbed exchange in December 2009 about whether or not climate change was the product of human activity, while flat-earth conservatives like James Inhofe accused Democrats of manipulating scientific data based on an email leak about flawed climate models.[176] Gore's response to Palin lacked detail, but on MSNBC he retorted that she was living in "an era of unreality."[177] The absence of decorum in the Palin-Gore exchange is an example of what literary theorist Timothy Clark calls the "derangements of scale," which often mark diverging views on the environmental crisis, with "ecological facts" quickly morphing into "moral imperatives on how to live."[178]

Gore was not alone in his concerns about temperature rises in Alaska. Activist musician Neil Young focuses on the forty-ninth state in the closing eco-anthem "Be the Rain" of his 2003 album *Greendale*; Marla Cone in *Silent Snow* reports the extinction threat to sea otters due to pollutants in the nearby Aleutian Islands; and *New Yorker* writer Elizabeth Kolbert has pointed out that fires near Fairbanks have increased with warmer summers and lower rainfall causing deep holes to appear in the permafrost.[179] Environmental changes in Alaska and Greenland led Kolbert to view the Anthropocene in near apocalyptic terms: "a disruption in monsoon patterns, a shift in ocean currents, a major drought—any one of these could easily produce streams of refugees numbering in the millions."[180] Although Gore rarely uses the term Anthropocene, *An Inconvenient Truth* echoes Kolbert's words through the lens of computer-generated imagery that show how rising ocean levels would completely alter the topographies of southern Florida, Manhattan, the Bangladeshi coast, and Shanghai and Beijing, among many other areas.

Gore's interest in Alaska is in counterpoint to his focus on Florida, perhaps ironically given that he narrowly lost the 2000 presidential election to George W. Bush on a vote recount in the Sunshine State, leading Bush to pull back from some of the climate agreements of the Clinton administration. Both Bush and Gore approved the bipartisan plan in 2000 to spend $7.8 billion during the election season to restore the ecosystem of the Everglades but, as political adversaries, they had very different views on the causes of global warming and the science that underpinned it. In late 1997, Gore visited the Everglades to help celebrate its fiftieth year as a national park, and he spearheaded a campaign to ensure that the ecosystem sustained its freshwater habitat. Perhaps because the Everglades' restoration projects soon fell behind schedule he refers to Florida infrequently in *An Inconvenient Truth*, making only passing mention of the unusual 2004 Atlantic hurricane season when fierce storms hit the state four times.

In contrast, *An Inconvenient Sequel* reflects on grassroots activism that in 2016 prevented a Florida utility company from restricting the use of solar panels, but instead of Gore conveying efforts to protect southern Florida from coastal erosion he focuses on the spectacle of floodwaters. We see him wading through an underwater Miami Beach accompanied by the Democratic mayor of Miami Beach Philip Levine, and he also includes a photograph of a stranded octopus in a parking garage following a king tide to illustrate the rising ocean level.[181] Gore comments in a folksy manner, "it's kind of hard to pump the ocean," before reverting to his instructor role, pointing out that the state's Republican governor, Rick Scott, refused to meet with scientists because he does not believe in global warming.[182]

An Inconvenient Sequel emphasizes the health threats of climate change more than the first film, though it is still a secondary focus. There might have been more in this film, for example, on respiratory illnesses and air pollution, or on working-class health risks of expanding urbanization and the global recession (what Thomas Friedman calls the "destabilization of both the Market and Mother Nature to a degree that can no longer be finessed or ignored"), or on the intersections between social, economic, and geographical vulnerabilities, though Gore does stress that hot southern states are at particular risk from new superbugs like SARS and Zika.[183] The roots of this secondary focus on health security can be traced back to a January 2000 speech to the United Nations Security Council in which Vice President Gore argued for a "new, more expansive definition" of security that would include protection from AIDS and infectious diseases as a means to "protect lives" from virulent health threats.[184] This UN speech of January 2000 (a speech Gore refers to in *An Inconvenient Sequel*) wavers between different kinds of threats "in defending our nation's health against all enemies, foreign and domestic" eighteen months before the aerial attacks of 9/11.

It is surprising, then, that there is not more on public health, especially as during September 2016 the Florida Department of Health aerially sprayed mosquito repellent in Wynwood, a trendy area just north of downtown Miami, after twenty-eight people were identified as being infected by the Zika virus.[185] Gore does not focus on this public health threat, except for commenting on the shifting balance between microbes and humans in warm climates like Miami where incubation rates are speeding up. In fact, Gore seemed to avoid the questions of border security, which is odd because the Paris terrorist attack of November 2015 is an important feature of *An Inconvenient Sequel*, though perhaps this tactic is understandable given the nationalist rhetoric of the Trump campaign and the escalation of extremist politics in Europe. Instead, the film embodies the globalist ideal of "collective will" from his UN speech that can "truly unite nations" and bend the moment "in the direction of life, not death; justice, not oppression; opportunity not deprivation."

This second film follows the format and tone of its predecessor, and, although Gore appears distinctly older, he retains his optimism and call to action. One of the reasons that *An Inconvenient Truth* was so successful and that *An Inconvenient Sequel* repeated the formula is its varied presentational mode. Yet Gore's leaps in perspective in the two films, despite being well meaning, are open to criticism as another example of derangements of scale. Take, for example, Michael Pollan's view that Gore's recommendation in the closing credits that viewers switch to energy-efficient light bulbs and reusable bags is incommensurate with the magnitude of the climate problem laid out over the previous ninety minutes.[186] Pollan does not take issue with Gore's ethic of personal responsibility, but he argues that this is too little too late "because the climate-change crisis is at its very bottom a crisis of lifestyle— of character, even" based on consumer choices that direct "countless little everyday choices." Pollan's criticism of Gore is not a matter of kind but one of scale.[187] The image of "vibrant connections" that Al and Tipper Gore wrote about in their 2002 book *Joined at the Heart* is quite similar to Pollan's image late in his *New York Times* piece in which he envisaged "a chain reaction of behavioral change" that would lead to a proliferation of green products and alternative technologies. Pollan's concept of "viral social change" replaces Gore's idea of an endangered ecosystem with a chain reaction of radical lifestyle change. Nevertheless, in Pollan's case this radical change is also about tending and caring for the planetary home to restore its vitality. He ends "Why Bother?" with the example of planting a vegetable garden: "at least in this one corner of your yard and life, you will have begun to heal the split between what you think and what you do, to commingle your identities as consumer and producer as citizen."

Even though Pollan arguably conflates domestic and planetary scales in the phrase "corner of your yard and life," his ethos and commitment to a green lifestyle in his 2008 book *In Defense of Food* is persuasive. In contrast, Pollan stereotypes Gore as a figure with a static rather than a dynamic vision of the planet, though Gore's praise in 2019 of the leadership and eloquence of the teenage Swedish activist Greta Thunberg illustrates his recognition that tackling climate change is a multigenerational task.[188] Gore is also open to criticism that his is a politician's view of global warming. Much of *An Inconvenient Sequel* focuses on Gore's diplomatic role in the Paris Climate Accord of December 2015, while his argument for net zero pollution by midcentury is in contrast to the repeated threats of Donald Trump to pull the United States out of the treaty during his successful presidential run. It is a view shared across the Democratic Party, illustrated by Barack Obama's sentiments in his 2016 Earth Day speech, in which he returned to the "common cause" of the inaugural Earth Day of 1970 as well as reaffirming the "shared purpose" of the Paris Agreement as a means to combat climate uncertainty.[189] This same environmental goal shapes *An Inconvenient Sequel*, and it juxtaposes with the tragedy of the Paris terrorist attack, suggesting that high-level agreements are a necessary means of imposing rational order in an unpredictable post-9/11 world.

Gore's vision of clean and smart technologies that will transform the energy market is also in tension in some respects with Naomi Klein's left-wing view that bottom up protest and citizen activism are the only real mechanisms for change. Echoing Pollan and Gore in her emphasis of living "non-extractively" but taking swipes at Gore's wealth, his odd rhetoric of "inconvenience," and his downplaying of economic injustice, as well as questioning whether an animated polar bear is an appropriate symbol for the seriousness of climate change, Klein's vision is one of dynamic transformation.[190] In her 2015 book *This Changes Everything* and documentary of the same name (directed by Avi Lewis), Klein goes further than these others in tackling the economic base as well as the cultural and social superstructure. In stressing regeneration over resilience and a desire to represent communities from within, Klein arguably misreads Gore as someone who speaks to the nation from on high. He would respond by claiming he is equally interested in measured diplomacy, as in equipping future global leaders with the knowledge, skills, and confidence to take on multinational corporations through educational programs like GLOBE and the Climate Reality Leadership Corps. This mode of transnational education is an example of putting humanistic planning over panic, but it is open to charges of elitism from the left and liberal indoctrination from the right.

In essence, Klein's and Gore's views pivot on their political persuasions. Alongside other high-profile Canadians such as Neil Young, Klein's leftist task is to seize back power for the people against business interests, such as in the case of the Tar Sands Gigaproject near Fort McMurray in northern Alberta, which has encroached on the treaty rights of the local First Nations peoples. (Young argued that pollution is killing the local Athabasca Chipewyan community, but he was widely criticized for likening the tar sands to the devastation of Hiroshima.)[191] Less eager to discuss contested land rights, Gore's centrist view fuses his scientific and spiritual respect for the planet with a program of activities, both big and small, that could preserve a rational liberal order at a time when expedient business decisions are appearing to accelerate global warming. Whereas Klein uses the environmental crisis as a call to revolution, Gore avoids alarmism and instead grasps these two moments (2006, 2017) as activist opportunities to put nature back in balance and preserve the planet for future generations.

Klein's and Gore's outspoken views are an indication of how important debates about fossil fuel emissions were in the mid-2010s, especially when Trump was promising a return to coal, as well as undoing environmental protections established by the Clinton and Obama administrations, and was attacking Greta Thunberg's global grassroots activism on social media. One could argue that Gore might have made health issues more visible if he wanted to be persuasive about the climate crisis, in line with the view of Massachusetts senator Edward Kennedy (speaking at a congressional hearing in April 2008) that "public health must be a central part of the discussion about climate change" especially for vulnerable communities.[192] Gore realized this when, in February 2017, he opened the Climate and Health Meeting at the Carter Center in Atlanta (organized in conjunction with the American Public Health Association [APHA]) and noted "many would argue that too little attention has been paid by many to the health consequences of the climate crisis"—it was clear that this "many" included himself.[193] As well as starting to tackle challenges that link climate and health pressures (embodied by the APHA's slogan at their November annual meeting, "Health Equity Now"), Gore took a longer view. Without resorting to the apocalyptic rhetoric of the Anthropocene, he focused on what communities can achieve, yet without the radical reterritorialization that Klein proposes. This stance returns us to the question of authenticity posed by the Crying Indian ad and the need to challenge political strangleholds on the public conversation (such as the EPA director Scott

Pruitt's pro-fossil-fuel agenda early in the Trump administration) and forward to the ideal of a "Green New Deal" as promoted by progressive Democrats in 2019–20.[194]

Gore and Klein have a broader set of communication platforms than they would have had in the 1950s or 1970s. But they are operating in a social-media-saturated culture where reasoned scientific and economic arguments are easily lost in sound bites and where the deep-seated nationalist backlash of the 2010s has swallowed the promises of a globalized future that Klein, writing in the early century, called meaningful windows that open onto fresh opportunities to renew human contact through citizen activism and transnational protest.[195] The medium is as potent as the message though, and their documentaries offer examples of the power of words and visuals in a supposedly post-truth decade. Thus, the two *Inconvenient Truth* films and *This Changes Everything*—alongside the 2017 *Flint* film—are examples of authentic commitment to futurity at a moment when combative polarization is straining the public sphere, though Gore believes that even in this squeezed space meaningful dialogues are still possible.

To return to this chapter's introductory remarks, Gore argues for a similar platform to Robert Bellah in *The Good Society* of "the middle range between the local and the global level" in which public health can thrive through a mixture of vertical and horizontal—as well as grassroots—discourses, communications, and interventions. Gore shows that a commitment to this middle range is akin to the habitats of most Americans, even as he draws on extreme examples of the polar arctic and subarctic Alaska in the Northwest and the humid subtropical climate of Florida in the Southeast. Just as *The China Syndrome* and the No Nukes concerts of the late 1970s brought public attention to the health and safety threats of nuclear power, so the documentaries fronted by Gore and Klein are purposeful guides for this critical phase of ecological health that pivot on the "geographies of vulnerability" that run through the first half of this book. We might criticize these public figures for performing authenticity rather than truly embodying it and for playing on fears of homelessness. Yet it would be cynical simply to take this view. Instead, these films are emblematic of a historical phase when the intersecting environmental threats of these first three chapters—disasters, poverty, and pollution—mean that for liberals like Gore it is more important than ever to speak out on issues relating to public health.

PART TWO

States of Vulnerability

Crises of Prevention and Treatment

.

CHAPTER 4

Virus

Influenza, Polio, HIV/AIDS

Three of the most consequential American health crises began with a virus. The influenza pandemic that swept through North America in 1918–19, seasonal episodes of poliomyelitis that affected hundreds of thousands of American children between the mid-1910s and the mid-1950s, and the upwards of 700,000 HIV/AIDS-related deaths in the United States since the earliest reported cases of 1980–81 each have a critical pitch. These crises were of different kinds and durations, but all three pose searching questions about health security and health communications at both federal and local levels. Initial neglect by the federal government more obviously exacerbated the threats of influenza in the late 1910s and the human immunodeficiency virus in the early 1980s than was the case for poliomyelitis. This was, in large part, because Franklin D. Roosevelt gave polio visible form following "a terribly serious" episode he experienced in 1921 and via his advocacy work for the philanthropic National Foundation for Infantile Paralysis from 1938.[1] The discovery by virologist Jonas E. Salk of an effective polio vaccine in 1952 is often hailed as a high point of medical history. Yet this heroic story masks a more complex history that links FDR's decision to hide physical effects of his polio from public view during his presidency, to the stigma of being a "cripple" in the early century, to mishaps during the vaccine trials and national rollout in 1954–55.

It is open to debate as to whether swifter action could have prevented influenza and AIDS from becoming major crises and whether

Woodrow Wilson and Ronald Reagan were themselves culpable for failing to invest in preventive medicine and better public health education at an earlier stage. Nevertheless, the lack of preparedness of their administrations and the tendency to accuse others—blaming Europeans for spreading "Spanish flu" and gay urban subcultures for the spread of HIV/AIDS—revealed the nation in the 1910s and 1980s to be inadequately equipped to contend with these escalating health emergencies.

For this reason, the second half of the book develops my argument about how health crises expose the structures and sites of vulnerability by telescoping out from specific geographies to organizational and institutional issues of prevention and intervention at the federal level. In doing so, I develop the concept "states of vulnerability" from cultural theorist Pramod Nayar's 2017 book *The Extreme in Contemporary Culture: States of Vulnerability* by viewing vulnerability as a "social ontology" in which health is refracted equally through personal experience, medical practice, and social policy.[2] As Andrew Lakoff argues, it is also an ontology that is "brought into being through contingent and often-overlooked historical processes."[3] This explains the temporal span of the case studies in the second half that return us to the inaugural moment of public health in the shape of the Great Influenza pandemic of 1918–19 through to the most acute health crisis of 2018 with the sharp increase of opioid-related deaths. As my introduction outlines, on a structural level these "states of vulnerability" inhabit a middle space between polarizing views of the nation-state seen either as a purveyor of sympathy or as a perpetrator of structural violence. At times, national responsibility for health is inflected positively in terms of caregiving and nurturance (values that Michele Landis Dauber associates with a "sympathetic state"); at others, it takes on a more negative cast, relating to invasive medical treatment, techniques of aggressive governmentality, and the perpetuation of stigmatizing language (all versions of Paul Farmer's reading of "structural violence").[4]

Even though federal politics and national stories figure prominently in the following three chapters, I bring into dialogue a macrolevel study of viruses, care, and drugs from an organizational perspective with the ways these phenomena play out in everyday life. With this in mind, I steer between interpreting "states of vulnerability" as *realities* that governmental aid or medical care might alleviate in crisis situations and *latencies* in which grassroots activities might prove better at tackling local health problems than grand federal interventions that can sometimes blur national security, economic interests, and public health—as is the case for the COVID-19 pandemic of 2020 that features in this chapter's closing pages, and to which I return in the book's coda. Taken together, the case studies in the second half of the book prompt searching questions about how much agency individuals and communities have over their health and what responsibility the state should assume for its citizens. These questions help us to investigate the "middle range" that relates closely to Robert Bellah's theory of moral balancing, positioned between the practices of institutions and the needs of individuals and communities. This topic underpins a reenergized notion of health citizenship that runs through the book's second half and to which I turn explicitly in my conclusion.[5]

This chapter marks a conceptual shift in the book from "geographies of vulnerability" of the first part to "states of vulnerability" in this second part, but in its focus on viral outbreaks it forms a pair with the first chapter's emphasis on health security with respect to environmental disasters. Given that viruses tend to infect large populations, only localized outbreaks can easily be contained, but often by the point of detection the virus has infected another host. To this end, William McNeill argues that the movement of peoples is the primary factor in the transfer of infectious disease, which requires forms of density control and proximity control to mitigate the spread, whereas John Barry focuses on the slippery language of viruses:

> unlike other life forms (if a virus is considered a life form), a virus...invades cells that have energy and then, like some alien puppet master, it subverts them, takes them over, forces them to make thousands, and in some cases hundreds of thousands, of new viruses.[6]

Barry's description amplifies the tenor of Jonas Salk's remarks of the early 1960s, in which Salk describes viruses as being "like radioactive fallout in the effect they may have on our cells," with repeat attacks or "re-awakenings" possible throughout a life.[7]

Priscilla Wald also draws on metaphors of invasion and border crossing in her 2008 study *Contagious: Cultures, Carriers, and the Outbreak Narrative*. Viruses exist, Wald argues, "in a liminal state, a kind of suspended animation, when outside the host cell"; because they take on new life inside the host's body, on this reading viruses impart "a mythical cast to their battle with human beings."[8] Extending this notion of the infiltrating outsider, Steven Kruger likens the virus to a "suspect 'foreign' language, a language in contest with the 'proper' language of cells and cellular function," replicating inside the host's body to further its invasion strategy.[9] Such a view helps to explain the spate of invasion stories and films that emerged during the early Cold War years in which human behavior is open to control by alien agents as they assail the foundations of democracy that are already under strain from suspect terrestrial activity. Even though the "science" of Cold War science fiction was often speculative, these films swing between portraying the host as the unwitting victim of invading forces to someone whose lifestyle opens them to or makes them complicit in the attack.

In her 2008 book *Life as Surplus*, Melinda Cooper shifts the historical frame slightly to theorize contagion in the post–Cold War years in respect to national security risks, triggered by "the irruption of so-called complex emergencies...characterized by the implosion of the state, the breakdown of essential public infrastructures (sanitation, water, power, and food supplies), and the prevalence of infectious disease."[10] The emergence of this paradigm for Cooper began in the 1980s during the HIV/AIDS epidemic and then intensified in the early 2000s, but it was also present in the late 1910s when influenza sufferers were tacitly—at times openly—blamed for not looking after themselves. From this ideological perspective, vulnerability links to a lack of self-care or even moral laxity. National and local media reports helped citizens negotiate these crises by explaining preventive measures and reporting the health risks of these viruses. However, as my three case studies show, mythmaking also played out in print and broadcast media, even as news coverage of influenza and AIDS was slow to emerge and variable in its objectivity. Given these multiple layers, the cultural signification, historical expression, and biomedical understanding of viruses are equally pivotal in this chapter, aligned with what Paula Treichler calls "an epidemic of meanings, definitions, and attributions" that play out in each of these historical cases, as well as in twenty-first-century disease outbreaks.[11]

The major difference between polio and the other two viruses is that the early 1950s witnessed the discovery of an effective vaccine for poliomyelitis after decades of endeavor. Polio had reemerged seasonally since the early century when it led to 18 percent of childhood deaths, but the discovery of two separate vaccines suggested medicine could ultimately be adaptive, a view that prompted the authors of a pair of 2004 books to choose triumphalist titles: *The Death of a Disease* and *Splendid Solution*.[12] This "conquest of polio" story hides unfortunate episodes, though, including what has been called "one of the worst pharmaceutical disasters in U.S. history," the Cutter incident, in which two hundred children in California and Idaho who were given the vaccine in April 1955 suffered from muscle weakness, paralysis, and for ten of them death.[13] As well as raising questions about the roles of the Public Health Service and the Department of Health, Education, and Welfare in ethical oversight and testing, the Cutter incident prompts broader questions about the politics of vaccination. These questions have always been troublesome, at least since the linking of citizenship rights to compulsory vaccinations on the US-Mexico border in the 1890s, the US Supreme Court's decision of 1905 that Henning Jacobson, a Boston pastor, could not refuse smallpox vaccine in the name of public health, and the founding of the Anti-Vaccination League of America in 1908.[14]

Even though public health campaigns invariably promote vaccination as good for individuals and the country, they often play on base fears about disease. This can generate a sense of panic born out of the fear of loss. However, rather than only assessing the channels by which governments, institutions, and the media convey top-down health information to patients and high-risk groups, it is important to attend to the tone, symbolism, and structure of health texts—both government texts issued in the name of the public good and more exploratory cultural texts—to understand their rhetorical and narrative construction. Charles Rosenberg discerns that these texts often have a "dramaturgic form" that combines storytelling (the etiology, escalation, and closure of the epidemic), pageantry ("mobilizing communities to act out propitiatory rituals"), and "dramatic intensity" (posing questions about the relationship between "ideology, social structure, and the construction of particular selves").[15] Whether it is in terms of instruction, persuasion, illustration, or framing—or even silence at key moments—such mediations shape the public understanding of critical health conditions, sometimes in alignment with and at other times at arm's length from medical science.

Take the 1995 disaster movie *Outbreak*, for example. The film focuses on an Ebola-type virus carried from Zaire to the West Coast of the United States by a stolen capuchin monkey. There the virus mutates and becomes airborne, evoking both the AIDS crisis (in the symptomology of the infected patients) and the 1918 influenza pandemic (in terms of the negligence and self-interest of authorities). Even though *Outbreak* is based loosely on *New Yorker* journalist Richard Preston's well-informed 1992 article "Crisis in the Hot Zone," and it seeks to accurately portray the international and domestic activities of the Centers for Disease Control and Prevention, we should not expect popular cultural texts to be precise on epidemiology and virology, especially when they are driven by a dramatic outbreak or pandemic narrative.[16] Yet, such examples reveal how medical knowledge, health journalism, and cultural accounts converge and how readers encounter their often-mixed messages. In this space of convergence, the panic that often ensues when an invisible virus spreads through vulnerable communities cannot simply be assigned wholly to medical fact, or to scientifically informed disease films like *Outbreak* and *Contagion* (2011), or to the apocalyptic tenor of science-fiction accounts such as the dystopian film *Aeon Flux* (2005) and Margaret Atwood's post-pandemic MaddAddam trilogy (2003–13), which imagine a struggling human future in the face of unrelenting forces. Each instance of viral outbreak has its own arc, but I would argue that the historical experience of the three viruses that feature here continue to inflect present-day viral panics.

A NATION IN DENIAL: THE INFLUENZA PANDEMIC, 1918–1919

Pneumonia, tuberculosis, and enteritis were the three great killers at the turn of the twentieth century. A short bout of influenza leading to pneumonia was nothing new (the first recorded influenza epidemic in North America was in 1647), yet the deadly virus that hit Massachusetts in August 1918 threatened not only the young and frail with sickness and death but also the whole nation. By that time "Spanish flu," as it was dubbed, was nearly six months old—the primary reason that this label caught on was that newspapers in Spain (a neutral country during World War I) freely reported on early cases in Madrid and Barcelona.[17] The virus lingered in Boston and infected around 85,000 residents of Massachusetts in September 1918, before moving through New England to New York City and Philadelphia, across the Midwest and on to the West Coast—and it even emerged on the Alaskan Peninsula.[18] The local effects of the virus varied. New York City, for example, with its well-developed public health infrastructure, experienced much lower mortality levels than did Boston and Philadelphia; there were only two student deaths at Columbia University among 248 cases of flu and pneumonia, due in large part to good hygienic practice and the tight organization of the Student Army Training Corps.[19] Yet globally the virus traveled far and wide as it moved east and south from Europe, through Africa, the Asian subcontinent, and into Australasia. With a fatality rate of at least 2.5 percent, the 1918–19 influenza was more consequential than the war that gave rise to it, leading to over five hundred million infections and over fifty million deaths worldwide (675,000 in the United States).[20]

This should not have been the case based on early twentieth-century medical confidence.[21] Advances in bacteriological science, germ theory, and urban sanitation made the nation better equipped to deal with infectious disease, with public health leaflets and popular magazines encouraging citizens to be vigilant about eradicating germs in their homes and how to avoid spreading them in communal spaces.[22] In 1922, Cary Grayson, Woodrow Wilson's physician, wrote about the power of modern science:

> vaccination, inoculation for typhoid, the extermination of the stegomyia mosquito which carries yellow fever, of the anopheles mosquito which carries malaria, of rats which carry fleas which carry bubonic plague, the war on promiscuous drinking cups, and spitting in public conveyances and streets whereby the spread of tuberculosis has been materially checked—all of these things, and half a hundred others, show what modern science can do and has done.[23]

Given the rise of new public health agenda in the 1910s, it is ironic that the federal government might have slowed the spread of the influenza virus through the United States in autumn 1918 by releasing earlier reports and planning a more responsive public health approach.[24] A deliberative response was also true of the governments of Canada and Great Britain, and what might otherwise have been a containable epidemic became a pandemic due to the conditions of war, the cautious decisions of leaders, and scrambled public health responses.

Surgeon General Rupert Blue did not begin making public statements on influenza until October 2, 1918, three months after he had persuaded President Wilson that the Treasury should supervise "all sanitary or public health activities." The following day he released a plan of cooperation for the Public Health Service and the American Red Cross, though he admitted that a vaccine was still at an "experimental stage."[25] The American Journal of Public Health published a special October issue on influenza that took a somber tone. This was perhaps because of the postponement of the annual meeting of the American Public Health Association due to the national crisis, but also because it recognized that "very few health officers, and no communities, appreciate the terrific devastation of the epidemic until it strikes them."[26] When first called on a few weeks earlier, the American Red Cross acted quickly to provide supplies and facilities, to mobilize nurses (though many were involved in the war effort) and volunteers with as little as three days hospital experience, and to distribute information about the risks of influenza. However, by the second week of October the strain was virulent—the lungs of some patients quickly filled with catarrh and their skin color turned purple or blue—and by December Rupert Blue issued a public warning to take all precautionary measures.[27]

There had been four previous waves of influenza between the 1830s and 1890s, including one strain that swept across Russia and Europe between 1889 and 1892 that helped scientists to develop a better understanding of its microbiology, though its origin remained mysterious.[28] The genesis of the 1918–19 pandemic and the number of strains that circulated globally in those two years are uncertain, although it is accepted that the virus would not have traveled as far or as fast had it not been for the Great War. Although one theory suggests that the influenza virus began in China in winter 1917–18 and then spread through Europe during the war, the most plausible origin is an outbreak in Haskell County in southwestern Kansas in early February 1918 that likely derived from farm animals—birds, pigs, or cows, given that scientific studies after the Civil War had inferred links between tuberculosis in cattle and humans.[29] John Barry has examined competing theories that suggest the virus might have originated in France, Spain, or Asia, but his epidemiological study of this rural Kansas community is persuasive. For many who contracted influenza in Kansas in February and March it was a three-day or four-day illness, but for others it led to pneumonia and even death. Local physician Loring Miner worked long hours to treat patients in Haskell County because Kansas, like many other states, was short of medical personnel due to many having mobilized to aid the war effort.[30] A possible vector was Private Albert Gitchell, a Haskell County resident and mess cook stationed at the Camp Funston military base in Fort Riley, 250 miles northeast of his home. Gitchell reported flu-like symptoms when he returned to the camp from leave in early March, and within three weeks a thousand soldiers were being treated in tent hospitals, with forty-eight cases leading to death.

Most likely American Expeditionary Forces carried the virus that spring from Camp Funston to the battlefields of France, and from there it was transmitted by personnel moving between camps, infecting around a million US soldiers.[31] The timeline was actually much tighter than the two waves imply, a theory that suggests there was a six-month hiatus between the Kansas outbreak and the reemergence of the virus on the Atlantic seaboard in October, at a time when early cases of influenza were detected in Puerto Rico, Cuba, and Jamaica, probably carried by ships from New York.[32] Counter to this successive wave theory, a US Army hospital in Bordeaux reported outbreaks in mid-April and at Saint-Nazaire and along the Somme in May 1918.[33] That month influenza broke out among French troops at Fontainebleau, and multiple reports of cases across France and Algeria emerged a few weeks later, before an August outbreak in Lorraine. German troops also suffered from summer influenza in June, and they quickly constructed relief hospitals, yet this did not prevent the virus spreading to the civilian population. The *New York Times* speculated that malnutrition exacerbated civilian cases of influenza in Berlin, but unseasonable winter conditions certainly did not help the vulnerable. This *Times* report of June 1918 is neutral in tone, yet it is emblematic of other second-wave reports that implicitly blamed the sufferer for not taking due care.[34]

The US Public Health Service documented these European outbreaks and attempted to intervene in August when officials demanded inspections of cargo arriving from the Atlantic. But it was surprising then that port cities were not more prepared when a month later the next major outbreak occurred in Boston (four thousand deaths were reported over a five-week period) and the Massachusetts training camp of Fort Devens (where over ten thousand cases were reported).[35] The Public Health Service began publishing weekly bulletins in September, a month in which influenza cases in New York hit triple figures, including the thirty-six-year-old Franklin Roosevelt. Alfred Crosby argues that the advice of the surgeon general on September 13 about how to treat the sick did not lead to urgent action in Massachusetts because the victory of the Boston Red Sox in the American League distracted many Bostonians.[36] It was not just Boston and other port cities taken by surprise. By the end of September, influenza had taken hold in army camps from New Jersey to California and had spread to Georgia by early October (city officials in Atlanta were quick to introduce preventive measures).[37] The US Congress allocated $1 million in emergency funds and commissioned a Public Health Service Reserve Corps in an effort to contain the virus, but local health boards and authorities were left to devise precautionary plans and curb public gatherings.[38] Such was the scale of the autumn influenza, including high mortality rates among pregnant women and the young, that when a third wave hit in early 1919 many regions were short of medical resources and personnel.[39]

The rapid spread of the virus between training camps was one crisis, but it also posed a grave threat to American soldiers stationed in Europe. Overcrowded barracks both at home and in France meant that physical contact was tricky to prevent, particularly during the winter months when pneumonia was more likely.[40] Despite rapid developments in medical personnel and better organization under the leadership of the US Army's surgeon general William Crawford Gorgas, the army's medical department was ill-equipped to deal with these successive waves, and in the absence of a prevention plan its officers were eager to blame the soldiers' living conditions. The mortality rate was higher among recruits serving in domestic training camps than those serving in France who tended to work in smaller units, yet this statistic overlooks the theory that trench warfare made the virus deadlier. Indeed, physicians and nurses in crowded hospitals, such as one in Vaubecourt in northeastern France, found it difficult to prevent influenza from spreading—this hospital received 34,000 patients within a six-week period in fall 1918, 70 percent of whom had influenza.[41] Nevertheless, when President Wilson, who was remarkably quiet on the viral threat, visited the American Hospital of Paris in December, following the armistice, he talked up the patients' spirits: "I found the men admirably taken care of and almost without exception in excellent spirits. Only a very few of them looked really ill, and I think their mothers and friends would have been entirely pleased by their surroundings and by the alert look in their eyes and the keen interest they took in everything about them."[42]

The documentation for the centenary exhibition at the CDC headquarters in Atlanta, *Remembering the 1918 Influenza Pandemic*, notes that this was the first epidemic to be captured in photographs, such as the *Locust Avenue, Masks On* image on the cover of this book of Marin County, California, residents taken in early November 1918 by Oakland amateur photographer Raymond Coyne.[43] Press reports of the second and third waves of influenza are also instructive for determining how seriously citizens were treating the virus and what preventive measures were being practiced in communities and schools. The peak of mainstream US media interest fell in October. Debra E. Blakely notes that during this peak season between October 1918 and March 1919 the *New York Times* released 219 influenza stories (compared to forty-seven and thirty-six respectively in the nine months before and after), whereas the *Times* of London published 148 stories (compared to twenty-eight and twenty-nine immediately before and after).[44] An early piece in the *New York Times* identified the illness among African Americans who were supporting the war effort—"a considerable number of American negroes, who have gone to France on horse transports, have contracted Spanish influenza on shore and died in the French hospitals of pneumonia"—although no statistics are offered, nor analysis of comparable cases among white US soldiers.[45] More broadly, Blakely identifies September 1918 as marking a pivot point from a muted government response toward a marked emphasis on "individual responsibility" partly, it seemed, to exonerate federal and state governments for not taking earlier action.[46] On this argument, the Wilson administration did not wish to shoulder the responsibility for a half million American lives lost to influenza so soon after the war.

Newspaper reports tended to focus on statistics and precautions and rarely spent time on symptomology or patient-centered accounts. Elizabeth Schlabach has shown that public health information in the Chicago press, for example, emphasized right living and tended to reinforce racial segregation as a form of quarantine, both as a lived reality for African Americans in the city and as a metaphor of social containment.[47] In the years following the third wave of influenza there was some recognition that more effective governance and public health information were needed at both national and community levels, with a 1927 American Medical Association publication offering the clearest markers when it came to a retrospective evaluation of the causes and consequences of the 1918–19 pandemic. Written by the Chicago bacteriologist Edwin O. Jordan, *Epidemic Influenza: A Survey* collated 1,300 sources to show how the aftereffects of influenza lingered on into 1926, but the text also acknowledged that the origins of the pandemic were "largely shrouded in obscurity" even though it may have resembled previous influenza outbreaks.[48] Using an epidemiological model, Jordan was the first scientist to establish Haskell County, Kansas, as the possible starting point, but medical science was not at a stage at that time when he would have been able to identify a viral cause. Jordan's account appeared a few years prior to the results of new bacteriological research provided a fuller understanding of virology, followed by vaccination trials in the early 1940s under the aegis of the Commission on Influenza of the Armed Forces Epidemiological Board.[49]

Beyond the newspapers and Jordan's medical summary, it is notable that war writing of the 1920s rarely addressed the 1918–19 influenza let alone made a strong narrative of it, even though both the American and British leaders were affected. Prime Minister David Lloyd George contracted influenza in September, a month before the British government released a statement about the pandemic, and Woodrow Wilson caught the flu in spring 1919, leading to a high fever and "paroxysms of coughing," a condition that weakened his "powers of resistance" and arguably permanently damaged his already precarious health.[50] This absence is evident in two major postwar novels by John Dos Passos, *Three Soldiers* (1921) and *U.S.A.* (1930–36), in which he mentions influenza only once, and then only in passing. It took a decade before the virus featured prominently in literary works that more often linked influenza to personal and familial suffering than to social transformation. Most notably, it emerged in Thomas Wolfe's re-creation of his brother Ben's death from pneumonia toward the end of his 1929 semifictional novel *Look Homeward, Angel*, and in two stories by Katherine Anne Porter. Wolfe found his brother's death, age twenty-five, at the family home in Asheville, North Carolina, deeply distressing, an experience that gave him the resolve to become a writer, whereas Porter drew on her own case of influenza that she contracted following a bout of tuberculosis for the title story of her 1939 collection *Pale Horse, Pale Rider*. In its exploration of loyalty, guilt, and pain in Denver, Colorado, "Pale Horse, Pale Rider" depicts the pandemic in both mythical and medical terms by focusing on local journalist Miranda's existential travails when she contracts influenza. Miranda becomes delirious as she discovers her suitor Adam has died from pneumonia after he had tended her sickbed; the story ends with her imagining "he was there beside her, invisible but urgently present, a ghost more alive than she was," before she sinks into "dazed silence."[51]

Laura Spinney's centenary study of the pandemic, *Pale Rider* (2017), takes its title from Porter's book, but the sense of personal and historical rupture in the story of "Pale Horse, Pale Rider" is sharpened in recent literary efforts to recover a historical episode that was both devastating but strangely lost in time.[52] Among revisionist novels written in the early twenty-first century are Reina James's *This Time of Dying* (2006), Thomas Mullen's *The Last Town on Earth* (2006), and Cat Winters's *The Uninvited* (2015). The first of these, *This Time of Dying*, dramatizes how ineffective were the belated attempts to contain the virus by imposing a hygiene regime in war-torn London. The opening of James's novel focuses on the physical suffering of the physician Dr. Thomas Wey who we see on the verge of collapse: "A sharp pain in his chest was beginning to interfere with his breathing; the cough was producing a rusty-orange phlegm that made him retch. By the time he reached the front door he was barely conscious."[53] An unposted letter is found in Wey's jacket pocket, revealing his attempts to alert the Local Government Board that "a plague is now among us which may well leave the earth to the animals."[54] Throughout *This Time of Dying*, this pervading sense of doom links warfare to miscommunication about a disease that threatens the whole of civilization.

The Uninvited further develops the crumbling of Edwardian values in the face of infection in *This Time of Dying*. Here, the protagonist Ivy Rowan wakens in small-town Illinois in October 1918 after contracting influenza, only to feel caught between the ghosts of the past and a hedonistic present that mixes the excitement of reawakening with deep anti-German sentiments embodied by the Espionage and Sedition Acts of 1917–18.[55] Rather than a personal ordeal, influenza cuts through Ivy's life and sharpens her suspicion of authorities who use the epidemic to curb public gatherings, to punish antisocial behavior (echoing a 1918 report that Chicago police would arrest anyone spitting or sneezing without a handkerchief), and to seal off the town from unwelcome visitors.[56] This is also a strong theme in Mullen's *The Last Town on Earth*, in which public officials of the Pacific Northwest town of Commonwealth enforce quarantine measures in the face of influenza, but in their effort to do so they make it an inhospitable place for returning soldiers. Rather than viewing the virus through a strictly medical lens, the crises in all three of these retrospective literary accounts pivot on crumbling Progressive-era values that seemed so secure at the turn of the twentieth century.

The fact that the pandemic did not receive much attention until the 1970s was surprising given that the high death toll and two further waves of influenza in 1929–30 and 1932–33—and again in 1957–58 (Asian flu) and 1968 (Hong Kong flu). A collaborative approach to influenza research began in 1947 at a new Information Center on Influenza in the US Public Health Service. The primary aim of this international collaboration was "to set up the machinery necessary to protect the world population in so far as feasible against recurrence of another disastrous pandemic of influenza such as was last experienced in 1918" and to identify a vaccine that could prevent such disasters.[57] Scholarship on the 1918–19 influenza pandemic did not appear in earnest until the mid-1970s though, when historian Alfred Crosby's *Epidemic and Peace, 1918* marked a new wave of research from epidemiological, military, and civilian perspectives, followed by his 1989 book *America's Forgotten Pandemic*. Crosby's 1976 study was timely because an outbreak of swine flu prompted the Ford administration to act when a soldier died and thirteen were hospitalized at an army base in Trenton, New Jersey.[58]

This theme of retrieving lost lives and breaking silence in the face of a devastating disease was also key to the British neurologist Oliver Sacks's book *Awakenings*, a 1973 account of his work with a community of in-patients in New York City who had developed encephalitis lethargica. Some reports claim that this type of encephalitis was an independent epidemic that spread from east to west, but others identify a close link between it and patients who contracted influenza between 1918 and 1920 (Woodrow Wilson may have suffered from encephalitis follow-ing his 1919 bout of influenza).[59] Even though many of Sacks's patients recovered in the 1920s, they experienced severe Parkinson's symptoms later in life and an inability to communicate. An experimental treatment of L-DOPA (administered to increase the neurotransmitter dopamine) briefly brought some patients back to life in the mid-1960s and helped to revive their stories, which had lain unspoken for many years, but this was only a brief awakening before their degenerative symptoms and near-catatonic state returned.

Sacks's neurological account echoes the silence and ghostliness of lit-erary reflections on the Great Influenza and its mysterious etiology, but it also suggests that there were lessons to be learned about prepared-ness, organization, communication, and the illness experience itself. For example, in preparing a *Pandemic Influenza Plan* in 2005, the De-partment of Homeland Security admitted that the country would face another pandemic in the twenty-first century in the face of the avian influenza outbreak that spread from Asia to east Europe.[60] That same year the Congressional Budget Office modeled what a severe flu pan-demic would look like in terms of infections and mortality rates. HHS updated the *Pandemic Influenza Plan* for a second and third time in 2009 and 2017, and in 2013 the federal government instituted a pub-lic health watch on human-animal interaction at agricultural fairs and zoos. Though preparations for virulent flu strains are at an advanced stage, as I will discuss later, there is strong evidence to show how disin-vestment in global health security within the National Security Council in the late 2010s has heightened the risk of a new pandemic catching the nation unawares.[61]

ONE NATION UNDER POLIO: VACCINE TRIALS AND ROLLOUT, 1952–1955

One of the high points of twentieth-century medicine was the success of New York virologist Jonas E. Salk's polio vaccine in eradicating po-liomyelitis as a common disease in the United States. By the time that

Salk had cultured his vaccine and the Truman administration had established an Epidemic Intelligence Service in the early 1950s, polio had scoured North American life for over half a century, causing disability and death among countless young children and some adults. Until the late 1890s "infantile paralysis," as it was then called, was a rare disease, and when it attracted the attention of physicians its causation and etiology often caused puzzlement.[62] However, following seventeen outbreaks over a fifteen-year period, in 1910 the US Public Health Service designated poliomyelitis a reportable disease. Two further epidemics in 1912 and 1916 made polio a health priority, especially between the months of July and October 1916, which saw public health officials declaring a state of emergency in New York City. Such seasonal crises were particularly acute because no medical cure existed for a virus that caused spinal paralysis in up to 10 percent of those infected, and in the summer of 1916 led to nine thousand cases of polio in New York and to 448 deaths.[63]

The Ohio Department of Health was especially concerned about the 1912 epidemic that ravaged the cities of Cincinnati and Cleveland; city officials demanded all cases were reported and blood samples taken, insisting that the source and breeding ground of polio needed identifying with some urgency.[64] An epidemic in New York City four years later reopened the debate as to whether improving urban conditions would be effective in reducing the virulence, but advocates of sanitation measures could not easily prove that environmental factors were critical, especially as the virus did not just infect poor and crowded communities but wealthy areas too. The Commissioner of Health in New York City's Health Department, Haven Emerson, admitted in 1916 that the "present ignorance of facts" was one reason for deploying containment methods to try to halt the spread of the virus.[65] In addition to antispitting laws introduced in the 1890s to contain tuberculosis, regulations included quarantining infected children, cleaning up streets and yards, disinfecting pets, creating no-go areas, closing swimming pools, delaying the opening of schools, and establishing a travel ban for children without a certificate that could guarantee them a clean bill of health. New York City health officials were taking public health education very seriously in 1916, introducing milk distribution centers to educate parents about hygiene and the welfare of their babies.

The philosophy of disinfection was more circumstantial than evidential, but it led New York City health officials and newspapers to blame poor immigrant groups such as an Italian community in the Pigtown area of Brooklyn, a neighborhood vilified for its swine, squalor, and crime.[66] Polio's racial politics were complex. Evidence suggested that the virus disproportionately infected white middle-class children, yet officials seized on the epidemic to justify the "filth theory of disease" and to impose behavioral regulations on poor minority communities in a year that saw more immigrants arrive in the Northeast than ever before.[67] This is explained in part by anti-immigrant stigma in the late 1910s and the resistance of some immigrant groups to public health regimes, and in part by early twentieth-century discourses that linked the tuberculosis virus to African American communities.[68] Samuel Kelton Roberts Jr. argues in his 2009 book *Infectious Fear* that "white reactionaries" saw "black tuberculosis as a harbinger of racial degeneration," tempering progressive health policies that embodied "a modern, responsible, public health state [that] owed care to all citizens."[69] Yet when it came to naming public health crises, the politics of ethnic and racial exclusion often held sway.

Haven Emerson doubted it was possible to eradicate polio, even as he and other health officials targeted flies and cats as likely vectors. A 1911 study, *House Fly, Disease Carrier*, noted that the term "house fly" domesticated what others were calling "filth flies" and "typhoid flies," a species that "multiples with startling rapidity" and has breeding places everywhere.[70] The realism of Emerson and the entomologist Leland O. Howard, the author of the *House Fly* book, was not shared by the physician Simon Flexner of the University of Philadelphia, who in 1901 became the first director of the Rockefeller Institute for Medical Research. Flexner set the ground for polio research over the next twenty years; he agreed about the airborne fly theory (a theory that persisted into the 1940s) but was optimistic about the possibility of an imminent breakthrough.[71] Flexner began a project to isolate the virus in 1907 after the first New York outbreak, and, in 1910, he claimed to have identified its basic properties, aided by the Japanese bacteriologist Hideyo Noguchi. A year later, the *New York Times* hailed this heroic fight against "the New Scourge of Infantile Paralysis," and the paper praised the Rockefeller Institute in its "War against Meningitis, Tuberculosis and Other Terrors."[72] Through the 1910s, Flexner experimented with injecting the poliomyelitis virus into rhesus monkeys and used lumbar puncture to assess its effects on the central nervous system.[73] But this was not the breakthrough the *New York Times* touted, and Flexner faced challenges during the 1920s for privileging his theory of spinal fluid over competing theories relating to blood and intestines.

Rockefeller Institute scientists produced a new wave of polio research in the early 1930s alongside a health awareness campaign symbolized by the launch of the National Foundation for Infantile Paralysis in January 1938. This campaign linked to Roosevelt's own experience of hydrotherapy treatment at Warm Springs, Georgia; he first visited Warm Springs in 1924 and returned regularly during his presidency to bathe in the 88-degree spring water, though whether the water had therapeutic properties was open to debate.[74] Despite the founding of the Georgia Warm Springs Foundation in 1927 as a place for treatment and research, the urgency of polio campaigners stemmed from a dearth of accurate health information and new polio outbreaks in New York City in 1931 (which spread to upstate communities "along lines of travel") and Los Angeles in 1934 (the infection spread to doctors and nurses dealing with hundreds of inpatients).[75] The focus of the National Foundation was fundraising, most prominently via the President's Birthday Ball held annually on January 30. At the inaugural event of 1938, Roosevelt announced that the Birthday Ball and the new National Foundation were fundamental aspects of a "solid front against an insidious but deadly enemy," and he encouraged donations, small and large, that could fund research and ameliorate "suffering and crippling among infantile paralysis victims wherever they are found."[76]

The comedian Eddie Cantor helped to publicize the fundraising drive, coining the phrase "March of Dimes" and urging his radio listeners to send in small change directly to the White House, while Hollywood stars such as Judy Garland and Mickey Rooney appeared in featurettes to convince their captive audience to channel their fears into donations.[77] The foundation contributed to health education in two broad ways: first, formal publications of urban incidences of polio categorized by age, gender, race, and recovery rates; second, posters and newsreels designed to teach parents to look for warning signs and to help their children take care. The campaign had the objective of countering crisis headlines with informed medical perspectives, but it also indulged in its own brand of fearmongering. This included short films like *The Crippler* (1940), in which a dark cloud metamorphoses into a health menace and a girl played by Nancy Davis (later Nancy Reagan) volunteers for the foundation, and the RKO Pathé film *In Daily Battle* (1947), in which "Virus Poliomyelitis" anthropomorphizes into its own character. In fact, the foundation did little to allay anxieties about this summer menace and neither did it dispel the unproven theory that some minority groups were more susceptible to catching polio, at least until the 1950s following pressure by civil rights activists.[78]

Up until World War II, polio seemed to be an uncontrollable "disease of modern life," the "insidious but deadly enemy" Roosevelt had described in 1938, even if it did not provoke the intense panic of the 1918–19 influenza pandemic.[79] The president insisted a "united effort on a national scale" would bring polio "under control" as it had for tuberculosis, smallpox, and diphtheria.[80] However, its cause remained difficult to determine despite Flexner's confidence twenty years earlier, and beneath Roosevelt's public conviction his rhetoric revealed worries about "the constantly increasing accumulation of ruined lives."[81] The president's projection of an increasingly sick nation in this September 1937 speech justified the formation of the foundation early in 1938, but that did not mean his anxieties evaporated. He returned to the topic of polio as "an enemy which neither slumbers nor sleeps" in his January 1939 Birthday Ball radio address, a speech in which the fight was drawn in militaristic terms.[82]

The seasonal pattern of polio meant the summer months were particularly worrisome for middle-class parents whose children could easily be "cheerful Catherine" or "vivacious Christine," characters that *Good Housekeeping* and the *Saturday Evening Post* presented as innocent survivors despite the physical limitations they faced as polio victims. Peter Oshinsky points out that the letters that President Roosevelt received in the 1930s (among the thirty million letters and telegrams he received over a fifteen-year period) were rarely as optimistic as these magazine exemplars. Instead, common themes of the letters were shame, stigma, fear, and sadness—including one sent to Mrs. Roosevelt in August 1935 by a fifteen-year-old Chicago girl who had contracted polio the previous summer: "My legs are paralyzed—I am heart broken...I get so lonely and depressed some days....I pray dear God will soon help me walk again."[83] Such letters were an important channel between the president, the first lady, and the people. Rather than seeing polio only as a crippler, Roosevelt's public emphasis on "useful citizenship" tallied with the discourse of "grace and redemption" of many polio magazine stories and with innovations in care such as portable hospital units, which helped cities like Jackson, Mississippi, that were suffering from inadequate or overcrowded facilities.[84] This restoration narrative often grated with the brute reality of a disease for which there was no obvious cure and that could strike even the cleanest of households.[85]

The use of prosthetic iron lungs in the 1930s and 1940s proved a lifesaver for polio patients experiencing muscle control loss but also brought a new type of stigma, prompting one first-person account to describe iron lungs as "monstrous tanks that looked like medieval instruments of torture."[86] After the war, the "iron lung" respirator—as featured in an October 1951 issue of *Life* and Charles Andrews's 1951 novel *No Time for Tears*—was both "reassuring and troubling" because it symbolized medical progress yet drew visual attention to the paralysis.[87] Less invasive techniques for alleviating the symptoms included the hot compress and muscle manipulation favored by Sister Elizabeth Kenny, an Australian nurse who came over to Minnesota in 1940 and remained opposed to iron-lung therapy and prosthetic devices, instead preferring gentle manipulation and heat to treat muscle spasms.[88]

Given that Sister Kenny and the medical establishment held divergent perspectives on how best to treat the virus, initially at least, it is instructive to view the disease from a health communications perspective alongside the lenses of epidemiology and virology. Naomi Rogers outlines different types of literature on polio that circulated in the 1930s and 1940s: "guides to prevention" that focused on hygiene, "therapeutic manuals for the care of paralyzed patients," and "inspirational tales of the disabled overcoming social stigma and achieving success in school, the workplace, or romance."[89] It is difficult to separate out fact from myth in many of these texts. This logic was mirrored by the fact that polio was embodied by the president, but also disembodied in his attempts to hide the condition from public view. On the one hand, Roosevelt was lauded for his "Come-back from Invalidism" (as *Physical Culture* magazine described it in 1932 as a supreme symbol of restoration) and, on the other hand, his polio was a reminder of what modern medicine could not conquer.[90]

Polio literature usually focused on a formulaic recovery narrative, even as it preyed on the emotions of potential donors. Much of the literature linked to the National Foundation's public-relations campaign that sought to raise morale and donations, for which there was a pressing need given that cases had climbed from 8 per 100,000 in 1940 to 37 per 100,000 in 1952. Epidemics in summer 1944 (19,000 polio cases in the Northeast and South), 1949 (40,000 cases), and 1952 (over 52,000 cases, including 3,000 deaths) tempered confidence that an effective polio vaccine was imminent.[91] For example, Wichita Falls General Hospital in northern Texas had been using an iron lung (an Emerson Respirator) since 1937 following outbreaks over the previous three years, but the polio threat continued after the war, such that in summer 1948 inspectors targeted uncovered garbage where rats and flies could breed.[92]

It was not until the 1952 polio scare seven years after the end of the war that clinical trials started to test the safety and validity of Jonas Salk's vaccine. This was one of two vaccines that emerged from US laboratories: Salk's work at the University of Pittsburgh generated a killed-virus vaccine in injectable form (it having been tested on the kidneys of monkeys), whereas Albert Sabin of the University of Cincinnati produced a live oral vaccine that did not become available medically until the early 1960s. The major public health issue that surrounded Salk's clinical trials of 1954 focused on the 1.8 million children who received the vaccine in its field trial, after an initial round of five thousand tests. These volunteers were often pictured as pioneers (the National Foundation issued "Polio Pioneer" certificates and badges), but most parents were just desperate to protect their own children.[93] This fear factor chimed not only with the National Foundation's advertising campaign (such as a 1942 billboard in which a girl in a wheelchair and a brace is juxtaposed with two slogans, "I could be *your* child" and "*Fight* Infantile Paralysis") and the findings of a Polio Project at the University of Maryland in the mid-1950s that focused on parents' fears and their feelings of guilt about children who had contracted the virus.[94] What Fred Davis, the lead researcher of the Baltimore Polio Project, called the "crisis experience" explained why families were eager to involve their children in the tests, buoyed by a "faith in the future" as a central aspect of the postwar polio story.[95]

Literary critic Jacqueline Foertsch shows how this kind of optimism was embedded in a number of early 1950s magazine accounts of polio, in which "bad news" about further victims of the virus is framed by "insistent optimism, or attempts to relegate what is most disturbing about the story" to the margins.[96] Even so, Foertsch chimes with Fred Davis in seeing such optimism to be in tension with "persisting fears, contradictions, and unanswered," questions that nag at edifying articles such as "I Had Polio" and "The Girl Who Never Gave Up," published in the popular middle-class magazines *True Experiences* in October 1949 and *Redbook* in June 1952. This leads Foertsch to wonder if this was just "irresponsible journalism" or consolatory news-making that spoke to the lack of certainty about the causes and occurrences of polio that still circulated in the early 1950s.[97] There was certainly a frequent element of fantasy—if not a recovery of body then a restoration of spirit—that lends both nonfiction and fictional accounts of polio a "see-saw effect," swinging between an emphasis on the patients' inner strength and their physical weakness.[98] Mark Shell argues that this strength-weakness dyad was embodied in popular culture in the figure of the rusted Tin Man in *The Wizard of Oz* (1939), who is reanimated by Dorothy with magic oil and friendship, and by a series of immobile characters in Hollywood films of the 1940s and early 1950s.[99] But the seeming reconciliation of these polarities also links to Roosevelt's magic spin on the slow progress in identifying and testing an effective vaccine and in the theater of his radio Fireside Chats in which the president's disembodied voice, transmitted into the nation's homes via radio, "emerged seemingly from another body, not his actual one" with its muscular frailty.[100] These tensions between presence and absence, between reality and fantasy, and between veracity and theatricality run through accounts of polio in the 1940s and early 1950s.

Such reassuring authority went a long way to mask the controversy around the testing of vaccines, which began in 1935 when the clinical trials conducted by the British-born Maurice Brodie of New York University (in conjunction with William Park of the New York City Department of Health) and John Kolmer at Temple University led to two vaccines being rushed out.[101] In August 1934, the *Los Angeles Times* proclaimed that Kolmer's "vaccine discovery may end search of the century," but the tests of summer 1935 actually led to nine deaths, and Brodie's vaccine also led to deleterious side effects.[102] Concerns that the Brodie and Kolmer tests were using orphans (following initial trials on monkeys) worried the Roosevelts, but vaccination ethics did not improve markedly in the following years, with the polio trials of the early 1950s skirting around issues of informed consent.[103]

As well as publishing scientific papers, Salk was always very willing to discuss the experiments of his team at the University of Pittsburgh, whether it was talking to the *New York Times*, appearing on the *Adventures in Science* CBS radio show, sitting for interviews for *See It Now* and *Good Housekeeping*, or giving press releases.[104] In Salk's dedication of a Pittsburgh high school in October 1954, we see an example of his heroic yet realistic style:

> while man has achieved so remarkably...we see far too much evidence of the great job still to be done, both in the art as well as the science of living together, to say nothing of living happily with oneself....Just as we have come to recognize that poliomyelitis, as a world problem, is a by-product of improvements in living, particularly improvements in sanitation which were designed to eliminate other diseases, such as typhoid and dysentery, so we

must recognize that still other advances in civilization which have made life pleasanter have also made it more complex. Advancement is not an unmixed blessing.[105]

The mantle of Salk as the heroic vanquisher of polio through what the chief of the Children's Bureau called his "health and life giving discovery" is part of golden-age mythmaking, epitomized by the portrait of Salk on the cover of *Time* magazine on March 29, 1954.[106] However, the semiotics of this cover image are quite complex. To the right of Salk's head are seven hypodermic needles poised over crutches and body and leg braces; there is no human form in this half of the image, just a white mass in the background to represent the creeping virus itself. This twin image is both heroic and clinical, shifting the focus away from lost and crippled lives to assert medical control over both the virus and prewar technologies that are pictured in a state of bodily fragmentation. The caption in the bottom left-hand corner of the cover "Polio Fighter Salk: Is This the Year?" is expectant but with a hint of desperation, given that the previous February *Time* had proclaimed that Salk "was ready for the big attack."[107]

The FDA finally approved the national roll out of the Salk vaccine in April 1955 following a successful trial at the University of Michigan. However, the Cutter incident that same month, when a faulty vaccine infected a group of children with polio, suspended the rollout in May, although the PHS managed to limit the damage when they publicly stated that the Cutter Laboratories of Berkeley, California, had mistakenly used a live rather than a killed virus in their tests.[108] The momentum of the National Foundation was a major reason why the American polio story often skirts around these mishaps and crises in favor of a heroic narrative, but there was a political dimension too. Even though President Eisenhower recognized the people's "debt of gratitude" to the work of the foundation when he presented it with a special citation in April 1955, the pressure that the sustained national campaign placed on the Eisenhower administration meant that it had to be more involved than it would have desired.[109] This federal intervention led to the first national immunization act, the Poliomyelitis Vaccination Assistance Act of August 1955, which complemented the fundraising of the foundation by allocating $30 million in grants to individual states to inoculate all children under twenty and pregnant mothers.

The national press hailed the readiness of the vaccine in April 1955 with titles such as "A Hero's Great Discovery Is Put to Work," although a delay in rolling out the vaccine nearly turned into a political crisis.[110] Eisenhower was keen for it to be available to all American children. However, Oveta Culp Hobby, secretary of the newly established Department of Health, Education, and Welfare, was worried that this would be the start of socialized medicine, given that only six years had passed since Truman's national health insurance bill had been pushed back by Congress and the AMA (see chapter 5).[111] Hobby wanted the forty-eight states or the public to pay for the vaccine, and only after the Cutter incident (for which she accepted no blame) did she implement a national distribution program, focusing initially on children between five and nine years of age. Hobby passed the responsibility to Surgeon General Leonard A. Scheele and the Public Health Service—even though the PHS was a major section within her own department. She stated to the Senate Committee on Labor and Public Welfare on May 16, 1955, that "no one could have foreseen the public demand" given that this was a "unique" phase of medical history, seeking to reassure the committee that "no child will be denied this vaccine."[112] The committee grilled Hobby on the balance between speed and safety, especially in the light of the Cutter incident. Among criticisms she faced was former President Truman's view that the federal polio program had been bungled and the 1952 Democratic presidential candidate Adlai Stevenson's claim in a public speech at New York University's Bellevue Medical Center that it "did not take any special clairvoyance to estimate the demand for the vaccine, the supply and the hazards of production and distribution" or to predict that "here was a situation above all others that called for foresight and meticulous planning and preparation."[113]

Such was the fallout from Hobby's reluctance to execute Eisenhower's pledge to protect American children that she resigned on July 13, 1955, only a few months into the vaccination program, just a few weeks before *Harper's Magazine* described it as "the Great Vaccine Mess." *Harper's* science reporter Leonard Engel recognized that this mess was due to "a tangled compound of many factors," to which "oversensationalism" in the media, "demagogy and political expediency," and "timidity and lack of leadership" all contributed.[114] Eisenhower defended Hobby but accepted her resignation, arguing that "in this great anxiety to do the thing rapidly and broadly" there were mixed political and scientific agendas, and Hobby was caught in the crossfire.[115] This was unconvincing, as was the stated reason why she resigned, ironically given that the courts exonerated Cutter Laboratories a month later.

These incidents took the shine off this golden moment in medical history, epitomized by Eisenhower dubbing Salk the "benefactor of mankind" in an April 1955 public citation. Eleanor Roosevelt echoed this heroic mood three years later; speaking from Warm Springs, Georgia, in January 1958, Mrs. Roosevelt introduced Salk as "one of the outstanding scientists of our time" whose work was bound up with the National Foundation for Infantile Paralysis.[116] On this occasion, the foundation was marking its twentieth year, at a time when national cases of polio were dropping sharply, with an estimated seven thousand lives in the 1950s saved in the process.[117] The year 1961 saw the lowest level of cases of polio recorded since reporting began in 1912, by which time 75 percent of children between ages one and five had received inoculations. Opening in the early 1960s, the Salk Institute for Biological Studies in La Jolla, California, has helped to carry the mythmaking of this golden moment into the twenty-first century. Yet concerns about the virus persisted into the 1960s, as did political wrangles at the federal level: President Kennedy signed the Vaccination Assistance Act in August 1962 to support intensive vaccination programs, but his administration preferred Sabin's oral vaccine, putting it at odds with the National Foundation's preference for the Salk vaccine.[118]

SILENCE, WHISPERS, VOICES: HIV/AIDS, 1981–1992

If influenza threw the country into half a year of panic and if polio had a *longue durée* with a seasonal pattern, then HIV/AIDS emerged in 1979–80 in local urban communities, when New York City and Los Angeles health officials detected lesions on the skin of dying patients, before escalating into a national and global crisis. The danger of focusing primarily on the United States is that it overlooks a global story in which AIDS remains a deadly disease, especially in sub-Saharan Africa. Though the discussion here frames the crisis in domestic terms, this is not to ignore threats to other countries or "global interdependence" when it comes to HIV/AIDS.[119]

The receding of the American AIDS epidemic was not as clear cut as the polio crisis, though panic levels had started to ebb by the late 1990s, so much so that President Clinton began his AIDS Day speech of December 1, 1998, with a celebratory story of an orphaned HIV positive baby from Iowa City, Jimiya Poisel, who was now a reasonably healthy six-year-old adopted girl. In a year when deaths from HIV were declining for the first time, Jimiya reminded Clinton "what the whole thing is about" and stirred his belief that AIDS was "no longer a death sentence."[120] Despite this symbolic moment of closure, it is far from a neat narrative: AIDS-related deaths remain high in California, and an outbreak of the virus in rural Indiana in 2015 (linked to contaminated opioid needles) illustrates the continuing threat.

This third case study builds on the previous two by focusing on the escalation of HIV/AIDS from early reported outbreaks in New York, Los Angeles, and San Francisco to the reluctance of the mainstream media in the early 1980s to cover the virus, through the Ronald Reagan and George H. W. Bush administrations, and up to 1992 when a combination of drug therapies were showing positive results and media stories on AIDS started to fall in number, after peaking in 1987.[121] Arguably, perhaps more than the viruses in the previous two case studies, this public health crisis poses the ontological, ethical, biopolitical, and cultural questions outlined in the book's preface, largely because AIDS was such a polarizing illness, at least up until the early 1990s.[122] For example, in November 1993, the *New York Times* published an impassioned piece, "Whatever Happened to AIDS?," claiming it was now "everywhere and nowhere, the leading cause of death among young men nationwide, but little threat to the core of American political power, the white heterosexual suburbanite."[123]

This national story should never ignore the fact that globally the 1990s and 2000s were *the* decades of the AIDS crisis, but in terms of the dynamic of silence and disclosure in the histories of influenza and polio, the earlier phase of the 1980s and turn of the 1990s offers one of the most instructive health stories of the century. There were differences of tone between the health messages of the Reagan and Bush administrations, but marked continuities too and similar criticisms leveled at the presidents by patients, health workers, activists, and celebrities. My discussion here focuses on federal AIDS policy over the course of a decade, but it also features cultural figures and literary voices who contested silences and reactionary views to speak out against inertia, fear, and misinformation in the years before AIDS entered the cultural mainstream. This mainstream entry point is symbolized by Tom Hanks's Oscar for Best Actor for his performance in the 1993 movie *Philadelphia* as the AIDS patient Andrew Beckett who takes on a prejudiced and inert corporate establishment, but also by Paul Farmer's opinion that "fantasies and junk science have often dominated public discussions of AIDS."[124]

It is not entirely clear when HIV/AIDS became a crisis in the United States. This was because the Reagan administration was slow to realize its impact, there was little discussion of the subject between the president and his first two secretaries of Health and Human Services Richard Schweiker (1981–83) and Margaret Heckler (1983–85), and when the White House finally acknowledged AIDS it was often tangled with discourses of drug use. In summer 1981, the CDC established a task force to study Kaposi's sarcoma, a rare type of skin cancer that was erupting on the skin of gay patients hospitalized for a combination of herpes and pneumonia, and the agency started to issue precautions in November 1982 and published prevention guidelines in March 1983.[125] Even though the goal of the CDC task force was to ascertain to what extent this was or might become an epidemic, the stigma that Sander Gilman traces through the history of sexually transmitted diseases clung to AIDS from the outset.[126]

In contrast to this faltering top-down governmental response were a series of bottom-up literary, sociological, and autobiographical texts on AIDS published between 1987 and 1989 that helped to raise consciousness and challenged the troubling tone of early press reports like "A Disease's Spread Provokes Anxiety," a *New York Times* piece of August 1982.[127] Susan Sontag, in her widely read 1989 book *AIDS and Its Metaphors*, recognized that such a crisis tone could often verge on the apocalyptic, as did David Holleran in his 1988 essay collection *Ground Zero* in which New York City is pictured as a "cemetery" that "haunts the mind as a sort of doppelgänger" of the glitzy city that visitors think they know.[128] The metaphor of zero in Holleran's title was one that *San Francisco Chronicle* journalist Randy Shilts introduced in his acclaimed 1987 book *And the Band Played On*, though this was a mistranslation of the concept of "Patient O," a term introduced by the CDC to identify an early HIV sufferer, the Air Canada flight attendant Gaëtan Dugas. Despite the importance of *And the Band Played On* in raising public awareness, exposing the disregard of the Reagan administration, and posing questions about the robustness of airport health security, in promulgating the "Patient Zero" discourse Shilts stigmatized both Dugas and communities most at risk from the virus.[129]

Until mid-decade the Reagan administration, just like the mainstream media, downplayed the AIDS threat because it conflicted with its fiscal priorities (as Reagan's second HHS secretary Margaret Heckler notes), but also arguably because the early cases were limited to the gay communities of San Francisco and New York City that were unlikely to ever vote Republican.[130] Despite NBC's early effort to dramatize the consequences of AIDS in the 1985 television film *An Early Frost* about an HIV-infected male lawyer, misinformation circulated widely about women being biologically unable to contract the virus. A December 1985 article in *Discover* magazine, for example, claimed to embody the "latest scientific facts" yet it promulgated the myth that the vagina was less likely to be infected than the anus.[131]

Federal officials also engaged in mythmaking and kept making public gaffes. For example, in the fall of 1986 Carlton E. Turner, Reagan's deputy assistant for drug-abuse policy, argued there was a direct connection between marijuana and AIDS and that extensive inhalation of cannabis permanently weakens the immune system. Following these remarks, Turner was forced to resign when *Newsweek* covered the story, yet two years later Vice President Bush continued to claim "the AIDS crisis and the drug crisis are intertwined."[132] Randy Shilts was a harsh critic both of Reagan's disregard for the suffering of AIDS patients and the failure of Congress to inject research funding into the National Institutes of Health. Californian Democratic congressman Henry Waxman was declaring AIDS a crisis as early as 1983, after calling for a federal hearing the previous year when reports started to emerge from Los Angeles. Yet although the PHS launched a National AIDS Hotline that February to offer health information and to ease the fears of callers, little federal funding went into research and prevention in the mid-1980s, leading Shilts to muse: "Henry Waxman shuddered as he read all the news stories about the nation's number-one health priority. If this was how they treated their number-one priority, he wondered, what do they do with number two or three?"[133]

By 1987, it was widely accepted that AIDS was a public health crisis. One would not know that from listening to the Christian Right though, some of whom saw AIDS as a punishment for homosexuality, or President Reagan who was largely silent on the topic despite HHS and CDC launching an "America Responds to AIDS" campaign in 1987 and the PHS producing a college and university video *AIDS: Why Should I Care?* the following year. Reagan's first full public mention of AIDS was in September 1985. When asked at a press conference whether the president would "support a massive government research program against AIDS," Reagan went on the defensive, saying that he had supported it for four years and it was one of his administration's top priorities. He cited the budget figures for AIDS research, and when pushed on the matter replied that $126 million, his allocation for 1986, "has got to be something of a vital contribution."[134] When pressed again, Reagan did not state that if he had young children he would send them into a classroom with a child who had AIDS.[135] Although he underestimated the public health challenge (twelve thousand New York students boy-cotted school the previous week), Reagan acknowledged both sides of the argument. Yet his response was symptomatic of unfounded rumors about how the virus was spreading, following the expulsion of thirteen-year-old Ryan White from his Indiana school in June 1985 after con-tracting HIV following a blood transfusion (he was reinstated to his class by the Indiana Department of Education the following April after a health check by the local board).[136] The reactions of anxious parents on behalf of their children were captured in "The New Untouchables," a *Time* article of September 1985 that echoed other forms of moral panic such as that of the Indiana representative Dan Burton who took his own scissors to the barber to prevent him coming into contact with anyone else's hair.[137] Robert Bellah notes that it was "not surprising that the reaction" to AIDS in its early days was "often irrational," with "fear and anger...on every side," but Bellah would have rejected such extreme individualistic reactions to what he called the shared domain of "common problems."[138]

Although far from acknowledging this shared domain, Reagan took the situation more seriously from 1986 onward, after *Time* had run a cover article "AIDS: A Growing Threat" in August 1985 and the shock-ing death of Rock Hudson in October 1985, a film actor fourteen years younger than Reagan.[139] Reagan's third HHS secretary, Otis R. Bowen, was more vocal than the previous two secretaries and, in the wake of Surgeon General C. Everett Koop's *Report on Acquired Immune De-ficiency Syndrome* of October 1986, the Reagan administration recog-nized the need for better preventive measures and vaccination research. This was in part because Koop's report was shaped by his friendship with the immunologist Anthony S. Fauci, the recently appointed direc-tor of the National Institute of Allergy and Infectious Diseases. With Koop's desire to "prevent the spread of AIDS while at the same time preserving our humanity and intimacy," the report seemed like a break-through moment, prompting the president to recognize HIV as a "ma-jor epidemic public health threat," though it disappointed many Repub-licans in prioritizing safe sex and sex education instead of promoting normative family values.[140] However, Reagan often returned to the ex-cuse of tight budgets. When questioned four months later by the *Los Angeles Times* about the "scary" PHS figures relating to the escalation of AIDS cases, Reagan said there was no leeway in the federal budget, and the Social Security Administration was keen to limit access to wel-fare benefits by adhering to the narrow CDC classification of AIDS as a disabling syndrome, thereby disqualifying other claimants with AIDS-related conditions.[141] In fact, throughout this period, Reagan seemed largely uninformed about the spread of the virus, from 239 cases in 1981 to 50,000 in 1987, as it moved far beyond the specific localities of the early cases, including a high prevalence among poor African American communities.[142]

Reagan mentioned AIDS only three times in his public speeches in 1986, and then more frequently in 1987, the peak year for media stories on the illness. He announced a collaborative health initiative with France in March 1987, and in late May spoke in heroic terms about the "breathtaking advances" in medicine, increases in spending, and "tearing down regulatory barriers" to move AIDS from the "laboratory to the marketplace as quickly as possible."[143] This AIDS Research Awards Dinner on May 31 was the stage for an important speech by Reagan in which he dispelled the rumor that the HIV virus is airborne, called for "urgency, not panic," "compassion, not blame" and "understanding, not ignorance," and set out a plan for a President's Commission on the HIV Epidemic. Despite efforts to avoid stigmatizing groups, Reagan's remarks veered toward the moralistic, and he again linked AIDS to "drug abuse and sexual promiscuity," proclaiming that it would be added "to the list of contagious diseases for which immigrants and aliens seeking permanent residence in the United States can be denied entry."[144] He received a chorus of boos for this comment, but he repeated the point, linking the virus to a foreign element that threatens "innocent, unknowing people."

Vice President Bush reprised this surface theme of "dignity and kindness" the following day, June 1, in his keynote address at the Third International Conference on AIDS. Bush's speech focused on the need to develop a confidential system of testing for AIDS and for better health education, leading to the distribution the following year of the Department of Education leaflet *AIDS and the Education of Our Children* and the CDC brochure *Understanding AIDS*. These publications reinforced the surgeon general's emphasis on safe sex and condom use. Avoiding such details and playing to the Republican base, the vice president mixed neutral points with an ideological statement about the need to strengthen family bonds: "this kind of education should teach traditional values. It should teach morality. It should help develop the child's sense of personal responsibility. And it should strengthen the concept of family."[145] Reagan himself returned to this point, stating that responsibility rests with the individual, and the "best way to prevent AIDS is to abstain from sex until marriage and then to maintain a faithful relationship, as well as to avoid illicit drugs altogether."[146] At least by then he had met HIV positive patients, during a visit to the National Institutes of Health in July 1987.

Significantly, the landmark *Report of the Presidential Commission on the Human Immunodeficiency Virus Epidemic*, released in June 1988, did not echo this conservative agenda. The head of the commission, Navy Admiral James D. Watkins, saw the epidemic as lifting the lid on "many of the problems our society faces today" that made it "much more than a medical crisis or a public health threat."[147] Watkins was concerned about poor health education in schools and a sluggish drug development system, but his letter to the president stated his worry about the signs of kneejerk moral panic to a complex terrain. He expressed this in terms of "a society in which some members [are] still too quick to reject, deny, condemn, and discriminate, resulting in a situation that neither bodes well for the individual nor the public health when dealing with this epidemic."[148] Instead of a bleak report, Watkins's letter emphasizes the "the spark of human spirit" and the benevolence of HIV researchers, marking this as a moment for change for health care and health education. The commission made a number of specific recommendations: AIDS should be referred to as "HIV infection," nurses should receive better incentives for working in areas of high HIV density, and robust ethical and antidiscrimination protocols and coordinated international cooperation were needed.

Watkins did not mention that new drugs had come onto the market that year with a swifter FDA approval schedule in a move to make treatments available to patients with life-threating conditions.[149] Approved in October 1987, the antiviral drug Zidovudine (or AZT) gave hope to those diagnosed as HIV-positive because it had the potential to reduce the risk of HIV infection after exposure and also lower the risk of mothers passing on the virus in utero. AZT was made available four months later, prior to the FDA licensing it as a drug to treat AIDS-related pneumonia, but activists railed against its high price and what they viewed as the profiteering instincts of its manufacturer Burroughs Wellcome (the price of AZT came down by 20 percent in October 1989 following a high-profile protest outside the New York Stock Exchange).

The recommendation of the commission for sweeping measures may not have been what Reagan envisaged when he appointed Watkins as head of the project. Although activists accused the president of ignoring the report's antidiscrimination recommendation, it nevertheless led to the development of a ten-point action plan, a significant hike in federal funding, and a shift in tone that George Bush adopted during his 1988 presidential campaign.[150] Importantly, the commission report stimulated a broader recognition of social, psychological, ethical, and cultural issues and a more integrated approach to HIV/AIDS. For example, Louis Wade Sullivan, President Bush's health secretary, closed the Sixth International AIDS Conference in June 1990, while being heckled by activists, by affirming "culturally relevant and sensitive programs" for minority communities affected by AIDS, and three months later Congress passed the Ryan White Comprehensive AIDS Resources Emergency Act to increase federal funding for poorer communities (White had died that April, age eighteen).[151]

The media oscillated between apocalyptic headlines and attempts to tell a narrative of progress, echoing the national story of polio in the late 1930s and 1940s once the National Foundation for Infantile Paralysis had formed. Bush contributed to this media cycle. On the one hand he continued to view AIDS as a "horrible national crisis," but on the other he argued for better health education, to reduce discrimination (he called AIDS a "disease not a disgrace"), for intelligent rather than superficial answers, and to dispel myths about contact with individuals with the virus.[152] His most important speech on the issue was to the National Coalition on AIDS in March 1990 in which he compared AIDS to polio:

> As with AIDS, regarding polio, there was a lot of ignorance—thousands of stray cats and dogs put to death, kids sleeping with camphor inhalers, and at least one town was fumigated with DDT....And then suddenly, it was over—the dreaded iron lung, unused, cluttering hospital hallways; children again growing up in a world without fear....There was a lot of ignorance. Let's learn from that. And in the darkest hours, hope came unexpectedly, powerfully, and with finality.[153]

This comparison was based on a supreme faith in laboratory science, but it also reflects Bush's wish to return to a mythical "kinder, gentler nation" of the 1950s (as he expressed during his 1988 presidential campaign) before the new social movements of the 1960s set the grounds for a more pluralistic culture that Republicans blamed for hastening the AIDS epidemic.

Whatever the ideological underpinning, Bush's words and the pace of change at the start of the 1990s were not enough for many AIDS activists and patients, despite the passage through Congress with an overwhelming majority of the Comprehensive AIDS Resource Emergency

Act of 1990.[154] Visibility and audibility were vital for activists and advocates. When artist Mary Fisher gave an impassioned speech at the Republican National Convention in Houston in 1992, she emphasized the theme of silence. In what is referred to as "The Whisper of AIDS" speech, Fisher spoke of the heartache she and her children experienced when she discovered she had contracted AIDS from her (now divorced) second husband. The fact that this was a Republican convention, and that later Fisher called Bush's response to AIDS "personally sympathetic but publicly lame," was poignant.[155] Fisher's speech was soon followed by the resignation from the National Commission on AIDS of the HIV-positive Los Angeles Lakers star Magic Johnson, whose reason was that Bush had "dropped the ball" on research and advocacy after promising much more early in his presidency, even though the NIH received a bigger budgetary hike than most other federal departments, as Bush was keen to point out in the election year of 1992. Nevertheless, Fisher and Johnson are instructive examples of public figures keen to call out federal negligence and to highlight the invisibility of women and African Americans within the AIDS crisis.[156]

If the federal government was slow to move in the 1980s, had mixed agendas, did not always separate science from rumor, tried to limit the state benefits available to HIV-positive citizens, mixed the war on AIDS with a war on drugs when news stories of needle sharing in inner cities came to light in 1986–87, and often relied on crude stereotypes, then the *truth* about AIDS—its health impact on lives and its cultural significance—was left to grassroots health organizations, lobby groups, and writers of fiction and memoir to explore and uncover.[157] Prominent among these community initiatives was the Gay Men's Health Crisis, a grassroots group established in Manhattan in 1982 to share information on AIDS within the gay community, to offer a counseling service, and to push community-based funding initiatives.[158] ACT UP (AIDS Coalition to Unleash Power) was by far the most vocal of the lobby groups. Formed in New York the year that Shilts published *And the Band Played On*, ACT UP focused on guerrilla-style public activities that could attract media attention. ACT UP activists targeted pharmaceutical companies such as Burroughs Wellcome and the federal government, and their strategies veered between anarchist demonstrations and installations, as also practiced after 1988 through the work of the eleven-member artist collective Gran Fury.[159]

The main slogan of ACT UP, "Silence = Death," was a potent symbol of activist practice, such as the demonstration targeted at making trial drugs more immediately available in front of the FDA building in Silver Spring, Maryland in October 1988 and the occupation of the nearby National Institutes of Health campus in May 1990. Though the National Institute of Allergy and Infectious Diseases director Anthony Fauci was one NIH scientist who sought a productive dialogue with ACT UP activists (following their criticism that he was trying to restrict access to AZT), the coalition stimulated widespread rule-breaking such as the noisy and anarchic writing style of the New Yorker David B. Feinberg in his 1988 and 1991 AIDS-related books *Eighty-Sixed* and *Spontaneous Combustion*, the second of which affirms another ACT UP slogan "Action = Life."[160] Just as the street theater of ACT UP and the installations of Gran Fury smashed the borders of politics and art (President Bush called ACT UP "crazy"), so authors like Feinberg sought to collapse boundaries between biography and fiction. In doing so, Feinberg incorporated gonzo journalism techniques and first-person testimonies by HIV-positive men in an effort to move beyond "stunned, confused silence," to tackle "the collective mood of emergency," and to develop a mixed-mode aesthetic that could trace the diverse experiences of AIDS culture and could challenge medical, political, moral, and cultural categories that, on their own, are inadequate for understanding the multiple meanings of the disease.[161]

Despite the efforts of experimental writers like Feinberg to subvert literary conventions, conventional domestic narratives on the subject also appeared, such as Alice Hoffman's *At Risk* (1988) in which an eleven-year-old suburban girl from Massachusetts contracts AIDS from a blood transfusion during a surgery procedure. The risk is that the act of writing about a fatal illness becomes a solitary pursuit framed in individualistic or familial terms rather than tackling the socioeconomic implications of the virus and the ways in which uneven medical categorization can often disenfranchise gay men and women.[162] The Los Angeles–based writer Paul Monette, for example, finds himself trapped in a domestic story when he finds that he is HIV-positive following the death of his partner in 1986. Monette's crisis is founded on loss as he searches for a medium through which to express his condition, yet words and structures fall short of what he needs in his two books of 1988, *Love Alone* and *Borrowed Time*, before his own death in 1995.[163] Loss and mourning are common themes in early AIDS writing, but Feinberg and fellow New Yorker John Weir, in his 1989 novel *The Irreversible Decline of Eddie Socket*, took a different tack, using humor and dark comedy to question medicalized narratives and control structures. This variance of tone presages a much broader range of AIDS texts and storytelling since the mid-1990s that has led writers and bloggers to explore racial, sexual, economic, and community dynamics that go far beyond the narrower frame of personalized life stories.[164]

In tracing what Seth Mnookin has called the "panic virus" from the early twentieth century through to the contemporary moment, one is struck by the themes of repetition, denial, and deep-rooted tension between medical and mythic discourses.[165] Each of the three viruses discussed here may not have been as devastating had the federal government acted with greater speed and sensitivity to public health. However, this begs the question about what aspects of health information could have been improved and how to safeguard civil liberties while establishing mitigation strategies, especially as there was no guarantee that scientists would have discovered an effective vaccine any quicker had federal interventions been more nuanced. Nonetheless, at least in the third case, the viral spread was exacerbated by what the *Los Angeles Times* journalist Robert Scheer calls "indifference" in "the years when governmental and medical bureaucracies comforted themselves with the illusion that AIDS was an illness peculiar to homosexuals" and not a national emergency.[166] As all three case studies show, media outlets treated the three viruses ambivalently, ignoring the diseases until they had reached crisis proportions, before often settling on steady narratives of medical progress. Against this grain, literary and autobiographical accounts have proved to be a crucial corrective in questioning silences by exploring the situated illness experience from the inside out.

The mixed meanings of viruses have heightened in our own time when viral metaphors are often unmoored from virology, whether it is in the "disease generation" video games (such as Pandemic 2.5 and Plague, Inc., two games launched in 2012 that are especially popular during epidemics), or in the cyber-realm where viruses provoke a different kind of security panic based on fears of infiltration.[167] Tony Sampson uses network theory in his 2012 book *Virality* to argue that the moral charge that is often superimposed on viral activity is not intrinsic to it, though this recognition rarely alleviates fears about a fast-moving invisible submicroscopic agent.[168] The US federal government's efforts to improve disease surveillance at home via CDC's Epidemic Intelligence Service and to make containment interventions abroad did not quell predictions that Atlantic nations would soon face another pandemic in the wake of the SARS, Ebola, H1N1, and Zika outbreaks.[169] This likelihood became a grim reality in early 2020 in the form of COVID-19, realizing President Obama's fears of 2014 that "there may and likely will come at time" when the world would experience a deadly airborne disease that would demand we "see it quickly, isolate it quickly, respond to it quickly."[170]

The stakes were high, therefore, when the World Health Organization prevaricated for a number of days before, on January 30, 2020, calling the highly contagious novel coronavirus SARS-CoV-2 a global health emergency, and announcing on March 11 that COVID-19 was now a pandemic.[171] The initial risk within the United States at the time was thought to be low, despite forty-three cases and two deaths across nine states by the end of February, among three thousand deaths worldwide at that time. The CDC director Robert Redfield was clear that the country should adopt an aggressive containment mode, including the quarantining of US nationals returning from East Asia, plus a federal ban on direct flights from China for visitors (given that the virus originated in Wuhan, Hubei province), followed by a mitigation phase of contact tracing and testing to limit community-based transmission. Yet these measures did little to slow the rapid spread from initial cases in Washington and California in late January to dense clusters in New York, New Jersey, Michigan, and Louisiana by late March and then a resurgence of the virus in the South, Midwest, and West in high summer. One reason for the initial acceleration was that scientists discerned only later that the virus had emerged undetected in a number of metropolitan areas during the first half of February. State governors and medical leaders scrambled to expand hospital facilities and to mobilize sufficient personal protective equipment for frontline health workers. Yet cases of COVID-19 rose to over 930 deaths across thirty-four US states by March 10 and climbed to nearly 190,000 confirmed cases and four thousand deaths in all fifty states by the end of March, before skyrocketing to over sixty thousand deaths by the end of April and passing the grim death toll of six figures by the end of May.

It took several weeks after the Wuhan report in late December for the White House to escalate its Coronavirus Task Force, led from late February by Vice President Mike Pence to offer "a whole of government approach." In contrast, in the midst of a presidential campaign and with an eye to falling markets, Trump contradicted the scientific views of the Task Force, including that of NIH immunologist Anthony Fauci, about the likely time frame for an effective vaccine. The president downplayed the spread of what he called a "foreign virus," blamed China and the World Health Organization for poor containment strategies, bragged about US government preparedness and the availability of testing kits, and marginalized Robert Redfield (the CDC director) and Alex Azar (the HSS secretary) as the crisis peaked, perhaps because CDC and HSS had given early warnings about biodefense security. Nevertheless, by mid-March the US death toll was climbing steeply, compelling the president to announce a national emergency, to mobilize FEMA, and to sign a $2 billion stimulus package as the Coronavirus Aid, Relief, and Economic Security (CARES) Act, but he remained reluctant to endorse mask wearing and was eager to quickly reopen businesses and schools against scientific advice.[172]

I return to the COVID-19 emergency in the book's coda because its threat to global health is so profound, though at present it is too early to assess fully its impact on nearly two hundred countries with varying population densities, border controls, and degrees of economic resilience. Nonetheless, this latest pandemic, like the Great Influenza a century earlier, reveals just how quickly hidden and new vulnerabilities can emerge. Both then and now, conflicting domestic priorities can skew public health responses to cross-border viral threats, yet global cooperation remains our best hope for ensuring continental preparedness, for combating drug-resistant diseases such as the spread of malaria in Southeast Asia, and for ameliorating fragmented national response systems.[173] International science-based accords are crucial for border health security. These include the International Health Regulations, adopted in 2005 by all members of the World Health Organization as a legal framework for the cross-border disease control, and the North American Plan for Avian and Pandemic Influenza of 2007, an agreement between Canada, Mexico, and the United States updated in 2012 following the H1N1 pandemic.[174] However, it is also important to prevent stigmatizing attitudes from spreading virally in the face of epidemics, to improve the candor and clarity of official communications, to coordinate more sensitively domestic support services, and to ensure the continuity of supply chains. And, on a national and regional level, there are chastening health security lessons to be learned from modern American history, where memories, narratives, and reports of outbreaks can help us to better understand the impact of viral mobility on vulnerable individuals and communities.

CHAPTER 5

Care

Postwar Hospitals, Community Action,
Vet Centers

On February 26, 1962, the Office of the White House issued a press release to major newspapers, radio stations, and television channels on behalf of President John F. Kennedy. Its subject was national health needs. The president noted with "justifiable pride" "our achievements in the field of medicine," notably the overcoming of epidemics and an increase in life expectancy, but he expressed unease that "this nation still falls far short of its responsibility" to the American people.[1] His particular concerns were infectious disease, infant mortality, the elderly, and treatment of "the mentally ill and mentally retarded." He also worried about shortages in medical personnel and saw it as the responsibility of the federal government to share the burden of health care with local and state authorities, as well as with diverse communities. Cooperative partnership and "creative change" were keynotes of Kennedy's and Johnson's domestic policies and mark out the 1960s as a high point for those health care initiatives geared to assisting vulnerable citizens.[2] This model was not a centrist one despite increased federal investment and criticism from Richard Nixon and Ronald Reagan that a pact between the Democrats and labor unions meant that this was socialized medicine through the back door. Neither Kennedy nor Johnson after 1963 had a blueprint to achieve these "effective procedures" and improve health education, except through an ongoing pluralist commitment to "joint activities most appropriate and acceptable to each community."[3]

As the second chapter discussed in the case of the Model Cities

Program, which arguably did little to improve urban deprivation in the 1960s, there is always a gap between plans and realities when it comes to the reform of health care systems. Nonetheless, the idea of breaking new frontiers in health research and treatment lends a heroic cast to such reformist aspirations. For example, Kennedy's emphasis on improving medical facilities reflected his new frontier philosophy, taking health into the atomic age at a time of a rapidly expanding population that jumped by three million between 1960 and 1961.[4] This vision linked to Kennedy's effort to get the nation moving economically and technologically via new partnerships. The Atomedic Research Center in Alabama also embraced the vision, a company that aimed to harness technologies from the US space program to improve the cost effectiveness and contemporary relevance of hospitals.[5] The plan was for a lightweight circular aluminum hospital powered by atomic energy that could be airlifted to where it was needed, with the estimation that this would halve the cost of hospital construction and cut operating costs by 30 percent. The atomic design attracted the interest of the president of the American Medical Association, Louis M. Orr, who thought that it was "geared to the coming space age."[6]

This Atomedic design was not mass produced, even though it led to a twenty-two-bed prototype being built in Montgomery, Alabama, in 1963 and a functional exhibition display at the 1964 New York World's Fair. Launched at a time when another aluminum Cold War structure—the family survival shelter—was waning in popularity, the aims of Atomedic nevertheless echoed and amplified the modernizing ethos of the 1946 Hospital Survey and Construction Act and the design drive toward flexible structures.[7] During the Truman and Eisenhower presidencies hospital construction and the development of new training facilities for nurses (overseen by the Division of Nursing Resources from 1949 and the Division of Nursing from 1960) only partially succeeded in modernizing state hospitals. Typically, these facilities were often in aging buildings without up-to-date medical equipment or adequate electric power and plumbing facilities, and they tended to have insufficiently trained hospital staff at a time when the nation lacked 25 percent of the estimated required nurses.[8] While this new emphasis on community services was not as innovative as the Atomedic design, congressional Democrats viewed these plans positively as a commitment to the needs of underserved communities, just as some Republicans saw the initiative as an unwelcome example of big government.

Of all the groups with health needs, the president was especially concerned about those diagnosed with mental illness or with an intellectual or developmental disability, categories often conflated unhelpfully and at times harmfully. He was not the only one. In May 1960, *Time* magazine cited the view of a New York City judge, Nathaniel Kaplan, that the dearth of mental health facilities was a "new shame of the states," a view that was especially pertinent in a year that was designated World Mental Health Year by the World Federation for Mental Health. With the phrase "new shame of the states," Kaplan echoed the title of journalist Albert Deutsch's exposé of the "snake pit" conditions of many 1940s state hospitals. Kaplan estimated that five hundred thousand children experienced mental illness, yet there were fewer than four thousand spaces in special facilities, with twenty-six states having no public facilities at all and an additional seventeen lacking private facilities. For Kaplan, the results were dire: "the usual fate of mentally ill children...is to be hidden away at home" or "dumped into institutions for victims of mental retardation" or "committed to questionable custodial care in state hospital mental wards."[9] In response to such criticism, Kennedy assembled the President's Panel on Mental Retardation in 1961, to which he appointed his sister Eunice as a special consultant. The focus of the twenty-seven-member panel was on prevention, education, public awareness, and research, and in an October 1962 national action report it sketched out improved coordination between federal, state, and local authorities and the private sector.[10] However, six years later, in 1968, the federal government acknowledged that the nation was still only at "the edge of change" on this issue.[11]

The first two case studies here focus on the "shame of the states" moments in the late 1940s and the mid-1960s. The first phase relates to attempts by the Truman administration to initiate infrastructure and insurance reforms in the face of congressional resistance; the second links to the reformist spirit of the Johnson administration's Great Society legislation of 1964–66 that developed Kennedy's plans for community health care. Rather than revisit the Kennedy family story in which health plays a pivotal role, this chapter takes a longer historical look at the problems and promises of health care institutions over a forty-year period, from 1945 to 1985, in response to alarmist accounts in the media about the substance and sustainability of US health care. The first case study focuses on the development of a modern hospital system after World War II that was in part to update inadequate state facilities and in part to address a lack of access based on region, race, and economic status. In the second section, I turn to the rise of community facilities in the mid-1960s as a responsive health care model, as well as to their partial demise in the 1970s and 1980s. The third case spotlights organizational and leadership concerns that beset the Veterans Health Administration through to the ten-year anniversary of the fall of Saigon, especially uneven care that Vietnam-era veterans faced, but it also shows examples of community health citizenship that chime with earlier case studies.

These cases each focus on an eight-year period, 1945–53, 1964–71, and 1977–85, which marked a transition between Democratic and Republican administrations. The three periods witnessed intense phases of health care policy at the federal level that capitalized in turn on Roosevelt's germinal national health program; the opening of the Department of Health, Education, and Welfare early in Eisenhower's presidency; and Nixon's concerns about drug taking by Vietnam-era soldiers that skewed public attitudes toward veterans and their health needs. Importantly, the three studies highlight the challenges faced by Democratic leaders as well as illustrate what Theda Skocpol calls a boomerang effect with respect to seismic shifts in national health priorities when administrations shift from one political party to another.

My emphasis on the crisis in post–World War II health care systems diverges from the acute panic and planning cycles of earlier chapters; it has moments of rising tensions but also much background debate, media noise, and frustration at the hands of party politics, congressional procedures, and the tricky task of enforcing policy, especially the desegregation of medical facilities. This forty-year span does not mean the crisis in hospital provision ceased in the mid-1980s (in 1988 the *New York Times* was declaring "Crisis in Emergency Rooms"), but this time frame enables me to assess the mix of progress and stasis over a prolonged phase in which budgetary priorities and responsive health care facilities were often fiercely in tension.[12] I touch on health finance and insurance here too, though my primary focus is on the structures and spaces of health care that, as Kennedy believed, need to be responsive to diverse communities if they stand a chance of averting organizational and environmental crises.

THE STATE OF POSTWAR HOSPITALS, 1945–1953

For three days in July 1938, the Mayflower Hotel in Washington, DC, witnessed a landmark event, the National Conference on Health and Medical Care, the aim of which was to establish a national health program. The chief organizer was the Interdepartmental Committee to Coordinate Health and Welfare Activities, which was then in its third year as a federal committee. Its members were keen to overhaul a health care system that had lost its Progressive-era optimism in the face of an expanding population, a creaky diagnostic system, poor record keeping, and outdated facilities. The Interdepartmental Committee set out five recommendations: first, to focus the Public Health Service on children's health; second, to develop a ten-year program of hospital expansion especially in rural areas; third, to increase care for the "medically needy"; fourth, to develop a health insurance system underpinned by grants-in-aid; and, fifth, to work on disability compensation for industrial accidents. These recommendations had equal weighting, but the delegates shared the belief that the development of a modern hospital system was the most urgent. Robert E. Neff, the president of the American Hospital Association for 1937–38 and administrator of the state university hospitals in Iowa, described the modern hospital as an "indispensable agency" that suffered from inadequate funding and unevenness of spread.[13] As a midwesterner, Neff called for better regional distribution, but he realized the cost of specialized equipment meant it would be difficult to create a perfectly calibrated system without introducing another layer of "tributary hospitals" from which patients who needed specialist care would be referred to metropolitan facilities. Neff's other rather idealistic point was the hospital should not cease being responsible for patients once they leave its doors, a task that would require cooperation across a range of agencies that should share with the modern hospital a "watchfulness over public health."[14]

The estimated cost of adequately overhauling the hospital system was $850 million per year in the late 1930s, and it was proposed this would be split equally between the federal and state governments, yet the condition of the hospital system varied considerably across regions and between urban and rural areas. The National Health Survey of 1935–36 had indicated that among poor citizens receiving relief aid there was an annual hospitalization rate of 63 per 1,000 persons compared to 49 per 1,000 in families earning more than $3,000 per year. Larger cities could cope with this volume, but "deficiency of hospitalization" was more typical in smaller cities and rural areas, with only 15 percent of poor patients receiving hospital treatment. The Public Health Service was aware of this deficiency and stated in the survey that hospital facilities were inadequate for low-income groups who lived away from metropolitan centers. This, it concluded, was a "problem of very serious proportions."[15] The president of the Associated Women of the American Farm Bureau Federation, H. W. Ahart, restated this mood of a looming crisis by arguing that a typical rural health center had "poorer medical facilities at its disposal today than it had a generation ago." Picturing the entwining of "economic and human waste," she claimed "human life in the United States today is being wasted recklessly."[16]

Poverty and regional services were prominent topics at the conference, whereas race was confined to a couple of talks that lamented the neglected health of African Americans as a reminder to the delegates that "disease draws no color line." Of these, Louis T. Wright, chair of the board of directors of the National Association for the Advancement of Colored People, argued that modern organized medicine "has ignored the health of my people," both as patients and as physicians.[17] In this short speech, Wright highlighted a key issue that organized medicine had been reluctant to tackle: how to integrate a creaking yet segregated hospital service, particularly in small southern towns and rural areas. The Interdepartmental Committee certainly recognized the limitations of the hospital systems, even if it did not couch this explicitly in terms of region, class, or race. In the 1939 pamphlet *Toward Better National Health*, which stemmed from the conference, the committee posed a series of questions:

> How far is it to the nearest hospital? Does it have laboratory, X-ray, surgical facilities? Is it operated entirely on fees from patients, or are there any free beds for those that cannot pay? Does it run clinics? Is there an out-patient department? Where can a case of tuberculosis be sent? How overcrowded are the State institutions for mental cases?[18]

Partially answering these questions, the pamphlet noted that only sixteen of the forty-eight states met the standard of 5.6 general hospital beds per 1,000 residents and that the country as a whole was 400,000 beds short. The pamphlet looked ahead to the 1940s and made the pressing case for five hundred new hospitals, a requirement that was acute for many rural areas, where eighteen million lived in counties without a general hospital. Significantly, then, *Toward Better National Health* sketched a much bleaker picture than the one Robert Neff portrayed at the conference in his proposed integration of metropolitan and tributary hospitals.

Echoing the conference themes, President Roosevelt took the view that national health security and health inequalities required urgent attention.[19] He focused on small hospitals in poor rural areas yet was adamant that they should be built "only where they are most needed." In a January 1940 speech on small hospitals in "needy areas," he mentioned African Americans only once with respect to improving regional facilities and care for tuberculosis sufferers. Roosevelt's belief that these new hospitals should be "simple, functional structures, utilizing inexpensive materials" reflected his wariness of federal overspending, but this might also have been a strategy to convince Congress that fifty hospitals could be built for less than $10 million, with the federal government only being responsible for construction and not operational costs.[20] However, this executive branch recommendation failed to gain traction in Congress, and Roosevelt noted this was still awaiting approval in summer 1941.[21]

It was the task of Roosevelt's vice president, Harry Truman, to take up the cause of the New Deal health plans when the bombing of Pearl Harbor in December 1941 shifted Roosevelt's attention to foreign policy. Speaking to Congress in November 1945, seven months after Roosevelt's death, Truman asserted that "every American citizen" has "the right to adequate medical care and the opportunity to achieve and enjoy good health," as well as the "right to adequate protection from the economic fears of . . . sickness."[22] Responding to data gathered in a 1929–32 study by the Committee on the Costs of Medical Care and the mid-1930s National Health Survey, Truman spoke with urgency in the face of a looming health crisis.[23] Around fifty million Americans lacked access to adequate facilities, but medical examinations conducted by the Selective Service System revealed a third of potential recruits were unfit for military service, a statistic that led Truman to surmise that there is a "widespread physical and mental incapacity among the young people of our nation."[24] The president was less interested in why some recruits were deemed unfit than in the belief that "no American child shall come to adult life with diseases or defects which can be prevented or corrected at an early age."[25] In this 1945 speech, Truman echoed the "national concern" of the 1938 conference in his commitment to "health security for all, regardless of residence, station, or race."[26]

Truman's and Roosevelt's agendas were similar, but the thirty-third US president's emphasis on improving the hospital system was the first point of his administration's five-point health proposal. In this respect, Truman agreed with Roosevelt and his surgeon general Thomas Parran, who was concerned that the hospital system was disorganized and needed integrating with public health agencies, specialist treatment facilities, and local health centers.[27] As chair and president-elect of the

American Public Health Association in the mid-1930s, Parran was a passionate champion of public health and in developing the research and training infrastructure that could underpin it, but he was not a believer in universal health insurance, fearing that this would create a monolithic system without flexibility.[28] He preferred instead to see "diversity of form" in the nation's health services, noting in the mid-1930s that it is "precisely the lack of regimentation which is to be expected from a nation of individualists" and a decade later, at the end of the war, arguing that the nation's mental health services had made great strides.[29] Yet, although psychiatric services were available to veterans and for many civilians in rural and semirural regions, appropriate modern facilities were lacking in many regions of the country.[30] In recognition of this, Truman was keen to ensure that the sixty thousand doctors demobilizing from the armed forces might be attracted to work as civilian doctors in underserved areas. Simply building more hospitals was not the answer, as a 1942 National Committee for Mental Hygiene report on nongovernment psychiatric facilities affirmed.[31] According to the report, hospitals should be better equipped and preferably linked to research units, while staff needed to be better trained and more numerous.[32]

In his State of the Union address two months later, Truman laid out the budgetary priorities for the 1947 fiscal year and spared a few words for new health facilities. Following from the first of his five-point health program, Truman stated plainly that "for an adequate national health program," new "hospitals, sanitation works, and additional facilities at medical schools will be required."[33] However, it took until August 1946 for the bill to pass through Congress. Truman signed the legislation on August 13 as the Hospital Survey and Construction Act, commonly referred to as the Hill-Burton Act named after its congressional sponsors from Ohio and Alabama, senators Harold Burton and Lester Hill. One aim of the Hill-Burton Act was to provide 4.5 beds per 1,000 residents in all states (lower than the aspiration of 5.6 beds per 1,000 a decade earlier), including a certain amount of "free care" for those unable to pay for treatment.[34] Another was to ensure hospitals did not operate under a segregation policy based on race or religion that served to ration health care by limiting or denying access to minority groups.[35] Many southern hospitals operated a separate but equal system with little fear of reprisal, and this lack of regulation meant that poor and non-whites continued to receive second-class treatment in many facilities. Despite the historic passage of Hill-Burton, things became harder for Truman when the Republicans gained a majority in Congress a few months later, for the first time since 1930. Given the GOP's sixteen-year wait to regain a majority in both chambers, many congressmen tried to prevent Truman from doing anything to extend what they saw as Roosevelt's socialist agenda on domestic policy.

There were two major reasons why the Hill-Burton Act passed through Congress: it stressed the progress of science rather than an explicit public works plan, and it required that states pay two dollars for every federal dollar spent on hospital construction. (This proportion was amended in October 1949 when it became apparent the rule was preventing construction in some priority areas, leading to states being required to pay a minimum of a third of the cost).[36] The idea was that hospitals should not be built haphazardly but within a regional system, connecting general with specialist facilities and, where possible, to university medical training and research facilities. The act was a success in stimulating new buildings, including more than 10,500 projects between 1947 and 1971, many of them in underserved areas. In the first five years of the program, Georgia, Mississippi, Montana, Nebraska, and Texas received most approvals, with thirty-two states benefiting from construction; in those five years the federal budget gave $3 million for surveys and $75 million per year for new builds and improvements.

In this respect, medical historian Karen Kruse Thomas calls the Hill-Burton program "perhaps the most progressive expression of redistributive midcentury liberalism," following the assessment by the Johnson administration in the late 1960s that through its "activities in planning, design, research, operation and organization" Hill-Burton upgraded the country's health care system.[37] However, Thomas shows how the program was built on compromise. Not only was the final version of the Hospital Survey and Construction Bill more palatable to Republicans than earlier iterations, it also had less "administrative authority" than originally intended, and it disappointed the aspirations of the National Medical Association and African American medical leaders.[38] The construction work often created new facilities for predominantly white communities and refurbished older building for blacks. For example, the Carver Memorial Hospital in Chattanooga, Tennessee, opened in 1947 as a repurposed fifty-bed municipally owned and fully accredited black hospital, one of the first of its kind in the country. A second example was the newly built Moses H. Cone Memorial Hospital in Greensboro, North Carolina. Despite the condition of the memorial funding that "none shall be turned away on account of inability to pay for medical or surgical treatment," this Greensboro hospital opened in 1953 as a private whites-only facility until the hospital was forced to desegregate in 1964 following two years of litigation.[39] If Hill-Burton helped to stimulate the growth of African American practicing and training facilities (even though fewer than two hundred physicians graduated in 1960 from the two dedicated African American medical schools in Nashville and Washington, DC), then it was difficult to legislate against ward segregation in biracial facilities and to ensure institutional compliance. For Howard University anthropologist W. Montague Cobb it represented what Cobb called an "entrenched ghetto hospital system" at a remove from the liberal-progressive spirit that Hill-Burton initially symbolized for Democratic members of Congress.[40] A lack of regulatory power over discriminatory practices was a major concern for legislators and civil rights advocates, an issue not fully addressed until the mid-1970s when the Hill-Burton program morphed into the Public Health Service Act.

The problem of racial integration in hospitals rumbled through the 1950s, but that was only part of the problem. Even though some aspects of his administration's health focus were successful, such as the instituting of a National Public Health Week in 1950 (which grew out of the long-standing National Negro Health Week), the president was finding it difficult to push his overall health program through Congress. In some ways, 1948 was a triumphant year for Truman given the surprise retention of his executive branch office when many including the national press had written him off. However, it was a bad year for his health agenda. In May 1948 he outlined a ten-year health program and affirmed his commitment to health and welfare as "fundamental" and "vital" for the well-being and prosperity of "the greatest republic the sun has every shone upon."[41] Two deep problems punctured this optimism. The first was a growing awareness of the dire conditions of many state hospitals and their treatment of the mentally ill; the second pivoted on health insurance, an issue that Truman saw as a moral imperative. In this regard, he fought an ideological battle not only with congressional Republicans but also with the American Medical Association, whose members saw Truman's universal health insurance plans as an attack on the AMA's professional status and as a potential shift of power to government agencies. These two health challenges help to illustrate the critical issues in health care in the postwar period under Democratic leadership, especially the difficulties of finding a path forward that could lead to equitable access to facilities and health security for the poor.

In November 1948, the month of Truman's reelection, the *New York Post* journalist and social historian Albert Deutsch published a scathing critique of state hospitals. His book *The Shame of the States* pictured them as understaffed, badly organized, unsanitary, and with provision far below the minimum standard set by the American Psychiatric Association. The reality of care for the close to 7.5 million people (one in twenty Americans) thought to need inpatient care for mental health conditions at some point in their life was very different from hospital architect Edward Stevens's view in the 1920s that "the Hospital has forever passed out of the class of grim, ugly structures representing the necessities of communities into a class of important buildings requiring definite architectural expression and design."[42] Stevens had first published *The American Hospital of the Twentieth Century* in 1918, and in this 1928 edition he stressed the importance of design for the effective delivery of medical services and for patient well-being. Not only was the treatment of the typical inpatient in the mid-1940s in stark contrast to Stevens's utopian vision, but it was also in tension with the historical journey "from the ideal of repression to the ideal of prevention...from manacles to mental disorder" that Deutsch traced in the updated edition of his 1937 book *Mentally Ill in America*. This 1949 version ends with Deutsch praising the newly founded National Institute of Mental Health (NIMH) located ten miles northwest of Washington, DC. He claimed "for the first time" the nation has "an organized, nation-wide long-range program for controlling mental disease," although Deutsch's word "manacles" belies a chronic neglect for African American mental health and culturally congruent training and caring facilities in the postwar years.[43]

Careful not to be overoptimistic and recognizing that overcrowding in state hospitals had increased markedly since the mid-1930s, Deutsch warned at the end of this 1949 edition of *Mentally Ill in America* that there was no room for complacency and that "a mantle of mystery still hangs over a large area of mental disorder."[44] Instead of championing a modern hospital system with sophisticated equipment and well-trained staff, *The Shame of the States* uses emotive and violent language and includes interior photographs of state hospitals, from Georgia to Ohio, to portray crumbling establishments full of incarcerated ghosts who are misdiagnosed, mistreated, and unlikely to regain independence. In this respect, Deutsch dedicates his 1948 book "to the sick and the sorrowing in the hope that the mists will be lifted and the shame erased," and he tries to lift the stigma from mental illness by challenging what

he describes as "popular ignorance" and "popular apathy," which together allow this health crisis to go on behind closed doors with little
recognition by "Mr. Average Citizen."[45]

Truman was also concerned about the lack of recognition of mental
health issues. He mentioned it a number of times in speeches in and
after 1946, linked to the passing of the National Mental Health Act
that year that established mental health as a countrywide priority. Truman believed mental illness was "the most heart-rending of the chronic
afflictions," and his administration estimated that patients diagnosed
with mental illness were occupying half of hospital beds, 87 percent of
which were in state hospitals.[46] The founding of the NIMH was a major
federal commitment toward research into the causes and prevention of
mental illness, but the institute did not become fully operational for a
few years, and as a research facility it could not alleviate the crisis in
care at a time when the Public Health Service was spending only 83
cents per mental health inpatient out of a budget of $527,600 for fiscal
year 1948, compared with a budget of $30 million for the Department
of Agriculture.[47]

Another text to raise consciousness about the fate of inpatients was
the Indiana novelist Mary Jane Ward's semiautobiographical 1946
book *The Snake Pit*. The narrative focuses on Virginia Cunningham,
a patient in an all-female facility who suffers from amnesia and possibly schizophrenia. Based on Ward's experiences as an inpatient in
Rockland State Hospital in Orangeburg, New York, *The Snake Pit* was
widely read, especially in its condensed *Reader's Digest* republication
that May. Released in November 1948, in the 20th Century Fox film
adaptation of Ward's book the melodramatic elements are heightened,
such as the description of electroconvulsive therapy: "They were going
to electrocute her, not operate upon her....Dare they kill me without
a trial?" The film, directed by Anatole Litvak, was dubbed "one of
the most challenging pictures of all time" due to its disturbing noir
lighting and the intense acting of Olivia de Havilland.[48] For her role as
Virginia, de Havilland wore no makeup and based her acting style on
the research she conducted at a California state facility.[49] Though the
ending implies Virginia may be able to regain good health, de Havilland's piercing screams and her profile image in *Time* magazine, with
the face of a tortured spectral double behind her, pushes the film closer
to Deutsch's gruesome account than to Ward's more nuanced novel.[50]

The Shame of the States followed a 1946 photojournalistic article in
Life magazine titled "Bedlam 1946," which exposed the conditions of

incarceration that Deutsch found at many of the hospitals he visited. For example, Deutsch found Ward N7 in Bellevue Hospital Center in Manhattan to be overflowing with female patients. Many of them were restrained in straitjackets and gave him the impression of the Black Hole of Calcutta, only to further challenge his expectations when he witnesses a schizophrenic patient choking another to death.[51] He was particularly concerned that inpatients seemed to be "thrown together indiscriminately" and subject to violence either at the hands of fellow patients or by attendants.[52] Not all hospital conditions were as dire (Brooklyn State Hospital is portrayed as exemplary), but Deutsch uses muckraking techniques to paint a bleak picture of the whole system. Although he and his photographer were not always permitted access to wards, the book makes visible deeply distressing scenes that pose questions about whether "therapy" was a custodial technique exacted to control perceived unruliness or, instead, a healing practice that could potentially cure patients and help them to return to fulfilling lives.

It is likely that Truman or his advisors read Deutsch—or at least the "Bedlam 1946" *Life* report—and we know Truman was in correspondence periodically through 1946–49 about the severe overcrowding of mental health patients and lack of access for local veterans at St. Elizabeth's Hospital in Washington, DC.[53] But Truman most often focused on macrolevel issues that would fulfill Roosevelt's New Deal plans and elevate the quality of the total system. He was particularly frustrated by the 80th Congress, which sat with a Republican majority in both the House and Senate between 1947 and 1949 and which was keen to question the role and size of the state, so much so that Truman famously called it the "Do-Nothing Congress" during his reelection campaign.[54] He was more successful in pushing through his foreign-policy agenda, but domestic initiatives were routinely blocked, especially a commitment to a universal health insurance scheme. Truman attempted to win over his congressional colleagues in his May 1947 speech by agreeing that the administration of personal health service benefits could be decentralized, but he continued to argue for public assistance to help cover medical costs and protect "against loss of earnings during illness."[55] The argument for the development of the hospital system was easier to win in Congress than the debate over health insurance, an issue that Truman believed would benefit all Americans except for the very rich.

Truman's vision of a national medical insurance program was part of what in 1949 he called his Fair Deal to the country as "the logical extension" of Roosevelt's social security system, with "sickness" being the missing element among other protections for unemployment, old age, and death.[56] In the background of the Fair Deal was the Wagner National Health Bill drafted by the New York senator Robert F. Wagner in the late 1930s; this formed the basis of the National Health Act of 1939 (which made provision for grants-in-aid to states to improve maternal and child health services) and was followed by a bill that Wagner cosponsored with the Montana senator James Murray and John Dingell, the House representative from Michigan, on health insurance for American workers and their families (sometimes referred to as the Truman plan).[57] President Truman spoke with conviction about the need for universal insurance, but for many congressmen the financial burden of the scheme was too heavy, while for others (including the AMA) it encroached on the right to choose. In fact, the Hill-Burton Act was the only health bill that made it into legislation during the Truman presidency.[58] The version of the Wagner bill the Republicans proposed was in contrast to Truman's ambitious health insurance plan in that it was wedded to charitable help for the poor. To the president and Democratic allies such as the Rhode Island senator J. Howard McGrath this proposal was backward-looking and out of step with the development of a modern medical system committed to combating heart disease and other life-threatening conditions.[59]

Truman had other allies, such as Oscar R. Ewing, the head of the Federal Security Agency, which housed the Public Health Service from 1939 to 1953. Ewing argued for the need for health professions to collaborate with one another and with voluntary organizations and local government; he prepared the ten-year health report for the president in August 1948; and three years later he argued the nation was taking health for granted, stating "public health programs protect the health of the people in a thousand ways, often so silently and efficiently that most people do not realize that without them they would hardly last out a week."[60] This argument was insufficient to sway either the 80th or 81st Congress on the health security question, particularly as Republicans in Congress and the AMA were highly critical of the United Kingdom's planned economy model.[61] In fact, AMA launched a national campaign against the insurance bill, claiming that "the Government proposes to assume control not only of the medical profession, but of hospitals—both public and private—the drug and appliance industries, dentistry, pharmacy, nursing and allied professions."[62] The AMA charged each of its members $25 to raise a fund designed to resist Truman's proposals via the lobbying body the National Physicians Committee, and by

1951 it had spent $4.5 million on antifederal activities. AMA members even contributed to cartoon-strip propaganda in the form of the character Waiting-Room Willie who in 1950 became a populist tool to stoke fears of a socialist future: Willie's travails proved that free-choice medicine is much better than a nationalized system.[63] What might at another time have been rebutted by the administration was heightened by the anticommunist and antistatist climate on which the AMA was keen to capitalize.[64]

Much of Truman's attention was focused on the new war in Korea, but he nevertheless established a President's Commission on the Health Needs of the Nation in December 1951 to study the nation's "total health requirements" and to devise an action plan that would give a clear role for the state. The Illinois surgeon Paul Magnuson, who was chosen to lead the commission, did not favor the president's health insurance plans, but he was committed to a holistic health survey in order to build the capacity and leadership that Surgeon General Parran was demanding before the war.[65] Based on thirty meetings in 1952, the report upheld health as one of the "well spring[s] of the nation's strength," arguing the government "must participate in the expansion of the means to achieve health," in part through better health promotion and "social action" and in part by better organization and regional coordination of the hospital system—fourteen years after the 1938 National Conference on Health and Medical Care had made the same point.[66] Quality of care is a major theme of this report in its insistence that physicians should act ethically and responsibly in order to ensure they remain "arbiters of communities," echoing Woodrow Wilson's phrase "guardians of communities" exactly forty years earlier by which he sketched out a moral agenda for the medical community.[67]

The main problem was that when Truman decided not to run for reelection in March 1952, and when Dwight Eisenhower beat the Democratic nominee Adlai Stevenson in the presidential election, the recommendations of the Magnuson 1,600-page report *Building America's Health* lost momentum. Recognizing that modern medical provision continued "to lag behind need," President Eisenhower proclaimed a national Medical Education Week in April 1956 to promote medical science and responsible health care, and his officials were committed to nonprofit hospital construction in observance of Hill-Burton.[68] Although Eisenhower believed that it was the government's responsibility to provide basic social services and safeguards against disasters, the health challenges for the poor, those living in rural areas, and those diagnosed with mental illnesses changed little, and the holistic view of health in *Building America's Health* did not resurface on the federal agenda until the 1960s.

COMMUNITY ACTION AND COMMUNITY HEALTH, 1964–1971

In his January 1954 speech to Congress, Eisenhower invoked an image of community health that was to become the progressive face of health care in the 1960s. Buoyed by recent breakthroughs in polio and tuberculosis, yet tempered by the realization that there was a significant lag in large-scale hospital construction, Eisenhower's reformist inclinations were markedly different from his two Democratic successors in the White House, especially as he did not share Truman's enthusiasm for compulsory health insurance.[69] His overriding concern was to avoid excessive federal spending:

> Certain non-acute illness conditions, including those of our hospitalized aged people, requiring institutional bed care can be handled in facilities more economical to build and operate than a general hospital, with its diagnostic, surgical and treatment equipment and its full staff of professional personnel.[70]

The Eisenhower plan was to extend the Hospital Survey and Construction Act by building specialist hospitals, "supervised nursing and convalescent homes," "rehabilitation facilities for the disabled," and "diagnostic or treatment centers for ambulatory patients."[71] The president reflected the growing opinion that some inpatient treatments could be conducted more effectively through outpatient facilities. Even though the first two years of the Eisenhower administration saw significant cuts to the health budget from the levels that Truman envisaged, a Democratic-led Congress from January 1955 earmarked funds to help individual states assess their needs, mindful that rural and remote communities remained underserved.[72]

In speaking of the "health of our people" as "the very essence of our vitality," Eisenhower's warnings about avoiding unnecessary bureaucracy sometimes sounded a lot like Truman, and his emphasis on community and outpatients could have been voiced by a Democratic leader despite his middle-way conservatism.[73] In recognizing that "mental illness is one of our most serious national problems," Eisenhower believed that community mental health services could help combat drug addiction (a view espoused by surgeon general Leonard Sheele), and he was as concerned as Truman that the young were fit and healthy (the Department of Agriculture reimbursed schools for the cost of milk for schoolchildren as an extension of the National School Lunch Program).[74] In addition to Eisenhower's admiration of the new "forceful leadership" of the World Health Organization, the founding of the Department of Health, Education, and Welfare in spring 1953 (the only major health-oriented legislation in Eisenhower's first two years of working with the Republican-led 84th Congress) was symbolically and organizationally important, given that there had been calls for federal oversight of the nation's health in every decade of the century.[75] Eisenhower appointed Oveta Culp Hobby as the first health secretary based on her work as director of the Women's Army Auxiliary Corps during World War II. The president's comment in a television address that a woman had been chosen because health "is the woman's job in the home" could be read in two ways: she was only the second woman in such a high office and yet Eisenhower did not favor equal rights for women.[76] Nevertheless, two effective wartime leaders overseeing the nation's health seemed sensible enough, though the twin emphasis on government enterprise and nonprofit private health insurance was a departure from the previous two administrations.[77]

Eisenhower and Hobby wanted to ensure a better organized health system, an effective Public Health Service, and more accessible grants-in-aid, yet without reviving the specter of socialized medicine that undermined Truman's universal health insurance plans.[78] There were some positives, such as a report out of Kansas (the president's home state) that eight out of ten patients had been released from its three state mental hospitals, that inpatients had fallen by eight hundred between 1948 and 1956, and that there was closer attention to the cultural specificities of and information channels for community health, such as a three-year project at Howard University with funding from the National Institutes of Health.[79] However, given the Cold War warnings about germ warfare and radioactive fallout, the nation's health was often framed as a national security risk rather than a domestic priority in its own right.

There was also a crisis in the newly formed health department. Hobby was arguably ineffective in coordinating the national roll-out of Salk's polio vaccine, and in 1955 she found herself embroiled in the Cutter incident when five children died and more than fifty developed a paralytic form of polio after being injected accidently with a live strain of the vaccine (see chapter 4).[80] Her resignation in July, allegedly because her husband was ill, followed a wave of negative press coverage that questioned her commitment to children's health. The fact that Hobby was succeeded as health secretary by two nonspecialists, Marion B. Folsom (1955–58) and Arthur S. Flemming (1958–61), suggested that Eisenhower's plan for a coordinated health system that was sensitive to the needs of rural and urban communities—that could challenge the racially divisive "separate but equal" health facilities and would care for the nation's youth rather than branding them "juvenile delinquents"—was unlikely to come to fruition in the 1950s.[81]

It was not until the final year of Kennedy's truncated presidency, in 1963, that the community health center program was fully articulated at a federal level, following advances in the understanding of patient care and rehabilitation in the late 1950s. Community health had a long genealogy that can be traced to urban volunteer organizations in the 1890s, but in Kennedy's case it linked to a professional and personal interest in mental illness and mental retardation given that his sister Rosemary had been institutionalized in 1941 after an enforced lobotomy. Kennedy was also aware of the primitive and often barbaric treatment that sometimes went on behind closed doors, practices that often seemed worse in the southern states. Two examples of this were presented by the leprosy patient Stanley Stein in his account of a thirty-year incarceration behind barbed wire in the Marine Hospital in Carville, Louisiana (Stein sent a copy of his book to Kennedy in June 1963) and an exposé of the squalid conditions in Milledgeville State Hospital, Georgia, that journalist Jack Nelson featured in the *Atlanta Constitution* in 1959 (Nelson was awarded the Pulitzer Prize, and he was featured on the cover of *Time* in April 1963 set against the title "Psychiatry: Out of the Snake Pits").[82]

Kennedy's twin commitment to improving preventive medicine and developing humane health services led him in October 1963 to sign the Mental Retardation and Community Mental Health Centers Construction Act, which followed the Mental Health Planning Grant program that Congress had approved the previous year. The Community Mental Health Act, as it was commonly called, stemmed from the recommendations of the Joint Commission on Mental Illness and Mental Health, a committee established by Eisenhower in 1955 and coordinated by the American Medical and Psychiatric Associations, which resulted in a 374-page report, *Action for Mental Health*. A feature of this act was to increase research into the causes of congenital and early onset conditions, but it also marked a shift of emphasis away from "custodial mental institutions" toward "therapeutic centers," which Kennedy hoped would release half of inpatients in state facilities within ten to twenty years.[83] This initiative may also have been partly a response to New York judge Nathaniel Kaplan's revival of the incendiary phrase "shame of the states" in 1960, suggesting that despite the flurry of hospital construction, the health care infrastructure was still a long way behind where it could or should be.

The *Action for Mental Health* report was important both in surveying current human and physical resources and in its recommendations to further basic science and advanced medical research through the university system and at the NIMH. This was vital, it assessed, for improving responsible public health education on mental illness in order for the country to "arrive at an informed opinion in its responsibility toward the mentally ill."[84] The report began by acknowledging that "mental illness involves so many complexities—biological, chemical, psychological, and social" that it was impossible to arrive at simple solutions, and it adopted flexibility and diversification as its strategic goals.[85] *Action for Mental Health* actually placed more emphasis on research than on treatment, but its authors recommended that "no further State hospitals of more than 1000 beds should be built" and that patients should not be an added burden on overflowing state facilities. Two points on which the report was most progressive were the recognition that "socialization, relearning, group living" cannot occur in a state of incarceration, and its authors' belief that connections with the patient's community are typically far more therapeutic than long-term inpatient care. It recognized that aftercare services were especially "primitive" and lacked integration into broader care programs.[86]

Action for Mental Health proved to be consequential in spite of Kennedy's untimely assassination. Just as Truman helped to implement some of Roosevelt's domestic policy plans, so Johnson sought to fulfil Kennedy's aspirations for health care and in providing for the elderly and the poor. Johnson even chose the Truman Presidential Library in Independence, Missouri, to sign Medicare and Medicaid into law on July 30, 1965, although, as Julian Zelizer points out, the legislation differed from Truman's proposal.[87] The plans of the Johnson administration were initially effective in kick-starting local health centers, drawing on the $150 million that Congress had agreed in 1963 to fund two-thirds of the construction costs.

Johnson went further than Kennedy. He boldly declared on November 1, 1964, three weeks before his landslide election victory over Barry Goldwater, that "we have hardly begun to meet our responsibilities" in developing a flexible health system with suitably trained staff that could sustain for the long term. He pledged his "wholehearted energies" to community health, stating that "the Great Society which we mean to build in America must be a healthy society," and he convinced the 89th Congress to allocate appropriate levels of funding for his health program.[88] Johnson was publicly optimistic in 1964–65, and Gallup polls suggested that nearly two-thirds of the population was in favor of the Medicare reforms, even if the American Medical Association was initially resistant, before caving in three months after Johnson signed the Medicare bill. Johnson and the AMA were both concerned about the shortage of doctors, nurses, medical technologists, and public health workers; in a stimulus effort the president set targets to increase the number of medical workers up to 60 percent by 1970 and to ensure that health professionals did not simply migrate to metropolitan areas. More immediately, Johnson was desperate to grasp the moment, stating to his cabinet that "I've just been elected by an overwhelming vote, but every day that I will be in office, I will be losing some of my ability to convert that victory into legislative reality."[89]

A prime example is the Community Action Program launched in the mid-1960s. The program took its impetus from the Economic Opportunity Act of August 1964 and efforts to decentralize the health department in order to extend its reach. Community action funding was channeled through nonprofit Community Action agencies to ensure coordination, while membership of the agencies was split into thirds to be shared between the public sector, private business leaders, and community members—a division that gave activists and economically disadvantaged groups a say in funding allocations. The community health center was a potent symbol for the federal government in its attempt to be responsive to localities through the Office of Economic Opportunity and the Public Health Service. This was in essence a distributive model. It embodied the ideal of health care as a moral commitment toward underserved citizens, the reaffirmation of consumer rights within a participatory democracy ("the right to safety, the right to be informed, the right to choose, the right to be heard"), and the spirt of "new fellowship" given momentum by Johnson's landslide election victory.[90]

The concept of the outpatient was key to this ethos, not because this offered a cheaper form of medicine (though it lessened the demand on emergency hospital beds), but because active connection to the community was seen to be part of the therapeutic process. On a theoretical level, this holistic view tallied with the belief of Mitchell Sviridoff, the antipoverty leader and president of the National Association for Community Development, that "human development problems" need to be tackled as a "whole and not in fragments."[91] On an organizational level, the PHS booklet *The Comprehensive Community Mental Health Center* noted that the number of outpatients treated at clinics had grown 100 percent between 1955 and 1963, and it envisioned the neighborhood clinic as a place of responsive therapeutic contact with doors that permitted patients to go out as well as come in. This challenge to custodial care was not entirely new. It reflected a Boston-based Community Health Project, initiated by the Harvard School of Public Health in 1953, that focused on "optimal restoration of social roles and social functioning," helped in part by "doors used by both the sick and the well—and revolving doors at that."[92] This model did not mean that hospitals and centers should be "way stations or holding operations" but part of the "complete circle of treatment" in which the posthospital experience is vital for sustained well-being.[93] The Community Health Project conducted a survey of this posthospital experience in the 1950s and identified some predictive patterns but also acknowledged variance, especially with respect to race and gender.

Public health officials recognized that even the most "efficiently administered" and "brilliantly staffed" health centers would not be effective without buy-in from the community, and they encouraged local cooperation and more focused health education.[94] The role of advocacy groups at the state and national level, including the National Association of Mental Health Planning and Advisory Councils, was vital to ensure that communities did not feel hospitals were imposing inpatients on them or that local health and welfare services would suffer strain. The Supreme Court ruling of March 1964 against the "separate but equal" provision made racially integrated services more feasible, even if the Public Health Service may have been more active in enforcing desegregation, before the mechanism for Medicare payments (as initiated in July 1966) demanded each state comply before they received grant funding.[95] The task of "reducing or removing barriers to good health and medical care" was paramount, even though Republicans criticized Johnson for what some saw as an exponential growth in entitlements.[96]

As well as embarking on the fight against the stigma of mental illness and cognitive disability, Johnson realized that a single burst of activity in 1964–65 would be insufficient. It needed long-term commitment to progressive reform and to both basic and advanced research. Not only did the role of the Department of Health, Education, and

Welfare expand dramatically in the mid-1960s (its spending level was raised second only to the Department of Defense), but the president also wanted to push the concept of community health beyond its starting premise of improving mental health facilities. He did this by working with his second health secretary John W. Gardner and surgeon general William H. Stewart on the Comprehensive Health Planning Act of 1966 (to ensure that all levels of government were collaborating effectively with the private sector and voluntary organizations) and to develop a broader neighborhood health project in line with the Regional Medical Program of the Public Health Service.[97] Among early initiatives was the Delta Health Center in the all-black community of Mound Bayou in the Mississippi Delta that, on opening in 1965, collaborated with local hospitals on emergency care, provided mental health and substance abuse facilities, and financially assisted health care for a rural outpatient community, many of whom were under the poverty line.[98] By 1967, thirteen family health centers had opened, including the Pilot City Health Center in Minneapolis (one of fourteen cities chosen for pilots), while poor and predominately African American rural counties like Lowndes County, Alabama (which witnessed deadly racial violence during the slow process of integrating public facilities) received a grant in 1968 for a health center in Hayneville, a year in which Johnson hoped to see fifty in operation.

Not all was well though. As chapter 2 discussed, the goals of the Office for Economic Opportunity (OEO), when it was launched in spring 1964, were not clearly defined, except to "cut across Departmental lines to facilitate coordination" and across a "multi-faceted constellation of projects."[99] The Neighborhood Center Project is a case in point. It involved cooperation between HUD, OEO, HEW, and the Department of Labor and was to be delivered by Neighborhood Health Councils that were expected, first, to encourage maximum participation in the community by providing health, education, and employment services, and, second, to embody nondiscriminatory policies by also providing information on citizens' rights and legal services. In early 1967, the federal government issued principled guidelines to codify community health initiatives, including the drive to accessibility and building strong interpersonal relationships between patients and health workers.[100] However, while such initiatives are arguably an example of what Richard Couto calls "heroic bureaucracies" in that they aimed to "break bottlenecks," address inequalities, and increase access through small storefront facilities, critics argued they undermined free choice of services for others.[101] There were two additional problems: one bottom up, the other top down. Activists involved in some Community Action Programs were keen to grasp decision-making rather than complying with federal rules, and some saw the Great Society as paternalistic in that it distorted the idea of community participation.[102] As well as local struggles around inclusion and exclusion with respect to minority groups, financial constraints limited the long-term prospects of these federally backed initiatives. It became trickier to sustain funding for antipoverty programs in 1967, despite the 90th Congress retaining a Democratic majority in both chambers.[103]

There were other aspects for officials to worry about when exposés of the poor or damaging treatment of patients started to appear in print and on screen. These included the sadistic behavior of Nurse Ratched in Ken Kesey's novel *One Flew over the Cuckoo's Nest* (1962), based on Kesey's experiences working in Menlo Park, California, and his knowledge of the Oregon State Hospital; the gruesome treatment of patients in the southern psychiatric hospital in Sam Fuller's darkly cynical film *Shock Corridor* (1963); the overcrowded, fetid, and inhumane institution of Frank Leonard's novel *City Psychiatric* (1965) based on his experiences as an attendant at Bellevue State Hospital; and Frederick Wiseman's cinema verité project *The Titicut Follies* (1967) of incarcerated individuals at Bridgewater State Hospital in Massachusetts. *Life* magazine promoted *The Titicut Follies*, and Wiseman's notoriety heightened when the film was banned for purportedly violating Massachusetts privacy laws even though Bridgewater staff and patients had cleared the filming.[104]

Even if Wiseman showed the worst of a creaking state facility, it was clear that primitive treatment continued despite efforts by the Johnson administration to ensure that the nation's health care system was modern, accessible, flexible, and humane. The National Advisory Commission on Health Manpower encapsulated this crisis in its report of November 1967, recommending wide-ranging changes to avert these acute conditions, including better educational opportunities for health officials, new health care programs for "the disadvantaged," and ensuring that health systems were less complex and easier to negotiate.[105] Taken together, these cultural representations and health service recommendations underscored the urgency of Johnson's reforms. Yet for some on the right, community and neighborhood projects seemed like a "monstrous, consuming outrage," as Richard Nixon called the welfare system in his 1971 State of the Union address.[106] Were it not for the entrenched war in Vietnam, the community health program might have been dismantled sooner and more aggressively.

The federal community health projects were a mixed success. On the one hand, the program represented a line of continuity from the 1955 presidential commission report, and it responded to the underserved, spreading to the establishment of eighty community health centers by 1973. On the other hand, some health professionals worried about a lack of coordination and thought that some centers were ineffective and lacked accountability.[107] On balance, the initiative was a partial success, both on its own terms and for what one commentator called "the chain reaction this social experiment will set off."[108] The most obvious sign was the free clinic movement that bubbled up from communities at an ideological remove from federal programs and often in collaboration with other voluntary services. This grassroots trend arguably gained energy from the federal stimulus, even though countercultural leaders like David E. Smith, the chair of the National Free Clinic Council, would not have admitted so, given that these centers were a safety net for the uninsured and underinsured run by the people for the people and with a "respect for personhood" as their core.[109]

The two community initiatives aimed to personalize medicine and tapped into the drive for social justice that aligned with the health activism of the civil rights, women's, and gay liberation movements. There were fifty-nine free clinics in North America by 1969 and 135 by 1971, with a concentration on the Pacific Coast, including dedicated African American centers such as the Black Man's Free Clinic, which opened in 1968 in the Fillmore neighborhood of San Francisco. The crisis in black health care did not abate in other urban centers though, centers that had "long lines and crowded waiting rooms, with no hope of immediate respite...and no 'cure' in sight," as the *New York Amsterdam News* reported in 1971.[110]

One could argue either way about whether spiraling health costs and ongoing concerns about a lack of coordination and unevenness of spread meant that the community health project was ultimately a failure or actually the culmination of the New Deal and Fair Deal reforms. Even if "the possibilities of the Great Society" had been "shattered" by the close of the 1960s, as Mark Krasovic argues, "the struggle to pull and stretch its mechanisms toward local desires and goals continued apace."[111] Endemic problems in mental health provision were not easy to solve, especially when psychiatry was being recast by French social critic Michel Foucault and other intellectuals of the late 1960s and early 1970s as a facet of the micropolitics of power rather than a force of good that could help patients get better and return to active lives. The process of rapid deinstitutionalization heightened these antagonistic views, regardless of whether or not outpatient community facilities were available to support former inpatients.

Looking back twenty years later, Gerald Grob concluded that the "many chronically and severely mental ill persons...were often cast adrift in communities without access to support services or the basic necessities of life."[112] This assault on the liberal politics of the Great Society by Republicans like Nixon and Reagan on the one hand and by so-called antipsychiatrist thinkers like Thomas Szasz on the other, meant that all federal health projects were seen as a form of state control in conservative quarters. Grob is not wrong in his view, but this characterization paints an overly bleak picture of what happened to community action after the 1960s. It is the development of veterans' health services at federal and local levels in response to the traumatic experiences that many recruits faced, in and beyond combat in Vietnam, that a more balanced assessment of community health is possible.

VIETNAM VETERANS AND THE VET CENTER PROGRAM, 1976–1984

This third case study switches to an issue that always seems to be in a state of crisis: veterans' health care. One could take headlines from any decade since the 1950s to suggest that the Veterans Administration was undergoing a crisis. Established during the Hoover presidency in 1930 and restructured as the US Department of Veterans Affairs in 1989, the VA offers free or heavily subsidized health care for retired servicemen and women. Discernible problems in the Veterans Health Administration emerged in the 1950s and early 1960s about how to deal with neuropsychological conditions that emerged during World War II and the Korean War but did not align with the rudimentary psychiatric terminology of the Army Medical Service. A 1956 report of a presidential commission highlighted organizational problems in the VA and inequities in veterans' benefits, but there were no major VA capacity issues at that time, and it was not until the height of the Vietnam War during 1967–71 that strain on their health services started to become critical.[113] The number and complexity of debilitating neuropsychiatric conditions that correlated with the experiences of recruits stationed in or near the combat zone crested in 1968, one of the bloodiest years of combat, and this trend continued through the 1970s as many veterans experienced traumatic symptoms years after active service.

The final section of this chapter takes the account of postwar health care into the 1970s and early 1980s when the crisis in the Veterans Administration peaked. It also addresses the development of a Vet Center Program in 1979 as a structural alternative to a huge federal system that had 172 hospitals and 226,000 employees by 1976 yet that lacked the capacity to adequately deal with cases of war trauma or the flexibility to integrate with other health and outreach services.[114] If health care at large was entering what a later report called a "maze of services, treatments, and supports," then the VA creaked and stumbled into the early 1980s.[115] By 1983–84, the VA was spending a third of its budget ($8.8 billion) on medical care; 1.4 million patients were receiving hospital care; and 18 million received treatment as outpatients, augmented by the Vet Center Program that stood at arm's length from the VA.[116] It is tempting to extend this case study into recent years, including a 2014 scandal when forty veterans died awaiting VA care in Phoenix, Arizona, though in order to retain my historical focus I close the discussion here in the mid-1980s. This was at the end of Reagan's first term when the threat to close the Vet Center Program was averted after a period of budgetary uncertainty, and at a moment when a four-year National Vietnam Veterans' Readjustment Study was underway that sought to understand the nature and consequences of posttraumatic stress disorder.

It is first useful to return to mass demobilization at the end of World War II and the concerns of medical leaders in the US Armed Forces about the unprecedented number of neuropsychological conditions that had arisen among combatants during the war. Making sense of neuropsychological symptoms was most pressing for practitioners, although opinion divided on whether warfare triggered ingrained conditions or whether combat situations had a deleterious effect on otherwise healthy recruits, especially as the American Psychiatric Association estimated only 10 percent "fell into any of the categories ordinarily seen in public mental hospitals."[117] This led the authors of the first edition of the *Diagnostic and Statistical Manual of Mental Disorders* (*DSM-I*) to extend the work of the Committee on Veterans' Medical Problems by refining diagnostic categories. The National Research Council added this committee in 1946 to account for veterans' experiences within a "uniform nomenclature of disease," though in its first edition of 1952 *DSM* included a general category for nonspecific conditions.[118] Truman offered a less technical perspective, but he was convinced from his experience of two wars (serving as an artillery officer of the National Guard in France in 1918) that a more robust health system could have detected such conditions earlier in life.

The benefits framework for veterans represented a major federal investment, but there was widespread concern that VA hospitals required investment and modernization. This was covered by Hill-Burton to an extent, and the relatively light number of casualties that US armed forces sustained in the Korean War did not place significant strain on the system, in large part because soldiers were treated in well-equipped hospitals in Japan that could tend to the wounded in proximity to the field of combat. However, the Vietnam War was a very different proposition. Even though MASH units continued to offer close-range medical care, as had been trialed in Korea, the bloody realities of a protracted war generated many more injuries to US recruits than expected, over 300,000, together with 58,000 deaths. The situation was compounded because the VA's budgetary allocations never seemed to be sufficient at a time when balkanized programs were competing for limited resources, especially in 1968, the bloodiest year of warfare, when demand for emergency treatment rose dramatically.[119]

In April 1971, the Senate Subcommittee on Health and Hospitals of the Committee on Veterans' Affairs met to discuss the hospital crisis. Not only did the subcommittee members recognize the inadequacy of existing facilities, but also budgetary threats meant that "thousands of beds and numerous wards" might close in the 165 VA hospitals—this would reduce capacity by 47,000 patients, the equivalent of closing fourteen hospitals.[120] The system experienced further strain in 1970 due to congressional approval that all veterans over sixty-five (many of them having served during World War II) should have access to Veterans Health Administration services regardless of their means to pay. Evidence showed that the use of hospital beds was efficient, even though veterans tended to require significantly longer periods as inpatients than did civilians. On top of this, *Life* magazine published an exposé in May 1970 of the horrendous conditions that wounded soldiers faced in the Bronx VA Hospital. Disabled marine Ron Kovic was a patient in the Bronx hospital in 1968, and in his memoir *Hurricane Street* he recalls that there were "men left dying in their own excrement, sometimes for hours, pushing call buttons for aides who never come."[121] This was not an isolated case, as Kovic found conditions little better on transferring to the VA Hospital in Long Beach, California.

It was not just facilities and conditions though. Waiting lists for VA hospitals in 1970–71 were close to five thousand with little sign of this number decreasing. Although it was not easy to shorten waiting lists, VA officials recognized the "unique, complex, and major challenge" that the war posed and made efforts to understand the welfare and health needs of Vietnam-era veterans by running a series of regional seminars through spring 1971.[122] The seminars sought to enact "attitudinal, operational, and institutional policies" that could improve services and benefits and combat the "indifference and outright hostility" that many veterans faced in civilian life.[123] The VA was keen to portray itself as responsive, and it sought to add informal rap groups to the formal seminars, but that did little to change public perception that the VA was failing to discharge the responsibility of the federal government or that its hospital system was adequate to the task, particularly for dealing with war trauma.

Ron Kovic made the most of television cameras at the August 1972 Republican Convention to highlight the critical state of the VA hospitals, using guerrilla tactics he had learned from the Vietnam Veterans against the War (VVAW) to ensure his voice would be heard. His primary target was President Nixon, who was campaigning for a second term on the promise of withdrawing troops from Vietnam, but Kovic was also disgusted by the inadequate medical treatment he had experienced. He argued that in VA hospitals "paralyzed men cried to be treated like human beings," such as the stroke victim Erwin Pawelski, who was stuck for twenty-seven hours in an elevator of Hines Veterans Hospital near Los Angeles, "strapped in his wheelchair, unable to talk or move."[124] Nixon seemed unwilling to acknowledge the psychological toll the war had taken on young veterans, portraying some soldiers as heroin junkies and lumping together countercultural protestors with all veterans who had become disillusioned with the war or spoke out against mistreatment. Alarmist stories in the media about drug pushing in VA hospitals and headlines such as "Addict Runs Amuck with Rifle in Clinic" did not help and raised fears that the war had permanently damaged veterans.[125]

The activist spirit of VVAW gained intellectually the following year from the publication of psychiatrist Robert Jay Lifton's book *Home from the War* and the Nader Report, *The Discarded Army*, which each highlighted the many ways the nation was failing its veterans. Lifton, who had served for two years in the US Air Force during the Korean War, was keen to identify the psychological, moral, and social dilemmas faced by veterans, seeking a middle way between polarizing and stigmatizing labels that he captured in the book's subtitle: *Vietnam Veterans neither Victims nor Executioners.* The Nader Report similarly tried to adopt a balanced perspective. On the one side, it argued that VA hospitals needed "greater integration" with community health centers to maximize the chances that veterans could successfully readjust to civilian life and to combat the suspicion that the government was secretly planning to do away with the VA.[126] On the other side, it acknowledged the deep hurt that some veterans felt and the pain of returning home to a divided nation. Yet it also noted signs of "resilience, vitality, and good humor," traits often overlooked in the face of public anger against what many felt had been mass betrayal by both the Johnson and Nixon administrations.[127]

Research published in 1973–75 revealed a delay of up to two years between withdrawal from combat and the emergence of nightmares, anxiety, and restlessness. For his 1973 report "The Grief of Soldiers," the Polish-born Canadian psychiatrist Chaim Shatan drew data from a series of rap groups for Vietnam-era veterans that Lifton and he held in New York City in autumn 1970. In the report Shatan described varied symptoms that could be traced back to the war: guilt, "the feeling of being scapegoated," indiscriminate violence, "psychic numbing," alienation, and lack of trust, among others.[128] To counter the view of veterans as victims of psychic numbness, Lifton and Shatan ran rap groups to help veterans "initiate their own process and conduct it largely on their own terms so that ... they retain major responsibility for the shape and direction of their enterprise"[129] These groups spanned four years, from 1970 to 1974, as a form of "street-corner psychiatry" that encouraged openness within an enabling group structure in which the psychiatrist was the veteran's coequal.[130]

This therapeutic project was compensatory and in some respects oppositional, given that the Nixon administration was not only largely inert on the subject of veterans' health and welfare but that it was vindictive, unfairly blaming the new heroin epidemic on veterans and dismissing antiwar protests out of hand, prompting the dark satire of Peter Watkins's 1971 dystopian film *Punishment Park*, which imagines the Nixon administration hunting protestors for sport. Support for veterans became more precarious in 1974 when President Ford attempted to veto the Vietnam Era Veterans Readjustment Assistance bill that sought to increase educational assistance for veterans and provide more vocational aid for those with a disability. Fortunately, Ford's veto failed, but when Jimmy Carter became president in January 1977 he was faced with Ford's fiscal cuts and a badly organized VA run by inept leaders. Newspapers were critical of the VA, noting its "spiraling growth has come at the expense of efficiency."[131] Yet it was tough to envisage a quick infrastructural fix after years of underfunding and with a polarized nation unsure how to come to terms with the war and how to treat those who fought in it.

Carter and his advisors tried a number of tactics: the President's Commission on Mental Health of 1978 included a study of the mental health of veterans; the president proclaimed the fourth week of May 1979 Vietnam Veterans Week so that the nation could "remember" the war "honestly, realistically, with humility"; and the administration tried to stimulate a jobs program to help veterans whose depression was exacerbated by redundancy.[132] The years 1978–79 were important ones as the Carter administration conducted a comprehensive review of veteran support programs. The president's emphasis was on physical disability ("there is no legislation that can...restore arms, legs, eyes to those who lost them in service"), but he also recommended counseling programs, collaborative research between the VA and NIH, and halfway houses to better treat veterans who faced alcohol and drug challenges.[133] Carter realized that work was needed to correct shortfalls in health care, to address the unique circumstances of the war, and to affirm "human rights as a fundamental tenet" of both foreign and domestic policy.[134] This included a review of cultural portrayals of veterans that underpinned Carter's view that the stereotypical "image of the Vietnam Veteran as unbalanced, unstable and drug-dependent is simply not borne out by available information."[135]

This endeavor did not satisfy angry and disillusioned veterans, such as activists who complained about a lack of employment opportunities and the weak leadership of the VA, including the *Washington Post* reporter Ward Sinclair who published a scathing attack on the Carter administration in April 1979.[136] Sinclair claimed that Vietnam veterans saw themselves as scorned strangers and the targets of lingering resentment over "a war that pleased no one." He blamed Carter for not delivering the "special help" that veterans deserved.[137] The problem with this view, however, is it pushed veterans into the role of helpless victims awaiting a supportive hand or handout. Congress sought to launch a counseling and follow-up program for an estimated 1.7 million veterans suffering from anxiety, depression, alcohol dependency, and sustained drug use, but many felt that this was too slow in coming, while the

VVAW vehemently rejected the president's claim that the majority of veterans had "successfully joined the mainstream of American life."[138] This was highlighted by the prominent themes of readjustment and stigma at the National Conference on Vietnam Era Veterans held that April, prompting the head of the Council of Vietnam Veterans Robert Muller to announce that "the day of the voiceless Vietnam veteran is coming to a close."[139]

Carter heeded Muller's view. The president marked Vietnam Veterans Week at the end of May by holding a reception at which he unveiled a commemorative Vietnam veterans' postage stamp and read from Philip Caputo's 1977 memoir *A Rumor of War*. In response to a question about the long-term effects of the herbicide Agent Orange (a defoliation agent used by US troops stationed in Vietnam up to 1971), Carter highlighted the appointment of the triplegic veteran Max Cleland as the administrator of veteran affairs who Carter had known in the Georgia senate. The president spoke passionately when he said that Cleland was the veterans' voice in the federal government as well as a voice in his "consciousness and heart"—a sentiment that tallied with his belief that the nation had a "moral debt" to veterans.[140] The efforts of Cleland and Alan Cranston, chair of the Veterans' Affairs Committee, were influential for showing veterans' groups that the Carter administration recognized the shortcomings of the VA, with Cleland noting that "the VA had a 43 percent error rate in the computer system for the millions of checks sent every year to veterans on the GI Bill."[141] As well as leading to epidemiological studies on the deleterious health effects of the dioxin element of Agent Orange, the Veterans Health Care Amendments of 1979 laid out plans "to address the psychological and social sequela of combat and armed conflict related problems," and in early 1980 the Vet Center Program was launched. Reflecting the spirit of community health, Cleland states that the letters "VA" were deliberately kept off the signage to encourage disenfranchised veterans to use the storefront facilities, even if the VA ultimately funded them.[142]

Designed with *health* rather than *medicine* in mind and run by paraprofessionals, the vet centers embodied a street-based model of care that could "respond more ably and flexibly to the psychological, stress-related problems so unique to this segment of our society," as a congressional hearing described it in 1981.[143] Employing an ethnically diverse mix of staff and veterans, many of whom had disabilities, the centers ran extended opening hours.[144] The focus on counseling echoed the spirit of the rap groups held by Lifton and Shatan a few years earlier, and their design countered criticisms of Johnson's community action plans by coordinating with community mental health centers and VA hospitals when medical treatment was required. The first vet center opened in California in February 1980 as the Van Nuys Vet Center, one of four in the Los Angeles metropolitan area, and within a year there were ninety-one centers serving eighty thousand veterans—this number rose to 137 by 1981. Cleland was pleased that he was able to dodge the bureaucracy of the VA and that media outlets were promoting the new storefront services that were reminiscent of the community facilities of the Neighborhood Center Project in the mid-1960s. Yet there were problems too. The $16.2 million that Congress approved for Operation Outreach for fiscal years 1980 and 1981 was slow to come through from the VA to the Vet Center Program; Cleland met resistance by officials who thought some veterans using the centers did not have legitimate health needs; and members of Congress were annoyed he was operating outside the system rather than improving it from within.

The vet centers were not an instant solution to the symptoms that many ex-soldiers were encountering, such as Illinois army veteran Larry Howard whose story of blurred vision, abdominal pain, nervousness, and paranoia featured in a *Los Angeles Times* column in March 1980. In addition to his own symptoms, Howard's daughter was born in 1973 with a malformed foot that appeared to stem from his exposure to Agent Orange in Vietnam, given the correlation between birth defects and exposure to the dioxin element of the herbicide. With his relationship under strain, Howard was forced to leave his Illinois hometown for California after trying to kidnap his daughter. His life did not improve on the West Coast though. He suffered from meager VA benefits, near poverty conditions, and haunting memories: "I come unglued hearing a car backfire and a thunderstorm will drive me almost completely mad."[145] Howard's pain is obvious in this interview, but he felt the new Van Nuys Vet Center offered valuable support and a safety net when all else failed. There was no panacea though—he could not see a bright future and believed he would die prematurely. This *Los Angeles Times* piece is instructive in helping to shift readers' perceptions, but it would most likely have reinforced the prejudices of some conservatives about drifting veterans who did not deserve VA support.[146]

The Vet Center Program was an important phase of activity that echoed and extended Johnson's and Truman's health reforms, but there were other positive consequences. The VA's recognition of posttraumatic stress disorder in the late 1970s informed the third edition of

DSM, whose authors shifted away from the psychoanalytic categories of the 1968 edition to more organic symptomology, and for the first time included PTSD as a clinical disorder in its own right. This was in large part due to the work of Lifton and Shatan and the Vietnam Veterans Working Group that put pressure on the American Psychiatric Association during the drafting of *DSM-III* and raised public awareness of delayed stress syndromes.[147]

However, just like Carter's plans to develop a more responsive and integrated mental health service, as embodied in the Mental Health Systems Act of October 1980, the progressive reforms of the VA suffered a major blow when Carter lost the 1980 presidential election. Rather like Nixon's attempt to scale back the health dollars appropriated by Congress in the mid-1960s, instead of following through on Carter's health plans, the 97th Congress, in collaboration with the Reagan administration, recalibrated the health budget by designating block grants to states to determine their own spending priorities. Moreover, Operation Outreach was also under threat with the initial three-year funding allocation expiring in 1982. The Reagan administration disliked the fact that the vet centers did not reflect the identity of the VA, and congressional Republicans thought that some veterans using community services embodied the "Vietnam syndrome" of which the president wished to rid the country. The head of Reagan's Veterans Affairs transition team, William H. Ayers, stated that he wanted to focus on "the deserving veteran," downplaying their long-term mental health needs, especially those who had become disillusioned with the war and were aligning their cause with resistance movements.[148] Thus, the threat to cut Operation Outreach by freezing plans for thirty further vet centers was arguably more for ideological than budgetary reasons.

The response to these closures came from within the veterans' community when a wave of sit-ins and hunger strikes triggered a crisis (or series of crises) with the aim of bringing the media's attention to Reagan's budgetary plans. The pressure was such that the president did an about-face. He promised to push Congress to fund the centers through to 1984 and pledged interagency cooperation and additional funding for research into "the effects of delayed stress," but this was arguably lip service; Reagan refused to meet hunger strikers in 1981, and he did not mention the plan to establish a national research center for PTSD when he signed the Veterans' Health Care Act in October 1984, despite it being a key element.[149] Even when he formally extended the Vet Center Program in a speech of November 1983 he did so ambivalently.

Beginning with positive words about the need to increase disability care and residential services for aging veterans, Reagan only briefly mentioned vet centers and the requirement that the VA should start to cater for "gender-specific health care needs of women veterans."[150] Reagan did not end the speech on a progressive note; instead, he griped about costs and procedures and implied strongly that the VA was receiving "special treatment" that spared it from executive branch rules. Rather than the speech embodying the sympathetic state, to recall Michele Landis Dauber's concept, this was a disgruntled and begrudging state.

It is difficult to identify a coherent health policy during Reagan's first term, yet there were significant gains during those years, particularly a more nuanced recognition of the health needs of Vietnam-era veterans and reparations for many veterans once the effects of Agent Orange were acknowledged in the courts in 1984, years after the public had been made aware of the link between dioxin and skin cancer via the March 1978 CBS documentary *Agent Orange: Vietnam's Deadly Fog.*[151] The cause of the vet centers was assisted by figures on both the outside and inside of the system. Outsider veterans like Ron Kovic had demonstrated the activist effects of hunger striking since 1974, while congressional insiders like Alan Cranston in his role as chair for the bipartisan Committee on Veterans Affairs pressured the Reagan administration to act responsibly.[152] This did not mean the Vet Center Program was secure on a long-term basis or that readjustment challenges and what Cranston called the "tragic reality" of homelessness were taken as seriously or "compassionately" as they might.[153]

The correlation between homelessness and veterans with chronic mental illness particularly concerned Cranston, who prepared a bill for a Homeless Veterans Assistance Act, a version of which Reagan, again begrudgingly, signed into law that July. In fact, this 1987 act deemed homelessness not only a major health and welfare problem but also an "unprecedented crisis."[154] The crisis first became apparent in 1983–84 and ran through the decade, such that by 1991 there were an estimated 150,000 to 200,000 homeless veterans on the streets set against a national homeless figure of 600,000.[155] The causes of this sudden increase of homeless veterans were complex, including the failure of retraining and reemployment programs, a recession in the early 1980s, a crisis in affordable housing, an overbureaucratic VA system when it came to deciding on veterans' benefits, deinstitutionalization, and higher levels of divorce.[156] When newly elected George H. W. Bush acknowledged in January 1989 that the specter of the Vietnam War "cleaves us still," it was with the tacit admission that the social and health problems laid bare the need for urgent action.[157] It was for this reason that Bush established a Task Force on Homelessness and Severe Mental Illness to improve housing, shelters, safe havens, and therapeutic programs run by the VA. This was embodied in the 1992 report *Outcasts on Main Street*, although, despite the urgency of the report ("the time to begin is now"), many veterans had already been homeless for ten to fifteen years.[158]

On balance, the case of the Veterans Center Program shows that that there can be creative solutions to critical strains on the vastly complex health care system that might better value and respond to the needs of veterans. The program was in decent health in 2018, encompassing a national network of centers and mobile units, open to veterans and their families of all major active military duties from World War II to the Iraq War. Avoiding the medicalized language of biopower and instead focusing on adjusting to civilian life, the tagline of the Veterans Center Program "We understand, and most of all, we care" shows that together sympathy and effective services can empower patients rather than propel them into a state of dependency.[159] This might seem to be only an incremental gain given that the VA still faces organizational problems and periodic crises on regional levels.[160] President Trump went some way to acknowledge this in June 2018 when he signed the VA MISSION Act, an expansion of a 2014 Obama-era act to improve continuity of care, though the consequences of this bipartisan 2018 legislation to increase private care options aroused the suspicions of veterans' groups that this might presage wholesale privatization of veterans' care.[161] There is no substitute for a properly funded, well-functioning, and carefully managed VA, but the fact that the Veterans Center Program was designed on a community health model that integrates with other services is evidence that Truman's and Johnson's clarion calls have a strong legacy.[162]

There is no easy fix to the system though, and bandage measures have not silenced critics such as Edward Kennedy in his 1990 *Health Care Crisis* report "to the American people," or psychiatrist E. Fuller Torrey who argued later that decade that the federal government is critically failing those diagnosed with mental illness.[163] Nor does it eradicate the limited access for some rural communities or language barriers encountered by Latinx communities or the inadequacy of medical equipment in some facilities or the lingering health problems encountered by veterans often years after combat. Yet the Vet Center Program has been widely accepted as a relatively ideologically free community initiative with much less of the stigma of its early phase. Perhaps uniquely, the program appeals to both idealists and realists, breaking down the polarization that is typical of congressional wrangles when it comes to health finance. As such, the Vet Center Program goes some way to resolve the tension that cuts through debates about health care reform, showing that progress is possible "when the vision of idealists [is] coupled with the creative and strategic activities of the realists, who take advantage of political opportunities to produce change."[164] Nevertheless, what health activist Bonnie Leftowitz calls the "jarring disconnect" between "the rich, emotional legacy" of community health and the need for such centers "to compete in a modern marketplace as sophisticated providers," marks a deep tension that runs through postwar health care policy.[165] Periodic emergencies in provision and shortages in facilities also frames the focus of my final chapter on the arguably most persistent crisis of the last fifty years: the war on drugs.

CHAPTER 6

Drugs

Methadone, Diazepam, Fentanyl

Minneapolis, April 21, 2016. Late that afternoon the celebrity news website TMZ broke the story that the Twin Cities' most famous musician, Prince Rogers Nelson, had died just after 10:00 a.m. from unknown causes.[1] A week earlier, news had leaked that Prince was suffering from a bout of flu so severe that his private plane made an emergency landing in Moline in western Illinois on the way home from a concert in Atlanta.[2] Two days after the incident he was back at his recording studio, Paisley Park, in the southern Minneapolis suburb of Chanhassen, showing off his new piano at a dance party. This would be his last public appearance. Local and national coverage followed minutes after TMZ announced his death: Minnesota Public Radio reported that fans were already gathering outside Paisley Park Studios, President Obama called him "one of the most gifted and most prolific musicians of our time," and he was on the front page of most morning papers.[3] Following a routine statement by Prince's publicist on the evening of April 21, no cause of death was proposed until the following afternoon when TMZ reported he had been treated at the Moline airport six days earlier for an overdose of the opiate Percocet, which he had been taking for hip pain over a number of years. Rumors circulated during the next few months about the most enigmatic of rock stars, including a report that Prince's doctor had been administering oxycodone and that he was discovered wearing his clothes backward in an elevator by a practitioner from a local rehab center (who happened to be the son of an opioid addiction specialist).[4] The cause of death was confirmed at the end of May, when the Midwest Medical Examiner's Office reported the potent synthetic opioid fentanyl had been found in Prince's body, a drug that caused nearly a hundred deaths in Minnesota that year (an increase of 80 percent from 2015), among 395 opioid-related deaths in the state.[5]

The long-term management of pain was a major cause of this drugs crisis, of which Prince was by no means the only well-known casualty. In 2016 around 20 percent of Americans were thought to be vulnerable to chronic pain and 8 percent were living with "high-impact chronic pain." A 2011 *Relieving Pain in America* report estimated this was costing the country $300 billion each year.[6] It is not just physical pain that needs managing via routines and analgesics, but also the range of emotions that it provokes: fear, anxiety, anger, withdrawal, and depression.[7] Pain is often a very private experience that can elude language and can even destroy "the capacity for speech," as Elaine Scarry asserted in 1985, yet this 2011 report asserts that pain is also a major public health challenge "to do with prevalence, seriousness, disparities, vulnerable populations...and the importance of prevention."[8] Keith Wailoo argues that pain not only links private and public spheres but also poses wide-ranging practical, ethical, and political questions about care and compassion as well as trickier questions about veracity, dependency, and fraud. Taken together, these factors make pain "not just a clinical or scientific problem, but a legal puzzle, a heated cultural concern, and an enduring partisan issue."[9]

So, while the high-profile deaths of Prince in spring 2016 and the Florida singer-songwriter Tom Petty in late 2017 were triggered by the long-term use of opioids (acquired through a combination of licit and illicit means) taken to manage hip complications, chronic pain is an everyday occurrence for nearly 40 percent of adult Americans. The intense spotlight on contemporary celebrities might seem at odds with the private experience of pain. But Scarry argues in *The Body in Pain* that there is often "an ugly inverting" of the public and private, bringing "all the solitude of absolute privacy with none of its safety, all the self-exposure of the utterly public with none of its possibility for camaraderie or shared experience."[10] Other celebrities like Whitney Houston and Philip Seymour Hoffman were the fatal casualties of addictions in 2012 and 2014, addictions that blurred their public and private lives in different but equally erosive ways. This inversion of personal and public worlds is also true of noncelebrity users, especially when pain management kick-starts a vicious cycle of drug maintenance that can lead some users to deceive their employer, their doctor, their family, and ultimately themselves. This pattern of addiction escalation also reflects the existential logic of living with chronic pain: "terrifying for its narrowness," Scarry writes, pain "nevertheless exhausts and displaces all else until it seems to become the single broad and omnipresent fact of existence."[11] The media rarely notice this intertwining though, leading Judy Foreman to argue in *The Global Pain Crisis* that there is not one but actually "two colliding epidemics": "the epidemic of chronic pain, which receives almost no media coverage, and the epidemic of opioid abuse, which receives a lot."[12] Physicians have prescribed opioids as painkillers for over a century. But the potency of twenty-first-century opioids has been exacerbated in recent years by their availability through "doctor shopping," on the black market, and via sites on the dark web such as Silk Road, an anonymous drug marketplace that the FBI traced and shut down in October 2013, yet only after it had sold street and prescription drugs for thirty months (a second-generation version of this cryptomarket faced federal charges the following November).

The most notorious of these new opioids, fentanyl is fifty to a hundred times stronger than heroin. Though fentanyl has been administered via skin patches since the early 1990s to help control chronic pain, it became the street drug of choice in the 2010s. The Centers for Disease Control and Prevention identified it as having the sharpest spike in overdose-related deaths of all opioids, rising 54 percent each year between 2011 and 2016.[13] Fentanyl features prominently in my third case study, but the story goes back much further than the near fifty years this chapter spans. When President Nixon focused on heroin in the first war on drugs of summer 1971, he was not the first leader to associate narcotics as a public health problem with border control and criminalization. It was also there at the inaugural moment of modern US public health that the introduction to this book outlines in the shape of the Harrison Narcotics Tax Act of December 1914. The act established what Tim Hickman calls a "cultural crisis," dividing drug users into the categories of "criminals and patients while also helping to expand the roles of professional medicine and federal police authority."[14] Yet as an antivice law, the Harrison Act was ineffective. Quacks and dope doctors increased in number in the years following the act, as did illicit opiate trafficking, and it took further legislation by the Coolidge administration, the Anti-Heroin Act of 1924, to prevent the synthesis and distribution of diamorphine.[15]

That the morally loaded concept of addiction links "street abusers" to "pain patients" is a major reason why medical and criminal discourses often blur in public discourses.[16] Prince fell into both categories of pain patient and street abuser. His doctor prescribed him oxycodone, usually written out to an alias, and the police found many prescription drugs in Paisley Park in mislabeled bottles. Some medications were made out to Prince's former drummer Kirk Johnson, and insiders suggested Prince had bought six-month supplies of Dilaudid periodically since the mid-1980s from a drug pusher (these transactions may have given rise to the counterfeit Vicodin pill laced with fentanyl that was assumed to be the cause of death).[17]

The overdose statistics in Minnesota the year of Prince's death mirrored this mixed picture: of the 395 opioid-related deaths, 194 were from prescription opioids and 150 involved heroin acquired illegally and taken in injectable or oral form, sometimes laced with fentanyl. Such health statistics are rarely neutral though and can often mask demographic disparities within the state, such as alarming levels of opioid use and opioid-related overdoses among the eleven Native American tribes of Minnesota. Nonetheless, the Minnesota Department of Health attempted to tackle opioid misuse on three fronts in the late 2010s. First, in emergency response mode, including a syringe exchange program at five centers in Minneapolis and naloxone for rapid-response overdose recovery (administered in the form of the nasal spray Narcan). Second, intervention and treatment, including screenings and services for substance abuse and mental health. Third, primary prevention involving regulation of prescriptions and public health education to reduce risks, especially for vulnerable demographic groups.[18] Improving data collection in urban and rural areas is vital for agencies to know how to respond to overdose trends, but officials at the Minnesota health department recognized that it is important to twin data analysis with responsive care legislation. An example of this is the move in July 2015 to make medical cannabis legally available through one of eight Minnesotan distribution centers to offer pain relief for seriously ill patients with qualifying conditions: cancer, HIV/AIDS, multiple sclerosis, epilepsy, and patients with a life expectancy of under a year.[19]

Such progressive programs for curbing drug dependency often depend on medical, pharmaceutical, and health professionals being honest actors and putting patient welfare ahead of profits. One example of when patient welfare was only recognized belatedly is OxyContin, which arrived on the market in January 1996 as a slow-release opioid painkiller. Because OxyContin pills could be decomposed easily, as powder OxyContin became a "gateway drug" for some users to an underworld of narcotics use, leading to exposés in the *New York Times* in 2001 that highlighted cases in which prescription patients misused OxyContin or switched to self-injecting heroin.[20] With stark headlines like "Overdoses of Painkiller Are Linked to 282 Deaths," these reports did lead to action. In summer 2001 the New York manufacturer Purdue Pharma removed its highest-strength dose (160 mg) from the market and made it clearer on packaging of lower-strength pills that it had the potential to be abused; in 2003 Purdue reformulated OxyContin to make it more difficult to inject; and in 2004 it started to prioritize drug education programs. However, by that time Purdue had made a profit of $31 billion from a drug it had advertised as non-habit-forming, leading Sam Quinones to argue that had it been reformulated in 1996 the story of addiction "might be different. But now there was a swollen population of OxyContin addicts nationwide."[21] Purdue's decision to prioritize drug education only occurred in late 2004 following a lengthy court case in West Virginia that charged the company for giving favorable rebates to pharmacy benefit managers who made OxyContin available without requiring prior authorization from a prescribing doctor.[22] Even so, Purdue aggressively marketed the drug well into the 2010s despite knowing its addictive qualities, creating what the Massachusetts attorney general called a "man-made disaster."[23]

In early 2018 Purdue ceased marketing the drug to doctors. But this was little more than a rear-guard action following an intense wave of scrutiny. This scrutiny included further exposés in the *Los Angeles Times* focusing on the zombifying effect of OxyContin and the inclusion in the *New York Times* of photographer Nan Goldin's images of her three-year addiction to the drug, which she first started taking for tendonitis in her wrists.[24] Rather than the evocative and colorful urban images of her famous AIDS-generation visual diary of 1986, *The Ballad of Sexual Dependency*, in which Goldin strove for "clarity and emotional connection," her OxyContin photographs (published in 2017–18 and showcased in her 2019–20 digital slideshow *Memory Lost*) reveal the blurring of licit and illicit drug-taking, with its numbing effects on Goldin's tired and glazed features depicting the banal face of addiction.[25] Federal statistics estimated that seven million patients had abused OxyContin by 2016, a year that saw over sixty thousand opioid-related deaths nationally. This led New Jersey governor Chris Christie, as chair of the President's Commission on Combating Drug Addiction, to call the opioid crisis "the AIDS epidemic of our generation, but even worse."[26] At a time when the White House was using the opioid crisis as a pretext for tough border security, Goldin was railing against big pharma. In January 2018, she stated, "most of my community was lost to AIDS. I can't stand by and watch another generation disappear," and two months later she staged a "Shame on Sackler" demonstration in the Sackler Wing of the Metropolitan Museum of Art to highlight links between the multi-billion-dollar owners of Purdue and the art world, reviving the direct-action action of ACT UP in the late 1980s and early 1990s.[27]

Goldin's addiction experience informs the focus of the book's final case study on how the current opioid crisis has registered politically, medically, and culturally. This crisis did not arrive in a vacuum and is shaped by the structural and geographical vulnerabilities that link this chapter to the preceding ones. Three high-profile wars on drugs during the Nixon, Reagan, and Trump presidencies mark the chapter's timeline, from the early 1970s to the late 2010s, and show how three Republican administrations that favored small government were compelled to expand the state apparatus to deal with these crises, albeit in limited ways. I would contend that the rise of polydrug use within this near fifty-year period distinguishes it from earlier critical moments in the US history of drug use and trafficking, framed by what Simon Strick calls the "biopolitics of pain."[28] This chapter's three case studies assess, first, the promotion of methadone by the Nixon administration in the early 1970s in an effort to combat a heroin crisis; second, the downturn in the popularity of Valium as the best known benzodiazepine in the late 1970s during a period of congressional and media scrutiny; and, third, the epidemic of new opioids that skyrocketed in the mid-2010s through a combination of overprescription and availability on the black market. In order to understand more fully the public health crisis triggered by opioid overuse, this chapter also discusses pharmaceutical deregulation in the 1980s and the incendiary yet confusing statements of President Reagan's deputy assistant for drug-abuse policy, Carlton E. Turner. However, I only touch briefly on Reagan's war on drugs (in the first and third case studies) because his antidrug campaign has limited use for appraising the relationship between licit and illicit drugs that links my three case studies.[29]

As well as assessing three historical phases when the national conversation took a drug turn, this chapter develops the theme of health security from chapter 4 and the prolonged crisis of health care from chapter 5, especially how the system is failing many vulnerable Americans, including the young and the elderly. Teenagers and young adults have long been associated with drug abuse, the elderly much less frequently. Yet the American Association of Retired People (AARP) estimated that 2.7 million Americans over the age of fifty were misusing painkillers in 2015, and the AARP statistics suggest hospitalization for the over-sixty-fives has quintupled since the mid-1990s.[30] This chapter also addresses gender and drugs, a topic that is often eclipsed in accounts of law enforcement efforts to tackle inner-city crime and border trafficking. While female addicts are frequently portrayed as victims of licit or illicit drug systems, longitudinal studies reveal how American women have been negotiating and in some instances resisting medical regimes and heavily interventionist programs. This experiential aspect is highlighted in the third case study in its move from a discussion of top-down interventions to the opioid crisis to an analysis of two literary texts that reveal a social and moral void to which policy—at least at the federal level—seems largely oblivious.

The final case study builds on the first two to illuminate what David Healy calls "the eclipse of care" by highlighting local stories in regional cities and small towns of the Midwest and Northeast. This focus is important because the opioid epidemic has spread inversely to the drug crime that President Reagan spotlighted in his September 11, 1986, television address in which he dubbed drugs a menace to society as they moved out from metropolitan centers into the suburbs.[31] Instead, as Beth Macy traces in her 2018 book *Dopesick*, opioids have since the mid-1990s grabbed a "toehold in isolated Appalachia, Midwestern rust belt counties, and rural Maine... in politically unimportant places, hollows and towns and fishing villages where the treatment options were likely to be hours from home," especially for "dislocated workers" and those with "work-related disability claims."[32] Even as the nativist discourse of infiltration was a signature aspect of the Reagan and Trump administrations, the chapter reveals ongoing and unresolved tensions between health provision at state and federal levels, particularly when it comes to dealing with the creeping progression of opioid use.

Taken together, the three case studies offer further evidence that only the middle range that Robert Bellah outlines in *The Good Society*—conceptually positioned between the perception of the state as a sympathetic bulwark on the one hand and a punitive apparatus on the other—is an effective space for addressing the intersecting public and personal challenges posed by a mixed economy of drug use, though the moral balancing between high ideals and practical realities that Bellah recommends offers no quick fixes. Moreover, as the final case study and the book's conclusion make apparent, with increased partisanship in Congress in the 2010s and an eroding of civic discourse in the public sphere, the possibility of establishing this middle ground at the national level has become more uncertain than ever.

NIXON'S FEAR OF HEROIN: THE METHADONE EXPERIMENT, 1971–1975

The synthetic opioid methadone was first tested in the United States in the late 1940s by two pharmaceutical companies, Eli Lilly and Winthrop-Stearns, after being synthesized initially in Germany in 1939. These tests ran alongside early experiments involving addicts housed at the US Public Health Service Hospital, which opened to much optimism in Lexington, Kentucky, in May 1935 on a thousand-acre site. The Lexington hospital served as a treatment facility for voluntary patients and a prison that engaged convicts in recreation and sports, agricultural labor and vocational training, and music and art therapy, together with psychotherapy and more interventionist treatments, including drug tests conducted at the hospital's Addiction Research Center.[33] Putting aside the very questionable ethics of human experimentation, scientists based at the US Narcotic Farm, or Narco as it was often called, established evidence by 1947 that methadone could be effectively administered as a detoxification substitute for heroin.[34] The therapeutic properties of methadone did not just spark local interest. Lawrence Kolb, the first director of the Lexington hospital, discussed the benefits of different synthetic analgesics as a member of the National Academy of Sciences' Advisory Committee on Drug Addiction up to 1947 (the committee reported directly to the surgeon general of the US Public Health Service), while *Life* magazine noted in August 1948 that methadone is habit-forming but can help to break a heroin habit without "intense suffering" and "violent reactions."[35]

Self-styled heroin addict William Burroughs portrayed his own experiences with methadone in his 1953 quasi-autobiography *Junky*. Alluding to methadone by its early trade name Dolophine, Burroughs recounts his first visit to the Lexington Narcotic Farm in summer 1946 where he took an eight-day course of methadone followed by a three-day prescription of barbiturates. Clinically, the narcotic effects of methadone last five times longer than heroin (thirty compared to six hours), and it has the potential to level out intense cravings, but the treatment was not so clinical for Burroughs. He could not sleep despite sedatives, he

lost his appetite and had mobility problems, commenting that "the dolophine suspends the sickness, but when the medication stops the sickness returns."[36] Burroughs became interested in the chemical properties
of drugs after taking medical classes in Austria, and he often linked his
personal experimentation to a scathing critique of the US medical-industrial complex and its covert association with law enforcement. That
he was regularly using methadone (supplied by the Kansas City Metro
Methadone Program) prior to his death in 1997, shows that—at least
in this case—it was not the quick fix methadone champions proposed.

There may be reasons why methadone treatment did not work for
Burroughs given that his life was laced with phases of polydrug use,
especially when we compare the clinical view that without "lifestyle
changes, transferring addiction from heroin to clinic doses of methadone is difficult if not impossible."[37] In tracing the rise of methadone,
David Bellis cites an important clinical trial of 1963–64 that involved
twenty-two patients overseen by Vincent Dole and Marie Nyswander
at Rockefeller University on the Upper East Side of Manhattan. Published in August 1965, a few months after *Life* magazine featured a
graphic photo essay on heroin use in the city, the results of the initial
trials framed addiction as a metabolic condition, following a *New York
Times* report that the tests substituted "good addiction for bad."[38] However, when the sample size of patients for the Manhattan trial increased
to 120, of the 107 patients who stayed with the treatment program 45
percent had heroin traces in their urine. Critics of the Dole-Nyswander
trial argued they were not administering the minimum oral dose but
were actually increasing the dose to mimic the euphoria of heroin in an
effort to retain patients in the trial, even though the investigators argued
the blocking of euphoric feelings made methadone an effective substitute for heroin.[39] Dole declared that the follow-up program was helping
to lower crime rates, yet questions remained about the patient sample.
The average age was thirty-three compared to twenty-eight in the city's
registry of addicts; it was 48 percent white and 33 percent black (compared to 25 and 47 percent in the registry); and this patient group was
"less involved with criminal activities than the total pool of known addicts in New York City."[40]

Marie Nyswander played an important if indirect role in the endorsement of methadone by the Nixon administration in response to the
president's proclamation of June 1971 that heroin had "assumed the
dimensions of a national health emergency."[41] That summer, Nixon's
health secretary, Elliot Richardson, set out a coordinated plan for HEW

in collaboration with the FDA and other federal agencies that balanced research, education, and rehabilitation, including methadone maintenance pilot studies alongside composite treatment programs.[42] But the impetus behind methadone came from Jerome H. Jaffe, a psychiatrist at the University of Chicago and the director of the Illinois Drug Abuse Program, who Nixon appointed as his drug czar the following April to deal with sharply escalating heroin use among young Americans and recruits of the US Army, enflamed by such headlines as "The Heroin Plague: What Can Be Done?" and "G.I. Heroin Addiction Epidemic in Vietnam."[43] Jaffe convinced the president that a methadone program was an effective treatment to wean addicts off heroin. This view was informed by Nyswander's positive accounts of methadone maintenance while serving as a navy doctor at the Lexington Narcotic Farm in 1945 and during her work on the New York City Narcotic Addiction Research Project in the mid-1950s.[44] Nyswander referred patients to Jaffe during his stint as a postdoctoral fellow at the Albert Einstein College of Medicine in the Bronx, including one patient who refused methadone because it did not generate the euphoric effect of heroin for him. Jaffe reported that this outpatient reacted successfully to injectable oxymorphone, but Jaffe found methadone worked for many of his clients. He retained this view when he moved to Chicago in 1966, where he continued to favor Nyswander's multimodal approach, which sought to combine psychotherapy, art therapy, and drug treatment.[45]

Countering positive views of methadone maintenance were others who argued that methadone and heroin were equally addictive, and methadone should be administered only when other analgesics have failed. The Bureau of Narcotics and Dangerous Drugs claimed initially that methadone contravened the 1916 Harrison Act, only for the bureau to reclassify methadone as a research drug in 1970 in an effort to increase its usability as an alternative to street-level addiction at a time when other "non-addictive" heroin substitutes such as cyclazocine and naloxone were being trialed.[46] Jaffe asserted that methadone might not turn a heroin addict into the "most productive" of citizens, but it could reduce "crime, disease, social degradation, and human misery" by substituting an illicit drug with a licit one.[47] The FDA established regulations in which participants must agree to volunteer, have a two-year history of dependence, and be over eighteen. However, the results lacked absolute clarity, especially when dealers were waiting outside clinics in an effort to tempt patients with heroin or higher doses of methadone. The political left and right both mounted criticisms: those on the left argued the root problem was socioeconomic, while those on the right felt uncomfortable with the idea of a federal drug regime. But Jaffe's confidence in methadone held sway in the White House for the best part of three years, especially in the months following Nixon's naming of Jaffe as director of the Special Action Office for Drug Abuse Prevention in April 1972.[48] Nixon hoped that Jaffe's "controversial, blunt, abrasive stance" in combination with his compassion would "establish a new attitude among our people" toward recreational drugs.[49]

This federal emphasis on methadone treatment emerged out of the alarming statistics that there were between a quarter and half a million heroin users in the United States in 1973.[50] Nixon included drug abuse as a prominent theme of his two successful presidential campaigns of 1968 and 1972, during which he twice pledged to bring law and order to a divided nation.[51] Reports of heroin use among schoolchildren and soldiers mobilized in Vietnam concerned him the most. In March 1970, for example, the president cited two twelve-year-olds who overdosed (one died, one received treatment for addiction), just days before *Time* magazine ran a feature with the headline "Heroin Hits the Young."[52] Though he was following the precedents of the 1951 Boggs Act and the 1956 Narcotics Control Act, Nixon's fearmongering speeches often elided law enforcement and health, most famously in his "public enemy number one" speech of June 1971 and during his 1972 campaign when he stirred in addiction, crime, and deviancy, prompted by media stories of drug pushing in VA hospitals and of violent veterans. Even his first public mention of methadone in August 1970, while recognizing the success of a Denver rehabilitation program, was framed by a primary focus on crime prevention.[53]

Occasionally, Nixon teased out issues. One example was the president's remarks on rehabilitation in a June 1971 speech in which he called for congressional support to broaden the Narcotic Addict Rehabilitation Act of 1966 to allow for methadone programs and research. He mentioned a $10 million hike in federal funding for drug education and training. But a moralistic stance crept in when he used the hip phrase "turned on," by which Nixon tacitly blamed addiction escalation on the countercultural youth and disillusioned veterans—two groups who were among the president's most vocal critics.[54] Absent from Nixon's speeches was any explicit racial coding of heroin addiction, a topic he avoided at a time of urban unrest, which we must assume was to avoid the ghetto stereotypes discussed in chapter 2.[55]

In his 2009 revisionist account of the perceived drug crisis among soldiers and veterans *The Myth of the Addicted Army*, Jeremy Kuzmarov blames the media for exaggerating the heroin epidemic and argues that Nixon responded positively to the wave of sensational media headlines.[56] The president was certainly keen for Jaffe's Special Action Office to coordinate drug research and implementation across federal agencies, and soon after Nixon's reelection Jaffe instituted a Drug Enforcement Administration (DEA) to oversee new health dollars for drug and alcohol treatment.[57] Claire Clark argues that the view that Nixon simply grabbed methadone treatment as a single-step solution to the heroin crisis oversimplifies the policy. Yet the argument that methadone maintenance could lower crime rates was a major factor in finding bipartisan support and an increase in congressional funding that led to eighty thousand heroin addicts receiving methadone treatment across private and public facilities by 1974. This was the year the National Institute on Drug Abuse joined the National Institute on Alcohol Abuse and Alcoholism in focusing NIH research on the effects and prevention of addiction.[58]

In fact, Nixon subtly revealed potential problems with methadone as early as spring 1972. In his speech that accompanied the signing of the Drug Abuse Office and Treatment Act, he mentioned that the daily visits to the clinics stymied the control process, but he then doubled down on the need for more research into "long-lasting methadone."[59] Nixon's claim in a September 1972 speech on narcotics control that the methadone program could be expanded to treat a quarter of a million addicts seemed far-fetched, especially as this was an emotive speech in which he called for "unconditional surrender of the merchants of death who traffic in heroin" and the "total banishment of drug abuse from American life."[60] In this speech, at least, planning and organization were at the service of the fearmongering that entangled law enforcement with health research.

The full-scale federal backing of methadone maintenance was short-lived. In June 1973, Jaffe resigned from his post as drug czar, faced with the fact that methadone was being sold and traded on the black market just as heroin was. After Nixon's reelection, Jaffe's office shifted into HEW, and the Bureau of Narcotics and Dangerous Drugs morphed into the DEA. In his 1977 book *Agency of Fear*, Edward Epstein argues that the seemingly progressive move to distinguish the punitive and medical sides of drug control actually revealed the Special Action Office to be a publicity stunt in an election year, especially as Nixon did not reference methadone treatment in public speeches beyond September 1972 after mentioning it frequently over a two-year period.[61] A commitment to addiction treatment retained momentum though. By 1974, Congress had allocated $300 million of federal funds to one thousand centers, in a year that saw the passing of the Narcotic Addict Treatment Act to control methadone prescriptions in response to criticisms of the effectiveness of methadone programs.

A World Health Organization report of 1974 returned to the problems of the early clinical trials.[62] It noted the federal sanction for the program might prove counterproductive by making it overly bureaucratic and in "discouraging patients from continued participation," thereby turning therapy into an arm of the state. The report is data-driven and includes statistics that go deeper than Nixon's rhetoric. It identifies addiction to be of acute concern in New York City (around half of the nation's heroin addicts lived in the metropolitan area, with a concentration among African Americans) and San Francisco where one thousand addicts (many of them Hispanic American) each year received methadone treatment in five Bay Area clinics. The report is not detailed enough to deal sensitively with local initiatives across the country, such as the opening of the Project CURE methadone center in Dayton, Ohio, in 1970, which largely treated African American residents from West Dayton in its early years.[63]

While the Nixon administration focused on returning veterans and urban youth, there was also a gender aspect to methadone maintenance, with the consensus being that methadone was not an appropriate treatment for pregnant women.[64] Following the 2001 study by Jennifer Friedman and Marixsa Alicea, *Surviving Heroin: Interviews with Women in Methadone Clinics*, in which they teased out the medical and moralistic discourses that often equated "addicted women" and "bad mothers," Suzanne Fraser argues that the methadone treatment not only normalized illicit drug-taking but was also bound up with gender expectations around domesticity and motherhood.[65] If methadone was a less risky option, then it also tugged the user back into the role of patient, turning them into "safe deviants." Although Fraser engages with questions of agency and autonomy, in the case of young mothers it was sometimes difficult to reconcile childcare responsibilities and the requirement of daily visits to a methadone clinic.[66] Friedman and Alicea take up the topic of agency. Drawing on interviews with thirty-seven female heroin addicts receiving treatment via three methadone-user group programs in the early 1990s, the two authors note that some female patients refused to be subjugated to a rigid therapeutic discourse, using techniques of "undermining, sidestepping, resisting" as ways of refusing normative expectations of class, gender, race, and sexuality.[67]

Another problem with the methadone treatment model is that it is predicated on heroin misuse being the root cause. Given the spike in polydrug use in the 1970s, single-step treatments were rarely effective. Detoxification methods proved even trickier, especially when some addicts began using alcohol and phencyclidine (PCP), an animal tranquilizer that stimulates hallucinations. Just as in the 1910s when the Harrison Narcotics Tax Act pushed up the price of morphine, so in the early 1970s PCP use was on the rise due to the decrease in quality of street heroin and the scarcity of marijuana following police crackdowns in Baltimore among other cities. In 1971, Maryland's secretary of Health and Mental Hygiene, Neil Solomon, tried to expose two physicians working in Washington, DC, who he believed were responsible for the availability of street methadone in Baltimore.[68] Three years later the *Baltimore Sun* reported that methadone was replacing heroin in the city as the primary cause of death through overdose, noting that narcotic-related deaths were down in Baltimore from a peak in 1971.[69]

However, in 1977 Richard Lane, the director of Baltimore's non-profit methadone outpatient center Man Alive (the first of its kind in Maryland), saw the drug scene as more complex: "hardly ever do we have anyone come in here now who just shows a positive [test] for heroin alone."[70] Lane was a former heroin addict who had used methadone since 1967 when Man Alive opened its doors. Half of Man Alive's income was drawn from the state of Maryland and the other half from patient fees, and its practice combined detoxification (in hospital) with a course of methadone (in the clinic). Lane personally witnessed positive results from methadone maintenance, but he was concerned that a number of clients were combining low-grade heroin from Mexico with antidepressants like Valium or hallucinogenics like PCP in order to increase the potency of their highs. The case of Baltimore is interesting as a localized story, but it was by no means isolated in the collision of economic, medical, and lifestyle issues in the mid-1970s—and beyond, given that President Obama's surgeon general Vivek Murthy upheld Man Alive as an exemplar of comprehensive treatment during the opioid crisis.[71]

So why didn't the Nixon administration's methadone experiment work? It would be hard to blame Jaffe given that he practiced a multimodal technique in the 1960s in which he administered methadone alongside forms of psychotherapy, even though Epstein argued that Jaffe "effectively masked the methadone program from political criticism" by including drug-free therapies.[72] Partly it was down to the blurred agendas that Nixon occasionally separated out but that more often muddied debates. Epstein's critique of the methadone experiment, as published in his *Public Interest* essay "Methadone: The Forlorn Hope" of summer 1974, gets to the heart of the problem. His three critiques were that "the methadone by itself did not reduce crime," "it did not blockade addicts against heroin," and heroin addiction was not a "metabolic disease" as Dole and Nyswander thought.[73] Given the delegates of the 1974 National Drug Abuse Conference were arguing that methadone could be more addictive than heroin, this position implicates Jaffe in an experiment for which there was not enough robust data or a reliable longitudinal study. This means that Nixon's decision to invest massively in methadone maintenance was at best short-sighted and at worst opportunistic, particularly in his reelection campaign of 1972 when he wanted to show the nation that he had an effective state apparatus to tackle the war on drugs at home and abroad, before soon shunting Jaffe on.

It also fundamentally did not take account of different types of heroin addiction—varying patterns of use and misuse sometimes mixed up with other prescription drugs as well as psychological difficulties that methadone maintenance often masked. But we should note that journalist Michael Massing credits the Nixon administration with bringing the heroin epidemic "under control" via a combination of tough law-enforcement measures and "affordable, accessible, and effective treatment."[74] The unraveling of the Nixon presidency in 1973–74 saw Gerald Ford continuing tough measures on imported drugs and using similar inflammatory rhetoric, such as the phrase "merchants of death" to describe drug traffickers.[75] Yet Ford acknowledged that, whereas the previous administration had thought it had "turned the corner" in the war on drugs, by 1975 "it was clear that drug use was increasing, that the gains of prior years were being lost, that in human terms, narcotics had become a national tragedy. Today, drug abuse constitutes a clear and present threat to the health and future of our Nation."[76] This was a prelude to a "new and more aggressive campaign," accompanied by a resolve that suggested Ford had learned a brief flirtation with a single-solution program was insufficient for tackling a socially complex problem. In this 1976 speech, Ford vacillated between foreign and domestic policy and between punitive and medical discourses, but he placed a new emphasis on community action and vocational rehabilitation in an effort "to alter the fundamental conditions which led the individual to seek escape through drug use."[77]

Ford's drug abuse message of 1976 was certainly no panacea, but, as the next case study shows, it revealed a more variegated understanding of the complex role of drugs in American life in the second half of the 1970s, rather than buying into what a Johns Hopkins University pharmacologist and drug-free treatment center worker (in a cowritten piece for the *Baltimore Sun*) called the "methadone gimmick" with "its fill 'er up gas-station philosophy" that the authors believed was "no answer to the underlying causes of drug addiction."[78] Peter Bourne, President Carter's choice as his special advisor on drugs, admired Jaffe, had practiced methadone treatment as a physician in Georgia in the early 1970s, and favored the continued support for methadone programs.[79] But Bourne pushed for a more nuanced policy on drugs, separating out public health problems from law enforcement, meaning that by the late 1970s methadone maintenance did not have the federal sanction it had during Nixon's presidency.

This did not mean that methadone maintenance programs vanished or that humanitarian initiatives were easily separable from what Claire Clark calls a "compromised treatment infrastructure."[80] Nor was the argument always heeded that methadone was the best available and cost-effective method for treating heroin addiction, despite efforts by the New York City Committee of Methadone Program Administrators (COMPA) to challenge misinformation and looming budget cuts in 1979–80.[81] And nor did it mean younger methadone patients were less vulnerable to backsliding or immune to drugs pushers, although COMPA and the National Alliance of Methadone Advocates were keen to preserve patient rights via education programs and community support. By 1980, the federal regulation of treatment periods was tighter, with clients expected to take mandatory urine tests, and, by 1989, methadone was widely seen as an interim measure rather than an end-therapy solution. Media headlines like "Methadone Linked to Addicts Deaths" decreased in frequency in the 1980s, perhaps because crack cocaine and then crystal meth had become the new urban drug problems by the end of the decade, together with a new moral panic involving racially charged discourses of "crack babies."[82] Yet, with the spread of new networks of heroin trafficking through the West and Midwest, the Bush administration admitted that the war on drugs would not be won in the president's generation.

"CHEMICAL TRANQUILITY": CONGRESS AND THE VALIUM CRISIS, 1978–1982

The 1974 World Health Organization report on methadone maintenance made a surprising claim. Preferring the phrase "drug dependence" to "addiction," the authors of the report argued, "we cannot see any meaningful distinction between the person dependent on a drug of morphine type, who may not be able to function adequately in its absence... and the patient dependent upon anticonvulsants, antidepressants, tranquilizers, or other legitimately prescribed drugs."[83] Calling for a more "accepting attitude" to drug dependence, this report opened a pharmacological window on the overuse of prescription drugs. The national visibility of such dependency was occluded for at least two decades, but in the mid-1970s it was emerging in a new form, as a kind of artificial "chemical tranquility" for which suppliers, regulators, doctors, and patients all shared responsibility, as Richard Hughes and Robert Brewin argued in their popular 1979 book *The Tranquilizing of America: Pill Popping and the American Way of Life*. The story of Carol, an airline stewardess who became dependent on a range of drugs (Librium, Valium, Tuinal, Midol, Excedrin), was to Hughes and Brewin illustrative of many Americans who were seeking chemical tranquility because they cannot find "real tranquility."[84]

Valium was at the center of what Hughes and Brewin called the "new health crisis" of sedativism based on "dual or poly addiction."[85] As the most commonly recognized market name for diazepam, Valium had been available as a prescription in the United States since 1963 when it quickly surpassed two popular drugs for treating anxiety and depression, Miltown (a meprobamate produced in 1956 by Wallace Laboratories in New Jersey) and Librium (a first-generation benzodiazepine produced in 1960 by the Swiss company Hoffmann-La Roche, synthesized in New Jersey by the Polish émigré chemist Leo Sternbach in 1955). *Time* magazine was optimistic about the benefits of Miltown in its June 1956 piece "Pills for the Mind," and four months earlier *Time* described it as a "pacifier for the frustrated and frenetic."[86] Rather than tackle the psychosociological roots of unease via lengthy courses of therapy, the attraction of tranquilizers was that they smoothed over "fissures that, left unattended, threatened to widen into more serious chasms" that could undermine domestic order.[87] Wallace claimed that 70 to 95 percent of nervous patients "recovered or improved" after taking Miltown, making it easier "to lead a normal family life" and for mothers to "carry on their usual work" because its effects lasted eight times longer than the common muscle relaxant mephenesin.[88] Little was known about the addictive properties of Miltown at a time when Wallace was claiming that the drug could relieve "*both* mental and muscular tension" without impairing "mental faculties, motor control or normal behavior," and it could be taken to alleviate "insomnia, anxiety and emotional upsets" associated with pregnancy.

With Wallace looking to target its advertising at middle-class housewives and white-collar male workers, the addictive properties of Miltown were not widely recognized until the 1960s. This delayed recognition was despite the claims of psychiatrists at a 1956 national conference that pills "were no substitute for compassion or psychotherapy," and a 1957 *JAMA* letter written by two doctors working at the US Public Health Service Hospital in Lexington, Kentucky, arguing that sudden withdrawal could result in convulsions and heightened postwithdrawal anxiety (they noted, too, that it was thought to be addictive only to a "small proportion of persons who receive the drug therapeutically").[89] A 1959 congressional investigation into drug pricing, overseen by Senator Estes Kefauver, sowed distrust in the media toward the aggressive advertising of pharmaceutical companies, including a 1965 exposé by the *Washington Post* journalist Morton Mintz, appropriately titled *The Therapeutic Nightmare.*[90] That same year Miltown was reclassified as a sedative, and the FDA withdrew it two years later for addictive qualities that made it open to abuse.[91] By 1967, the year that Hollywood released *Valley of the Dolls*, its lurid adaptation of Jacqueline Susann's popular novel of drug and alcohol dependency, *Look* magazine claimed drug addiction had moved from the streets to suburban homes where it was thought to be propping up the lives of many middle-class Americans who now "can't sleep, wake up or feel comfortable without drugs."[92]

One may think that this narrative of Miltown's rise and fall would have given physicians and regulators pause for thought at a time when Valium was becoming the most prescribed drug in the country. Instead, when it was launched by Hoffmann-La Roche following FDA approval in 1963, Valium was promoted as a more potent upgrade to Librium. Both drugs were synthesized by Leo Sternbach at the New Jersey Roche Laboratory alongside a group of benzodiazepines that were thought to act safely and without toxicity. Roche advertised Valium as a minor tranquilizer that could counter the "emotional storms of psychoneurotic tension," as displayed in a 1970 magazine ad alongside images of a thirty-five-year-old spinster whose life is described as being "in a losing pattern." This same ad details precautions and possible side effects but plays on the stereotype of a lonely unmarried middle-aged woman, as did other Roche ads targeted at medical practitioners, in which Valium is touted to alleviate "undue psychic tension" and is effective in combination with therapy.[93] In contrast to the mind-expanding potential of recreational drugs favored by the 1960s counterculture, many women thought that taking Valium helped them to maintain the "traditional female role of wife and housemaker" and to preserve domestic order, literally and metaphorically.[94]

Despite the pharmaceutical confidence of these magazine ads (including one in which a placid and becalmed face is pasted over a grimacing and anguished one), there were some early warning signs. One of these was a letter in the *British Medical Journal* that detailed the case of a twenty-three-year-old female patient taking Valium over the course of a year. This patient's dose was now four times the original in order to achieve the same effect; after several days in the hospital without the drug she exhibited cravings, "agitation, tremulousness, and hyperhidrosis" for a few days more though continued to show signs of psychological dependence.[95] A *JAMA* article of March 1968 noted the possibility that suicidal thoughts might increase for patients taking diazepam (two out of a group of eight test patients who were receiving treatment actually committed suicide), but critical clinical studies on the effects of Valium in the 1960s were sparse.[96] Hoffmann-La Roche sold Valium as a benign drug that could soothe everyday stresses, but the FDA thought there was cause for concern when it clashed with the company in the mid-1960s in an effort to regulate Librium and Valium. Roche pushed back on the threat of regulation during hearings in the autumn of 1966, and when the Controlled Substances Act of 1970 sought to classify Valium as a Schedule III drug with potential for abuse, aggressive lobbying by Roche together with congressional support meant that it was omitted from classification for three years. Eventually, in 1973, the DEA placed Valium in the Schedule IV category (along with Miltown) as a substance with low abuse potential.[97]

Set against this account of inertia in the face of business interests was the emergence of advocacy and lobbying groups (including Ralph Nader's Public Citizen group); a startling National Institute on Drug Abuse "Monitoring the Future" survey (the first in an annual series) that estimated in 1974 that 42 percent of American women had taken psychoactive drugs on prescription; and a number of stories that tackled

Roche's exaggerated claims about Valium's therapeutic benefits, despite an estimated 15 percent of the country having taken Valium in shorter or longer forms.[98] Two revealing accounts appeared in *Vogue* in February 1975 and *Ladies' Home Journal* in November 1976. Sandwiched between an article on vegetarian diets and columns on the benefits of milk and how to treat wounds and burns, the *Vogue* piece begins by quoting Marie Nyswander's view that Valium addiction is far worse than heroin—she recommends that Valium should only be taken for a month: "when they're used for a chronic or long-lasting condition, you get into trouble—addiction, tolerance, often an agonizing withdrawal."[99] Nyswander's language is panic provoking: she calls the drug a "disaster" in waiting, long-term courses "lash back," and "the person looks and acts like a zombie" during withdrawal. The *Ladies' Home Journal* piece, published the following November, was billed as a special report on "Women and Tranquilizers." Even though this report also draws on expert opinion to argue that mild tranquilizers can have an anesthetizing effect on everyday activities and can suppress sexual desires, it differs in tone from the *Vogue* piece.[100] Countering the crude stereotypes of the Roche ads, it takes a sociocultural perspective on why Valium is targeted at women, looking at how shifting gender roles were posing questions about prescriptions on demand and if tranquilizers are actually the answer to life's worries or chronic conditions.

An increasing number of confessional accounts in popular magazines in the mid-1970s prompted others to tell their stories, most famously the journalist Barbara Gordon in her autobiographical *I'm Dancing as Fast as I Can* (1978), which recounts the terrible withdrawal symptoms from Valium she experienced after a long-term prescription. As well as documenting the unraveling of her life, Gordon's narrative blames her "treat-the-symptom" physician (her partner calls him a "Valium-dispensing machine") who insists that long-term use of Valium was safe despite the "feverish intensity" she feels.[101] When Gordon decides to stop taking pills suddenly (something that Nyswander warned against in the 1975 *Vogue* piece), her withdrawal symptoms include a burning scalp, spasms and tremors, dizziness, hot flushes, insatiable thirst, constant anxiety, insomnia, and loss of self-esteem as she loses the will to undress or leave the house. These intense experiences do not just affect her physical being but also her ability to speak, and when she is treated for depression and cyclothymia in the hospital with the antidepressant Sinequan, her memories are "jumbled" and her words "incoherent."[102] She eventually finds some stability, but only after consulting numerous doctors, undergoing inpatient therapy, taking megavitamins, and reorienting her whole life outlook.

While accounts of drug addiction to diazepam were still rare in medical literature at the time, 1978 was a key year for the mounting crisis. Not only had over fifty million prescriptions for Valium been written by 1978, but that year also revealed how cross-addiction had permeated national life when, in April, former First Lady Betty Ford announced her addiction to Valium and alcohol and her decision to seek rehabilitation treatment at Long Beach Naval Hospital.[103] Betty Ford started taking painkillers and drinking liberally in the mid-1960s for an inoperable pinched nerve and osteoarthritis. When she underwent an operation for breast cancer as first lady in September 1974, popular household magazines started to draw the public's attention to signs of her addiction, with *McCall's* speculating that "the open and natural Mrs. Ford" was often "frozen stiffly into a post that leads some observers to wonder if she isn't dazed on tranquilizers" based on rumors that she was "at times overly drugged."[104]

In her two autobiographies of 1978 and 1987, Ford finds it easier to accept her dependence on prescription medication than alcohol, perhaps because it is easier to blame a health system that failed her.[105] She was particularly critical of physicians who prescribed drugs in combination but, instead of simply pointing her figure at medical negligence, she admits "there was enough blame for all of us, the doctors and me."[106] Ford does not make drug taking a feminist issue, but her feeling that she should be a "Bionic woman" in her professional and private lives, and that pills were one way of insuring this, hints that medical bias was stacked against women. This belief echoed the views of psychiatrist Robert Seidenberg and the authors of *The Tranquilizing of America* that advertising played on gender stereotypes in targeting women's anxieties about their capabilities.[107] Nevertheless, when Ford disclosed the reason she decided to enter Long Beach Hospital, she was hailed as a brave sixty-year-old public figure willing to share her painful story. First Lady Rosalynn Carter praised her predecessor, stating "it's the kind of thing we are hoping well-known Americans will do—speak out about such problems."[108] Yet Ford's two written accounts offer only limited details of the biological and psychological aspects of dependency. Instead, she frames her journey in moral and spiritual terms, while in her second autobiography *A Glad Awakening* she promotes the Betty Ford Center, the eighty-bed rehabilitation facility that opened in 1982 in Palm Springs, California.

The scattered published accounts on the deleterious effects of Valium caught the eye of Edward Kennedy, chair of the Senate Subcommittee on Health and Scientific Research. Kennedy had been vocal about the need for pharmaceutical reform since the early 1970s, based on his belief that patients were the victims rather than the beneficiaries of drugs that were sometimes "irrationally prescribed," as he stated in a 1974 hearing. The Kennedy hearings of the mid-1970s caused disquiet in the medical and pharmaceutical sectors because the hearings seemed to them to be a sign of a creeping government takeover. Against warnings that the country was quickly becoming a "chemical society served by a 'psychem supermarket,'" the hearing of September 10, 1979, on the addictive effects and health consequences of Valium prescriptions was historic and consequential.[109] Yet, given that diazepam had been on the market for sixteen years, this seems like a rear-guard action to a public health threat, only reaching serious proportions after a series of media reports on the deleterious effects of tranquilizers.

Kennedy began the hearing by stating that, although he could easily cite the number of prescriptions for Valium in any given year (44.6 million in 1978), the nation was ill-equipped to determine appropriate use because it had no surveillance mechanism by which to measure effective prescription versus addiction, despite the introduction of the Drug Abuse Warning Network (DAWN) in 1974. Funded by the DEA and the National Institute on Drug Abuse, DAWN drew its data from reported visits to hospital emergency rooms and medical examinations, though it was difficult to produce adequate statistics for all regions, and polydrug addition was especially tricky to quantify. At root, Kennedy wanted wholesale change rather than short-term fixes to "the crisis in America's health care," as he subtitled his 1972 book *In Critical Condition*. He first introduced to Congress the proposal for a Drug Regulation Reform Act in March 1978 as a "consensus bill." Yet when it was discussed at a national conference in Washington, DC, four months later (sponsored by the Center for the Study of Drug Development at the University of Rochester), there were marked disagreements about the cost and purpose of such legislation.[110] By the time of the September 1979 subcommittee hearing, a revised and more modest version of the proposed Drug Regulation Reform Act looked like it might gain congressional approval with its emphasis on patient information inserts, improved postmarketing surveillance, and data collection.[111] The Senate backed the proposal (there were very few senators on the floor for the vote), but then it died in the House following a fierce backlash from the AMA and the Pharmaceutical Manufacturers Association.[112]

Despite these broader policy wrangles, the September 1979 subcommittee hearing was an important event in identifying and articulating Valium as the "number one drug problem in the United States today" behind alcohol.[113] The first two panels to testify were a mixed group of patients and health specialists. The patients included two medical doctors, a Catholic priest, two white-collar workers, and two housewives from New Jersey and Delaware who had all taken Valium, for some along with other prescription drugs and for others in combination with alcohol over varying periods. Each of them had experienced debilitating withdrawal symptoms, especially the California physician Bill Thomas, who chose to go cold turkey like Barbara Gordon after increasing his dose of Valium regularly over a decade. Thomas's story was similar to the others: coming off Valium he experienced insomnia, loss of appetite, delusions, and skin burning; he needed a month in the hospital to detoxify; and it was another eighteen months before regular sleep returned. Kennedy echoed three themes that all these individuals touched on: the drug is indubitably addictive but they had little knowledge of this; the withdrawal experience is "extremely harsh" and symptoms tend to linger after detoxification; and yet there is "a real sense of hope" in these stories, and especially in their courage to speak out.[114]

The health professionals' panel included Lowell Anderson, a New York professor of psychology; Captain Joseph A. Pursch, head of the alcohol rehabilitation service at Long Beach Naval Regional Medical Center (where Betty Ford had received treatment); Frederick Glaser, a psychiatrist and addiction specialist from the University of Toronto; and Nelson Hendler, a chronic pain treatment specialist from Johns Hopkins University Hospital. Anderson's view was that the use of the drug by this group of patients (all of them were professionals) "seemed no more frequent than one would expect from a random sampling of business people," but he concluded that "Valium worked too well," dissuading professionals from working less or learning relaxation techniques.[115] Anderson shared the others' view that the drug was often misprescribed or overprescribed. The pain specialist Nelson Hendler, for example, bemoaned that 40 to 60 percent of pain patients were taking benzodiazepines, even though there was little evidence they were an effective medication. In his formal statement, Joseph Pursch drew from his extensive knowledge of alcohol addiction, claiming "the longer we look, the more cases we find" of diazepam addiction whatever the reason for starting, whether it is

> physical injury, postoperative pain, or emotional trauma such as divorce, rape, mourning or moving to a new location [or] because of a chronic disorder manifested by anxiety, depression, insomnia, psychosomatic symptoms...or to ameliorate some other drug addiction including alcoholism.[116]

With this kind of testimony and medical reports that doctors only have "the sketchiest knowledge of where, or what, and precisely how such drugs work," the panel concluded too little is known about cross-addiction and the precise ways Valium works on the brain, including concerns that it may lead to long-term impairment of cognitive functioning.[117]

Some positive messages emerged from the daylong hearing, especially the need for more highly educated physicians and patients who would enable them to detect biases in public health information. To this end, PHS director J. Richard Crout informed the subcommittee that since August 1978 Roche had invested funds in a two-year educational campaign, "The Consequences of Stress: The Medical and Social Implications of Prescribing Tranquilizers," that they had entrusted to a private New Jersey firm, distributed by Cornell University Medical College.[118] Crout confirmed that such material was not in tension with FDA regulations, but it highlighted the fine line between company advertising and health education.[119] Roche's president defended this initiative, but Crout's reservations echoed those of the National Consumers League, particularly the influence of big pharmaceutical companies on medical schools, the limited psychopharmacological knowledge possessed by many physicians, and the fearmongering in drug advertising, "showing patients, mostly women, to be weak, neurotic, fearful of old age, unable to make decisive decisions."[120] The FDA was slow to address the concerns of the National Consumers League, including the view that due to slow metabolisms seniors were prone to addiction, a point raised with respect to the "pacifying" effects of diazepam by Robert Butler in his widely read 1975 book *Why Survive? Being Old in America* and by Hughes and Brewin in *The Tranquilizing of America*.[121]

The Kennedy hearing heightened awareness of the need for better FDA oversight of patient inserts and drugs education and for pharmaceutical companies to be more responsible in their targeting of patient groups. This included moves to stop prescribing Valium and drugs like Dalmane to elderly patients in the light of studies revealing a dramatic increase in the likelihood of sleep apnea. It also included the need to work with support and advocacy groups, such as the Women's Center in Washington, DC (which focused on female polydrug use) and the Women in Crisis project (between 1977 and 1979), which saw the Department of Alcohol and Drug Abuse working with eleven women's programs in California (across a range of racial groups in rural and urban areas) to assess the relationship between drug abuse and "domestic violence, rape, economic survival, medical and emotional problems."[122]

The following three years were a watershed for tightening prescription regulations on Valium, although, in truth, its medical use had been decreasing year by year since 1974–76, from sixty-one million in 1975 to thirty-four million by 1980.[123] This did not prevent an estimated eight thousand patients paying visits to emergency rooms in 1981 due to diazepam addiction (down from 21,000 in 1977) and 4,500 entering drug treatment centers for the first time that year.[124] These statistics are provided on the opening page of the 1982 Public Citizen Health Research Group report *Stopping Valium*, a publication that presents an overview of the public health issues, advice to patients about the effects and risks of Valium, sources of information at the state level, and a long final chapter exposing the tricks of tranquilizer advertising, highlighting in particular Roche's Valium campaigns. The emphasis in the report is on clear and unbiased public health information where individuals are empowered to "practice intelligent, well-informed defensive consumerism" and to spot the mechanisms of pharmaceutical control.

Valium was far from the only drug to experience tighter regulations in the early 1980s. The example of benoxaprofen, launched in the United States by Eli Lilly as Oraflex in May 1982 as a drug that could significantly reduce the pain and inhibit inflammation of arthritic joints, serves as a useful comparative case. In less than three months Oraflex was withdrawn on both sides of the Atlantic when seventy-two elderly patients died (most of them British) from toxicity in their liver and kidney (benoxaprofen had been available in the United Kingdom for two years under the European brand name Opren). The FDA was concerned that Oraflex had not been thoroughly tested for potential carcinogenicity, but Eli Lilly retorted that the drug had been withdrawn in an "environment of hysteria," implying that deaths are inevitable before the efficacy of a new drug can be fully tested. However, a *New York Times* report argued that the company "must bear the burden of a product that turned sour," just as Roche had to do with Valium.[125]

These controversies made a dent in the profits of Roche and Eli Lilly but did little to slow the influence of pharmaceutical giants despite the expiry of the Roche patent on Valium in 1985. There were some legislative attempts to tackle monopolies, such as the Hatch-Waxman Act of 1984 that moved to ensure that cheaper generic equivalents were not prevented from reaching the market quickly due to long-standing patents. Not only could physicians and patients choose from three near equivalents to Valium by 1985 but there were new tranquilizers too, such as Xanax, specifically designed to counter panic attacks. Yet even though in July 1980 Hoffmann-La Roche and other companies agreed to issue more specific information to physicians about minor tranquilizers and antianxiety drugs, public health information was less tightly regulated after February 1982 when the FDA was pressured to lift its ruling that prescription drug packages must contain patient inserts.[126] Keith Wailoo argues that this deregulated "drug market revolution" contributed to the rise of opioids in the following decades, even though Valium was on the wane as the prescription drug of choice by 1982.[127] Nevertheless, debates about regulation and addiction were far from over in the year that John Hinckley Jr., loaded up on diazepam, attempted to assassinate President Reagan.[128]

SUPER-STRENGTH OPIOIDS: THE THIRD WAR ON DRUGS, 2014–2018

What lessons might be learned from these two drug epidemics? There are at least five conclusions one could draw from the federally backed methadone experiment of 1972–73 and the congressional benzodiazepine hearings of 1979. First, a one-step chemical solution is not the answer to a multifaceted issue that is at once social, cultural, and medical, especially when it relates to polydrug use. Second, US public health information on drugs tends to be inflammatory or skewed—or patchy in the case of patient packaging inserts. Third, there was often a clouding of punitive and medical discourses that blurred the lines between the criminal and the patient, particularly the attempts on behalf of the Nixon-Ford and Reagan-Bush administrations to make surgical strikes on dealers and traffickers, just as they were seeking to deregulate aspects of health care governance. Fourth, the patient was often propelled into the role of passive recipient rather than an active agent, a position that advocacy groups for women, the elderly, and minorities, and the 1982 Public Citizen Health Research Group report *Stopping Valium*, all tried to redress. And, fifth, there was clear evidence of what Muriel

Nellis calls "industry-government incest" between interdependent sectors. A prime example of this is Joseph Califano's influential role as a private lawyer in lobbying for Valium to be exempt from drug scheduling in the early 1970s; this work (which Califano later regretted) was sandwiched between his role as President Johnson's special assistant (1965–68) and as President Carter's health secretary (1977–79) up until just before the benzodiazepine hearings.[129]

The tendency to ignore misuse of prescription medication during the Reagan years or to blame patients for fabricating or exaggerating a condition in order to claim more from the state (what Keith Wailoo calls "pain fraud") was exacerbated by the idiosyncratic views of Carlton E. Turner, President Reagan's deputy assistant for drug abuse policy.[130] Just as Wailoo argues that the rise in the 1980s of cases of chronic pain linked a lack of adequate welfare support for vulnerable Americans, so in a number of television appearances Turner cast the blame for drug dependency squarely on the individual, arguing that there should be no distinction between hard and soft drugs.[131] Turner worked closely with First Lady Nancy Reagan on the Just Say No campaign aimed at school kids; commencing in 1982, the campaign escalated into a series of network television appearances in 1983 and a proliferation of anti-drug school clubs by the summer of 1984. Although the Department of Health and Human Services began publishing an educational newsletter in 1985, the Reagans and Turner treated recreational drug use as a moral issue, in contrast to Nancy Reagan's predecessor Rosalynn Carter, who emphasized the importance of caregiving as a central aspect of her mental health advocacy.

Turner viewed all treatment models as morally suspect compared to a regime of abstinence and resorted to inflammatory rhetoric such as "when you buy drugs, you buy terror; when you buy a high, you buy a nightmare. Drugs are a threat to our national security, our health, our future."[132] The Reagans closely echoed Turner's view when they portrayed all drugs as a menace to society on national television in September 1986, but just one month later Turner resigned after making an unsubstantiated connection between marijuana use and HIV/AIDS.[133] The moralism that characterized this second War on Drugs continued through the George H. W. Bush administration as the nation's "gravest domestic threat," albeit in slightly milder form given the cost of federal interventions and in recognition that recreational use of other drugs such as antidepressants, methamphetamine, and crystal meth was on the rise.

Writing toward the end of the Clinton administration, Michael Massing made three recommendations. First, he recommended a special action office along the lines of Jerome Jaffe's appointment by Nixon; second, a coordinated outreach program for addicts; and third, a respected medical figure to lead on national policy such as C. Everett Koop, Reagan's surgeon general, who acknowledged systemic weaknesses in the health care infrastructure, as well as assessing the autoimmune dangers of AIDS and the risks of in utero complications.[134] Yet when the opioid epidemic reemerged in the national conversation in 2016–17, neither Obama nor Trump heeded Massing's three recommendations, as clearly illustrated when in February 2020 Trump put Vice President Mike Pence in charge of the federal Coronavirus Task Force to displace the more circumspect yet more specialized HHS secretary Alex M. Azar II.[135]

This case study focuses on the final two years of the Obama administration and the first two years of the Trump presidency when a third war on drugs became a domestic priority that echoed and in some ways exaggerated the mistakes of the early drug wars. This escalation is ironic given that the 106th Congress (at the end of Clinton's presidency) declared the first years of the century as the "Decade on Pain Control and Research," and a congressional inquiry launched by the 107th Congress (toward the start of Bush's presidency) described OxyContin as "the angel of mercy" for some users in bringing "welcome relief" from pain, whereas for others it "is the angel of death" due to its highly addictive properties.[136] Yet bipartisan consensus on what best to do was hard to reach. An example of congressional inertia is the National Pain Care Policy Act sponsored by Republican senator Michael J. Rogers of Michigan. The aim of the spring 2003 bill was to make pain care a national public health priority via a dedicated White House conference and an NIH National Center for Pain and Palliative Care Research, but it did not reach a vote in the Republican-controlled Congress. A variation of the bill was reintroduced six years later by Lois Capps, the Democratic representative from California; this time the proposal received approval by the House, but it died in the Senate even though the Democrats had majorities in both chambers.

Set against such paralysis, this final case study illustrates the escalating crisis—or "crises" to recall Judy Foreman's idea of "two colliding epidemics" of chronic pain and opioid abuse—by assessing the relationship between the national drug crisis of the mid-2010s and drug use and treatment at state and local levels. Here I bring into dialogue health surveys, policy reports, and congressional hearings with cultural theory and two 2018 novels by Nico Walker and Stephen Markley set in Ohio, a midwestern state that saw the highest number of opioid-related deaths in the mid-2010s alongside West Virginia and New Hampshire.

When did the opioid crisis begin? One might trace it back to 2003–4 with the publication of the investigative journalist Barry Meier's 2003 book *Pain Killer: A Wonder Drug's Trail of Addiction and Death* and when a court ruling forced Purdue to reformulate OxyContin to make it more difficult to inject, or to early 2001 when the *New York Times* published Meier's front-page story describing a massive drug raid across five Kentucky counties.[137] There is a case to be made about the federal neglect of opioid use during the George W. Bush and Obama years when a more forthright and integrated public health and education program might have reduced the overdose threat "to a far more manageable scale" before it reached the kind of crisis levels outlined in the introduction to this chapter.[138]

A decade after Meier's accounts the threat was high in the national conversation. This coincided with the publication of the 2011 report of the Office of National Drug Control Policy, *Epidemic: Responding to America's Drug Abuse Crisis*, followed by statistics in 2014 about rising death counts from heroin overdoses in New York and New England, and with lawsuits being taken out against pharmaceutical companies in Chicago and California.[139] A January 2015 article, "The Prescription Opioid and Heroin Crisis," in the *Annual Review of Public Health* centered the conversation on the relationship between opioids and narcotics, two months before a series of congressional hearings took a broad-ranging look at the economic, legislative, medical, and security aspects of the looming epidemic.[140] The first hearing in this sequence began with the bleak statement that "despite all of our science and public health agencies, and despite the billions of dollars devoted to fighting the opioid problem, the situation is no better than it was 100 years ago" at a time when the opium problem first started to ring political alarm bells.[141] These hearings foregrounded the mounting crisis but offered few innovate solutions for polydrug use. Although deaths from overdoses continued to rise in the early 2010s, there were some successes. Florida, for example, saw a marked drop in opioid-related deaths after 2011 due in part to the state introducing tougher prescription laws, though this appeared to be temporary given a sharp rise in 2016–17, and there were reports that Florida was a "pill mill pipeline" in distributing black-market opioids through Kentucky and farther north.[142]

Despite congressional hearings and intelligence gathering between spring 2015 and autumn 2016, would it have been possible to slow the growing threat with a more interventionist approach? This is a difficult question to answer. The 2004 view of Senator Barack Obama of Illinois was that the previous federal wars on drugs had "been an utter failure."[143] A few years later it was clear that President Obama was committed to a nuanced health agenda instead of the rhetoric of war; in March 2009 he attempted to separate the law enforcement from the public health aspects of drugs, promoting a "both/and" rather than an "either/or" approach, but in this instance he was speaking of marijuana rather than a combination of prescription and street drugs.[144] Following a February 2010 meeting on Drug Demand Reduction held by the US and Mexican governments in which it was acknowledged that illicit drug use in the United States was not on the statistical rise (stable at twenty million users), presidents Obama and Hinojosa jointly affirmed that addiction treatment should be "a part of mainstream medical practice," supported by screening, referral, and prevention.[145] Obama continued to advocate "harm reduction": in July 2011 he stated that poverty should not be a bar to those seeking drug rehabilitation and in April 2012 he announced $30 billion for health education on drug awareness and treatment. Obama's second health secretary, Sylvia Burwell, prioritized opioids in 2016, arguing for more training and educational resources, increasing the use of naloxone, and expanding Medication-Assisted Treatment as encoded in CDC's Prescription Drug Overdose: Prevention for States program launched in 2015. This integrated public health context was amplified in *Facing Addiction in America*, the surgeon general's report of November 2016 that includes a chapter on "the many paths to wellness," but for critics these measures either came too late or were seen as the tentacles of big government.[146]

Balanced assessments of the effectiveness of the Obama administration in curbing the volume of high strength opioids are rather sparse. For the liberal critic Kathleen Frydl, who judges many of Obama's domestic policies as progressive, the growing opioid threat was his "worst failure."[147] She bases this assessment on a lack of federal attention to the sharp upswing in prescription drug abuse and for allowing the FDA and the DEA to become ineffective in their regulatory roles. Not only did the early 2010s see the escalating overprescription of the FDA-approved OxyContin, but also the Obama administration seemed content with easy wins rather than delving into the relationship between licit and illicit drug use and into improving public health education about "opiophobia" to ensure that pain patients were not prevented from receiving the most effective drugs because of stigma and panic discourses about drug abuse.[148] This is as an example of structural violence by the pharmaceutical industry in which the federal government was unable or unwilling to intervene. There were attempts at public health education such as the FBI and Department of Drug Enforcement film *Chasing the Dragon: The Life of an Opiate Addict* of February 2016, designed for use in schools and in communities both as a deterrent and to stimulate conversation.[149] But even two pieces of legislation Obama signed in 2016—the Comprehensive Addiction and Recovery Act in July (on prevention and treatment) and the 21st Century Cures Act in December (to ensure that treatments for debilitating conditions, both physical and mental, appear on the market swiftly)—were at best end-stage interventions that did little to reduce the public health threat, and at worst further empowered the pharmaceutical companies.[150] In the year of Prince's death, it was clear the opioid threat was in a critical phase. But Obama mentioned drugs only briefly in his January 2016 State of the Union address, and at year's end his emphasis on creative innovation and community support did little to mask a lack of tightly coordinated strategy.[151]

Obama's decision not to declare a war on drugs was a self-conscious choice given the zealous legacy of the Nixon and Reagan campaigns as well as the view that the first two wars on drugs disproportionately targeted African American users rather than serving to demolish cartels. Frydl notes that the Nixon and Reagan administrations embraced "a minimal state presence" on many domestic matters but "supported aggressive state actions of interdiction and punishment" when it came to illicit drugs, which to her mind shows that the federal government in general is ill-equipped to win a war on drugs.[152] Options were limited though: either a noisy crusade against drugs or the quieter war of the Clinton administration that continued some of the law enforcement tactics of the Bush years but without the inflammatory rhetoric. What is clear, as Frydl and Foreman argue, is the need for a central role for public health in developing patient-centered initiatives (including complementary and alternative medicine), more funding for pain research, and strengthening community networks. Regardless of whether this approach entails either an opioid-free "exit strategy" or a "government-approved drugs" maintenance program, it is vital to sustain coordination and resources across successive administrations.[153]

There was clearly much more that the Obama administration and the

Republican-controlled Congress in Obama's second term might have done, as pointed out by Massachusetts senator Elizabeth Warren, who was critical of the 21st Century Cures Act, and Vermont senator Bernie Sanders, who argued (in a January 2016 Democratic primary debate in Charleston, South Carolina) that the pharmaceutical industry was failing to scope the public health consequences of drug production and marketization. Although Sanders sparred with Hillary Clinton throughout the 2016 Democratic primaries, the pair agreed that opioid use must be tackled as primarily a health rather than a criminal issue. In the Charleston debate, for example, Clinton claimed "we need to divert more people from the criminal justice system into drug courts, into treatment, and recovery" by increasing the amount of federal funds available to each state for prevention and treatment.[154] Despite his defeat in the Democratic primaries, Sanders's impassioned stance on universal health care and critique of big pharma continued through the 2016 and 2020 election cycles. In February 2018, for example, he called on Congress to investigate the industry's failure to accept responsibility for the opioid epidemic and to assess to what extent "pharmaceutical companies lied about the additive impacts of the drugs."[155] What Clinton and Sanders did not discuss, though, is how high-strength pain medication such as OxyContin turns many poor patients to heroin, especially when heroin producers become "simply more competitive" than licit suppliers.[156]

The preoccupation of the 45th president with winning meant that it was inevitable that Donald Trump would declare a third war on drugs, but arguably one in which the inherent tensions of the previous two wars were intensified, especially as the new president cared little for historical or scientific evidence. He made some obvious moves though, such as the appointment in March 2017 of New Jersey governor Chris Christie to chair a President's Commission on Combating Drug Addiction and the Opioid Crisis. The commission's interim report, published that July, recognized that the opioid situation was a public health emergency, though Trump delayed the announcement until October 26, when he delivered a White House address that evoked the "very real complexity" of the situation. Trump followed a speech aimed at heightening public awareness and channeling resources by veering off into familiar combative rhetoric, blaming Obama for not being tough enough on drug trafficking and China as the major importer of fentanyl, before signing a memorandum that centered on fentanyl as the most dangerous of the synthetic opioids.[157] In his focus on border security, harsher drug laws, and cuts to entitlements, the president disregarded many of the recommendations in the commission's final November report. He did not promise new funds and he dodged the enforcement of the Mental Health Parity and Addiction Equity Act (passed initially in 1996 as the Mental Health Parity Act and signed in 2008) geared to ensuring that mental health conditions and substance abuse are treated with equal seriousness to physical health.[158]

By appointing his counselor Kellyanne Conway to head up his opioid campaign instead of the kind of respected medical figure recommended by Michael Massing, Trump ensured that the focus was on optics and public relations rather than a carefully scoped initiative or even continuity with the presidential commission.[159] In a number of television appearances in February 2018, Conway outlined a three-pronged approach to medication, law enforcement, and health education, but she was habitually light on detail, unlike Christie, who as New Jersey governor had made progressive moves to tackle drug-use escalation, funding methadone maintenance treatment via Medicaid and a prisoner reentry program in eight New Jersey locations in late summer 2017. Conway tended to ignore experienced and expert voices in the Drug Enforcement Agency (DEA) and the Office of National Drug Control Policy, she said little about how the pharmaceutical and medical professions could be brought into responsible dialogue, and did not reflect on current medical research that showed, for example, how methadone in tapered doses can be used to ease opioid withdrawal. At the heart of these aspirations was the national rollout of an Rx Awareness campaign that had been trialed in autumn 2017 in four states with high levels of opioids, but this campaign had already had tangible effects across a number of states without requiring a public-relations drive.

The Department of Health and Human Services remained in the background in 2017–18 when it came to communications about the new drugs crisis. This was in part because Tom Price, Trump's first health secretary, resigned due to an expense scandal only eight months into office. His replacement in early 2018, Alex Azar, a former Eli Lilly president, had a different agenda, focusing on making prescription drugs more affordable via the American Patients First initiative and assisting the president and the Republican-controlled Congress in attempting to repeal and replace core elements of the Affordable Care Act.[160] In spring 2018, Azar outlined a range of approaches to curbing the opioid epidemic; these included destigmatization of opioid users, medication-assisted treatment such as methadone, encouraging doctors to seek alternatives to prescribing opioids, and finding ways to recall drugs left in family medicine cabinets that might tempt children and teenagers to experiment.[161]

On April 29, 2018, the Department of Justice ran a National Prescription Drug Take Back Day in collaboration with Google Maps that enabled users to see where to take their unused prescription drugs; this continued a program that began over five years with the passing of the Secure and Responsible Drug Disposal Act in September 2010. Conway bragged ahead of the 2018 National Take Back Day that the Trump administration had delivered 900,000 pounds of out-of-date prescription drugs, and a few days later she declared April 29 the most successful Take Back Day. Yet the DEA had no hard evidence to prove that this method was effective in quelling the opioid crisis, especially given that drop-offs spanned a range of drugs with varying expiry dates. Repeatedly through 2018 and into 2020 Azar was forced to renew his public health emergency declaration about the opioid crisis.[162] Trump's and Azar's stress on tougher penalties for dealers (Trump even mentioned the death penalty) overshadowed progressive aspects that were not markedly different from Azar's predecessor Sylvia Burwell, although Burwell was keen to emphasize that the "critical and complex public health challenge" of opioid dependency "demands a multifaceted approach."[163]

The fact that opioid prescriptions dropped by 10 percent nationally in 2017 gave the illusion that Trump's campaign was effective, but this could equally be attributed to the late-stage interventions of the previous administration.[164] There were some new developments such as Operation S.O.S. (Synthetic Opioid Surge) launched by the Department of Justice in summer 2018 that targeted ten districts with high overdose levels (including two districts in Ohio and two in West Virginia), but there was much the administration failed to acknowledge that occurred before Trump's inauguration: the congressional hearings on opioids in 2015–16; the limitations of the Reagan administration's drug education programs; the complex relationship between prescription and street drugs; and broader cultural issues that contribute to what Simon Strick calls "late modern pain." In his 2014 book *American Dolorologies*, Strick argues that "speaking pain" has emerged from the treatment room into mass entertainment via chat shows and talk radio, with the public sphere becoming "a site of intimate 'affect' exchange" through "confession, testimony, and other articulations of traumatized selfhood."[165] Marvin Seppala of the Hazleden Betty Ford Foundation expressed a similar, if less theoretical, point at an April 2015 congressional hearing. Seppala stated that doctors were prescribing opioids to numb both physical and psychological pain, but the risk of addiction was high for vulnerable patients "in a culture that promotes quick fixes, instant gratification, and escapism."[166] This tension between an increasingly surveilled public sphere and a furtive private sphere returns us to the shuttling between public and private worlds of Elaine Scarry's *Body in Pain*, and it is also emblematic of the Trump presidency that shadowboxed with a national drug policy as a public relations exercise rather than as an integrated public health strategy.

An example of the public relations aspect was Melania Trump's Be Best platform. Launched in early May 2018, this initiative was an effort to integrate "social, emotional, and physical health" by focusing on three pillars in the lives of children: well-being, social media use, and the rise in opioid use. The first lady's emphasis was on developing "positive relationship skills" and "responsible decision-making" in order to heighten "mutual respect, compassion, and self-esteem." She referred to schools' pilot projects that tackled social inclusion, the need to confront cyberbullying, and the "true crisis" of opioid addiction. On this topic, she drew on two visits she had made to facilities: in October 2017 she visited the infant recovery center Lily's Place in Huntington, West Virginia, and four months later the Cincinnati Children's Hospital where she was briefed on Neonatal Abstinence Syndrome. For an administration struggling with clear yet nuanced messages, Be Best had a carefully choreographed launch, combining health education programs with an awareness that attention to "well-being" was a counterpoint to the combative rhetoric and name-calling that peppered her husband's tweets. Rather than the rhetoric of war, the first lady spoke of the "victories and difficult realties" that children experience as they grow up. The implicit competitiveness of the slogan "Be Best" aroused some skepticism, but it was a softer message than the abstinence regime Nancy Reagan and Carlton Turner promoted in the 1980s.[167] However, almost immediately there were calls that the campaign—at least the social media part—was no different from a 2014 Obama-era program (including strong echoes of a Federal Trade Commission pamphlet on the online behavior of children), and the "Be Best" slogan was eerily reminiscent of Michelle Obama's 2016 call to American men to "be better."[168]

While the first lady pinpointed local initiatives in West Virginia and Ohio, the two worst hit states for opioid overdose deaths in 2016, the chance to establish a strong message floundered in the controversy about the originality of the messaging. It also was not at all clear from the White House posturing in late 2017 and early 2018 how the federal government would address the reality of opioid addiction and the stigma that went with it. Indeed, when it came to New Hampshire (the third most affected state in 2016), federal messages were again mixed.[169] In contrast to Hillary Clinton's comments in April 2015 that opioid misuse in the state had been "hidden" and was just beginning to surface, twenty months later President Trump was telling President Peña Nieto of Mexico that New Hampshire was a "drug infested den" and that drugs were streaming across the US-Mexico border, despite its principal city Manchester being located over two thousand miles from the southern border.[170] There was a fierce backlash from Democrats and Republicans in the state. Democratic representative Annie Kuster demanded an apology for the president's "nasty rhetoric and cruel policies," and the local paper in Nashua—a city hit hard by opioid addiction—expressed indignation and disbelief that the whole state could be so crudely stereotyped.[171] Nashua (the most racially varied city in the state, though 83 percent white in the 2010 Census) and the nearby city of Manchester (86 percent white) had both witnessed opioid overdoses since 2014, even though the semirural state was home to the Dartmouth-Hitchcock Medical Center in Lebanon, which was conducting research into pain management and launching public health projects, including "Moms in Recovery," which spanned seven maternity centers and coordinated local services for pregnant women with addictions. This research did not register on the president's radar, though Tom Price visited Somersworth on the New Hampshire–Maine border to pledge £200 million for in-state community health centers to improve opioid and mental health treatment.[172]

Notably, Trump chose Manchester Community College to deliver his administration's formal response to the opioid epidemic, four months after the final report of the President's Commission on Combating Drug Addiction and the Opioid Crisis. Trump's "Opioids: The Crisis Next Door" speech, delivered on March 19, 2018, was a mixture of initiatives not so distinct from the Obama era, mixed together with posturing about the need to be tough, largely irrelevant comments about prescription drug prices, and blame directed toward nearby Hispanic communities for being distributers of fentanyl.[173] This was a major national speech, including contributions from Melania Trump and Alex Azar, but it did nothing to recognize or sensitively address regional or local issues. Had it done so, Trump's speech might have referenced attempts to combat the stigma of addiction via rallies and walks, a toll-free addiction crisis hotline, the Safe Station initiatives in Manchester and Nashua where medical assistance is offered by firefighters around the clock, recently discontinued programs such as the drug recovery provider Hope for New Hampshire, or attempts to improve neonatal care and offer a professional cuddling service to help combat Neonatal Abstinence Syndrome for both mothers and affected babies.[174] Nor did Trump acknowledge the role of the previous New Hampshire Republican senator Kelly Ayotte in co-drafting the Comprehensive Addiction and Recovery Act (though this was less surprising because Ayotte had criticized Trump during the presidential election). Trump's idiosyncratic statements led the *New Yorker* to report that he habitually "talked past" the reality of addiction, using supercharged rhetoric that failed to acknowledge lessons learned from earlier wars on drugs about the need to be regionally sensitive and to work in collaboration with existing community-facing programs.[175]

Ohio is a similarly instructive case. The area around Cincinnati has a strong medical infrastructure for clinical research and addiction treatment, but this has not prevented alarming statistics emerging in urban and suburban areas across the state, particularly in Dayton, Columbus, and Akron. Ohio has become a paradigmatic case for gauging the extent of the crisis, which is partly attributed to the crossroads of two major interstates, 70 and 75, just north of Dayton, making it a "source city" with an easy and cheap supply of drugs via these "heroin highways."[176] However, it is the combination of heroin and fentanyl that has been particularly destructive—71 percent of Ohio's 349 deaths by drug overdoses in 2016 were thought to involve fentanyl and no trace of heroin.[177] The *New York Times* used the state as a national litmus test in a June 2017 feature on drug deaths, as did Sam Quinones in his award-winning *Dreamland*, which focuses on the postindustrial city of Portsmouth, Ohio, near the Kentucky border. Quinones attributes high levels of use to the overprescription of OxyContin in the late 1990s and early 2000s. To this he adds two other factors: the illegal distribution of narcotics by pill mills (such as the pain management clinic Advanced Urgent Care operating out of Philadelphia) and the availability of highly potent black tar heroin that he traces to Nayarit, Mexico, a town nearly 1,400 miles south of San Diego.[178] The narrative of *Dreamland* follows a therapeutic arc of addiction, reckoning, and recovery that draws on communal resources and a survivalist instinct. However, CDC statistics since *Dreamland* was published in spring 2015 show that this crisis cannot be overcome simply by perseverance, and the fact that local newspapers were reporting overdoses due to a mixture of fentanyl and heroin as early as 2006 shows how ingrained were drug problems in the Midwest by the mid-2010s.[179]

In early 2017, opioid-related deaths in Ohio were nearly triple the national average, with more than fourteen deaths a day during the CDC census period.[180] That summer, carfentanil, an extremely potent version of fentanyl, hit Akron, leading to 140 deaths from overdose of a drug estimated to be five thousand times stronger than heroin.[181] In Montgomery County, home of Dayton, the majority of deaths from opioids in early 2017 were male (64.4 percent) and overwhelmingly white (91.5 percent), with nearly 58 percent of deaths in the twenty-five-year-old to forty-four-year-old category.[182] Things were no better in Butler County, north of Cincinnati, where a combination of methamphetamine, cocaine, and fentanyl was the major cause of death by overdose in 2017, while Columbus saw a 47 percent growth of opioid overdoses that year, two-thirds from fentanyl.[183] The opening of new addiction treatment centers to supplement Ohio's twelve licensed methadone clinics did little to stem overdose threats, though practices of "kinship care" by relatives and friends offered some respite for children of addicted parents.[184]

On the legislative front, in 2016 Ohio senator Rob Portman had worked with Kelly Ayotte to introduce legislation that became the Comprehensive Addiction and Recovery Act, and in 2017 Portman developed the Synthetics Trafficking and Overdose Prevention (STOP) Act to balance medical concerns with crime prevention, with a special focus on catching fentanyl sent from overseas through the postal service. Another initiative was the long-term effort of the Veterans Administration to provide better pain management guidelines, improve accountability (via the 2016 Jason Simcakoski Memorial Opioid Safety Act), and to reduce the number of veterans legally receiving opioids at a time when dependency among veterans was rising rapidly.[185] A case in point is the Louis Stokes Cleveland VA Medical Center, which encourages nondrug pain treatment and exercise regimes among its military patients (it was treating 2,210 veterans by 2007), together with improved health education and training for its medical staff based in its ambulatory care clinic and its community outpatient clinics.[186]

Trying to make sense of the overdose spike in Ohio was not just the task of the state government and health providers—or journalism such as the "Faces of an Epidemic" feature in the *New Yorker* in December 2017 that focused on the health toll across Ohio and featured haunting images by freelance photographer Philip Montgomery.[187] In August

2018, two months before the FDA approved the medical use of sufentanil, or Dsuvia (ten times stronger than fentanyl), two quite different novels were published with northeastern Ohio as their setting.[188] The first, written by Iraq War veteran and felon Nico Walker (he wrote the novel between 2013 and 2017 from a jail in Ashland, Kentucky, after being convicted for multiple bank robberies in northeast Ohio), is a first-person account of drug addiction and crime that the young narrator falls into after returning from Iraq. Echoing Walker's life experiences, in the early part of the book the narrator uses drugs periodically before he drops out of college and drifts into the army as a medic.[189] Life becomes more intense and fragmentary for him when he returns to Cleveland after his tour of duty. There he experiences PTSD symptoms, an inability to focus, the demise of his marriage, and full-scale drug addiction to heroin and opioids, having been initially exposed to Percocet and OxyContin during active service.

The book is a meditation on physical and mental health but also on moral choice as the narrator hovers between knowing he is making a mess of his life and not being able to summon the conviction to make a change. This ambivalent tone is established early on when he reflects on his life with his girlfriend Emily ("we're happy enough, though we're often sad because we feel like we're losing everything") and on his drugs regime ("somewhere along the way I got into this...one thing leads to another, leads to another. Things get better, they get worse").[190] This oscillation between declarative positions makes his limited agency in a world of empty values a major theme of the novel at a far remove from the "Be Better" and "Be Best" slogans of first ladies Michelle Obama and Melania Trump with respect to moral character. With phrases like "I tried to be good. But I was fucked up," *Cherry* is a series of uncertain descents in which moments of moral clarity are quickly lost.[191]

In contrast to the singularly idiosyncratic yet symptomatic life of Walker's narrator, in *Ohio* Stephen Markley interweaves four stories in the symbolically named and economically challenged Rust Belt town of New Canaan. *Ohio* takes a longer temporal frame than *Cherry*, stretching back to 9/11 when its central characters were attending high school, but the two novels share the theme of emptiness. This is symbolized at the beginning of *Ohio* with an eerie November 2007 funeral parade to honor a corporal killed in action in Iraq; his body had actually been buried in July but the town parade was postponed due to a flash flood. Significantly for the theme of absence, none of the book's four central characters from the same high-school year group are present at this parade. The narrator, who wavers between a distant storyteller and an active presence, breaks the frame on the final page of the prelude to state that all four characters were "missing for reasons all their own" but that each will return to New Canaan six years after the funeral, in summer 2013. The narrator warns the reader that these will not be linear stories but rather a "wild, fucked-up flamethrower of a collective dream," suggesting a shared yet disjointed consciousness in a postrecession country that no longer makes sense, particularly in a state scarred by "social dislocation" and "the carcasses of dying industrial towns— Dayton, Toledo, Mansfield, Youngstown, Akron."[192]

The opioid theme of the two novels is striking. In *Cherry*, after snorting low doses of Percocet and OxyContin while in the US Army, Walker's narrator goes on a drinking spree on returning to Ohio, and he takes Xanax and OxyContin too, acquired illicitly and sometimes snorted with cocaine or injected with heroin. This shields him from the hurt of a broken relationship and helps him hold at bay postwar hallucinations and suicidal thoughts, given that very little infrastructural or therapeutic support seem to be on offer.[193] It is unclear to what extent the drug taking affects his decision-making, yet by the final page of the novel the narrator associates shooting up with the good life even as he knows these are merely fleeting moments within his now-abject life. This is a version of what Sam Quinones calls a "narcissistic, self-absorbed, solitary" life, emphasized by the quasi-confessional tone of Walker's novel, even as the narrator retains self-knowing irony in places.[194]

Some of Walker's character traits are paralleled in two of the four central characters of Markley's *Ohio*. The antiwar activist Bill Ashcraft had been drinking heavily and taking drugs for over a decade to numb the pain of what he saw as the travesty of the Iraq War, which the nation controversially entered in the wake of the terrorist attacks of 9/11. Bill had experimented with opioids in high school as "coping mechanisms"—these are listed by their street names, "Vic, Val, Oxy, Hydro, Norco," together with LSD and methamphetamine—but now he deals drugs as well.[195] The other main male character, Dan Eaton, has served three tours of duty in Iraq, has lost an eye, and is now suffering from PTSD. Bill describes Dan as "looking like a ghost crawled up his ass and into his eyes," but this condition runs deeper than a physical injury or combat trauma, described as "an ancient human hurt written in the bones, sung in the sinew of muscle, ground out in the anamnesis of cells."[196] The pain felt by *Ohio*'s characters is a collective anguish of loss and emptiness that recalls the trope of ghostliness (as discussed in chapter 2) and links laterally to what Simon Strick calls "late modern pain," which in these novels is both biological and cultural in linking to the symptomology of PTSD. Markley's novel joins a tradition of literary jeremiads focusing on cultural malaise and an erosion of values, but he deliberately sets *Ohio* during Obama's second term when the surge in opioid use was labeled a national crisis. Yet, just as importantly, *Ohio* and *Cherry* do not offer a healing space or seek a sentimental resolution, in contrast to the sentimentalism that Strick associates with liberal attempts to ameliorate pain via "integration, understanding, and recognition."[197]

These two novels emphasize there is no single-step solution to an issue that crosses so many borders of American life. As we have seen, often the federal government looks to winning the war on drugs with a grand but often simplistic vertical approach, rather than analyzing the interplay of historical, cultural, sociological, and health factors. This vertical approach tends to underestimate the time and labor required by educators, health workers, and patients to bring about long-term sustainable change. It also sometimes overlooks the need to regulate pharmaceutical companies: Purdue Pharma filed for bankruptcy in 2019 and pleaded guilty to federal criminal charges in fall 2020, and high-street drug stores CVS and Walgreens both faced civil trials in 2019 for aiding the spread of opioid use by not reporting suspicious orders.[198]

Even in instances of marked local success in tackling opioid abuse via noninvasive techniques, the danger of the "balloon effect" where combating the addiction crisis on one front simply means it reemerges on another suggests that this is a long-term endeavor. It is certainly not a linear success story. For example, though there were encouraging signs of a decrease in opioid-related deaths in Ohio in 2018, deaths spiked again in Cleveland and Columbus in 2019, and the opioid crisis returned to Ohio and West Virginia in 2020 due, in part, to rising unemployment in the wake of the COVID-19 pandemic.[199] The fact that by that time a number of states had adopted an integrated outpatient approach to addiction—relapse prevention, cognitive-behavioral therapy, a twelve-step program, family education, and social support networks—suggests that multipronged treatment models can be effective within a horizontal public health philosophy.[200] Such responsive initiatives, together with the bipartisan SUPPORT Act that included a Medicaid and Medicare provision for financing addiction recovery, gives hope that a layered approach is possible, yet without the illusion that the state can create what Simon Strick calls a "pain-free space."[201]

Conclusion

2018

*Obama, Trump, and the Future of Health
Citizenship*

Each of the health crises charted in these six chapters has wide-ranging
national and regional implications. However, it is individuals, families,
and local communities for whom threats to well-being and health—and
sometimes to raw existence—registers most profoundly, even when a
national emergency prompts us to adopt a panoramic perspective. Individuals still matter at the federal level despite differing views about
whether health systems should be largely determined by the congressional and executive branches, or whether the upgrading of medical
technologies and facilities matter most in making health care effective
and responsive. These two views are equally valid. Yet, as medical historian Charles Rosenberg has noted, they are often in fierce opposition:
"even those Americans least critical in their attitude toward the benefits
of continued medical progress are concerned about the monetary cost.
Others who are more skeptical, but still willing to concede the real advances of contemporary medical practice, deplore the ethical and human costs of bureaucratic, episodic, high-technology care."[1]

Rosenberg was writing in the mid-1980s, at a time when the sluggish
federal response to HIV/AIDS prompted what he calls a "multisided
crisis in public expectation," reinforcing his view that "we live in a
fragmented society."[2] The possibility of a single even-handed system
that caters to diverse and underserved communities seemed like a mi-
rage to Rosenberg in the 1980s, but such a belief should not lead to
us to conclude that the system is broken and cannot be fixed or that

individuals and groups cannot help stimulate structural change. In fact, health causes are often championed by individuals who have experienced firsthand or via a close encounter the kinds of health issues that motivate them to challenge stasis. This isn't to suggest that heroism offers a route out of systemic crisis, even when it is heroism on a communal scale such as first responders putting the lives of others first at times of emergency. Nor does it mean that focusing on the humanistic aspects of cultivating good health should be at the expense of tending to the environments and structures of health care, as I have discussed in the book's two halves with respect to intersecting geographies and states of vulnerability. This double-jointedness is why the Johnson administration's model in the mid-1960s had so much potential, even as the proliferation of intergovernmental programs and increasing pressure from Congress not to overspend on public works made it difficult to deliver on the Great Society promises. Regardless of historic results though, actors and agency always matter for health.

A major, perhaps unique, case in point is the Massachusetts senator Edward Kennedy. Health issues and personal tragedy profoundly affected Kennedy's life as a child and a young man, including the committal of his sister Rosemary following an enforced lobotomy in 1941 (when Ted was age nine), the death of his oldest brother Joe in combat during World War II (when Ted was twelve), and his father Joe's aphasia and reliance on a wheelchair following a stroke in 1961. Ted Kennedy himself experienced alcohol dependency throughout his long career as Massachusetts senator, and possibly PTSD too, linked to the assassinations of his brothers John and Bobby in 1963 and 1968, as his son Patrick Kennedy claims.[3] Writing as a mental health advocate, Patrick argues that his father repressed his tragedies and difficulties, including a broken back from a near fatal plane crash in 1964, cancer scares faced by two of his children (that looped back to his role in the "cancer crusade" as a Massachusetts lawyer in the early 1960s), and his first wife Joan receiving treatment for alcohol addiction. This leads Patrick to speculate that Ted might have been even more effective in the arena of health care had he accepted more support in the 1960s and early 1970s. It is a matter of judgment as to what extent these aspects motivated his father to revive the FDR-era idea of "health care for all" as a "living and functioning reality" and to champion workers' rights for family and medical leave.[4] However, it is clear that at least some of these factors intensified Ted Kennedy's drive to challenge Jimmy Carter's more incremental approach to health care reform, to tackle the big pharma monopoly over the prescription drugs market, to lead a congressional inquiry on addictive benzodiazepine in the late 1970s, and to return repeatedly to sponsor progressive bills that culminated in the passing of the Patient Protection and Affordable Care Act of 2010—landmark legislation approved by Congress a year after Kennedy's death.[5]

Kennedy's grand-sweep politics grated with most every Republican and with moderate Democrats like Carter too, but it is unarguable that his efforts facilitated change in tackling health care crises like no other legislator in the twentieth century. We might assign these efforts to what Edward Shorter calls "the exercise of power: of the power that accrues from celebrity, from effectiveness in Senate, and from systematic and determined lobbying," but that does not make them any less meaningful. In fact, there was arguably more invisible graft than there was visible celebrity in Kennedy's efforts to ensure that health care is better coordinated and more equitable.[6] Kennedy's 1972 book on the national health crisis, *In Critical Condition*, written in response to a series of congressional hearings he led in spring 1971, concludes with a short paragraph: "We have a choice of conscience to make in America. It is a choice of whether we will assure each other and all Americans good health care at a cost they can afford....I urge Americans to search their hearts to choose and to make their choice known."[7] This "choice of conscience" is one that Kennedy continued to urge Congress and nine US presidents, from Johnson to Obama, to keep at the forefront of their minds.

The Affordable Care Act was in many ways the fulfilment and in other ways the frustration of Kennedy's efforts during his half century of public service. In its early years the ACA did not resolve the "medical maze" of services that Kennedy labeled a crisis—and it arguably hit the middle class hardest in better serving the poor—but its congressional champions believed that it was a comprehensive move to ensure all Americans had health insurance at a basic level.[8] Yet Kennedy's death in August 2009 following a diagnosis of aggressive brain cancer meant that these reform plans lurched into crisis mode. When the Republican Scott Brown won the now vacant Massachusetts senatorial seat it became easier for congressional Republicans to block what many of them feared was a socialist agenda or, at least, a move in that direction from which it would be difficult to scale back.

In late August 2008, at the Democratic National Convention, Kennedy spoke of health care reform as "the cause of my life" in his sustained effort to break the "old gridlock" that he believed incremental reform would not improve and may well just exacerbate.[9] He remained hopeful in the final year of his life that this was achievable, especially because Barack Obama made it a priority during his early months as president.[10] When Kennedy wrote to Obama (Kennedy's widow delivered the letter to the president in early September 2009), it was clear that in describing health care reform as "the great unfinished business of our society" the youngest Kennedy son's work was both personal and political:

> For me, this cause stretched across decades; it has been disappointed, but never finally defeated. It was the cause of my life.... You have reminded all of us that it concerns more than material things; that what we face is above all a moral issue; that at stake are not just the details of policy, but fundamental principles of social justice and the character of our country.[11]

Obama quoted these final two lines from Kennedy's letter in his September 9, 2009, speech to Congress on systemic reform, one of the most powerful by a US president on the topic of American health, even though Obama and his speechwriter Jon Favreau heavily revised it at the last minute.[12] The evocation of Kennedy by the new president served three ends. First, it enabled Obama to justify his bipartisan point that rugged individualism and "figuring out the appropriate size and role of government" were not mutually exclusive. Second, it enabled him to contrast the "bold and decisive action" of progressive reform with the recent fear that the country's "financial system was on the verge of collapse." Third, it gave the plans an authenticity and historical weight that allowed him to push back on oppositional views that government-backed health insurance would lead to "death panels" and "forced vaccinations," conspiracies that the Tea Party spread in town hall meetings that summer.[13] Kennedy's emphasis on social justice shaped Obama's belief that this debate would be pivotal in defining the country's character by yoking pragmatic effort to idealistic reform, one of the objectives of which was to avert the crisis of thirty million legal citizens who lacked health insurance. Seeking a high moral register in an effort to reorient this fraught and long-running debate—and evoking the reformist ambitions of Franklin Roosevelt in the mid-1930s and Lyndon Johnson in the mid-1960s—Obama pictured health care as central to the future of the country, stating that "we did not come here just to clean up crises, we came here to build a future."[14]

What this future looks like a century after the inaugural moment of modern public health during the Woodrow Wilson presidency was fiercely contested in the 2010s. It was clear that the Affordable Care

Act, in its troubled passing and implementation, was always likely to be a compromise solution as a national health care model, even as it sought to fulfill earlier failed attempts to institute a government-backed health insurance system that would offer some protection to vulnerable Americans. Toward the close of his September 2009 speech Obama invoked the politics of vulnerability: "our predecessors understood that the danger of too much government is matched by the perils of too little, that without the leavening hand of wise policy, markets can crash, monopolies can stifle competition, the vulnerable can be exploited." In this respect, Obama saw the health question as fundamentally an American question:

> They knew that when any government measure, no matter how carefully crafted and beneficial, is subject to scorn, when any efforts to help people in need are attacked as un-American, when facts and reason are thrown overboard and only timidity passes for wisdom, and we can no longer engage in a civil conversation with each other over the things that truly matter, that at that point, we don't merely lose our capacity to solve big challenges, we lose something essential about ourselves.[15]

On these grounds, legislators fashioned ACA to be responsive to vulnerable communities, the poor, and the unemployed, but the act retained markets and did not look to government to "solve every problem."[16] The ACA's individual mandate that required everyone to purchase health insurance or pay a tax penalty remained controversial. Yet, in his speech, Obama sketched out a middle ground between the global and the local—as Robert Bellah did in *The Good Society* seventeen years earlier—in which it is possible to navigate competing agendas and where active citizenship can lead to meaningful action at all societal levels.

Such idealism was sorely tested, though, when it came to launching a robust enrollment system at HealthCare.gov on October 1, 2013, because the website kept crashing and the Department of Health and Human Services had limited oversight of the technology (this public-relations disaster led to the resignation of health secretary Kathleen Sebelius in June 2014). Even for its supporters, the ACA did not fix the crisis in health care delivery or the underinvestment in public health, particularly when Congress began to make budget cuts to the ACA Prevention and Public Health Fund from 2013. The ACA certainly did not satisfy the outspoken independent Vermont senator Bernie Sanders, whose emphasis on universal health care as a human right during his two bids to become the Democratic presidential nominee found momentum among congressional progressives as a model of economic redistribution.

Sanders's long-term commitment to Medicare for All (legislation he unsuccessfully introduced to the Senate in September 2017) built on the aspirations of his mentor Ted Kennedy and his ardent belief that "a for-profit health care system distorts medical priorities" because it prioritizes prescription drugs and "high-tech procedures" over disease prevention and health education.[17] Suspicions remained—not only on the political right—that Medicare for All was socialized medicine that would delimit or eliminate choice, even though some versions of it retained supplemental private insurance.[18] The cost of a single-payer system is highly contested; its champions claim that it would slightly lower health care spending, while detractors believe it would cost an additional $32.6 trillion over a decade, to 2030.[19]

Disagreement and conflict through the Obama years paled into insignificance when President Trump launched an unrelenting attack on the central tenets of Obamacare in his first year in the White House. Trump had started to discredit Obamacare as a candidate back in 2015; using the language of disaster, he called the "un-Affordable" Care Act a "catastrophe."[20] As president, Trump was quick to declare the ACA prematurely dead at a time he was pushing HHS to spend less on promoting insurance choices and to minimize the open-enrollment season as ploys to reduce its take-up.[21] In this respect, the declared crisis was largely a manufactured one, given that congressional Republicans predicated tax reform and increased Department of Defense spending on the dismantling of the ACA. This was in part an ideological project (even though their own health care plans were very vague) and partly a personal attack on the legacy of Obama shaped by what *Vanity Fair* called Trump's "dangerously limited" awareness of health care reform that the article claimed was contributing to the "national crisis."[22] Just as Obama saw the ACA as defining the nation's future, Trump saw its dismantling as pivotal to reducing entitlement spending and in realizing the Republican plan to replace the ACA with a marketized model. For Robert Bellah, to whom I return in the following sections, Trump's emphasis would represent a resurgence of hyperindividualism over the "moral balancing" and "cultivation" exemplified by Obama's 2009 speech to Congress.[23]

HEALTH PROMOTION AND HEALTH SECURITY

As an example of what Bellah calls global interdependence, the World Health Organization accord is a major benchmark in early twenty-first-century health practice in its promotion of basic standards of health and committing nations with advanced economies to provide aid for poor and postconflict countries.[24] The accord stemmed from the Ottawa Charter, drafted in 1986 at the first international conference for health promotion as "a process of enabling people to increase control over, and to improve, their health," at a time when the WHO was starting to regroup in response to the needs of developing nations.[25] Embodied by the slogan "Health for All," the view of WHO members that health should be "a resource for everyday life, not the objective of living" was reaffirmed at the Jakarta Conference of 1997. That conference added to the list of vital resources required for good health a better understanding of infectious diseases and mental health as well as transnational factors including "the integration of the global economy, financial markets and trade, wide access to media and communications technology, and environmental degradation."[26] Global health governance poses important questions about accountability, human rights, sustainability, and a careful balancing of sociological and biomedical perspectives.[27] But these national and global commitments are also strong examples of what Robert Bellah calls the need to balance "high ideals" with a "soberly realistic stance" to vulnerabilities and inequalities in health potentiality.[28]

Bill Clinton half echoed the WHO "Health for All" slogan in his late-1990s speeches, following his pronouncement of a National Public Health Week on March 13, 1995. This slogan chimed with the links Clinton drew between "the health of all Americans" and the protection of ecosystems in his 1996 book *Between Hope and History* as an example of what Bellah (writing four years earlier) called an "inclusive rallying point that brings together concerns for social justice, economic vitality, and environmental integrity."[29] Though he was keen to develop global markets to advance US economic interests, most notable was Clinton's program to eradicate racial discrimination in health by the year 2010, a feature of his "One America for the 21st Century: Forging a New Future" commission of 1997–99.[30] His presidential speeches very often focused on economic opportunity, but the report of this commission (chaired by the African American studies scholar John Hope Franklin) contains a section on race and health (based on a July 10, 1998, meeting) that spans structural inequities, discrimination, culturally competent care, and data gathering about health access for underserved communities.[31]

However, Clinton's speeches of the late 1990s did little to frame health topics in internationalist terms, except occasionally in respect to HIV/AIDS. And when President Bush turned his attention to global health and AIDS relief in his January 2003 State of the Union address (in part prompted by a 2000 report by the National Intelligence Council on AIDS and global security), it was framed primarily as a security risk to the United States rather than in strictly humanitarian terms. Bush tried to strike a compassionate chord for answering pressing global health needs, and he described his $15 billion President's Emergency Plan for AIDS Relief (PEPFAR) in Africa and the Caribbean over a five-year period as "a work of mercy beyond all international efforts."[32] Clinical trials in Africa overseen by NIH immunologist Anthony Fauci and AIDS work in rural Haiti conducted by Paul Farmer shaped this ambitious project of treating two million people and implementing far-reaching prevention plans across these economically poor regions by 2008.[33] PEPFAR is an emblem of long-term investment in a public health model that can operate effectively at home and abroad and that can complement WHO's International Health Regulations, established in 2005 to ensure cross-border disease control. Conversely, though, we might be tempted to view Bush's language of compassion as a ploy to take the edge off his emphasis on national security risks that the Bush administration believed the country was facing in 2003 in the wake of 9/11 and other terrorist threats.

On this evidence, international health emergencies tend to enter the national conversation only when they become domestic threats. They can also sometimes cast a panicky shadow over less visible domestic crises such as obesity, which the *Healthy People 2000* report acknowledged was on the rise in the 1990s and that (according to the WHO) put the United States a lowly twenty-fourth in the world for health attainment at that time.[34] This on-off focus on international health is true of other nation-states, but it has been particularly resonant over the last twenty years when the intertwining of national destinies suggests that the WHO slogan "Health for All" also means "Care for All" regardless of how close or distant the geographical threat is to American shores. This perspective is captured by the emphasis on planetary health in the 2018 Smithsonian Natural History Museum exhibition *Outbreak: Epidemics in a Connected World*, cosponsored by the Centers for Disease Control and Prevention and the National Foundation for Infectious Diseases, among others, and with contributions from WHO and EcoHealth Alliance. The exhibition charts epidemics from the 1918–19 influenza pandemic to the Zika outbreak of 2015–16, and it advocates for more effective vaccines, increased community involvement, and international collaboration between interdisciplinary teams of experts, first responders, and aid workers. The *Outbreak* exhibition seems politically neutral. However, with its visual emphasis on interconnectivity and rhetoric of "working together" and "one health," it offers a retort to the partisan politics of 2016–18 when antiscience, nationalist, and nativist agendas were jeopardizing long-standing international agreements on health and environmental standards, the need for which were revealed so starkly during the COVID-19 world emergency of 2020. The exhibition documents the threat of epidemics but steers away from fearmongering "state of emergency" language that can erode citizens' rights in the name of a national cause or that normalizes a crisis mindset within everyday life.

A case in point is the US presidential race of 2016 in which the Republican nominee Donald Trump took repeated opportunities to label Obamacare a catastrophe, relied on the politics of denunciation rather than concrete campaign commitments on health care, and did not address international health topics at all. This is perhaps unsurprising as Trump ran on a nationalist "Make American Great Again" agenda that was as nostalgic as Bill Clinton's "One America in the 21st Century" initiative was aspirational—a hopeful mood that Obama amplified in his 2008 presidential campaign.[35] The 2016 Democratic nominee Hillary Clinton was more convincing than Trump on health promotion and health security in her election manifesto *Stronger Together: A Blueprint for America's Future*, released midway through her presidential campaign. The short section in the manifesto on "Global Health and Pandemics" was the strongest Democratic platform statement of 2016 of the need for the United States to nurture health security across national borders. Citing new threats that stemmed from climate change, globalization, and waves of epidemics—Zika, SARS, MERS, Ebola, H1N1—Clinton and her vice presidential running mate Tim Kaine mapped out the public health implications.[36]

Claiming that the United States acted decisively in stopping the spread of Ebola beyond West Africa (itself a contestable claim), Clinton and Kaine emphasized the risks of failing to respond rapidly to, if not predict, the next epidemic.[37] They list destabilized regions, political unrest, and biological warfare as the chief threats to strong public health both at home and abroad. They recognized consistent foreign policy is required to provide overseas aid and to ensure the stability of developing and postconflict countries and that domestic health infrastructure needs to be robust yet flexible enough to deal with emergencies without lurching into crisis mode. These pledges to safeguard the nation and to grow capacity in "emerging economies to protect public health, track cases of disease, and rapidly scale emergency medical equipment" echoed the Grand Challenges for Development of the US Agency for International Development (USAID), a humanitarian initiative launched by President Kennedy in 1961 to tackle poverty and "promote resilient, democratic societies."[38] It is notable that Hillary Clinton's daughter, Chelsea, channeled these views in early 2020. In responding to Donald Trump's initially dismissive attitude to the COVID-19 outbreak, Chelsea Clinton claimed the "Trump administration is chronically inept at, and seemingly uninterested in, any type of long-term planning," especially as it had, in 2018, scaled back the National Security Council's global security unit.[39]

All these points are sound ones with regard to long-term planning, resilience, and interconnecting health and environmental agendas to offset more kneejerk or panic reactions, even though the dual emphasis on technological solutions and health advocacy was not markedly different from the Clinton administration's agenda in the late 1990s. For example, Bill Clinton's Richard Dimbleby Lecture, delivered in London in December 2001 nearly a year after he had departed the White House, focused on the opportunities that globalization could bring to a range of civic commitments and business enterprises. The lecture, titled "Struggle for the Soul of the 21st Century," tried to recapture the optimism that saw his administration balance the budget at the end of the 1990s and avoid any large-scale war, despite a controversial military intervention in Bosnia. That is not the say that the lecture was without warnings, given that Clinton's tone was sobered by the recent terrorist attacks of 9/11. He focused on the looming threat of global warming and the breakdown of stable ecosystems, and then went on to talk about an imminent crisis in public health triggered by the rise of transcontinental epidemics. His emphasis was on global and domestic concerns alike. Citing "one in four of all the people on earth who die, will die of AIDS, TB, malaria and infections related to diarrhoea. Most of them, little kids that never get clean water," he was concerned about the spread of AIDS in African countries, India, China, and the Caribbean.[40] As a warning to Republican politicians who tended to downplay the threat—or considered it a unique health problem faced by developing countries—the former president pointed out that as New York senator his wife was dealing with similar issues. It is revealing, though, that he mentioned immigrants from the Dominican Republic living in New York City. He was perhaps recalling a race riot of July 1992 a few months before his presidency began (the riot was in response to the fatal shooting of a Dominican youth by a white Manhattan policeman), or implying that white American communities were again victims of an outsider epidemic.

On the evidence of the public service of Jimmy and Rosalynn Carter, which is geared toward humanitarian aid abroad and better public understanding of health threats at home, perhaps it is the province of foundations such as the Carter Center in Atlanta, in collaboration with NGOs, to ensure that an awareness of international health threats enters the national conversation. In his 2007 book *Beyond the White House*, Jimmy Carter spoke about his postpresidential focus on peacekeeping, fighting disease, and supporting developmental work in the Global South. He wrote specifically of his "Closing the Gap" initiative of the mid-1980s in collaboration with CDC that sought to tackle "unnecessary disease" and "premature death" domestically and to eradicate smallpox and guinea worm disease around the world.[41] This twin focus on domestic and international health linked directly to Rosalynn Carter's mental health advocacy, which extended her primary focus as first lady and honorary chair of the 1978 President's Commission on Mental Health (as I discuss in chapter 5). As well as the Carter Center hosting an annual conference since 1985, the Carter Foundation has awarded over two hundred fellowships to encourage scientifically and culturally informed domestic health journalism, fellowships for international health journalists in South America and the Middle East, and a public health training initiative to support critical gaps in care in Sudan and Nigeria.[42] Rosalynn Carter's work from the mid-1980s through the 2010s is a potent example of what can be done via local and international collaboration to challenge mental health stigma and encourage active citizenship by raising awareness of health conditions that affect a quarter of Americans.[43]

The most obvious reason for the effectiveness of championing public health concerns beyond Congress and the White House is to put partisan politics aside. This was the aim of Bill Clinton's and George H. W. Bush's collaboration to establish a Bush-Clinton Katrina Fund of over $100 million in December 2005 for aid relief in Louisiana, Mississippi, and Alabama to help local faith-based and educational institutions.[44] Well-meaning celebrity interventions are not always effective though. One example is actor Brad Pitt's Make It Right Foundation, which worked with the Clinton Global Initiative and a New Orleans architect to design new affordable housing in the Lower Ninth Ward following the mass damage caused by Hurricane Katrina, but only for the new residents to find many homes had been constructed from substandard materials.[45]

Humanitarian causes invariably carry ideological freight, especially when it comes to environmental health. For instance, President Trump misjudged the scale and tenor of the crisis when deadly wildfires swept through California in November 2018, choosing to blame poor forest floor practices even when the worsening situation was labeled a public health emergency, while the Trump administration's immigration policy on the southern border was widely criticized for inflaming critical health conditions, especially for children separated from their migrant parents.[46] Whatever the belief about the provenance of climate change or disease, the effects on public health should go beyond partisanship. Yet when it comes to relief efforts at home and abroad budgetary constraints are often the bottom line—especially at times of escalating defense and military spending—rather than seen as one-third of a triple bottom line where people and planet are equal priorities. This makes private fundraising, as in the case of the Bush-Clinton Katrina Fund, all the more important. It also returns us to this book's initial case study, the Mississippi River Flood of 1927 when President Coolidge was keen to stay at arm's length from the relief effort for fear of setting a precedent, relying instead on Herbert Hoover and the Red Cross to oversee aid in the Delta. Nevertheless, as this section shows, the relationship between health promotion and health security is as complex as it is enduring, raising profound questions about health education, citizenship, welfare, and what Joseph Masco describes as the relationship between public health and escalating risk.

PUBLIC HEALTH AND HEALTH CITIZENSHIP

This emphasis on social justice returns us to the status of public health as we approach the first quarter mark of the twenty-first century for reducing the risks and the scale of health crises. Writing in 1998, Richard Levinson argues that public health at the federal level is often caught between being "an institution of social control" and a service in "a quest for social justice," but at the nongovernmental level Nancy Stepan argues "human agency" and "the role of deliberate political choices" are of equal importance within the arena of health care.[47] This agency spans a spectrum of rights linked to critical or potentially critical conditions of health and well-being. These include the right to choose with respect to reproductive health (a heated topic in 2018 with renewed calls by Republicans to repeal the landmark *Roe v. Wade* legislation of 1973); sex protection and rights for self-identifying LGBTQ+ Americans at a time when Trump's health department was looking to redefine sex in strictly biological terms; long-term federal and state commitment to health care facilities; access to public health information and mobile platforms; and culturally congruent health services that cater to diverse communities and do not overlook traditional healing practices in favor of biomedical solutions.[48]

In addition, most would agree that an independent and well-informed press is equally important for promoting health rights and for preserving first amendment rights. However, when set against the recent rise in regional and residential health disparities and growing numbers of babies born with low birth weights, Stepan argues that the rhetoric of eradication—wars on drugs, on poverty, and on epidemics—frequently misses the broader public health implications. Instead, Stepan argues that what is required is the long-term cultivation of an ecology of differing yet coordinated public health approaches rather than a one-step solution.[49] To this, CNN's medical correspondent Elizabeth Cohen would add that patients should be empowered with the knowledge and tactics to navigate a paternalistic health care system that at times gives faulty diagnoses and does not present the fullest range of options. Marc Siegel, as medical correspondent for the rival network Fox News, takes a more conspiratorial tone, arguing that patients need to inoculate themselves against the fear tactics often deployed by government, big pharma, and in some parts of the media.[50]

Stepan's insights suggest that the rhetoric is as important as the substance of public health policy, especially in 2018—a year in which 41 percent of voters put health care as the number one issue in the national midterm election, and when Democrats and Republicans were each claiming they were the best party to protect preexisting conditions.[51] The need for informed and understandable health journalism that does not simplify complex issues is just one aspect of better communication and openness in the sphere of public health. This aligns with David Rosner's and Gerald Markowitz's argument that twenty-first-century national emergencies show that not only does crisis preparedness need to be improved, but that the government's "failure to communicate honestly about uncertainty is a big mistake" because silence and misinformation can worsen a crisis as much as inflammatory rhetoric can.[52] There is no silver bullet, of course, and any model is open to the criticism that there is either too much or too little state control, and also that health journalism is either too passive in echoing orthodox medical opinion or unnecessarily antagonistic in its ideological critique of government.

Robert Bellah's emphasis on localism and citizen participation offers some answers, but only when federal oversight is responsive and when competing spending priorities do not squeeze state health budgets. An example of transparent communication at the federal level is the commitment since 2012 to increase public access to government data via the Open Data Initiatives program, which interfaces with the Health Data Initiative that HHS launched in 2010 as a public-private partnership. Yet there is always a danger with controversial issues such as climate change, unemployment, and reproductive health that data is at times skewed for ideological reasons. This was a heated topic during the culture wars of the 1990s, especially when in 1993 Bill Clinton lifted the "gag rule" that meant that HHS had for five previous years prohibited companies that received Title X funding (funding targeted at uninsured individuals or those on low incomes) "from providing their patients with full information and counseling concerning pregnancy."[53] Clinton was keen that there should be no censors on medical information aligned with his prochoice beliefs, but this was again a key issue for the Trump administration when in summer 2019 a court ruling again restricted Title X funding, during a phase that has seen the principles of open data neglected or even undermined.

These differing priorities also raise questions about the relationship between health and citizenship that runs through this book: from environmental activism, to the lobbying efforts of ex-patient groups and veterans for more responsive services, to advocacy around women's and minority health, to informed news reporting, and to community volunteerism. One instance of such a citizenship intervention is First Lady Michelle Obama's Let's Move! Campaign, which began in 2010 to raise nutritional awareness among children with the goal of reducing obesity. Obama describes this as a campaign with a "fun public face" designed to "making a human appeal as opposed to a regulatory one."[54] A second example is the work of Chirlane McCray, chairwoman of the Mayor's Fund to Advance the City of New York, to implement a mental health support network across the city, though both the cost and governance of ThriveNYC have proved controversial.[55] Whether fronted by a public figure and backed by government funding or stirring from grassroots levels, a strong model of health citizenship offers a commitment to the health of diverse communities and a middle ground for thinking about health neither as the state's ultimate responsibility nor solely in individualistic terms.[56]

While "health for all" remains an idealistic aspiration and has waxed and waned in US presidential rhetoric, the WHO priority of cultivating community involvement via bottom-up approaches that improve health literacy and access to health services are equally as vital as responsible governance attentive to diverse health needs, cross-border health regulations, and independent media platforms. To return to Robert Bellah, these aspects suggest that health is understood best as a search for interpersonal meaning and something fundamental on which life and ecosystems depend. To abandon this quest for a deeper communal language is to risk ignoring that US citizens form the active body of the state rather than being its subjects, or reducing a complex and variegated health landscape to a financial and bureaucratic calculus, or provoking panic-inducing fears about epidemics, invasion, and loss.

Bellah argues in *Habits of the Heart* that "the fullest conception of civic politics that emerges from a citizens' movement" is to interlink "local participation to a national dialogue."[57] This is a much broader notion of polity than a "politics of interest" that can often motivate a group cause but is hard to sustain long term, especially as alliances between groups are often fleeting and contingent. In terms of public health, this notion of "fullest conception" would be a moral ecology that is sensitive to multiple scales and responds to vulnerability on both geographical and structural levels. Nevertheless, there is something utopian—as well as exceptionalist—in this notion of "fullest conception" through which personal and group interest is subordinate to a span of relationships with others "in a society organized through public dialogue." Bellah elaborates on this point in *The Good Society*:

> Such politics is premised on active citizen involvement and discussion—with issues of long-term purpose and consequence taking precedence over the simpler indices upon which current policy analysis focuses—public participation in administrative decisions, constituency involvement in corporate decisions, and a closer public monitoring of legislative action, through review commissions and public debates.[58]

Even though Bellah admits that "this vision remains sporadic and largely local in scope," health citizenship can nevertheless emerge from and strengthen the "middle ground" to "open up spaces for reflection, participation, and the transformation of our institutions."[59] Such a goal is always vulnerable to new critical health challenges that problematize community participation (such as the social distancing measures implemented to stem the COVID-19 pandemic) or where constituency involvement wins out on a rhetorical level but does not significantly change social institutions or the behaviors with respect to class, race, gender, and sexuality of those that manage and finance them.[60] Yet this model offers a conceptual and creative space with the potential to move beyond panic and planning crisis cycles by cultivating what Bellah calls a "common moral grounding" that gives "witness to the enormous possibilities in human experience," a view informed by his liberal Episcopalian beliefs and his commitment to social justice.[61] As well as offering a space to reflect on the experience of health and illness via histories, narratives, music, and images—all aspects of Bellah's notion of a "politics of imagination"—he puts faith in localism and in citizens becoming more attentive to and participating in their shared environment.

There are dangers in conceiving of health as a form of what Bellah terms "civil religion" in privileging certain kinds of social networks and marginalizing others, but this concept nonetheless informs the idea of a moral commitment to public health that was circulating eighty years earlier during Woodrow Wilson's presidency.[62] Viewed progressively, this dovetails with what Bellah describes as a common culture that embraces difference and gives impetus to "citizenship-oriented care" initiatives for vulnerable Americans, such as the Citizens Project facilitated by the Connecticut Department of Mental Health and Addiction that addresses "community disconnection among people in recovery who have experienced incarceration."[63] One might argue that this impetus veers toward socialized medicine, which is more in keeping with Central and South American countries than the economic, political, and social strata of the United States, arousing the suspicions on the right that health care is part of a deep state conspiracy that will delimit or undermine freedoms. These conspiratorial fears aside, the ethical dimension of public health inflects a number of federal plans and aspirations I have traced through a turbulent century, especially the ideal of community health and what Charles Rosenberg calls the "process of interaction between phenomenon, perception, and policy."[64]

If only, as the antipoverty leader Mitchell Sviridoff claimed in 1966, "human development problems" could be tackled as a "whole and not in fragments," then a less piecemeal and reactive approach to health security and health promotion might be achieved without the sharp

disinvestment between programs that is common with changes in political leadership.[65] For Paul Farmer this would be "making public health
matter," by reaching "across boundaries of state and ethnicity and language to make common cause with those who bear the microbial burdens of poverty," whereas in Robert Bellah's thought it would connect
a "politics of imagination" to a "politics of generativity" that "takes
social inclusion and participation as a key theme."[66] When cultivated
over the long term, this social ontology has the dual potential to bring
about the moral reform of social institutions and to reestablish public
trust in democratic forms of government that are seen neither as the
enactor of structural violence nor the sympathetic answer to everyone's
health needs. This might, as I have argued, not only foster a longer-
term historical perspective on health reform but also prevent a failure
of imagination that Farmer claims often impedes the tackling of health
and development problems.[67] It should also lead to careful use of crisis
rhetoric, as the CDC recognized by avoiding the word "crisis" in its
2018 publication *Health, United States, 2017* despite alarming mortality statistics. We need to return to the 1918–19 influenza pandemic to
see a comparable downward turn in US life expectancy, this time due to
opioid-related overdoses, suicide, and chronic liver disease, a trend that
worsened dramatically in 2020 with mass deaths due to COVID-19.[68]

There is always a gap between *is* and *ought* when it comes to health
care, but Bellah's concept of moral balancing and the yoking of resilient ideals to sober realities is instructive for thinking through responsive crisis management, in tandem with what in 2018 the CDC director Robert Redfield called putting "science into action to protect U.S.
health."[69] This possibility, it seems, pivots on the revival of participatory democracy. The ideal may have lost the potency of the mid-1960s,
but it nonetheless continues to reveal itself through the political collec-
tivism of grassroots groups that, at least in terms of a politics of interest,
pressure state and federal governments to act responsibly. At the dawn
of this third decade of the twenty-first century, with partisanship and
paralysis gripping the US Congress and with a new public health emergency engulfing the world, the cultivation of an imaginative and genera-
tive politics might lessen the risk of future crises and help to transform
panic into participation.

Coda 2020

On March 31, 2020, the White House Coronavirus Task Force held its daily briefing for selected press reporters. President Trump was increasingly visible and vocal at the press briefings during the month of March. It was a surprise, then, that following initial remarks in which he spoke about this "great national trial" against a "deadly virus," outlined a small business loan scheme, and praised the nation's medical capability, Trump gave over the podium to Deborah Birx. As the Coronavirus Response Coordinator, Birx was one of two prominent scientific figures who regularly joined the president to face the press. The other figure was Anthony Fauci, the widely respected director of the National Institute of Allergy and Infectious Diseases. Other health leaders on the task force—Secretary of Health and Human Services Alex Azar II, Director of the Centers for Disease Control and Prevention Robert Redfield, and Surgeon General of the United States Jerome Adams—appeared at the podium less frequently as the crisis mounted, from early isolated cases in Washington and California in late January to initial hospitalized deaths by late February to a full-scale national emergency by mid-March.

The importance of the March 31 briefing was that Birx displayed a series of dramatic charts to illustrate the rapid spread and trajectory of the coronavirus SARS-CoV-2 across all fifty states. Trump gave Birx the podium to offer medical justification for temporarily shutting down parts of the economy, extending an initial "15 Days to Slow the Spread" strategy to another thirty days. Birx emphasized the importance of community spirit before introducing her first slide. Titled "Goals of Community Mitigation," the slide featured an ominous dark blue bell curve to illustrate how the COVID-19 pandemic may have killed up to 2.2 million Americans without a full mitigation strategy. Superimposed on this heavily marked "blue mountain" was a shallower and lighter arc: a "stippled hill," as she called it. This flatter hill projected between 100,000 to 240,000 deaths over a longer period, even with interventions aimed at reducing the strain on the health care infrastructure and flattening the curve of regional infections. These graphics marked a sobering end to a turbulent month, reinforced by Fauci's reasoned scientific case for pursuing a national mitigation strategy. Vice President Mike Pence, who the president had charged with leading the Task Force at the end of February, adopted a different, more heroic tone. Pence praised the president's foresight and ability to communicate effectively with state governors, medical leaders, and chief executives, and he urged Americans not to be discouraged, thanking them for observing travel and self-quarantining guidelines.

As the most visible faces of the federal response to this latest American health crisis, Trump, Birx, Fauci, and Pence were four contrasting figures who appeared regularly at the White House coronavirus press briefings in spring 2020, offering a dramatic early-evening backdrop to one of the grimmest emergencies in global history. Trump's prepared remarks had more substance than his freewheeling replies to reporters, in which he displayed his displeasure when pushed to say why the federal government did not act earlier, seemingly doing little proactively in February to isolate early cases and conduct rigorous contact tracing. Though the president was quick to stop flights from China for non-US citizens, the administration lost valuable weeks before extending flight restrictions to Europe and working with state governors to promote social distancing. The "miracle" and "burst of light" that the president wished for "in a relatively short period of time" contrasted with the mounting death toll that represented arguably the worst viral crisis since the Great Influenza pandemic of 1918–19.[1]

Between them, Fauci and Birx had a distinguished history of dealing with infectious disease, collaborating fifteen years earlier on George W. Bush's President's Emergency Plan for AIDS Relief. Their influential work on PEPFAR reprised Fauci's leadership role at the National Institutes of Health in the mid-1980s, when he advised President Reagan's surgeon general C. Everett Koop to adopt a holistic and responsive HIV/AIDS policy that helped to shift the tone after years of federal neglect. Previously serving under five administrations (three Republican, two Democratic), Fauci was a bipartisan public health leader, an experienced immunologist, and a talented speaker. He was aware that what Mike Pence called a "whole of government" response meant that a risk-adverse "pure public health standpoint" needs to be balanced with other priorities, so as not to ignore broader policy issues by focusing narrowly on the immediate task of saving lives and eliminating disease. However, neither Birx nor Fauci had faced a national crisis of such rapid escalation, nor had they previously worked this intimately with an administration that placed economic interests above all else.

From April onward, the confirmed death toll in the United States was higher than any other country, but Trump was keen to stress, in an election year, that the United States was doing better per capita than most European nations and that China was likely underreporting its death count. By mid-April, the Institute of Health Metrics and Evaluation (IHME) had optimistically scaled down its mortality prediction to 60,000 with full mitigation.[2] However, by April 30 official deaths had already exceeded this number, leading the IHME to nudge projections upward. The IHME more than doubled its mortality predictions to 147,000 on May 12, based on a range of states reopening their nonessential businesses before the dates that CDC recommended, and by September the institute was making the prediction of around 400,000 American deaths by early 2021.[3]

As the initial epicenter of the domestic crisis, New York witnessed between 30 to 40 percent of the nation's hospitalized deaths through April. This was despite the mitigation work of Governor Andrew Cuomo who, in his own televised daily briefings, mixed a keen awareness of medical science with operational detail. Cuomo recognized the physical and psychological aspects of the virus, given that high fever and hallucinations often accompanied the respiratory illness and that social distancing could easily lead to social isolation, with cases of addiction relapse and domestic violence rising during the lockdown.[4] In their public responses, Fauci and Cuomo enacted the words of Woodrow Wilson 108 years earlier when, in his address to the American Medical Association of June 1912, he claimed that medical leaders should be the "guardians of communities not only with regard to those general sanitary problems...but of a great many moral problems also."[5] For example, in a CNN interview on Easter Sunday, Fauci recognized the moral weight of this "historic ordeal": "people are going to write about it as a terrible affront on us as a nation, to our heath and our well-being."[6]

When pressed on his personal beliefs, the immunologist gave a persuasive response that faith "will take an important role" in dialogue with scientific reason, echoing Robert Bellah's concept of civil religion, with a strong moral orientation toward public service and community well-being.

In contrast, Trump switched between espousing a blind faith in miracles and a supreme faith in his administration's ability to respond effectively and with sufficient resources to fight COVID-19, a conflict he often portrayed in militaristic terms. The president was eager to keep the economy as buoyant as possible during the lockdown period, including working with Congress on a stimulus package that awarded $1,200 to up to 150 million taxpayers below individual and household earning thresholds. We might credit the Coronavirus Aid, Relief, and Economic Security (CARES) Act, passed in bipartisan fashion by Congress in late March, as an example of the sympathetic state in action, in recognition of the mental and physical health toll of economic hardship. Equally, though, we might view these payments as tokenistic given they barely scratched the surface of systemic structural violence at the juncture of precarity, poverty, and poor health (the act arguably did more to offer tax breaks to corporations than to protect the vulnerable).

On most counts, Trump was the wrong kind of president for such an emergency. This was not only in his inability to grasp urgency and scale, but also because he had little experience of responsible governance, lacked empathy, and seemed unaware of Dwight Eisenhower's conviction of 1953 that federal government officials should make every effort to show they are "loyal in their motives and reliable in the discharge of their duties. Only a combination of both loyalty and reliability promises genuine security."[7]

In truth, an earlier and more tightly coordinated federal response may not have decreased cases, given that Italy, Spain, France, and the United Kingdom all had major death counts by mid-April, though these countries were also "playing a tragic game of catch-up," as the New Yorker called it, after being slow to act in February.[8] Yet, the examples of New Zealand, Germany, and Denmark show that an early response, a firm mitigation strategy, strong yet compassionate leadership from above and below, and consistent public health messaging could help flatten the infection and death curves. We can be reasonably certain that both curves would have been flatter had Trump listened to the advice of HHS and CDC officials in January to prepare a federal response ahead of the first US deaths in late February.

If this grave public health emergency revealed a crisis of national leadership, then Trump had an added problem because he refused to take ultimate responsibility for an initially slow and then erratic response. This echoed previous US presidential responses to natural disasters as a tactic to deflect blame and to avoid full responsibility for the recovery process. Despite the mobilization in mid-March of the Federal Emergency Management Agency to coordinate operations, the president seemed to lack a national plan.[9] Trump was quick to find scapegoats. Most notably, he blamed the World Health Organization for failing to give early enough warnings and for being favorable to China, leading him to suspend federal funding to the WHO, even as he ignored the domestic intelligence that gave time to prepare and the view of CDC that global health surveillance and international cooperation was now more important than ever.

In reality, Trump prevaricated before following Fauci's and Birx's recommendations, yet he bristled when probed by the press, bragging about the availability of tests and how he could instruct governors to reopen states on his timetable, some of whom, like Governor Cuomo, were struggling for equipment and to keep their health force operational. At a Senate hearing of mid-May, Robert Redfield and Anthony Fauci affirmed that coordination between CDC, NIH, and the White House had been productive. Yet the Trump administration seemed to ignore the guidelines of the CDC for safely opening up states, and medical professionals thought the president was reckless when he promoted the antimalaria drugs chloroquine and hydroxychloroquine (unverified for COVID-19, and which might exacerbate heart conditions), speculated about bogus medical theories, and was personally reluctant to endorse the health benefits of wearing masks in public.[10] It was ironic, though not entirely surprising, when Trump contracted COVID-19 in early October after disregarding health and safety guidelines, prompting the editors of the *New England Journal of Medicine* to claim that national leadership had "failed at almost every step.[11]

Given Trump's propensity to use "disaster" to refer to things he does not like, it was noticeable that he was keen to avoid panic discourses. Nevertheless, Trump embodied what Jackie Orr in *The Panic Diaries* (2006) calls "contagions of suggestion" by tweeting regularly to stir his political base and speaking in vague and conspiratorial tones, implicating, in turn, the liberal media, congressional progressives, Democratic governors, HHS inspectors, and Communist China.[12] When the president criticized WHO in mid-April, he did so by means of insinuation, blaming the humanitarian organization without evidence for "unleashing the contagion around the world" by failing to control borders: "That was a horrible, tragic mistake, or perhaps they knew. Because if they knew the gravity, that would be an even worse offense."[13] Although it is vital that WHO remains vigilant, impartial, and transparent, Fauci's public statements epitomized what Orr calls "reasonable truths" in contrast to Trump's "contagions of suggestion" that the president continued to peddle when he revived the coronavirus press briefings in July, but this time without his health officials at the podium. Trump dodged questions of accountability in his self-professed role of national cheerleader and he appeared to ignore the state-by-state reports of the Coronavirus Task Force that identified widespread danger zones.[14] In contrast, Fauci echoed Robert Oppenheimer's belief of the mid-1950s (see chapter 3) regarding the importance of being candid about what is known and honest about what is unknown: in this instance, accurately predicting viral behavior, antibody immunity, and a reliable vaccine time frame. For his ability to triangulate between public health, politics, and the media, Fauci embodied what Senator Richard J. Durbin of Illinois calls "the north star for America in terms of finding our way through this dangerous journey."[15]

Fauci realized it is premature to judge the resilience of a public health system in the midst of a crisis and that, soon enough, there would be many books written about the uncertain causes and global consequences of COVID-19. Yet, the early months of 2020 offer a paradigmatic crisis that returns me to this book's three arguments, as outlined in the preface: it enables us to reflect on types and scales of health crises, the vulnerabilities they reveal, and the possibility of an active public health culture that can be both responsive and reflective.

As a novel and highly infectious coronavirus, thought to have first transmitted between animals (possibly a bat) and humans, the COVID-19 crisis was different from the others documented in his book. Fauci was keen to correct journalists who made erroneous parallels to other viral outbreaks and recognized that its health impact was both physical and psychological, while keeping his responses proportionate to avoid "derangements of scale" that fuel rumor and speculation.[16] The transmissibility of the virus and the scale of social distancing across the globe distinguished this from previous pandemics, but there were also resonances. For example, the possibility that a second and third wave of the coronavirus could occur into 2021 would, if realized, follow the rhythm of the Great Influenza pandemic. That the virus emerged in

Wuhan, China, in December 2019 and spread from East Asia led to instances of xenophobia, including abuse and hate crimes leveled at Asian Americans, echoing the stigmatizing attitudes toward groups often falsely blamed for escalating historic health crises (given its prevalence, the virus may have come to the Atlantic coastal states from Europe).[17] Difficulties in devising a national strategy for reliable and timely virus testing echoed the logistical problems faced by the Eisenhower administration in the 1950s with respect to the polio vaccine. Finally, given that the CDC had been ramping up pandemic preparedness for seasonal influenza over nearly two decades, and that international cooperation was a trusted model for slowing viral spread, it was surprising that proactive containment and mitigation strategies were not in place in the early weeks of 2020.

All the crises explored in this book reveal social vulnerabilities that often hide in plain sight. In the book's first half, we saw that environmental disasters disproportionately affect poor minority communities. Surgeon General Jerome Adams recognized this was also the case for the coronavirus, given that African American patients represented around 30 percent of total hospitalizations by mid-April, closely followed by Hispanic patients, far in excess of population demographics, and the federal government did nothing to protect Native American reservations from the viral spread. That the prevalence was particularly high in the cities of Detroit and New Orleans (the latter probably spread during Mardi Gras) reveals the virus disproportionately affected communities that were already under economic strain and with a prevalence of preexisting comorbidities such as hypertension, cardiovascular disease, and diabetes.[18] In addition to health threats among prison communities, inside homeless shelters, and for social groups facing food insecurity, seniors over seventy years old were particularly vulnerable, especially those contracting COVID-19 in nursing homes who were not included in initial official statistics (from April care homes were required to inform CDC and families if they were experiencing infections). Health workers were also highly vulnerable because of the dearth of personal protective equipment in some states; without fast and reliable tests in the early weeks, doctors and nurses could not be sure if they were reinfecting the patients they were treating. The psychological toll of social distancing was unprecedented for many Americans, but the traumatic strain on care workers was immeasurable as the body count escalated in hospitals, with dying patients typically isolated from their families.

The widely repeated phrase "We're all in this together" was

emblematic of fragmented yet hopeful communities living under the shadow of COVID-19. With this in mind, on March 17, Joe Biden, the presumptive Democratic presidential nominee, used the phrase during a video broadcast from his Delaware home in which he thanked all working Americans, especially health care professionals, as an aspect of his progressive labor policy. However, by revealing deep structural inequalities the crisis posed profound questions about the possibility of an active model of health citizenship that aligns with Robert Bellah's concept of a moral ecology.[19] Helping to bind together virtual communities were telehealth and mobile health interventions to support patients and digital communications to connect families and work colleagues. As such, technology provided some—though by no means all—of the answers on a level unimaginable twenty-five years earlier.[20] Yet, on a human scale, it was difficult at the height of the crisis for many citizens who did not work in emergency and health services to be proactive or to embody the kind of "politics of imagination"—as Bellah recommended—that took them far beyond self-care. Among ethically attuned practices were disciplined social distancing and mask wearing, refraining from panic buying, donating to food banks, participating in a network of phone check-ins for seniors, and volunteering to drop off food and medicine for isolated citizens, but these were fairly modest practices in restricted public spaces.[21]

With protestors clamoring for states to reopen before sustained decreases in infections, fears that new surveillance measures would infringe civil liberties, the perpetuation of stigmatizing attitudes, and likely midterm cuts in public spending, it is too early to say if this episode will force a step change in tackling health vulnerabilities and encouraging health citizenship, linking responsible state interventions to a renewed social contract between individuals and institutions. If the US government's actions during the COVID-19 emergency reveal similar mistakes to responses by previous administrations to the health crises discussed in these pages, then with a renewal of moral leadership we must hope that the lessons of 2020 mark a turning point that will transform fear into fellowship longer term.

October 2020

Acknowledgments

I am particularly grateful to the Lyndon B. Johnson Foundation for the award of a Moody Research Grant in summer 2018 and to the University of Leicester's Wellcome Trust Institutional Strategic Support Fund for financial support in spring 2018 and summer 2019, which made possible the research that informs this study. Librarians and archivists, too numerous to mention here by name, have been very generous with their time and expertise over the last eight years, which has enabled me to deepen and contour this study. I want to offer special thanks to Allen Fisher and Brian McNerney of the LBJ Presidential Library for helping me identify health and social policy material and for guiding me to the Administrative History Collection written in the final months of the Johnson administration. I would also like to thank Courtney Christman, who in 2017–18 recataloged the administrative history of the Department of Health, Education, and Welfare 1963–69, which makes it much easier for LBJ Library researchers to navigate the records of a time when the responsibility of HEW was expanding rapidly.

My thanks go to library staff at the Mississippi Department of Archives and History in Jackson; the New Orleans Public Library; the Archives and Special Collections at the Consortium Library, University of Alaska Anchorage; and the Barbara A. Matheson Special Collections Department, Gerald R. Sherratt Library, Southern Utah University, Cedar City. I am particularly grateful for the help I received from Martha DeMarre, manager of the Nuclear Testing Archive in Las Vegas;

Andrew Goldstein at the Valdez Museum Historical Archive, Alaska; Becky Butler at the Alaska and Polar Regions Collections and Archives, University of Alaska Fairbanks; Keith Shuler and Brittany Parris at the Jimmy Carter Presidential Library and Museum in Atlanta; Sandra Stillman, the museum coordinator for Greenville-Washington County, Mississippi; Francis Zavadil, chair of the Addiction Studies Program at the University of South Dakota; Daniel Weddington of the Special Collections Research Center at the University of Kentucky, Lexington; Alex Toner of the Special Collections and Archives at the University of Pittsburgh; Natalie Snoyman, the supervising librarian and archivist of the Lucretia Little History Room, Mill Valley Public Library, and Carrie Bond of Rapid City Public Library for her gracious assistance both during and following my visit to South Dakota in April 2018.

A number of friends and colleagues have helped me to improve the range, detail, and ambition of this book, though any mistakes are my own. For commenting on drafts, assisting me with sources, and pushing me to think and feel more deeply, I am indebted to Clare Anderson, Tammy Ayres, Queenela Cameron, Joanna Carson, Courtney Christian, Lucy Evans, Zalfa Feghali, Corinne Fowler, Ignatius T. Goosen, Paul Hegarty, Michelle Houston, Andrew Johnstone, Liz Jones, Rob Jones II, Sophie Jones, Will Kaufman, Dylan Kerrigan, Zuzanna Ladyga, Gavan Lennon, George Lewis, Danny Lutz, Daniel Matlin, Beatriz Meireles, Catherine Morley, Carl Nelson, Michelle O'Reilly, Joy Porter, Laraine Porter, Jon Powell, Joel Rasmussen, Rachel Rich, Jude Riley, Mikko Saikku, Emma Staniland, Joe Street, Alex Waddan, Casey Wallace, Brian Ward, Kristy Warren, Stephen Whitfield, and Alex Zagaria. Sincere gratitude goes to the two readers whose reports allowed me to refine the typescript, and to my editor Niels Hooper for his enthusiastic support. I especially wish to thank Kristen for her love and for her game-changing one-liners; my family for always being there for me; staff at the Library of Congress for their assistance even when I had too many books piled up on Desk 110; and for helping me improve as a thinker and writer my life-long gratitude goes to Richard King and Andy Mousley.

"I lost some people I was traveling with" (as Neil Young said) during the writing of this book, most significantly Mary Donovan in 2018 and John Heath in 2017, to whom I pay tribute. This publication coincides with the ten-year anniversary of the passing of my cousin Kathryn Ward. For all the laughs we shared, I dedicate this book to Kathryn.

Notes

PREFACE

1. "American Life and Times, 1900–1950," *Life*, January 2, 1950. John C. Burnham, *Health Care in America* (Baltimore: Johns Hopkins University Press, 2015).

2. Julian E. Zelizer, *The Fierce Urgency of Now: Lyndon Johnson, Congress, and the Battle for the Great Society* (New York: Penguin, 2015), 3, 10.

3. See Julius B. Richmond, *Currents in American Medicine: A Developmental View of Medical Care and Education* (Cambridge, MA: Harvard University Press, 1969).

4. Robert N. Bellah, Richard Madsen, William M. Sullivan, Ann Swidler, and Steven M. Tipton, *Habits of the Heart: Individualism and Commitment in American Life*, updated edition with a new introduction (1985; Berkeley: University of California Press, 1996), and Robert N. Bellah, Richard Madsen, William M. Sullivan, Ann Swidler, and Steven M. Tipton, *The Good Society* (New York: Vintage, 1992).

5. Donald J. Trump, "Remarks by President Trump in Meeting with African American Leaders," February 27, 2020, www.whitehouse.gov/briefings-sta tements/remarks-president-trump-meeting-african-american-leaders.

6. Laurie B. Green, John McKiernan-González, and Martin Summers, eds., *Precarious Prescriptions: Contested Histories of Race and Health in North America* (Minneapolis: University of Minnesota Press, 2012), xii.

INTRODUCTION

1. Executive Order 2899: "Public Health Activities of All War Agencies Placed Under the Treasury Secretary" (July 1, 1918); reprinted in the *Annual*

Report of the Surgeon General of the Public Health Service (Washington, DC: US Government Printing Office, 1918), 10, https://archive.org/details/annualre portofsu1918unit/page/10.

2. For developments in the US Public Health Service, see Laurence F. Schmeckebier, *The Public Health Service: Its History, Activities, and Organization* (Baltimore: Johns Hopkins University Press, 1923), 1–75; Wilson G. Smillie, *Public Health: Its Promise for the Future* (New York: Macmillan, 1955); George Rosen, *A History of Public Health* (1958; Baltimore: Johns Hopkins University Press, 1993); Bess Furman, *A Profile of the United States Public Health Service, 1798–1948* (Washington, DC: National Institutes of Health, 1973); and Fitzhugh Mullan, *Plagues and Politics: The Story of the United States Public Health Service* (New York: Basic Books, 1989).

3. Ernest C. Levy, "Some Public Health Lessons of the War," *American Journal of Public Health* 8, no. 9 (September 1918): 667.

4. Letter from William Gibbs McAdoo to Woodrow Wilson, August 29, 1918, in *The Papers of Woodrow Wilson*, ed. Arthur S. Link (Princeton, NJ: Princeton University Press, 1985), 49: 379. For an overview of public health activities in 1918, see Secretary to the Treasury, *Public Health Activities of the Public Health Service* (December 1, 1919), House of Representatives, 66th Congress, Second Session, Document 486.

5. See Upton Sinclair, *The Jungle* (London: Doubleday, Page & Co., 1906), and Upton Sinclair and Michael Williams, *Good Health and How We Won It, with an Account of the New Hygiene* (New York: Frederick A. Stokes, 1909). For context, see James Harvey Young, *Pure Food: Securing the Federal Food and Drugs Act of 1906* (Princeton, NJ: Princeton University Press, 1989).

6. See James G. Burrow, *Organized Medicine in the Progressive Era: The Move toward Monopoly* (Baltimore: Johns Hopkins University Press, 1977), 101–2.

7. On the Flexner Report, see "The Council on Medical Education and Hospitals," in *A History of the American Medical Association, 1847 to 1947*, ed. Morris Fishbein (Philadelphia: Saunders, 1947), 898–99, and Burrow, *Organized Medicine in the Progressive Era*, 33–47. The modernizing drive of the Flexner Report had some unfortunate consequences. It supported medical education for black physicians but was critical of African American training facilities, which as a consequence reduced in number from ten in 1900 to just two by 1924: Meharry Medical College, Nashville, and Howard University, Washington, DC. See Vanessa Northington Gamble, *Making a Place for Ourselves: The Black Hospital Movement, 1920–1945* (New York: Oxford University Press, 1995), 124; Kenneth M. Ludmerer, *Time to Heal: American Medical Education from the Turn of the Century to the Era of Managed Care* (Oxford: Oxford University Press, 1999), 46–47; Michael W. Byrd and Linda A. Clayton, *An American Health Dilemma*, vol. 2, *Race, Medicine, and Health Care in the United States, 1900–2000* (New York: Routledge, 2002), 35–84; and Todd L. Savitt, *Race and Medicine in Nineteenth- and Early-Twentieth-Century America* (Kent, OH: Kent State University Press, 2007), 252–66.

8. Editorial, "The Harrison Anti-Narcotic Law," *Journal of the American Medical Association*, 64, no. 11 (March 13, 1915): 912. See also C. E. Terry,

"The Harrison Anti-Narcotic Act," *American Journal of Public Health* 5, no. 6 (June 1915): 518.

9. Extra-cantonment zones were used to control malaria, typhoid, influenza, and syphilis: "Extra-Cantonment Zone Sanitation," *Municipal Journal* (November 30, 1918); Charles Lynch, Frank W. Weed, and Loy McAfee, *The Medical Department of the United States Army in the World War*, vol. 1 (Washington, DC: US Government Printing Office, 1923), 808–9, 998; and Lucy S. Morgan, "Health Education in Extra-Cantonment Zones," *American Journal of Public Health and the Nation's Health* 32, no. 1 (November 1942): 1209–14.

10. The quotations are from the *Fit to Fight* pamphlet released by the surgeon general's office (Washington, DC: US Government Printing Office, 1918), and "Blue Issues Warning," *New York Times*, December 4, 1918. See also *Keeping Fit* (Washington, DC: US Public Health Service, 1919); Robin E. Jensen, *Dirty Words: The Rhetoric of Public Sex Education, 1870–1924* (Urbana: University of Illinois Press, 2010), 115–47; Benjamin S. Warren and Charles F. Bolduan, "War Activities of the United States Public Health Service," *Public Health Reports* 34, no. 23 (June 6, 1919): 1243–67; and Bobby A. Wintermute, *Public Health and the U.S. Military: A History of the Army Medical Department* (London: Routledge, 2011), 189–218.

11. Cited in Scott Wasserman Stern, "The Long American Plan: The U.S. Government's Campaign against Venereal Disease and Its Carriers," *Harvard Journal of Law and Gender* 38, no. 2 (Summer 2015): 387. For context, see Allan Brandt, *No Magic Bullet: A Social History of Venereal Disease in the United States since 1880* (New York: Oxford University Press, 1985), and Terra Ziporyn, *Disease in the Popular American Press: The Case of Diphtheria, Typhoid Fever, and Syphilis, 1870–1920* (New York: Praeger, 1988), 128–32.

12. Grover Cleveland, "Second Annual Message to the Congress of the United States," December 3,1894, *A Compilation of the Messages and Papers of the Presidents* (New York: Bureau of National Literature, 1897), 12: 5983.

13. On the first National Board of Health, see Jerrold M. Michael, "The National Board of Health: 1879–1883," *Public Health Reports* 126, no. 1 (January/February 2011): 123–29.

14. "Free Vaccination against Smallpox and Typhoid Fever," *Official Bulletin*, 2, no. 355 (July 9, 1918).

15. William H. Taft, "Second Annual Message to Congress," December 6, 1910, in *The Collected Works of William Howard Taft*, vol. 4, *Presidential Messages to Congress*, ed. David H. Burton (Athens: Ohio University Press, 2002), 64. On efforts to contain yellow fever, see Margaret Humphreys, *Yellow Fever and the South* (New Brunswick, NJ: Rutgers University Press, 1992).

16. See the press release of April 13,1954: "Press Releases—Office of the Secretary," Box 30, Papers of Oveta Culp Hobby, Secretary of Health, Education, and Welfare, Dwight D. Eisenhower Presidential Library, Abilene, Kansas.

17. Theda Skocpol, *Protecting Soldiers and Mothers: The Political Origins of Social Policy in the United States* (Cambridge, MA: Harvard University Press, 1992), 302–4. For the second quotation, see Franklin D. Roosevelt, "Presidential Statement on Appointment of Interdepartmental Committee for Coordina-

tion of Federal Health Activities," August 15, 1935, *The Public Papers and Addresses of Franklin D. Roosevelt*, vol. 4, *The Court Disapproves, 1935* (New York: Random House, 1938), 327. Eisenhower recalled the Hoover-era campaigns of 1928 and 1930 when in spring 1953 he established the Department of Health, Education, and Welfare: Dwight D. Eisenhower, "Special Mention to the Congress Transmitting Reorganization Plan 1 of 1953 Creating the Department of Health, Education, and Welfare," March 12, 1953, *Public Papers of the Presidents of the United States, Dwight D. Eisenhower, 1953* (Washington, DC: US Government Printing Office, 1960), 94–98 (further citations from this series are shortened to *Public Papers of the Presidents*).

18. For the quotation, see President Roosevelt's letter to Josephine Roche, chair of the Interdepartmental Committee to Coordinate Health and Welfare Activities, included in Roche's opening address of the National Health Conference, *Proceedings of the National Health Conference* (Washington, DC: US Government Printing Office, 1938). On federal health plans in the 1930s, see Wilson G. Smillie, *Public Health Administration in the United States* (New York: Macmillan, 1935); "A National Health Program," *Journal of the American Medical Association* (February 26, 1938): 652–65; and Franklin D. Roosevelt, "A Call for a Coordinated National Health Program, July 15, 1938, in *The Public Papers and Addresses of Franklin D. Roosevelt, 1938 Volume: The Continuing Struggle for Liberalism* (New York: Random House, 1941), 459–62. On ill health and poverty, see Harriet Silverman, "Your Health, America! Notes on an Epochal Conference," *New Masses* (August 2, 1938): 3–5. For the National Negro Health Week and the PHS publication *National Negro Health News*, see Phoebe Pollitt, "From National Negro Health Week to National Public Health Week, *Journal of Community Health* 21, no. 6 (December 1996): 401–7.

19. Bertram M. Bernheim, *Medicine at the Crossroads* (New York: Morrow, 1939), 13, 255–56.

20. The Woodrow Wilson quotation is from his September 3, 1917, statement, "To the Soldiers of the National Army," quoted in the free pamphlet *Sexual Hygiene for Young Men* (n.d.) held in "Newspaper Clippings Collected by the Venereal Disease Division, 1919–1925," Box 345, Records of the Public Health Service, General Records, Record Group 90, National Archives and Records Administration, College Park, Maryland. On the National Institutes of Health, see Manfred Waserman, "The Quest for a National Health Department in the Progressive Era," *Bulletin of the History of Medicine* 49, no. 3 (Fall 1975): 353–80, and Victoria A. Harden, *Inventing the NIH: Federal Biomedical Research Policy, 1887–1937* (Baltimore: Johns Hopkins University Press, 1986). On prostitution near armed forces camps, see "New Regulations in Support of Policy of Absolute Repression of Prostitution in the Vicinity of Army and Navy Camps," *Official U.S. Bulletin* (August 13, 1918).

21. Letter from William G. McAdoo to President Wilson, November 2, 1917, *Papers of Woodrow Wilson*, 45: 27. Rupert Blue called universal health insurance the "next big step in American labor legislation": "Fine Progress in Labor Legislation during Year 1918," *Labor Journal* (September 6, 1918). On health insurance developments, see Paul Starr, *Remedy and Reaction: The*

Peculiar American Struggle over Health Care Reform (New Haven, CT: Yale University Press, 2013), 29–34, and for a comparative perspective, see Daniel M. Fox, *Health Policies, Health Politics: The British and American Experience, 1911–1965* (Princeton, NJ: Princeton University Press, 1986). On the American Association for Labor Legislation, see Alan Derickson, *Health Security for All: Dreams of Universal Health Care in America* (Baltimore: Johns Hopkins University Press, 2005), 26–29. On the political economy of health care after 1910, see Colin Gordon, *Dead on Arrival: The Politics of Health Care in Twentieth-Century America* (Princeton, NJ: Princeton University Press, 2003), 12–45.

22. See Jeanne E. Abrams, "Spitting Is Dangerous, Indecent, and Against the Law! Legislating Health Behavior during the American Tuberculosis Crusade," *Journal of the History of Medicine and Allied Sciences* 68, no. 3 (July 2013): 419, and John McKiernan-González, *Fevered Measures: Public Health and Race at the Texas-Mexico Border, 1848–1942* (Durham, NC: Duke University Press, 2012), 2, 64–65.

23. See Hibbert Winslow Hill, *The New Public Health* (Minneapolis, MN: Press of the Journal Lancet, 1913). On bacteriological research, see Amy L. Fairchild, Ronald Bayer, and James Colgrove, *Searching Eyes: Privacy, the State, and Disease Surveillance in America* (Berkeley: University of California Press, 2007), 3–5, and Nancy Tomes, *The Gospel of Germs: Men, Women, and the Microbe in American Life* (Cambridge, MA: Harvard University Press, 1998), 237–55.

24. Letter from A. Prescot Folwell to Rupert Blue (December 3, 1918), File Number 5017, Folder 5, Box 542, Central File, 1897–1923, Records of the Public Health Service, RG 90, National Archives, College Park.

25. See James Jay Carafano and Richard Weitz, *Mismanaging Mayhem: How Washington Responds to Crisis* (Westport, CT: Praeger, 2008), 7–13.

26. Amy L. Fairchild, David Merritt Johns, and Kavita Sivaramakrishnan, "A Brief History of Panic," *New York Times*, January 28, 2013. See also Amy L. Fairchild and David Merritt Johns, "Don't Panic! 'The Excited and Terrified' Public Mind from Yellow Fever to Bioterrorism," in *Empires of Panic: Epidemics and Colonial Anxieties*, ed. Robert Peckham (Hong Kong: Hong Kong University Press, 2015), 155–79.

27. For these different kinds of panic, see "Corona Virus Is Causing Panic but not Lawlessness," *New Yorker*, March 2, 2020.

28. Stanley Cohen, *Folk Devils and Moral Panics*, 3rd ed. (1972; New York: Routledge, 2011), viii.

29. "Gov. Andrew Cuomo: 'It's Making Sure We Live Through This,'" *New York Times*, Daily Podcast, March 18, 2020, www.nytimes.com/2020 /03/18/podcasts/the-daily/cuomo-new-york-coronavirus.amp.html. Cuomo expanded on these COVID-19 remarks in his Democratic National Convention speech of August 17, 2020, in which he claimed effective government is "our immune system," https://m.youtube.com/watch?v=jaBx2mOEbdE.

30. John G. Bowman, *General Hospitals of 100 Beds or More: Report of 1919* (Chicago: American College of Surgeons, 1919).

31. "Dr. Grayson Tells of Great Progress in Navy Medical Corps under Wilson," *Atlanta Constitution*, November 15, 1916. The keynote speech appeared

as Cary T. Grayson, "The Doctor's Work for Naval Preparedness," *Southern Medical Journal* (January 1917): 6–12. For Grayson's views of Wilson, see Cary T. Grayson, *Woodrow Wilson: An Intimate Memoir* (1960; Washington, DC: Potomac Books, 1977).

32. John C. Burnham, *Health Care in America* (Baltimore: Johns Hopkins University Press, 2015), 214–20. See also Charles E. Rosenberg, *The Care of Strangers: The Rise of America's Hospital System* (New York: Basic Books, 1987), and Joel D. Howell, "Machines and Medicine: Technology Transforms the American Hospital," in *The American Hospital: Communities and Social Contexts*, ed. Diana Long and Janet Golden (Ithaca, NY: Cornell University Press, 1989), 109–34.

33. See Karen Kruse Thomas, *Health and Humanity: A History of the Johns Hopkins Bloomberg School of Public Health, 1935–1985* (Baltimore: Johns Hopkins University Press, 2016).

34. See *The Modern Health Crusade: A National Program of Health Instruction in Schools* (New York: National Tuberculosis Association, 1922), and Michael E. Teller, *The Tuberculosis Movement: A Public Health Campaign in the Progressive Era* (Westport, CT: Greenwood, 1988), 109–19. See also Charles M. De Forest, "The Crusade Method of Health Training," *Journal of Education* 98, no. 1 (July 5, 1923): 7–8.

35. On the conservation movement and infant mortality, see Laura L. Lovett, *Conceiving the Future: Pronatalism, Reproduction, and the Family in the United States, 1890–1938* (Chapel Hill: University of North Carolina Press, 2007), 122–24. For Wilson's view of the Red Cross, see "Address of President Wilson, Opening the Campaign in New York for the Second Red Cross Fund," May 18, 1918 (Washington, DC: US Government Printing Office, 1918), 6.

36. *Modern Health Crusaders Manual* (New York: National Tuberculosis Association, 1918), 1–2. On citizen cooperation, see Daniel Eli Burnstein, *Next to Godliness: Confronting Dirt and Despair in Progressive Era New York City* (Urbana: University of Illinois Press, 2006), 91–139.

37. See Richard A. Meckel, *Save the Babies: American Public Health Reform and the Prevention of Infant Mortality, 1850–1929* (1998; Ann Arbor: University of Michigan Press, 1998), 200–201, and Cynthia A. Connolly and Janet Golden, " 'Save 100,000 Babies': The 1918 Children's Year and Its Legacy," *American Journal of Public Health* 108, no. 7 (July 2018): 902–7.

38. J. Stanley Lemons, "The Sheppard-Towner Act: Progressivism in the 1920s," *Journal of American History* 55, no. 4 (March 1969): 776–86. A Children's Charter emerged from the November 19, 1930, White House Conference on Child Health and Protection.

39. Woodrow Wilson, "Address of Welcome to the Members of the American Medical Association by Gov. Woodrow Wilson, June 4, 1912," *Congressional Record* (August 13, 1912), 11692.

40. Wilson, "Address of Welcome to the Members of the American Medical Association," 11693. On Wilson's grappling with moral problems, see Patricia O'Toole, *The Moralist: Woodrow Wilson and the World He Made* (New York: Simon and Schuster, 2018).

41. The interest in eugenics ranged from physician William J. Robinson's

1922 study *Eugenics, Marriage and Birth Control* to university programs and popular eugenics education such as "Fitter Families" contests at state fairs. See Ann Gibson Winfield, *Eugenics and Education in America: Institutionalized Racism and the Implications of History, Ideology, and Memory* (New York: Peter Lang, 2007), and Ruth Clifford Engs, "Eugenics, Immigration Restriction, and the Birth Control Movements," in *A Companion to Warren G. Harding, Calvin Coolidge, and Herbert Hoover*, ed. Katherine A. S. Sibley (Oxford: Wiley Blackwell, 2014), 313–37.

42. The two quotations are from Woodrow Wilson, "A Credo," *Papers of Woodrow Wilson*, vol. 17, 337, and from a public speech of November 1921 by H. L. Shaw, the president of the American Child Hygiene Association, as reported in the *American Journal of Nursing* 22 (Rochester, NY: American Journal of Nursing Company, 1922), 217. For the response to outbreaks of yellow fever, see Margaret Humphreys, *Yellow Fever and the South* (New Brunswick, NJ: Rutgers University Press, 1992), and Daniel Sledge, *Health Divided: Public Health and Individual Medicine in the Making of the Modern American State* (Lawrence: University Press of Kansas, 2017), 1–2. On new public health, see John Duffy, *The Sanitarians: A History of American Public Health* (Urbana: University of Illinois Press, 1990), 205–20, and Martin V. Melosi, *The Sanitary City: Urban Infrastructure in America from Colonial Times to the Present* (Baltimore: Johns Hopkins University Press, 2000), 103–16. For concerns about the number and capacity of trained medical personnel, see "Records of a Conference on the Future of the Public Health Program in the United States and on the Education of Sanitarians, March 14–15, 1922," Boxes 1–2, Records of the Public Health Service, General Records, RG 90, National Archives, College Park, MD.

43. See Barbara Gutmann Rosenkrantz, *Public Health and the State: Changing Views in Massachusetts, 1842–1936* (Cambridge, MA: Harvard University Press, 1972), 129. See also Dorothy Porter, *Health, Civilization, and the State: A History of Public Health from Ancient to Modern Times* (London: Routledge, 1999), 147–62.

44. Cited in George Rosen, *Preventive Medicine in the United States, 1900–1975: Trends and Interpretations* (New York: Science History Publications, 1975), 18.

45. "Need Department National Health, Physicians Assert," *Atlanta Constitution*, November 15, 1916.

46. Letter from McAdoo to Wilson, August 29, 1918, *Papers of Woodrow Wilson*, 49: 380. McAdoo resigned from the US Treasury in December, declaring he desired a quieter life after being exposed for insider trading on the stock exchange.

47. Woodrow Wilson, "A Statement," December 22, 1918, *Papers of Woodrow Wilson*, 53: 469.

48. "Wilson Visits 1,200 of Our Wounded," *New York Times*, December 22, 1918. "Mr. and Mrs. Wilson Give Day to Cheering the Wounded in Paris Military Hospital," *New York Herald*, December 23, 1918.

49. The *Manchester Guardian* documented Woodrow and Mrs. Wilson's trip to Manchester for Christmas and New Year's Eve 1918, noting that the

director general of the American Medical Services in France was claiming that "news of the armistice" immediately restored 2,000 shell-shocked soldiers to health, even though many had been "shaken to their marrow and atrophied in their limbs": "Fear and Health," *Manchester Guardian*, December 30, 1918, and "Speech at the Royal Exchange, Manchester," *Manchester Guardian*, December 31, 1918.

50. Grayson, "Doctor's Work for Naval Preparedness," 8.

51. Wilson, "An Annual Message on the State of the Union," December 7, 1920, *Papers of Woodrow Wilson*, 66: 488.

52. Letter from William Bauchop Wilson to Woodrow Wilson, March 1, 1921, *Papers of Woodrow Wilson*, 67: 179. For context, see Alan M. Kraut, *Silent Travelers: Germs, Genes, and the Immigrant Menace* (New York: Basic Books, 1994).

53. On Grayson's relationship with Wilson, see A. Scott Berg, *Wilson* (New York: Putnam's, 2013), 282–83, 613–20, and on Wilson's erratic decision-making, see Edwin A. Weinstein, *Woodrow Wilson: A Medical and Psychological Biography* (Berkeley: University of California Press, 1981).

54. For context, see David Blumenthal and James Monroe, *The Heart of Power: Health and Politics in the Oval Office* (Berkeley: University of California Press, 2010). See also Rosalynn Carter, with Susan K. Golant and Kathryn E. Cade, *Within Our Reach: Ending the Mental Health Crisis* (New York: Rodale, 2010), 99–100, and Rosalynn Carter, *Helping Someone with Mental Illness* (New York: Three Rivers Press, 1999).

55. The "calm man" persona presented in the *Saturday Evening Post* ("A Calm Review of a Calm Man," July 28, 1922) belied Harding's precarious health: see Robert H. Ferrell, *The Strange Deaths of President Harding* (Columbia: University of Missouri Press, 1996). On Roosevelt's worsening health complications, see Hugh E. Evans, *The Hidden Campaign: FDR's Health and the 1944 Election* (New York: Routledge, 2002), and Steven Lomazow and Eric Fettmann, *FDR's Deadly Secret* (New York: PublicAffairs, 2009).

56. There was little media coverage of the Tuskegee Syphilis Experiment until an exposé in July 1972, followed by the Belmont Report of 1979 and a presidential apology in 1997. See "Syphilis Victims in U.S. Study Went Untreated for 40 Years," *New York Times*, July 16, 1972; James H. Jones, *Bad Blood: The Tuskegee Syphilis Experiment* (New York: Free Press, 1981), and Susan Reverby, *Examining Tuskegee: The Infamous Syphilis Study and Its Legacy* (Chapel Hill: University of North Carolina Press, 2009). On the Henrietta Lacks case, see Rebecca Skloot, *The Immortal Lives of Henrietta Lacks* (New York: Crown, 2010).

57. Sledge, *Health Divided*, 3.

58. Nancy Tomes, "Speaking for the Public: The Ambivalent Quest of Twentieth-Century Public Health," in *The Contested Boundaries of American Public Health*, ed. James Colgrove, Gerald Markowitz, and David Rosner (New Brunswick, NJ: Rutgers University Press, 2008), 57. For a similar argument, see Geof Rayner and Tim Lang, *Ecological Public Health: Reshaping the Conditions for Good Health* (London: Routledge, 2013), 13–15.

59. On socialized medicine, see Gordon, *Dead on Arrival*, 136–71; on

health care finance reform, see Philip J. Funigiello, *Chronic Politics: Health Care Security from FDR to George W. Bush* (Lawrence: University Press of Kansas, 2005); on health care as a subgovernmental structure, see Douglass Cater and Philip R. Lee, *Politics of Health* (Huntington, NY: Robert E. Krieger, 1979), 1–7.

60. Uwe E. Reinhardt, *Priced Out: The Economic and Ethical Costs of American Health Care* (Princeton, NJ: Princeton University Press, 2019), 1–9, 81–84.

61. The Department of Health and Human Services succeeded HEW in May 1980 in line with the Department of Education Organization Act. President Carter emphasized the benefits of a separate education department but also recognized that a discrete health department would offer "assistance," "compassion," and "opportunity" to millions: "8/3/79—Swearing in of Patricia Roberts Harris as Secretary of HEW," Staff Offices Speechwriters—Chron Files, Box 51, Jimmy Carter Presidential Library and Museum, Atlanta, Georgia.

62. "Growth of the Department of Health, Education, and Welfare," April 23,1965, "FG 165, Department of Health, Education and Welfare, 3/28/65–6/5/65," EX FG, White House Central Files, Box 238, LBJ Library, Austin, Texas. CDC took ownership of the *Morbidity and Mortality Weekly Report* in the early 1960s, a report that began life in 1878 as *The Bulletin of Public Health* linked to the National Quarantine Act.

63. Lyndon B. Johnson, "Remarks upon Signing Bills Relating to Health and Education," November 3, 1966, *Public Papers of the Presidents, Lyndon B. Johnson, 1966*, Book 2 (Washington, DC: US Government Printing Office, 1967), 1308.

64. Lyndon B. Johnson, "Special Message to the Congress: 'Education and Health in America,'" February 28, 1967, *Public Papers of the Presidents, Lyndon B. Johnson, 1967*, Book 1 (Washington, DC: US Government Printing Office, 1968), 245. For the 1964 quotation, see Johnson, "Special Message to the Congress on the Nation's Health," February 10, 1964, *Public Papers of the Presidents, Lyndon B. Johnson, 1963–64*, Book 1 (Washington, DC: US Government Printing Office, 1968), 275.

65. "Nixon Links Humphrey with Administration 'Fiscal Blunders,'" *Los Angeles Times*, July 7, 1968, and Richard M. Nixon, "Annual Message to Congress on the State of the Union," January 22, 1971, *Public Papers of the Presidents: Richard M. Nixon, 1971* (Washington, DC: US Government Printing Office, 1974), 51.

66. On the regional spread of health crises, see Jonathan Cohn, *Sick: The Untold Story of America's Health Care Crisis* (New York: HarperCollins, 2007).

67. See Andrew Lakoff, *Unprepared: Global Health in a Time of Emergency* (Berkeley: University of California Press, 2017).

68. See the Association of State and Territorial Health Officials' "Emergency Authority and Immunity Toolkit," www.astho.org/Programs/Preparedness/Public-Health-Emergency-Law/Emergency-Authority-and-Immunity-Toolkit/Emergency-Declarations-and-Authorities-Fact-Sheet/.

69. On legal aspects of emergency declarations, see Lawrence O. Gostin and

Lindsay F. Wiley, *Public Health Law* (Berkeley: University of California Press, 2016), 396–402.

70. See the World Health Organization website, www.who.int/hac/crises.

71. For example, see Donald J. Trump, *Crippled America: How to Make America Great Again* (New York: Simon and Schuster, 2015), 70.

72. Naomi Klein's keynote speech at the Labour Party Convention, Brighton, UK, September 26, 2017, https://labour.org.uk/press/author-naomi-klein -speech-to-labour-party. See also Naomi Klein, *The Shock Doctrine: The Rise of Disaster Capitalism* (New York: Metropolitan Books, 2007).

73. Timothy Clark, "Scale," in *Telemorphosis: Theory in the Era of Climate Change*, vol. 1, ed. Tom Cohen (Ann Arbor: Open Humanities Press, an imprint of MPublishing—University of Michigan Library, 2012), 148–66.

74. Cohen, *Moral Panic and Folk Devils*, xxv. Albert Ellis and Robert A. Harper, *A New Guide to Rational Living* (New York: Wilshire, 1975), 12, 38, 174. On apocalyptic discourses, see Thomas L. Long, *AIDS and American Apocalypticism: The Cultural Semiotics of an Epidemic* (Albany: State University of New York Press, 2004), and Philip Alcabes, *Dread: How Fear and Fantasy Have Fueled Epidemics from the Black Death to Avian Flu* (New York: PublicAffairs, 2010).

75. Wolfgang Streeck, *Buying Time: The Delayed Crisis of Democratic Capitalism*, 2nd ed. (2014; London: Verso, 2017), vi.

76. See Matthew Pressman, *On Press: The Liberal Values That Shaped the News* (Cambridge, MA: Harvard University Press, 2018), 40–41, 188–91.

77. See Barbara and John Ehrenreich, *The American Health Empire: Power, Profits and Politics* (New York: Random House, 1970); John Ehrenreich, ed., *The Cultural Crisis of Modern Medicine* (New York: Monthly Review Press, 1978); and Carl F. Ameringer, *The Health Care Revolution: From Medical Monopoly to Market Competition* (Berkeley: University of California Press, 2008). For the multidimensional dynamic of crises on a global scale, see Paul Crosthwaite, ed., *Criticism, Crisis, and Contemporary Narrative: Textual Horizons in an Age of Global Risk* (New York: Routledge, 2011).

78. Streeck, *Buying Time*, xii.

79. See Donald A. Barr, *Health Disparities in the United States: Social Class, Race, Ethnicity, and the Social Determinants of Health* (Baltimore: Johns Hopkins University Press, 2008), and Kant Patel and Mark E. Rushefsky, *Health Care in America: Separate and Unequal* (Armonk, NY: M. E. Sharpe, 2008).

80. Streeck, *Buying Time*, 119.

81. On vertical versus horizontal approaches to health security on an international scale, see Chelsea Clinton and Devi Sridhar, *Governing Global Health: Who Runs the World and Why* (Oxford: Oxford University Press, 2017), 8–12.

82. Kathleen J. Tierney and Barbara Baisden, *Crisis Intervention Programs for Disaster Victims: A Source Book and Manual for Smaller Communities*, Miscellaneous Report 22 (Disaster Research Center, Ohio State University, 1977), 1, http://dspace.udel.edu/bitstream/handle/19716/1278/MR22.pdf?se quence=1. The Disaster Research Center was cofounded by sociologist Enrico Quarantelli at Ohio State University in 1963; it has been housed at the University of Delaware since 1985.

83. See "Vaccine Issue arises at Republican Debate, to Doctors' Dismay, *New York Times*, September 17, 2015, and Seth Mnookin, *The Panic Virus: The True Story behind the Vaccine-Autism Controversy* (New York: Simon and Schuster, 2012). For the MMR controversy, see "The Message of Measles," *New Yorker*, September 2, 2019, 38–47.

84. See Jon D. Lee, *An Epidemic of Rumors: How Stories Shape Our Perception of Disease* (Boulder: University Press of Colorado, published by Utah State University Press, 2014).

85. On contemporary health journalism, see Institute of Medicine, *The Future of the Public's Health in the 21st Century* (Washington, DC: National Academies Press, 2003), 307–57.

86. See the "Bad Blood: The Stealth Epidemic" series in the *New York Times*, especially "Diabetes and Its Awful Toll Quietly Emerge as a Crisis," *New York Times*, January 9, 2006. For obesity statistics, see National Center for Health Statistics, *Health People 2010: Final Review* (Hyattsville, MD: US Department of Health and Human Services, 2012), iii.

87. Alison Bashford, "Epilogue: Panic's Past and Global Futures," in *Empires of Panic: Epidemics and Colonial Anxieties*, ed. Robert Peckham (Hong Kong: Hong Kong University Press, 2015), 204. Jackie Orr, *Panic Diaries: A Genealogy of Panic Disorder* (Durham, NC: Duke University Press, 2006), 45.

88. See "Novel Coronavirus (2019-nCoV) Situation Report—13," February 2, 2020, www.who.int/docs/default-source/coronaviruse/situation-reports/20200202-sitrep-13-ncov-v3.pdf, and "W.H.O. Fights a Pandemic besides Coronavirus: An 'Infodemic,'" *New York Times*, February 6, 2020. For the use of "infodemic" during the SARS outbreak, see David J. Rothkopf, "When the Buzz Bites Back," *Washington Post*, May 11, 2003, and for the echo chamber effect, see Adam Kucharski, *The Rules of Contagion: Why Things Spread—and Why They Stop* (London: Profile Books, 2020), 161–69.

89. See Kevin B. Wright, Lisa Sparks, and H. Dan O'Hair, *Health Communication in the 21st Century* (Oxford: Blackwell, 2008), 155–204, and Elizabeth Rosenthal, *An American Sickness: How Healthcare Became Big Business and How You Can Take It Back* (New York: Penguin, 2017), 321–27.

90. On narrow and broad conceptions of public health, see Institute of Medicine, *The Future of Public Health* (Washington, DC: National Academy Press, 1988), 40, and Verina Wild and Angus Dawson, "Migration: A Core Public Health Ethics Issue," *Public Health* 158 (May 2018): 67. For millennial fears about the effectiveness of public health, see Laurie Garrett, *Betrayal of Trust: The Collapse of Global Public Health* (New York: Hyperion, 2000).

91. Theda Skocpol, *Boomerang: Health Care Reform and the Turn against Government* (New York: Norton, 1996). Jonathan Engel, *Poor People's Medicine: Medicaid and American Charity Care since 1965* (Durham, NC: Duke University Press, 2006), xi.

92. Michele Landis Dauber, *The Sympathetic State: Disaster Relief and the Origins of the American Welfare State* (Chicago: University of Chicago Press, 2013); Paul Farmer, "On Suffering and Structural Violence: A View from Below," *Daedalus* 125, no. 1 (Winter 1996): 261–83. Farmer develops the concept of structural violence from the Norwegian sociologist Johan Galtung's es-

say "Violence, Peace, and Peace Research," *Journal of Peace Research* 6 (1969): 167–91.

93. Robert N. Bellah, Richard Madsen, William M. Sullivan, Ann Swidler, and Steven M. Tipton, *The Good Society* (New York: Vintage, 1992), 14.

94. Bellah et al., *Good Society*, 14–15.

95. Bellah's afterword to Donald L. Gelpi, ed., *Beyond Individualism: Toward a Retrieval of Moral Discourse in America* (Notre Dame, IN: University of Notre Dame Press, 1989), 219. See also Michael D. Stein and Sandro Galea, *Pained: Uncomfortable Conversations about the Public's Health* (New York: Oxford University Press, 2020).

96. On this golden age model, see John C. Burnham, "American Medicine's Golden Age: What Happened to It?" *Science* 215 (March 1982): 1474–79.

97. For federal underinvestment in public health, see the nonprofit organization Trust for America's Health report of April 2020: *The Impact of Chronic Underfunding on America's Public Health System: Trends, Risks, and Recommendations*, 2020, www.tfah.org/wp-content/uploads/2020/04/TFAH2020PublicHealthFunding.pdf.

CHAPTER 1: DISASTER

1. See Hans-Georg Bohle, *Living with Vulnerability: Livelihoods and Human Security in Risky Environments* (Bonn: InterSections, 2007). See also Andrew Curtis, Jacqueline Warren Mills, and Michael Leitner, "Katrina and Vulnerability: The Geography of Stress," *Journal of Health Care for the Poor and Underserved* 18, no. 2 (June 2007): 315–30, and Victoria Basolo, "Environmental Change, Disasters, and Vulnerability: The Case of Hurricane Katrina and New Orleans," in *Global Environmental Change and Human Security*, ed. Richard A. Matthew, Jon Barnett, Bryan McDonald, and Karen L. O'Brien (Cambridge, MA: MIT Press, 2010), 97–116.

2. For the quotation, see Jason David Rivera and DeMond Shondell Miller, "Continually Neglected: Situating Natural Disasters in the African American Experience," *Journal of Black Studies* 37, no. 4 (March 2007): 503.

3. See Erik Larson, *Isaac's Storm: A Man, a Time, and the Deadliest Hurricane in History* (New York: Vintage, 2000), and John Edward Weems, *A Weekend in September* (1957; College Station: Texas A&M University Press, 1970), 167–70.

4. On blues and the Mississippi River Flood, see Paul Oliver, *Blues Fell This Morning: Meaning in the Blues* (1960; Cambridge: Cambridge University Press, 1990), 215–26.

5. See, for example, *Emerging Systemic Risks in the 21st Century: An Agenda for Action*, Organisation for Economic Co-Operation and Development, 2003.

6. William Faulkner, *The Wild Palms* (1939; London: Penguin, 1970), 46–47.

7. Ari Kelman, "Water Damaged: Disaster History in New Orleans and on the Gulf Coast," *Reviews in American History* 34, no. 2 (June 2006): 223.

8. Mark Monmonier, *Cartographies of Danger: Mapping Hazards in America* (Chicago: University of Chicago Press, 1997), 105.

9. Martyn Bone, "Introduction: Old/New/Post/Real/Global/No South," in *Creating and Consuming the American South*, ed. Martyn Bone, Brian Ward, and William A. Link (Gainesville: University Press of Florida, 2015), 2.

10. On disaster mythology, see James Kendra and Tricia Wachtendorf, *American Dunkirk: The Waterborne Evacuation of Manhattan on 9/11* (Philadelphia: Temple University Press, 2016), 25.

11. Kate Parker Horigan, *Consuming Katrina: Public Disaster and Personal Narrative* (Jackson: University Press of Mississippi, 2018), 6.

12. Timothy Philip Schwartz-Barcott, *After the Disaster: Re-creating Community and Well-Being at Buffalo Creek since the Notorious Coal Mining Disaster in 1972* (Amherst, NY: Cambria Press, 2008), xxi.

13. Michelle Obama, *Becoming* (New York: Penguin, 2018), 220–21.

14. Ben Wisner, Piers Blaikie, Terry Cannon, and Ian Davis, *At Risk: Natural Hazards, People's Vulnerability, and Disasters* (London: Routledge, 1994), 14, 79–122.

15. Patricia Yaeger, *Dirt and Desire: Reconstructing Southern Women's Writing, 1930–1990* (Chicago: University of Chicago Press, 2000), 15; Karin H. deGravelles, "The Global Meets the Local: The Third-Worlding of New Orleans," *Journal of Curriculum and Pedagogy* 6, no. 1 (June 2009): 139–55. See also Anthony Carrigan, "Towards a Postcolonial Disaster Studies," in *Global Ecologies and the Environmental Humanities: Postcolonial Approaches*, ed. Elizabeth DeLoughrey, Jill Didur, and Anthony Carrigan (London: Routledge, 2015), 117–39.

16. Edwin L. McIntosh, "After the Flood," *New York Herald Tribune*, January 29, 1928. The press frequently used the word "calamity" ("Mastering the Mississippi," *Washington Post*, May 2, 1927), but it also appeared in the subtitle of J. P. Kemper's *Floods in the Valley of the Mississippi* (New Orleans: National Flood Commission, 1928) and early in the text of *The Mississippi Valley Flood Disaster of 1927: Official Report of the Relief Operations* (Washington, DC: American National Red Cross, 1929), 5.

17. See Adam Fairclough, *Race and Democracy: The Civil Rights Struggle in Louisiana, 1915–1972* (1995; Athens: University of Georgia Press, 1999), 123, 327–28, 388.

18. "Coolidge Refuses Special Session for Flood Aid," *Times-Picayune*, April 30, 1927. On Coolidge's reluctance to act, see John M. Barry, *Rising Tide: The Great Mississippi Flood of 1927 and How It Change America* (New York: Simon and Schuster, 1997), 286–87.

19. Calvin Coolidge, "Address at the Annual Meeting of the American Red Cross, Washington, D.C.," October 3, 1927, www.presidency.ucsb.edu/ws/index.php?pid=430.

20. Amity Shlaes, *Coolidge* (New York: HarperCollins, 2013), 358. "Coolidge Tour Hinges on Hoover," *Times-Picayune*, May 1, 1927.

21. "House Concurrent Resolution No. 36," March 29, 1928, "Missio–Mississippi Steamboating," Box 388, Commerce Papers, Herbert Hoover Presidential Library and Museum, West Branch, Iowa (hereafter Commerce Papers).

22. "Hoover to Flood Relief Duty," *Times-Picayune*, April 26, 1927. Kendrick A. Clements, *The Life of Herbert Hoover*, vol. 4, *Imperfect Visionary, 1918–1928* (New York: Palgrave Macmillan, 2010), 378–82.

23. Herbert Hoover, "Inaugural Address," March 4, 1929, *Public Papers of the President, 1929* (Washington, DC: US Government Printing Office, 1974), 6.

24. For this statistic, see *Losses and Damages Resulting from the Flood of 1927* (Memphis, TN: Mississippi River Flood Control Association, 1927), 3.

25. See Bruce A. Lohof, "Herbert Hoover, Spokesman of Humane Efficiency: The Mississippi Flood of 1927," *American Quarterly* 22, no. 3 (Fall 1970): 690–700.

26. Michele Landis Dauber, *The Sympathetic State: Disaster Relief and the Origins of the American Welfare State* (Chicago: University of Chicago Press, 2013), 3.

27. Letter from Sally Bell to Herbert Hoover, April 25, 1927, "Mississippi Valley Flood—Relief Work, Miscellaneous, 1927 April," Box 388, Commerce Papers.

28. Letters from George Long to Joseph E. Ransdell, April 26, 1927, and from George Long to Edwin S. Broussard, April 26, 1927, Box 388, Commerce Papers.

29. "Two Louisiana Disasters—The Flood and Hoover," *Seattle Post-Intelligencer*, May 16, 1927.

30. See the interview with James Hand Jr. of Rolling Fork, Mississippi, December 29, 1970, in Henry Kline, *The Flood of 1927* (Jackson: Mississippi Department of Archives and History, 1970), 108. For praise of the Red Cross in Vicksburg, Mississippi, see " 'We Have a Fighting Spirit …': Recollections of the Flood of 1927 by South Deltans," *Delta Scene* (Spring 1980): 24–25. "Red Cross Blues" was first recorded in summer 1933 and then was re-recorded variously with different lyrics; see Oliver, *Blues Fell This Morning*, 222–23.

31. Clements, *Life of Herbert Hoover*, 4: 373. Glen Jeansonne, *Herbert Hoover: A Life* (New York: New American Library, 2016), 182.

32. Isaac Monroe Cline, *Storms, Floods, and Sunshine: A Book of Memoirs* (New Orleans: Pelican, 1945), 197. "Colony from Lower Parishes Living Comfortably," *Times-Picayune*, May 8, 1927, and "Food Committee Makes Inspection of Crevasse Area," *Times-Picayune*, May 9, 1927.

33. "Red Cross Reconstruction Fund," "Mississippi Valley Flood—Relief Work, Miscellaneous, 1927 May 21–25," Box 388, Commerce Papers. The Red Cross documented the function of the relief camps (called "refugee camps") in *The Mississippi Valley Flood Disaster of 1927*, 38–48.

34. On Memphis newspapers, see Patrick O'Daniel, *When the Levee Breaks: Memphis and the Mississippi Valley Flood of 1927* (Charleston, SC: History Press, 2013).

35. This letter closes by asking if the millions of dollars of expense in white bread is "really doing millions of dollars' worth of good, or is it causing still further wretchedness, disease and death?": Lieutenant Rex E. Keller, "Why Add Insult to Injury? Mississippi Flood Sufferers Have Enough Now!" May

20, 1927, "Mississippi Valley Flood—Relief Work, Miscellaneous, 1927 May 16–20," Box 388, Commerce Papers.

36. Hoover, "Bible #751," Box 388, Commerce Papers. On venereal disease, see Pete Daniel, *Deep'n as It Come: The 1927 Mississippi River Flood* (Fayetteville: University of Arkansas Press, 1996), 170–75.

37. Clements, *Life of Herbert Hoover*, 378; Barry, *Rising Tide*, 238–58.

38. Gifford Pinchot, "Prevention First," *Survey Graphic* (July 1927): 367. For rediscovered footage of the disaster, see Bill Morrison's 2014 documentary *The Great Flood*.

39. For the headline, see Washington, DC's *Sunday Star*, May 8, 1927. On aid camps, see Arthur Kellogg, "Up from the Bottom Lands," *Survey Graphic* (July 1927): 360–61, and Barry, *Rising Tide*, 274–75. On pellagra, see Joseph Goldberger and Edgar Sydenstricker, "Pellagra in the Mississippi Flood Area," *Public Health Reports* 42, no. 44 (November 1927): 2706–25; "Use Yeast to Combat Flood Area Disease," *New York Times*, August 24, 1927; George Brown Tindall, *The Emergence of the New South, 1913–1945* (Baton Rouge: Louisiana State University Press, 1967), 276–84; and Elizabeth Etheridge, *The Butterfly Caste: A Social History of Pellagra in the South* (Westport, CT: Greenwood Press, 1972).

40. For vaccination statistics, see "Information Relative to Public Health Activities in the Flooded Area of Mississippi," "Public Health Activities—Flooded Area of Miss, 1927," Flood Control and Relief Files, 1927–1937, Mississippi State Department of Health, Series 2182, Box 19306, Mississippi Department of Archives and History, Jackson.

41. See the *Daily Democrat-Times* of Greenville, Mississippi (April 25, 1927). "Hoover Comes out of the Mud" featured in many newspapers on September 28, 1928: "Mississippi Valley Flood—Relief Work Clippings 1927, September (2), Box 391, Commerce Papers, Herbert Hoover Presidential Library and Museum. For mistreatment in relief camps, see "Refugees Herded Like Cattle to Stop Escape from Peonage" and "Use Troops in Flood Area to Imprison Farm Hands," *Chicago Defender*, May 7, 1927.

42. "Levee Breaks at Stops Landing," *Daily Democrat-Times*, April 21, 1927. "150 or More Dead in Flood, Is Belief," *New York Times*, April 24, 1927. Barry, *Rising Tide*, 199–209.

43. William Percy, *Lanterns on the Levee: Recollections of a Planter's Son* (New York: Knopf, 1941), 249–50, 257–59.

44. "Scores of Hysterical Refugees Scream in Attics of Clarendon; Four Cling to Roof as Boat Sinks," *Times-Picayune*, April 22, 1927.

45. "No Cause to Fear for City, States Major Holcombe," *Times-Picayune*, April 22, 1927.

46. "Hoover Tells of Terrific Disaster," *Boston Daily Globe*, May 1, 1927.

47. "Refugees Pour into Camp Here from the Lowlands" and "Flood Conditions in Southeast Ark. Are Growing Acute," *Natchez Democrat*, April 27, 1927, and "Catastrophe: Deluge," *Time*, May 2, 1927.

48. Memphis itself flooded in 1937. On the racial politics of this relief effort, see David Welkym "'There Will Be No More Discrimination: Race, Power, and the Memphis Flood of 1937," in *An Unseen Light: Black Struggles for Freedom*

in Memphis, Tennessee, ed. Aram Goudsouzian and Charles W. McKinney Jr. (Lexington: University Press of Kentucky, 2018), 86–106.

49. See Franklin D. Roosevelt, "The President Transmits to the Congress a Report on Control and Use of Headwaters to Conserve Water and Control Floods," May 12, 1937, *The Public Papers and Addresses of Franklin D. Roosevelt, 1937 Volume: The Constitution Prevails* (New York: Macmillan, 1941), 193–96.

50. Robert E. Park, "Human Migration and the Marginal Man," *American Journal of Sociology* 33, no. 6 (May 1928): 881–93; Richard Wright, *Down by the Riverside*, in *Uncle Tom's Children* (1938; New York: HarperCollins, 2004), 75.

51. Wright, *Down by the Riverside*, 63.

52. Wright described his childhood memories of the river near Natchez as "yellow, dreaming waters" (due to the river's sandy sedimentation) that gave "the vague sense of the infinite." He was pleased to leave for Memphis though, returning to his boyhood Delta town only once, briefly, in 1940. Richard Wright, *Black Boy* (1945; New York: Vintage, 2000), 8–9.

53. Wright, *Down by the Riverside*, 124.

54. See "Deny Food to Flood Victims in Mississippi," *Chicago Defender*, June 4, 1927, and "See Attempt to Hide Facts as Committee Starts Flood Probe," *Chicago Defender*, July 16, 1927. Will Percy recounts the *Chicago Defender* criticisms of his role as Greenville's chair of the flood relief: Percy, *Lanterns on the Levee*, 263–65.

55. Wright, *Down by the Riverside*, 69. For criticism of the Red Cross along racial lines, see "The Flood, the Red Cross, and the National Guard," *The Crisis* 35, nos. 1–3 (January–March 1928): 5–7, 26–28, 41–43, 64, 100–102.

56. William Howard, "Richard Wright's Flood Stories and the Great Mississippi Flood of 1927: Social and Historical Backgrounds," *Southern Literary Journal* 16, no. 2 (Spring 1984): 47. The second story, "Silt," appeared in the *New Masses* (August 24, 1937) and was republished as "The Man Who Saw the Flood" in *Eight Men* (Cleveland: World, 1961).

57. Wright, *Uncle Tom's Children*, 74.

58. Howard, "Richard Wright's Flood Stories," 48.

59. Percy, *Lanterns on the Levee*, 268.

60. Kai T. Erikson, *Everything in Its Path: Destruction of Community in the Buffalo Creek Flood* (New York: Simon and Schuster, 1976), i.

61. Erikson, *Everything in Its Path*, ii, v.

62. Kathleen J. Tierney and Barbara Baisden, *Crisis Intervention Programs for Disaster Victims: A Source Book and Manual for Smaller Communities*, Miscellaneous Report 22 (Disaster Research Center, Ohio State University, 1977), 28–29.

63. Tierney and Baisden, *Crisis Intervention Programs for Disaster Victims*, 30. Following the flood, West Virginia's Republican governor, Arch A. Moore Jr., banned what he called irresponsible reporters from the vicinity; see Harry M. Caudhill, "Buffalo Creek Disaster," *Saturday Review*, August 26, 1972, 16. For radio reports, see "Anatomy of a Disaster: Hope to Agony, Tested Logan Residents Caught by Surprise," *Charleston Daily Mail*, February 28, 1972.

64. Commission to Investigate the Buffalo Creek Disaster, *Disaster on Buffalo Creek, 1972* (Charleston, WV: Citizens' Commission), 5.

65. Erikson, *Everything in Its Path*, 22, 251.

66. Erikson, *Everything in Its Path*, vi. On the psychological impact of disasters, see Kai T. Erikson, *A New Species of Trouble: Explorations in Disaster, Trauma, and Community* (New York: Norton, 1994).

67. Erikson, *Everything in Its Path*, 48.

68. Richard A. Couto, "Appalachian Innovation in Health Care," in *Appalachia and America: Autonomy and Regional Dependence*, ed. Allen Batteau (Lexington: University Press of Kentucky, 1983), 168.

69. Erikson, *Everything in Its Path*, 11.

70. Erikson, *Everything in Its Path*, 14–15.

71. "The Warning, If Any, Was Not Enough...All Lost, Many Thankful for Their Lives," *Bluefield Daily Telegraph*, March 5, 1972.

72. See Tom Nugent, "After Buffalo Creek: Bureaucracy of Disaster," *The Nation*, June 18, 1973, 785–88.

73. See Barbara Ellen Smith, *Digging Our Own Graves: Coal Miners and the Struggle over Black Lung Disease* (Philadelphia: Temple University Press, 1987); Alan Derickson, *Black Lung: Anatomy of a Public Health Disaster* (Ithaca, NY: Cornell University Press, 2014), 154–56; Wendy Welch, ed., *Public Health in Appalachia: Essays from the Clinic and the Field* (Jefferson, NC: McFarland, 2014).

74. On the need for a Coal Mine Health and Safety Bill, see the letter from Hubert H. Humphrey to Lyndon B. Johnson, September 11, 1968, "HE 3-2 Occupational Health," EX HE 3, Box 14, Paper of Lyndon Baines Johnson, LBJ Library, Austin, Texas.

75. See Richard Fry, "Making Amends: Coal Miners, the Black Lung Association, and Federal Compensation Reform, 1969–1972," *Federal History* 5 (January 2013), www.shfg.org/resources/Documents/FH%205%20(2013)%20Fry.pdf.

76. Richard M. Nixon, "Message to the Congress Proposing Additional Disaster Relief Measures Following Tropical Storm Agnes," July 17, 1972, *Public Papers of the Presidents, Richard Nixon, 1972* (Washington, DC: US Government Printing Office, 1974), 735.

77. See Andrew J. F. Morris, "Psychic Aftershocks, Crisis Counseling, and Disaster Relief Policy," *History of Psychology* 14, no. 3 (August 2011): 264–86.

78. *The Buffalo Creek Flood: An Act of Man* (dir. Mimi Pickering, 1975) appears on a 2006 Appalshop DVD alongside a 1985 documentary, *Buffalo Creek Revisited*, which focuses on the process of rebuilding the communities along Buffalo Creek Valley.

79. Just a fortnight after the flood Governor Moore demanded that the one hundred or so coal waste impoundments in West Virginia be pumped dry to prevent a repeat of the slurry spill: "Arch's Orders: Pump All Dams Dry," *Raleigh Register*, March 7, 1972.

80. Subcommittee on Labor of the Committee on Labor and Public Welfare, *Buffalo Creek (W. Va.) Disaster, 1972*, United States Senate, 92nd Congress,

2nd Session (Washington, DC: US Government Printing Office, 1972), Appendix A, Part 1, 1220, 1234.

81. Commission to Investigate the Buffalo Creek Disaster, *Disaster on Buffalo Creek 1972*, 2.

82. Commission to Investigate the Buffalo Creek Disaster, *Disaster on Buffalo Creek 1972*, 6.

83. Commission to Investigate the Buffalo Creek Disaster, *Disaster on Buffalo Creek 1972*, 7.

84. Commission to Investigate the Buffalo Creek Disaster, *Disaster on Buffalo Creek 1972*, 30.

85. Gerald M. Stern, *The Buffalo Creek Disaster: The Story of the Survivors' Unprecedented Lawsuit* (New York: Vintage, 1976), x.

86. Bill Clinton's foreword to the 2008 edition of Stern, *Buffalo Creek Disaster*, n.p.

87. James L. Titchener and Frederic T. Kapp, "Family and Character Change at Buffalo Creek," *American Journal of Psychiatry* 133, no. 3 (March 1976): 295.

88. Titchener and Kapp, "Family and Character Change at Buffalo Creek," 296, 298.

89. Erikson, *Everything in Its Path*, 48, 136.

90. Erikson, *Everything in Its Path*, 146, and Stern, *Buffalo Creek Disaster*, 177.

91. See *Delayed Redevelopment Was Reasonable after Flood Disaster in West Virginia* (Washington, DC: US General Accounting Office, 1976).

92. See Goldine C. Gleser, Bonnie L. Green, and Carolyn Winget, *Prolonged Psychosocial Effects of Disaster: A Study of Buffalo Creek* (New York: Academic Press, 1981), 121–36.

93. Erikson, *Everything in Its Path*, 130.

94. Robert Jay Lifton and Eric Olson, "The Human Meaning of Total Disaster," *Psychiatry* 39, no. 1 (February 1976): 1–18, and for Gerald M. Stern, "From Chaos to Responsibility," *American Journal of Psychiatry* 133, no. 3 (March 1976): 300–301.

95. See the two reviews in *Social Forces* 57, no. 2 (December 1978): 721–23, and Lynda Ann Ewen and Julia Lewis, "Revisiting Buffalo Creek and *Everything in Its Path*: Deconstructing an Outsider's Stereotypes, *Appalachian Journal* 27, no. 1 (Fall 1999): 22–45.

96. Erin R. Eldridge, "The Continuum of Coal Violence and Post-Coal Possibilities in the Appalachian South," *Journal of Political Ecology* 22, no. 1 (2015): 279–98.

97. American Minor, "Buffalo Creek," *Buffalo Creek* EP (2004). Mining blues have a long history going back to the Carter Family's "Coal Miner's Blues" of 1938. Two songs of 1972, the Kentucky trade union organizer Nimrod Workman's "Coal Black Mining Blues" and Arkansas folk singer Jim Ringer's "Black Waters," spotlight the intensifying labor disputes.

98. For the Martin County slurry spill, see Robert Salyer's 2005 Appalshop film *Sludge*, and on regional environmental health threats, see Drew A.

Swanson, *Beyond the Mountains: Commodifying Appalachian Environments* (Athens: University of Georgia Press, 2018).

99. Schwartz-Barcott's *After the Disaster* informs my reading of the song.

100. Denise Giardina, *The Unquiet Earth: A Novel* (New York: Norton, 1992), 351–67.

101. "Last Full Measure of Love: 3 Unclaimed Flood Toddlers Rest in Peace," *Charleston Daily Mail*, March 28, 1972.

102. The 2006 Mine Improvement and New Emergency Response Act (the MINER Act) required that mining companies take their health and safety responsibilities seriously. Health care benefits remain precarious for mining families, though, while the adverse health effects of mountaintop removal include the contamination of public water supplies. See, for example, Shirley Stewart Burns, *Bringing Down the Mountains: The Impact of Mountaintop Removal on Southern West Virginia Communities* (Charleston: West Virginia University Press, 2007).

103. See Lisa A. Eckenwiler, "Emergency Health Professionals and the Ethics of Crisis," in *In the Wake of Terror: Medicine and Morality in a Time of Crisis*, ed. Jonathan D. Moreno (Cambridge, MA: MIT Press, 2003), 111.

104. See "A Flood of Emotion in Song," *New York Times*, April 27, 2008. Plaquemines Parish itself experienced fourteen-foot storm surges when Katrina hit land.

105. Anna Hartnell, *Rewriting Exodus: American Futures from Du Bois to Obama* (London: Pluto, 2011), 1.

106. See Andrew S. Jessen, "Louisiana and the Coastal Zone Management Act in the Wake of Hurricane Katrina," *Ocean and Coastal Law Journal* 12, no. 1 (January 2006): 133–60.

107. Jed Horne, *Breach of Faith: Hurricane Katrina and the Near Death of a Great American City* (New York: Random House, 2008), 19. On Katrina and its aftermath, see, for example, Douglas Brinkley's *The Great Deluge: Hurricane Katrina, New Orleans, and the Mississippi Gulf Coast* (New York: HarperCollins, 2006).

108. On Mayor Nagin's role, see Robert Draper, *Dead Certain: The Presidency of George W. Bush* (New York: Free Press, 2007), 329–30.

109. "10 Years after Katrina," *New York Times*, August 16, 2015.

110. See Beverly H. Wright, "New Orleans: A City That Care Forgot," in *In Search of the New South: The Black Urban Experience in the 1970s and 1980s*, ed. Robert D. Bullard (Tuscaloosa: University of Alabama Press, 1987), 45–74.

111. See Evangeline Franklin, "A New Kind of Medical Disaster in the United States," in *There Is No Such Thing as a Natural Disaster: Race, Class, and Hurricane Katrina*, ed. Chester Hartman and Gregory D. Squires (New York: Routledge, 2006), 187–89, and Bradford H. Gray and Kathy Hebert, "Hospitals in Hurricane Katrina," in *Natural Disasters and Public Health: Hurricanes Katrina, Rita, and Wilma*, ed. Virginia M. Brennan (Baltimore: Johns Hopkins University Press, 2009), 70–85.

112. Rumor merged with fact when it came to accounts of rioting at and near the Convention Center and Superdome. John R. Brinkerhoff, "In the Wake of the Storm: The National Response to Hurricane Katrina," in *Mismanaging*

Mayhem: How Washington Responds to Crisis, ed. James Jay Carafano and Richard Weitz (Westport, CT: Praeger, 2008), 226–29.

113. Franklin, "New Kind of Medical Disaster," 190. Havidán Rodríguez, Joseph Trainor, and Enrico L. Quarantelli, "Rising to the Challenges of a Catastrophe: The Emergent and Prosocial Behavior Following Hurricane Katrina," *Annals of the American Academy of Political and Social Science* 604, no. 1 (March 2006): 82–101.

114. "A Crisis Agency in Crisis," *U.S. News and World Report*, September 19, 2005.

115. "Individuals with Disabilities in Emergency Preparedness: Executive Order 13347" (Washington, DC: Department of Homeland Security, 2005), 3. This July 21, 2005, report is available at www.dhs.gov/disabilityprepared nessicc. In September 2005 the chair of the National Council of Disability wrote to the secretary of Homeland Security to argue for better coordination for those with disabilities affected by Katrina; Letter from Lex Friedan to Michael Chertoff (September 19, 2005), Folder "NCD–Katrina," Box 3, Domestic Policy Council: Susan Buckland—Subject File, George W. Bush Presidential Library and Museum. It is worth noting that in February 2003 the DHS launched a Ready Campaign (www.ready.gov) "to promote preparedness through public involvement" in the face of a range of "natural and man-made disasters."

116. "Individuals with Disabilities in Emergency Preparedness," 22–23.

117. Anderson Cooper, *Dispatches from the Edge: A Memoir of War, Disasters, and Survival* (New York: Harper, 2007), 142–43. Cooper was, at that time, best known for his foreign dispatches from Africa and Asia; as he observes the "shell-shock" of New Orleans residents and squints at the carnage, he says "for a second I'm back in Somalia" (153). For the othering of the Katrina-hit Gulf Coast, see DeGravelles, "The Global Meets the Local," 139–55. Whereas Biloxi recovered reasonably quickly after the hurricane, Waveland and Bay St. Louis were "largely obliterated"; see "Recovery Is Taking Shape on Mississippi Coast," *Times-Picayune*, March 12, 2006, and Ellis Anderson, *Under Surge, Under Siege: The Odyssey of Bay St. Louis and Katrina* (Jackson: University Press of Mississippi, 2010).

118. "National Hurricane Preparedness Week, 2005: A Proclamation," May 15, 2005, "National Hurricane Preparedness Week," Box 7, White House Office of Presidential Correspondence, Presidential Proclamations, George W. Bush Presidential Library and Museum.

119. See Jean Edward Smith, *Bush* (New York: Simon and Schuster, 2016), 431–34. First Lady Laura Bush defended the president's decision not to visit the disaster zone immediately, believing it would have diverted attention from the relief effort. Laura Bush, *Spoken from the Heart* (New York: Scribner's, 2010), 339.

120. George W. Bush, "Remarks on the Relief Efforts for Hurricane Katrina," August 31, 2005, *Public Papers of the Presidents, George W. Bush, 2005*, Book 2 (Washington, DC: US Government Printing Office, 2009), 1379.

121. George W. Bush, "The President's Radio Address," August 26, 2006, *Public Papers of the Presidents, George W. Bush, 2006*, Book 2 (Washington, DC: US Government Printing Office, 2010), 1555.

122. Bush, "Remarks Following a Meeting with Former President George H. W. Bush and Former President William J. Clinton," September 1, 2005, *Public Papers, George W. Bush, 2005*, Book 2, 1381.

123. "Waiting for a Leader," *New York Times*, September 1, 2005.

124. "Barbara Bush Calls Evacuees Better Off," *New York Times*, September 7, 2005.

125. George W. Bush, "Remarks Following a Walking Tour of Areas Damaged by Hurricane Katrina" and "Remarks on Hurricane Katrina Recovery Efforts in Kenner, Louisiana," *Public Papers of the Presidents, George W. Bush, 2005*, Book 2, 1386, 1390.

126. See Paul Martin Lester, *On Floods and Photo Ops: How Herbert Hoover and George W. Bush Exploited Catastrophes* (Jackson: University Press of Mississippi, 2010).

127. Bush, "The President's Radio Address," *Public Papers, 2006*, Book 2, 1555–56. George W. Bush, *Decision Points* (New York: Crown, 2010), 330.

128. Henry A. Giroux, *Stormy Weather: Katrina and the Politics of Disposability* (Boulder, CO: Paradigm, 2006), 22. On the "biopolitics of disposability," see Christopher Lloyd, *Rooting Memory, Rooting Place: Regionalism in the Twenty-First-Century American South* (London: Palgrave Macmillan, 2015), 53–84.

129. Raymond Scurfield, "Post-Katrina Storm Disorder and Recovery in Mississippi More Than 2 Years Later," *Traumatology* 14, no. 2 (June 2008): 88–106.

130. Michael Casserly, "Double Jeopardy: Public Education in New Orleans Before and After the Storm," in *There Is No Such Thing as a Natural Disaster*, 206–7.

131. See Nancy Boyd-Franklin, "Working with African Americans and Trauma: Lessons for Clinicians from Hurricane Katrina," in *Re-visioning Family Therapy: Race, Culture, and Gender in Clinical Practice*, 2nd ed., ed. Monica McGoldrick and Kenneth V. Hardy (New York: Guilford, 2008), 244–56.

132. "HSS Efforts to Help Persons with Disabilities Impacted by Hurricane Katrina," Folder "Hurricane Katrina," Box 2, Domestic Policy Council: Susan Buckland—Subject File, George W. Bush Presidential Library and Museum.

133. Casserly, "Double Jeopardy," 207–8. Keith Elder et al., "African Americans' Decisions Not to Evacuate New Orleans before Hurricane Katrina: A Qualitative Study," *American Journal of Public Health* 97, no. 1 (April 2007): S129.

134. On the psychological impact of the evacuation, see Howard J. Osofsky, "Posttraumatic Stress Symptoms in Children after Hurricane Katrina: Predicting the Need for Mental Health Services," *American Journal of Orthopsychiatry* 79, no. 2 (April 2009): 212–20, and "The Lost Children of Katrina," *The Atlantic*, April 2, 2015.

135. Marline Otte, "The Mourning After: Languages and Loss and Grief in Post-Katrina New Orleans," *Journal of American History* 94, no. 3 (December 2007): 828.

136. Chris Rose, *1 Dead in Attic: After Katrina* (New York: Simon and Schuster, 2007), 16–18.

137. Rose, *1 Dead in Attic*, 63.

138. Rose, *1 Dead in Attic*, 64.

139. Rose, *1 Dead in Attic*, 327–39.

140. "Post-Katrina Depression Triples Suicide Rate in New Orleans," *New Orleans City Business*, July 3, 2006, and "A Legacy of the Storm: Depression and Suicide," *New York Times*, June 21, 2006.

141. See Jean Rhodes et al., "The Impact of Hurricane Katrina on the Mental and Physical Health of Low-Income Parents in New Orleans," *American Journal of Orthopsychiatry* 80, no. 2 (April 2010): 237–47.

142. See Gary Rivlin, *Katrina: After the Flood* (New York: Simon and Schuster, 2015), 368, and Ronald C. Kessler et al., "Trends in Mental Illness and Suicidality after Hurricane Katrina," *Molecular Psychiatry* 13, no. 4 (April 2008): 373–84.

143. Ronald C. Kessler et al., "Mental Illness and Suicidality after Hurricane Katrina," *Bulletin of the World Health Organization* 84, no. 12 (December 2006): 936.

144. See Susan M. Sterett, "New Orleans Everywhere: Bureaucratic Accountability and Housing Policy after Katrina," in *Catastrophe: Law, Politics, and the Humanitarian Impulse*, ed. Austin Sarat and Javier Lezaun (Amherst: University of Massachusetts Press, 2009), 83–115.

145. *Post-catastrophic Crisis: Addressing the Dramatic Need and Scant Availability of Mental Health Care in the Gulf Coast*, Congressional Hearing Before the Ad Hoc Subcommittee on Disaster Recovery, October 31, 2007 (Washington, DC: US Government Printing Office, 2008), 2.

146. For the controversial closure of Charity Hospital, see *Big Charity: The Death of America's Oldest Hospital* (dir. Alex Glustrom, 2017). Another medical controversy was the forty-five bodies found in the aftermath of Katrina in the uptown Memorial Medical Center that raised suspicions of second-degree murder, see "The Deadly Choices at Memorial," *New York Times*, August 25, 2009, and Sheri Fink, *Five Days at Memorial: Life and Death in a Storm-Ravaged Hospital* (New York: Crown, 2013).

147. For the patient statistics, see the hospital display in the Living with Hurricanes exhibition at the Presbytère, Louisiana State Museum, which emphasizes the shift from crisis to resilience and renewal across an extended timeline, going back to Hurricane Betsy of 1965.

148. *Post-catastrophic Crisis*, 32, 37.

149. See, for example, Arjen Boin, Christer Brown, and James A. Richardson, *Managing Hurricane Katrina: Lessons from a Megacrisis* (Baton Rouge: Louisiana State University Press, 2019).

150. On tourist areas as "political combat zones," see Tara McPherson, *Reconstructing Dixie: Race, Gender, and Nostalgia in the Imagined South* (Durham, NC: Duke University Press, 2003), 99. On cheap labor, see Allison Graham, "Free at Last: Post-Katrina New Orleans and the Future of Conspiracy," *Journal of American Studies* 4, no. 3 (December 2010): 601–11.

151. *Trouble the Water* (dir. Tia Lessin and Carl Deal, 2008) does not deal explicitly with health, but its website raises awareness of NGO and community partners tackling poverty and homelessness, www.troublethewaterfilm.com.

Kimberly Rivers Roberts's follow-up film *Fear No Gumbo* (2018) tackles challenges in the Lower Ninth Ward a decade after Katrina.

152. Jesmyn Ward, *Salvage the Bones: A Novel* (New York: Bloomsbury, 2011), 255. "Mississippi's Recovery after Katrina Holds Lessons for Policy Makers," *New York Times*, August 28, 2015. On race and renewal, see Robert D. Bullard and Beverly Wright, *Race, Place, and Environmental Justice after Hurricane Katrina* (Boulder, CO: Westview, 2009), and Anna Hartnell, *After Katrina: Race, Neoliberalism, and the End of the American Century* (Albany: State University of New York Press, 2017).

153. Spike Lee's documentaries aired on HBO on August 16, 2006, and August 23, 2010, respectively.

154. Lloyd, *Rooting Memory, Rooting Place*, 71, 75–84.

155. Kent B. Germany, *New Orleans after the Promises: Poverty, Citizenship, and the Search for the Great Society* (Athens: University of Georgia Press, 2007), 310.

156. Anissa Janine Wardi, *Water and African American Memory: An Ecocritical Perspective* (Gainesville: University Press of Florida, 2011), 140.

157. For the statistics, see Aaron Schneider, *Renew Orleans?: Globalized Development and Worker Resistance after Katrina* (Minneapolis: University of Minnesota Press, 2018), 99.

158. *United Nations Plan of Action on Disaster Risk Reduction for Resilience* (2017), www.preventionweb.net/files/49076_unplanofaction.pdf.

159. George Luber and Jay Lemery, *Global Climate Change and Human Health* (San Francisco: Jossey-Bass, 2015), 57–66.

160. George W. Doherty, ed., *Being There When It Counts* (Laramie, WY: Rocky Mountain DMH Institute Press, 2010), 104–5.

161. See Dauber, *Sympathetic State*, 14; Bohle, *Living with Vulnerability*, 9.

162. See Sara Le Menestrel's essay "Memory Lives in New Orleans: The Process and Politics of Commemoration," in *Hurricane Katrina in Transatlantic Perspective*, ed. Romain Huret and Randy J. Sparks (Baton Rouge: Louisiana State University Press, 2014), 153–77. See also "Remembering Katrina and Its Unlearned Lessons, 15 Years On," *New York Times*, August 21, 2020.

163. Ward, *Salvage the Bones*, 255. Flash flooding in summer 2017 exposed the city's creaky drainage system; "New Orleans Braces for More Rain, Watchful for Flash Floods," *New York Times*, August 10, 2017.

164. Al Gore, *An Inconvenient Truth: The Crisis of Global Warming* (New York: Viking, 2007), 65.

165. "Where Harvey Is Hitting Hardest, 80 percent Lack Flood Insurance," *Washington Post*, August 29, 2017; "Where Did Harvey Hit Houston the Hardest?" *Houston Chronicle*, September 28, 2017.

166. These headlines are from the CNN evening broadcast of August 27, 2017.

167. "And Then the Rain Came," *New York Times*, August 27, 2017.

168. "Houston's Hospitals Treat Storm Victims and Become Victims Themselves," *New York Times*, August 28, 2017.

169. "Hurricane Harvey's Public-Health Nightmare," *The Atlantic*, Sep-

tember 2, 2017; "Life after the Storm: Children Who Survived Katrina Offer Lessons," *New York Times*, September 8, 2017.

170. On Louise Walker, see "Flood Traps Houston Apartment Residents," August 27, 2018, www.cnn.com/videos/tv/2017/08/27/houston-apartment-flood-survivors-cabrera-segment-nr.cnn.

171. "The Health App That Beat Hurricane Harvey," *Politico*, January 18, 2018, www.politico.com/magazine/story/2018/01/18/what-works-health-app-harvey-216479.

172. See Nishant Kishore et al., "Mortality in Puerto Rico after Hurricane Maria," *New England Journal of Medicine* 379 (May 2018): 162–70; "The New Estimate of Deaths in Puerto Rico Reflects a Broader and Shameful Neglect," *New Yorker*, May 31, 2018; and "Why Are the Death Tolls in Puerto Rico from Hurricane Maria So Different?" *New York Times*, June 2, 2018. For the autumn 2018 report, see *Transformation and Innovation in the Wake of Devastation: An Economic and Disaster Recovery Plan for Puerto Rico*, www.p3.pr.gov/assets/pr-draft-recovery-plan-for-comment-july-9-2018.pdf.

173. The Deep from the Heart concert featured five Points of Light awards (a scheme established by George H. W. Bush in 1989) for volunteer storm-relief workers.

174. "100 Days of Darkness," *New York*, December 25, 2017–January 7, 2018, 16–29, 86–88.

175. Carmen Yulín Cruz speaking on CNN's *New Day*, August 29, 2018. See also "Trump's False Claims Rejecting Puerto Rico's Death Toll from Hurricane Maria," *New York Times*, September 13, 2018. On structural violence in Puerto Rico, see Marisol LeBrón, *Policing Life and Death: Race, Violence, and Resistance in Puerto Rico* (Berkeley: University of California Press, 2019).

176. See the foreword by the Professors Self-Assembled in Solidarity Resistance (PAReS) to Naomi Klein, *The Battle for Paradise: Puerto Rico Takes on Disaster Capitalists* (Chicago: Haymarket, 2018), vii–xi.

177. Al Gore, *The Assault on Reason* (New York: Penguin, 2007), 2. See also "Walker Percy's Theory of Hurricanes," *New York Times*, August 4, 2015.

178. See "Hurricane Barry and the New Normal," *New York Times*, July 14, 2019, and the Climate Central report "Flooded Future: Global Vulnerability to Sea Level Rise Worse Than Previously Understood," October 29, 2019, www.climatecentral.org/news/report-flooded-future-global-vulnerability-to-sea-level-rise-worse-than-previously-understood.

CHAPTER 2: POVERTY

1. George W. Bush, "The President's Radio Address," August 26, 2006, *Public Papers of the Presidents, George W. Bush, 2006*, Book 2 (Washington, DC: US Government Printing Office, 2010), 1556.

2. "Hurricane Katrina: Emergency Support Function 15—External Affairs, September 16, 2005, Folder: "Hurricane Katrina," Box 2, Domestic Policy Council: Susan Buckland—Subject Files, George W. Bush Presidential Library and Museum, Dallas, Texas.

3. "Lots of Blame, But It's No Game," *U.S. News and World Report*, Sep-

tember 19, 2005, cited in Kevin Rozario, *The Culture of Calamity: Disaster and the Making of Modern America* (Chicago: University of Chicago Press, 2007), 213. *The Dust Bowl* (dir. Ken Burns, 2012).

4. Thomas Fisher, "Are Hurricanes Our Next Dust Bowl?" *Huffington Post*, February 4, 2013, www.huffpost.com/entry/hurricane-sandy_b_2207228.

5. David K. Shipler, *The Working Poor: Invisible in America* (New York: Vintage, 2005), xi.

6. "Extreme Poverty Returns to America," *Washington Post*, December 21, 2017.

7. Shipler, *Working Poor*, 11. See Alisha Coleman-Jensen, Mark Nord, and Anita Singh, *Household Food Security in the United States in 2012* (US Department of Agriculture, Economic Research Council, 2012). In 2018, this food insecure figure was calculated at 11.1 percent.

8. *One America in the 21st Century: Forging a New Future; The President's Initiative on Race* (Washington, DC: US Government Printing Office, 1998), 89.

9. Timothy Noah, *The Great Divergence: America's Growing Inequality Crisis and What We Can Do about It* (New York: Bloomsbury, 2012), 24. For the relationship between chronic poverty and ill health, see Kathryn J. Edin and H. Luke Shaefer, *$2.00 a Day: Living on Almost Nothing in America* (Boston: Houghton Mifflin, 2015).

10. Michael Harrington, *The Other America* (1962; New York: Collier, 1994), 2. Dwight Macdonald, "Our Invisible Poor," *New Yorker*, January 19, 1963, 82–132.

11. *Harvest of Shame* aired on CBS on November 25, 1960, directed by Fred W. Friendly. Eisenhower formed a President's Committee on Migratory Labor in late November 1960, just ten days before *Harvest of Shame* screened.

12. On the rhetoric and tactics of the War on Poverty, see Carl M. Brauer, "Kennedy, Johnson, and the War on Poverty," *Journal of American History* 69, no. 1 (June 1982): 98–119. Polls suggested that the nation was favorable to the campaign in 1964–66, but the mood had changed by late 1966: "The People: The Dimming of the Dream," *Time*, December 9, 1966, and "Has the Imposing Vision Faded?" *Washington Post*, January 15, 1967.

13. Documents relating to the National Health Survey are held at the National Archives and Records Administration, College Park, Maryland, in the National Institutes of Health holdings (Record Group 443, A1 44), including local newspaper and radio coverage. National articles such as "Illness Rises with Poverty in U.S. Index," *Washington Post*, January 17, 1938, and "6,000,000 Found Ill in Day by Survey of National Health," *New York Times*, January 17, 1938, responded to the Public Health Service press release of January 17, "Press Releases, 1935–1940," Box 26, President's Interdepartmental Committee to Coordinate Health and Welfare Activities, 1935–41, General Records, Franklin D. Roosevelt Presidential Library and Museum, Hyde Park, New York. See also George St. J. Perrott, Clark Tibbitts, and Rollo H. Britten, "The National Health Survey—Scope and Method of the Nation-wide Canvass of Sickness in Relation to Its Social and Economic Setting," *Public Health Reports* 54, no. 37 (September 1939): 1663–87.

14. See Kevin Fitzpatrick and Mark LaGory, *Unhealthy Cities: Poverty, Race, and Place in America* (New York: Routledge, 2011).

15. Richard A. Couto, *Ain't Gonna Let Nobody Turn Me Around: The Pursuit of Racial Justice in the Rural South* (Philadelphia: Temple University Press, 1991), 306–10, cited in Michael R. Grey, *New Deal Medicine: The Rural Health Programs of the Farm Security Administration* (Baltimore: Johns Hopkins University Press, 2002), 4.

16. Lyndon B. Johnson, "Statement by the President upon Signing Bill Providing for District of Columbia Participation in the Medicaid Program," December 27, 1967, *Public Papers of the Presidents, Lyndon B. Johnson, 1967*, Book 2 (Washington, DC: US Government Printing Office, 1968), 1192. Department of Health, Education and Welfare, Public Hearing on Medicaid, Atlanta, Georgia, December 20, 1968, "Hearings: Atlanta," Box 1, Papers of Wilbur J. Cohen, Lyndon Baines Johnson Library, Austin, Texas, 5.

17. On the legal aspects of Medicaid, see Sheri I. David, *With Dignity: The Search for Medicare and Medicaid* (Westport, CT: Greenwood Press, 1985), and for the history of Medicaid, see Jonathan Engel, *Poor People's Medicine: Medicaid and American Charity Care since 1965* (Durham, NC: Duke University Press, 2006), 48–53.

18. "Black America's Exploding Health Crisis," CBS, July 24, 2008, www .cbsnews.com/news/black-americas-exploding-health-crisis. Tim Giago, "Indian Health Care: A National Tragedy," *Huffington Post*, April 20, 2008, www .huffpost.com/entry/indian-health-care-a-nati_b_97666.

19. Hollis Godfrey, *The Health of the City* (Boston: Houghton Mifflin, 1910), 303.

20. John C. Dawson Sr., *High Plains Yesterdays: From XIT Days through Drouth and Depression* (Austin, TX: Eakin Press, 1985), 74.

21. Advertisement, *Texoma Times*, July 3, 1914.

22. Timothy Egan, *The Worst Hard Time: The Untold Story of Those Who Survived the Great American Dust Bowl* (Boston: Houghton Mifflin, 2006), 28–29, 91–92, 230, 261–62.

23. Dawson, *High Plains Yesterdays*, 87.

24. J. Russell Smith, "The Drought—Act of God and Freedom," *Survey Graphic* 23, no. 9 (September 1934): 412.

25. See Hugh H. Bennett and W. R. Chapline, *Soil Erosion: A National Menace* (Washington, DC: US Department of Agriculture, 1928), and Paul Bonnifield, *The Dust Bowl: Men, Dirt, and Depression* (Albuquerque: University of New Mexico Press, 1979), 87–118.

26. See Beatrix Hoffman, *Health Care for Some: Rights and Rationing in the United States since 1930* (Chicago: University of Chicago Press, 2012), 17–19.

27. See T. H. Watkins, *The Hungry Years: A Narrative History of the Great Depression in America* (New York: Henry Holt, 1999), 443.

28. Dawson, *High Plains Yesterday*, 178.

29. The Library of Congress holds Rothstein's untitled 1935 photograph of the Wilson plantation in Mississippi County, Arkansas. Dorothea Lange and Paul S. Taylor, *An American Exodus: A Record of Human Erosion* (New York: Reynal and Hitchcock, 1939).

30. Paul S. Taylor, "Statement in Support of Project to Establish Camps for Migrants in California," August 22, 1935, Taylor (Paul S.) Papers, Box 15, Folder 25, Bancroft Library, University of California, Berkeley.

31. See Bourke-White's draft introduction to Erskine Caldwell and Margaret Bourke-White, *You Have Seen Their Faces* (New York: Modern Age Book, 1937), from the manuscript held in the Margaret Bourke-White Archives, Syracuse University, Syracuse, New York.

32. Dorothea Lange, "The Assignment I'll Never Forget: Migrant Mother," *Popular Photography* 46, no. 2 (February 1960): 42–43; "When Biting Dust Sweeps Across the Land," *New York Times*, April 11, 1937. For context, see Brad D. Lookingbill, *Dust Bowl, USA: Depression America and the Ecological Imagination, 1929–1941* (Athens: Ohio University Press, 2001).

33. Franklin D. Roosevelt, "The Philosophy of Social Justice through Social Action," Campaign Address at Detroit, Michigan, October 2, 1932, *The Public Papers and Addresses of Franklin D. Roosevelt*, vol. 1, *The Genesis of the New Deal, 1928–1932* (New York: Random House, 1938), 771. "Gov. Roosevelt's Address at Detroit Asking Greater Efforts in Cause of Social Justice," *Washington Post*, October 3, 1932.

34. Franklin D. Roosevelt, "The 'Forgotten Man' Speech," Radio Address, Albany, NY, April 7, 1932, *The Public Papers and Addresses of Franklin D. Roosevelt*, 1: 625.

35. Roosevelt, "Philosophy of Social Justice through Social Action," 772.

36. See Committee on the Costs of Medical Care, *Medical Care for the American People: The Final Report of the Committee on the Costs of Medical Care* (Chicago: University of Chicago Press, 1932).

37. Michele Landis Dauber, *The Sympathetic State: Disaster Relief and the Origins of the American Welfare State* (Chicago: University of Chicago Press, 2013), 13.

38. E. L. Bishop, "Public Health at the Cross-Roads," *American Journal of Public Health* 25, no. 11 (November 1935): 1176.

39. "The Red Cross and the Great Drought," *Social Service Review* 6, no. 2 (June 1932): 297–300. See also Roger Lambert, "Hoover and the Red Cross in the Arkansas Drought of 1930," *Arkansas Historical Quarterly* 29, no. 1 (Spring 1970): 3–19.

40. Anthony J. Badger, *The New Deal: The Depression Years, 1933–1940* (Basingstoke: Macmillan, 1989), 236.

41. "When Biting Dust Sweeps Across the Land."

42. "How to Keep Well: The Effect of Dust on Health," *Chicago Daily Tribune*, April 13, 1936.

43. The first quotation is from the *Kansas City Times*, March 20, 1935, cited in Donald Worster, *Dust Bowl: The Southern Plains in the 1930s* (1979; Oxford: Oxford University Press, 2004), 17. The second is from a June 30, 1935, letter by Caroline Henderson published in the May 1936 issue of *The Atlantic*: Caroline Henderson, *Letters from the Dust Bowl*, ed. Alvin O. Turner (Norman: University of Oklahoma Press, 2001), 147–50. See also "Black Gale Sweeps Panhandle Territory Sunday Night," *Dalhart Texan*, April 15, 1935.

44. Woody Guthrie, "The Great Dust Storm," *Dust Bowl Ballads* (Victor Records, 1940).

45. Worster, *Dust Bowl*, 20–22; Egan, *Worst Hard Time*, 171–75.

46. See the letter from Senator William G. McAdoo to President Roosevelt, September 7, 1933, "Health 1933–37," OF 103, President's Central File, Franklin D. Roosevelt Presidential Library.

47. Woody Guthrie, "Dusty Old Dust," *Dust Bowl Ballads*. Guthrie, "Dead from the Dust," Series 1: Songs—1, Box 2, Woody Guthrie Center, Tulsa, Oklahoma.

48. "Silicosis Is Killin' Me," *Hard Hitting Songs for Hard-Hit People*, compiled by Alan Lomax (1967; Lincoln: University of Nebraska Press, 1999), 134. For Guthrie's view of Black Sunday, see Woody Guthrie, *Pastures of Plenty: A Self Portrait of Woody Guthrie*, ed. David Marsh and Harold Levanthol (New York: Harper, 1990), 43–44. On Guthrie's environmental songs, see Will Kaufman, *Woody Guthrie's Modern World Blues* (Norman: University of Oklahoma Press, 2018), 101–4.

49. Dorothea Lange and Daniel Dixon, "Photographing the Familiar," *Aperture* 1 (1952): 4–15, 68–72.

50. Gerald W. Johnson, "The Average American and the Depression," *Current History* 35 (February 1932): 671–75. On the psychological effects of migration and displacement, see Glen H. Elder Jr., *Children of the Great Depression: Social Change in Life Experience* (1974; Boulder, CO: Westview Press, 1999).

51. John Steinbeck, *The Grapes of Wrath* (1939; New York: Penguin, 2002), 51, 52, 110.

52. On Steinbeck's and Lange's political motives, see Dauber, *Sympathetic State*, 104–11. Lawrence Svobida, *An Empire of Dust*, republished as *Farming the Dust Bowl: A First-Hand Account from Kansas* (1940; Lawrence: University Press of Kansas, 1986), 37. The second quotation is from Svobida's dedication.

53. Svobida, *Farming the Dust Bowl*, 240, 34. Although Meade County had four small hospitals, it could not easily contend with the respiratory problems caused by the dust storms. Svobida notes that often doctors encouraged locals to evacuate if they had an "organic weakness" (234).

54. Svobida, *Farming the Dust Bowl*, 33.

55. Svobida, *Farming the Dust Bowl*, 238, 233.

56. Franklin D. Roosevelt, "The First 'Fireside Chat' of 1936," September 6, 1936, *The Public Papers and Addresses of Franklin D. Roosevelt*, vol. 5, *The People Approve, 1936* (New York: Random House, 1938), 332.

57. Roosevelt, "First 'Fireside Chat' of 1936," 331. For Roosevelt's account of the trip, see "Invitation of the Governors of the Drought States for a Drought Conference with the President," August 21, 1936, *Papers and Addresses of Franklin D. Roosevelt*, vol. 5, *The People Approve, 1936*, 293–95. Rexford G. Tugwell, head of Roosevelt's Resettlement Administration, visited the two panhandles in August 1936, and Roosevelt gave a speech in Oklahoma City in July 1938, stopping briefly at Wichita Falls, Texas, en route to San Diego (he had visited Dallas in 1936 and the Texas coast in 1937). For complaints he was neglecting the South, see Al Percy Garrot's telegram to France B. Sayre, July 22,

1936, "Louisiana (Dust Bowl Trip)," OF 200-EE, Trips of the President, Box 23, Franklin D. Roosevelt Presidential Library.

58. On Martha Friesen's diary, see Pamela Riney-Kehrberg, "Separation and Sorrow: A Farm Women's Life, 1935–1941," *Agricultural History* 67, no. 2 (Spring 1993): 185–96.

59. Letter from Caroline Henderson to Henry A. Wallace (Secretary of Agriculture), July 26, 1935, in Henderson, *Letters from the Dust Bowl*, 140.

60. The precursor to *The Grapes of Wrath*, Steinbeck's October 1936 series "The Harvest Gypsies," published in the *San Francisco News*, was possibly based on Sanora Babb's unpublished local reports on federal migrant camps.

61. See Keith L. Bryant Jr., "Oklahoma and the New Deal," in *The New Deal*, vol. 2, *The State and Local Levels*, ed. John Braeman, Robert H. Bremner, and David Brody (Columbus: Ohio State University Press, 1975), 166–97.

62. Sanora Babb, *Whose Names Are Unknown: A Novel* (Norman: University of Oklahoma Press, 2004), 44.

63. Babb, *Whose Names Are Unknown*, 90–91.

64. "Illness Rises with Poverty in U.S. Index," *Washington Post*, January 17, 1938.

65. "When Biting Dust Sweeps Across the Land."

66. US Department of Labor, *How American Buying Habits Changed* (Washington, DC: US Government Printing Office, 1959), 44. James T. Patterson, *America's Struggle against Poverty in the Twentieth Century* (1995; Cambridge, MA: Harvard University Press, 2000), 38.

67. See C. E. Waller, "The Social Security Act in Its Relation to Public Health," *American Journal of Public Health* 25, no. 11 (November 1935): 1186–94.

68. On "social security without health security," see Hoffman, *Health Care for Some*, 21–36, and Paul Starr, *Remedy and Reaction: The Peculiar American Struggle over Health Care Reform* (New Haven, CT: Yale University Press, 2013), 35–41. On the FSA's work to improve rural health following Roosevelt's reelection of 1937, see Grey, *New Deal Medicine*, 20–108. (The FSA helped 650,000 farmers to enroll into cooperative medical plans by 1942.)

69. *The Great Plains of the Future: Report of the Great Plains Committee* (December 1936), OF 2285, Box 2, Great Plains Drought Committee, December 1936–45, Franklin D. Roosevelt Library.

70. Godfrey, *Health of the City*, 302, 305.

71. Godfrey, *Health of the City*, 303, 305.

72. See *Where Shall We Live? Report on the Commission on Race and Housing* (Berkeley: University of California Press, 1958), 4. See also Davis McEntire, *Residence and Race: Final and Comprehensive Report to the Commission on Race and Housing* (Berkeley: University of California Press, 1960), Commission on Race and Housing documents held in the University of Chicago Library's Department of Special Collections.

73. Speech by Florence Greenberg, July 19, 1938, *Proceedings of the National Health Conference* (Washington, DC: US Government Printing Office, 1938), 84.

74. Vern L. Bullough and Bonnie Bullough, *Health Care for the Other Americans* (New York: Appleton-Century-Crofts, 1982), 4.

75. Bullough and Bullough, *Health Care for the Other Americans*, 6.

76. Lorraine Hansberry, *A Raisin in the Sun* (1959; London: Methuen, 2001), 28.

77. Hansberry, *A Raisin in the Sun*, 28.

78. Hansberry, *A Raisin in the Sun*, 62.

79. Stokely Carmichael and Charles V. Hamilton, *Black Power: The Politics of Liberation in America* (New York: Random House, 1967), 155.

80. Michelle Obama, *Becoming* (New York: Penguin, 2018), 44, 385.

81. Memo, Wilbur J. Cohen (Under Secretary of Health) to Douglass Cater (Special Assistant to the President), September 20, 1965, "HE Health, 11/22/63–9/2/65," EX HE Box 1, White House Central Files, LBJ Library.

82. See "Health & Nutrition (Tab 3)," "Aid to the Cities and the Urban Poor," Office Files of Joseph A. Califano, Box 34, Papers of Lyndon B. Johnson, LBJ Library.

83. Lyndon Johnson, "Special Message to the Congress on the Nation's Cities," March 2, 1965, *Public Papers of the Presidents, Lyndon B. Johnson, 1965*, Book 1 (Washington, DC: US Government Printing Office, 1966), 232–33.

84. On the "urban snake pit," see Lewis Herber, *Crisis in Our Cities* (Englewood Cliffs, NJ: Prentice-Hall, 1965), 10–16.

85. For the administration's efforts to experience ghetto life firsthand in spring 1967, see "Pricing Files: Ghetto Visit," Box 8, Office Files of John E. Robson and Stanford G. Ross, Papers of Lyndon Baines Johnson, LBJ Library.

86. On sending a copy of *Youth in the Ghetto* to the White House, Kenneth Clark received a reply from the president's special assistant to say, "it is clear that the real answers to our nation's youth problems must come from local groups like HARYOU which seek long-range solutions to basic problems": letter from Ralph A. Dungan to Kenneth B. Clark, April 14, 1964, "Clark, K," Name File, WHCF, LBJ Library. (Clark sent the president a signed copy of *Dark Ghetto* in 1965.) On HARYOU, see Kenneth B. Clark, *Dark Ghetto: Dilemmas of Social Power*, 2nd ed. (1965; Middletown, CT: Wesleyan University Press, 1989), xxvii.

87. *Youth in the Ghetto: A Study of the Consequences of Powerlessness and a Blueprint for Change* (New York: Harlem Youth Opportunities Unlimited, 1964), 313. Clark, *Dark Ghetto*, xxix–xxx.

88. Clark, *Dark Ghetto*, xxx.

89. Clark, *Dark Ghetto*, xxxvi.

90. See Gerald Markowitz and David Rosner, *Children, Race, and Power: Kenneth and Mamie Clark's Northside Center* (Charlottesville: University of Virginia Press, 1999).

91. James Baldwin, "The Harlem Ghetto" (1948), in *Notes of a Native Son* (1955; London: Penguin, 1991), 57.

92. Baldwin, "Fifth Avenue, Uptown," *Esquire*, July 1960, 72.

93. Baldwin, "The Harlem Ghetto," 72. Clark, *Dark Ghetto*, 82.

94. Ralph Ellison, "Harlem Is Nowhere" (1952), in *Shadow and Act* (New

York: Random House, 1964), 296. The nameless narrator of Ellison's 1952 novel *Invisible Man* describes himself as a "spook."

95. Clark, *Dark Ghetto*, 84. On anxiety among the urban poor, see Louis Harris, *Living Sick: How the Poor View Their Health Sources* (New York: Blue Cross Association, 1969).

96. Clark, *Dark Ghetto*, 62.

97. Clark, *Dark Ghetto*, 47, 57. See Erving Goffman, *Asylums: Essays on the Social Situation of Mental Patients and Other Inmates* (New York: Anchor, 1961).

98. The first volume of the Office of Economic Opportunity's three-volume survey *Maps of Poverty*, xi–xiii (table 3) shows that Chicago and New York City had nineteen of the 193 designated urban poverty areas for cities over 250,000 in population (based on the 1960 Census) or 10 percent of the nation's urban poverty areas. Office Files of Frederick Panzer, Boxes 26–27, Papers of Lyndon Baines Johnson, LBJ Library.

99. See Gabriel N. Mendes, *Under the Strain of Color: Harlem's Lafargue Clinic and the Promise of an Antiracist Psychiatry* (Ithaca, NY: Cornell University Press, 2015), 4, 9. For community action in Chicago, see Clifford R. Shaw, *Bright Shadows in Bronzetown: The Story of the Southside Community Committee* (1949; Los Angeles: HardPress, 2012).

100. Richard Wright, "Psychiatry Comes to Harlem," *Free World* (September 1946). Ellison discusses Lafargue Clinic in "Harlem Is Nowhere." For Ellison's collaboration with *Life* photographer Gordon Parks, see *Invisible Man: Gordon Parks and Ralph Ellison in Harlem*, ed. Michael Raz-Russo (Chicago: Art Institute of Chicago, 2017), and for an example of Parks's sociological imagination, see the March 8, 1968, issue of *Life*: "The Cry That Will Be Heard: The Negro and the Cities."

101. Kevin Robins, "Prisoners of the City: Whatever Could a Postmodern City Be?" in *Space and Place: Theories of Identity and Location*, ed. Erica Carter, James Donald, and Judith Squires (London: Lawrence and Wishart, 1993), 323.

102. See Dennis A. Doyle, *Psychiatry and Radical Liberalism in Harlem, 1936–1968* (Rochester, NY: University of Rochester Press, 2016), 128–33.

103. Hansberry, *A Raisin in the Sun*, 28.

104. E. Franklin Frazier, *The Negro in the United States* (New York: Macmillan, 1949), 636.

105. Abram Kardiner and Lionel Ovesey, *The Mark of Oppression: Explorations in the Personality of the American Negro*, 2nd ed. (1951; Cleveland: Meridian, 1962), ix.

106. *The People Left Behind: A Report by the National Advisory Commission on Rural Poverty* (Washington, DC: US Government Printing Office, 1967), ix–xii.

107. See John Dittmer, *Good Doctors: The Medical Committee of Human Rights and the Struggle for Social Justice in Health Care* (New York: Bloomsbury, 2009), and Thomas J. Ward, *Out in the Rural: A Mississippi Health Center and Its War on Poverty* (New York: Oxford University Press, 2017).

108. Fannie Lou Hamer's foreword to Tracy Sugarman, *Stranger at the Gates: A Summer in Mississippi* (New York: Hill and Wang, 1966), ix.

109. See Alan D. Berg, "Malnutrition and National Development," *Foreign Affairs* (October 1967): 126–36.

110. The headline of the July 28, 1967, issue of *Life* was "Newark: The Predictable Insurrection," and the inside feature was "Revolt in the Newark Ghetto."

111. See Thomas J. Hrach, *The Riot Report and the News: How the Kerner Commission Changed Media Coverage of Black America* (Amherst: University of Massachusetts Press, 2016), 4–10, and Julian E. Zelizer's introduction to the National Advisory Commission on Civil Disorder, *The Kerner Report* (1968; Princeton, NJ: Princeton University Press, 2016), xv. For the final point, see "OEO and the Riots—A Summary," Office for Economic Opportunity, Box 2, Volume II—Documentary Supplement, Chapters III–IV, Administrative History Collection, LBJ Library, 3.

112. "Office of the Assistant Secretary for Community and Field Services [1 of 2]," Box 2, Department of Health, Education, and Welfare, 1963–69, Administrative History Collection, LBJ Library, 9.

113. Lyndon B. Johnson, "Special Message to the Congress Recommending a Program for Cities and Metropolitan Areas," January 26, 1966, *Public Papers, Lyndon B. Johnson, 1966*, Book 1, 82. For a critique of Johnson's claim, see "'The Year of Rebirth for U.S. Cities' Turned Out to Be a 1966 Stillbirth," *Washington Post*, January 23, 1967.

114. Lyndon B. Johnson, "Special Message to the Congress Proposing a Nationwide War on the Sources of Poverty," March 16, 1964, and "Remarks to the Labor Advisory Council to the President's Committee on Equal Employment Opportunity, March 16, 1964, *Public Papers of the Presidents, Lyndon B. Johnson, 1963–64*, Book 1 (Washington, DC: US Government Printing Office, 1965), 375–80, 384–86. For the quotations, see "Administrative History of the Department of Housing and Urban Development," Volume I, Part I, Chapter 1 and Chapter IV, Box 1, Administrative History Collection, LBJ Library, 1, 5–6.

115. "Office of the Assistant Secretary for Community and Field Services [1 of 2]," 1–7.

116. For problems faced by OEO, see Patterson, *America's Struggle against Poverty*, 142–54, and John A. Andrew III, *Lyndon Johnson and the Great Society* (Chicago: Ivan R. Dee, 1998), 144–45, 149–50.

117. "Nixon Links Humphrey with Administration 'Fiscal Blunders,'" *Los Angeles Times*, July 7, 1968.

118. Lyndon B. Johnson, "Special Message to the Congress: America's Unfinished Business, Urban and Rural Poverty," March 14, 1967, *Public Papers of the Presidents, Lyndon B. Johnson, 1967*, Book 1 (Washington, DC: US Government Printing Office, 1968), 332.

119. Public Health Service, *Securing Health in Our Urban Future: A Report to the Surgeon General* (Washington, DC: US Department of Health, Education, and Welfare, 1967).

120. Department of Health, Education, and Welfare, Medicaid Public Hearing, Chicago, December 30, 1968, "Hearings: Chicago," Papers of Wilbur

J. Cohen, LBJ Library, 143–48. For the argument that Head Start perpetuated stigmatizing categories, see Mical Raz, *What's Wrong with the Poor? Psychiatry, Race, and the War on Poverty* (Chapel Hill: University of North Carolina Press, 2013), 99–109.

121. Johnson, "Special Message to the Congress: America's Unfinished Business," 346.

122. See Gerald D. Suttles, *The Social Order of the Slum: Ethnicity and Territory in the Inner City* (Chicago: University of Chicago Press, 1968).

123. William Julius Wilson, *The Truly Disadvantaged: The Inner City, the Underclass, and Public Policy* (1987; Chicago: University of Chicago Press, 2012), 117.

124. On this point, Paul Farmer discusses Wilson's 1980 book *The Declining Significance of Race: Blacks and Changing American Institutions* (1978; Chicago: University of Chicago Press, 2012). See Paul Farmer, "On Suffering and Structural Violence: A View from Below," *Daedalus* 125, no. 1 (Winter 1996): 276.

125. Sometimes "inhuman" is quoted as "inhumane" in King's speech, as reported on March 29, 1966, in the *Woodlawn Booster* (a newspaper based in Woodlawn, Illinois). See Dittmer, *Good Doctors*, 144–47, and James R. Ralph, *Northern Protest: Martin Luther King Jr., Chicago, and the Civil Rights Movement* (Cambridge, MA: Harvard University Press, 1993).

126. See "Dr. King Is Felled by Rock," *Chicago Tribune*, August 6, 1966.

127. King spoke about the "radical redistribution of economic power" in speeches through summer 1967 and early 1968, including a February 1968 speech in Mississippi that features in episode ten of *Eyes on the Prize* (dir. Henry Hampton, 1987). For King's views on slum shock, see "The Chicago Plan," January 7, 1966, www.crmvet.org/docs/6601_sclc_mlk_chicagoplan.pdf, and "Address by Dr. Martin Luther King, Jr.," Chicago Freedom Festival, March 12, 1966, www.crmvet.org/docs/6603_sclc_mlk_cfm.pdf. For the cited poverty statistics, see Senator Fred R. Harris's speech "The American Negro Today," in *The Urban Crisis: A Symposium* (New York: Da Capo Press, 1971), 29.

128. Huey P. Newton and David Hilliard, eds., *The Huey P. Newton Reader* (New York: Seven Stories Press, 2002), 229.

129. The statistics are based on 1970–90 census data, cited in Paul A. Jargowsky, *Poverty and Place: Ghettos, Barrios, and the American City* (New York: Russell Sage Foundation, 1997), 42.

130. See Mary T. Bassett, "Beyond Berets: The Black Panthers as Health Activists," *American Journal of Public Health* 106, no. 10 (October 2016): 1741–43.

131. "Address by Dr. Martin Luther King, Jr.," Chicago Freedom Festival.

132. J. David Greenstone and Paul E. Peterson, *Race and Authority in Urban Politics: Community Participation and the War on Poverty* (Chicago: University of Chicago Press, 1973), xv.

133. Pierre DeVise, *Misused and Misplaced Hospitals and Doctors: A Locational Analysis of the Urban Health Care Crisis* (Washington, DC: Association of American Geographers, 1973), 79.

134. Johnson made this commitment in "Advancing the Nation's Health," January 7, 1965, *Public Papers, Lyndon B. Johnson, 1965*, Book 1, 12.

135. See Alondra Nelson, *Body and Soul: The Black Panther Party and the Fight against Medical Discrimination* (Minneapolis: University of Minnesota Press, 2011), 6, and Alyosha Goldstein, *Poverty in Common: The Politics of Community Action during the American Century* (Durham, NC: Duke University Press, 2012), 217–20.

136. See Robert Park, "The City: Suggestions for the Investigation of Human Behavior in the City Environment," *American Journal of Sociology* 20, no. 5 (March 1915): 577–612.

137. Loïc Wacquant, "The Body, the Ghetto, and the Penal State," *Qualitative Sociology* 32, no. 1 (March 2009): 107.

138. Loïc Wacquant, *Urban Outcasts: A Comparative Sociology of Advanced Marginality* (New York: Polity, 2007), 45. See also Loïc Wacquant and William Julius Wilson, "The Cost of Racial and Class Exclusion in the Inner City," *Annals of the American Academy of Political and Social Science* 501 (January 1989): 8–25.

139. Jill Quadagno, *The Color of Welfare: How Racism Undermined the War on Poverty* (New York: Oxford University Press, 1996), 11.

140. See "Statement by Bertrand M. Harding before the Permanent Subcommittee on Investigation, October, 10–11, 1968," "Conference File: Washington, D.C. McClellan Hearing," Box 43, Personal Papers of Bertrand M. Harding, LBJ Library. For press coverage, see "OEO Director Backs Giving Aid to Gangs," *Chicago Tribune*, October 11, 1968. For context, see John Hall Fish, *Black Power/White Control: The Struggle of the Woodlawn Organization in Chicago* (Princeton, NJ: Princeton University Press, 1973), 159–64.

141. Loïc Wacquant, "Class, Race, and Hyperincarceration in Revanchist America," *Daedalus* 139, no. 3 (Summer 2010): 81. On hypersegregation and incarceration, see Michelle Alexander, *The New Jim Crow: Mass Incarceration in the Age of Colorblindness* (New York: New Press, 2012), 122.

142. Wacquant, "Class, Race, and Hyperincarceration," 81. For the report, see Alice Goffman, *On the Run: Fugitive Life in an American City* (Chicago: University of Chicago Press, 2014), 3.

143. The South Side Healthcare Collaborative, devised in 2005 by Michelle Obama, sought to improve access to hospitals for low-income patients in the South Side area, though critics on the right were quick to brand it a patient-dumping scheme.

144. Sherman Alexie, *You Don't Have to Say You Love Me: A Memoir* (New York: Little, Brown, 2017), 7. Alexie explores hydrocephalus in his novel for young readers, *The Absolutely True Diary of a Part-Time Indian* (Boston: Little, Brown, 2007).

145. "Reservation's Despair Takes Greatest Toll," *Washington Post*, December 16, 1997.

146. Kalpesh Lathigra's foreword to *Lost in the Wilderness* (self-published, 2015).

147. Alexie, *You Don't Have to Say You Love Me*, 7.

148. See "President Clinton's New Markets Tour," White House Archives,

July 7, 1999, https://clintonwhitehouse2.archives.gov/WH/New/New_Markets/cities/pine_ridge_reservation_facts.html.

149. Robert H. Ruby, *Doctor among the Oglala Sioux Tribe: The Letters of Robert H. Ruby, 1953–1954*, ed. Cary C. Collins and Charles V. Mutschler (Lincoln: University of Nebraska Press, 2010), xxxiv–xxxvii.

150. Sherman Alexie, *Indian Killer* (New York: Atlantic Month Press, 1996), 3.

151. See Jane E. Smith and Jonathan Krejci, "Minorities Join the Majority: Eating Disturbances among Hispanic and Native American Youth," *International Journal of Eating Disorders* 10, no. 2 (March 1991): 179–86.

152. "Clinton to See Poorest of Poor," *Rapid City Journal*, July 7, 1999.

153. See David Hugh Bunnell, *Good Friday on the Rez: A Pine Ridge Odyssey* (New York: St. Martin's Press, 2017), 36–42. *On a Knife Edge* (dir. Jeremy Williams, 2017) portrays the consequences of alcohol sales in Whiteclay on the Oglala Sioux. On the 2006 roadblock, see "White Clay Road Blocks to Start June 28," *Lakota Country Times*, June 7, 2006.

154. Office for Economic Opportunity, Volume II—Documentary Supplement, Box 2, Administrative History Collection, LBJ Library, 2–17.

155. Preface to *Community Health and Mental Health Care Delivery for North American Indians* (New York: MSS Information Corp., 1974), 7. See the *Health Care Crisis at Rosebud* documentary held at the University of South Dakota Library, Vermillion.

156. William J. Clinton, "Remarks to the Community at Pine Ridge Indian Reservation," July 7, 1999, *Public Papers of the Presidents, William J. Clinton, 1999*, Book 2, 1149–53.

157. Memos on Native American Mental Health, May 1999, Box 43, 206-0197-F Segment 3, Records on President Clinton's Indian Native American Policy, Mary Smith Files, William J. Clinton Presidential Library, Little Rock, Arkansas.

158. "President to Make History on Reservation" and "Clinton to See Poorest of Poor," *Rapid City Journal*, July 7, 1999. "Clinton Looks at Poverty and Sees Promise" and "Indian Country Economic Growth Catches on with BIA," *Indian Country Today*, July 19–26, 1999.

159. "Salway Says Oglala Vision Can Tap into Initiatives," and "Housing: Some Have Doubts," *Indian Country Today*, July 19–26, 1999.

160. "President Coolidge in the Black Hills," *Black Hills Engineer* 15, no. 4 (November 1927): 205, 234–35.

161. "Coolidge Addresses 10,000 Sioux Indians as Supreme Chief," *New York Times*, August 18, 1927.

162. Institute for Government Research, *The Problem of Indian Administration* (Baltimore: Johns Hopkins Press, 1928), 3.

163. On trachoma, see Todd Benson, "Race, Health, and Power: The Federal Government and American Indian Health, 1909–1955" (unpublished PhD thesis, Stanford University, 1994), 42–108. For early Indian health surveys, see the Treasury Department publication *Observations on Indian Health Problems and Facilities* (Washington, DC: US Government Printing Office, 1936).

164. Institute for Government Research, *Problem of Indian Administration*, 52–53.

165. Institute for Government Research, *Problem of Indian Administration*, 189.

166. Herbert Hoover, "Statement on Indian Affairs," January 3, 1930, *Public Papers of the Presidents, Herbert Hoover, 1930* (Washington, DC: US Government Printing Office, 1976), 6.

167. See Benson, "Race, Health, and Power," xiii. On the Indian New Deal, see Thomas Biolsi, *Organizing the Lakota: The Political Economy of the New Deal on the Pine Ridge and Rosebud Reservations* (Tucson: University of Arizona Press, 1992).

168. "Report of the Committee on Indian Nutrition," "Office of Defense Health and Welfare Services, Nutrition Division, 1942–43," Box OF 4563–4565, President's Official File, Franklin D. Roosevelt Presidential Library, Hyde Park, New York. On diabetes, see Charlton Wilson et al., "Diabetes Outcomes in the Indian Health System during the Era of the Special Diabetes Program for Indians and the Government Performance and Results Act," *American Journal of Public Health* 95, no. 9 (September 2005): 1518–22. On fetal alcohol syndrome, see Michael Dorris, *The Broken Cord* (New York: Harper and Row, 1989), and "Tragedy at Pine Ridge: Fetal Alcohol Syndrome," *NBC Nightly News*, November 20–21, 1989.

169. For the quotation, see the letter from Senator John F. Kennedy to Mr. Oliver La Farge, President, Association of American Indian Affairs (October 28, 1960), American Presidency Project, www.presidency.ucsb.edu/documents /letter-indian-affairs-from-senator-john-f-kennedy-mr-oliver-la-farge-president -association.

170. For the statistic, see Akim D. Reinhardt, *Ruling Pine Ridge: Oglala Lakota Politics from the IRA to Wounded Knee* (Lubbock: Texas Tech University Press, 2009), 118. By the 1990s, unemployment among the Oglala Sioux was as high as 73 percent: see *Indian Labor Force Report* (Washington, DC: Bureau of Indian Affairs, 1997).

171. See Attorney General Robert Kennedy's address to the National Congress of American Indians, Bismarck, North Dakota, September 13, 1963, www.justice.gov/sites/default/files/ag/legacy/2011/01/20/09-13-1963.pdf. On Robert Kennedy's 1968 trip, see "Kennedy Greeted Warmly in South Dakota: Indian Boy Rides Along," *Minneapolis Tribune*, May 17, 1968. See also "Cost of Maintaining Poor People's 'Resurrection City' Are Spelled Out," *Rapid City Journal*, May 16, 1968.

172. Lyndon B. Johnson, "Special Message to the Congress on the Problem of the American Indian: 'The Forgotten American,'" March 6, 1968, *Public Papers of the Presidents, Lyndon B. Johnson, 1968–69*, Book 1 (Washington, DC: US Government Printing Office, 1970), 335–44.

173. Ellen Maynard and Gayla Twiss, *Hechel Lena Oyate Kin Nipi Kte: That These People May Live* (Pine Ridge, SD: Community Mental Health Program, 1969), 104.

174. Johnson, "Special Message to the Congress on the Problem of the American Indian," 343.

175. "A Report to the President's Commission on Mental Health from the American Indian and Alaska Native Task Panel," January 1978, Office of Public Liaison–Costanza, Ethnic Experience: Publication 1977 through Mental Health: Native Americans 1/78, Presidential Papers of Jimmy Carter, Jimmy Carter Presidential Library and Museum, Atlanta, Georgia.

176. Nancy Lande, *Words, Wounds, Chasms: Native American Health Care Encounters*, 2nd ed. (2005; Bozeman, MT: Windy Creek Press, 2016), 39.

177. Jennifer F. Clarke et al., eds., *A Gathering of Wisdoms: Tribal Mental Health, a Cultural Perspective*, 2nd ed. (1991; LaConner, WA: Swinomish Indian Tribal Community, 2002), 108–20.

178. "Electronic Smoke Signals: Native American Radio in the United States," *Cultural Survival*, June 1998, www.culturalsurvival.org/publications/cultural-survival-quarterly/electronic-smoke-signals-native-american-radio-united.

179. See Don Coyhis and William White, *Alcohol Problems in Native America: The Untold Story* (Colorado Springs, CO: White Bison, 2006), and White Bison Inc., *The Red Road to Wellbriety: In the Native American Way* (Colorado Springs, CO: White Bison, 2002).

180. *Surveillance of Health Status in Minority Communities: Racial and Ethnic Approaches to Community Health across the U.S. (REACH U.S.), Risk Factor Survey, United States, 2009* (Atlanta: Centers for Disease Control and Prevention, 2011), 1. On REACH U.S., see the CDC website, www.cdc.gov/nccdphp/dnpao/state-local-programs/reach/index.htm.

181. Indian Health Care Service, "Indian Health Care Improvement Act Made Permanent," March 27, 2010, www.ihs.gov/newsroom/pressreleases/2010pressreleases/indianhealthcareimprovementactmadepermanent. For the largely inconsequential economic initiatives that followed from Clinton's visit to the reservation: "On Pine Ridge, a String of Broken Promises: Politicians' Talk Means Little on Troubled S.D. Reservation," *Washington Post*, October 21, 2004.

182. "Sherman Alexie on How Trump Is Turning the US into a Reservation," *BuzzFeed*, June 25, 2017, www.buzzfeed.com/annehelenpetersen/sherman-alexie-is-not-the-indian-you-expected?utm_term=.nxxMoZvlO#.uc5x69Yqz.

183. Terese Mailhot, "Native American Lives Are Tragic, But Probably Not in the Way You Think," *Mother Jones*, November/December 2018, www.motherjones.com/media/2018/11/native-american-story-tragic-terese-mailhot-tommy-orange-poverty-porn/. Alexie features here because of his literary focus on health and identity, but it is important to note that in spring 2018 he released a public statement responding to multiple charges of sexual harassment, which has led to a reevaluation of his writing. See, for example, "Do Works by Men Implicated by #MeToo Belong in the Classroom," *New York Times*, October 7, 2019.

184. Clinton signed the Native American Housing Assistance and Self-Determination Act in October 1996 and Executive Order 13007 on May 24, 1996, on Indian Sacred Sites.

185. Elissa Washuta, *My Body Is a Book of Rules* (Pasadena, CA: Ren Hen

Press, 2014), and Terese Marie Mailhot, *Heart Berries* (New York: Counterpoint, 2018).

186. William J. Clinton, "Remarks to Native American and Native Alaskan Tribal Leaders," April 29, 1994, *Public Papers of the Presidents, William J. Clinton, 1994*, Book 1 (Washington, DC: US Government Printing Office, 1995), 800–803. Despite the opening of a Suicide Prevention Resource Center at the Oglala Lakota College in 2012, suicide rates at Pine Ridge remain a major concern: see "Pine Ridge Indian Reservation Struggles with Suicides among Its Young," *New York Times*, May 1, 2015.

187. Alexie, *You Don't Have to Say You Love Me*, 11, 297.

188. Adrian C. Louis, *Skins* (Granite Falls, MN: Ellis Press, 2002), 37, 1. Whiteclay features prominently in Louis's novel as a border town profiting "from Indian misery" (57).

189. Louis, *Skins*, 268, 305.

190. On the Ghost Dance, see James R. Walker, *Lakota Belief and Ritual*, ed. Raymond J. De Mallie and Elaine A. Jahner (Lincoln: University of Nebraska Press, 1991), 142–43. On the 1973 occupation, see Pekka Hämäläinen, *Lakota America: A New History of Indigenous Power* (New Haven, CT: Yale University Press, 2019), 386–88.

191. See Leonard Crow Dog and Richard Erdoes, *Crow Dog: Four Generations of Sioux Medicine Men* (New York: Harper, 1995), 125–31.

192. Carole Gallagher, *American Ground Zero: The Secret Nuclear War* (Cambridge, MA: MIT Press, 1993), xiii.

193. Walker, *Lakota Belief and Ritual*, 165. Danielle T. Raudenbush, *Health Care Off the Books: Poverty, Illness, and Strategies for Survival in Urban America* (Berkeley: University of California Press, 2020).

194. See Gavin Cologne-Brookes, "The Ghost of Tom Joad: Steinbeck's Legacy in the Songs of Bruce Springsteen," in *John Steinbeck's The Grapes of Wrath*, ed. Harold Bloom (New York: Infobase, 2007), 159–69.

CHAPTER 3: POLLUTION

1. Finis Dunaway, *Seeing Green: The Use and Abuse of American Environmental Images* (Chicago: University of Chicago Press, 2015), 79.

2. "Ways to Beautify America—Exclusive Interview with the First Lady," *U.S. News and World Report*, February 22, 1965. See President Johnson's foreword of November 5, 1965, to the President's Science Advisory Committee Report of the Environmental Pollution Panel, *Restoring the Quality of Our Environment* (Washington, DC: The White House, 1965).

3. Wendy Melilla, *How McGruff and the Crying Indian Changed America: A History of Ad Council Campaigns* (Washington, DC: Smithsonian Institution Press 2013), 104.

4. Bruno Latour, *We Have Never Been Modern*, trans. Catherine Porter (1991; Cambridge, MA: Harvard University Press, 1993).

5. Dunaway, *Seeing Green*, 81, 92–94. See Kate Davies, *The Rise of the U.S. Environmental Health Movement* (Lanham, MD: Rowman and Littlefield, 2013).

6. Richard M. Nixon, "Annual Message to Congress on the State of the Union," January 22, 1970, in *Public Papers of the Presidents, Richard M. Nixon, 1970* (Washington, DC: US Government Printing Office, 1971), 12.

7. On Nixon's new federalism, see Michael R. Vickery, "Conservative Politics and the Politics of Conservation: Richard Nixon and the Environmental Protection Agency," in *Green Talk in the White House: The Rhetorical Presidency Encounters Ecology*, ed. Tarla Rai Peterson (College Station: Texas A&M University Press, 2004), 113–33.

8. See *The Environmental Protection Agency's Research Program, with Primary Emphasis on the Community Health and Environmental Surveillance System (CHESS): An Investigative Report* (Washington, DC: US Government Printing Office, 1976).

9. Contrast the lofty ideals of the international Water for Peace conference held in Washington, DC, in May 1967 and the header of the August 1, 1969, *Time* magazine piece "America's Sewage System and the Price of Optimism." See Alex Prud'homme, *The Ripple Effect: The Fate of Freshwater in the Twenty-First Century* (New York: Scribner's, 2011), 18–19, 43.

10. Lenore Marshall, "The Nuclear Sword of Damocles," *Living Wilderness* (Spring 1971): 17–19. For the emergence of these groups, see Luke W. Cole and Sheila R. Foster, *From the Ground Up: Environmental Racism and the Rise of the Environmental Justice Movement* (New York: New York University Press, 2001).

11. For this life expectancy statistic, see the Center for Rural Health report, "Prevalence of Chronic Disease among American Indian and Alaska Native Elders," University of North Dakota, Bismarck (October 2005), www.nrcnaa.org/pdf/chronic_disease1005.pdf.

12. Jennifer Thomson, *The Wild and the Toxic: American Environmentalism and the Politics of Health* (Chapel Hill: University of North Carolina Press, 2019), 130.

13. Miriam Lee Kaplow, "Manufacturing Danger: Fear and Pollution in Industrial Society," *American Anthropologist* 87, no. 2 (June 1985): 343.

14. Nixon, "Annual Message to Congress on the State of the Union," 13.

15. Douglas M. Costle, "Pollution's 'Invisible' Victims: Why Environmental Regulation Cannot Wait for Scientific Certainty," April 28, 1980, "Environmental Protection—Douglas M. Costle on Pollution's Invisible Victims," Box 85, Records of the Office of the Assistant to the President for Women's Affairs (Sarah Weddington), Jimmy Carter Presidential Library and Museum, Atlanta, Georgia.

16. Rob Nixon, *Slow Violence and the Environmentalism of the Poor* (Cambridge, MA: Harvard University Press, 2011), 2–3.

17. Paul Crutzen and Eugene Stoermer, "The Anthropocene," *IGBP Global Change Newsletter* 41 (May 2000): 17–18.

18. See Elizabeth M. Whelan, *Toxic Terror: The Truth behind the Cancer Scares* (1985; New York: Prometheus Books, 1993).

19. See Barbara and John Ehrenreich, *The American Health Empire: Power, Profits, and Politics* (New York: Random House, 1970).

20. Gregg Mitman, Michelle Murphy, and Christopher Sellers, eds., *Land-*

scapes of Exposure: Knowledge and Illness in Modern Environments (Chicago: University of Chicago Press, 2004), 13.

21. Intergovernmental Panel on Climate Change, *Global Warming of 1.5°C*, October 2018, www.ipcc.ch/report/sr15.

22. See Steve Lerner, *Sacrifice Zones: The Front Lines of Toxic Chemical Exposure in the United States* (Cambridge, MA: MIT Press, 2010).

23. Lady Bird Johnson, *A White House Diary* (1970; Austin: University of Texas Press, 2007), 234. The quotation is from a diary entry of February 3, 1965. Robert N. Bellah, Richard Madsen, William M. Sullivan, Ann Swidler, and Steven M. Tipton, *The Good Society* (New York: Knopf, 1991), 14–15.

24. Dwight D. Eisenhower, "Address before the General Assembly of the United Nations on Peaceful Uses of Atomic Energy, New York City," December 8, 1953, in *Public Papers of the Presidents, Dwight D. Eisenhower, 1955* (Washington, DC: US Government Printing Office, 1960), 822.

25. David McCullough, *Truman* (New York: Simon and Schuster, 1992), 456–57.

26. Truman established the Atomic Bomb Casualty Commission in 1946 to assess the long-term impact of nuclear weaponry on the health of Japanese survivors.

27. Joseph Masco, "Atomic Health, or How the Bomb Altered American Notions of Death," in *Against Health: How Health Became the New Morality*, ed. Jonathan M. Metzl and Anna Kirkland (New York: New York University Press, 2010), 133.

28. See Robert Coles, *The Privileged Ones: The Well-Off and the Rich in America* (New York: Little, Brown, 1977).

29. For Eisenhower on air pollution, see "Special Message to the Congress Recommending a Health Program," January 31, 1955, *Public Papers of the Presidents, Dwight D. Eisenhower, 1955* (Washington, DC: US Government Printing Office, 1959), 216–23. An interdepartmental Committee on Community Air Pollution was established by the Department of Health, Education, and Welfare in 1954 and a Division of Air Pollution in 1960. On civil defense, see Tracy C. Davis, *Stages of Emergency: Cold War Nuclear Civil Defense* (Durham, NC: Duke University Press, 2007), 106–7.

30. Ira Chernus, *Eisenhower's Atoms for Peace* (College Station: Texas A&M University Press, 2002), 29–30.

31. See Lester B. Lave and Eugene P. Seskin, *Air Pollution and Human Health* (Washington, DC: RFF Press, 1977); the original article with the same title was published in *Science* (August 21, 1970): 723–33. On the "great acceleration," see Will Steffen et al., *Global Change and the Earth System: A Planet under Pressure* (Berlin: Springer, 2004).

32. Barton C. Hacker " 'Hotter Than a $2 Pistol': Fallout, Sheep, and the Atomic Energy Commission, 1953–1986," in *The Atomic West*, ed. Bruce W. Hevly and John M. Findlay (Seattle: University of Washington Press, 1998), 160.

33. For Oppenheimer's resignation speech and his October 1945 meeting with President Truman, see Kai Bird and Martin J. Sherwin, *American Prometheus: The Triumph and Tragedy of J. Robert Oppenheimer* (New York:

Knopf, 2005), 328–33. For the letter from Oppenheimer to Truman (dated May 3, 1946) and Truman's response in a memo to Dean Acheson, see Dennis Merrill, ed., *Documentary History of the Truman Presidency*, vol. 21 (Lanham, MD: University Publications of America, 1998), 44–47.

34. J. Robert Oppenheimer, interview by Edward R. Murrow, *See It Now*, CBS, January 4, 1955. On the Atomic Energy Commission, see Gerard H. Clarfield and William M. Wiecek, *Nuclear America: Military and Civilian Nuclear Power in the United States, 1940–1980* (New York: Harper and Row, 1984), and Richard G. Hewlett and Jack M. Holl, *Atoms for Peace and War, 1953–1961: Eisenhower and the Atomic Energy Commission* (Berkeley: University of California Press, 1989). On Cold War medical experimentation, see Eileen Welsome, *The Plutonium Files: America's Secret Medical Experiments in the Cold War* (New York: Random House, 1999), and Gerald Kutcher, *Contested Medicine: Cancer Research and the Military* (Chicago: University of Chicago Press, 2009).

35. Donald Worster, *Nature's Economy: A History of Ecological Ideas* (Cambridge: Cambridge University Press, 1977), 339.

36. Chernus, *Eisenhower's Atoms for Peace*, 16–24.

37. On tensions between Lewis Strauss and Robert Oppenheimer with respect to Operation Candor, see Hewlett and Holl, *Atoms for Peace and War*, 52–57.

38. See "Nuclear Weapons (Testing)," *Life*, March 30, 1953, and "Eisenhower Pushed Operation Candor," *Washington Post*, September 21, 1953. A 1953 Federal Civil Defense Administration chart emphasized that civil defense measures "depend on the prevention of panic among the survivors in the first 90 seconds" on the basis that "panic is fissionable" and can "produce a chain reaction more deeply destructive than any explosive known": "Panic: The Ultimate Weapon?" *Collier's*, August 21, 1953.

39. Atomic Energy Commission, *Major Activities in the Atomic Energy Programs, January–June 1953* (Washington, DC: US Government Printing Office, 1953), 48–49, 52. For context, see Philip L. Fradkin, *Fallout: An American Nuclear Tragedy* (1989; Boulder, CO: Johnson Books, 2004), 80–81, 97–98. On the AEC's efforts to navigate between public information and national security, see Corbin Allardice and Edward R. Trapnell, *The Atomic Energy Commission* (New York: Praeger, 1974), 134–62.

40. Corinne Clegg Hales, "Covenant: Atomic Energy Commission, 1950s," in *Separate Escapes* (Ashland, OR: Ashland Poetry Press, 2002), 16.

41. See Anna Tsing, Heather Swanson, Elain Gan, and Nils Bubandt, eds., *Arts of Living on a Damaged Planet: Ghosts and Monsters of the Anthropocene* (Minneapolis: University of Minnesota Press, 2017).

42. The Atomic Energy Commission announcement of January 11, 1951, as quoted in Gerard J. DeGroot, *The Bomb: A Life* (Cambridge, MA: Harvard University Press, 2005), 238.

43. The *Salt Lake Times* did not start reporting on fallout until 1959; see, for example, "Is the Truth Told about Fallout," *Salt Lake Times*, April 3, 1959, and "Senate Says Reports of Fallout Are 'Greatly Exaggerated,'" *Salt Lake Times*, July 2, 1959.

44. "Effects of Atom Blasts on Southern Utah Discussed by U. of U. Student," *Iron County Record*, May 7, 1953. This series of eleven explosions at the Nevada Test Site between March and June 1953 was called Operation Upshot-Knothole.

45. "Atomic Winds—Fall-Out," *Iron County Record*, May 21, 1953.

46. Hacker, "Hotter Than a $2 Pistol," 161–62.

47. The AEC issued a pamphlet to coincide with the spring 1955 test series (Operation Teapot), which claimed radiation was not hazardous, that it had not affected crops and water, and that "fall-out of significance in animals has been experienced only close to the site of the detonation." Atomic Energy Commission, *Atomic Test Effects in the Nevada Test Site Region*, January 1955, 18. For local reporting in southern Utah on the 1955 test series, see the *Iron County Record* from March 3, 1955, April 21, 1955, and May 1, 1956. For context, see Daniel W. Miles, *Radioactive Clouds of Death over Utah: Downwinders' Fallout Cancer Epidemic* (Bloomington, IN: Trafford Publishing, 2013).

48. Dwight D. Eisenhower, "Statement by the President Concerning Disclosure of Information on Fallout," March 25, 1959, *Public Papers of the Presidents: Dwight D. Eisenhower, 1959* (Washington, DC: US Government Printing Office, 1960), 302. "Clouds from Nevada," *The Reporter*, May 16, 1957, and "We Were Trapped by Radioactive Fallout," *Saturday Evening Post*, July 20, 1957.

49. Edward S. Weiss, "Leukemia Mortality in Southwestern Utah," July 23, 1965, NV0178397, NNSA/NSO Nuclear Testing Archive, Las Vegas, Nevada. On Weiss's research, see Fradkin, *Fallout*, 203–4, and Barton C. Hacker, *Elements of Controversy: The Atomic Energy Commission and Radiation Safety in Nuclear Weapons Testing, 1947–1974* (Berkeley: University of California Press, 1994), 229.

50. See Edward S. Weiss et al., "Surgically Treated Thyroid Disease among Young People in Utah, 1948–1962," *American Journal of Public Health* 57, no. 10 (October 1967): 1807–14. A study of mortality rates from leukemia in the region by Joseph Lyon of the Utah Cancer Registry Committee preceded a congressional hearing on radiation. Subcommittee on Oversight and Investigations of the Committee on Interstate and Foreign Commerce, *Low-Level Radiation Effects on Health*, House of Representatives, 96th Congress, First Session, April 23–August 1, 1979. For local reporting, see "Fallout Levels Understated, Data Indicate," *Deseret News*, February 7, 1979, and "U. Study Confirms Fallout Caused Leukemia Deaths," *Deseret News*, February 13, 1979. A *Deseret News* journalist wrote to the White House for information on the Nevada Test Site and expressed astonishment that "the documents the Atomic Energy Commission furnished Truman are startling in their total omission of any reference to possible long-range effects of radiation to off-site civilians": letter from Gordon Eliot White to Jody Powell, February 24, 1979, "HE 8, 1/20/77–1/20/81," Box HE-20 White House Central File Health, Carter Presidential Library.

51. "Draft Report of Task Force on Compensation of Radiation-Related Illnesses," December 17, 1979, "Radiation—[Compensation for Radiation-Related Illnesses, 1979]," Box 24, Domestic Policy Staff Human Resources, Diana Elmes's Subject Files, Carter Presidential Library.

52. "Judge Says U.S. Lied in Fallout Case," *New York Times*, August 5, 1982. "Trial to Open Today in Lawsuit over Nuclear Fallout," *New York Times*, September 14, 1982.

53. Howard Ball, *Justice Downwind: America's Atomic Testing Program in the 1950s* (New York: Oxford University Press, 1986), 195. For recent clusters of leukemia in Nevada potentially linked to nuclear testing, see Lerner, *Sacrifice Zones*, 267–95.

54. Carole Gallagher, *American Ground Zero: The Secret Nuclear War* (New York: Random House, 1993), xxiv. For this phrase, "low-use segment," see a public meeting of the Advisory Committee on Human Radiation Experiments, Washington, DC, March 15, 1995, https://nsarchive2.gwu.edu/radi ation/dir/mstreet/commeet/meet12/trnsc12a.txt.

55. For these 1993 disclosures, see David Henry "'We're Coming Clean': Clinton, Public Advocacy, and the Human Radiation Experiments," in Peterson, *Green Talk in the White House*, 207–29.

56. Gallagher, *American Ground Zero*, xxiv–xxv. Gallagher covers a wide demographic range, but she does not address the health consequences of Navajo communities in southeastern Utah and western Colorado who suffered sickness and death from uranium mining; see Sarah Alisabeth Fox, *Downwind: A People's History of the Nuclear West* (Lincoln: University of Nebraska Press, 2014).

57. Scott Kirsch, "Harold Knapp and the Geography of Normal Controversy: Radioiodine in the Historical Environment," in Mitman, Murphy, and Sellers, *Landscapes of Exposure*, 170. See also Carolyn Kopp, "The Origins of the American Scientific Debate over Fallout Hazards," *Social Studies of Science* 9, no. 4 (November 1979): 403–22.

58. Cited by Ball, *Justice Downwind*, 109.

59. See Special Task Force Report to Gov. Nelson B. Rockefeller, *Protection from Radioactive Fallout* (State of New York, 1959).

60. See Janet Burton Seegmiller, *A History of Iron County: Community above Self* (Salt Lake City: Utah State Historical Society, 1998), 143–50, and Douglas D. Alder and Karl F. Brooks, *A History of Washington County: From Isolation to Destination* (Salt Lake City: Utah State Historical Society, 1996), 285–88.

61. See *Estimated Exposures and Thyroid Doses Received by the American People from Iodine-131 in Fallout Following Nevada Atmospheric Nuclear Bomb Tests: A Report from the National Cancer Institute* (Washington, DC: US Department of Health and Human Services, 1997). The National Cancer Institute began working with the Centers for Disease Control and Prevention in 1998 to estimate the health effects of the Nevada nuclear tests.

62. On stomach ulcers, see "Anti-Cancer Drugs Held a Possibility," *New York Times*, March 6, 1952. On radiation and aggressive surgery, see Ellen Leopold, *Under the Radar: Cancer and the Cold War* (New Brunswick, NJ: Rutgers University Press, 2009), 36–41.

63. Letter from a National Institutes of Health administrator to Senator Herbert H. Lehman, February 15, 1951, "National Institutes of Health, Bethesda, MD," Box 42, Oscar R. Ewing Papers, Harry S. Truman Presidential

Library. For cancer research and medical plutonium tests at the University of Chicago, see Peter Bacon Hales, *Atomic Spaces: Living on the Manhattan Project* (Urbana: University of Illinois Press, 1997), 273–98.

64. See "The Danger of Radiation at the Portsmouth Shipyard," *Boston Globe*, February 19, 1978, and Thomas Najarian, "The Controversy over the Health Effects of Radiation," *Technology Review* 81 (November 1978): 74–82.

65. Audre Lorde, "The Transformation of Silence into Language and Action" (1977), in *Sister Outsider: Essays and Speeches* (1984; New York: Ten Speed Press, 2007), 40.

66. Lorde, "Transformation of Silence into Language and Action," 42.

67. Lorde, "Poetry Is Not a Luxury" (1977), in *Sister Outsider*, 37.

68. Audre Lorde, *I Am Your Sister: Collected and Unpublished Writings of Audre Lorde*, ed. Rudolph P. Byrd, Johnetta Betson Cole, and Beverly Guy-Shetfall (Oxford: Oxford University Press, 2009), 130, 175, 221.

69. Leopold, *Under the Radar*, 208.

70. Richard Peto, "Distorting the Epidemiology of Cancer: The Need for a More Balanced Overview," *Nature* 284 (March 1980): 297–300.

71. Joseph Califano Jr., "Address by Joseph A. Califano, Jr., Secretary of Health Education and Welfare before the National Interagency Council on Smoking and Health," Shoreham Hotel, Washington, DC, 1978, www.industrydocumentslibrary.ucsf.edu/tobacco/docs/#id=mfnp0094.

72. Governor's Fact Finding Committee, *Shippingport Nuclear Power Station: Alleged Health Effects* (1974), Three Mile Island Health Research and Studies, RG-11, Box 1, Department of Health, Bureau of Epidemiology, Pennsylvania State Archives, Harrisburg.

73. See, for example, "Nuclear Power's Role: The Debate Must Begin," *Philadelphia Inquirer*, April 4, 1979.

74. "Talk of the Town: Notes and Comment," *New Yorker*, April 16, 1979.

75. See Jimmy Carter, "Middletown, Pennsylvania: Remarks to Reporters Following a Visit to the Three Mile Island Nuclear Facility," April 1, 1979, in *Public Papers of the Presidents: Jimmy Carter, 1979*, Book 1 (Washington, DC: US Government Printing Office, 1980), 578.

76. "Anti-Nuclear Group Protests; 11 Arrested," *Philadelphia Tribune*, April 3, 1979. "Nuclear Energy Opponents Rally," *Patriot-News*, April 2, 1979.

77. *Report of the President's Commission on the Accident at Three Mile Island, the Need for Change: The Legacy of TMI* (Washington, DC: US Government Printing Office, 1979), http://large.stanford.edu/courses/2012/ph241/tran1/docs/188.pdf. On milk safety, see "Radioactivity Found in Pa. Milk," *Philadelphia Daily*, April 4, 1979. For a historical account of the reactor failure, see Samuel J. Walker, *Three Mile Island: A Nuclear Crisis in Historical Perspective* (Berkeley: University of California Press, 2004).

78. See Peter S. Houts, Paul D. Cleary, and Teh-Wei Hu, *The Three Mile Island Crisis: Psychological, Social, and Economic Impacts on the Surrounding Population* (University Park: Pennsylvania State University Press, 1988), ix–x. On public mistrust, see "Record Shows Public Misled in Nuclear Crisis," *Philadelphia Inquirer*, April 9, 1979.

79. Cited in Michael Gallantz, "*The China Syndrome*: Meltdown in Hollywood," *Jump Cut* 22 (May 1980): 3–4. For links between the film and the incident, see "Nuke Plant Spews Radiation in Pa. Syndrome Review?" *Philadelphia Daily News*, March 29, 1979, and John Wills, *The Conservation Fallout: Nuclear Protest at Diablo Canyon* (Reno: University of Nevada Press, 2006), 91–94.

80. *Report of the President's Commission on the Accident at Three Mile Island*, 12–13. Houts, Cleary, and Hu, *Three Mile Island Crisis*, 47–48.

81. "TMI Studies," Three Mile Island Health Research and Studies, RG-11, Box 1, Department of Health, Bureau of Epidemiology, Pennsylvania State Archives. These psychological studies were conducted by Penn State Health Milton S. Hershey Medical Center and the Western Psychiatric Institute at the University of Pittsburgh. See also Maureen C. Hatch et al., "Cancer Near the Three Mile Island Nuclear Plant: Radiation Emissions," *American Journal of Epidemiology* 132, no. 3 (September 1990): 397–412.

82. Houts, Cleary, and Hu, *Three Mile Island Crisis*, 54, 77.

83. See Adriana Petryna, *Life Exposed: Biological Citizens after Chernobyl* (Princeton, NJ: Princeton University Press, 2002).

84. *Report of the President's Commission on the Accident at Three Mile Island*, 78–79.

85. Anna Gyorgy, *No Nukes: Everyone's Guide to Nuclear Power* (Boston: South End Press, 1979), 71. On the Clamshell Alliance, see Michael Stewart Foley, *Front Porch Politics: The Forgotten Heyday of American Activism in the 1970s and 1980s* (New York: Farrar, Straus and Giroux, 2013), 121–49.

86. The Radiation Exposure Compensation Act was eventually signed into law in 1990 by George H. W. Bush.

87. Kai T. Erikson, *A New Species of Trouble: The Human Experience of Modern Disasters* (New York: Norton, 1994), 155.

88. "Undefinable Fear Has Residents Stocking Up on Guns, Foodstuffs," *Philadelphia Inquirer*, April 4, 1979.

89. *Report of the President's Commission on the Accident at Three Mile Island*, 79. The Kemeny Commission's task force on public information concluded that media coverage of the Three Mile Island incident was relatively balanced: *Staff Report to the President's Commission on the Accident at Three Mile Island: Report of the Public's Right to Information Task Force* (Washington, DC: US Government Printing Office, 1979), 182–225.

90. Jimmy Carter, "President's Commission on the Accident at Three Mile Island," December 7, 1979, *Public Papers of the Presidents: Jimmy Carter, 1979*, Book 2 (Washington, DC: US Government Printing Office, 1980), 2202–4.

91. Jimmy Carter, "Radioactive Waste Management Program," February 12, 1980, *Public Papers of the Presidents: Jimmy Carter, 1980*, Book 1 (Washington, DC: US Government Printing Office, 1981), 296.

92. "Doomsday: Grim Observances Kick Off Ground Zero Week," *Pittsburgh Post-Gazette*, April 19, 1982.

93. "Throngs Fill Manhattan to Protest Nuclear Weapons," *New York Times*, June 13, 1982.

94. Ken Butigan, *Pilgrimage through a Burning World: Spiritual Practice and Nonviolent Protest at the Nevada Test Site* (Albany: State University of New York Press, 2003), ix.

95. "Three Mile Island Represented the Power and Peril of Nuclear Energy: Now It's Closed," *Washington Post*, September 26, 2019.

96. See Paolo Bacigalupi, "The Tamarisk Hunter," *High Country News*, June 26, 2006, and Paolo Bacigalupi, *The Water Knife* (New York: Knopf, 2015).

97. Public Health Service Committee on Environmental Health Problems, *Report to the Surgeon General* (Washington, DC: US Department of Health, Education, and Welfare, 1961), 256. On water scarcity, see Peter Rogers and Susan Leal, *Running Out of Water: The Looming Crisis and Solutions to Conserve Our Most Precious Resource* (New York: Palgrave Macmillan, 2010).

98. "CA Senator Harris Introduces $250 Billion Water Justice Act to Address National Water Crisis," *California Water News Daily*, July 25, 2019, http://californiawaternewsdaily.com/legislation/ca-senator-harris-introduces-250-billion-water-justice-act-to-address-national-water-crisis.

99. Tom Perreault, "What Kind of Governance for What Kind of Equity? Towards a Theorization of Justice in Water Governance," *Water International* 39, no. 2 (February 2014): 233–45.

100. Rutgerd Boelens et al., "Hydrosocial Territories: A Political Ecology," *Water International* 41, no. 1 (January 2016): 10.

101. American Dental Association, ADA Statement Commemorating the 60th Anniversary of Community Water Fluoridation, ADA, Washington, DC, 2005. See R. Allan Freeze and Jay H. Lehr, *The Fluoride Wars: How a Modest Public Health Measure Become America's Longest Running Political Melodrama* (London: John Wiley, 2009), 1–6.

102. Letter from Oveta Culp Hobby to Congressman Gardner R. Withrow, June 20, 1955, "Water Fluoridation," Box 24, Papers of Oveta Culp Hobby, Dwight D. Eisenhower Presidential Library.

103. The quotation is from an open letter to Congress on "Fluoridation of Water" dated May 31, 1955, by Arthur W. Ginsky of La Crosse, Wisconsin, a letter that Wisconsin Congressman Withrow sent to Oveta Culp Hobby; "Water Fluoridation," Box 24, Papers of Oveta Culp Hobby.

104. H. V. Smith, "Potability of Water from the Standpoint of Fluorine Content," *American Journal of Public Health* 25, no. 4 (April 1935): 434–41. See also Margaret Cammack Smith, "Fluorine Toxicosis: A Public Health Problem," *American Journal of Public Health* 25, no. 5 (May 1935): 696–702.

105. For a fuller study, see Catherine Carstairs, "Debating Water Fluoridation before Dr. Strangelove," *American Journal of Public Health* 105, no. 8 (August 2015): 1559–69. On the fluoride controversy, see "Fluoridation, Pro and Con," *New York Times*, March 3, 1957, and "Fluoride or No: An Emotional Debate," *New York Times*, May 25, 1958.

106. "The Fluoridation Fight: Dr. Stare Calls Foes 'Quacks and Charlatans,'" *Boston Globe*, November 4, 1963.

107. Memo from Thomas L. Hagan, Chief of the Division of Dental Public Health, to Regional Directors, Department of Health, Education, and Welfare,

August 10, 1956, "Statements and Resolutions in Regard to Fluoridation," General Records Relating to Fluoridation Studies, 1951–1969, RG90, National Archives.

108. Louis Parkes and Henry Kenwood, *Hygiene and Public Health* (Philadelphia: P. Blakiston's Son, 1902), 1, 49.

109. Parkes and Kenwood, *Hygiene and Public Health*, 50.

110. Parkes and Kenwood, *Hygiene and Public Health*, 51, 67.

111. Werner Troesken, *The Great Lead Water Pipe Disaster* (Cambridge, MA: MIT Press, 2006), 16.

112. Troesken, *Great Lead Water Pipe Disaster*, 17.

113. See Douglas Brinkley, *Rightful Heritage: Franklin D. Roosevelt and the Land of America* (New York: Harper, 2016), 334–35.

114. Letter from John D. Dingell to President Roosevelt, June 4, 1935, Box 13, OF 216 Public Health Service 1933–36, Department of the Treasury, Franklin D. Roosevelt Presidential Library and Museum, Hyde Park, New York.

115. See the February 1935 issue of the *American Journal of Public Health* 25, no. 2, 119–46.

116. Martin V. Melosi, *The Sanitary City: Urban Infrastructure in America from Colonial Times to the Present* (Baltimore: Johns Hopkins University Press, 2000), 149–74.

117. See Robert A. Shanley, "Franklin D. Roosevelt and Water Pollution Control Policy," *Presidential Studies Quarterly* 18, no. 2 (Spring 1988): 319–30.

118. Published as *Water Pollution in the United States* (Washington, DC: US Government Printing Office, 1939).

119. Letter from Wayne Taylor to President Roosevelt, September 15, 1937, OF 216 Public Health Service 1933–36, Department of the Treasury, Box 13, Franklin D. Roosevelt Library. *Report of a Survey of the Health Department and Other Health Agencies in the District of Columbia* (Washington, DC: US Government Printing Office, 1939), 307.

120. President Roosevelt, "A Recommendation That the Federal Government Aid in the Solution of the Problems of Water Pollution," February 16, 1939, in *The Public Papers and Addresses of Franklin D. Roosevelt, 1939 Volume, War—And Neutrality* (New York: Macmillan, 1941), 137.

121. *Water Pollution in the United States*, 83.

122. H. R. Crohurst, "Water Pollution Abatement in the United States," *American Journal of Public Health* 26, no. 2 (February 1936): 180.

123. See Charles Gilman Hyde, "The Trained Public Health Engineer in Public Health Departments," *American Journal of Public Health* 26, no. 7 (July 1936): 709.

124. G. N. Quam and Arthur Klein, "Lead Pipes as a Source of Lead in Drinking Water," *American Journal of Public Health* 26, no. 8 (August 1936): 778–80, and "Warning on Lead Danger," *New York Times*, August 17, 1936.

125. See "Lead Levels in Water Misrepresented across US," *Washington Post*, October 5, 2004.

126. Barbara Demeneix, *Losing Our Minds: How Environmental Pollution Impairs Human Intelligence and Mental Health* (Oxford: Oxford University

Press, 2014), 12–16; Gerald Markowitz and David Rosner, *Deceit and Denial: The Deadly Politics of Industrial Pollution* (Berkeley: University of California Press, 2002), 36–63; Gerald Markowitz and David Rosner, *Lead Wars: The Politics of Science and the Fate of America's Children* (Berkeley: University of California Press, 2013), 44–51.

127. Phil Brown, "Environmental Health as a Core Public Health Component," in *The Contested Boundaries of American Public Health*, ed. James Colgrove, Gerald Markowitz, and David Rosner (New Brunswick, NJ: Rutgers University Press, 2008), 85.

128. See Phil Brown, *Toxic Exposures: Contested Illnesses and the Environmental Health Movement* (New York: Columbia University Press, 2007).

129. See Jim Gash, "Beyond Erin Brockovich and a Civil Action: Should Strict Products Liability Be the Next Frontier for Water Contamination Lawsuits?" *Washington University Law Review* 80, no. 1 (January 2002): 51–117.

130. Sandra Steingraber, *Living Downstream: An Ecologist's Personal Investigation of Cancer and the Environment* (1997; New York: Da Capo, 2010), xx. See also the activist documentary of the same name featuring Steingraber (dir. Chanda Chevannes, 2010), www.livingdownstream.com.

131. Andrew R. Highsmith, *Demolition Means Progress: Flint, Michigan, and the Fate of the American Metropolis* (Chicago: University of Chicago Press, 2015), 107–8; Anna Clark, *Poisoned City: Flint's Water and the American Urban Tragedy* (New York: Picador, 2019).

132. "Detroit's Plan to Profit on Its Water, by Selling to Its Neighbors, Looks Half Empty," *New York Times*, May 26, 2014.

133. For casualty statistics, see "Legionnaires'-associated Deaths Grow to 12 in Flint Area," *Detroit Free Press*, April 11, 2016.

134. For a time line, see "Lead-Laced Water in Flint: A Step-by-Step Look at the Makings of a Crisis," *The Two Way*, NPR (April 20, 2016). See "Flint's Water Crisis Still Isn't Over: Here's Where Things Stand a Year Later," *Time*, January 18, 2017.

135. Barack Obama, "Remarks in Detroit, Michigan" January 20, 2016, www.presidency.ucsb.edu/documents/remarks-detroit-michigan-0.

136. "Flint's Children Suffer in Class after Years of Drinking the Lead-Poisoned Water," *New York Times*, November 6, 2019.

137. On dirty water and high African American mortality rates, see Werner Troesken, *Water, Race, and Disease* (Cambridge, MA: MIT Press, 2004).

138. "How Hillary Clinton Put the Flint Water Crisis on the Front Page," *Washington Post*, January 20, 2016.

139. "Transcript of the Democratic Presidential Debate in Flint, Michigan," *New York Times*, March 6, 2016.

140. "Flint Mayor Announces Program for Youth," *Detroit News*, March 6, 2016. On Bill Clinton's executive order, see David M. Konisky, *Failed Promises: Evaluating the Federal Government's Response to Environmental Justice* (Cambridge, MA: MIT Press, 2015).

141. "Clinton Just Vowed to Eliminate the Lead Threat in Five Years," *Washington Post*, April 13, 2016. See the CDC report, *Eliminating Childhood*

Lead Poisoning: A Federal Strategy Targeting Lead Paint Hazards, February 2000, www.cdc.gov/nceh/lead/about/fedstrategy2000.pdf.

142. "Trump Plans Wednesday Trip to Flint, Water Plant," *Detroit News*, September 13, 2016.

143. InfoWars.com, February 24, 2016, accessed on YouTube July 2016, but no longer available (from summer 2018) for violating hate speech policies.

144. Michel Moore, "Flint Poisoning Is a Racial Crime," *Time*, January 21, 2016.

145. Barack Obama, "Remarks at Kettering University in Flint, Michigan," May 4, 2016, www.presidency.ucsb.edu/documents/remarks-flint-michigan.

146. "The Toxic Tap," *Time*, February 1, 2016. In 2018, LeeAnne Walters was awarded the Goldman Environmental Prize for her environmental activism.

147. For arguably the best overview of the Flint crisis, see Siddharta Roy and Marc Edwards, "Citizen Science during the Flint, Michigan, Federal Water Emergency: Ethical Dilemmas and Lessons Learned," *Citizen Science: Theory and Practice* 4, no. 1 (March 2019): 1–28.

148. Dorceta E. Taylor, *Toxic Communities: Environmental Racism, Industrial Pollution, and Residential Mobility* (New York: New York University Press, 2014). On the discontinuance of the bottled water program, see "Michigan Will No Longer Provide Free Bottled Water to Flint," *New York Times*, April 8, 2018.

149. For the Black Lives Matter statement, see "Black Lives Matters Calls the Flint Water Crisis an Act of 'State Violence,'" *Grist*, January 25, 2016, https://grist.org/living/black-lives-matters-calls-the-flint-water-crisis-an-act-of-state-violence/amp/. For context, see Chelsea Grimmer, "Racial Microbiopolitics: Flint Lead Poisoning, Detroit Water Shut Offs, and the 'Matter' of Enfleshment," *Comparatist* 41 (October 2017): 19–40.

150. House Subcommittee on Investigation and Oversight of the Committee on Science and Technology, *A Public Health Tragedy: How Flawed CDC Data and Faulty Assumptions Endangered Children's Health in the Nation's Capital*, May 20, 2010, www.dcwatch.com/wasa/100520.pdf.

151. Perreault, "What Kind of Governance," 237.

152. James Inhofe attacks Gore and climate change believers in *The Greatest Hoax: How the Global Warming Conspiracy Threatens Your Future* (Washington, DC: WND Books, 2012).

153. Thomson, *The Wild and the Toxic*, 10.

154. Rachel Carson, *Silent Spring*, 40th anniversary ed. (1962; New York: Houghton Mifflin, 2002), 188, 268. The Johnson administration responded to Carson's research on pesticides via the President's Science Advisory Committee report *The Use of Pesticides*. Johnson paid tribute to Carson on the signing of the Pesticide Control Bill in May 1964 (she had died the previous month from a heart attack after suffering from breast cancer).

155. Al Gore, *An Inconvenient Truth: The Crisis of Global Warming* (New York: Viking, 2007), 10.

156. For discussion of this 1979 study by the Ad Hoc Study Group on Carbon Dioxide and Climate, see Elizabeth Kolbert, *Field Notes from a Catastrophe: Man, Nature, and Climate Change* (New York: Bloomsbury, 2006),

10–13. On the importance of 1988 in the climate debate, see Peter Newell, *Climate for Change: Non-State Actors and the Global Politics of the Greenhouse* (Cambridge: Cambridge University Press, 2008), 74–75.

157. The Senate ratified the Kyoto Treaty in 1998. Two years later George W. Bush proposed instead a Clear Skies initiative to place limits on gases from pollution that Al Gore dubbed "the dirty skies initiative": http://ens-newswire .com/wp-content/uploads/2010/05/2002-04-23-01.html.

158. Al Gore, *Earth in the Balance* (Boston: Houghton Mifflin, 1992), 221. Gore recounts his exposure to Rachel Carson and Roger Revelle in the introduction to *Earth in the Balance*.

159. "The 2000 Campaign: Spiritual Seeker," *New York Times*, October 22, 2000. Gore, *Earth in the Balance*, 265.

160. Gore, *Earth in the Balance*, 360.

161. Gore, *Earth in the Balance*, 269–94. Gore recounts his son's accident in his introductory remarks to the first edition of *An Inconvenient Truth* (New York: Rodale, 2006), 8.

162. Bill Clinton and Al Gore, *Putting People First: How We Can All Change America* (New York: Times Books, 1992), 93, 212. The second quotation is from Gore's July 16, 1992, speech "A Vision for America" at the Democratic National Convention in Madison Square Garden, as quoted in J. Robert Cox, "The (Re)Making of the 'Environmental President': Clinton/Gore and the Rhetoric of U.S. Environmental Politics, 1992–1996," in Peterson, *Green Talk in the White House*, 160.

163. Al and Tipper Gore, *Joined at the Heart: The Transformation of the American Family* (New York: Henry Holt, 2002), 296.

164. Gore, *An Inconvenient Truth*, 11, 166–69.

165. Ralph Nader, "The Greens and the Presidency: A Voice, Not an Echo," *The Nation*, July 8, 1996.

166. Gore, *An Inconvenient Truth*, 180.

167. Al Gore, *The Assault on Reason* (New York: Penguin, 2007), 25. For the first quotation, see Philip Smith and Nicolas Howe, *Climate Change as Social Drama: Global Warming in the Public Sphere* (New York: Cambridge University Press, 2015), 76.

168. See Nancy Lord, *Early Warming: Crisis and Response in the Climate-Changed North* (Berkeley, CA: Counterpoint, 2011), 2–3.

169. The Florida panther was in danger of extinction in the 1990s, but twenty years later conservationists noted that numbers were rising even though extinction threats continue: "This Florida Predator Is Making a Comeback," *Miami Herald*, February 22, 2017; "Florida Has 1,036 Animals Scientists Think Could Vanish," *Miami Herald*, March 29, 2018.

170. See *Spill: The Wreck of the* Exxon Valdez: *Report of the Alaska Oil Spill Commission* (State of Alaska, January 1990); Dunaway, *Seeing Green*, 223–38; and Michael Burgen, Exxon Valdez: *How a Massive Oil Spill Triggered an Environmental Catastrophe* (North Mankato, MN: Compass Point, 2018).

171. For the quotation, see Grant Sims, "A Clot in the Heart of the Earth," *Outside*, June 1989, 40. For these criticisms of Exxon and a comparison to

the Three Mile Island incident, see "Preparing for Crisis: Being Ready Is Part of Business," and "Corporate American Botches It Again," *Anchorage Daily News*, April 30, 1989. Lawrence Rawl did not himself go to Alaska but published a full-page advertisement by way of an apology in national newspapers on April 3. President Bush sent two White House officials to visit the site five days after the spill, followed by Vice President Dan Quayle on May 5, over a month later.

172. On the environmental health risks of the spill, see "Recovery: Ability of Species to Rebound from Oil Differs Sharply," *Anchorage Daily News*, May 6, 1989, and "Images of the Spill," *Anchorage Daily News*, May 7, 1989. On the public health risks of the spill, see State of Alaska Division of Emergency Services, *Soundings* May 2, 1989, Box 3, Folder 4, Exxon Valdez Oil Spill Collection, Valdez Museum Historical Archive, Valdez, Alaska. For personal stories of the Tatitlek and Chenega Bay communities, see Sharon Bushell and Stan Jones, *The Spill: Personal Stories from the* Exxon Valdez *Disaster* (Kenmore, WA: Epicenter Press, 2009), 242–55. For the efforts of the nonprofit Alaska Health Project to improve the health of native communities, see Alaska Health Project records, Box 5, Folder 39 and Box 13, Folder 50, Archives and Special Collections, Consortium Library, University of Alaska Anchorage.

173. "Alaska Changes View on Carter after 20 Years," *New York Times*, August 25, 2000.

174. Gore, *An Inconvenient Truth*, 135.

175. "'Frozen Gore' Sculpture Returns in Fairbanks to Fuel Climate Change Debate," *Fairbanks Daily News-Miner*, January 5, 2010.

176. Sarah Palin, "The Politicization of the Copenhagen Climate Conference," *Washington Post*, December 9, 2009. See Inhofe, *Greatest Hoax*, 119–36. Naomi Klein dismisses "Climategate," as it was called, for being a right-wing distortion of hacked scientific data: Naomi Klein, *This Changes Everything* (New York: Simon and Schuster, 2015), 41.

177. "Al Gore Blasts Sarah Palin and GOP for Irrational Denial of Climate Change," *News and Politics Examiner*, December 9, 2009.

178. Timothy Clark, "Scale," in *Telemorphosis: Theory in the Era of Climate Change*, vol. 1, ed. Tom Cohen (Open Humanities Press, 2012), 148–66.

179. Marla Cone, *Silent Snow: The Slow Poisoning of the Arctic* (New York: Grove, 2005), 35–36. The University of Alaska Fairbanks hosted a congressional hearing on climate change in the Arctic on May 29, 2001, which raised many points made by Gore, Cone, and Kolbert: *Global Climate Change* (Washington, DC: US Government Printing Office, 2002). See also "Extreme Climate Change Has Arrived in America," *Washington Post*, August 13, 2019.

180. Kolbert, *Field Notes from a Catastrophe*, 14.

181. Al Gore, *An Inconvenient Sequel: Truth to Power* (New York: Rodale, 2017), 63, 132–33. See also Elizabeth Kolbert, "The Siege of Miami," *New Yorker*, December 21/28, 2015, and "Octopus in the Parking Garage Is Climate Change's Canary in the Coal Mine," *Miami Herald*, November 18, 2016.

182. On environmental threats and sustainability projects in Miami-Dade County, see the US Army Corps of Engineers' report *Beach Erosion Control*

and Hurricane Protection Project, Dade County, Florida, 1995 (held at the Miami Beach Public Library).

183. Thomas Friedman, *Hot, Flat, and Crowded: Why the World Needs a Green Revolution—And How We Can Renew Our Global Future* (New York: Penguin, 2008).

184. Vice President Al Gore, United Nations Security Council Opening Session January 10, 2000), https://clintonwhitehouse3.archives.gov/WH/EOP/OVP/speeches/unopen_fp.html.

185. "Zika Virus Spreading in Miami as New Local Case Reported outside of Wynwood," *Miami Herald*, August 2, 2016.

186. Michael Pollan, "Why Bother?" *New York Times*, April 20, 2008. See also Howe, *Behind the Curve*, 201–3.

187. See Michael Pollan, *In Defense of Food: An Eater's Manifesto* (London: Penguin, 2008).

188. Al Gore, "Youth Activists Are Demanding Action against Climate Change: It's Time for Us to Listen," *Time*, September 19, 2019.

189. Barack Obama, Proclamation 9426, "Earth Day, 2016," www.presidency.ucsb.edu/documents/proclamation-9426-earth-day-2016.

190. Klein, *This Changes Everything*, 41, 155, 447.

191. "Neil Young: Tar Sands Site 'Looks Like Hiroshima,'" *Democracy Now*, September 11, 2013.

192. *Climate Change: A Challenge for Public Health* (Washington, DC: US Government Printing Office, 2009), 2. On the public health consequences of climate change, see, for example, William N. Rom, *Environmental Policy and Public Health: Air Pollution, Global Climate Change, and Wilderness* (San Francisco: Jossey-Bass, 2012).

193. Climate and Health Meeting, Carter Center, Atlanta, February 16, 2017, www.climaterealityproject.org/health.

194. See Michael Burger and Justin Gundlach, eds., *Climate Change, Public Health, and the Law* (Cambridge: Cambridge University Press, 2018), and Bill McKibben, *Falter: Has the Human Game Begun to Play Itself Out?* (London: Headline, 2019), 118–27.

195. Naomi Klein, *Fences and Windows: Dispatches from the Frontline of the Globalization Debate* (London: HarperCollins, 2002), xiii–xiv.

CHAPTER 4: VIRUS

1. For this quotation, see a letter from Lily Norton to Helen Whidden, November 14, 1921, "Lily Norton," Anna Eleanor and Franklin D. Roosevelt, Reminiscences by Contemporaries, Franklin D. Roosevelt Library, Hyde Park, New York.

2. Pramod K. Nayar, *The Extreme in Contemporary Culture: States of Vulnerability* (Lanham, MD: Rowman and Littlefield, 2017), xiii–xv.

3. Andrew Lakoff, *Unprepared: Global Health in a Time of Emergency* (Berkeley: University of California Press, 2017), 7.

4. See Michele Landis Dauber, *The Sympathetic State: Disaster Relief and the Origins of the American Welfare State* (Chicago: University of Chicago

Press, 2013), and Paul Farmer, *Infections and Inequalities: The Modern Plagues* (Berkeley: University of California Press, 1999).

5. Robert N. Bellah, "Citizenship, Diversity, and the Search for the Common Good" (1987), in *The Robert Bellah Reader*, ed. Robert N. Bellah and Steven M. Tipton (Durham, NC: Duke University Press, 2006), 303–18.

6. William H. McNeill, "Patterns of Disease Emergence in History," in *Emerging Viruses*, ed. Stephen S. Morse (New York: Oxford University Press, 1993), 29–45, and John M. Barry, *The Great Influenza: The Epic Story of the Deadliest Plague in History* (New York: Viking, 2004), 99.

7. "Coming: A 100-Virus Vaccine; Interview with Dr. Jonas Salk," *This Week*, July 8, 1962.

8. Priscilla Wald, *Contagious: Cultures, Carriers, and the Outbreak Narrative* (Durham, NC: Duke University Press, 2008), 42–43.

9. Steven F. Kruger, *AIDS Narratives: Gender and Sexuality, Fiction and Science* (New York: Routledge, 2011), 13–14.

10. Melinda Cooper, *Life as Surplus: Biotechnology and Capitalism in the Neoliberal Era* (Seattle: University of Washington Press, 2008), 51–52.

11. See Paula A. Treichler, "AIDS, Homophobia, and Biomedical Discourse: An Epidemic of Signification," *October* 43 (Winter 1987): 31–70, and Paula A. Treichler, *How to Have Theory in an Epidemic: Cultural Chronicles of AIDS* (1999; Durham, NC: Duke University Press, 2004), 1–10.

12. See Jeffrey Kluger, *Splendid Solution: Jonas Salk and the Conquest of Polio* (New York: Putnam's, 2004), and Bernard Seytre and Mary Shaffer, *The Death of a Disease: A History of the Eradication of Poliomyelitis* (New Brunswick, NJ: Rutgers University Press, 2005; first published in French in 2004).

13. Neal Nathanson and Alexander D. Langmuir, "The Cutter Incident: Poliomyelitis Following Formaldehyde-Activated Poliovirus Vaccination in the United States during the Spring of 1955," *American Journal of Tropical Medicine and Hygiene* 78, no. 1 (July 1963): 29–60. See also Paul A. Offit, *The Cutter Incident: How America's First Polio Vaccine Led to the Growing Vaccine Crisis* (New Haven, CT: Yale University Press, 2005).

14. See John McKiernan-González, *Fevered Measures: Public Health and Race at the Texas-Mexico Border, 1848–1942* (Durham, NC: Duke University Press, 2012), 64–66; James Colgrove, *State of Immunity: The Politics of Vaccination in Twentieth-Century America* (Berkeley: University of California Press, 2006), 38–44; and Mark A. Largent, *Vaccine: The Debate in Modern America* (Baltimore: Johns Hopkins University Press, 2012), 15–36.

15. Charles E. Rosenberg, "What Is an Epidemic? AIDS in Historical Perspective" (1989), in *Explaining Epidemics and Other Stories in the History of Medicine* (Cambridge: Cambridge University Press, 1992), 279.

16. Richard Preston, "Crisis in the Hot Zone," *New Yorker*, October 26, 1992, and Richard Preston, *The Hot Zone* (New York: Corgi, 1994). On these narrative types, see Neil Allen Gerlach, "From Outbreak to Pandemic Narrative: Reading Newspaper Coverage of the 2014 Ebola Outbreak," *Canadian Journal of Communication* 41, no. 4 (November 2016): 611–30.

17. See George Dehner, *Influenza: A Century of Science and Public Health Response* (Pittsburgh, PA: University of Pittsburgh Press, 2012), 42–43. See

also Nancy K. Bristow, *American Pandemic: The Lost Worlds of the 1918 Influenza Epidemic* (Oxford: Oxford University Press, 2012), 32, and Sandra Opdycke, *The Flu Epidemic of 1918: America's Experience in the Global Health Crisis* (New York: Routledge, 2014), 26–30.

18. On the statistic, see Oscar Jewell Harvey, *The Spanish Influenza Pandemic of 1918* (Philadelphia: Weyland Easterbrook, 1920).

19. For the Columbia University statistic, see the *Annual Report of the President and Treasurer to the Trustees for the Year Ending June 30, 1919* (New York: Columbia University, 1920), 183, 254–56. For the New York City context, see "Influenza Has Reached Crest Here," *New York Tribune*, October 20, 1918, and Francesco Aimone, "The 1918 Influenza Epidemic in New York City: A Review of the Public Health Response," *Public Health Reports* 125, supplement 3 (2010): 71–79.

20. Lois N. Magner, *A History of Infectious Diseases and the Microbial World* (Westport, CT: Praeger, 2009), 178. For global mortality estimates of between twenty-one and fifty million, see Niall P. Johnson and Juergen Mueller, "Updating the Accounts: Global Mortality of the 1918–1920 'Spanish' Influenza Pandemic," *Bulletin of the History of Medicine* 76, no. 1 (Spring 2002): 105–10. On the first two waves of influenza, see David K. Patterson and Gerald F. Pyle, "The Geography and Mortality of the 1918 Influenza Epidemic," *Bulletin of the History of Medicine* 65, no. 1 (Spring 1991): 4–21.

21. Nancy Tomes, *The Gospel of Germs: Men, Women, and the Microbe in American Life* (Cambridge, MA: Harvard University Press, 1998), 6; Sonia Shah, *Pandemic: Tracking Contagions; From Cholera to Ebola and Beyond* (New York: Farrar, Straus and Giroux, 2016), 133–37.

22. See Andrew McClary, "Germs Are Everywhere: The Germ Threat as Seen in Magazine Articles, 1890–1920," *Journal of American Culture* 3, no. 1 (Spring 1980): 32–46.

23. Cary T. Grayson, "The Heritage of the Presidents," "Health Hints from the White House, 1922," Box 1, Cary T. Grayson Papers: Articles by Cary T. Grayson, 1920–1927, Woodrow Wilson Presidential Library and Museum, Staunton, VA, 7.

24. Grayson, "Heritage of the Presidents," 8.

25. *Annual Report of the Surgeon General of the Public Health Service* (Washington, DC: US Government Printing Office, 1918), 10. Letter from Oscar Dowling to Rupert Blue (October 3, 1918), File Number 1712, Folder 1, Box 157, Central File, 1897–1923, Records of the Public Health Service, Record Group 90, National Archives and Records Administration, College Park, Maryland. For the surgeon general's recommendations to armed forces surgeons on the control of influenza, see Charles Lynch, Frank W. Weed, and Loy McAfee, *The Medical Department of the United States Army in the World War*, vol. 1 (Washington, DC: US Government Printing Office, 1923), 998–1004. The joint Public Health Service and American Red Cross coordination plan is reprinted in Lavinia L. Dock et al., *History of American Red Cross Nursing* (New York: Macmillan, 1922), 973–74.

26. Editorial, "Weapons against Influenza," *American Journal of Public Health* 8, no. 10 (October 1918): 787.

27. "'Flu' Again a Danger," *Washington Post*, December 13, 1918. See Alfred W. Crosby, *America's Forgotten Pandemic: The Influenza of 1918*, 2nd ed. (1989; Cambridge: Cambridge University Press, 2003), 51–52, and Marian Moser Jones, "The American Red Cross and Local Response to the 1918 Influenza Pandemic: A Four City Case Study," *Public Health Reports* 125, supplement 3 (April 2010): 92–104.

28. Esteban Rodríguez-Ocaña, "Barcelona's Influenza: A Comparison of the 1889–1890 and 1918 Autumn Outbreaks," in *Influenza and Public Health: Learning from Past Pandemics*, ed. Tamara Giles-Vernick and Susan Craddock (London: Earthscan, 2010), 44.

29. See Mark Osborne Humphries, "Paths of Infection: The First World War and the Origins of the 1918 Influenza Pandemic," *War in History* 21, no. 1 (January 2014): 55–81, and Keir Waddington, *The Bovine Scourge: Meat, Tuberculosis, and Public Health, 1850–1914* (Woodbridge: Boydell Press, 2006), 30–61.

30. Loring Miner recorded these cases in the PHS journal *Public Health Reports* once the immediate threat of the outbreak was over. See John M. Barry, "The Site of Origin of the 1918 Influenza Pandemic and Its Public Health Implications," *Journal of Translational Medicine* 2, no. 3 (January 2004), www.ncbi.nlm.nih.gov/pmc/articles/PMC340389. Barry follows A. A. Hoehling's earlier account of the Kansas outbreak in *The Great Epidemic: When the Spanish Influenza Struck* (Boston: Little, Brown, 1961).

31. Gerald F. Pyle, *The Diffusion of Influenza: Patterns and Paradigms* (Lanham, MD: Rowman and Littlefield, 1986), 40. On Camp Funston, influenza, and quarantining, see Judith R. Johnson, "Kansas in the 'Grippe': The Spanish Influenza Epidemic of 1918," *Kansas History* 15, no. 1 (Spring 1992): 44–55.

32. For influenza in the Caribbean, see David Killingray, "The Influenza Pandemic of 1918–1919 in the British Caribbean," *Social History of Medicine* 7, no. 1 (April 1994): 39–87.

33. Carol R. Byerly, *Fever of War: The Influenza Epidemic in the U.S. Army during World War I* (New York: New York University Press, 2005), 70–71.

34. "Spanish Influenza Is Raging in the German Army; Grip and Typhus also Prevalent among Soldiers," *New York Times*, June 17, 1918.

35. "Weapons against Influenza," 787. On the effects of the virus on Massachusetts, see Alan C. Swedlund, "Everyday Mortality in the Time of Plague: Ordinary People in Massachusetts before and during the 1918 Influenza Epidemic," in *Plagues and Epidemics: Infected Spaces Past and Present*, ed. D. Ann Herring and Alan C. Swedlund (Oxford: Berg, 2010), 153–77.

36. Crosby, *America's Forgotten Pandemic*, 45–47. The surgeon general's comments are quoted in "Takes Steps to Stop Influenza Spread," *New York Times*, September 14, 1918.

37. Byerly, *Fever of War*, 75. Francine King, "Atlanta," in *The 1918–1919 Pandemic of Influenza*, 105–18.

38. See David L. Cockrell, "'A Blessing in Disguise': The Influenza Pandemic of 1918 and North Carolina's Medical and Public Health Communities," *North Carolina Historical Review* 73, no. 3 (July 1996): 309–27.

39. Byerly, *Fever of War*, 388.

40. On pneumonia research at the time, see the "Annual Report of the Director of the Hospital of the Rockefeller Institute for Medical Research," October 1918, https://profiles.nlm.nih.gov/spotlight/cc/catalog/nlm:nlmuid-10158 4575X286-doc.

41. Paul W. Ewald, *Evolution of Infectious Disease* (Oxford: Oxford University Press, 1994), 111.

42. "President Visits Wounded," *Red Cross Bulletin* 3, no. 1 (December 30, 1930): 3.

43. *Remembering the 1918 Influenza Pandemic*, David J. Sencer CDC Museum, Centers for Disease Control and Prevention, Atlanta, Georgia (2018–19). It is unlikely that Raymond Coyne's *Locust Avenue, Masks On* photograph of November 3, 1918, would have been published at the time (the photographic negative was donated to the Mill Valley Public Library in 2011), but the sentiment of the "Wear a Mask or Go to Jail" sign around the neck of the woman on the right of the image was echoed in a contemporary piece in the *Mill Valley Record* that carried the subtitle "Violators Will Be Made to Pay Full Penalty." See "The Mask Ordinance," *Mill Valley Record*, November 9, 1918. I would like to thank archivist and librarian Natalie Snoyman of the Lucretia Little History Room at the Mill Valley Public Library for assistance in contextualizing Coyne's photograph.

44. See Debra Blakely, *Mass Mediated Disease: A Case Study Analysis of Three Flu Pandemics and Public Health Policy* (Lanham, MD: Lexington Books, 2006).

45. Quoted in Dorothy A. Pettit and Janice Bailie, *A Cruel Wind: Pandemic Flu in America, 1918–1920* (Murfreesboro, TN: Timberlake Books, 2008), 81.

46. Debra E. Blakely, "Mass Mediated Disease: A Case Study Analysis of News Reporting and Three Influenza Pandemics and Public Health Policy" (unpublished PhD thesis, University of Southern Mississippi, 2001), 54.

47. Elizabeth Schlabach, "A Measure of Race Relations: Influenza and Chicago's Public Health Ordinances, 1910–1918," paper presented at the American Studies Association Conference, Chicago, November 10, 2017.

48. See Edwin O. Jordan, *Epidemic Influenza: A Survey* (Chicago: American Medical Association, 1927), 60.

49. See Fred M. Davenport, "Role of the Commission on Influenza: Studies of Epidemiology and Prevention," *Public Health Reports* 73, no. 2 (February 1958): 133–39, and John M. Eyler, "Influenza and the Remaking of Epidemiology, 1918–1960," in Giles-Vernick and Craddock, *Influenza and Public Health*, 156–79.

50. On Wilson's influenza of April 1919, see Cary T. Grayson's letter to Joseph P. Tumulty, April 10, 1919, Cary T. Grayson Correspondence, Box 93, Woodrow Wilson Presidential Library. For the phrase "his powers of resistance were weakened," see Grayson's "Personal Notes on Woodrow Wilson's Health" (undated), Box 2, Cary T. Grayson Papers: Articles by Cary T. Grayson, 1920–1927, Woodrow Wilson Presidential Library. The *Public Health* journal, published by the Society of Medical Officers of Health in the United Kingdom, was also fairly quiet on influenza in late 1918 and early 1919,

focusing instead on venereal disease and tuberculosis: "Influenza Epidemic," *Public Health* 32, no. 3 (December 1918): 33, and "The Carrier Problem on Demobilisation," *Public Health* 32, no. 7 (April 1919): 76–79). From a British perspective, see Niall Johnson, *Britain and the 1918–19 Influenza Pandemic: A Dark Epilogue* (London: Routledge, 2006), 192–93, and from a Canadian perspective, see Mark Osborne Humphries, *The Last Plague: Spanish Influenza and the Politics of Public Health in Canada* (Toronto: University of Toronto Press, 2013), 79–83.

51. Katherine Anne Porter, *Pale Horse, Pale Rider: Three Short Novels* (1936; New York: Penguin, 2011), 363. For broader literary studies of influenza, see Jane Elizabeth Fisher, *Envisioning Disease, Gender, and War: Women's Narratives of the 1918 Influenza Pandemic* (London: Palgrave Macmillan, 2012).

52. Laura Spinney, *Pale Rider: The Spanish Flu of 1918 and How It Changed the World* (London: Jonathan Cape, 2017), 261–71.

53. Reina James, *This Time of Dying* (London: Portobello, 2006), 3–4.

54. James, *This Time of Dying*, 6.

55. Winters notes that she based her study of the fictional Buchanan, Illinois, on Patricia J. Fanning's study of Norwood, Massachusetts, in *Influenza and Inequality: One Town's Tragic Response to the Great Epidemic of 1918* (Amherst: University of Massachusetts Press, 2010).

56. Cat Winters, *The Uninvited: A Novel* (New York: HarperCollins, 2015), 289. For the report, see "Drastic Rule in Chicago," *New York Times*, October 4, 1918. A more recent evocative literary revisioning of the influenza pandemic is Emma Donoghue's Dublin-set novel *The Pull of the Stars* (London: Picador, 2020).

57. Letter from James T. Culbertson (of the Influenza Information Center) to Max A. Lauffer (of the University of Pittsburgh), September 20, 1948, Box 5, Folder 15, Correspondence—U.S. Public Health Service, 1948, Max A. Lauffer Papers, 1915–2013, UA.90.F99, Archives and Special Collections, University of Pittsburgh, Pennsylvania.

58. On the Ford administration's response to the swine flu, see Max J. Skidmore, *Presidents, Pandemics, and Politics* (New York: Palgrave Macmillan, 2016), 53–76.

59. On Wilson's illness, see Rose McDermott, *Presidential Leadership, Illness, and Decision Making* (Cambridge: Cambridge University Press, 2008), 72–73. For debates about possible connections between the two epidemics, see Paul Bernard Foley, "Encephalitis Lethargica and the Influenza Virus," *Journal of Neural Transmission* 116, no. 10 (October 2009): 1295–308, and Molly Caldwell Crosby, *Asleep: The Forgotten Epidemic That Remains One of Medicine's Greatest Mysteries* (New York: Berkley Books, 2010).

60. Homeland Security Council, "National Strategy for Pandemic Influenza," November 2005, www.cdc.gov/flu/pandemic-resources/pdf/pandemic-infl uenza-strategy-2005.pdf.

61. "Top White House Official in Charge of Pandemic Response Exits Abruptly," *Washington Post*, May 11, 2018. On the plans of the Congressional Budget Office, see Lakoff, *Unprepared*, 112. On preparedness for the 2017–18

flu season, see US Department of Health and Human Services, *Pandemic Influenza Plan, 2017 Update*, www.cdc.gov/flu/pandemic-resources/pdf/pan-flu-report-2017v2.pdf, and CDC's *Morbidity and Mortality Weekly Report*, September 28, 2018, 1050–59, and October 26, 2018, 1169–72.

62. See, for example, "Infantile Paralysis," *Medical and Surgical Reporter* 67, no. 3, July 16, 1892, and "More Infantile Paralysis," *New York Times*, August 5, 1899. For press coverage, see Richard J. Altenbaugh, *The Last Children's Plague: Poliomyelitis, Disability, and Twentieth-Century American Culture* (London: Palgrave Macmillan, 2015), 4–7.

63. Stephen E. Mawdsley, *Selling Science: Polio and the Promise of Gamma Globulin* (New Brunswick, NJ: Rutgers University Press, 2016), 2.

64. Morris Fishbein, ed., *A Bibliography of Infantile Paralysis, 1789–1944* (Philadelphia: J. B. Lippincott, 1946), 117, 120.

65. Haven Emerson's introduction to *The Epidemic of Poliomyelitis (Infantile Paralysis) in New York City in 1916* (New York: Department of Health of New York City, 1917), 9. On responsible health behavior in New York City, see Anne Hardy, *The Epidemic Streets: Infectious Disease and the Rise of Preventive Medicine, 1856–1900* (Oxford: Oxford University Press, 1993), and David Rosner, *Hives of Sickness: Epidemics and Public Health in New York City* (New Brunswick, NJ: Rutgers University Press, 1995).

66. See Gareth Williams, *Paralysed with Fear: The Story of Polio* (London: Palgrave Macmillan, 2013), 117. On the racialization of health in New York City at the time, see Emily K. Abel, *Hearts of Wisdom: American Women Caring for Kin, 1850–1940* (Cambridge, MA: Harvard University Press, 2000), 154–59, and Tanya Hart, *Health in the City: Race, Poverty, and the Negotiation of Women's Health in New York City, 1915–1930* (New York: New York University Press, 2015), 110–13, 147–48.

67. Naomi Rogers, *Dirt and Disease: Polio before FDR* (New Brunswick, NJ: Rutgers University Press, 1992), 20, 16.

68. Alan M. Kraut, *Silent Travelers: Germs, Genes, and the Immigrant Menace* (New York: Basic Books, 1994), 110–12.

69. Samuel Kelton Roberts Jr., *Infectious Fear: Politics, Death, and the Health Effects of Segregation* (Chapel Hill: University of North Carolina Press, 2009), 5.

70. Leland O. Howard, *The House Fly, Disease Carrier*, 2nd ed. (New York: Frederick A. Stokes, 1911), xvii–xviii. Philip Roth lightly satirizes the attempt to exterminate easy domestic animal targets in the opening pages of his novel *Nemesis*, which focuses on the 1944 outbreak of polio: Philip Roth, *Nemesis* (London: Vintage, 2010), 4–5.

71. See "Infantile Paralysis a Scourge and a Puzzle," *New York Times*, July 9, 1916. For discussion of Flexner, see David M. Oshinsky, *Polio: An American Story* (Oxford: Oxford University Press, 2005), 17–19, 124–25. A Philadelphia Department of Public Health poster of the early 1940s depicts a fly dropping bombs over an American city with the caption, "The Fly Is as Deadly as a Bomber!!" See Ennis Carter, *Posters for the People: Art of the WPA* (New York: Quirk Books, 2008), 62.

72. "Fighting the New Scourge of Infantile Paralysis," *New York Times*, August 20, 2011.

73. For this 1910 discovery, see Simon Flexner, "The Contribution of Experimental to Human Poliomyelitis," *Journal of the American Medical Association* 55, no. 13 (September 1910): 1105–13.

74. See "Franklin D. Roosevelt Will Swim to Health," *Atlanta Journal*, October 26, 1924, and " 'Polio-Physio' Follies Staged for Roosevelt," *Chicago Daily Tribune*, December 3, 1933. The Little White House Museum and the Historic Pools Museum at Warm Springs, Georgia, are useful sources for the Roosevelt polio narrative.

75. "Statement Concerning Poliomyelitis in New York State," August 28, 1931, Box 10, Folder 83, Thomas Parran Papers, 1892–1968, UA.90.F14, Archives and Special Collections, University of Pittsburgh Library System. George M. Stevens, "The 1934 Epidemic of Poliomyelitis in Southern California," *American Journal of Public Health* 24, no. 12 (December 1934): 1213–14.

76. President Roosevelt, "Radio Address on the Occasion of the President's Fifth Birthday Ball for the Benefit of Crippled Children," January 29, 1938, *The Public Papers and Addresses of Franklin D. Roosevelt, 1938 Volume: The Continuing Struggle for Liberalism* (New York: Random House, 1941), 72.

77. See Charlotte DeCroes Jacobs, *Jonas Salk: A Life* (Oxford: Oxford University Press, 2015), 71–72. On the National Foundation's role in funding polio research, see D. J. Wilson, "Basil O'Connor, the National Foundation for Infantile Paralysis, and the Reorganization of Polio Research in the United States, 1935–41," *Journal of the History of Medicine and Allied Sciences* 70, no. 3 (July 2015): 394–424.

78. Daniel J. Wilson, *Living with Polio: The Epidemic and Its Survivors* (Chicago: University of Chicago Press, 2005), 16–17; Jane S. Smith, *Patenting the Sun: Polio and the Salk Vaccine* (New York: William Morrow, 1990), 83–85. Naomi Rogers, "Race and the Politics of Polio: Warm Springs, Tuskegee, and the March of Dimes," *American Journal of Public Health* 97, no. 5 (May 2007): 785. On the racial politics of campaigning, see Gregg Mitman, "The Color of Money: Campaigning for Health in Black and White America," in *Imagining Illness: Public Health and Visual Culture*, ed. David Serlin (Minneapolis: University of Minnesota Press, 2010), 52–57.

79. Arthur Allen, *Vaccine: The Controversial Story of Medicine's Greatest Lifesaver* (New York: Norton, 2007), 178–79. Naomi Rogers, "Polio Can Be Conquered: Science and Health Propaganda in the United States from Polio Polly to Jonas Salk," in *Silent Victories: The History and Practice of Public Health in Twentieth-Century America*, ed. John W. Ward and Christian Warren (Oxford: Oxford University Press, 2007), 82.

80. Roosevelt, "Radio Address on the Occasion of the President's Fifth Birthday Ball," 72.

81. Roosevelt, "Presidential Statement on the New National Foundation for Infantile Paralysis," September 23, 1937, *The Public Papers and Addresses of Franklin D. Roosevelt, 1937 Volume: The Constitution Prevails* (New York: Random House, 1941), 374.

82. Roosevelt, "Radio Address on the Occasion of the President's Sixth

Birthday Ball for the Benefit of Crippled Children," January 30, 1939, *The Public Papers and Addresses of Franklin D. Roosevelt, 1939 Volume: War—And Neutrality* (New York: Macmillan, 1941), 104. Roosevelt built on these militaristic metaphors in his 1944 Birthday Ball radio address.

83. Oshinsky, *Polio: An American Story*, 45–46. Robert Cohen, ed., *Dear Mrs. Roosevelt: Letters from Children of the Great Depression* (Chapel Hill: University of North Carolina Press, 2002), 232.

84. On "useful citizenship," see Roosevelt, "Informal Remarks on Reception of Fund Raised by Birthday Ball in [sic] Behalf of Crippled Children," May 9, 1934, *The Public Papers and Addresses of Franklin D. Roosevelt, Volume 3: The Advance of Recovery and Reform, 1935* (New York: Random House, 1938), 226. On the Jackson polio clinic, see "Children's Hospital Takes Over Polio Clinic," *Jackson Daily News*, July 21, 1946.

85. See Amy L. Fairchild, "The Polio Narratives: Dialogues with FDR," *Bulletin of the History of Medicine* 75, no. 3 (Fall 2001): 488–524.

86. Lawrence Alexander, *The Iron Cradle* (New York: Crowell, 1954), 10.

87. Bert Hansen, *Picturing Medical Progress from Pasteur to Polio: A History of Mass Media Images and Popular Attitudes in America* (New Brunswick, NJ: Rutgers University Press, 2009), 245.

88. See Tony Gould, *A Summer Plague: Polio and Its Survivors* (New Haven, CT: Yale University Press, 1995), 96–100, and Naomi Rogers, *Polio Wars: Sister Kenny and the Golden Age of American Medicine* (Oxford: Oxford University Press, 2013), 364–66.

89. Rogers, "Polio Can Be Conquered," 82.

90. For links between Roosevelt's partial recovery from polio in 1932 and a narrative of national restoration, see Susan Currell, "Eugenic Decline and Recovery in Self-Improvement Literature of the Thirties," in *Popular Eugenics: National Efficiency and American Mass Culture in the 1930s*, ed. Susan Currell and Christian Cogell (Athens: Ohio University Press, 2006), 45–49.

91. The statistics are cited in Paul Langford Adams, "Health of the State: British and American Public Health Policies in the Depression and World War II" (unpublished PhD thesis, University of California, Berkeley, 1979), 226.

92. " 'Iron Lung' Is Shipped Here," *Wichita Falls Record News*, September 4, 1937, and "Checkers Spot Polio Hazards," *Wichita Falls Record News*, June 25, 1948.

93. "Local Second Graders Make History," *Wichita Falls Record News*, May 5, 1954.

94. For the 1942 billboard image, see www.fdrlibrary.marist.edu/archives /collections/franklin/index.php?p=digitallibrary/digitalcontent&id=4281ntent &id=4281.

95. See Fred Davis, *Passage through Crisis: Polio Victims and Their Families* (1963; New Brunswick, NJ: Transaction, 1991), xv.

96. Jacqueline Foertsch, *Bracing Accounts: The Literature and Culture of Polio in Postwar America* (Madison, NJ: Fairleigh Dickinson University Press, 2008), 29.

97. Foertsch, *Bracing Accounts*, 31.

98. Foertsch, *Bracing Accounts*, 94–96.

99. See Mark Shell, *Polio and Its Aftermath: The Paralysis of Culture* (Cambridge, MA: Harvard University Press, 2005).

100. Edward D. Miller, *Emergency Broadcasting and 1930s American Radio* (Philadelphia: Temple University Press, 2003), 80. On federal radio broadcasts, see Robert Park, "Morale and the News," *American Journal of Sociology* 47, no. 3 (November 1941): 360–77.

101. "Paralysis Vaccine Discontinued Here," *New York Times*, December 27, 1935.

102. "Vaccine Discovery May End Search of Century," *Los Angeles Times*, August 18, 1934, and Maurice Brodie, "Active Immunization against Poliomyelitis," *American Journal of Public Health* 25, no. 1 (January 1935): 54–67.

103. See Susan Lederer, *Subjected to Science: Human Experimentation in America before World War II* (Baltimore,: Johns Hopkins University Press, 1995), 108–9.

104. See Smith, *Patenting the Sun*, 255, and Jacobs, *Jonas Salk*, 86. For an example of Salk's scientific publications, see Jonas E. Salk, "Studies in Human Subjects on Active Immunization against Poliomyelitis," *JAMA* 151, no. 13 (March 1953): 1081–98. For newspaper clippings relating to Salk's work, see Series II of the Jonas Salk Vaccine Collection, 1954–2005, UA.90.F89, Archives and Special Collections, University of Pittsburgh Library System. On vaccine distribution and promotion, see the PHS Polio Vaccine Collection 1951–62, Series III, US National Library of Medicine, Bethesda, Maryland.

105. "News from the University of Pittsburgh," October 25, 1954, Box 1, Folder 2, Press Releases, 1952–2005, Jonas Salk Polio Vaccine Collection, 1917–2005, UA.90.F89, Archives and Special Collections, University of Pittsburgh Library System.

106. For the quotation, see the Chief of the Children's Bureau Martha M. Eliot's remarks at Citizens' Conference on the Polio Vaccine, Department of Health, Education, and Welfare, Washington, DC, April 27, 1955, "Salk Vaccine—April & May 1955," Box 23, Papers of Oveta Culp Hobby, Dwight D. Eisenhower Library, Abilene, Kansas.

107. "Medicine," *Time*, February 9, 1953.

108. See Kluger, *Splendid Solution*, 309–12. A HEW report on the Cutter incident of August 1955 concluded that the "trouble was inadequate inactivation coupled with failure of the safety tests"; see "Scheele, Leonard A., Surgeon General, Public Health Service," Box 31, Papers of Oveta Culp Hobby, Eisenhower Library.

109. President Eisenhower, "Citation Presented to the National Foundation for Infantile Paralysis and Accompanying Remarks," April 22, 1955, *Public Papers of the Presidents, Dwight D. Eisenhower, 1955* (Washington, DC: US Government Printing Office, 1959), 415.

110. "A Hero's Great Discovery Is Put to Work," *Life*, May 2, 1955. See also "Statement by the President on the Polio Vaccine Situation," May 31, 1955, *Public Papers of the Presidents, Dwight D. Eisenhower, 1955*, 559–63.

111. Eisenhower emphasized, "I don't like the word 'compulsory.' I am against the word 'socialized'" as these terms were, to his mind, against "our traditional system of free enterprise": Dwight D. Eisenhower, "Remarks to the

Members of the House of Delegates of the American Medical Association," March 14, 1953, *Public Papers of the Presidents, Dwight D. Eisenhower, 1953* (Washington, DC: US Government Printing Office, 1960), 98.

112. Committee on Labor and Public Welfare, *Hearings on the Poliomyelitis Vaccine*, United States Senate, 84th Congress, First Session, May 16, 1955, 149. See also "Mrs. Hobby Says Responsibility for Vaccine Plan Is Dr. Scheele's," *New York Times*, June 21, 1955.

113. "Text of Stevenson's Address at Dedication of Medical Science Building," *New York Times*, June 3, 1955.

114. "The Salk Vaccine: What Caused the Mess," *Harper's Magazine*, August 1955, 27–33.

115. Eisenhower, "The President's News Conference of May 18, 1955," *Public Papers of the Presidents, Dwight D. Eisenhower, 1955*, 505.

116. "U.S. Clears Cutter Lab in Polio Vaccine Fizzle," *Washington Post*, August 26, 1955. Eisenhower ,"Citation Presented to Dr. Jonas Salk and Accompanying Remarks," April 22, 1955, *Public Papers of the Presidents, Dwight D. Eisenhower, 1955*, 414.

117. Eleanor Roosevelt, "Statement on Polio Research and Treatment," January 2, 1958, and "Introduction of Dr. Jonas E. Salk," Box 1422, Eleanor Roosevelt Papers Speech and Article File, 1957–1962, Franklin D. Roosevelt Library. For the estimation of seven thousand lives saved, see Basil O'Connor to John F. Kennedy, February 28, 1962, Folder: "HE 1, 11-1-61–3-31-62," Papers of John F. Kennedy, White House Central Files, John F. Kennedy Presidential Library, Boston, Massachusetts.

118. *Health, Education, and Welfare Trends: 1962 Edition* (Washington, DC: US Department of Health, Education, and Welfare, 1962), xi. On the Vaccination Assistance Act of 1962 and the development of vaccination in the 1960s, see "Immunization Program," "National Communicable Disease Center [1 of 4]," Box 6, Department of Health, Education, and Welfare, 1963–1969, Administrative History Collection, Lyndon Baines Johnson Library, Austin, Texas. On the politics of vaccination in the early 1960s, see Elizabeth W. Etheridge, *Sentinel for Health: A History of the Centers for Disease Control* (Berkeley: University of California Press, 1992), 140–48, and "How the Poor Get Blamed for Disease," *The Atlantic*, November 9, 2014.

119. On global interdependence, see Helen Epstein, *The Invisible Cure: Africa, the West, and the Fight against AIDS* (New York: Farrar, Straus and Giroux, 2007).

120. Bill Clinton, "Remarks Announcing AIDS Initiatives," December 1, 1998, *Public Papers of the Presidents, William J. Clinton, 1998*, Book 2 (Washington, DC: US Government Printing Office, 2000), 2104. Clinton mentioned Jimiya Poisel again eighteen years later, in 2016, when she was in the audience for an Iowa City stump speech to promote Hillary Clinton in the Democratic primaries.

121. For media coverage of AIDS, see James Kinsella, *Covering the Plague: AIDS and the American Media* (New Brunswick, NJ: Rutgers University Press, 1989), and Mollyann Brodie et al., "AIDS at 21: Media Coverage of the HIV

Epidemic, 1981–2002," supplement to the *Columbia Journal Review* (March/April 2004): 2.

122. For this ontological threat, see Catherine Waldby, *AIDS and the Body Politic: Biomedicine and Sexual Difference* (London: Routledge, 1996), 1–10.

123. "Whatever Happened to AIDS?" *New York Times*, November 28, 1993.

124. Farmer, *Infections and Inequalities*, 60.

125. Elizabeth W. Etheridge, *Sentinel for Health: A History of the Centers for Disease Control* (Berkeley: University of California Press, 1992), 321–40. The first CDC report on what the following year became known as AIDS was June 5, 1981.

126. Sander Gilman, *Disease and Representation: Images of Illness from Madness to AIDS* (Ithaca, NY: Cornell University Press, 1988), 266.

127. "A Disease's Spread Provokes Anxiety," *New York Times*, August 8, 1982. This followed a piece by Lawrence Altman three months earlier: "New Homosexual Disorder Worries Health Officials," *New York Times*, May 11, 1982.

128. Susan Sontag, *AIDS and Its Metaphors* (New York: Farrar, Straus and Giroux, 1989), 86. David Holleran, *Ground Zero* (New York: Morrow, 1988), 19.

129. See Richard A. McKay, " 'Patient Zero': The Absence of a Patient's View of the Early North American AIDS Epidemic," *Bulletin of the History of Medicine* 88, no. 1 (Spring 2014): 161–94. For context, see Timothy Murphy, *Ethics in an Epidemic: AIDS, Morality, and Culture* (Berkeley: University of California Press, 1994); Stefan Elbe, *Virus Alert: Security, Governmentality, and the AIDS Pandemic* (New York: Columbia University Press, 2009), 78–85; and Michelle Cochrane, *When AIDS Began: San Francisco and the Making of an Epidemic* (New York: Routledge, 2004).

130. For Margaret Heckler's view of the Reagan administration's response to HIV/AIDS, see www.pbs.org/wgbh/pages/frontline/aids/interviews/heckler .html.

131. "AIDS: The Latest Scientific Facts," *Discover* (December 1985). Cited by Farmer, *Infections and Inequalities*, 61.

132. "Reagan Aide: Pot Can Make You Gay," *Newsweek*, October 27, 1986, 95. "Statement by the Vice-President on the AIDS Commission Report, 28 June 1988," OA/ID 23344, Emily Mead Files, George Bush Presidential Library, College Station, Texas.

133. Randy Shilts, *And the Band Played On: Politics, People, and the AIDS Epidemic* (New York: St Martin's Press, 1987), 298. On the National AIDS Hotline, see Timothy Edgar, Anne Fitzpatrick, and Vicki S. Freimuth, *AIDS: A Communication Perspective* (Hillsdale, NJ: Erlbaum, 1992), 137–39. See also Henry Waxman and Joshua Green, *The Waxman Report: How Congress Really Works* (New York: Twelve, 2009), 35–52.

134. Ronald Reagan, "The President's News Conference" (September 17, 1985), *Public Papers of the Presidents, Ronald Reagan, 1985*, Book 2 (Washington, DC: US Government Printing Office, 1988), 1104–5.

135. Reagan, "President's News Conference," 1108.

136. "Student Victims, Terrified Parents: Reagan Sympathizes with Both Sides in AIDS Furor," *Los Angeles Times*, September 18, 1985.

137. "The New Untouchables," *Time*, September 23, 1985.

138. Robert N. Bellah's foreword to Richard L. Smith, *AIDS, Gays, and the American Catholic Church* (Cleveland, OH: Pilgrim Press, 1994), xiii. Robert N. Bellah, "America's Cultural Conversation," in *Individualism and Commitment in American Life*, ed. Robert N. Bellah et al. (New York: Harper and Row, 1987), 4.

139. An almost unrecognizable photo of Rock Hudson appeared on the cover of the August 12, 1985, edition of *Newsweek* juxtaposed with the stark headline "AIDS."

140. *Surgeon General's Report on Acquired Immune Deficiency Syndrome* (Washington, DC: US Department of Health and Human Services, 1986), 6, www.nlm.nih.gov/exhibition/survivingandthriving/education/Activity-Surgeon -General/Surgeon-Generals-Report-on-AIDS.pdf. See C. Everett Koop, *Koop: The Memoirs of America's Family Doctor* (New York: HarperCollins, 1992), 248, and for Republican reactions to the report, see Jennifer Brier, *Infectious Ideas: U.S. Political Responses to the AIDS Crisis* (Chapel Hill: University of North Carolina Press, 2009), 88–101.

141. Reagan, "Interview with Eleanor Clift, Jack Nelson, and Joel Havemann of the Los Angeles Times," June 23, 1986, *Public Papers of the Presidents, Ronald Reagan, 1986*, Book 1, 831. For restrictions on welfare benefits, see Jonathan Bell, "Rethinking the 'Straight State': Welfare Politics, Health Care, and Public Policy in the Shadow of AIDS," *Journal of American History* 104, no. 4 (March 2018): 931–52.

142. Jeffrey A. Kelly and Janet S. St. Lawrence, *The AIDS Health Crisis: Psychological and Social Interventions* (New York: Plenum Press, 1988), 15.

143. Reagan, "Remarks at the American Foundation for AIDS Research Awards Dinner," May 31, 1987, *Public Papers of the Presidents, Ronald Reagan, 1987*, Book 1, 585.

144. Reagan, "Remarks at the American Foundation for AIDS Research Awards Dinner," 586. See "Reagan Asks Expansion of AIDS Virus Testing: Inmates, Aliens, Marriage Licensees Cited," *Washington Post*, June 1, 1987.

145. "Remarks for Vice President George Bush, Third International Conference on AIDS," June 1, 1987, Third International Conference on AIDS, Washington, DC, Speechwriter Files, George H. W. Vice Presidential Records Office, George Bush Presidential Library.

146. Ronald Reagan, "1988 Legislative and Administrative Message: A Union of Individuals," January 25, 1988, *Public Papers of the Presidents, Ronald Reagan, 1988*, Book 1, 109.

147. James D. Watkins, "Letter of Transmittal," *Report of the Presidential Commission on the Human Immunodeficiency Virus Epidemic: Submitted to the President of the United States* (Washington, DC: US Government Printing Office, 1988), vi. Later that year, the Institute of Medicine released a landmark report that revealed a worrying fragmentation of public health services. See Institute of Medicine, *The Future of Public Health* (Washington, DC: National Academy Press, 1988).

148. Watkins, "Letter of Transmittal," vi.

149. "How AIDS Has Changed FDA," *FDA Consumer* (February 1990): 14–17.

150. See "Reagan, AIDS and Discrimination," *Chicago Tribune*, August 10, 1988.

151. "Remarks by Louise W. Sullivan, M.D., Sixth International Conference on AIDS," Health (File A)—AIDS 1, Domestic Policy Council Files, George Bush Presidential Library.

152. George H. W. Bush, "Remarks at a Fundraising Dinner for Gubernatorial Candidate Jim Edgar in Chicago, Illinois," March 29, 1990, *Public Papers of the Presidents, George Bush, 1990*, Book 1 (Washington, DC: US Government Printing Office, 1991), 788; "Remarks at the Presentation Ceremony for the National Medals of Science and Technology," November 13, 1990, *Public Papers of the Presidents, George Bush, 1990*, Book 2 (Washington, DC: US Government Printing Office, 1991), 1591.

153. Bush, "Remarks to the National Leadership Coalition on AIDS," March 29, 1990, *Public Papers of the Presidents, George Bush, 1990*, Book 1, 434.

154. See Ronald Bayer, "The Dependent Center: The First Decade of the AIDS Epidemic in New York City," in Rosner, *Hives of Sickness*, 145–46. Bayer cites a February 1990 letter by Edward Kennedy (who cosponsored the Resource Emergency Act) that describes "the unfolding AIDS tragedy [as] already a hundredfold greater than any natural disaster to strike our nation in this century" (146). See also Ronald Bayer, *Private Acts, Social Consequences: AIDS and the Politics of Public Health* (New York: Free Press, 1989).

155. See the 2012 foreword to Mary Fisher, *My Name Is Mary: A Memoir* (1995; New York: Scribner's, 2012), n.p.

156. "Magic Johnson Quits Panel on AIDS," *New York Times*, September 26, 1992. Johnson features in the 2012 PBS *Frontline* documentary *Endgame: AIDS in Black America*. For Bush's comments on Johnson, see "Presidential Debate in St. Louis," October 11, 1992, *Public Papers of the Presidents, George Bush, 1992–93*, Book 2 (Washington, DC: US Government Printing Office, 1993), 1803.

157. On needle sharing, see "In State-Funded Project, Ex-Drug Addicts Take AIDS Warnings to the Streets," *Baltimore Sun*, April 15, 1986, and "Spread of AIDS Virus Is Unabated among Intravenous Drug Takers," *New York Times*, June 4, 1987.

158. On community-based HIV/AIDS activism on a global scale, see Jennifer Chan, *Politics in the Corridor of Dying: AIDS Activism and Global Health Governance* (Baltimore: Johns Hopkins University Press, 2015), 189–253.

159. ACT UP NY/Gran Fury artists were included in the 2015–16 *Art AIDS America* exhibition organized by the Tacoma Art Museum and the Bronx Museum of the Arts. On activist efforts, see Deborah B. Gould, *Moving Politics: Emotion and ACT UP's Fight against AIDS* (Chicago: University of Chicago Press, 2009), and David France, *How to Survive a Plague: The Story of How Activists and Scientists Tamed AIDS* (New York: Knopf, 2016).

160. Feinberg criticizes the FDA and HHS in "Queer and Loathing at the

FDA: Revolt of the Perverts," *Tribe* 1, no. 1 (Winter 1989), reprinted in David B. Feinberg, *Queer and Loathing: Rants and Raves of a Raging AIDS Clone* (New York: Penguin, 1995), 3–53.

161. Emmanuel S. Nelson, ed., *AIDS: The Literary Response* (New York: Twayne, 1992), 2. For Bush's statement, see "Question-and-Answer Session in Grand Rapids," October 29, 1992, *Public Papers of the Presidents, George Bush, 1992–93*, Book 2, 2086.

162. See Joe Rhatigan et al., "Rereading Public Health," in *Women, Poverty, and AIDS: Sex, Drugs, and Structural Violence*, ed. Paul Farmer, Margaret Connors, and Janie Simmons (Monroe, ME: Common Courage Press, 1996), 208. See also Emma-Louise Anderson, *Gender, HIV, and Risk: Navigating Structural Violence* (London: Palgrave Macmillan, 2015), 21–23, and Jonathan Bell, ed., *Beyond the Politics of the Closet: Gay Rights and the American State since the 1970s* (Philadelphia: University of Pennsylvania Press, 2020).

163. See Lisa Diedrich, "'Without us all told': Paul Monette's Vigilant Witnessing to the AIDS Crisis," in *Difference and Identity: A Special Issue of Literature and Medicine* (Baltimore: Johns Hopkins University Press, 1995), 112–13.

164. See Andrew Blades, "'The Past Is Not a Foreign Country': John Weir's AIDS Fiction," *Studies in American Fiction* 44, no. 1 (Spring 2017): 139–60. On community AIDS narratives, see Sonja Mackenzie, *Structural Intimacies: Sexual Stories in the Black AIDS Epidemic* (New Brunswick, NJ: Rutgers University Press, 2014). For an example of AIDS blogging, see the Critical Path Project launched in Philadelphia in 1989.

165. See Seth Mnookin, *The Panic Virus: A True Story of Medicine, Science, and Fear* (New York: Simon and Schuster, 2011).

166. "Early Indifference to AIDS Is Blamed for Its Spread," *Los Angeles Times*, November 29, 1986. See also Daniel M. Fox, "Chronic Disease and Disadvantage: The New Politics of HIV Infection," *Journal of Health Politics, Policy, and the Law* 15, no. 2 (April 1990): 341–55.

167. "When a Gaming Fantasy Is Eerily Close to Reality," *New York Times*, April 8, 2020.

168. See Tony Sampson, *Virality: Contagion Theory in the Age of Networks* (Minneapolis: University of Minnesota Press, 2012).

169. See Michael T. Osterholm and Mark Olshaker, *Deadliest Enemy: Our War against Killer Germs* (Boston: Little, Brown, 2017); the World Health Organization's 2019 report *Global Influenza Strategy, 2019–2030: Prevent, Control, Prepare*, www.who.int/influenza/global_influenza_strategy_2019_203 0/en; and Debora MacKenzie, *COVID-19: The Pandemic That Never Should Have Happened and How to Stop the Next One* (New York: Hachette, 2020).

170. Barack Obama, "Remarks at the National Institutes of Health in Bethesda, Maryland," December 2, 2014, www.presidency.ucsb.edu/docu ments/remarks-the-national-institutes-health-bethesda-maryland-0. The National Security Council left the Trump administration a playbook for early responses to infectious disease, https://assets.documentcloud.org/documents/681 9268/Pandemic-Playbook.pdf.

171. On crisis rhetoric in George W. Bush's January 2003 State of the Union

Address, see "Bush Proposal on AIDS Funds Shows Concern about Security," *New York Times*, January 29, 2003, and Elbe, *Virus Alert*, 101–2. For the HHS report on local preparedness, see *State and Local Pandemic Influenza Preparedness: Medical Surge* (Washington, DC: Department of Health and Human Services, 2009). On SARS, see Tim Brookes and Omar A. Khan, *Behind the Mask: How the World Survived SARS, the First Epidemic of the 21st Century* (Washington, DC: American Public Health Association, 2005). For the Center for Strategic and International Studies symposium on "Pandemic Policy and Preparedness: Policy and Practice in the 21st Century" (May 17, 2018), see https://soundcloud.com/csis-57169780/pandemic-preparedness-policy-and-pr actice-in-the-21st-century.

172. Alex Azar declared a nationwide public health emergency on January 31, 2020, followed by President Trump's pronouncement of a national emergency on March 13. Trump used "foreign virus" in a televised message from the Oval Office on March 11 when he banned air travel for non-US citizens from many European countries for thirty days. For early media coverage, see "As Global Health Crisis Grows, Governments Engage in 'Blame Game,'" *New York Times*, March 7, 2020, and "Squandered Time: How the Trump Administration Lost Control of the Coronavirus, *Washington Post*, March 7, 2020.

173. See "Now Arriving: The Deadly Ebola Virus Lands in America," *Time*, October 13, 2014, and Pardis Sabeti and Lara Salahi, *Outbreak Culture: The Ebola Crisis and the Next Epidemic* (Cambridge, MA: Harvard University Press, 2018).

174. World Health Organization, *International Health Regulations* (2005, updated 2016), www.who.int/ihr/publications/9789241580496/en, and *North American Plan for Animal and Pandemic Influenza* (2007, updated 2012), www.phe.gov/Preparedness/international/Documents/napapi.pdf.

CHAPTER 5: CARE

1. John F. Kennedy, "Special Message to Congress on National Health Needs," February 27, 1962, *Public Papers of the Presidents, John F. Kennedy, 1962* (Washington, DC: US Government Printing Office, 1963), 165. See also the Office of the White House Press Secretary's press release, Folder "HE, 8-1-61–7-25-62," Box 336, Papers of John F. Kennedy, White House Central Files, John F. Kennedy Presidential Library and Museum, Boston, Massachusetts.

2. Lyndon Johnson, "Special Message to the Congress: 'Education and Health in America,'" February 28 1967, *Public Papers of the Presidents, Lyndon B. Johnson, 1967*, Book 1 (Washington, DC: US Government Printing Office, 1968), 245.

3. Letter from Frederick G. Dutton (Special Assistant to the President) to Joseph P. Coco (New York Health Commissioner), May 6, 1961, Folder "HE, 1-20-61–5-10-61," Box 336, Papers of John F. Kennedy, White House Central Files, Kennedy Presidential Library.

4. *Health, Education, and Welfare Trends: 1962 Edition* (Washington, DC: US Department of Health, Education, and Welfare, 1962), ix.

5. The Director of the Atomedic Research Center, Hugh C. McGuire, wrote

to President Kennedy on March 25, 1961, and was referred to HEW. He published a piece with Orion P. South, "Atomedics—A Medical Program for Our Times," in the *Journal of the Maine Medical Association* in January 1961.

6. Lincoln Cushing, "Atomedics—The Future Hospital That Never Was," March 4, 2015, http://kaiserpermanentehistory.org/latest/atomedics-the-future -hospital-that-never-was. For the plans of the Atomedic Research Center, see "The Hospital of Tomorrow," *This Week*, January 17, 1960, a piece that included the endorsement of Lewis Orr.

7. "World's Fair to Operate Hospital-in-the-Round: Prefabricated Building," *Washington Post*, July 21, 1963; "Hospital Makes Dream a Reality," *New York Times*, November 17, 1963.

8. On federal hospital and training initiatives, see the HEW correspondence in "Hospital Survey and Construction Act," Box 22, Papers of Oveta Culp Hobby, Dwight D. Eisenhower Library, Abilene, Kansas. On the shortage of nurses in the early 1960s, see Paul W. Sanger, "The Nursing Shortage," February 1961, Folder "HE, 12-1-62-," Box 337, Papers of John F. Kennedy, White House Central Files, Kennedy Presidential Library. Comments about power supplies, plumbing, and toilets were made by an HEW special committee that in summer 1965 inspected five PHS hospitals built in the 1930s: "Health Services and Mental Health Administration [1 of 4]," Box 4, Department of Health, Education, and Welfare, 1963–1969, Administrative History Collection, Lyndon Baines Johnson Library, Austin, Texas, 10–15.

9. "Medicine: Nowhere to Go," *Time*, May 30, 1960.

10. "Presidential Action Relative to the Report of the Joint Commission on Mental Illness and Health," April 30, 1962, Folder "HE-1-1 11-16-61-5-20-62," Box 338, Papers of John F. Kennedy, White House Central Files, Kennedy Presidential Library.

11. Lyndon Johnson followed Kennedy's initiative by establishing a President's Committee on Mental Retardation in May 1966. The phrase "the edge of change" is the title of the commission's second report, *MR68*, published in October 1968.

12. "Crisis in Emergency Rooms: More Symptoms Than Cures," *New York Times*, July 18, 1988.

13. Speech by Robert E. Neff, July 19, 1939, *Proceedings of the National Health Conference, July 18, 19, 20, 1938, Washington, D.C.* (Washington, DC: US Government Printing Office, 1938), 78.

14. Speech by Robert E. Neff, 81.

15. Public Health Service, Press Release, January 17, 1938, "Press Releases, 1935–1940," Box 26, President's Interdepartmental Committee to Coordinate Health and Welfare Activities, 1935–41, General Records, Franklin D. Roosevelt Presidential Library and Museum, Hyde Park, New York.

16. Speech by H. W. Ahart, July 18, 1938, in *Proceedings of the National Health Conference*, 18. See Jennifer Klein, *For All These Rights: Business, Labor, and the Shaping of America's Public-Private Welfare State* (Princeton, NJ: Princeton University Press, 2010), 143–44.

17. Speech by Louis T. Wright, July 19, 1938, in *Proceedings of the National Health Conference*, 87.

18. *Toward Better National Health* (Washington, DC: US Government Printing Office, 1939), 8.

19. Franklin D. Roosevelt, "A Recommendation for the Construction by the Federal Government of Small Hospitals in Needy Areas of the Country Presently without Such Facilities," January 30, 1940, *The Public Papers and Addresses of Franklin D. Roosevelt, 1940 Volume: War—and Aid to Democracies* (New York: Macmillan, 1941), 66.

20. Roosevelt, "Recommendation," 67. "Roosevelt Asks 50 Hospitals in Poor Areas," *Washington Post*, January 31, 1940.

21. Roosevelt, "Recommendation," 68.

22. Harry S. Truman, "Special Message to the Congress Recommending a Comprehensive Health Program," *Public Papers of the Presidents of the United States, Harry S. Truman, 1945* (Washington, DC: US Government Printing Office, 1961), 475–76.

23. For Truman as a "crisis president," see Harold S. Gosnell, *Truman's Crises: A Political Biography of Harry S. Truman* (Westport, CT: Greenwood Press, 1980).

24. Truman, "Special Message to the Congress Recommending a Comprehensive Health Program," 476. See George St. J. Perrott, "Physical Status of Young Men, 1918 and 1941," *Milbank Memorial Fund Quarterly* 19, no. 4 (October 1941): 337–44.

25. Truman, "Special Message to the Congress Recommending a Comprehensive Health Program," 477.

26. Truman, "Special Message to the Congress Recommending a Comprehensive Health Program," 477. For context, see Alan Derickson, *Health Security for All: Dreams of Universal Health Care in America* (Baltimore: Johns Hopkins University Press, 2005), 92–100.

27. See Rosemary Stevens, *In Sickness and in Wealth: American Hospitals in the Twentieth Century* (1989; Baltimore: Johns Hopkins University Press, 1999), 207.

28. On Parran's advocacy for a robust public health infrastructure, see Karen Kruse Thomas, *Health and Humanity: A History of the Johns Hopkins Bloomberg School of Public Health 1935–1985* (Baltimore: Johns Hopkins University Press, 2016).

29. Thomas Parran, *Health Services of Tomorrow* (Washington, DC: US Government Printing Office, 1934), 2.

30. Thomas Parran, *Over the Horizon in Public Health* (Washington, DC: US Government Printing Office, 1945), 3–4. The Thomas Parran Papers, 1892–1968, are held at the Archives and Special Collections (UA.90.F14), University of Pittsburgh Library System, Pennsylvania.

31. For this National Committee for Mental Hygiene report of 1942, see Gerald N. Grob, ed., *Psychiatric Research in America: Two Studies, 1936–1941* (New York: Arno Press, 1980).

32. A hospital study panel of 1952 (as part of President Truman's Commission on the Health Needs of the Nation) affirmed these views on equipment and research.

33. Harry S. Truman, "Message to the Congress on the State of the Union

and the Budget for 1947," January 21, 1946, *Public Papers of the Presidents, Harry S. Truman, 1946* (Washington, DC: US Government Printing Office, 1962), 83. The five-point program was elaborated in "Special Message to Congress Recommending a Comprehensive Health Program," November 19, 1945, *Public Papers of the Presidents, Harry S. Truman, 1945*, 475–91.

34. Truman, "Statement by the President upon Signing the Hospital Survey and Construction Act," August 13, 1946, *Public Papers of the Presidents, Harry S. Truman, 1945*, 413.

35. Beatrix Hoffman, *Health Care for Some: Rights and Rationing in the United States since 1930* (Chicago: University of Chicago Press, 2012), xxix–xxx.

36. Stevens, *In Sickness and in Wealth*, 218, 224.

37. Karen Kruse Thomas, *Deluxe Jim Crow: Civil Rights and American Health Policy, 1935–1954* (Athens: University of Georgia Press, 2011), 181. "Health Services and Mental Health Administration [3 of 4]," Box 4, Department of Health, Education, and Welfare, 1963–1969, Administrative History Collection, LBJ Library, 3–6.

38. Thomas, *Deluxe Jim Crow*, 176, 166–67. For the argument that Hill-Burton was "a weak attempt to address the problem of hospital segregation," see Vanessa Northington Gamble, *Making a Place for Ourselves: The Black Hospital Movement, 1920–1945* (Oxford: Oxford University Press, 1995), 186–88.

39. "Greensboro, N.C. Hospital Drops Racial Barriers," *Chicago Defender*, December 20, 1962; "Color Bar Tested in Hospital Suit: North Caroline Case Involves U.S. Construction Funds," *New York Times*, August 15, 1963; "South Faces Hospital Desegregation Drive," *Washington Post*, March 4, 1964. The Carver hospital was demolished in 1962, prior to the desegregation of Chattanooga's hospital system in 1964.

40. W. Montague Cobb, "The National Health Program of the N.A.A.C.P," *Journal of the National Medical Association* 45, no. 4 (September 1953): 333–39; quoted in Thomas, *Deluxe Jim Crow*, 174. See David Barton Smith, *Health Care Divided: Race and Healing a Nation* (Ann Arbor: University of Michigan Press, 1999), 15, and John Dittmer, *Good Doctors: The Medical Committee of Human Rights and the Struggle for Social Justice in Health Care* (New York: Bloomsbury, 2009), 5, 13.

41. Truman, "Remarks at the National Health Assembly Dinner," May 1, 1948, *Public Papers of the Presidents, Harry S. Truman, 1948* (Washington, DC: US Government Printing Office, 1964), 241.

42. See Thomas Parran, "One out of Ten," *This Week*, November 17, 1946, and "What Is the Mental Health Situation in the United States Today: Fact Sheet I," "Mental Health Act, 1949, Proposed Legislation—Senatorial," Box 30, Howard J. McGrath Papers, Harry S. Truman Presidential Library. Edward F. Stevens, *The American Hospital of the Twentieth Century*, 2nd rev. ed. (New York: F. W. Dodge, 1928), iv.

43. Albert Deutsch, *The Mentally Ill in America: A History of Their Care and Treatment from Colonial Times*, 2nd rev. ed. (1937; New York: Columbia University Press, 1949), 518, 513.

44. Deutsch, *Mentally Ill in America*, 518.

45. Deutsch, *The Shame of the States* (New York: Harcourt Brace, 1948), 4, 16–17. On the violence of Deutsch's language, see "Lunacy, Like the Rain," *New York Times*, November 14, 1948.

46. Truman, "Address at the Dedication of the National Institutes of Health Clinical Center, June 22, 1951, *Public Papers of the Presidents, Harry S. Truman, 1951* (Washington, DC: US Government Printing Office, 1965), 350.

47. For the development of the National Institute of Mental Health, see Richard Mintzer, *The National Institutes of Health* (Philadelphia, PA: Chelsea House, 2002).

48. Mary Jane Ward, *The Snake Pit* (New York: Random House, 1946), 43. " 'Snake Pit' Powerful Film Event," *Los Angeles Times*, December 27, 1948.

49. "An Oscar for Olivia? Looking at Hollywood," *Chicago Daily Tribune*, December 12, 1948.

50. "Cinema: Shocker," *Time*, December 20, 1948, 44–52.

51. Deutsch, *Shame of the States*, 104. For this observation, see "Books and Things," *New York Tribune Herald*, November 17, 1948. See also Albert Maisel, "Bedlam 1946: Most US Mental Hospitals Are a Shame and a Disgrace," *Life*, May 6, 1946.

52. Deutsch, *Shame of the States*, 50, 58.

53. See letters to and from President Truman in the "St Elizabeth's Hospital" folder, OF 7-H, Papers of Harry S. Truman Official File, Harry S. Truman Presidential Library.

54. For Truman's frustrations with Congress, see Susan M. Hartmann, *Truman and the 80th Congress* (Columbia: University of Missouri Press, 1971), and Donald A. Ritchie, *Congress and Harry S. Truman: A Conflicted Legacy* (Kirksville, MO: Truman State University Press, 2011). On debates during the 80th Congress on the role of the state, see Jonathan Bell, *The Liberal State on Trial: The Cold War and American Politics in the Truman Years* (New York: Columbia University Press, 2004), 47–55.

55. Truman, "Special Message to the Congress on Health and Disability Insurance," May 19, 1947, *Public Papers of the President, Harry S. Truman, 1947* (Washington, DC: US Government Printing Office, 1963), 250–51.

56. Truman, "Special Message to the Congress," 252. For a longer view of health insurance, see Daniel S. Hirshfield, *The Lost Reform: The Campaign for Compulsory Health Insurance in the United States from 1932 to 1943* (Cambridge, MA: Harvard University Press, 1970).

57. See Harold Maslow, "The Background of the Wagner National Health Bill," *Law and Contemporary Problems* 6 (Fall 1939): 606–18; Michael R. Grey, *New Deal Medicine: The Rural Health Programs of the Farm Security Administration* (Baltimore: Johns Hopkins University Press, 2002), 158–63; and Bell, *Liberal State on Trial*, 67–77.

58. See Michael A. Dowell, "Hill Burton: The Unfulfilled Promise," *Journal of Health Politics, Policy, and Law* 12, no. 1 (Spring 1987): 153–75.

59. Hartmann, *Truman and the 80th Congress*, 72–73.

60. "A National Health Program," *Medical Annals of the District of Columbia* 17, no. 2 (February 1948): 105–7, and Oscar R. Ewing, "Speech to

the FSA Regional Staff Meeting," December 10, 1951, Box 43, Oscar Ewing Papers, Harry S. Truman Presidential Library. For the report, see *The Nation's Health: A Report to the President by Oscar R. Ewing* (Washington, DC: US Government Printing Office, 1948), and the National Health Assembly, *America's Health: A Report to the Nation* (New York: Harper, 1949).

61. Theodore R. Marmor, *The Politics of Medicare* (1970; Chicago: Aldine, 1973), 12–14. Bell, *Liberal State on Trial*, 76, 162.

62. National Education Campaign, *The Voluntary Way Is the American Way: 50 Questions You Want Answered* (Chicago: American Medical Association, 1949). For context, see Monte M. Poen, *Harry S. Truman versus the Medical Lobby: The Genesis of Medicare* (Columbia: University of Missouri Press, 1979).

63. "A.M.A. Forms Political Combine with Taft and Byrd," *Industrial Democracy*, December 15, 1951. *The Sad Case of Waiting-Room Willie* (Baltimore: American Visuals, 1950).

64. See "President Truman's Health Plan," "National Health Insurance, 1947: Proposed Legislation—Senatorial," Box 32, J. Howard McGrath Papers, Harry S. Truman Presidential Library. See also "Medical Lobby's Scheme to 'Fix' Cartoonists Backfires," *Labor*, March 27, 1948. On the media's failure to engage with the insurance debate, see Donna Allen, "Inadequate Media and the Failure of the National Health Insurance Proposal in the Late 1940s" (unpublished PhD thesis, Howard University, 1971). For criticisms of the AMA, see Michael M. Davis, *Medical Care for Tomorrow* (New York: Harper, 1955), 95–110.

65. Thomas Parran, *The Health of the Nation* (Washington, DC: US Government Printing Office, 1939), 7. On the commission, see Paul B. Magnuson, "The President's Commission on the Health Needs of the Nation," *Journal of the American Medical Association* 150, no. 15 (December 1952): 1509–10.

66. "The President's Commission on the Health Needs of the Nation: Panel on Promotion of Health" (April 22, 1952), "Study Panel on Promotion of Health, 4/22/52 transcript, Panel File, Box 2, PCHNN, Harry S. Truman Presidential Library, 1735. *Building America's Health* (Washington, DC: US Government Printing Office, 1952–53), vol. 1: 1–2, 38.

67. *Building America's Health*, 30.

68. Dwight D. Eisenhower, "Special Message to the Congress on the Health Needs of the American People," January 18, 1954, *Public Papers of the Presidents, Dwight D. Eisenhower, 1954* (Washington, DC: US Government Printing Office, 1960), 75.

69. "Ike on Medical Care," *Washington Post*, September 16, 1952.

70. Eisenhower, "Special Message to the Congress on the Health Needs of the American People," 75–76.

71. Eisenhower, "Special Message to the Congress on the Health Needs of the American People," 76.

72. "Mrs. Hobby Deplores Drastic Cuts in HEW," *Washington Post*, May 21, 1953.

73. Eisenhower, "Special Message to the Congress on the Health Needs of the American People," 75–76.

74. For the quotation, see Dwight D. Eisenhower, "Special Message to the Congress on the Nation's Health Program," January 26, 1956, *Public Papers of the Presidents, Dwight D. Eisenhower, 1956* (Washington, DC: US Government Printing Office, 1958), 202. See also Leonard Scheele's testimony before the Subcommittee on Improvements in the Federal Criminal Code of the Committee of the Judiciary, September 19, 1955, "Scheele, Leonard A., Surgeon General, Public Health Service," Box 31, Papers of Oveta Culp Hobby, Eisenhower Presidential Library, Abilene, Kansas.

75. For Eisenhower's view on the World Health Organization, see his "Special Message to the Congress Recommending a Health Program," January 31, 1955, *Public Papers of the Presidents, Dwight D. Eisenhower, 1955* (Washington, DC: US Government Printing Office, 1955), 223.

76. Eisenhower, "Television Report to the American People by the President and Members of the Cabinet," June 3, 1953, *Public Papers of the Presidents, Dwight D. Eisenhower, 1953* (Washington, DC: US Government Printing Office, 1960), 365.

77. Eisenhower, "Special Message to the Congress on the Nation's Health Program," 197.

78. On the new Department for Health, Education, and Welfare, see Hobby's press statement of March 11, 1954: "Speech—Press Conference on Administration's Health Proposals—2 p.m., March 11, 1954," Box 38, Papers of Oveta Culp Hobby, Eisenhower Presidential Library.

79. Margaret Cram, *Mental Health in Kansas: Community Action* (Lawrence, KS: Governmental Research Center, 1956), 9.

80. For a defense of Hobby's record and on the Cutter incident, see Debra L. Winegarten, *Oveta Culp Hobby: Colonel, Cabinet Member, Philanthropist* (Austin: University of Texas Press, 2014), 61–77.

81. The White House held a conference on juvenile delinquency in June 1954, even though Eisenhower had publicly expressed his dislike for this term just a few weeks before. Eisenhower wrote a self-congratulatory letter to Arthur Flemming at the end of the administration that praised the work of HEW for expanding health facilities, for developing radiological research, for "fighting air and water pollution," and for advancing education and social security reforms. Letter from Dwight Eisenhower to Arthur Flemming, January 13, 1961, "Flemming, Arthur S. 1959–61 (1)," Box 15, Dwight D. Eisenhower: Papers as President of the United States, Administration Series, Eisenhower Presidential Library.

82. Stein sent President Kennedy a copy of his book in late June 1963: Stanley Stein with Lawrence G. Blochman, *Alone No Longer: The Story of A Man Who Refused to Be One of the Living Dead* (Carville, LA: The Star, 1963). For Jack Nelson's exposés, see "$14.1 Million Asked for Mental Health," *Atlanta Constitution*, January 12, 1960, and "Psychiatry: Out of the Snake Pits," *Time*, April 5, 1963, 82.

83. John F. Kennedy, "Remarks upon Signing Bill for the Construction of Mental Retardation Facilities and Community Mental Health Centers," October 31, 1964, *Public Papers of the Presidents, John F. Kennedy, 1963* (Washington, DC: US Government Printing Office, 1963), 825–26.

84. *Action for Mental Health: Final Report of the Joint Commission on Mental Illness and Health* (New York: Basic Books, 1961), xviii.

85. *Action for Mental Health*, v, viii.

86. *Action for Mental Health*, xvi–xvii.

87. For comparison of Truman and Johnson on health insurance, see Edward Berkowitz, "Medicare: The Great Society's Enduring National Health Insurance Program," in *The Great Society and the High Tide of Liberalism*, ed. Sidney M. Milkis and Jerome M. Mileur (Amherst: University of Massachusetts Press, 2005), 320–50, and Julian E. Zelizer, *The Fierce Urgency of Now: Lyndon Johnson, Congress, and the Battle for the Great Society* (New York: Penguin, 2015), 200–201.

88. Lyndon B. Johnson, "Presidential Policy Paper No. 2: The Nation's Problems of Health," November 1, 1964, *Public Papers of the Presidents, Lyndon B. Johnson, 1963–64*, Book 2 (Washington, DC: US Government Printing Office, 1965), 1565. See also Johnson, "Special Message to the Congress: Advancing the Nation's Health," January 7, 1965, *Public Papers of the Presidents, Lyndon B. Johnson, 1965*, Book 1 (Washington, DC: US Government Printing Office, 1966), 12–25.

89. Wilbur Cohen, interview by James Sargent, March 18, 1974, 130–31, Columbia University Oral History Project; cited in Zelizer, *Fierce Urgency of Now*, 166.

90. See Alice Sardell, *The U.S. Experiment in Social Medicine: The Community Health Center Program, 1965–1986* (Pittsburgh: University of Pittsburgh Press, 1988), 50–76. Johnson affirmed the consumer rights Kennedy set out in 1962 in a "Special Message to the Congress on Consumer Interests," February 5, 1964, *Public Papers of the Presidents, Lyndon B. Johnson, 1963–64*, Book 1 (Washington, DC: US Government Printing Office, 1965), 263. This moral commitment tallied with Johnson's idea of "common purpose" in his campaign book *My Hope for America* (New York: Random House, 1964), 11, 58–59.

91. Memo from Mitchell Sviridoff to Joseph A. Califano, June 29, 1966, "WE 9, 6/10/66–8/1/66," Box 27, Welfare Ex WE9, Papers of Lyndon Baines Johnson, LBJ Library.

92. Howard E. Freeman and Ozzie G. Simmons, *The Mental Patient Comes Home* (New York: John Wiley, 1963), viii– ix, 2.

93. Freeman and Simmons, *Mental Patient Comes Home*, 2. *The Comprehensive Community Mental Health Center: Concept and Challenge* (Washington, DC: US Department of Health, Education, and Welfare, 1964), 14.

94. *The Comprehensive Community Mental Health Center*, 22.

95. On hospital desegregation, see Daniel Sledge, *Health Divided: Public Health and Individual Medicine in the Making of the Modern American State* (Lawrence: University Press of Kansas, 2017), 190–92. On links between Medicare and desegregation, see Jill Quadagno, "Promoting Civil Rights through the Welfare State: How Medicare Integrated Southern Hospitals," *Social Problems* 47, no. 1 (February 2000): 68–89.

96. Letter from Lyndon Johnson to William Kissick, December 15, 1964, "11/1/64–12/31/64," Box 238, White House Central Files EX FG 165, Papers of Lyndon B. Johnson, LBJ Library.

97. See the Regional Medical Programs Collection 1948–1993, History of Medicine Division, US National Library of Medicine, Bethesda, MD.

98. On the Delta Health Center, see Thomas J. Ward Jr., *Out in the Rural: A Mississippi Health Center and Its War on Poverty* (New York: Oxford University Press, 2016).

99. For the quotation, see the administrative history of the Office for Economic Opportunity, Box 1, Volume I, Part I, Administrative History Collection, LBJ Library, 35–36.

100. Office for Economic Opportunity, Box 1, Volume I, Part II, 335–36. On neighborhood centers, see "Pilot Program for Multipurpose Neighborhood Centers," "Neighborhood Centers," Box 14, Office Files of Fred Bohen, Papers of Lyndon Baines Johnson, LBJ Library.

101. Richard A. Couto, *Ain't Gonna Let Nobody Turn Me Around: The Pursuit of Racial Justice in the Rural South* (Philadelphia: Temple University Press, 1991), 306–10. For this criticism of neighborhood health centers, see Judith Randal, "The Bright Promise of Neighborhood Health Centers," *Reporter*, March 21, 1968, 15–18. For achievements (such as fifty Head Start programs operating on reservations in 1967) and plans to improve facilities for Native Americans, see the January 1968 PHS publication *Mental Health Activities in the Indian Health Program*, "Bureau of Health Services, Division of Indian Health," Box 10, Department of Health, Education, and Welfare, Administrative History Collection, LBJ Library.

102. Randall B. Woods, *Prisoners of Hope: Lyndon B. Johnson, the Great Society, and the Limits of Liberalism* (New York: Perseus, 2016), 284–85.

103. Alyosha Goldstein, *Poverty in Common: The Politics of Community Action during the American Century* (Durham, NC: Duke University Press, 2012), 155–98. On cuts to the antipoverty programs, see "A Promise to the Poor," *New York Times*, November 4, 1967, and "The War against the War on Poverty," *Washington Post*, November 8, 1967.

104. See Richard Schickel, "The Frightful Follies of Bedlam," *Life*, December 1967, 12. See also Thomas Szasz, "*The Titicut Follies*: The Forgotten Story of a Case of Psychiatric Censorship," *History of Psychiatry* 18, no. 1 (April 2007): 123–25.

105. *Report of the National Advisory Committee on Health Manpower* (Washington, DC: US Government Printing Office, 1967), vol. 1, https://files.eric.ed.gov/fulltext/ED029108.pdf. See also "Nation Is Warned of Health Crisis," *Washington Post*, November 21, 1967.

106. Richard M. Nixon, "Annual Message to the Congress on the State of the Union," January 22, 1971, *Public Papers of the Presidents, Richard M. Nixon, 1971*, Book 1 (Washington, DC: US Government Printing Office, 1972), 51.

107. For these points, see an internal 1972 report by the National Institute of Mental Health, cited in E. Fuller Torrey, *American Psychosis: How the Federal Government Destroyed the Mental Illness Treatment System* (Oxford: Oxford University Press, 2014), 83.

108. Randal, "The Bright Promise of Neighborhood Health Centers," 18.

109. Richard J. Alexander, "People's Free Clinic," *Texas Medicine* 68, no. 2 (February 1972): 94–100. See also David E. Smith et al., *The Free Clinic:*

A Community Approach to Health Care and Drug Abuse (Beloit, WI: Stash, 1971), xiv, and Virginia M. Brennan, ed., *Free Clinics: Local Responses to Health Care Needs* (Baltimore: Johns Hopkins University Press, 2013), 77–85. For broader discussion of the Free Clinic movement, see Gregory L. Weiss, *Grassroots Medicine: The Story of America's Free Health Clinics* (Lanham, MD: Rowman and Littlefield, 2006).

110. "Health Task Force: Mobilizing to Meet Crisis," *New York Amsterdam News*, July 3, 1971.

111. Mark Krasovic, *The Newark Frontier: Community Action in the Great Society* (Chicago: University of Chicago Press, 2016), 11. For an assessment of Johnson-era health care reforms, see Paul Starr, "The Health Legacy of the Great Society," in *LBJ's Neglected Legacy: How Lyndon Johnson Reshaped Domestic Policy and Government,* ed. Robert H. Wilson, Norman J. Glickman, and Laurence E. Lynn Jr. (Austin: University of Texas Press, 2015), 235–58.

112. Gerald N. Grob, *From Asylum to Community: Mental Health Policy in Modern America* (Princeton, NJ: Princeton University Press, 1991), 304. See also Gerald N. Grob, *The Mad among Us: A History of the Care of America's Mentally Ill* (New York: Free Press, 1994), 249–78.

113. See *Veterans' Benefits in the United States* (Washington, DC: US Government Printing Office, 1956), www.va.gov/vetdata/docs/Bradley_Report.pdf.

114. Max Cleland with Ben Raines, *Heart of a Patriot: How I Found the Courage to Survive Vietnam, Walter Reed, and Karl Rove* (New York: Random House, 2007), 128.

115. *Achieving the Promise: Transforming Mental Health Care in America* (Washington, DC: US Department of Health and Human Services, 2003), n.p.

116. *Veterans Administration Health Care: Planning for Future Years* (Washington, DC: Congressional Budget Office, 1984), 3. David E. Bonior, Steven M. Champlin, and Timothy S. Kolly, *The Vietnam Veteran: A History of Neglect* (New York: Praeger, 1984), 159.

117. "Veteran's Medical Care," *New York Times*, February 22, 1948.

118. *Diagnostic and Statistical Manual of Mental Disorders* (1952; Washington, DC: American Psychiatric Association, 1965), v–vi, 31–34.

119. See Galen L. Barbour et al., *Quality in the Veterans Health Administration* (San Francisco: Jossey-Bass, 1996), 22.

120. Subcommittee on Health and Hospitals of the Committee on Veterans' Affairs, *Oversight of VA Hospital Crisis*, United States Senate, 92nd Congress, First Session (Washington, DC: US Government Printing Office, 1971), 2.

121. Ron Kovic, *Hurricane Street* (Brooklyn, NY: Akashic, 2016), 184. For the *Life* cover story, see "Our Forgotten Wounded," *Life*, May 22, 1970.

122. *The Vietnam Era Veteran: Challenge for Change* (Washington, DC: Veterans Administration, 1972), 1.

123. *Vietnam Era Veteran*, 2, 49.

124. For Kovic's speech, see *The Official Proceedings of the Democratic National Convention* (Washington, DC: Library of Congress, 1976), 380. For the case of Erwin Pawelski, see "Helpless Patient 'Lost' for 27 Hours," *Los Angeles Times*, May 22, 1975.

125. "Addict Runs Amuck with Rifle in Clinic," *New York Times*, March 31, 1973.

126. Paul Starr, *The Discarded Army: Veterans after Vietnam, The Nader Report on Vietnam Veterans and the Veterans Administration* (New York: Charterhouse, 1973), 106–7.

127. Starr, *Discarded Army*, 2.

128. Chaim F. Shatan, "The Grief of Soldiers: Vietnam Combat Veterans Self-Help Movement," *American Journal of Orthopsychiatry* 43, no. 4 (July 1973): 645–46.

129. Robert Jay Lifton, *Home from the War: Vietnam Veterans, Neither Victim nor Executioner* (New York: Simon and Schuster, 1973), 78.

130. Lifton, *Home from the War*, 81. See Arthur Egendorf, "Vietnam Veteran Rap Groups and Themes of Postwar Life," *Journal of Social Issues* 31, no. 4 (Fall 1975): 111–24, and Patrick Hagopian, *The Vietnam War in American Memory: Veterans, Memorials, and the Politics of Healing* (Amherst: University of Massachusetts Press, 2011), 53–55.

131. "Vets the Victims of Clumsy VA Giant," *Chicago Tribune*, January 18, 1976.

132. Jimmy Carter, "Vietnam Veterans Week, 1979 Remarks at a White House Reception," May 30, 1979, *Public Papers of the Presidents, Jimmy Carter, 1979*, Book 1 (Washington, DC: US Government Printing Office, 1981), 445.

133. "Vietnam Era Veterans Update: Background Report by Office of Media Liaison," October 14, 1978, Box 39, Folder 3, Office of Counsel to the President, Jimmy Carter Presidential Library, Atlanta, Georgia.

134. Jimmy Carter, "Address at the University of Notre Dame," May 22, 1977, *Public Papers of the Presidents, Jimmy Carter, 1977* (Washington, DC: US Government Printing Office, 1977), 958.

135. Jimmy Carter, "Vietnam Era Veterans," *Public Papers of the Presidents, Jimmy Carter, 1978*, Book 2, 1741.

136. "Carter, and U.S., Forget Vietnam Vets," *Washington Post*, May 29, 1978.

137. "Vietnam Veterans Still Feel Chill from the White House," *Washington Post*, April 28, 1979.

138. Carter, "Veterans Health Care Amendments of 1979," June 14, 1979, *Public Papers of the Presidents: Jimmy Carter, 1979*, Book 1, 1039. See also "Aid Urged for Vietnam Veterans," *New York Times*, January 28, 1979.

139. "For Vietnam Veterans Week: Veterans, Stand Up and Be Counted," *The Veteran* 9 (Spring 1979): 1.

140. Carter, "Vietnam Veterans Week, 1979," May 30, 1979, *Public Papers of the Presidents: Jimmy Carter, 1979*, Book 1, 974. Carter, "Veterans Health Care Amendments of 1979," 1039.

141. Cleland, *Heart of a Patriot*, 129.

142. Cleland, *Heart of a Patriot*, 133.

143. Interview with William Mahedy by Wilbur J. Scott (November 22, 1988), cited in Wilbur J. Scott, *The Politics of Adjustment: Vietnam Veterans since the War* (New Brunswick, NJ: Aldine, 1993), 71. Subcommittee on Gov-

ernment Information and Individual Rights of the Committee on Government Operations, *VA Vietnam Veterans' Readjustment Counseling Program*, House of Representatives, 97th Congress, First Session, October 19, 1981, 1.

144. "Operation Outreach for 'Nam Vets," *New Pittsburgh Courier*, December 27, 1980.

145. "Veteran Haunted by Vietnam Horrors and Agent Orange," *Los Angeles Times*, March 16, 1980.

146. For a parody of this stereotype of Vietnam veterans, see Tim O'Brien, "The Violent Vet," *Esquire*, December 1979, 96.

147. Cleland, *Heart of a Patriot*, 132. On PTSD and *DSM-III*, see Scott, *The Politics of Adjustment*, 57–68, and Hannah S. Decker, *The Making of DSM-III: A Diagnostic Manual's Conquest of American Psychiatry* (Oxford: Oxford University Press, 1994), 274–75.

148. "Fight Looms over Veteran Aid Centers," *Los Angeles Times*, February 14, 1981.

149. Ronald Reagan, "Remarks on Signing a Veterans Medical Care Bill," June 17, 1981, *Public Papers of the President, Ronald Reagan, 1981* (Washington, DC: US Government Printing Office, 1982), 530.

150. Ronald Reagan, "Statement on Signing the Veterans' Health Care Amendments of 1983," November 21, 1983, *Public Papers of the Presidents, Ronald Reagan, 1983*, Book 2 (Washington, DC: US Government Printing Office, 1985), 1619–20.

151. See also "Across America, Dioxin," *New York Times*, March 7, 1983.

152. As Kovic re-creates in his 2016 memoir *Hurricane Street*, a group of fifteen veterans (six of them wheelchair users) staged a sit-in at Cranston's Washington, DC, office in early 1974 to protest "the national disgrace" of VA hospitals: "15 Veterans Occupy Cranston's Office," *Los Angeles Times*, February 13, 1974.

153. See Alan Cranston's opening statement in the Committee on Veteran's Affairs, *The Vet Center Program, and Homeless Veterans Issues*, United States Senate, 100th Congress, First Session, February 18–19, 1987 (Washington, DC: US Government Printing Office, 1988), 2, 126.

154. For the consequences of the 1987 Homeless Veterans Assistance Act, see the Congressional Service Report titled "Homelessness: Targeted Federal Programs and Recent Legislation," https://fas.org/sgp/crs/misc/RL30442.pdf.

155. See *Outcasts on Main Street: Report on the Federal Task Force on Homelessness and Severe Mental Illness* (Rockland, MD: Department of Health and Human Services, 1992), x.

156. For these causes, see "Nation's Homeless Veterans Battle a New Foe: Defeatism," *New York Times*, December 30, 1987, and Rob Rosenthal, *Homeless in Paradise: A Map of the Terrain* (Philadelphia: Temple University Press, 1993), 9–17.

157. George H. W. Bush, "Inaugural Address," January 20, 1989, *Public Papers of the Presidents of the United States, George Bush, 1988–89*, Book 1 (Washington, DC: US Government Printing Office, 1991), 3.

158. *Outcasts on Main Street*, xvii.

159. See the Vet Center Program website: www.vetcenter.va.gov/About_US.asp.

160. On regional crises in VA hospitals, see, for example, "Suspicious Insulin Injections, Nearly a Dozen Deaths: Inside an Unfolding Investigation at a VA Hospital in West Virginia," *Washington Post*, October 5, 2019.

161. "VA Is Gearing Up for a Massive Shift of Health Care to the Private Sector," *Washington Post*, March 21, 2019.

162. See the National Research Council's Gulf War report *Strategies to Protect the Health of Deployed U.S Forces: Detecting, Characterizing, and Documenting Exposures* (Washington, DC: National Academy Press, 2000).

163. See Edward M. Kennedy, *The Health Care Crisis: A Report to the American People* (Washington, DC: US Government Printing Office, 1990), and E. Fuller Torrey, *Out of the Shadows: Confronting America's Mental Illness Crisis* (New York: Wiley, 1997).

164. Gerald N. Grob and Howard H. Goldman, *The Dilemma of Federal Mental Health Policy: Radical Reform or Incremental Change?* (New Brunswick, NJ: Rutgers University Press, 2006), 182.

165. Bonnie Lefkowitz, *Community Health Centers: A Movement and the People Who Made It Happen* (New Brunswick, NJ: Rutgers University Press, 2007), 135.

CHAPTER 6: DRUGS

1. "Prince Dead at 57," TMZ (April 21, 2016), www.tmz.com/2016/04/21/prince-dead-at-57.

2. "Frantic Moments on Prince's Plane as He Seemed to Slip Away," *New York Times*, June 22, 2016.

3. Barack Obama, "Statement by the President on the Passing of Prince," April 21, 2016, https://obamawhitehouse.archives.gov/the-press-office/2016/04/21/statement-president-passing-prince.

4. See "Prince Died Amid Frantic Plans for Drug Addiction Treatment," *Star Tribune*, May 4, 2016, and "Prince's Addiction and an Intervention Too Late," *New York Times*, May 4, 2016. For a later report, see "Pills Seized from Paisley Park Contained Illicit Fentanyl, Same Drug That Killed Prince," *Star Tribune*, August 21, 2016.

5. Minnesota Department of Health News Release, "Minnesota's Drug Overdose Deaths Continued to Rise in 2016," September 7, 2017, www.health.state.mn.us/news/pressrel/2017/opioid090717.html.

6. Centers for Disease Control and Prevention, "Prevalence of Chronic Pain and High-Impact Chronic Pain among Adults—United States, 2016," *Morbidity and Mortality Weekly Report* 67, no. 36 (September 14, 2018): 1001–6. Institute of Medicine, *Relieving Pain in America: A Blueprint for Transforming Prevention, Care, Education, and Research* (Washington, DC: National Academies Press, 2011).

7. The World Health Organization works on a three-step "analgesic ladder" for controlling cancer-related pain, only the third step of which involves

strong opioids: *Cancer Pain Relief*, 2nd ed. (1986; Geneva: World Health Organization, 1996).

8. Elaine Scarry, *The Body in Pain: The Making and Unmaking of the World* (Oxford: Oxford University Press, 1985), 54.

9. Keith Wailoo, *Pain: A Political History* (Baltimore: Johns Hopkins University Press, 2014), 4.

10. Scarry, *Body in Pain*, 53.

11. Scarry, *Body in Pain*, 55.

12. Judy Foreman, *The Global Pain Crisis: What Everyone Needs to Know* (Oxford: Oxford University Press, 2017), 57.

13. Theodore Stanley, "The Fentanyl Story," *Journal of Pain* 15, no. 12 (December 2014): 1215–26. Centers for Disease Control and Prevention, *National Vital Statistics Reports*, December 12, 2018, www.cdc.gov/nchs/data/nvsr/nvsr67/nvsr67_09-508.pdf.

14. Timothy A. Hickman, *The Secret Leprosy of Modern Days: Narcotic Addiction and Cultural Crisis in the United States, 1870–1920* (Amherst: University of Massachusetts Press, 2007), 151.

15. David T. Courtwright, *Dark Paradise: A History of Opiate Addiction in America* (1982; Cambridge, MA: Harvard University Press, 2001), 104–5, and Stephen R. Kandall, *Substance and Shadow: Women and Addiction in the United States* (Cambridge, MA: Harvard University Press, 1996), 76–77.

16. Judy Foreman, *A Nation in Pain: Healing Our Biggest Health Problem* (Oxford: Oxford University Press, 2014), 127. See also Michael Kinch, *A Prescription for Change: The Looming Crisis in Drug Development* (Chapel Hill: University of North Carolina Press, 2016).

17. "Prince Alleged Drug Dealer Claims Late Star Had Secret Drug Addiction," *Hollywood Life* April 23, 2016; "Prince's Death Warrants Reveal Pills Hidden Everywhere," TMZ, April 17, 2017; "How Prince Concealed His Addiction: Aspirin Bottles of Opiates," *New York Times*, April 17, 2017.

18. For opioid-related deaths in Minnesota, see www.health.state.mn.us/divs/healthimprovement/opioid-dashboard/index.html#DeathTrends.

19. An example of public service at the national level is the publication in July 2019 by the *Washington Post* of the Drug Enforcement Administration's pain pill database, which tracks their regional distribution between 2006 and 2012.

20. Lauretta E. Grau et al., "Illicit Use of Opioids: Is OxyContin a 'Gateway Drug,'" *American Journal of Addiction* 16, no. 3 (May 2007): 166–73; "The Alchemy of OxyContin," *New York Times*, July 29, 2001, and "Overdoses of Painkiller Are Linked to 282 Deaths," *New York Times*, October 28, 2001.

21. Sam Quinones, *Dreamland: The True Tale of America's Opiate Epidemic* (2015; New York: Bloomsbury, 2016), 304. See also "Drug Is Harder to Abuse, but Users Persevere," *New York Times*, June 15, 2011. For context, see Barry Meier, *Pain Killer: An Empire of Deceit and the Origin of American's Opioid Epidemic* (2003; New York: Random House, 2018), and Robin Feldman and Evan Frondorf, *Drug Wars: How Big Pharma Raises Prices and Keeps Generics off the Market* (Cambridge: Cambridge University Press, 2017).

22. Wailoo, *Pain: A Political History*, 190.

23. The Massachusetts attorney general Maura Healey used the phrase "man-made disaster" in her official memo during a set of 2018–19 legal hearings to investigate Purdue's actions, https://d279m997dpfwgl.cloudfront.net/wp/2019/01/Mass_AGO_Pre-Hearing_Memo_and_Exhibits.pdf.

24. "You Want a Description of Hell? Oxycontin's 12-Hour Problem," *Los Angeles Times*, May 5, 2016, and "Don't Call Her a Victim," *New York Times*, January 22, 2018.

25. Nan Goldin, *The Ballad of Sexual Dependency* (1986; New York: Aperture, 1996), 6. *Memory Lost* was debuted at Nan Goldin's *Sirens* exhibition at the Marian Goodman Gallery, London, November 2019–January 2020.

26. For the Chris Christie quotation, see "Christie on Opioids," CNN, October 27, 2017. For the Nan Goldin quotation, see "Nan Goldin," *Art Forum* 56, no. 5 (January 2018), www.artforum.com/print/201801/nan-goldin-73181.

27. "The Family That Built an Empire of Pain," *New Yorker*, October 30, 2017; "Nan Goldin: I've Turned My Opioid Addiction into Activism," *Time*, February 22, 2018; "Nan Goldin's War on OxyContin," *Sleek*, March 12, 2018, www.sleek-mag.com/2018/03/12/nan-goldin-war-sackler. In June 2018, an eleven-foot bent heroin spoon sculpture by Boston metal artist Domenic Esposito was placed in front of Purdue Pharma's headquarters in Stamford, Connecticut, to protest the deceptive marketing of OxyContin. Evidence emerged in early 2019 that implicated the Sacklers in Purdue's aggressive marketing of OxyContin even though both the owners and company knew of its strongly addictive qualities: "Sacklers Directed Efforts to Mislead Public about OxyContin," *New York Times*, January 15, 2019.

28. Simon Strick, *American Dolorologies: Pain, Sentimentalism, Biopolitics* (Albany: State University of New York Press, 2014), 150. See also Daniel S. Goldberg, *The Bioethics of Pain Management: Beyond Opioids* (New York: Routledge, 2014).

29. By the mid-1980s it was estimated that there were 500,000 heroin users in the United States, two-fifths of whom were based in New York City: "Growth in Heroin Use Ending as City Users Turn to Crack," *New York Times*, September 13, 1986.

30. "Special Report: The Opioid Epidemic," *AARP Bulletin*, June 2017, www.aarp.org/health/drugs-supplements/info-2017/opioid-drug-addiction-pain-pills.html.

31. Ronald Reagan, "Address to the Nation on the Campaign against Drug Abuse," September 14, 1986, *Public Papers of the Presidents of the United States: Ronald Reagan, 1986*, Book 2 (Washington, DC: US Government Printing Office, 1989), 1181. On the mid-1980s crack crisis, see Steven R. Belenko, *Crack and the Evolution of Anti-Drug Policy* (Westport, CT: Greenwood Press, 1993), and Harry G. Levine, *Crack in America: Demon Drugs and Social Justice* (Berkeley: University of California Press, 1997). On the "eclipse of care," see David Healy, *Pharmageddon* (Berkeley: University of California Press, 2012), 195–233.

32. Beth Macy, *Dopesick: Dealers, Doctors, and the Drug Company That Addicted America* (New York: Little, Brown, 2018), 8, 32.

33. On the Addiction Research Center and the outlawing of human experi-

mentation in 1975, see Nancy Campbell, J. P. Olsen, and Luke Walden, *The Narcotic Farm: The Rise and Fall of America's First Prison for Drug Addicts* (New York: Abrams, 2008), 164–87. See also John A. O'Donnell, *Narcotic Addicts in Kentucky* (Washington, DC: US Government Printing Office, 1969); "Admissions of Narcotic Drug Addicts to Public Health Service Hospitals, 1935–63," *Public Health Reports* 80, no. 6 (June 1965): 471–75; and the Lexington Narcotic Farm Collection (MSS 222) held at Kentucky Historical Society in Frankfort, Kentucky. In 1967 the Narcotic Farm gave up its signature agricultural feature, and in 1974 the Bureau of Prisons took over the running of the estate following criticism of the drug experimentation, renaming it the Federal Medical Center.

34. Quinones, *Dreamland*, 76–79.

35. "Methadon[e]," *Life*, August 9, 1948, 87, 90. The archives at the National Academy of Sciences holds the papers of the Committee on Drug Addiction (1941–47) and the Committee of Drug Addiction and Narcotics (1947–65).

36. William S. Burroughs, *Junky* (1953; London: Penguin, 1977), 67–68. See also Burroughs, *Naked Lunch* (1959; New York: Grove, 2013), 204, 252–56. For more thorough patients' accounts of the US Public Health Service Hospital, see Alexander King's memoir *Mine Enemy Grows Older* (New York: Simon and Schuster, 1958), and Clarence L. Cooper Jr.'s experimental novel *The Farm* (New York: Crown, 1967).

37. David J. Bellis, *Heroin and Politicians: The Failure of Public Policy to Control Addiction in America* (Westport, CT: Greenwood Press, 1981), 105.

38. "The World of Needle Park," *Life*, February 26, 1965; *Vincent P. Dole and Marie E. Nyswander, "A Medical Treatment for Diacetylmorphine (Heroin) Addiction: A Clinical Trial with Methadone Hydrochloride," Journal of the American Medical Association 193, no. 8 (August 23, 1965): 646–50;* "Patients in Test Substitute Good Addiction for Bad," *New York Times*, December 8, 1964.

39. Vincent Dole and Marie Nyswander, "Heroin Addiction: A Metabolic Disease," *Archives of Internal Medicine* 120, no. 1 (July 1967): 19–24. For criticism that Dole and Nyswander did not address methadone addiction, see the letter from Victor H. Vogel (chair of the Narcotic Addict Evaluation Authority, Corona, CA) to John H. Talbott (editor of *JAMA*), September 3, 1965, "Bureau of Narcotics, General, 1961–1965," Series 6: Government Agencies, Committee on Drug Addiction and Narcotics, 1947–1965, National Academy of Science.

40. See Bellis, *Heroin and Politicians*, 101–2. Bellis takes these statistics from a report on "Methadone Maintenance Treatment of Narcotic Addiction" in the April 1976 issue of *American Journal of Drug and Alcohol Abuse*.

41. Richard M. Nixon, "Special Message to the Congress on Drug Abuse Prevention and Control," June 17, 1971, *Public Papers of the Presidents, Richard M. Nixon, 1971* (Washington, DC: US Government Printing Office, 1972), 739.

42. On Richardson's plans for HEW as the lead agency in coordinating the federal response to the drugs crisis, see "Domestic Council Decision Paper: Narcotic Addiction and Drug Abuse Programs," March 19, 1971, and "Draft

Testimony for the Secretary on Drug Abuse," July 5, 1971., "Drug Abuse," Department of Health, Education, and Welfare Subject File, Box 139, Elliot L. Richardson Papers, Manuscript Division, Library of Congress.

43. For Jaffe's work in establishing this Chicago program, see Claire D. Clark, *Recovery Revolution: The Battle over Addiction Treatment in the United States* (New York: Columbia University Press, 2017), 103–7.

44. Nat Hentoff, *A Doctor among the Addicts* (New York: Rand McNally, 1967), 57, 64–66, 71–73.

45. See Marie E. Nyswander, *The Drug Addict as a Patient* (New York: Grune and Stratton, 1956). On Jaffe's outpatient work with methadone, see Amitai Etzioni and Richard Remp, *Technological Shortcuts to Social Change* (New York: Russell Sage, 1973), 15. For Jaffe's comments, see his interview with Nancy Campbell (no date), Oral History of Substance Abuse Research, William White papers, Bentley Historical Library, University of Michigan, Ann Arbor, www.williamwhitepapers.com/pr/2013%20Dr.%20Jerome%20Jaffe .pdf.

46. Etzioni and Remp, *Technological Shortcuts*, 42–45. Peter Conrad and Joseph W. Schneider, *Deviance and Medicalization: From Badness to Sickness*, 2nd ed. (1980; Philadelphia: Temple University Press, 1992), 137. "Six Projects Started to Develop Nonaddictive Heroin Substitute," *New York Times*, September 20, 1971.

47. This quotation from Jaffe is included at the end of a chapter on the Harrison Narcotic Act in Edward M. Brecher, ed., *Licit and Illicit Drugs* (Boston: Little, Brown, 1972), 55.

48. Wailoo, *Pain: A Political History*, 86.

49. Richard M. Nixon, "Remarks to Eastern Media Executives Attending a Briefing on Domestic Policy in Rochester, New York," June 18, 1971, *Public Papers, Richard M. Nixon, 1971*, 755. Support for methadone maintenance came in the form of the Consumers Union report *Licit and Illicit Drugs*, 135–82.

50. For this statistic, see Stephen S. Wilmarth and Avram Goldstein, *Therapeutic Effectiveness of Methadone Maintenance Programs in the Management of Drug Dependence of Morphine Type in the USA* (Geneva: World Health Organization, 1974), 1.

51. On August 8, 1968, Nixon described "filth peddlers and narcotic peddlers…corrupting the lives of the children of this country": Richard M. Nixon, "Address Accepting the Presidential Nomination at the Republican National Convention in Miami Beach, Florida," www.presidency.ucsb.edu/documents /address-accepting-the-presidential-nomination-the-republican-national-conve ntion-miami.

52. Richard M. Nixon, "Statement Announcing an Expanded Federal Program to Combat Drug Abuse," March 11, 1970, *Public Papers of the Presidents, Richard M. Nixon, 1970* (Washington, DC: US Government Printing Office, 1971), 256–57. "Kids and Heroin: The Adolescent Epidemic," *Time*, March 16, 1970. On the perceived heroin crisis among the young, see Eric C. Schneider, *Smack: Heroin and the American City* (Philadelphia: University of Pennsylvania Press, 2009), 51–74, and on heroin and the Vietnam War, see David J. Bentel and David E. Smith, "Drug Abuse in Combat: The Crisis of Drugs

and Addiction among American Troops in Vietnam," *Journal of Psychedelic Drugs* 4, no. 1 (Fall 1971): 23–24.

53. Richard M. Nixon, "Remarks to Newsmen in Denver, Colorado," August 3, 1970, *Public Papers, Richard M. Nixon, 1970*, 641. See also Mical Raz, "Treating Addiction or Reducing Crime? Methadone Maintenance and Drug Policy under the Nixon Administration," *Journal of Policy History* 29, no. 1 (January 2017): 58–86.

54. Richard Nixon, "Special Message to the Congress on Drug Abuse Prevention and Control," June 17, 1971, *Public Papers of the Presidents, Richard M. Nixon, 1971*, 743–44.

55. Dan Baum, *Smoke and Mirrors: The War on Drugs and the Politics of Failure* (Boston: Little, Brown, 1996), 5.

56. Jeremy Kuzmarov, *The Myth of the Addicted Army: Vietnam and the Modern War on Drugs* (Amherst: University of Massachusetts Press, 2009), 44–45.

57. Richard M. Nixon, "Remarks to the American Medical Association's House of Delegates Meeting in Atlantic City, New Jersey," June 22, 1971, *Public Papers, Richard M. Nixon, 1971*, 765. Jaffe discussed the difficulties of coordinating a federal response to "one of the major social and health care issues of our society" in his foreword to Roger E. Meyer, *Guide to Drug Rehabilitation: A Public Health Approach* (Boston: Beacon Press, 1971), ix–xi.

58. Claire D. Clark, "'Chemistry Is the New Hope': Therapeutic Communities and Methadone Maintenance, 1965–71," *Social History of Alcohol and Drugs* 26, no. 2 (Summer 2012): 193–94.

59. Richard M. Nixon, "Statement about the Drug Abuse Office and Treatment Act of 1972," March 21, 1972, *Public Papers of the Presidents, Richard M. Nixon, 1972* (Washington, DC: US Government Printing Office, 1974), 456.

60. Richard M. Nixon, "Remarks to the Washington Conference on International Narcotics Control," September 18, 1972, *Public Papers, Richard M. Nixon, 1972*, 874–75. In 1974 the World Health Organization claimed there were 25,000 patients on methadone maintenance programs in 1973.

61. Edward Jay Epstein, *Agency of Fear: Opiates and Political Power in America* (1977; London: Verso, 1990), 249.

62. Wilmarth and Goldstein, *Therapeutic Effectiveness of Methadone Maintenance Programs*, 1. For the federal dollar statistic, see Bellis, *Heroin and Politicians*, xiv.

63. "Addicts at Project Cure 'Just Want to Be Normal,'" *Dayton Daily News*, May 16, 2010.

64. Wilmarth and Goldstein, *Therapeutic Effectiveness of Methadone Maintenance*, 17–18.

65. Suzanne Fraser, "Repetition and Rupture: The Gender of Agency in Methadone Maintenance Treatment," in *Rebirth of the Clinic: Places and Agents in Contemporary Health Care*, ed. Cindy Patton (Minneapolis: University of Minnesota Press, 2010), 71–73. Jennifer Friedman and Marixsa Alicea, *Surviving Heroin: Interviews with Women in Methadone Clinics* (Gainesville: University Press of Florida, 2001).

66. Suzanne Fraser and Kylie Valentine, *Substance and Substitution: Methadone Subjects in Liberal Societies* (Basingstoke: Palgrave, 2008), 169, 179.

67. Friedman and Alicea, *Surviving Heroin*, 4–5, 170.

68. "Health Chief Asks Help on Methadone," *Washington Post*, June 18, 1971.

69. "Methadone Deaths Rise, Heroin Overdoses Down," *Baltimore Sun*, March 28, 1974.

70. "Low-Grade Heroin Gives Rise to Addicts on Several Drugs Simultaneously," *Baltimore Sun*, May 8, 1977.

71. "Baltimore First Stop on Federal Drug Treatment Tour," *Baltimore Sun*, April 5, 2016.

72. Epstein, *Agency of Fear*, 127.

73. Epstein, *Agency of Fear*, 187. See Edward Jay Epstein, "Methadone: The Forlorn Hope," *Public Interest* 36 (Summer 1974): 3–24.

74. Michael Massing, *The Fix* (1998; Berkeley: University of California Press, 2000), 7.

75. Gerald R. Ford, "Remarks upon Signing the Drug Abuse Message," April 27, 1976, *Public Papers of the Presidents, Gerald R. Ford, 1976–77*, Book 2 (Washington, DC: US Government Printing Office, 1979), 1219.

76. Ford, "Remarks upon Signing the Drug Abuse Message," 1219.

77. Ford, "Remarks upon Signing the Drug Abuse Message," 1222, 1224.

78. "Methadone: Treatment, or a Worse Addiction?" *Baltimore Sun*, January 31, 1976.

79. See Peter G. Bourne and John Slade, "Methadone: The Mechanism of Its Success," *Journal of Nervous and Mental Disease* (November 1974): 371–75.

80. Clark, "Chemistry Is the New Hope," 192, 210.

81. "An Information Packet about Opioid Addiction and Treatment with Methadone," December 1978, held in the Archives and Manuscript Division of the Wellcome Library, London.

82. "Methadone Linked to Addicts Deaths," *New York Times*, February 2, 1982, and Jerome J. Platt et al., "Methadone Maintenance Treatment: Its Development and Effectiveness after 30 Years," in *Heroin in an Age of Crack-Cocaine*, ed. James A. Inciardi and Lana D. Harrison (Thousand Oaks, CA: Sage, 1998), 160–87. On the racial implications of the crack crisis, see Jason E. Glenn, "Making Crack Babies: Race Discourse and the Biologization of Behavior," in *Precarious Prescriptions: Contested Histories of Race and Health in North America*, ed. Laurie B. Green, John McKiernan-González, and Martin Summers (Minneapolis: University of Minnesota Press, 2012), 237–60.

83. Wilmarth and Goldstein, *Therapeutic Effectiveness of Methadone Maintenance*, 3.

84. Richard Hughes and Robert Brewin, *The Tranquilizing of America: Pill Popping and the American Way of Life* (New York: Harcourt Brace Jovanovich, 1978), 8.

85. Hughes and Brewin, *The Tranquilizing of America*, 27.

86. "Pills for the Mind," *Time*, June 11, 1956, and "Don't-Give-a-Damn Pills," *Time*, February 27, 1956. For media coverage of Miltown, see Mickey C.

Smith, *Small Comfort: A History of Minor Tranquilizers* (New York: Praeger, 1985), 64–82.

87. Andrea Tone, *The Age of Anxiety: A History of America's Turbulent Affair with Tranquilizers* (New York: Perseus, 2009), 115.

88. Quoted in *Medicine Avenue: The Story of Medical Advertising in America* (Huntingdon, NY: Medical Advertising Hall of Fame, 1999), 23.

89. "Happiness by Prescription," *Time*, March 11, 1957, 59. Carl F. Essig and John D. Ainslie, "Addiction to Meprobamate (Equanil, Miltown)," *Journal of the American Medical Association* 164, no. 12 (July 20, 1957): 1382.

90. Susan L. Speaker, "From 'Happiness Pills' to 'National Nightmare': Changing Cultural Assessment of Minor Tranquilizers in America, 1955–1980," *Journal of the History of Medicine and Allied Sciences* 52, no. 3 (July 1997): 347–50; David Herzberg, *Happy Pills in America: From Miltown to Prozac* (Baltimore: Johns Hopkins University Press, 2009), 127–28; Dominique A. Tobbell, *Pills, Power, and Policy: The Struggle for Drug Reform in Cold War America and Its Consequences* (Berkeley: University of California Press, 2012), 89–120.

91. "Letdown for Miltown," *Time*, April 30, 1965, 85.

92. "Drugs: The Mounting Menace of Abuse," *Look*, August 8, 1967, 11–28; cited in Herzberg, *Happy Pills in America*, 134.

93. Valium advertisement in *Hospital and Community Psychiatry* 22, no. 4 (1971). For an overview of Valium advertising, see Smith, *Small Comfort*, 118–22.

94. Ruth Cooperstock and Henry L. Lennard, "Some Social Meanings of Tranquilizer Use," *Sociology of Health and Illness* 1, no. 3 (December 1979): 335, 344.

95. E. B. Gordon, "Addiction to Diazepam (Valium)," *British Medical Journal* 5532, no. 1 (January 14, 1967): 112.

96. Hewitt F. Ryan et al., "Increase in Suicidal Thoughts and Tendencies: Association with Diazepam Therapy," *Journal of the American Medical Association* 203, no. 13 (March 25, 1968): 1137–39.

97. On the FDA clash with Hoffmann-La Roche in 1966, see Edward Shorter, *Before Prozac: The Troubled History of Mood Disorders in Psychiatry* (Oxford: Oxford University Press, 2009), 103–12. After serving as special assistant to President Johnson, Joseph Califano was centrally involved as Hoffmann-La Roche's legal representative, before reentering high office when he was made Carter's health secretary in 1977. Califano sees his legal work to prevent diazepam being classified as a "dark moment" in his career: Joseph A. Califano Jr., *Inside: A Public and Private Life* (New York: Public Affairs, 2004), 205.

98. For this statistic, see "Valium Potentially Addictive, Hill Told," *Washington Post*, September 11, 1979. The annual "Monitoring the Future" series is based on research at the Institute of Social Research at the University of Michigan. In 1982 Ralph Nader's Public Citizen Health Research Group published a report, *Stopping Valium*, that took critical swipes at many other minor tranquilizers.

99. "Danger Ahead! Valium: The Pill You Love Can Turn on You," *Vogue*, February 1975, 152–53.

100. Penelope McMillan, "Women and Tranquilizers," *Ladies' Home Journal*, November 1976, 164–67. For a digest of stories on Valium in popular US magazines from 1975 to 1980, see Herzberg, *Happy Pills in America*, 243.

101. Barbara Gordon, *I'm Dancing as Fast as I Can* (1978; New York: Beaufort, 2011), 34. Anton Holden, *Prince Valium* (New York: Stein and Day, 1982), 179.

102. Gordon, *I'm Dancing as Fast as I Can*, 94.

103. For the statistic, see Califano, *Inside: A Public and Private Life*, 205. For a review of medical literature on diazepam use in the mid-1970s, see John Marks, *Benzodiazepines: Use, Overuse, Misuse, Abuse* (Baltimore: University Park Press, 1985).

104. Myra MacPherson, "The Blooming of Betty Ford," *McCall's*, September 1975.

105. See "Betty Ford Says That She Is Addicted to Alcohol," *Washington Post*, April 22, 1978, and "Mrs. Ford, in Hospital Statement, Says: 'I Am Addicted to Alcohol,'" *New York Times*, April 22, 1978.

106. Betty Ford, *A Glad Awakening* (Garden City, NY: Doubleday, 1987), 163. For her treatment at the Long Beach Naval Hospital, see the final chapter of Betty Ford, *The Times of My Life* (New York: Harper Collins, 1978).

107. See Robert Seidenberg, "Drug Advertising and Perceptions of Mental Illness," *Mental Hygiene* 55, no. 1 (January 1971): 21–31.

108. "Carter Backs a $500 Million Plan to Improve Mental Health Care," *New York Times*, April 28, 1978.

109. Hughes and Brewin, *Tranquilizing of America*, 318. They take the term "psychem supermarket" from Gene Bylinsky's book *Mood Control* (New York: Scribner, 1978).

110. Subcommittee on Health and Scientific Research of the Committee of Human Resources, *Drug Regulation Reform Act of 1978*, United States Senate, 95th Congress, Second Session, March 17, 1978. Daniel S. Greenberg, "Drug Regulation Reform," *New England Journal of Medicine* 298 (April 1978): 979–80.

111. "Report of Washington Conference on the Drug Regulation Reform Act of 1978," *Journal of Clinical Pharmacy* 4 (1979): 167–73. See Tobbell, *Pills, Power, and Policy*, 142, 177.

112. Tobbell, *Pills, Power, and Policy*, 182.

113. Subcommittee on Health and Scientific Research of the Committee on Human Resources, *Use and Misuse of Benzodiazepines*, United States Senate, 96th Congress, First Session, 10 September 1979 (Washington DC: U.S. Government Printing Office, 1980), 53. "Senate Panel Is Told of Dangers of Valium Abuse," *New York Times*, September 11, 1979.

114. *Use and Misuse of Benzodiazepines*, 22.

115. *Use and Misuse of Benzodiazepines*, 24.

116. *Use and Misuse of Benzodiazepines*, 39. For Pursch's statement, see www.jimmycarterlibrary.gov/digital_library/sso/148878/129/SSO_148878 _129_10.pdf, 1–2.

117. "Beyond Valium," *New York*, February 5, 1979.

118. *Use and Misuse of Benzodiazepines*, 89–90, 108, 210, 228, 320–25.

119. *Use and Misuse of Benzodiazepines*, 108, 114, 205.

120. *Use and Misuse of Benzodiazepines*, 121. The National Consumers League letter is dated March 15, 1978.

121. *Use and Misuse of Benzodiazepines*, 123. Hughes and Brewin, *Tranquilizing of America*, 180–208.

122. Eve Bargmann et al., *Stopping Valium* (Washington, DC: Public Citizen's Health Research Group, 1982), 21. See also "Helping Troubled Women in an Era of Change," *New York Times*, May 21, 1979.

123. Bargmann et al., *Stopping Valium*, 5.

124. Bargmann et al., *Stopping Valium*, 1, 17.

125. "At Lilly, The Side-Effects of Oraflex," *New York Times*, August 15, 1982. The "environment of hysteria" statement was attributed to Eugene L. Step, president of Eli Lilly's pharmaceutical division.

126. Upjohn and NIH collaborated on a Cross-National Collaborative Panic Study in collaboration to assess the effectiveness of the new drug. On Upjohn's role in the study, see Jackie Orr, *Panic Diaries: A Genealogy of Panic Disorder* (Durham, NC: Duke University Press, 2006), 251–62, and on patient inserts, see Jeremy A. Greene and Elizabeth Siegel Watkins, *Prescribed: Writing, Filling, Using, and Abusing the Prescription in Modern America* (Baltimore: Johns Hopkins University Press, 2012), 112–14.

127. Wailoo, *Pain: A Political History*, 6.

128. "Valium and the New Normal," *New York Times*, September 12, 2012.

129. Muriel Nellis, *The Female Fix* (Boston: Houghton Mifflin, 1980), 115–17.

130. Wailoo, *Pain: A Political History*, 100.

131. Wailoo, *Pain: A Political History*, 110. Turner was a guest on the *Larry King Show* in October 1982 and a month later appeared on a television panel following a screening of the documentary *Epidemic: Why Your Kid Is on Drugs*.

132. Carlton Turner spoke on behalf of President Reagan at the Health Care Expo press conference, November 29, 1984, Box 30, Health Care Expo 1985, Washington, DC, Carlton E. Turner Files, Ronald Reagan Presidential Library, Simi Valley, California. For Turner's role in the Just Say No campaign, see Massing, *The Fix*, 158–64.

133. "Reagan Aide: Pot Can Make You Gay," *Newsweek*, October 27, 1985.

134. Massing, *The Fix*, 272.

135. Massing, *The Fix*, 189.

136. Subcommittee on Oversight and Investigations of the Committee on Energy and Commerce, *Oxycontin: Its Use and Abuse*, House of Representatives, 107th Congress, First Session, August 28, 2001 (Washington, DC: US Government Printing Office, 2001), 1. See also the Committee on Health, Education, Labor, and Pensions, *Oxycontin: Balancing Risks and Benefits*, United States Senate, 107th Congress, Second Session, February 12, 2002. See also Frank Brennan, "The US Congressional 'Decade on Pain Control and Research'

2001–2011: A Review," *Journal of Pain and Palliative Care Pharmacotherapy* 29, no. 3 (September 2015): 212–27.

137. "Cancer Painkillers Pose New Abuse Threat," *New York Times*, February 9, 2001.

138. Massing, *The Fix*, 275.

139. Office of National Drug Control Policy, *Epidemic: Responding to America's Prescription Drug Abuse Crisis* (2011), www.ncjrs.gov/pdffiles1/on dcp/rx_abuse_plan.pdf. See the Showtime series *Nurse Jackie* (2009–15).

140. Andrew Kolodny et al., "The Prescription Opioid and Heroin Crisis: A Public Health Approach to an Epidemic of Addiction," *Annual Review of Public Health* 36 (January 2015): 559–74.

141. This statement by the psychologist and Pennsylvania representative Tim Murphy opened the hearing conducted by the Subcommittee on Oversight and Investigation of the Committee on Energy and Commerce, *Examining the Growing Problems of Prescription Drug and Heroin Abuse: State and Local Perspectives*, House of Representatives, 114th Congress, First Session, March 26, 2015, https://energycommerce.house.gov/committee-activity/hearings/heari ng-on-examining-the-growing-problems-of-prescription-drug-and.

142. "Prescription Overdose Deaths in Florida Plunge after Tougher Measures," *New York Times*, July 2, 2014.

143. Fernando M. Perez, "Obama, Progressivism, Harm Reduction, and Drug Policy: From War to Health and Rights," in *Grading the 44th President: A Report Card on Barack Obama's First Term as Progressive Leader*, ed. Luigi Esposito and Laura L. Finley (Santa Barbara, CA: Praeger, 2012), 84.

144. Barack Obama, "Interview with Regional Reporters," March 11, 2009, *Public Papers of the Presidents, Barack Obama, 2009*, Book 1 (Washington, DC: US Government Printing Office, 2010), 224.

145. Joint Statement by President Barack Obama and President Felipe de Jesus Calderon Hinojosa of Mexico," May 19, 2010, *Public Papers of the Presidents, Barack Obama, 2010*, Book 1 (Washington, DC: US Government Printing Office, 2010), 680. See also remarks by the HSS Secretary Kathleen Sebelius (February 23, 2010), https://2009-2017.state.gov/j/inl/rls/rm/137270.htm.

146. *Facing Addiction in America: The Surgeon General's Report on Alcohol, Drugs, and Health* (Washington, DC: US Department of Health and Human Services, 2016), www.ncbi.nlm.nih.gov/pubmed/28252892.

147. Kathleen J. Frydl, "Barack Obama and the Opioid Crisis," *Medium* (October 17, 2017), https://medium.com/@kfrydl/obama-the-opioid-crisis-791 oce57d0b6. For the statistic, see Subcommittee on Oversight and Investigations of the Committee on Energy and Commerce, *Combating the Opioid Abuse Epidemic: Professional and Academic Perspectives*, House of Representatives, 114th Congress, First Session, April 23, 2015 (Washington, DC: US Government Printing Office, 2015), 6.

148. Foreman, *Global Pain Crisis*, 97. "The Other Opioid Crisis: Pain Patients Who Can't Access the Medicine We Need," *Washington Post*, March 9, 2018.

149. *Chasing the Dragon: The Life of an Opiate Addict*, www.fbi.gov/video -repository/newss-chasing-the-dragon-the-life-of-an-opiate-addict/view.

150. "Sweeping Health Measure, Backed by Obama, Passes Senate," *New York Times*, December 7, 2016.

151. Barack Obama, "Remarks on Signing the 21st Century Cures Act" (December 13, 2016), www.presidency.ucsb.edu/documents/remarks-signing -the-21st-century-cures-act.

152. Kathleen J. Frydl, *The Drug Wars in America, 1940–1973* (Cambridge: Cambridge University Press, 2013), 418.

153. Tim Murphy debated these options at the April 23, 2015, congressional hearing: *Combating the Opioid Abuse Epidemic*, 2–3.

154. "The 4th Democratic Debate Transcript, Annotated," *Washington Post*, January 17, 2016.

155. The quotation is from a February 5, 2018, letter from Bernie Sanders to the Tennessee senator Lamar Alexander: www.sanders.senate.gov/new sroom/press-releases/sanders-demands-investigation-into-pharmas-role-in-opio id-epidemic.

156. Frydl, *Drug Wars in America*, 422.

157. Donald J. Trump, "Remarks on Signing a Memorandum on Combatting the National Drug Demand and Opioid Crisis," October 26, 2017, www .presidency.ucsb.edu/documents/remarks-signing-memorandum-combatting -the-national-drug-demand-and-opioid-crisis. For one of Trump's many unsubstantiated criticisms of Obama, see "Vowing Again to Attack Opioids, Trump Faults Obama," *New York Times*, August 9, 2017. For a dramatization of fentanyl-laced heroin, see the Missouri-set Netflix drama *Ozark*, series 2, episode 8 ("The Big Sleep"), aired on August 31, 2018.

158. For the final report of the President's Commission, "On Combating Drug Addiction and the Opioid Crisis" (November 17, 2017) see www.whiteh ouse.gov/sites/whitehouse.gov/files/images/Final_Report_Draft_11-1-2017.pdf. Julie Hirschfield Davis, "Trump Declares Opioid Crisis a 'Health Emergency' but Requests No Funds," *New York Times*, October 26, 2017.

159. "Kellyanne Conway Might as Well Be 'Opioid Czar,'" *New York Times*, November 30, 2017.

160. For the HHS publication *American Patients First* of May 2018, see www.hhs.gov/sites/default/files/AmericanPatientsFirst.pdf.

161. "Drugs to Lull Opioid Urges Given Nod by F.D.A.," *New York Times*, February 26, 2018.

162. Kellyanne Conway speaking on CBS Philly on April 27, 2018. Her comment on the 2018 National Prescription Drug Take Back Day was on CNN's *State of the Nation*, May 6, 2018.

163. Sylvia Burwell emphasized "common ground" at a New America Foundation event in Washington, DC, on January 15, 2015, www.c-span.org /video/?323797-1/hhs-secretary-sylvia-burwell-health-care-policy-priorities.

164. "Opioid Prescriptions Fell 10 Percent Last Year Study Says," *Washington Post*, April 19, 2018.

165. Strick, *American Dolorologies*, 3, 149.

166. *Combating the Opioid Abuse Epidemic*, 23.

167. "Melania Trump Rolls Out 'Be Best,' a Children's Agenda with a Focus on Social Media," *New York Times*, May 7, 2018.

168. "As Melania Trump Faces Plagiarism Claims, Her Staff Lashes Out at News Media," *New York Times*, May 8, 2018. Michelle Obama's "be better" tagline was used in conversation with Oprah Winfrey at a White House United States of Women Summit, June 14, 2016, an aspect of which focused on health and well-being.

169. See www.cdc.gov/drugoverdose/data/statedeaths.html.

170. "Clinton Avoids Talk of Scandals in NH," *Nashua Telegraph*, April 22, 2015. "Trump Called New Hampshire a 'Drug-Infested Den,' Drawing the Ire of Its Politicians," *New York Times*, August 3, 2017. Trump's comment came to light in early August, and even the more conservative newspaper the *New Hampshire Union Leader* was critical of him: "Granite State Pushes Back at Trump Reference to NH Drug Crisis," *New Hampshire Union Leader*, August 4, 2017.

171. "New Hampshire not 'Drug Den,'" *Nashua Telegraph*, August 4, 2017.

172. "In N.H., HHS Secretary Price Announces Funding for Mental Health and Opioid Services," New Hampshire Public Radio, September 17, 2017, nhpr .org/post/nh-hhs-secretary-price-announces-funding-mental-health-and-opioid -services#stream/o.

173. Donald J. Trump, "Remarks in Manchester, New Hampshire," March 19, 2018, www.presidency.ucsb.edu/documents/remarks-manchester-new-ham pshire-5. For the "Opioids: The Crisis Next Door" website, which encourages the sharing of stories, see www.crisisnextdoor.gov. There was a slight drop in opioid-related deaths in 2017 in New Hampshire, but fentanyl (taken alone) caused nearly half the opioid overdose deaths in the state (200 out of 428), and fentanyl taken with other drugs (excluding heroin) totaled 82 percent of all opioid-related deaths in the state, www.doj.nh.gov/medical-examiner/docu ments/drug-data-update.pdf.

174. "Innovative Way of Dealing with Opioid Crisis," *Nashua Telegraph*, April 23, 2017. "Ahead of Trump's Visit, N.H. Officials Speak Up about Opioid Epidemic," WBUR News, March 19, 2018, www.wbur.org/news/2018/03 /19/trump-visit-nh-opioids.

175. "In New Hampshire, Trump Talks Past the Opioid Problem," *New Yorker*, March 20, 2018.

176. "Dayton's Overdose Crisis Has a Regrettable Easy Pipeline: Its Highways," *Dayton Daily News*, June 23, 2017. Five years earlier, in 2012, the availability of heroin in Dayton was marked as a 10 on a scale of 0 to 10 by an Ohio Substance Abuse Monitoring Network report: "Area Heroin Deaths Double in 2012," *Dayton Daily News*, March 1, 2013.

177. "Here, Heroin Spares No One, Not Even the Sheriff's Wife," CNN, August 8, 2017.

178. Quinones, *Dreamland*, 243–44.

179. See, for example, "New Drug Cocktail Causing Overdoses," *Cincinnati Enquirer*, May 28, 2006, and "Addicts Turn to Pain Patch, Sometimes Fatally," *Cincinnati Enquirer*, June 16, 2006.

180. "Ohio Drug Overdose Deaths up 39%—Nearly Triple US Average," *Columbus Dispatch*, February 12, 2018.

181. "Cincinnati Is Awash with a Drug That Kills in Miniscule Doses," *New York Times*, September 6, 2016. On carfentanil, see Macy, *Dopesick*, 4.

182. Centers for Disease Control and Prevention, "Overdose Deaths Related to Fentanyl and Its Analogs—Ohio, January–February 2017," *Morbidity and Mortality Weekly Report* 66, no. 34 (September 1, 2017): 904–8.

183. "New Surge of Meth, Cocaine Mixed with Powerful Opioids Pushes Ohio's Drug Overdose Death Toll Higher," *Akron Beacon Journal*, April 2, 2018.

184. "Services Grow in Dayton to Treat Opiate Addictions," *Dayton Daily News*, July 20, 2013. " 'They're My Safe Place': Children of Addicted Parents, Raised by Relatives," *New York Times*, December 26, 2019.

185. "Veterans Face Greater Risks amid Opioid Crisis," *Frontline* (March 28, 2016), www.pbs.org/wgbh/frontline/article/veterans-face-greater-risks -amid-opioid-crisis. Human Rights Watch released a 2014 report on drug dependence in the VA, *No Time to Waste*, recommending access to naloxone, methadone replacement treatment, and a Housing First initiative in an effort to improve well-being for homeless veterans. Megan McLemore, *No Time to Waste* (New York: Human Rights Watch, 2014).

186. "Area VA Seeing Consequences of Iraq War," *Akron Beacon Journal*, March 12, 2007, and "The Best Effort to Fight Opioid Addiction May Be at This VA Hospital in the Center of America's Epidemic," *Task and Purpose*, January 15, 2018, https://taskandpurpose.com/va-opiate-prescription-rates.

187. "Faces of an Epidemic," *New Yorker*, October 30, 2017.

188. "F.D.A. Clears Potent Opioid Despite Worry Abuse Is Likely," *Washington Post*, November 3, 2018.

189. See "How a Young War Veteran Became a Serial Bank Robber, Then a Novelist," *New York Times*, August 10, 2018.

190. Nico Walker, *Cherry* (New York: Knopf, 2018), 6, 8.

191. Walker, *Cherry*, 78.

192. Stephen Markley, *Ohio* (New York: Simon and Schuster, 2018), 18, 30, 70.

193. Walker, *Cherry*, 196.

194. Quinones, *Dreamland*, 353.

195. Markley, *Ohio*, 59.

196. Markley, *Ohio*, 114, 473.

197. Strick, *American Dolorologies*, 148.

198. "76 Billion Opioid Pills: Newly Released Federal Data Unmasks the Epidemic," *Washington Post*, July 17, 2019.

199. "Ohio Overdose Deaths Drop 21%," *Columbus Dispatch*, January 27, 2019, and "Ohio Approach to Battling Opioids Shows Promise," *Columbus Dispatch*, March 1, 2019. For three deaths in the area in January 2019 due to carfentanil overdoses, see "Deadly Opioid Resurfaces Locally," *Columbus Dispatch*, February 9, 2019. For a state-by-state summary of rising opioid cases in 2020, see the American Medical Association's issue brief "Reports of Increases in Opioid-Related Overdoses and Other Concerns during COVID Pandemic," updated August 14, 2020, www.ama-assn.org/system/files/2020-08/is sue-brief-increases-in-opioid-related-overdose.pdf.

200. This type of integrated model was pioneered in the 1980s by the Matrix Institute on Addictions based in Santa Monica, California. See Jeanne L. Obert et al., "The Matrix Model of Outpatient Stimulant Abuse Treatment: History and Description," *Journal of Psychoactive Drugs* 32, no. 2 (April–June 2000): 157–64. See also *Matrix Intensive Outpatient Treatment for People with Stimulant Use Disorders: Counselor's Treatment Manual* (Rockville, MD: Department of Health and Human Services, 2013).

201. Strick, *American Dolorologies*, 150. "Senate Easily Passes Sweeping Opioids Legislation, Sending to President Trump," *Washington Post*, October 3, 2018. Donald Trump signed the Substance Use-Disorder Prevention That Promotes Opioid Recovery and Treatment (SUPPORT) for Patients and Communities Act on October 24, 2018.

CONCLUSION

1. Charles E. Rosenberg, *Explaining Epidemics and Other Studies in the History of Medicine* (Cambridge: Cambridge University Press, 1992), 270.

2. Rosenberg, *Explaining Epidemics*, 275.

3. Patrick J. Kennedy and Stephen Fried, *A Common Struggle: A Personal Journey through the Past and Future of Mental Illness and Addiction* (New York: Blue Rider Press, 2015), 32–34.

4. Alan Derickson, *Health Security for All: Dreams of Universal Health Care in America* (Baltimore: Johns Hopkins University Press, 2005), 142.

5. On Ted Kennedy's criticisms of Jimmy Carter, see Burton Hersh, *Edward Kennedy: An Intimate Biography* (New York: Counterpoint, 2011), 465–67.

6. Edward Shorter, *The Kennedy Family and the Story of Mental Retardation* (Philadelphia: Temple University Press, 2000), 143.

7. Edward M. Kennedy, *In Critical Condition: The Crisis in America's Health Care* (New York: Simon and Schuster, 1972), 252. On the congressional hearings, see Committee on Labor and Public Welfare, *Health Care Crisis in America, 1971*, 92nd Congress, First Session (Washington, DC: US Government Printing Office, 1971).

8. Kennedy, *In Critical Condition*, 125–51. Hersh, *Edward Kennedy*, 394–95. For the argument that the Affordable Care Act neglects the middle class, see Uwe E. Reinhardt, *Priced Out: The Economic and Ethical Costs of American Health Care* (Princeton, NJ: Princeton University Press, 2019), 102–9.

9. For criticism of incremental health reform during George W. Bush's presidency, see "Desperate Measures: America's Health-Care Crisis," *The Economist*, January 26, 2006.

10. See "Ted Kennedy and Health Care Reform," *Newsweek*, July 19, 2009, and "Ted Kennedy's Speech at the DNC," *Newsweek*, August 26, 2009. For context, see Daniel E. Dawes, ed., *150 Years of Obamacare* (Baltimore: Johns Hopkins University Press, 2016), 93–94, 107–8. Kennedy was equally hopeful about health care reform when Bill Clinton became president; see Edward M. Kennedy, *True Compass: A Memoir* (New York: Twelve, 2009), 453–55.

11. Quoted in Steven Brill, *America's Bitter Pill: Money, Politics, Backroom*

Deals, and the Fight to Fix Our Broken Healthcare System (New York: Random House, 2015), 159.

12. Brian Abrams, *Obama: An Oral History 2009–2017* (New York: Little A, 2018), 130–32.

13. Barack Obama, "Address Before a Joint Session of the Congress on Health Care Reform," September 9, 2009, *Public Papers of the Presidents, Barack Obama, 2009*, Book 2 (Washington, DC: US National Archives and Records Administration, 2011), 1362–63, 1366, 1369. On the Tea Party backlash, see Anthony DiMaggio, *The Rise of the Tea Party: Political Discontent and Corporate Media in the Age of Obama* (New York: Monthly Review Press, 2011), 192–208, and John Dombrink, *The Twilight of Social Conservatism: American Culture Wars in the Obama Era* (New York: New York University Press, 2015), 43–53.

14. Obama, "Address Before a Joint Session of the Congress on Health Care Reform," 1363. For comparisons between Obama and Roosevelt, see "Franklin Delano Obama," *New York Times*, March 1, 2009, and the importance of this health care speech within Obama's early presidency, see "Aim of Obama Health Speech: Reigniting a Presidency," *New York Times*, September 9, 2009. See also Obama's *The Audacity of Hope: Thoughts on Reclaiming the American Dream* (New York: Crown, 2006), 183–87.

15. Obama, "Address Before a Joint Session of the Congress on Health Care Reform," 1369.

16. Obama, "Address Before a Joint Session of the Congress on Health Care Reform," 1369.

17. Bernie Sanders, *Our Revolution: A Future to Believe In* (New York: Macmillan, 2016), 325. Sanders worked with Kennedy on the Senate Health, Education, Labor, and Pensions Committee from 2007 to 2009.

18. See "Health Care and Insurance Industries Mobilize to Kill 'Medicare for All,'" *New York Times*, February 23, 2019.

19. The figure of $32.6 trillion was proposed in summer 2018 by the nonprofit Mercatus Center of George Mason University; "'Medicare for All' Could Cost $32.6 Trillion George Mason Study Says," *Time*, July 30, 2018.

20. Donald J. Trump, *Crippled America: How to Make America Great Again* (New York: Simon and Schuster, 2015), 71. The book was republished as *Great Again: How to Fix Our Crippled America* in July 2016 for Trump's presidential run.

21. On these stealth interventions, see, for example, "The Ongoing, Quiet Repeal: Despite Failed Votes, Obamacare Is Being Dismantled Internally," *The Atlantic*, September 28, 2017.

22. "Donald Trump's Ignorance Is Becoming a National Crisis," *Vanity Fair*, June 28, 2017.

23. Robert Bellah, Richard Madsen, William M. Sullivan, Ann Swidler, and Steven M. Tipton, *The Good Society* (New York: Vintage, 1992), 279, 231. Bellah takes the notion of "moral balancing" from the theologian and social critic Reinhold Niebuhr, whose 1952 book, *The Irony of American History*, Obama was reading the previous year.

24. Bellah et al., *Good Society*, 113, 221.

25. World Health Organization, "The Ottawa Charter for Health Promotion" (1986), www.who.int/healthpromotion/conferences/previous/ottawa/en.

26. World Health Organization, "Jakarta Declaration on Leading Health Promotion into the 21st Century" (1997), www.who.int/healthpromotion/con ferences/previous/jakarta/declaration/en/.

27. See Marcos Cueto, Theodore M. Brown, and Elizabeth Fee, *The World Health Organization: A History* (Cambridge: Cambridge University Press, 2019), 2.

28. Bellah et al., *Good Society*, 224. Another example of this global commitment is the One Health Initiative (onehealthinitiative.com) that, since 2006, has adopted a holistic and integrated approach to human, animal, and environmental health.

29. Bill Clinton, *Between Hope and History: Meeting America's Challenges for the 21st Century* (New York: Random House, 1996), 106–7. Bellah et al., *Good Society*, 271. Clinton's late-1990s views on global health broadly aligned with the Institute of Medicine publication *America's Vital Interest in Global Health: Protecting Our People, Embracing Our Economy, and Advancing Our International Interests* (Washington, DC: National Academy Press, 1997).

30. For the "One America" initiative, see Bill Clinton, "Commencement Address at the University of California San Diego in La Jolla, California," June 14, 1997, *Public Papers of the Presidents, William J. Clinton, 1997*, Book 1 (Washington, DC: US Government Printing Office, 1998), 739–40.

31. See Steven F. Lawson, ed., *One America in the 21st Century: The Report of President Bill Clinton's Initiative on Race* (New Haven, CT: Yale University Press, 2009), 79–83. In its preface, John Hope Franklin discusses public opposition to the commission and criticizes President Clinton for not engaging with it more closely (xi–xii). For the initial White House report of January 1999, *Pathways to One America in the 21st Century: Promising Practices for Racial Reconciliation*, see https://clintonwhitehouse2.archives.gov/Initiatives /OneAmerica/Practices/ppreport.pdf.

32. George W. Bush, "Address before a Joint Session of the Congress of the State of the Union," January 28, 2003, *Public Papers of the Presidents, George W. Bush, 2003*, Book 1 (Washington, DC: US Government Printing Office, 2006), 85.

33. See "The President's Emergency Plan for AIDS Relief: How George W. Bush and Aides Came to 'Think Big' on Battling HIV," *Health Affairs* 31, no. 7 (July 2012): 1389–96. Fauci and Farmer reflected on their roles in PEPFAR at "The Lazarus Effect, 15 Years Later," held in May 2018 at the George W. Bush Presidential Center, Dallas, www.bushcenter.org/exhibits-and-events/events/20 18/05/engage-lazarus-effect.html.

34. See the National Center for Health Statistics, *Healthy People 2000: Final Review* (Hyattsville, MD: US Department of Health and Human Services, 1997), www.cdc.gov/nchs/data/hp2000/hp2k01.pdf.

35. For links between Clinton's "One America in the 21st Century" initiative and Obama's campaign rhetoric, especially Obama's "A More Perfect Union" address of March 18, 2008, see Steven F. Lawson's introduction to *One America in the 21st Century*, xv–xxxviii. On the obesity epidemic, see Natalie

Boero, *Killer Fat: Media, Medicine, and Morals in the American "Obesity Epidemic"* (New Brunswick, NJ: Rutgers University Press, 2012), 6–7.

36. See Hillary Clinton and Tim Kaine, *Stronger Together: A Blueprint for America's Future* (New York: Simon and Schuster, 2016), 180–82, 89–95, 214–17, 141.

37. See Reid Wilson, *Epidemic: Ebola and the Global Scramble to Prevent the Next Killer Outbreak* (Washington, DC: Brookings Institution Press, 2018), and Pardis Sabeti and Lara Salahi, *Outbreak Culture: The Ebola Crisis and the Next Epidemic* (Cambridge, MA: Harvard University Press, 2018).

38. Mission statement of USAID, usaid.gov. Clinton and Kaine, *Stronger Together*, 152.

39. Chelsea Clinton and Devi Sridhar, "US May Pay Price of Trump's Ignorance on Global Health," CNN, February 24, 2020. See also Chelsea Clinton and Devi Sridhar, *Governing Global Health: Who Runs the World and Why* (Oxford: Oxford University Press, 2017).

40. Bill Clinton, "Struggle for the Soul of the 21st Century," *New Perspectives Quarterly* 19, no. 2 (Spring 2002): 27–35. For Clinton's December 14, 2001, Richard Dimbleby Lecture, see http://australianpolitics.com/2001/12/14 /bill-clinton-struggle-for-the-soul-of-the-21st-century.html.

41. Jimmy Carter, *Beyond the White House: Waging Peace, Fighting Disease, Building Hope* (New York: Simon and Schuster, 2007), 147–51, 158–77. On the Closing the Gap initiative, see Jimmy and Rosalynn Carter, *Everything to Gain: Making the Most of the Rest of Your Life*, rev. ed. (1987; Fayetteville: University of Arkansas Press, 1995), 29–58, and Robert W. Amler and H. Bruce Dull, *Closing the Gap: The Burden of Unnecessary Illness* (New York: Oxford University Press, 1987).

42. See www.cartercenter.org/health/phti/index.html.

43. See Christopher J. Murray and Alan D. Lopez, *The Global Burden of Disease* (Cambridge, MA: Harvard University Press, 1996), and Steven H. Woolf and Laudan Aron, eds., *U.S. Health in International Perspective: Shorter Lives, Poorer Health* (Washington, DC: National Academies Press, 2013).

44. "Raising Storm Relief Money, Ex-Presidents Try to Decide Where to Send It," *New York Times*, October 8, 2005, and "Former Presidents Announce First Storm Grants," *New York Times*, December 8, 2005.

45. Kaitlin Menza, "Where Did Brad Pitt's Make It Right Foundation Go Wrong?" *Architectural Digest*, January 18, 2019, www.architecturaldigest .com/story/brad-pitt-make-it-right-foundation-new-orleans-katrina-lawsuit.

46. See "Trump Blames Wildfires on California Forest Policy and Threatens to Withhold Funds from State," *Los Angeles Times*, October 17, 2018, "Wildfires Prompt Concern over Major Health Consequences," *Time*, November 16, 2018, and "Wildfires and Public Health Concerns," NPR, November 18, 2018, www.npr.org/2018/11/18/669007515/wildfires-and-public-health-concerns. On the cumulative effects of wildfires, see "4 Years of Catastrophic Fires in California: 'I'm Numb,'" *New York Times*, August 24, 2020, and for critical health conditions on the Texas-Mexico border, see "The Looming Health Crisis for Migrant Children," *Washington Post*, June 28, 2019.

47. Richard Levinson, "Issues at the Interface of Medical Sociology and

Public Health,'" in *Modernity, Medicine, and Health: Medical Sociology towards 2000*, ed. Graham Scambler and Paul Higgs (London: Routledge, 1998), 76. Nancy Leys Stepan, *Eradication: Ridding the World of Diseases Forever?* (London: Reaktion, 2011), 30.

48. On the uneven abortion coverage of insurance plans, see Katie Oliviero, *Vulnerability Politics: The Uses and Abuses of Precarity in Political Debate* (New York: New York University Press, 2018), 209–10. On LGBTQ+ health rights, see the Human Rights Watch report *You Don't Want Second Best: Anti-LGBT Discrimination in US Health Care*, July 2018, www.hrw.org/report/20 18/07/23/you-dont-want-second-best/anti-lgbt-discrimination-us-health-care. On culturally congruent care, see World Health Organization, *WHO Traditional Medicine Strategy, 2014–2023*, www.who.int/medicines/publications/tr aditional/trm_strategy14_23/en.

49. Stepan, *Emancipation*, 30–33. On widening health disparities, see National Center for Health Statistics, *Healthy People 2010: Final Review* (Hyattsville, MD: US Department of Health and Human Services, 2012), iii. On culturally sensitive mHealth interventions, see Stephanie Craig Rushing et al., "Using Technology to Promote Health and Wellbeing among American Indian and Alaska Native Teens and Young Adults," in *Indigenous People and Mobile Technologies*, ed. Laurel Evelyn Dyson, Stephen Grant, and Max Hendriks (New York: Routledge, 2016), 164–78.

50. Elizabeth Cohen, *The Empowered Patient* (New York: Ballantine, 2010). See also Marc Siegel, *False Alarm: The Truth about the Epidemic of Fear* (New York: Wiley, 2006).

51. The statistic is from a CNN Exit Poll published on November 6, 2018.

52. David Rosner and Gerald Markowitz, *Are We Ready? Public Health since 9/11* (Berkeley: University of California Press, 2006), 157.

53. William J. Clinton, "Remarks on Signing Memorandums on Medical Research and Reproductive Health and an Exchange with Reporters," January 22, 1993, *Public Papers of the Presidents, William J. Clinton, 1993*, Book 1 (Washington, DC: US Government Printing Office, 1994), 8.

54. Michelle Obama, *Becoming* (New York: Viking, 2018), 337. For coverage of Let's Move! see "Childhood Obesity Battle Is Taken Up by First Lady," *New York Times*, February 10, 2010. The initiative should be placed alongside the Obama administration's Task Force on Childhood Obesity of 2010 and the collaboration between HHS and Department of Agriculture on nutritional standards; see *Dietary Guidelines for Americans, 2015–2020* (December 2015), https://health.gov/dietaryguidelines/2015.

55. On ThriveNYC, see thrivenyc.cityofnewyork.us, and the 2016 report *ThriveNYC: Year One Update*, https://thrivenyc.cityofnewyork.us/wp-conte nt/uploads/2017/02/Thrive_Year_End_Updated-1.pdf. For press coverage, see "In New York, an Influential First Lady Redefines the Position," *New York Times*, October 20, 2017, and "Once-Thriving City Nonprofit Sputter under Mayor's Wife, Chirlane McCray," *New York Times*, May 29, 2018.

56. See Julie Cwikl, *Social Epidemiology: Strategies for Public Health Activism* (New York: Columbia University Press, 2006), and Glen Laverack, *Health Activism: Foundations and Strategies* (London: Sage, 2013).

57. Robert N. Bellah, Richard Madsen, William M. Sullivan, Ann Swidler, and Steven M. Tipton, *Habits of the Heart: Individualism and Commitment in American Life*, updated ed. with a new introduction (1985; Berkeley: University of California Press, 1996), 218.

58. Bellah et al., *Good Society*, 279.

59. Bellah et al., *Habits of the Heart*, 218.

60. On health activism at the intersection of these identity categories, see Celia Roberts and Richard Tutton, "The Rise of Health Activism: The Importance of Social Class to Biosociality," in *Bio-Citizenship: The Politics of Bodies, Governance, and Power*, ed. Kelly E. Happe, Jenell Johnson, and Marina Levina (New York: New York University Press, 2018), 204–21.

61. Bellah et al., *Good Society*, 26. See also Robert N. Bellah, *Beyond Belief: Essays on Religion in a Post-Traditional World* (New York: Harper and Row, 1970), xviii, and Roger Bowen, "Robert Bellah on Religion, Morality, and the Politics of Resentment," *Academe* 92, no. 1 (January–February 2006): 33–37. On public health imagination, see Geof Rayner and Tim Lang, *Ecological Public Health: Reshaping the Conditions for Good Health* (London: Routledge, 2013), 326–31.

62. On social networks, race, and economic status, see Danielle T. Raudenbush, *Health Care Off the Books: Poverty, Illness, and Strategies for Survival in Urban America* (Berkeley: University of California Pres, 2020), 10–14.

63. Robert N. Bellah, "Is There a Common American Culture?" in *The Robert Bellah Reader*, ed. Robert N. Bellah and Steven M. Tipton (Durham, NC: Duke University Press, 2006), 319–32. Bellah discusses criticisms of civil religion in his afterword to *The Broken Covenant: American Civil Religion in Time of Trial* (1975; Chicago: University of Chicago Press, 1992), 164–88. For the Citizens Project, see https://citizens.collaborative.yale.edu/programs/citizens-project, and on citizenship-oriented care and for context, see Michael Rowe, *Citizenship and Mental Health* (Oxford: Oxford University Press, 2015).

64. Rosenberg, *Explaining Epidemics*, 277.

65. Memo from Mitchell Sviridoff to Joseph A. Califano, June 29, 1966, "WE 9, 6/10/66–8/1/66," Box 27, Welfare Ex WE9, Papers of Lyndon Baines Johnson, LBJ Library, Austin, Texas.

66. Paul Farmer, *To Repair the World: Paul Farmer Speaks to the Next Generation*, ed. Jonathan Weigel (Berkeley: University of California Press, 2019), 143–55. Bellah et al., *Good Society*, 278.

67. Farmer, *To Repair the World*, 57–71.

68. National Center for Health Statistics, *Health, United States, 2017*, www.cdc.gov/nchs/hus/description.htm. See "US Life Expectancy Declines Again: A Dismal Trend Not Seen since World War I," *Washington Post*, November 29, 2018.

69. Robert R. Redfield, "CDC Director's Media Statement on U.S. Life Expectancy," November 29, 2018, www.cdc.gov/media/releases/2018/s1129-US-life-expectancy.html.

CODA 2020

1. Coronavirus Task Force Briefing, the White House, March 31, 2020, www.rev.com/blog/transcripts/donald-trump-coronavirus-task-force-briefing -transcript-march-31-painful-weeks-ahead.

2. See the disease modeling of University of Washington's Institute of Health Metrics and Evaluation, http://covid19.healthdata.org/united-state-of-america.

3. See www.whitehouse.gov/wp-content/uploads/2020/04/Guidelines-for-Op ening-Up-America-Again.pdf, accessed May 4, 2020.

4. See "The Coronavirus Pandemic Is Pushing America into a Mental Health Crisis," *Washington Post*, May 4, 2020. For a documentary account of the New York City pandemic experience, see Bill Hayes, *How We Live Now: Scenes from the Pandemic* (New York: Bloomsbury, 2020).

5. Woodrow Wilson, "Address of Welcome to the Members of the American Medical Association by Gov. Woodrow Wilson, June 4, 1912," *Congressional Record*, August 13, 1912, 11692. Fauci and Cuomo topped an Insider poll of April 2020 about whom the American public considered the most trusted leaders for this crisis.

6. Anthony Fauci interviewed on CNN's *State of the Union*, April 12, 2020.

7. Dwight D. Eisenhower, "Annual Message to the Congress on the State of the Union," February 2, 1953, *Public Papers of the Presidents, Dwight D. Eisenhower, 1953* (Washington, DC: US Government Printing Office, 1960), 24.

8. "The Politics of the Virus," *New Yorker*, April 27, 2020, 11.

9. Among critical views of the Trump administration, see "He Could Have Seen What Was Coming: Behind Trump's Failure on the Virus," *New York Times*, April 11, 2020; *The Pandemic and the President*, CNN, May 3, 2020; and "The Last Days of the Summer: How Trump Fell Short in Containing the Virus," *Washington Post*, August 8, 2020. On sustained underfunding of public health services, see "The Nation's Public Health Agencies Are Ailing When They're Needed Most," *Washington Post*, August 31, 2020.

10. *Covid-19: Safely Getting Back to Work and Back to School*, Hearings of the Committee on Health, Education, Labor, and Pensions, United States Senate, 116th Congress, Second Session, May 12, 2020. *CDC Activities and Initiatives Supporting the COVID-19 Response and the President's Plan for Opening Up American Again*, May 2020, www.cdc.gov/coronavirus/2019-nc ov/downloads/php/CDC-Activities-Initiatives-for-COVID-19-Response.pdf.

11. Editorial, "Dying in a Leadership Vacuum," *New England Journal of Medicine*, 383 (October 8, 2020): 1479–80.

12. Jackie Orr, *Panic Diaries: A Genealogy of Panic Disorder* (Durham, NC: Duke University Press, 2006), 45.

13. Donald Trump, Coronavirus Task Force Press Briefing, the White House, April 15, 2020, www.rev.com/blog/transcripts/donald-trump-coronavir us-press-briefing-transcript-april-15. The president's statement took on historical weight when audio tapes released in September confirmed that Trump knew of the virulence of COVID-19 as early as February 7, but he chose to downplay it in order not to create panic, as he said to journalist Bob Woodward on March 19. See Bob Woodward, *Rage* (New York: Simon and Schuster, 2020).

14. Press release by the Select Subcommittee on the Coronavirus Crisis, House of Representatives, August 31, 2020, https://coronavirus.house.gov /news/press-releases/select-subcommittee-releases-eight-weeks-coronavirus-task -force-reports-kept.

15. See "Trump Calls Fauci a 'Wonderful Guy,'" *Washington Post*, April 13, 2020, and "The Good Doctor," *New Yorker*, April 27, 2020, 39–45. Fauci was attacked by the right-wing media and by congressional Republicans through the late spring and summer for overstepping what they considered appropriate for a public health official to say. In October, in the closing weeks of his re-election campaign, Trump criticized Fauci for being over-cautious, instead favoring the more cavalier approach of Scott Atlas, a neuroradiologist who Trump had added to the Coronavirus Task Force in August.

16. Appearing on Fox News on April 16, Fauci corrected Laura Ingraham for making casual parallels between HIV/AIDS, SARS, and COVID-19.

17. See, for example, "Asian American Doctors and Nurses Are Fighting Racism and the Coronavirus," *Washington Post*, May 19, 2020.

18. See "How to Save Black and Hispanic Lives in a Pandemic," *New York Times*, April 11, 2020.

19. See Lisa Bowleg, "We're Not All in This Together: On COVID-19, Intersectionality, and Structural Inequality," *American Journal of Public Health* 110, no. 7 (July 2020): 927.

20. For differing views on the potential of digital health care, see "Expanded Telehealth Has Provided a Boost for Rural America. Will it Last?" *US News*, May 7, 2020, and Natalie C. Benda, Tiffany C. Veinot, Cynthia J. Sieck, and Jessica S. Ancker, "Broadband Internet Access Is a Social Determinant of Health!" *American Journal of Public Health* 110, no. 8 (August 2020): 1123–25.

21. See, for example, the California Volunteers network, promoted by the Office of the California Governor, www.californiavolunteers.ca.gov/get-involv ed/covid-19/.

Selected Bibliography

Altenbaugh, Richard J. *The Last Children's Plague: Poliomyelitis, Disability, and Twentieth-Century American Culture*. London: Palgrave Macmillan, 2015.

Anderson, Emma-Louise. *Gender, HIV, and Risk: Navigating Structural Violence*. London: Palgrave Macmillan, 2015.

Ball, Howard. *Justice Downwind: America's Atomic Testing Program in the 1950s*. New York: Oxford University Press, 1986.

Barr, Donald A. *Health Disparities in the United States: Social Class, Race, Ethnicity, and the Social Determinants of Health*. Baltimore: Johns Hopkins University Press, 2008.

Barry, John M. *The Great Influenza: The Epic Story of the Deadliest Plague in History*. New York: Viking, 2004.

———. *Rising Tide: The Great Mississippi Flood of 1927 and How It Changed America*. New York: Simon and Schuster, 1997.

Baum, Dan. *Smoke and Mirrors: The War on Drugs and the Politics of Failure*. Boston: Little, Brown, 1996.

Bayer, Ronald. *Private Acts, Social Consequences: AIDS and the Politics of Public Health*. New York: Free Press, 1989.

Bellah, Robert N., Richard Madsen, William M. Sullivan, Ann Swidler, and Steven M. Tipton. *The Good Society*. New York: Knopf, 1991.

———. *Habits of the Heart: Individualism and Commitment in American Life*. 1985. Updated edition with a new introduction. Berkeley: University of California Press, 1996.

Blakely, Debra E. *Mass Mediated Disease: A Case Study Analysis of Three Flu Pandemics and Public Health Policy*. Lanham, MD: Lexington Books, 2006.

Bohle, Hans-Georg. *Living with Vulnerability: Livelihoods and Human Security in Risky Environments*. Bonn: InterSections, 2007.

Bonnifield, Paul. *The Dust Bowl: Men, Dirt, and Depression*. Albuquerque: University of New Mexico Press, 1979.

Brennan, Virginia M., ed. *Natural Disasters and Public Health: Hurricanes Katrina, Rita, and Wilma*. Baltimore: Johns Hopkins University Press, 2009.

Brier, Jennifer. *Infectious Ideas: U.S. Political Responses to the AIDS Crisis*. Chapel Hill: University of North Carolina Press, 2009.

Bristow, Nancy K. *American Pandemic: The Lost Worlds of the 1918 Influenza Epidemic*. Oxford: Oxford University Press, 2012.

Brown, Phil. *Toxic Exposures: Contested Illnesses and the Environmental Health Movement*. New York: Columbia University Press, 2007.

Burnham, John C. *Health Care in America*. Baltimore: Johns Hopkins University Press, 2015.

Burrow, James G. *Organized Medicine in the Progressive Era: The Move toward Monopoly*. Baltimore: Johns Hopkins University Press, 1977.

Byerly, Carol R. *Fever of War: The Influenza Epidemic in the U.S. Army during World War I*. New York: New York University Press, 2005.

Byrd, Michael W., and Linda A. Clayton. *An American Health Dilemma*. Vol. 2, *Race, Medicine, and Health Care in the United States, 1900–2000*. New York: Routledge, 2002.

Chan, Jennifer. *Politics in the Corridor of Dying: AIDS Activism and Global Health Governance*. Baltimore: Johns Hopkins University Press, 2015.

Clark, Anna. *Poisoned City: Flint's Water and the American Urban Tragedy*. New York: Picador, 2019.

Clark, Claire D. *Recovery Revolution: The Battle over Addiction Treatment in the United States*. New York: Columbia University Press, 2017.

Clark, Kenneth B. *Dark Ghetto: Dilemmas of Social Power*. 1965. 2nd ed. Middletown, CT: Wesleyan University Press, 1989.

Clark, Timothy. "Scale." In *Telemorphosis: Theory in the Era of Climate Change*, vol. 1, edited by Tom Cohen. Ann Arbor: Open Humanities Press, an imprint of MPublishing—University of Michigan Library, 2012, 148–66.

Clinton, Chelsea, and Devi Sridhar. *Governing Global Health: Who Runs the World and Why*. Oxford: Oxford University Press, 2017.

Cohen, Alan B., David C. Colby, Keith Wailoo, and Julian E. Zelizer, eds. *Medicare and Medicaid at 50: America's Entitlement Programs in the Age of Affordable Care*. Oxford: Oxford University Press, 2015.

Cohen, Stanley. *Folk Devils and Moral Panics*. 1972. 3rd ed. New York: Routledge, 2011.

Colgrove, James, Gerald Markowitz, and David Rosner, eds. *The Contested Boundaries of American Public Health*. New Brunswick, NJ: Rutgers University Press, 2008.

Crosby, Alfred W. *America's Forgotten Pandemic: The Influenza of 1918*. 1989. 2nd ed. Cambridge: Cambridge University Press, 2003.

Crosby, Molly Caldwell. *Asleep: The Forgotten Epidemic That Remains One of Medicine's Greatest Mysteries*. New York: Berkley Books, 2010.

Crosthwaite, Paul, ed. *Criticism, Crisis, and Contemporary Narrative: Textual Horizons in an Age of Global Risk*. New York: Routledge, 2011.

Cueto, Marcos, Theodore M. Brown, and Elizabeth Fee. *The World Health Organization: A History*. Cambridge: Cambridge University Press, 2019.

Cwikel, Julie. *Social Epidemiology: Strategies for Public Health Activism*. New York: Columbia University Press, 2006.

Dauber, Michele Landis. *The Sympathetic State: Disaster Relief and the Origins of the American Welfare State*. Chicago: University of Chicago Press, 2013.

Davies, Kate. *The Rise of the U.S. Environmental Health Movement*. Lanham, MD: Rowman and Littlefield, 2013.

Davis, Karen, and Cathy Schoen. *Health and the War on Poverty: A Ten-Year Appraisal*. Washington, DC: Brookings Institution Press, 1978.

Derickson, Alan. *Black Lung: Anatomy of a Public Health Disaster*. Ithaca, NY: Cornell University Press, 2014.

———. *Health Security for All: Dreams of Universal Health Care in America*. Baltimore: Johns Hopkins University Press, 2005.

Deutsch, Albert. *The Mentally Ill in America: A History of Their Care and Treatment from Colonial Times*. 1937. Rev. ed. New York: Columbia University Press, 1949.

———. *The Shame of the States*. New York: Harcourt Brace, 1948.

Dittmer, John. *Good Doctors: The Medical Committee of Human Rights and the Struggle for Social Justice in Health Care*. New York: Bloomsbury, 2009.

Doyle, Dennis A. *Psychiatry and Radical Liberalism in Harlem, 1936–1968*. Rochester, NY: University of Rochester Press, 2016.

Duffy, John. *The Sanitarians: A History of American Public Health*. Urbana: University of Illinois Press, 1990.

Duncan, Cynthia M. *Worlds Apart: Poverty and Politics in Rural America*. 1999. 2nd ed. New Haven, CT: Yale University Press, 2014.

Egan, Timothy. *The Worst Hard Time: The Untold Story of Those Who Survived the Great American Dust Bowl*. Boston: Houghton Mifflin, 2006.

Ehrenreich, Barbara, and John Ehrenreich. *The American Health Empire: Power, Profits, and Politics*. New York: Random House, 1970.

Ehrenreich, John, ed., *The Cultural Crisis of Modern Medicine*. New York: Monthly Review Press, 1978.

Engel, Jonathan. *Poor People's Medicine: Medicaid and American Charity Care since 1965*. Durham, NC: Duke University Press, 2006.

Erikson, Kai T. *Everything in Its Path: Destruction of Community in the Buffalo Creek Flood*. New York: Simon and Schuster, 1976.

Etheridge, Elizabeth W. *Sentinel for Health: A History of the Centers for Disease Control*. Berkeley: University of California Press, 1992.

Fairchild, Amy L., Ronald Bayer, and James Colgrove. *Searching Eyes: Privacy, the State, and Disease Surveillance in America*. Berkeley: University of California Press, 2007.

Farmer, Paul. *Infections and Inequalities: The Modern Plagues*. Berkeley: University of California Press, 1999.

———. "On Suffering and Structural Violence: A View from Below." *Daedalus* 125, no. 1 (Winter 1996): 261–83.

Foreman, Judy. *The Global Pain Crisis: What Everyone Needs to Know*. Oxford: Oxford University Press, 2017.

———. *A Nation in Pain: Healing Our Biggest Health Problem*. Oxford: Oxford University Press, 2014.

Frydl, Kathleen J. *The Drug Wars in America, 1940–1973*. Cambridge: Cambridge University Press, 2013.

Gallagher, Carole. *American Ground Zero: The Secret Nuclear War*. Cambridge, MA: MIT Press, 1993.

Gamble, Vanessa Northington. *Making a Place for Ourselves: The Black Hospital Movement, 1920–1945*. Oxford: Oxford University Press, 1995.

Goldstein, Alyosha. *Poverty in Common: The Politics of Community Action during the American Century*. Durham, NC: Duke University Press, 2012.

Gordon, Colin. *Dead on Arrival: The Politics of Health Care in Twentieth-Century America*. Princeton, NJ: Princeton University Press, 2003.

Gore, Al. *An Inconvenient Sequel: Truth to Power*. New York: Rodale, 2017.

———. *An Inconvenient Truth: The Crisis of Global Warming*. New York: Viking, 2007.

Green, Laurie B., John McKiernan-González, and Martin Summers, eds. *Precarious Prescriptions: Contested Histories of Race and Health in North America*. Minneapolis: University of Minnesota Press, 2012.

Grey, Michael R. *New Deal Medicine: The Rural Health Programs of the Farm Security Administration*. Baltimore: Johns Hopkins University Press, 2002.

Grob, Gerald N. *From Asylum to Community: Mental Health Policy in Modern America*. Princeton, NJ: Princeton University Press, 1991.

Grob, Gerald N., and Howard H. Goldman. *The Dilemma of Federal Mental Health Policy: Radical Reform or Incremental Change?* New Brunswick, NJ: Rutgers University Press, 2006.

Hacker, Barton C. *Elements of Controversy: The Atomic Energy Commission and Radiation Safety in Nuclear Weapons Testing, 1947–1974*. Berkeley: University of California Press, 1994.

Halliwell, Martin. *Therapeutic Revolutions: Medicine, Psychiatry, and American Culture, 1945–1970*. New Brunswick, NJ: Rutgers University Press, 2013.

———. *Voices of Mental Health: Medicine, Politics, and American Culture, 1970–2000*. New Brunswick, NJ: Rutgers University Press, 2017.

Happe, Kelly E., Jenell Johnson, and Marina Levina, eds. *Bio-Citizenship: The Politics of Bodies, Governance, and Power*. New York: New York University Press, 2018.

Hardy, Anne. *The Epidemic Streets: Infectious Disease and the Rise of Preventive Medicine, 1856–1900*. Oxford: Oxford University Press, 1993.

Hoffman, Beatrix. *Health Care for Some: Rights and Rationing in the United States since 1930*. Chicago: University of Chicago Press, 2012.

Hughes, Richard, and Robert Brewin. *The Tranquilizing of America: Pill Popping and the American Way of Life*. New York: Harcourt Brace Jovanovich, 1978.

Jargowsky, Paul A. *Poverty and Place: Ghettos, Barrios, and the American City*. New York: Russell Sage Foundation, 1997.

Jensen, Robin E. *Dirty Words: The Rhetoric of Public Sex Education, 1870–1924.* Urbana: University of Illinois Press, 2010.

Kandall, Stephen R. *Substance and Shadow: Women and Addiction in the United States.* Cambridge, MA: Harvard University Press, 1996.

Kardiner, Abram, and Lionel Ovesey. *The Mark of Oppression: Explorations in the Personality of the American Negro.* 1951. 2nd ed. Cleveland: Meridian, 1962.

Kennedy, Edward M. *In Critical Condition: The Crisis in America's Health Care.* New York: Simon and Schuster, 1972.

———. *The Health Care Crisis: A Report to the American People.* Washington, DC: US Government Printing Office, 1990.

Klein, Naomi. *This Changes Everything.* New York: Simon and Schuster, 2015.

Kluger, Jeffrey. *Splendid Solution: Jonas Salk and the Conquest of Polio.* New York: Putnam's, 2004.

Kraut, Alan M. *Silent Travelers: Germs, Genes, and the Immigrant Menace.* New York: Basic Books, 1994.

Kucharski, Adam. *The Rules of Contagion: Why Things Spread—and Why They Stop.* London: Profile Books, 2020.

Kuzmarov, Jeremy. *The Myth of the Addicted Army: Vietnam and the Modern War on Drugs.* Amherst: University of Massachusetts Press, 2009.

Lakoff, Andrew. *Unprepared: Global Health in a Time of Emergency.* Berkeley: University of California Press, 2017.

Laverack, Glen. *Health Activism: Foundations and Strategies.* London: Sage, 2013.

Lee, Jon D. *An Epidemic of Rumors: How Stories Shape Our Perception of Disease.* Boulder: University Press of Colorado, published by Utah State University Press, 2014.

Lefkowitz, Bonnie. *Community Health Centers: A Movement and the People Who Made It Happen.* New Brunswick, NJ: Rutgers University Press, 2007.

Lerner, Steve. *Sacrifice Zones: The Front Lines of Toxic Chemical Exposure in the United States.* Cambridge, MA: MIT Press, 2010.

Lifton, Robert Jay. *Home from the War: Vietnam Veterans, Neither Victim nor Executioner.* New York: Simon and Schuster, 1973.

MacKenzie, Debora. *COVID-19: The Pandemic That Never Should Have Happened and How to Stop the Next One.* New York: Hachette, 2020.

Macy, Beth. *Dopesick: Dealers, Doctors, and the Drug Company That Addicted America.* New York: Little, Brown, 2018.

Markowitz, Gerald, and David Rosner. *Deceit and Denial: The Deadly Politics of Industrial Pollution.* Berkeley: University of California Press, 2002.

———. *Lead Wars: The Politics of Science and the Fate of America's Children.* Berkeley: University of California Press, 2013.

Massing, Michael. *The Fix.* 1998. Berkeley: University of California Press, 2000.

Metzl, Jonathan M., and Anna Kirkland, eds. *Against Health: How Health Became the New Morality.* New York: New York University Press, 2010.

Mitman, Gregg, Michelle Murphy, and Christopher Sellers, eds. *Landscapes of*

Exposure: Knowledge and Illness in Modern Environments. Chicago: University of Chicago Press, 2004.

Mnookin, Seth. *The Panic Virus: The True Story behind the Vaccine-Autism Controversy*. New York: Simon and Schuster, 2012.

Moreno, Jonathan, ed. *In the Wake of Terror: Medicine and Morality in a Time of Crisis*. Cambridge, MA: MIT Press, 2003.

Morgen, Sandra. *Into Our Own Hands: The Women's Health Movement in the United States, 1969–1990*. New Brunswick, NJ: Rutgers University Press, 2002.

Mullan, Fitzhugh. *Plagues and Politics: The Story of the United States Public Health Service*. New York: Basic Books, 1989.

Nixon, Rob. *Slow Violence and the Environmentalism of the Poor*. Cambridge, MA: Harvard University Press, 2011.

Noah, Timothy. *The Great Divergence: America's Growing Inequality Crisis and What We Can Do about It*. New York: Bloomsbury, 2012.

Oliviero, Katie. *Vulnerability Politics: The Uses and Abuses of Precarity in Political Debate*. New York: New York University Press, 2018.

Opdycke, Sandra. *The Flu Epidemic of 1918: America's Experience in the Global Health Crisis*. New York: Routledge, 2014.

Orr, Jackie. *Panic Diaries: A Genealogy of Panic Disorder*. Durham, NC: Duke University Press, 2006.

Oshinsky, David M. *Polio: An American Story*. Oxford: Oxford University Press, 2005.

Osterholm, Michael T., and Mark Olshaker. *Deadliest Enemy: Our War against Killer Germs*. Boston: Little, Brown, 2017.

Peckham, Robert, ed. *Empires of Panic: Epidemics and Colonial Anxieties*. Hong Kong: Hong Kong University Press, 2015.

Prud'homme, Alex. *The Ripple Effect: The Fate of Freshwater in the Twenty-First Century*. New York: Scribner's, 2011.

Quadagno, Jill. *The Color of Welfare: How Racism Undermined the War on Poverty*. New York: Oxford University Press, 1996.

Quinones, Sam. *Dreamland: The True Tale of America's Opiate Epidemic*. New York: Bloomsbury, 2016.

Raudenbush, Danielle T. *Health Care Off the Books: Poverty, Illness, and Strategies for Survival in Urban America*. Berkeley: University of California Press, 2020.

Rayner, Geof, and Tim Lang. *Ecological Public Health: Reshaping the Conditions for Good Health*. London: Routledge, 2013.

Reinhardt, Uwe E. *Priced Out: The Economic and Ethical Costs of American Health Care*. Princeton, NJ: Princeton University Press, 2019.

Rhoades, Everett R., ed. *American Indian Health: Innovations in Health Care, Promotion, and Policy*. Baltimore: Johns Hopkins University Press, 2000.

Richmond, Julius B. *Currents in American Medicine: A Developmental View of Medical Care and Education*. Cambridge, MA: Harvard University Press, 1969.

Roberts, Samuel Kelton, Jr. *Infectious Fear: Politics, Death, and the Health Effects of Segregation*. Chapel Hill: University of North Carolina Press, 2009.

Rogers, Naomi. *Dirt and Disease: Polio before FDR*. New Brunswick, NJ: Rutgers University Press, 1992.

Rosenberg, Charles E. *The Care of Strangers: The Rise of America's Hospital System*. New York: Basic Books, 1987.

———. *Explaining Epidemics and Other Stories in the History of Medicine*. Cambridge: Cambridge University Press, 1992.

Rosenthal, Elizabeth. *An American Sickness: How Healthcare Became Big Business and How You Can Take It Back*. New York: Penguin, 2017.

Rosenthal, Rob. *Homeless in Paradise: A Map of the Terrain*. Philadelphia: Temple University Press, 1993.

Rosner, David. *Hives of Sickness: Epidemics and Public Health in New York City*. New Brunswick, NJ: Rutgers University Press, 1995.

Rosner, David, and Gerald Markowitz. *Are We Ready? Public Health since 9/11*. Berkeley: University of California Press, 2006.

Rozario, Kevin. *The Culture of Calamity: Disaster and the Making of Modern America*. Chicago: University of Chicago Press, 2007.

Sabeti, Pardis, and Lara Salahi. *Outbreak Culture: The Ebola Crisis and the Next Epidemic*. Cambridge, MA: Harvard University Press, 2018.

Scarry, Elaine. *The Body in Pain: The Making and Unmaking of the World*. Oxford: Oxford University Press, 1985.

Scott, Wilbur J. *The Politics of Adjustment: Vietnam Veterans since the War*. New Brunswick, NJ: Aldine, 1993.

Shah, Sonia. *Pandemic: Tracking Contagions, from Cholera to Ebola and Beyond*. New York: Farrar, Straus and Giroux, 2016.

Shell, Mark. *Polio and Its Aftermath: The Paralysis of Culture*. Cambridge, MA: Harvard University Press, 2005.

Shilts, Randy. *And the Band Played On: Politics, People, and the AIDS Epidemic*. New York: St. Martin's Press, 1987.

Shipler, David K. *The Working Poor: Invisible in America*. New York: Vintage, 2005.

Siplon, Patricia D. *AIDS and the Policy Struggle in the United States*. Washington, DC: Georgetown University Press, 2002.

Skocpol, Theda. *Boomerang: Health Care Reform and the Turn against Government*. New York: Norton, 1996.

Sledge, Daniel. *Health Divided: Public Health and Individual Medicine in the Making of the Modern American State*. Lawrence: University Press of Kansas, 2017.

Smith, Barbara Ellen. *Digging Our Own Graves: Coal Miners and the Struggle over Black Lung Disease*. Philadelphia: Temple University Press, 1987.

Smith, Jane S. *Patenting the Sun: Polio and the Salk Vaccine*. New York: William Morrow, 1990.

Spinney, Laura. *Pale Rider: The Spanish Flu of 1918 and How It Changed the World*. London: Jonathan Cape, 2017.

Starr, Paul. *Remedy and Reaction: The Peculiar American Struggle over Health Care Reform*. New Haven, CT: Yale University Press, 2013.

Stein, Michael D., and Sandro Galea. *Pained: Uncomfortable Conversations about the Public's Health*. New York: Oxford University Press, 2020.

Stern, Gerald M. *The Buffalo Creek Disaster: The Story of the Survivors' Unprecedented Lawsuit.* New York: Vintage, 1976.

Stevens, Rosemary. *In Sickness and in Wealth: American Hospitals in the Twentieth Century.* 1989. Baltimore: Johns Hopkins University Press, 1999.

Streeck, Wolfgang. *Buying Time: The Delayed Crisis of Democratic Capitalism.* 2014. 2nd ed. London: Verso, 2017.

Strick, Simon. *American Dolorologies: Pain, Sentimentalism, Biopolitics.* Albany: State University of New York Press, 2014.

Taylor, Dorceta E. *Toxic Communities: Environmental Racism, Industrial Pollution, and Residential Mobility.* New York: New York University Press, 2014.

Thomas, Karen Kruse. *Deluxe Jim Crow: Civil Rights and American Health Policy, 1935–1954.* Athens: University of Georgia Press, 2011.

Thomson, Jennifer. *The Wild and the Toxic: American Environmentalism and the Politics of Health.* Chapel Hill: University of North Carolina Press, 2019.

Titus, A. Costandina. *Bombs in the Backyard: Atomic Testing and American Politics.* 1986. Reno: University of Nevada Press, 2001.

Tobbell, Dominique A. *Pills, Power, and Policy: The Struggle for Drug Reform in Cold War America and Its Consequences.* Berkeley: University of California Press, 2012.

Tomes, Nancy. *The Gospel of Germs: Men, Women, and the Microbe in American Life.* Cambridge, MA: Harvard University Press, 1998.

Torrey, E. Fuller. *Out of the Shadows: Confronting America's Mental Illness Crisis.* New York: Wiley, 1997.

Troesken, Werner. *The Great Lead Water Pipe Disaster.* Cambridge, MA: MIT Press, 2006.

Wacquant, Loïc. *Urban Outcasts: A Comparative Sociology of Advanced Marginality.* New York: Polity, 2007.

Wailoo, Keith. *Pain: A Political History.* Baltimore: Johns Hopkins University Press, 2014.

Wald, Priscilla. *Contagious: Cultures, Carriers, and the Outbreak Narrative.* Durham, NC: Duke University Press, 2008.

Ward, Thomas J., Jr. *Out in the Rural: A Mississippi Health Center and Its War on Poverty.* New York: Oxford University Press, 2017.

Weiss, Gregory L. *Grassroots Medicine: The Story of America's Free Health Clinics.* Lanham, MD: Rowman and Littlefield, 2006.

Wilson, William Julius. *The Truly Disadvantaged: The Inner City, the Underclass, and Public Policy.* 1987. Chicago: University of Chicago Press, 2012.

Wintermute, Bobby A. *Public Health and the U.S. Military: A History of the Army Medical Department.* London: Routledge, 2011.

Woods, Randall B. *Prisoners of Hope: Lyndon B. Johnson, the Great Society, and the Limits of Liberalism.* New York: Perseus, 2016.

Zarefsky, David. *President Johnson's War on Poverty: Rhetoric and History.* Tuscaloosa: University of Alabama Press, 1986.

Zelizer, Julian E. *The Fierce Urgency of Now: Lyndon Johnson, Congress, and the Battle for the Great Society.* New York: Penguin, 2015.

Index